THE AMERICAN AENEAS

George Sandys in 1626 reclining (lower right, foreground) on the Virginia Strand, translating Ovid's *Metamorphoses* while those around him transform the New World ambiance. Captain John Smith stands right foreground with ax in hand. Drawing by H. A. Ogden, 1939.

The American Aeneas

Classical Origins of the American Self

John C. Shields

The University of Tennessee Press
Knoxville

First Edition.

The paper used in this book meets the minimum requirements of ANSI/NISO Z39.48-1992 (R 1997) (Permanence of Paper). The binding materials have been chosen for strength and durability.

LIBRARY OF CONGRESS CATALOGING-IN-PUBLICATION DATA

Shields, John C., 1944–
The American Aeneas: classical origins of the American self /
John C. Shields—1st ed.
p. cm.
Includes bibliographical references (p.) and index.
ISBN 1-57233-132-1 (hardcover: alk. paper)
1. American literature—Roman influences.
2. American literature—Colonial period, ca. 1600–1775—History and criticism.
3. American literature—19th century—History and criticism.
4. National characteristics, American, in literature.
5. United States—Civilization—Roman influences.
6. Aeneas (Legendary character) in literature.
7. National characteristics, American.
8. Classicism—United States.
9. Virgil—Influence.
10. Virgil. Aeneas.
I. Title.
PS159.R6 S55 2001
810.9'358—dc21 00-012737

to Elizabeth Merle Shields
and Granville Blaine Shields Sr., my parents,
who always believed I could

and to
Mary Ruth Ryder,
my muse

Contents

Illustrations

Preface

At first glance, the title of this book may suggest that my aim is to resurrect an ancient Mediterranean cultural grid and then impose it on American thought and culture. In fact, I intend no such resurrection. Nor do I wish to burden the idea of America with some new cultural construct, external or otherwise. Instead, what I propose in this volume is the recovery of a heretofore lost key which unlocks the American self.

Few would dispute that the two modes of discourse which govern the cultures of Europe are the classical and the Judaeo-Christian. Yet conventional wisdom holds that, when Anglo-Europeans, excluding other races and/or ethnicities, colonized the Atlantic shores of what would become the United States of America, these colonizers brought with them only the strand of Judaeo-Christianity. Somehow the classical strand jumped ship on the way over. Many claim that true Americanness resides exclusively within the myth[1] of Adam.[2] At present these claimants, in a latter-day jeremiad, energetically urge the American public to "return" to what is alleged to have been the founding fathers' Christian values. However, I have found the tenets of the Adamic myth (the Judaeo-Christian mythos) insufficient to explain the obvious secularity of the American people.

This book argues that both the largely spiritual Adamic discourse and the largely secular classical discourse crossed over from Europe. These two modes have intermingled dynamically in such a way that both have become rearticulated, in a manner distinct from that of Europe, in order to meet the demands of the American adventure in freedom. This peculiar blending of classical and biblical mythoi on the American strand constitutes the

American cultural self. Recovery of this combination can mitigate what some have called America's fear of pastlessness, and perhaps allay that anxiety altogether.

Much of this fear of pastlessness may be attributed to the hegemonic effects of the Adamic myth. This hegemony has concealed the Aeneas myth, or the classical half of the American self, for so long a time that nothing less than a full-scale reclamation of the American Aeneas can address this loss satisfactorily. Recuperation of the forgotten classical half of the American cultural self, then, is this study's central concern. At the same time, this project interrogates the interconnectedness of the Adamic and the classical discourses. Such a recovery greatly strengthens arguments for an American exceptionalism, such as that made recently by Jack P. Greene in *Intellectual Construction of America*.

For a considerable time I resisted the notion of a classical half of Americanness. So stubborn and so long has been the denigration of the Aeneas myth that an extensive archaeology was required before I could accept this classical half. Eventually, as I recovered a huge quantity of startling evidence that classical thought and culture had contributed mightily to shaping the American self, my skepticism diminished. This previously unseen classical half did and does exist, and recuperation of that half explains much about how and why Americans have acted and thought as they have, and continue to act and to think as they do.

For example, in writing entries for Levernier and Wilmes, *American Writers Before 1800*, I found that two of my subjects, Joseph Green and Joseph Seccombe, were authors of pastoral elegies, an unrecovered genre of Early American poetry. This form allowed its practitioners to record in poetic mode a tradition. After further investigation, I concluded that neither of these writers sought out Milton's *Lycidas* as a paradigm for imitation; rather, each (like Milton before them) went directly to Vergil for instruction in this form. Looking farther, I determined that Green, writing later than Seccombe, had read Seccombe and borrowed some ideas from him. Green also borrowed from Jeremy Belknap, a consummate classicist and another Early American writer of pastoral elegy. Green, then, was writing as an Early American, not as an imitator of the British Milton, despite the undeniable fact that all of these writers (and virtually all Early American writers, from Cotton Mather to Phillis Wheatley) knew Milton, as well as many other British and Continental authors of this period.

This study advances a subordinate argument, too. When the tenets of the Aeneas myth are allowed to come into play along with those of the Adamic myth while reading the works of Early American writers, their writings (excluding those by Loyalists) do not display a dependence upon British authors. Rather, they demonstrate an originality and independence whose temper predicts the struggle for political and economic independence. Contrary to conventional wisdom, Early American writers were original thinkers, discovering for themselves an original identity.

Recovery of the American Aeneas and its interaction with the Adamic myth necessitates a reevaluation of the whole of American literature created before 1800. While this volume initiates such a reevaluation, in no way does it exhaust this undertaking.

But this combination of classical and Adamic myths is not merely a phenomenon of pre-Revolutionary America; indeed, it persists in a dialectical relationship even today. The chapters on Hawthorne and Melville demonstrate this persistence. Hawthorne's "My Kinsman, Major Molineaux" and Melville's *Billy Budd,* rather than other texts, have been selected because practically every person who has taught or taken a survey course in nineteenth-century American literature knows them. While the classical half of the American self persists in virtually all American authors of the nineteenth and twentieth centuries, from James Fenimore Cooper to Willa Cather and beyond, here I have attempted only to establish the presence and persistence of the Aeneas myth.

It would be impossible to treat, in this limited space, the full compass and consequence of the persistence of the Aeneas myth. Nevertheless, I shall suggest some plausible directions that such a reassessment may take. What *The American Aeneas* sets out to accomplish, then, is to restore America's missing classical half. Doing so will provide a more precise and accurate *paradeictic* (model used as argument) for the American self, one against which we, without anxiety, may productively and usefully interrogate our self/selves.

In a collection of essays entitled *Race, Discourse, and the Origin of the Americas: A New World View,* which was read at the Smithsonian Institution in 1991 in anticipation of the quincentenary of Columbus's first voyage to the Western Hemisphere, the editors, Vera L. Hyatt and Rex Nettleford, take the position that the only adequate process for evaluating the consequences of this voyage is to bring into the dialogue the cultures affected—those of European origin, certainly, but also those of Africa and Native America. The authors of these essays propose that only a syncretization of these three cultural matrices will enable the collective cultures of North America and the Caribbean to survive the vicissitudes augured by the onslaught of the twenty-first century.

The present volume participates in this aspiration. Taking seriously my own biological origins among the native peoples of the North American continent, I frequently point out negative interactions between Native Americans and European interlopers as those cultural exchanges occur. Much of my career has been devoted to improving our understanding of the author Phillis Wheatley, America's first African American to publish a book. Acknowledging Wheatley's contribution toward defining the American self spotlights the concerns of African Americans, as well as oppressed women. Issues concerning Native and African Americans are particularly pertinent here, because the period 1500–1800, on which this study concentrates, was the era in which oppressive policies toward these minorities became established.

In his conclusion to the Smithsonian collection, Rex Nettleford writes:

> A chaotic, turbulent twenty-first century that is even now upon us is likely to be grateful that the likes of us survived not only Columbus, the man, but the myth and metaphor of modern history his name has been used to symbolize. The discourse is nothing if it is not about survival and beyond. Therein lies the hope of a New World that will be able to eradicate the obscenities of racism and successfully engage the dilemma of difference. (Hyatt and Nettleford 289)

I offer this volume as a contribution to our struggle to "eradicate the obscenities of racism and successfully engage the dilemma of difference."

Acknowledgments

JUST AS VERGIL'S PROTAGONIST OF THE *AENEID* WAS MUCH BUFFETED ON LAND AND SEA, SO HAS *THE AMERICAN AENEAS* ENDURED SIMILAR VICISSItudes. I want to make clear, however, that that which has been difficult has never been the search, the conceiving or the writing; every particle of time and effort given to those processes marks only periods of joy brought on by ecstatic discovery. Amidst their celebratory mission, the following acknowledgments will, nevertheless, suggest moments of discomfiture but hardly the full extent of this book's troublesome, sixteen-year journey. An often perplexing and problematic gestation has, at last, yielded a welcome birth.

The title of this book owes obvious debt to R. W. B. Lewis's *The American Adam: Innocence, Tragedy and Tradition in the Nineteenth Century* and to Sacvan Bercovitch's *Puritan Origins of the American Self*. Invocation of these two significant works calls attention both to the hegemony of the Adamic myth (in no way to be understood as Lewis's exclusive construction; recall that he asked for new cultural conversations, of which *The American Aeneas* is one) and to signal a new direction in American cultural studies which restores the classical half to the American self.

Additional texts which gave me essential guidance, particularly in the early years of this project's development, are Richard Beale Davis's monumental *Intellectual Life in the Colonial South, 1585–1763* (3 vols.); Henry F. May's *The Enlightenment in America;* John W. Eadie's provocative collection of essays by such distinguished scholars as Meyer Reinhold, A. Owen Aldridge, David Stanley Wiesen, George Kennedy and J. G. A. Pocock,

Classical Traditions in Early America; and Meyer Reinhold's *Classica Americana: The Greek and Roman Heritage in the United States*, with which I have some misgivings (see chapter 7 and note 4).

The origins of this project go back many years to my high school Latin days when my instructor, Blanche McCall, called me the best translator she had ever taught. It was this initial confidence in my ability which eventually led to my decision to make, myself, all translations which appear in this book. While a student at the University of Tennessee, Knoxville, I came under the fortuitous guidance and influence of Classics Professors Arthur H. Moser, Albert Rapp, James E. Shelton and Harry C. Rutledge; these gentlemen have remained firmly in my mind as great sources of knowledge and inspiration regarding the vitality and value of classical languages and literatures. Because of their excellent example, I have, in my academic career, always been keenly prepared to recognize the undeniable impact the classical world has had and continues to have upon modern culture throughout the globe, especially upon the cultures of the United States and other regions of the Americas.

Those of the University of Tennessee's Department of English not only gave me the benefit of their excellent examples through the years, but the generosity of their time and professional counsel. I shall always remember with particular fondness Bain T. Stewart, Jack E. Reese, John A. Hansen (who directed my master's thesis), Kenneth Curry, Edward W. Bratton, Kenneth L. Knickerbocker, Nathalia Wright (always, in my mind, the finest scholar and the best teacher), Bobby J. Leggett, Samuel H. McMillan Jr., R. Baxter Miller (who directed my dissertation), and Mary P. Richards. All these superior professors allowed me at one time or another to pursue my interests regarding classicism in American and British authors. I recall on one occasion, for example, seeing on a paper, "Classical Allusions in Melville's Poetry," Professor Wright's comment, "I've always said a book should be written on Melville's classicism." Regrettably, such a book has yet to be published; perhaps the time draws near.

This past summer, D. Allen Carroll, head of UT's English Department, along with Edward Bratton, Michael Lofaro, and others were responsible for awarding me, under the auspices of the John C. Hodges Better English Fund (the same Fund that supported my receipt of the first John C. Hodges Excellence in Teaching Award given by UT's English Department), a subvention, matched by my home base, Illinois State University's English Department, to be applied toward the production of this volume's color figures and the color used for its dust jacket. Thank you all for endorsing my work and for giving it dignity.

Soon after accepting an assistant professorship with the English Department of Illinois State University, a colleague, Steven Kagle, put me in touch with James A. Levernier who, with Douglas Wilmes, was preparing a three-volume series, *American Writers Before 1800: A Biographical and Critical Dictionary*. Eventually I agreed to write sixteen entries for these volumes; as a result I was virtually transformed into an Early Americanist, and I became good friends with Jim Levernier. Besides finding from this experience the first four pastoral elegies of a genre I was unaware was practiced among Early Americans, I found Jim Levernier a supportive reader and valuable critic of several portions of *The American Aeneas* manuscript.

A National Endowment for the Humanities Summer Stipend for the summer of 1983 enabled me to have the time to begin to assimilate the many discoveries (pastoral elegies, pastorals, meditatios, epics, patterns of deference, not to Continental or British authors, but to other Early American authors, poems of literary independence and other cultural adaptations of classical elements to Early America—however recognizable these elements may be to others, these were all new to me) participation in Levernier's and Wilmes's project had led me to make. The following year I soon found that I was no longer teaching American literature the same way. That is, I began to recognize that classicism as employed by Early American authors, *and even later ones*, was much more significant than I had been led to believe. It was about this time that I began to learn that editors of journals for American literary criticism were not often friendly to essays which argued for a strong classical influence, but that journals leaning toward a comparatist approach were.

During the fall of 1983, nevertheless, I had unearthed enough strands of information to give shape to a proposal to Cornell University's Society for the Humanities and to construct a proposal for participation in an NEH Summer Seminar. I was fortunate enough to receive both, so now I was given the gift of twelve months of virtually uninterrupted time to devote to developing my certainly, at this stage, inchoate paradeictic of Adam and Aeneas. This time proved absolutely critical to *The American Aeneas* project. Had I not been released from a heavy teaching load of four classes a semester at this critical moment (i.e., when the evidence was just beginning to make sense to me), I think *The American Aeneas* would never have come about.

This kind of project does not come easily. That is, my experience has taught me that a project like *The American Aeneas* must be "teased out" through long investigation and research. The nurturing environments provided by Frances Ferguson, seminar director, then at UC Berkeley, and by Jonathan Culler, director of the Society for the Humanities, were pivotal to me in the shaping of my career. I am grateful both to these individuals and to the institutions which enabled their invaluable nurturing to take place. As well the summer at Berkeley and the year at Cornell made accessible to me the extensive collections of the Bancroft and Olin Libraries. The archival research I was able to carry out amidst these fine repositories both confirmed and extended my earlier conclusions. Text after text (and these were of course not all literary texts) supported my contention that the Adam and Aeneas model was not merely a literary pattern but a cultural phenomenon, one which has determined our behavior as a nation, even at the present moment.

In the earlier years of this evolving project, my inclination usually fell toward disbelief. I found myself often asking: can what I was seeing be credible? Why was I seeing it when virtually no one had done so before me? The facts are that many had patently denied even the possibility of a substantial classical influence, despite such obvious architectural marvels as Monticello and Washington, D.C.'s government buildings. The fortunate award of two more opportunities to participate in NEH Summer Seminars kept my head above water and inspired me to drive forward.

Immersing myself in Yale's Beinecke and Sterling Libraries, finding occasion to travel to Harvard's Houghton and Widener Libraries and pleased to discover the humane and most helpful staff of Princeton's Firestone Library, I made no turn in these repositories, once again, which did not support my earlier conclusions. But more importantly, in Paul H. Fry and Thomas P. Roche, I encountered generous consideration and sincere enthusiasm for my still evolving project. Without their encouragement and reinforcing criticism, I may well have given in to my predilection for disbelief and dropped the project. Once again, I find myself happily indebted to NEH, especially for creating the opportunity to make the acquaintance of Paul Fry, one of the most inspiring scholar/colleagues I have met. Without these wonderful opportunities to do research and to receive informed criticism made possible through the auspices of the NEH and Cornell's Society for the Humanities, this project could not have been completed.

Although the repositories named above house many texts which I was not able to find either at I.S.U.'s Milner Library or at the University of Illinois Library, these collections have, perhaps surprisingly, served me best through the years. The University of Illinois Library contains an especially rich variety and quantity of Early Americana, of African Americana, and of texts related to Early America. At my home institution, I have ever found the staff to be knowledgeable and generous with its knowledge. And the help and keen intelligence of Joan Winters (my friend through the years) have made my life much easier and relaxed than it ever could have been without her. She is a special person. Frederick Nash, formerly head librarian of the University of Illinois's Rare Book Room and Vera Mitchell, librarian of its Afro-American and African Studies Collections, and Diane Pye helped me solve many problems and always made me feel comfortable. I should like to take this opportunity once again to recall the many kindnesses extended to me personally and to my students by the late Hugh Atkinson, who served for many years as Illinois's University Librarian.

I should like, as well, to thank my Department and the College of Arts and Sciences for the space and time of two sabbatical leaves awarded me during the evolution of this project; these sabbaticals gave me the opportunity first to develop the backbone of this project and later to revise and refine the entire manuscript. I owe a special debt of gratitude to Marna Winters (a special friend), Carol Eagan, Dona Meador, Terri Mack, Diane L. Smith, and Irene Taylor. These fine women have, through the long years, made my life much more comfortable than it could have been without them.

Many other individuals have given me their generous professional support during the execution of this project, including Ronald Fortune, my department chair, who graciously took the time to scan the entire book onto disks; Lucia Getsi, whose strong example and personal interest have sustained me through some tough times; Carol Walker, Willard Spiegelman, and Henry Russell, members of NEH seminars who took particular interest in my work; Michael A. Lofaro, whose encouragement and guidance have proved invaluable; Rebecca Saunders, whose brilliant intellect and expansive knowledge enlighten us all; Greg Aloia, who, as my graduate school dean, supported me with mini-grants and copious praise; Virginia Owen, who, as dean of the College of Arts and Sciences, showed by her professional and often personal interest that she valued my work; Nina Baym, who took an early interest in this project; Ramsay MacMullen, who corrected some of my Latin translations in the chapter on George Washington; Avery Springer, who answered my queries about some finer points regarding Latin grammar; Michael Lind, whose *The Alamo* is a wondrous accomplishment and who wisely advised me to give more time to the South; Kendall Johnson, whose intellect soars and whose enthusiasm is contagious; William Morgan, who thoughtfully read the first draft of a long portion of this book; Raymond Dolle, David S. Shields, Peter White, Harrison T. Meserole, and Philip Gura, who encouraged me in the early stages of this project; and William P. Sisler, whose belief in this project has remained constant.

To certain of my colleagues—Timothy Twohill, Robert Epperson, Ethan Krase, Heath Martin, Louis Schroeder, Cheri Grizzard, and Carol Rose Clark—whom I have been lucky enough to have enroll in my classes, who have patiently listened to me drone on and on about this or that aspect of *The American Aeneas*, but who have substantially influenced, because of their sharp intelligence and insightfulness, the construction of this book, I extend my gratitude. Their consistent encouragement and invaluable criticism have helped make of the book what I think is a declaration of substance; as well their willingness to offer constructive criticism has made me a better teacher. Ethan Krase, Louis Schroeder, Tom O. McCulley, and Heath Martin have read the manuscript entire and made instructive commentary. Louis Schroeder's amazing linguistic abilities and familiarity with classical cultures and languages enabled him to read my entire manuscript with generosity, perspicacity, and sound, good judgment and to compile this book's bibliography. Heath Martin, moreover, edited the manuscript with the eagle eye of an experienced and professional editor; I can not thank him enough for his tireless efforts.

Then there are those faculty colleagues who took time away from their own busy careers to read and comment on the entire manuscript to whom any amount of praise and gratitude could never suffice. I take great pleasure, nevertheless, in thanking Richard Dammers, whose background in Classics was always reinforcing; Russell Rutter, who listened to me rant and rave about Aeneas through many years of evolution and who one day most happily surprised me by asking to read the whole manuscript (I thought my endless oral discourse had surely exhausted his curiosity, but Russ is a special treasure); and Carl Springer, whose abundant and comprehensive knowledge of the classical world have helped determine the shape of the entire project and whose humanity is boundless (his invitation, for example, to fill in for him as instructor of intermediate and advanced courses in Vergil at I.S.U. while he and Avery were on sabbatical leave one semester was crucial to whatever success this project may enjoy; for it was during this period that I was able to carry out close readings of the *Aeneid*, the *Eclogues*, and the *Georgics* in their original Latin).

I am particularly pleased to be able to thank publicly the members of my family, who have steadfastly maintained confidence in my ability to bring this project into being: my sisters, Ruth Ann and Rhonda Elizabeth; my brother, Granville Blaine Jr., who has read and commented insightfully on every stage of this project; and my brother-in-law, Samuel Ray Upton.

Sherry Sharp, my typist, has made me "look good" for almost fifteen years and has constantly given me moral support. Ronald D. Frazier made the professional reproduction of the art work used in the figures of this text look much easier than I am sure it was. Carol Wallace Orr, former director of the University of Tennessee Press, took a concerted interest in my work early on in the evolution of this project; her encouragement and counsel were a most welcome and positive influence at a formative stage. For their close attention to this manuscript I am most grateful to Stan Ivester, the press's managing editor, and to editors Scot Danforth and Mavis Bryant. But the person whose intelligence, wit, and wisdom have exercised a timely and most salubrious effect upon me and this text is the press's acquisitions editor, Joyce Harrison. The three distinguished readers of *The American Aeneas* for the press, Emory Elliott, Carl J. Richard, and George Hutchinson, demonstrated great concern in their evaluations for the improvement of this text, as I took to heart all of their most constructive and judicious suggestions.

Their insight and care have made of *The American Aeneas* a much more readable book. For his most healthy stewardship of this project (i.e., for his most benevolent and magnanimous attitude toward me and my work), I am grateful, beyond measure, to Emory Elliott, great soul that he is!

And finally I wish to express my heartfelt appreciation to the one person who has walked with me every step of the way since I began to carve the figure out of the stone and whose enthusiasm has matched my own, Mary Ruth Ryder. Mary has always been, and I can think of no better, more accurate description, my Muse.

For their kind permission to reprint portions of this manuscript which first appeared among their pages, I am grateful to several literary journals. As well I feel obligated to thank these journals for having faith in the value of my work, by allowing it to appear at all. Indeed, as I indicated earlier, my work has not often found a home in journals of American literary criticism. For example, one vehicle of American literary criticism reported I had "nothing new to offer" regarding interpretation of Hawthorne's "My Kinsman Major Molineau," when my own research had taught me that no one else had made a connection between Hawthorne's "Kinsman" and Vergil's *Aeneid*. I make much of this happenstance (there were many other such occurrences) because it is, I think, symptomatic of the present-day hegemony of the Adamic myth. In any event, *Studies in Philology* has permitted the reprinting of large portions of "Jerome in Colonial New England: Edward Taylor's Attitude Toward Classical Paganism" in chapter 2; *Eighteenth-Century Studies*, of "Phillis Wheatley's Subversive Pastoral" as a long section of chapter 4; and *Classical and Modern Literature, A Quarterly*, of a version of "Hawthorne's 'Kinsman' and Vergil's *Aeneid*" as Chapter 8. I am also grateful to the Yale University Art Gallery for permission to represent Eunice Bourne's *The Fishing Lady* and to Richard Hamilton, governor of the Penobscot Nation, for allowing me to reprint the "Penobscot Broadside," and for making me feel like a "brother" one winter day in Maine at the end of which he handed me a copy of the broadside.

All translations in this volume are my own, as so are all errors. I have chosen to use Loeb editions for most of the Latin authors—even though my colleagues in classical studies may have preferred me to have used more scholarly editions—because these editions are readily available to my colleagues in American studies.

Introduction

The Quest for the American Aeneas

This volume exposes a significant cultural blindness within American consciousness. At least since the mid 1780s, American culture has been dominated by a mode of discourse whose domination is the principal cause of this cultural blindness and which is commonly referred to by the phrase "the myth of Adam." This mode of discourse, or thought engaged as social praxis, derives its authority largely from the texts of the Judaeo-Christian tradition, the Old and New Testaments. Perhaps the best single explication of how the Adamic myth operates within American culture may be found in R. W. B. Lewis's *The American Adam: Innocence, Tragedy and Tradition in the Nineteenth Century* (1955). Among the many excellencies of this book is Lewis's declaration that "We stand in need of more stirring impulsions, of greater perspectives and more penetrating controversies" (10). Explicit in this statement is its author's own testimony that *The American Adam* does not address the range of the American self.

Yet many Americanists have proceeded as if the idea of an Adamic American self does suggest the totality of Americanness. For example, in the 1970s, Sacvan Bercovitch published two books, *The Puritan Origins of the American Self* (1975) and *The American Jeremiad* (1978). In these works, Bercovitch refines tenets of the Adamic myth, demonstrating that the jeremiad persisted into the nineteenth century as a positive mode of reaffirming the American adventure into the wilderness. In *The Puritan Ordeal* (1989), Andrew Delbanco burrows even more deeply into the Adamic myth when he resurrects Perry Miller's view of the jeremiad, in opposition to Bercovitch's, as a negative mode of admonitory lamentation.

In the 1990s, however, Bercovitch himself recognized that the Adamic myth is inadequate to explain the idea of Americanness. As editor of the new *Cambridge History of American Literature*, his stance is "to make a virtue of dissensus" (634) or to promote, for the time being, "a Babel of contending approaches" (633). From this contention may emerge, at some future time, "a new coherence in the study of American literature and culture" (653).

In "The Problem of Ideology in American Literary History," perhaps Bercovitch's most substantial apologia for dissensus, he argues eloquently:

> To denounce a king through precepts derived from the divine right of kings is to define government itself as monarchical; just as to denounce immoral Christians by contrast with the sacred example of Christ is to sacralize Christian morality. To define injustice through particular violations of free enterprise . . . is to consecrate free enterprise as *the* just society. (644)

If the above is true—that is, if defining a particular ideology in terms of that same ideology is to become entrapped within that particular ideology—then it follows that defining American literature and culture in terms of the Adamic myth is to legitimate the Judaeo-Christian *Weltanschauung* (world view) as *the* Weltanschauung for American literature and culture. To do so excludes alternative modes of discourse, producing a cultural blindness. Just such a cultural blindness has precluded recognition of the classical origins of the American self.

Bercovitch certainly is not alone in exemplifying this cultural blindness. Indeed, I myself had internalized this viewpoint. Some time ago, I wrote a twenty-page essay called "Classical Allusions in Edward Taylor's Poetry." In it I described what I thought was Taylor's essentially negative attitude toward all things classical (hardly guessing then that I had been programmed by the hegemonic Adamic myth to arrive at just such a determination). The response of one scholarly journal's reader was typical of all evaluations the essay received. It had

> nothing of importance to say, even anything that could not be predicted of Taylor. Taylor's use of classical material was quite in the standard Puritan manner: the old gods became devils, classical places are bad places, etc. Anyone who remembers a bit of Milton is prepared for that sort of relegation-usage.

This last comment left a lingering question in my mind. In my early study of Milton, I had thought that—in *Paradise Lost,* for example—his debt to classicism, and especially to Vergil's *Aeneid,* was self-avowedly considerable. At the same time, it began to dawn on me that a cursory reading of Taylor would not produce either a fair reading of the Puritan minister and physic of Westfield, Massachusetts, or a piece of scholarship to which I would wish to sign my name. Resolved not to lose the energy that I already had put into this project, and determined to produce a competent essay, I embarked on a regimen of preparation and reevaluation which led directly to the present volume. After a concentrated reading, during which I catalogued well over six dozen concrete, definitely classical references, I began to understand that the poems themselves contradicted my initial thesis. Taylor did *not* loathe all things classical. In fact, more often—much more often—he appeared to enjoy classical thought and letters, actually allowing this body of "pagan" knowledge to instruct and to shape many of his private colloquies with his God (I refer, of course, to his two series of *Preparatory Meditations*). Having completely altered my perspective on Taylor's assimilation of classicism, I constructed a wholly new essay emphasizing Taylor's positive attitude; this piece met with more favorable readings.

It occurred to me that, if I had been misled about Taylor, perhaps I had been misled about other authors or even literary and/or cultural paradigms. Why, for instance, does Cotton Mather, on the one hand, caution young ministers in *Manuductio ad Ministerium (Manual for Ministers)* not to converse "with muses that are no better than harlots" and, on the other, depend so unabashedly upon Vergil's *Aeneid* in the composition of his major publication, *Magnalia Christi Americana?* It appeared that the literature written by Early Americans, particularly, reflects more complex attitudes than students of Early American studies have recognized.

That Early Americanists and Americanists in general so concentrate their efforts within the boundaries of the Adamic myth's tenets has led several students of American Studies to lodge substantial objections to a perceived lack of balance in the field. In 1978, William C. Spengeman declared, "Each year we [in American Studies] have said more and more about less and less, until we now find ourselves left with a half-dozen masterpieces and little more to say about them" (131). At that time, American Studies as a field was arguably moribund.

More recent attempts to enlarge the canon of American literature to include writings by women, Native Americans, African Americans, and Hispanic Americans, among other minorities, promise some degree of healing. Bercovitch's "Babel of contending approaches," invigorating as it is, nevertheless has led at least one critic to express considerable skepticism regarding the future of a state of dissensus. In a significant collection of essays, *New Americanists: Revisionist Interventions into the Canon,* editor Donald E. Pease states in his introduction: "Without any context within which dissensus Americanists can argue among themselves over the outcomes of the conflicts among dominant and subordinate social groups, among the rhetorics most effective for the reconstruction of American history, or among the shapes emergent historical forces should assume, the new dissensus only continues the old consensus—but under the displaced form of its breakup into unrelated fragments" (22–23).[1] Perhaps a recognition of America's classical origins will help us discover new coherence and hence generate the balance so regrettably lacking in American Studies today.

An inevitable concomitant of an attempt to delineate the classical origins of the American self (in other words, to recover the discourse of the American Aeneas) is a critique of the hegemony of the Adamic mode of discourse. This critique, however, should not be construed as a negative assessment of the work of other students of American letters and culture. How could I censure the work of others when I myself have exemplified the dominance of the American Adam? Any recovery of America's classical mode of discourse must challenge the authority of the present, "ruling" mode. Only the hegemony of that ruling mode is at stake, not the mode itself; for these two modes, the Adamic and the classical, always stand in tension with one another, neither ever eliminating the other.

My desideratum is that this recovery will infuse the study of American letters and culture with new vitality. In *The Culture of Criticism and the Criticism of Culture*, Giles Gunn devotes a chapter to "American Studies as Cultural Criticism." In it he posits that "the particular field itself can only advance if one is able to measure the implications of particular [i.e., cultural] contributions to its practice for an understanding of the field's larger meaning and purpose" (148). Recovery of the particular contribution of classicism to Early American culture should enable Americanists "to measure the implications" suggested by the American Aeneas and so help delineate "the field's larger meaning and purpose."

Cultural Blindness

To judge by their titles, many recent works seem to herald a new recognition of the role of classical learning in Early American culture: Paul Lucas, *American Odyssey;* Meyer Reinhold, *Classica Americana;* Mary R. Ryder, *Willa Cather and Classical Myth;* William L. Vance, *America's Rome;* and Garry Wills, *Cincinnatus*. Yet, except for Ryder's learned volume,[2] none of these works is informed by an understanding of the dialectic of Adam and Aeneas.

For example, little could be farther from the truth than Vance's assertion that "Rome before 1870 was the place most alien to America" (xx). In fact, Rome was implicated in Peter Martyr's observation, in the first of his Latin *Decades* (1516), that Columbus and his band of sailors found conditions at Hispaniola (present-day Haiti and the Dominican Republic) "as when Eneas arrived in Italy, he founde *Latium* divided into many kyngedomes and provinces, as Latium, Mezeutium [*sic*], Turnum, and Tarchontem, which were seperated with narow boundes" (Eden, *First Three English Books* 66).

Indeed, Rome and her great poem, Vergil's *Aeneid*, were anything but alien to Early Americans, as this book will demonstrate. Vergil's land to the west, Hesperia (e.g., *Aeneid*, I, 530), which is the classical Greek (or Trojan) name for Italy, is not too far from Martyr's imagination, as he promises, in a passage preceding the above quote, to describe "the Ilandes of the West Ocean" (Eden 65).

The simple fact is that, years before the Puritan settlers identified their own errand in the American wilderness, Englishmen (not to mention Italians, Portuguese, Frenchmen, and Spaniards, among other Europeans) were disposed to see the New World in terms of Aeneas's perilous sea voyage to discover the land to the west. In book X of Martyr's second *Decade*, for example, he states, "I remember . . . when I was a chylde . . . I readde in the poet Virgyl howe . . . ," etc. (135). To young students of Europe during the late fifteenth and sixteenth centuries, Aeneas epitomized the sailor who struck out across dangerous, uncharted seas to discover a new land in which to build a new civilization.

Vance correctly points out that "the Roman Republic filled the imagination of Adams and Jefferson during the same decades that American artists were first seeing the actual ruins of the Empire" (xxiii). Admittedly, Vance's objective is to emphasize the preoccupation of American artists with ancient Rome, but, throughout his substantial two volumes, he makes authoritative observations regarding the incontestable influence of the ancient city's culture on American culture. Yet he appears unable to ask *why* Adams and Jefferson were so concerned with things classical. Nor does he investigate *why*, in his words, "often enough, in 1848 as in 1918 and 1948, American disciples of freedom could declare that only in Rome did they find their 'true America'" (xxiv). A major concern of this volume will be to pursue precisely such questions. Why were the imaginations of Jefferson and Adams fixed upon Roman republicanism? Why did and do "American disciples of freedom" locate their "true America" in Roman cultural values?

A cultural blindness prevents Vance and others from acknowledging the classical origins of the American self. From the earliest days when an "America" emerged as an idea, that entity, rather than being alienated from classicism, was conceived in terms classical as well as biblical. Vance, like most readers of earlier American culture and literature today, attempts to assess the field only in terms of the Adamic myth.

All the problems attendant upon identifying only half the dialectic and overlooking the classical component are already evident in R. W. B. Lewis's "Prologue: the Myth and the Dialogue," which introduces his highly influential *American Adam*. This book established the central terms according to which subsequent analysts of American culture have evaluated the products of the American creative imagination.

Lewis chooses to cover the period 1820–60 in America; this is the very period within which the Adamic myth *apparently* achieved absolute ascendancy over the classical mode of discourse. This ascendancy was achieved, it will be argued below, through a radical shift in discourse that valorized the Adamic myth. It is not surprising, then, that this period in American letters provides such fertile ground for the myth of Adam.

Lewis does not tell enough of the tale, however, when he focuses on the Adamic myth as having "finally yielded up its [the nineteenth-century American culture's] own special identifying 'myth'" (3). For, as will be shown, the myth of Aeneas then, and now, remained in place beneath the more visible Adamic myth. Ironically, Lewis selects illustrations from Cicero and Vergil as strong indicators that the ideals of Augustan Rome are foreign to the tenets of the Adamic myth and hence to those of America (4). In fact, to a great extent, those Roman ideals of political and moral action shaped the lives and characters of the authors of the United States Constitution, as Carl Richard in *The Founders and the Classics* (1994) vividly demonstrates.

Especially poignant is Lewis's explicit recognition, first, that the Adamic myth was "during earlier stages . . . somewhat submerged, making itself felt as an atmospheric presence, a motivating idea" (6); and, second, that it is necessary to

> distinguish between the notion of progress toward perfection and the notion of primitive Adamic perfection. Both ideas were current, and they overlapped and intertwined. On the whole, however, we may settle for the paradox that the more intense the belief in progress toward perfection, the more it stimulated a belief in a present primal perfection. (5n)

Here Lewis has conceded that his approach has its limitations—that the Adamic myth is insufficient to explain some observable characteristics. But why should critics of American literature be satisfied with paradox? The Vergilian mythic mode, which Lewis earlier discounted, explains why the Adamic myth lay submerged during an earlier time and also accounts for the urgency toward secular perfection inherent within the American character.

The tendency to conjure up the classical past (ultimately the source of two substantives within Lewis's subtitle, *tradition* and *tragedy*) and then to disavow it constitutes a pattern of acceptance and denial that we shall note repeatedly in this book. Here we see an entrenched refusal to entertain the possibility that the idea of "Americanness" might be rooted in classical sources. This pattern is characteristic of many later studies of American literature, with three notable exceptions: Leo Marx, *The Machine in the Garden: Technology and the Pastoral Ideal in America* (1964); Lewis P. Simpson, *The Dispossessed Garden: Pastoral and History in Southern Literature* (1975); and Richard, *The Founders and the Classics*.

By itself, Lewis's *American Adam* is a brilliant and essentially accurate (as far as it goes) examination of the conditions of nineteenth-century American letters. The quarrel here is not with that book or its author. The problems arise as functions of the decisive influence exerted by this approach—and by the example of Perry Miller—on American Studies in general.[3] So influential has this approach been that it (i.e., the approach, not the book or Lewis) has exercised a monolithic hegemony within the field. As a result, the myth of Aeneas, which has been at work shaping the American self since the early 1500s, has remained nearly invisible.

Some years ago, in a fine collection of essays entitled *Classical Traditions in Early America*, Meyer Reinhold issued a challenge: no study of classicism in Early America had yet investigated "the depth of the classical influences on Early Americans, and the extent to which this knowledge of the Classics was determinative of thought and action" (Eadie 14). While providing a wealth of knowledge and sources (these inform portions of the present volume), *Classical Traditions* does not arrive at any useful paradigm for getting at what Reinhold recognized was the crucial question: how did Early Americans internalize their classical knowledge in such a manner that this learning "was determinative of thought and action"? As one response to this question, the present book suggests how many literate Early Americans, from 1500 to 1800 in particular, internalized their classical learning.

In *Professing Literature*, Graff traces the post–World War I failure to discover a model for the field of American Studies and laments its lack of organization (209–25). Such a model is still lacking. Perhaps the dialectic between the myths of Aeneas and Adam can suggest a suitable paradeictic (model used as argument). Poirier, in *The Renewal of Literature*, offers a fascinating approach which uses Emerson's thought as a means toward rediscovering what literature and reading are and, more particularly, what American literature and American reading may become. One passage from Poirier's volume strikingly anticipates the gist of the present volume:

> Emerson's belief that Aristophanes [among other ancient authors] is "full of American history," that we are here not to read but to "become" Dante, that we can foresee ourselves while being part of the "old paternal mind"—the implication is that the New World offers an opportunity less to disown the Old than to rediscover its true origins otherwise obscured within encrustations of acquired culture. To be worthy of the New World, any "new world," it is necessary to imagine what it was like when the old world was also new. (45–46)

Perhaps one of those "encrustations of acquired culture," the hegemony of the Adamic myth, has impeded the effort to "imagine what it was like" for Early Americans to discover to themselves and to the entire globe the "newness" of the Old World in conjunction with the "newness" of their contemporary world.

Another interpreter of American culture who comes tantalizingly close to recovering the paradeictic of the American Aeneas is Sacvan Bercovitch. In "Puritan Vision of the New World," Bercovitch observes that the second and third generations of New Englanders "enshrined their forebears . . . as giants of a golden age, like Vergil's Legendary Trojans entering upon the future site of Rome" (39). Of Cotton Mather's *Magnalia Christi Americana*, Bercovitch says that Mather hoped to create a "New World epic" which would be greater than Vergil's *Aeneid* (42). In his earlier *Puritan Origins*, Bercovitch makes the same observation (that Mather "conceived the *Magnalia* as a greater *Aeneid*"); then he points to Mather's characterization of John Winthrop as an American Nehemiah, a pious, Christianized Aeneas, who is "destined by Jove/ Jehova [*sic*] to harrow hell, to rebuild the walls of Latium [Ilios/ Rome?] and change the course of civilization" (66). The powerful rhetoric Bercovitch adopts here is arresting; one might expect him to proceed apace toward discovery of the classical origins of the American self. Rather than unearth the American Aeneas, however, he soon drops the classical connection and invests his energies in tracing the Puritan origins of the American self.

Parallels to Aeneas

Despite their evident cultural blindness, the above authors eloquently set the stage for a thoroughgoing investigation of the classical origins of the American self. What precisely did Vergil's hero, Aeneas, and his poem, the *Aeneid*, suggest to migrating and settling Early Americans and to Americans of the Revolutionary era? One of the most obvious parallels between Vergil's poem and the colonization of the New World is the idea of founding a new land to the west. This theme pervades the *Aeneid*, as it does the thought and literature of Early America. This idea was not shared by Europeans who remained behind.

The designation of a land to the west describes what actually happened, whereas the Adamic myth's movement of the Israelites out of Egypt to the land of Canaan to the *east* demands a migration in the wrong direction. Recall that, even before Puritanism began in England, Eden (in 1555) "Englished" the *Decades* of Peter Martyr. Martyr, in the opening section of the *Decades*, vows to trace the voyages of Columbus to "the Ilandes of the West Ocean." This same Martyr narrates Columbus's landing in terms of Aeneas's arrival on the strand of Latium.

In a rather long Latin poem prefacing Cotton Mather's *Magnalia*, Henry Selyns, a New York minister of the Dutch Reformed Church, quotes a phrase from a passage of the *Aeneid* (II, 274). Here Aeneas recalls a dream in which the defeated Hector admonishes Vergil's hero to leave Troy immediately—i.e., to embark upon his journey to establish Rome. In this very dream, Hector, the epitome of Trojan virtue, invests Aeneas with virtue, or *pietas* (devotion to the gods, to family, and to country). Mather, too, quite early in his "General Introduction," quotes a passage from Vergil, but he alters the Mantuan's text. The original describes Aeneas as a man distinguished by his devotion ("insignem pietate virum"; I, 10), but Mather renders Vergil's singulars as plurals: "*men* distinguished by *their* devotion" ("Insignes Pietate Viros"; 1852, 25). Thus Mather appropriates Vergil's supreme virtue to characterize the New World settlers. Selyns's quotation serves as a prelude for Mather's, emphasizing the importance of Vergil's poem to *Magnalia*, an indispensable text in the search for the American self.

In August 1777, George Washington wrote of the American effort to counter General James Burgoyne's threat to New York State, "The associated armies in America act from the noblest motives, liberty. The same principles actuated the arms of Rome in the days of her glory; and the same object was the reward of Roman valour" (Gummere 18). The "Roman valour" of which Washington speaks may be identified as that same *pietas* which motivates Vergil's Aeneas.

In 1807, when Joel Barlow published *The Columbiad*, his revised and expanded version of the 1787 *The Vision of Columbus*, he opened the poem with the couplet: "I sing the Mariner who first unfurl'd/ An eastern banner o'er the western world" (Barlow, *Poetry* 413). The echo of Vergil's opening for the *Aeneid*, "Arma virumque cano" (Arms and the man I sing), is unmistakable.

Like Aeneas before him, Barlow's hero Columbus travels westward to open a new land. This land has as its guardian genius Hesper, or the West; this land, Barlow explains, may be called *Columbia* or *Hesperia* (420n.), this last noun echoing Vergil's naming of "Hesperia" or Italy (I, 530) as the object of Aeneas's quest. From the opening of the New World to Europe until the period of the Revolution, then, this momentous adventure was understood in terms of Vergil's text.

Many settlers among the first migrants to New England (largely Puritans at first) had a high moral purpose in carrying out their endeavor, much like Aeneas and his followers. Christian improvers upon the *Aeneid*, such as Bernardus Silvestris (the twelfth-century Christian humanist of Tours) and Cristoforo Landino (fifteenth century), formulated what became the standard moral interpretation of the *Aeneid* until the seventeenth century. The message was that Aeneas's journey from the burning towers of Ilios westward to the founding of Rome represented the process of maturation. In this schema, for example, even Aeneas's dalliance with Dido is explained away as but another step toward the hero's acquisition of wisdom. In Silvestris's view, Aeneas "leaves Dido and puts passion aside."[4] This sort of Christianizing of a pagan poem made more appealing, at least to the first generation of Puritans, the virtues evident in Vergil's work.

Before the 1650s, most authorities in fact took it for granted that the classical authors had purloined much of their material from the Bible (especially the Old Testament). In his 1632 commentary on the first book of Ovid's *Metamorphoses*, for instance, George Sandys identifies Ovid's description of the Creation as essentially derived from Genesis. The ancient poet appears "so consonant to the truth [i.e., the biblical rendering]," Sandys observes, that "he had either seene the Books of Moses, or receaved that doctrine by tradition" (49). At another point in this same commentary, Sandys reveals the standard mode of the Christian improver upon the ancient authors when he declares, "But to conforme the fable to the truth: Prometheus signifies Providence, and Minerva Heavenly Wisdom: by God's providence therefore and wisdome Man was created" (58). Indeed, in Sandys's view, Jove becomes "the counterfeit Jehovah" (61).

Sir Walter Raleigh, in his exceedingly popular *History of the World* (1614; well known to such authors as Edward Taylor and Cotton Mather), condemns this (alleged) theft of biblical material to flesh out pagan authors' concoctions: "Besides, whence had Homer his invention of Alcinous Gardens, as Justin Martyr noteth, but out of Moses his description of Paradise? Gen. 2. and whence are their praises of the Elizian fields, but out of the story of Paradise?" Gathering momentum, Raleigh continues:

> And it is manifest, that Orpheus, Linus, Pindarus, Hesiodus, and Homer, and after him Ovid, one out of another, and all these together with Pythagoras and Plato, and their Sectatours [disciples], did greatly enrich their inventions, by venting the stolne Treasures of Divine Letters, altered by prophane additions, and disguised by poetical conversions as if they had bin conceived out of their owne speculations and contemplations. (32–33)

Although there is no evidence proving that any of the classical authors named by Raleigh ever saw the Hebrew Holy Scriptures, and although the myth that Moses penned the first five books of the Old Testament later was debunked, great effort obviously was expended throughout the Middle Ages and the Renaissance to accommodate the pagan authors to Christian thought. This prevailing attitude (not shared by all) toward the rebirth of classical learning must have made it easy for the Early American adventurer to see his own perilous voyage to the land to the west as the trip of a Christianized Aeneas. Aeneas's perilous sea journey, his high moral purpose, and his pious determination to establish New Troy, or Rome, are not too distant from the struggle in the wilderness of the displaced children of Israel (here referring metaphorically to the Puritans), the high moral aspirations of the New England "Saints," and their stubborn resolve to found New Jerusalem.

One line from the *Aeneid* could have carried considerable weight in justifying the early settlers' seizure of land from Native Americans, this purpose not so moral. In book XI of Vergil's text, Aeneas answers the Native Italians' suit for peace. In the middle of a speech in which the hero acknowledges great losses on both sides, he makes this arresting declaration: "Nec veni, nisi fata locum sedemque dedissent" (XI, 112; Nor had I come, unless the fates had given [me this] particular place and [this] settlement [or foundation]). The line implies divine ordination and, by extension, justification for assuming ownership. Do the seeds of Manifest Destiny reside in this line? A final point deserves attention. The expression "locus et sedes" commonly appears in classical rhetorics, such as Cicero's *De oratore* and Quintilian's *Institutio oratoria;* both these works were standard texts in American grammar schools from their earliest days until the 1790s. As a rhetorical expression, this phrase denotes "place and source" for argument, an application which cannot have been unknown to the author of the *Aeneid*. Nor would its rhetorical application have escaped the more perceptive students of the Latin grammar schools, to whom it could have provided a convenient rationalization for their parents' seizure of land from Native Americans.

Another parallel to Vergil's text came into play at the moment when Americans began to call themselves citizens of the United States. In book XII, Juno pleads one last time with her husband Jupiter that he not require the Native Italians to give up either their language or their nationality as Latins (ll. 823–25). To this request Jupiter assents, declaring, "Sermonem Ausonii patrium moresque tenebunt,/ utque est nomen erit" (ll. 834–35; The Ausonians [inhabitants of central and southern Italy] shall retain the language and customs of [their] fathers, and as it is, so their name shall be). Jupiter continues, however: "Hinc genus Ausonio mixtum quod sanguine surget,/ supra homines, supra ire deos pietate videbis/ nec gens ulla tuos aeque celebrabit honores" (ll. 838–40; Hence a nation will arise mixed with Ausonian blood which by its devotion [*pietas*] you will observe to move above men, [even] above gods, nor shall any nation with equality [equal to yours] celebrate your honor).

Vergil's narrative of how Latin derived from the language of the peoples of Latium and how Aeneas's descendants would keep their identification as Latins directly parallels a campaign launched by Noah Webster almost immediately after the signing, in 1783, of the Treaty of Paris ending the American Revolution. Webster sought to promote, first, a distinctively *American* English and, second, a resolve on the part of citizens of the new Republic to retain their name as *Americans*. Of even greater moment is the clear parallel between Jupiter's mixed races and the undeniable mixture, on the American strand, of peoples whose origins were English, African, Dutch, French, Italian, Spanish, and others. Another parallel exists between Jupiter's prediction that the nation Aeneas founds will rise to exalted heights and the heart-felt conviction of many Americans that they were constructing a nation destined for greatness.

Jupiter's use of the noun *pietas* signals a particularly dynamic parallel; for, in an epic whose subject is Aeneas's manifestation of this supreme Roman virtue, such usage cannot be accidental. Nor could any serious student of Vergil's poem ignore a naming of pietas. As we are about to discover, the men who constructed the United States Constitution (all of whom had attained at least the equivalent of a Latin grammar school education) did not ignore this virtue either. Indeed, the most dramatic manifestation of the unacknowledged classical half of the American self may be the way our country's designers adapted the primary virtue of Vergil's hero to the so-called "American Way." Throughout the *Aeneid*, Aeneas repeatedly displays in valorous acts and thought this highest Roman virtue of pietas, or devotion to the gods, one's family, and one's country. For those who shaped the Constitution, all of them steeped in the myth of Aeneas, the distance from pietas to the American ideal of God, Mother, and Country was short indeed.

Many of these parallels between Vergil's epic and the establishment of the American self do not have biblical parallels and bespeak a largely secular orientation. In short, for a time, the mode of the American Adam explicated well the theme of American innocence thrust into a wilderness, the consequence being an irreversible loss of innocence. Now, however, the Adamic mode does not respond fully (if it ever really did) to the less vertical, heaven-bound, more practical side of the earlier (pre-1800) American self. The gift of the Adamic myth was (and remains) largely spiritual and theocratic (e.g., lost innocence engages in futile struggle to reclaim paradise). However, the myth of Aeneas suggested to Early American writers and thinkers a political, social, and cultural ideology tinged with a spirituality wholly compatible with the evolving deism of the Enlightenment and the Age of Reason. On the one hand, then, the Adamic myth provided a universal justification for coming to the New World in order to regain a vertical paradise (finally it is not essential that this idea of paradise be Christian). On the other hand, the myth of Aeneas provided a practical, secular justification for the pursuit of a horizontal paradise imbued with the moral and spiritual virtues of Roman republicanism, as represented by Vergil's hero.

The parallel advanced by the structure of the *Aeneid* is more compatible to the American adventure than that provided by the biblical narrative. William Bradford, John Wilson, John Cotton, and Richard Mather, forced out of an intolerant England, carried their idea of God with them to the New World. Vergil's epic hero Aeneas, too, carries his family gods on his back as he leaves the burning towers of Ilios. The Puritan Fathers left their homeland under duress; Aeneas, too, is forced out of his homeland. Aeneas does not rebuild in the ashes of Troy, because he is told that it is his destiny and that of his progeny to build again in another land. Upon arrival in this new land, Aeneas encounters a people who have to be supplanted before he can take possession of the new land.

As an epic, the *Aeneid* tells the story of a nation which came to dominate the world. What Aeneas learns in the Underworld of book VI is that he is in the process of establishing not a haven for the practice of religious conscience nor even a relatively free arena for the pursuit of economic self-aggrandizement, but rather a new civilization destined to rule the known world. This passage surely prefigures America's "manifest destiny." In the nineteenth century, the objective in promulgating this doctrine was the amassing not of souls for God but of new lands to satisfy a will to power. The doctrine thinly veiled an American imperialism.

This surfacing of the "grid" (underlying cognitive structure) of the American Aeneas represents but a single instance of this myth's persistence. Many others will be noted as this volume unfolds. The tenets of the Vergilian myth include an emphasis on devotion to God, to family, and to patria or country; the narrative of a dangerous sea voyage to a land to the west; an emphasis on retaining a self-earned, independent identity and name; a dynamic thrust toward a future age of supremacy; and a secular, horizontal orientation.

The illustration from Martyr's *Decades* reveals that the myths of Adam and Aeneas worked in tandem from the beginning of American settlement. But how were the tenets of the Aeneas myth transferred to the New World? The answer to this necessary question lies in the system of education which came to be established in all the thirteen colonies, and to a lesser extent in the other British possessions of North America.

For the most part, until about 1650, no Dame Schools or Petty Schools existed. Before 1650, then, the teaching of English was largely the province of parents, who, of course, had learned to read in Britain. When Dame Schools or Petty Schools were organized to teach reading and writing in the English language and some elementary arithmetic, both girls and boys attended. After the founding of Harvard College in Massachusetts in 1636, grammar schools had to be established, based largely on English models, to prepare boys for entry into the college. (Similar grammar schools were founded later in other colonies.) Those entering Harvard had to be able to parse Vergil and speak and/or write fluent Latin; it was expected that they would be able to read New Testament Greek as well. Virtually all colleges founded later—William and Mary, Yale, Princeton, the University of Pennsylvania, Columbia, and others—had these same requirements for admission. The grammar schools had seven forms (grades), corresponding roughly to seven years. In the early forms, the curriculum was devoted largely to the study of Latin. Vergil and Cicero were studied intensively in the later forms, and in the last form some Greek (and occasionally, on demand, even some Hebrew) was introduced.

Whereas the grammar schools emphasized the study of classical languages and literature, the content of the Dame and Petty schools centered upon the Geneva Bible (until around 1720—the King James Version thereafter) and catechetical tracts such as the *New England Primer,* which reproduced the Puritan catechism.

If one made it through the Petty Schools (about three years), then, one attained a reading knowledge of English and became thoroughly steeped in the tenets of the Adamic myth. If one passed through a grammar school, at least through the sixth form, then he (almost always such a student was male) could read and even speak Latin and was thoroughly imbued with classical thought (the myth of Aeneas). To be sure, Christian thought was reinforced with "appropriate training in piety and civility," says Cremin (186).[5] Perhaps surprisingly, this curriculum within the Petty and grammar schools remained constant, for the most part, until about 1783.

Some notion of the classical virtues of pietas (not Christian Piety) and Roman republicanism must have been impressed indelibly in the minds of those who strove so diligently to memorize lengthy passages from the *Aeneid* or from Cicero's *Orationes* or his *De officiis*. Nor can the tenets of the myth of Aeneas, described above, have been missed by the more perceptive students. Of course, only those who actually parsed and memorized Vergil (and Cicero) internalized the myth of Aeneas.

Those who went only to the Petty Schools, or who failed to attend the Petty Schools at all, did not internalize classicism, unless those who could read English committed to memory such classical handbooks as William King's *Heathen Gods and Heroes* or Andrew Tooke's *Pantheon of the Heathen Gods*. Still, those who were sent abroad to English schools and those who were tutored privately in their own homes must not be discounted.

A pattern regarding the myths of Adam and Aeneas begins to emerge. Those who had access to the myth of Aeneas clearly were those who stayed in school long enough to complete most of the grammar school training either in America or abroad, or who received private tutoring. The myth of Aeneas, then, was internalized by those whom one could identify as an intellectual elite, including virtually all persons who governed the American colonies, were largely responsible for establishing social precedent, and eventually shaped the United States Constitution. To draw this conclusion is to describe conditions only before the Revolution. The conditions of education differed radically after the American Revolution. Already evident, nevertheless, is the sliding tension between the myths of Adam and Aeneas.

Derivation of the Paradeictic

Other parallels between the New World adventure and Vergil's epic abound. Among these is Hector's exhortation (some may insist, command) to Aeneas in a dream that he take his Penates (household gods) and his "fatorum comites" (companions of fate) and seek "moenia magna" (great walls, or a city) for them after a lengthy sea-wandering comes to an end (see *Aeneid*, II, 293–95). This notion of transporting gods and companions and then building a city (country) for them closely parallels the Puritans' task of transporting their religion and families across a hostile sea in order to found New Zion or New Jerusalem "on a hill." In 1784, a poet of the Revolutionary era, Phillis Wheatley, in a celebration of peace, would address the new country as "newborn Rome." Thus she tied together the two modes of discourse, the Adamic and the classical.

Vergil's hero, Aeneas, repeatedly is called *pius* when he demonstrates his devotion through careful observance of ritual behavior in celebrations of the Roman godhead. At one moment early in the epic, Vergil describes Anchises, Aeneas's father, as "O felix nati pietate" (III, 480; O blessed by the devotion of [your] son). As if to insure Aeneas's bid for divinity, his mother Venus implores Jupiter to confirm her son's eventual apotheosis. Jupiter readily responds that she herself will bear great-souled Aeneas to the stars of heaven (I, 259–60; "Feres ad sidera caeli/ magnanimum Aenean"). The obvious parallels to pious biblical figures whose behavior warrants apotheoses hardly need remarking. Such parallels as these between the Adamic and classical modes of discourse gave the Christian "improvers" of Vergil's text much ground for accommodation. These parallels surely must have diminished Christian hostility toward Vergil's pagan text, particularly among seventeenth-century Puritans.

To continue to enumerate still other parallels at this juncture would be superfluous. That so many may be drawn, however, indicates the importance of the present undertaking. Vergil's epic functioned as a basic text in the education of numerous Early Americans. The more thoughtful among them must have noticed parallels between the *Aeneid* and their developing religious and cultural consciousness within the New World setting. Nor can those more perceptive students have failed to note that their cultural predicament was unique, wholly other than that of the Europe left behind. Yet most investigators of Early American literature and culture continue to insist that colonial Americans demonstrated only derivation and imitation, reflecting their subordinate status.

Contrary to the arguments of such Early American historians as David Cressy and Richard L. Bushman, for example, the tenets of the American Aeneas strongly suggest that the culture constructed in the New World by Early Americans did not derive wholly from that of London. Cressy states, "It seems to me more appropriate to consider seventeenth-century New England as an outlier of the old country, as a detached English province, than as the seed-bed of a new nation" (viii). Yet Stephen Webb, in his book, *1676*, argues, "King Philip's War had sapped the physical (and psychic) strength of Puritanism, limited the territorial frontiers of New England, and dramatically reduced the corporate colonies' ability to resist the rising tide of English empire either politically or economically" (412).

King Philip, the chief sachem of the Algonquin Confederacy, had threatened the very existence of the New World English colonies during the years 1675 and 1676 and consequently forced a severely weakened frontier military defensive to seek military and economic intervention by Charles II. The result was a legacy of *reaction against* the authority of the crown, including the establishment of such "institutions" as "the association of taxation with representation; the introduction of general elections and popular participation at every level of the extant government; [and] revolutionary rule by committees of associators, bound by oath to resist oligarchy, monarchy, and empire" (414). Hence the Revolution of 1776 was fought in large part to regain liberties already enjoyed more than a hundred years earlier, and never forgotten. This consideration challenges Cressy's insistence upon a derivative status as characteristic of seventeenth-century New England. Curiously, Cressy does not include Webb's *1676* in his bibliography of secondary sources (306–14), although Webb's volume appeared three years before Cressy's.

Bushman, in virtual accord with Cressy, states bluntly that "America was a cultural province of London, as most of England itself was, linked by nerves and arteries to the source of cultural ideas" (367). The present recovery of Early America's classical origins, however, establishes that London was hardly "*the* [emphasis mine] source of cultural ideas." In fact, a major source of American cultural self-definition may be traced to a rearticulation of classical culture, shaped by the vicissitudes and desiderata of those participating in the New World adventure.

The tension between the myths of Adam and Aeneas characterizes "Americanness" and yields new hope for recognizing or restructuring the field of American Studies. In other words, American exceptionalism is not dead—though it is incorrect to assume that this exceptionalism at any moment indicates an utter discontinuity with British and/or Continental culture. Exceptionalism does identify a creative reshaping of those cultures, providing an alternative to Bercovitch's recommendation that chaotic "dissensus" should rule the day in American Studies.

While this study reflects nothing more than a keen eye for the obvious, the Adamic myth has exercised such hegemony, particularly within the study of American literature, that it has obscured other mythical modes, particularly that of the American Aeneas. How came the Adamic myth to enjoy such hegemony? Nothing less than a Foucauldian "epistemic mutation" accounts for the radical shift in discourse that took place after the Revolutionary War. The era before and during that war emphasized the American Aeneas, while, in the era after that war, the Adamic myth achieved ascendancy. This shift corresponds, in part, to Foucault's delineation, in *The Order of Things*, of the shift from the "classical" *episteme* (conceptual grid or cognitive infrastructure exercising subliminal controls on social praxis) characterizing much of the eighteenth century toward the "modern" episteme describing the social practice of the nineteenth and twentieth centuries to about 1950.[6] While Foucault's epistemes correctly identify movements of thought in Europe which interact with those in the

American colonies and the Early American Republic, the shift in discourse which occurs in America (between, say, 1763 and 1800) is far more "determinative of thought and action," effecting not a gradual transformation but a radical metamorphosis. In that metamorphosis, however, the "grid" of the American Aeneas remained intact.

Foucault's model of epistemic mutation (what I usually refer to as a "radical shift in discourse") serves well as a description of the apparent "loss" of the Vergilian myth. However, his epistemes are inadequate to trace the course of the interaction between Adam and Aeneas. Another paradeictic is required, and a model resembling Hegelian dialectic appears to be most useful. To Hegel, the word *dialectic*, derived from the Greek word for *logic*, refers to logical necessity and applies to the patterning of ideas *and* to the patterning of events in the real world. One identifies (isolates) an idea, such as "A" and "not A," by noting a series of conflicts between "A" and "not A" which evolve into a pair of oppositions. Out of this pair of oppositions or contradictions evolves a resolution. Here let us cast "A" and "not A" as the American Aeneas and not the American Aeneas (or the American Adam). Out of this opposition comes a resolution, the American self, a blending of the two apparently contradictory strands of Adam and Aeneas. In the Adamic strand, clearly, there are elements not true of the Aeneas strand; the Adamic strand, for example, always strives vertically, toward a paradisiacal vision of the next world, while the Aeneas strand is predominantly horizontal, or oriented toward a happy vision realizable in the secular world of actual events.

These contradictions arise out of careful scrutiny of each strand. As a result of such scrutiny, differences or conflicts become noted which expand into contradictions. Thus, it comes about that complex social relations involve these real (but often concealed) contradictions and not merely conflicts—say, among rival subgroups within rival groups (ethnic groups, for example). As such historians as Garry Wills have demonstrated, America was *invented*, rather than evolving through centuries of cultural interaction. (One example of the latter evolution is Christianity's incorporation of many classical institutions, such as the hierarchical order of the Church.) That is to say, the myths of Adam and Aeneas were applied self-consciously to the cultural undergirding of what was to become North and South America. In this book we are most concerned with that portion of the Americas which became the United States, and with the cultural rearticulation of these apparently contradictory institutions.

America's evolutionary process, then, consists of two strands, Adam and Aeneas, standing in apparent contradiction. Certainly such Puritans as Anne Bradstreet, Edward Taylor, and Cotton Mather *declared* these two strands to be in opposition. In the interaction of these two strands, ever in dynamic tension one with another, one usually achieves ascendancy, but neither ever disappears. The effort in this book, in tracing the undulating courses of both strands, is not to describe literary development but to schematize the course of an evolving American culture.

Broadly, from 1492 to 1620, both myths run alongside each other, making fecund connections but neither privileged. Then, from 1620 to about 1720, the Adamic myth is slightly valorized by the Puritan adventure. From the 1720s through the time of the construction of the United States Constitution, the Vergilian or classical mode (in the form of secular Enlightenment and Deism) dominates, and Adam effectively becomes Aeneas. Finally, from about 1790 until the present, the Adamic myth is promoted to such a degree that Aeneas yields, leaving Adam in a position of dominance.[7]

Unlike the movement of Hegel's dialectic, the resolution between Adam and Aeneas, which results in the fullest expression of the American self, does not evolve into another new idea which eventually, as analysis brings forward new conflicts, yields yet another opposition (whose resolution, upon scrutiny, yields still another set of conflicts, resulting in another opposition, and so on). Instead, the dialectic of Adam and Aeneas seeks constantly, given infinite, three-dimensional possibilities for new interplay and recombinations, to address and to serve the needs of a constantly changing cultural condition that is distinctly American. The movement here, then, is not toward new dialectics, as in Hegel; rather, it should be understood as movement within the possibilities of interplay between two dynamic, recreative strands. In other words, virtually any ethnic and/or cultural group can inscribe itself within this capacious, all-embracing dialectic, if the members of that ethnic or cultural group wish to become identified as American citizens.

Like the American Adam, the American Aeneas is a cultural phenomenon. At the present time, the most useful and most honest definition of *culture*, as a subject for analysis, is the one used by such cultural critics as Clifford Geertz and Kenneth Burke and succinctly articulated by Gunn as "systems of symbolic meaning that serve an essential functional or heuristic purpose" (164). Poirier advances an instructive variant of this definition when he describes the form of "our social and cultural fate" as "ultimately . . . the language we use in learning to know ourselves" (72). The major "languages" used by Europeans as they began to open up the New World were those rhetorical "systems of symbolic meaning" provided by the myths of Adam and Aeneas. Indeed, the dialectic (or cultural conversation) between these two systems of thought enabled European explorers to discover to themselves their "social and cultural fate[s]" in this New World adventure.

Throughout the remainder of this work, the tenets of the American Adam, generally well known, will be accepted as *données*, while those of the

American Aeneas, not so familiar, will receive almost constant statement and refinement. Although other myths of cultural identification attend those of Adam and Aeneas—those of men and women, races, oppressed and relatively unoppressed (i.e., free and unfree), housed and unhoused, rich and poor, and a host of others which contemporary dissensus doubtless will reveal—these two embody the principal determinants of American cultural response. Both are characterized always by the dynamism of renewal. Always and immediately inherent in the Adamic myth's rearticulation in terms of the New World experiment in cultural transfer (or in the chance to do "it" again and get "it" right this time) has been the notion that change will lead to improvement. It matters not that failure may (and does) occur; the dynamism of renewal holds out an ineluctable promise of success. Such a cultural dynamic is no less viable (promising) for the rearticulation of the myth of Aeneas in the New World. Simply put, this dynamism of renewal distinguishes the articulation of both these myths in Europe from their rearticulations in the New World.

At this point a few brief illustrations of this cultural dynamic (particularly the classical half) in action may be helpful; many other demonstrations, these not so brief, will be given in the remainder of this work. In the several "Complimentary Verses" which preface John Smith's *Generall Historie of Virginia, New-England . . .* (1624), Smith is compared to Jason of the Argonauts, Vulcan ("He *Vulcan* like did forge a true Plantation" [J. Smith II, 45]), Achilles, and even Caesar. In his *Of Plymouth Plantation*, William Bradford cites a passage from Peter Martyr's fifth *Decade* to illustrate how difficult it was for the earliest Spaniards to find food in the New World, thereby showing that Martyr's work, replete with comparisons linking the New World adventure to classical images and events, was known among the first literate settlers of Plymouth.

Benjamin Tompson, poet, physician, sometime mathematician, and schoolmaster to Cotton Mather, in his extant poetry speaks twice of "Aeneas in his cloak of mist" (Tompson 94 and 105) and nods toward Vergil's Dido when he describes "A FORTIFICATION AT Boston begun by Women. *Dux Foemina Facti*" (98). Tompson refers to a grisly act by hostile Native Americans in terms of Vergil's depiction of Turnus's bloody assault on Aeneas and his band (111–12). Furthermore, Cotton Mather's use of Vergilian imagery throughout book VII of *Magnalia Christi Americana* to portray hostile Native American campaigns against colonists strikingly recalls his former schoolmaster's description of Turnus's assault. These examples hardly cover the territory, and surely any Early Americanist has her or his examples to add.

As noted above, American culture has shown a strong tendency to accept or to incorporate tenets of the Aeneas myth, while at the same time or very shortly thereafter denying this acceptance. Perhaps the most obvious illustration of this pattern is visible in the establishment of the "American Way." Writers such as Cotton Mather (whose portrait of William Phips, the longest in *Magnalia*, is entitled "Pietas in Patriam"), the authors of *Pietas et Gratulatio* (a 1761 celebration of the accession of George III), and the designers of the United States Constitution all were intimately familiar with the classical tripartite structure of devotion: to the gods, to the family, and to the country. Yet, shortly after ratification of the Constitution in 1789, the source of this national cultural imperative—God, Mother, and Country—was lost sight of for over two hundred years.

The work of Edward Taylor provides an early instance of the acceptance and denial pattern. For example, his private poetry displays a decided preference for classical references, while his public sermons exhibit hostility toward the ancient body of knowledge. To be sure, this pattern of acceptance and denial was visible most clearly during and following the radical shift in discourse, after which America's classical roots were all but forgotten by the People. As we shall see, these roots were not forgotten by such authors as Emerson, Hawthorne, Melville, Thoreau, and Whitman.

It must be apparent by now that this book, while not excluding classical texts other than Vergil's *Aeneid*, does emphasize the Mantuan's epic. Vergil's *Eclogues*, too, enjoy a privileged status in the pages that follow. The fact is that, in America before 1800, the *Aeneid* and the *Eclogues* were far better known than other classical works. The text of the *Aeneid* constituted the backbone of the grammar school curriculum, and the *Eclogues* were used by students as models for composition exercises. Particularly in the colonial era, most men and women who later would make contributions to literary and/or intellectual discourse, knew the texts of Rome's epic poet about as well as the Bible (during the eighteenth century, perhaps better). One could even argue that Vergil's *Aeneid* and *Eclogues* played the same central role in disseminating the myth of Aeneas as the Bible did in disseminating the myth of Adam. Therefore it is possible to speak with almost as much facility of classical "types" as of biblical types; that is, a classical typology manifests itself, especially within Early American literature, which parallels biblical typology.

This classical typology does not parallel that of the Bible precisely. There is no Old *Aeneid* and New *Aeneid*, so there can be no antitypes paralleling those of the Old Testament and New Testament. The idea of a classical typology, as applied to American literature, nonetheless can prove useful. The case of Edward Taylor is pertinent here. Taylor is fond of drawing out classical types which parallel biblical ones. In meditation 77 of the second series of his *Preparatory Meditations*, for example, the poet writes of "The pit wherein *is* no water" (from the Geneva Bible, Zechariah 9.11.383, verso),

"Here for Companions, are Fears, Heart-Aches, Grief/ Frogs, Toads, Newts, Bats, Horrid Hob-Goblins, Ghosts" (223). These "Companions" also greeted Aeneas as he approached the first threshold upon his descent into the Underworld, or Orcus; for here the epic hero encounters "Luctus" (Grief), "ultrices . . . Curae" (avenging cares or heartaches), "Metus" (Fear), and "mala mentis/ Gaudia" (evil delights of the mind) (*Aeneid*, VI, 274–79).

Yet Samuel Mather, uncle of Cotton Mather and author of the standard Puritan handbook for typology, *The Figures or Types of the Old Testament* (1683), states unequivocally in his *Figures* (a copy of which Taylor owned and annotated), "It is not safe to make any thing a Type meerly upon our own fansies and imaginations; it is *Gods* Prerogative to make *Types*" (55). Additionally, Samuel Mather's pronouncement that "the curse of Christ will fall upon such as endeavour to restore Rome again, and raise up the Ruines that he hath brought upon it" (102) would seem to discourage use of classical allusions, certainly in positive contexts. Taylor's habitual practice of employing classical references for the purpose of informing his poetry flies in the face of what one would expect of an orthodox, Puritan minister. At the same time, such praxis illustrates still another type of interplay between classical and Adamic modes of discourse. As well Taylor has here provided an additional example of an appropriation of Vergil's text.

The *Eclogues* exercised a less general influence on the evolution of Early American thought. Even so, their use gave rise to a particularly dramatic episode that is of interest here. Grammar school imitations of the *Eclogues* gradually became a sophisticated mode of preserving a measure of the evolving American past. Between the 1720s and the 1790s, adaptations of the *Eclogues* combined with the Puritan funeral elegy to give shape to a primary manifestation of the valorization of the Aeneas myth over that of Adam. These pastoral elegies also gave their authors opportunities to publish their political views regarding a popular eighteenth-century topic, liberty.

Even earlier, the sophistication of Vergil's pastorals had been captured in historical and/or promotional tracts, such as Robert Beverley's *The History and Present State of Virginia* (1705). Beverley's *History* led the way toward a particularly piquant application of classical pastoral. Such Early Americans as Beverley, first, and later St. Jean de Crèvecoeur and Phillis Wheatley employed this classical form as a means of subversion. Wheatley's praxis of pastoral as a mode of subversion dramatizes the predicament of any intelligent member of a minority oppressed by an insensitive majority.

Vergil's *Aeneid* and *Eclogues*, then, play decisive roles in the Early American struggle toward self-definition and self-determination, forcing us to recognize them as the principal texts in America's classical origins. At the same time, we shall not ignore the parts played by other classical texts—for example, Cicero's *De officiis*.

Another way in which Vergil's texts parallel the biblical text occurs in the classical discourse's secularization of spiritual values. During the mid-eighteenth century, it will be argued, classicism became so thoroughly internalized that, particularly among the intelligentsia, it manifested itself not so much in words as in behavior. This behavior, among America's political leaders before 1800, represents an enactment of Vergil's primary virtue, *pietas*. It also bespeaks a palpable anthropocentrism (placing human beings at the center of everything), somewhat after the manner of the Greek Protagoras's dictum, "Man is the measure of all things." This anthropocentrism, whose source assuredly is Vergil's text (among other texts of the classical ancients), opposes the undeniable logocentrism of the Adamic mode. The one centers on man in *this* world, while the other directs the focus of human beings to the *next* world.

This mode of behavior greatly resembles what Charles Norris Cochrane has described in *Christianity and Classical Culture* as the embodiment of a religion of this world which derives from Vergil's idea of history in the *Aeneid* and which carries "a hidden meaning which, while it may be dimly forecast in the utterances of seers and prophets . . . , is to be fully disclosed only with the culmination of secular process in the evolution of Eternal Rome" (68). Just as Vergil's *pietas* invokes a dynamic which remains horizontal and secular, the dynamic of the Adamic myth is vertical and preternatural. The implications of this distinction are vital, for one leads to latter-day political and religious orthodoxy, while the other, always more malleable because firmly grounded in the real world, has given America its Constitution and its essentially secular way of life.

One way in which the biblical and the Vergilian texts are not parallel is that Vergil is not himself so often invoked, quoted and touted abroad as an awesome admonition to keep a potentially rowdy populace in line. Quite the contrary, Vergil's secular spirituality appears as a factor of behavior among its adherents; that is, the classical mode manifests itself as what Cochrane calls *Romanitas*, a mode of behavior which in ancient Rome permitted all races and most religions to persist, enabling all "citizens of the empire" to discover "a bond of community with one another on the plane of natural reason" (73). Another way of stating the principal difference between how the biblical and the Vergilian texts were used in social discourse is to observe that the biblical could sometimes be wielded as a sort of bludgeon (e.g. the jeremiad) against behavior not in evidence, while the points of referentiality for the classical texts direct one's focus toward behavior in evidence.

Cochrane's description of all races enjoying the freedom "to lead their own lives and achieve their own destiny" signals a promise held out by American *libertas* which was never achieved. In 1784, when Phillis Wheatley penned the line, "And new-born *Rome* shall give *Britannia* Law" (*Collected*

Works 154), she had good reason to expect that the freedom gained for this new Rome carried with it the "Law" of a "generous Spirit" (155) which would extend to the manumission of blacks. Lorenzo J. Greene, in his unsurpassed *The Negro in Colonial New England,* notes that, in Providence, Rhode Island, on the eve of the Revolution, blacks who were the property of individuals dying intestate were given their freedom: "The town, sensible of its own struggle for liberty, could not with consistency, it is said, sell these slaves again into bondage" (175). Wheatley's longtime friend and soul mate, Obour Tanner, was a resident of Providence during this period.

Greene is careful to point out that, in New England and particularly in Massachusetts, blacks enjoyed most of the same privileges under the law as whites. "The liberal sentiment which marked the eve of the American Revolution," Greene continues, "further encouraged slaves to seek their liberty by bringing suits against their masters" (183). Greene then relates the case of a slave owned by a Caleb Dodge of Beverly, Massachusetts, who won his suit against his master in 1774. But the "most celebrated of all" such suits, Greene maintains, "was the *Walker v. Jennison* case which was decided at Worcester, Massachusetts, in 1783." Walker's victory against his master "finally resulted in the emancipation of the slaves in Massachusetts" (183–84). Greene also records that "some 3,000 Negroes fought in the American ranks during the Revolution" (190). As well Wheatley may have known that the British promised freedom to an equal number of blacks if they joined *their* cause. Surrounded by such a positive atmosphere for blacks, Wheatley had good reason to expect that the American government, not yet fully established, would award the gift of freedom to all citizens—blacks included.

Had Wheatley lived (her death occurred on December 5, 1784), she would have been chagrined—even devastated—by the failure of Congress to display any sort of "generous Spirit" toward blacks. The denial of citizenship to most blacks in America with ratification of the Constitution in 1789 sweeps into the center of the Adam and Aeneas dialectic the entire issue of racial oppression. In addition, Wheatley's career testifies clearly to the efforts of an interracial community of women to overcome patriarchal oppression of women authors. Composition of her poems was constantly encouraged by Susanna Wheatley, her mistress, and by Mary Wheatley, Susanna's daughter. It is also highly probable that Phillis Wheatley's volume, *Poems on Various Subjects, Religious and Moral* (1773), never would have been published, had it not been for the financial backing of Selina Hastings, Countess of Huntingdon. The nurture Obour Tanner offered the developing and mature poet may be discerned by examining Wheatley's extensive, extant correspondence with Tanner. Since historically each strand of the Adam and Aeneas dialectic is patriarchal and racist (but need not remain so), that dialectic embraces both racial and feminist issues.

The interplay, the tension, between the classical and Adamic strands promises to be capacious—to advance a model within which Americanness, in its infinite possibility, may be delineated. If the Adamic myth (which pervades American Studies at the present time) is perceived as intrinsically metaphorical, then the tension within this model must be maintained, always. Otherwise, use of this metaphor must become reduced to literalism or idolatry. Indeed, this reduction occurred long ago. Why? Because the Adamic myth has settled so deeply into American consciousness that it has achieved the status of liturgy. A powerful attitudinal imperative sustains the hegemony of the Adamic myth, making it the only mode of discourse accepted within the field of American Studies. Thus those who would study American culture move into the field already predisposed to a cultural blindness which militates against recognition of the Aeneas myth.

This narrowness of vision contributes mightily, I think, to a regrettable pattern which many (but not enough) identify in the United States today—that learning itself is being valued less highly. Perhaps this trend began when we set aside our classical heritage. The sea-room (after Melville) of the Adam and Aeneas dialectic, however, can infuse American Studies with renewed respect for our classical origins by promoting a new model. This model is not composed of a single strand which can only direct the struggle to explore the dimensions of American culture in a linear fashion—an inevitable dead end. The image of two strands coming together, intertwining and interconnecting so as to accommodate virtually infinite possibilities, more accurately captures the dynamic of Americanness. The metaphor in my mind for this dynamic is the double helix of human DNA. Alleles situate themselves and so create the conditions leading to the myriad results of such combinations. Such possibilities match the idea of humanity itself—not too distant, I suspect, from the possibilities the designers of our Constitution intended to accommodate. Perhaps this perdurable metaphor will invigorate American Studies. Borrowing the inimitable words of Edgar Allan Poe, perhaps just such a model will enable students of American culture to journey "home/ To the glory that was Greece/ And the grandeur that was Rome." ▩

PART I

Adam and Aeneas: Circa 1500–1720

1

Translatio Cultus

Ordinarily, when speaking of a transfer of knowledge from one locale to another, from the Old World to the New, Early Americanists employ the Latin phrase *translatio studii* (transfer of an enthusiasm for a particular pursuit of knowledge). For purposes of this investigation, however, I have adopted the Latin phrase *translatio cultus* because of its greater diversity of meanings and applications. To bring over the elements of either the Adamic myth or the Aeneas myth was not merely to transfer a body of knowledge. Indeed, both "transplantings" carried with them cultural imperatives that ultimately determined the idea of the American self. Besides describing the transfer of a "mode or standard of living," in a figurative sense, *translatio cultus* denotes transplanting "the action of dwelling in a place." The denotative meaning of *cultus* obviously bears a resemblance to Foucault's definition of (cultural) *discourse* as thought engaged as social praxis. More to the point, this last definition, taken directly from *The Oxford Latin Dictionary*, focuses immediately on a "process"—the daily conduct of an Old World populace functioning in a radically altered New World environment. This understanding of the phrase urges consideration of that process by which Old World citizens settle into patterns of cultural redefinition.

Translatio cultus also can refer to the transplanting of training or education (equivalent to *translatio studii*), the transfer of "elegance of design or orderliness," and "the refining or elaborating of standards of living." Relevant in this book is yet another application of *translatio cultus:* transfer of "the worship or veneration of a deity" or of "devotion (to a dignitary, friend, etc.), loyalty, respect." This last description of the concept closely resembles the cultural imperative of pietas, or the American Way of devotion to God, Mother, and Country. With such a collection of possible uses, the term *translatio cultus* efficiently captures a range of cultural characteristics germane to the present study.

Even before Old World citizens began to settle into patterns of cultural redefinition, Peter Martyr ascribed the myths of Adam and Aeneas to the New World adventure. Thus the outlines of the American *translatio cultus* began to emerge.

Peter Martyr (1457–1526), or Pietro Martire d'Anghiera, as he was known to his Italian countrymen, has been described by Henry R. Wagner, one of his biographers, as "a kind of funnel through which information and news from Spain and the Indies was [*sic*] transmitted to Italy and news of Italy to friends in Spain" (249). This Peter Martyr should not be confused with a later Peter Martyr, the Italian reformer (Pietro Martire Vermigli, 1500–1562). The former Martyr, who composed *De Orbe Novo Decades (The Decades Concerning the New World)*, may have been more than a mere acquaintance of Christopher Columbus; the two men certainly knew each other and carried on a correspondence (Thacker 1: 39–40). Martyr's *Decades* (eight tracts in all, each *Decade* divided into ten short books) was among the very first published material claiming to describe Columbus's explorations of the New World. The work became an overnight sensation when it was published complete in 1516 (some earlier portions had appeared before this date, without Martyr's permission). By 1628, at least twelve English-language translations had been printed, along with two editions each in German, Italian, and Spanish and one each in Dutch and French. During the same period, eleven editions appeared in Latin, the language of Martyr's original composition. Martyr's *Decades* were known to the American colonists of the seventeenth and early eighteenth centuries, for William Bradford, Benjamin Tompson, and Cotton Mather all refer to him.

The English displayed by far the greatest interest in printing and reprinting the *Decades*. Richard Eden (circa 1521–76), the first English translator of the *Decades*, issued the first three *Decades*, along with other tracts not by Martyr relating to the exploration of the New World, as *The Historie of Travayle in the West and East Indies* (1555). No other Englishmen undertook either to expand upon or to supersede Eden's work during his lifetime; for some time before his death, however, Eden had been at work on a revised and expanded version of the 1555 book. This second edition appeared in 1577, a year after Eden's death, having been completed by

Richard Willes. Also in 1577, an abridgment of Eden's second edition was printed. The task of completing an English translation of the other five *Decades* was left to Michael Lok, whose translation, along with Eden's version of the first three *Decades*, first appeared in 1612. These two translations were printed together as the complete *Decades* of Peter Martyr at least three times in 1612 alone and several more times thereafter.

Because of its availability at the present time (Lok's translation of the remaining five *Decades* is difficult to find) and because of its relative popularity, this discussion focuses on Eden's translated text of Martyr's first three *Decades*. Following a Latin dedication to Philip II of Spain and Mary Tudor (at the time Philip's wife and queen), Eden offers a preface, "Richard Eden to the Reader." As one might expect, this preface urges a combined English and Spanish move toward the New World for the purpose of aggressive, even militant, proselytizing of Native Americans:

> And if it were lawful for Israel accordynge to the flesshe, to use all meanes and pollicies to buylde up the walles of earthly Hierusalem, howe muche more then ought the spiritual Israelites to use all possible meanes to buylde up the walles and temples of spirituall Hierusalem, whose fundation is Christe, wyllynge all the nations of the worlde to be buylded uppon the same. (Eden 56–57)

Unquestionably, Eden promotes the Adamic myth, in this case replete with a stubborn resolve to avoid any sort of religious tolerance.

Nevertheless, in undeniable tension with this stern articulation of the Christian mythos, stands classicism. Eden opens his preface with a reference to "the moste famous oratoure and learned Phylosopher Marcus Tullius Cicero." On this same page, he cites "the Pyramides of Egypt" and "the Mazes cauled Labyrinthi" and extols Cicero's definition of true glory in terms of euhemeristic "goddes made of men" (49). These references are employed in arguing that the Spanish feats of exploration are superior to the achievements of the ancient pagans. At one point Eden maintains that "the navigations of the Spanyardes [have] excelled the v[o]yage of Iason and the *Argonautae*" (51). Elsewhere he defends Martyr as a credible authority of his subject, asserting that Martyr "hath seene a greate parte him self," much "as Vyrgyll wryteth of Eneas, *Et quorum pars magna fui*" (49–50; And I was a great part of these things). While appearing to denigrate the achievements of the ancients in order to raise up those of the Spaniards and thereby promote New World exploration, Eden still calls upon Vergil to bolster the validity of his text.

Eden, moreover, evokes the example or authority of such figures as Aesop, Horace, Pliny, Statius, and Strabo. And he concludes his preface by citing "auncient Romans and Greekes" who recognized men of "great enterprises as might bee profitable for mankynde" by constructing elaborate images of them for prominent display. Then he exhorts his readers:

> Surely if ever sense the begynnynge of the worlde any enterpryse have deserved greate prayse as a thynge atchyved by men of heroicall vertue, doubtlesse there was never any more woorthy commendation and admiration then is that whiche owre nation [i.e., England] have attempted by the north seas to discover the mightie and rich empire of Cathay. (59)

Celebration of "heroicall vertue" also pervades Martyr's own text of the *Decades*. The words *hero*, *heroic*, and *heroical* do not appear in the Bible. Clearly, they are derived from the context of classical epic and are designed to valorize secular people.[1] Eden's preface embodies a clear tension between the myths of Adam and Aeneas and therefore serves as a fitting preparation for Eden's translation of Martyr's text. (Although this tension points toward the idea of an American self, it does not yet identify it.)

Toward the end of the third *Decade*, Martyr repeats an observation concerning Columbus's arrival at Hispaniola that he made in book I of the first *Decade* (discussed in the introduction to this volume). In the third *Decade*, however, he gives the account a special twist. Instead of describing the advent of Columbus and his men in terms of the Troy story, Martyr says that the native population must have come to Hispaniola "as is redde in the begynnynge of the Romaynes that *Eneas* of Troye aryved in the region of Italy cauled *Latium* uppon the bankes of the ryver of Tiber" (Eden 166). At the first of this book, the seventh, Eden translates Martyr's urbane Latin description of Hispaniola's neighboring islands in terms of Roman deities in a passage which displays a most felicitous, linguistic muscle flexing of Early Modern English characteristic of the Renaissance:

> The beginnynge of this narration [of book VII], shal be the particular description of the Ilande of *Hispaniola*, forasmuche as it is the heade and as it weare the principall parte of all the lyberality of the Ocean, and hath a thousande and againe a thousande fayre, pleasaunt, bewtifule, and ryche *Nereides* whiche lye aboute it on every syde, adournynge this their ladye and moother, as it were an other *Tethis* the wyfe of *Neptunus*, envyronynge her aboute, and attendynge uppon her as their queene and patronesse. (165)

Following this charming passage, Martyr calls Hispaniola "moste lyke unto the earthly paradyse," despite the fact that this paradise on earth was inhabited first after a manner not at all biblical but wholly classical. In addition to describing the first native settlement in terms of Aeneas's arrival on the shores of Latium, Martyr compares this initial settlement to "howe *Dardanus* came from *Corytho*, and *Teucrus* [Dardanus and Teucrus are two ancestors of the people of Troy] from *Creta* into Asia, and that the regyon where they placed their habitacion, was afterwarde cauled *Troianum* [Troy]" (166). The "paradise" of Hispaniola, then, is to be understood in terms classical, yielding another instance of the tension between Adamic and classical myths.

When Eden wrote in his preface of the "heroical factes [deeds] of the Spaniardes of these days," asserting that their achievements were "above the famous actes of Hercules and Saturnus" whose "glorious and vertuous enterpryses were accoumpted as goddes amonge men" (50), he may have taken from Martyr's text the hint for this euhemeristic interpretation of these classical figures as compared to Spaniards. For Martyr draws almost exactly the same portrait when, at the conclusion of the last book of the first *Decade*, he writes:

> Wherefore the Spanyardes in these owre dayes, and theyre noble enterpryses, doo not gyve place eyther to the factes [deeds] of *Saturnus*, or *Hercules*, or any other of the ancient princes of famous memorie which were canonized amonge the goddes cauled *Heroes* for theyr searchinge of newe landes and regions, and bringinge the same to better culture and civilitie. Oh God: howe large and farre shal owre posteritie see the Christian Religion extended? (105)

As if to drive home this assertion that Spanish culture and the Roman Catholic religion are superior to the religion and culture of the classical world, Martyr declares at the conclusion of book IV of the third *Decade:*

> what so ever hath heretofore byn discovered by the famous travayles of *Saturnus* and *Hercules*, with such other whom the antiquitie for their heroical factes honoured as goddes, seemeth but lyttell and obscure if it be compared to the Spanyardes victorious laboures. (156)

This assumption of cultural and spiritual ascendancy over Vergil's world was characteristic of many throughout the Renaissance, and many Americans of the colonial and Revolutionary eras had a similar attitude. However, particularly among Early Americans, a somewhat less superior tone was equally prevalent. When Early Americans compared themselves to the ancients, as they were so fond of doing, more often than not (particularly during the deistic era from the 1720s until about 1800), they made such comparisons reverentially, for they recognized that classical models were integral to their own developing identity. Martyr approaches such an attitude when he relates this moving story:

> When I was a chylde, mee thowght my bowelles grated and that my spirites were marvelouslye troubeled for verye pitie, when I readde in the poet Virgyl howe *Achemenides* [Achaemenides] was lefte of Ulysses upon the sea bankes amonge the giantes cauled *Cyclopes* where for the space of many dayes from the departinge of Ulysses untyll the commynge of *Eneas* he eate none other meate but only berryes and hawes. (135)

In recalling this incident from the latter portion of book III of the *Aeneid*, Martyr's purpose is to emphasize that the suffering of a group of "unfortunate Spanyardes" was even more horrible. If Martyr could draw such an association while sitting at his writing desk thousands of miles from the site of these dire events, how much more poignant must Vergil's passage have seemed to the children of colonists, when their parents or families, or indeed they themselves, had undergone similar experiences! Martyr only wrote about such occurrences; many Early Americans lived them.

While Martyr offers a plethora of other classical references throughout his *Decades*, one final illustration is particularly pertinent to the Adam and Aeneas dialectic. In book IX of the third *Decade*, Martyr draws an arresting parallel between the New World adventure and the beginnings of several ancient civilizations, as such history was understood in Martyr's time:

> It may suffyce to understond that there are large landes and many regyons whiche shal hereafter receave owre nations, tounges, and maners: and therewith embrase owre relygion. The Troyans dydde not soodenly replynshe Asia, the Tyrians Libia, nor the Greekes and Phoenices Spayne. (177)

While being studious to promote "owre relygion," Martyr is not at all careful to cite any Old or New Testament parallels to the transfer of European cultures to the New World. Rather, all his instructive parallels are unabashedly classical. Such an illustration points up the tension between classical and biblical modes, except that in this case the role of Adamic discourse is muted by the pertinence of examples drawn from the classical mode. Can Martyr himself be yielding here to powerful cultural imperatives, so close to embodying *translatio cultus*, explicit in classical discourse?

In the commentary on his translation of Ovid's *Metamorphoses*, George Sandys clearly remains unaware of the cultural imperatives attendant upon the dynamics of *translatio cultus*. Nevertheless, he does display an elaborate awareness of the impact of the New World adventure on the composition of his prose. Peppered throughout Sandys's fifteen essays accompanying his translations of the fifteen books of the *Metamorphoses* are concrete references to Sandys's own firsthand experience of the Virginia colony from 1623 to 1626, when he served as treasurer of the Virginia Company. Sandys translated and published the first five books in 1621 without commentary; he added the commentary only in his 1632 edition. Two more books he translated aboard ship en route to Virginia. The last eight books he completed while witnessing and even participating in the metamorphosis of the American wilderness, as trees were razed, trenches dug, clearings created, and walls and other structures erected. How incredibly pertinent to the American adventure that Sandys should have been rendering into English at that precise moment Ovid's text on mutability (see frontispiece)!

For example, in the weaving contest between Athena and Arachne which opens book VI of the *Metamorphoses*, Athena's tapestry deals with her controversy with Neptune over the naming of Athens. Of this episode, Sandys writes, "This fable decides, and by the sentence of the Gods, that a City is not to be so much renowned for riches and empire, purchased by naval victories; as by civill arts and a peaceable government." Sandys applies this political counsel "to the planting and cultivating" of new cities or countries generally (286). Surely the "planting and cultivating" of the Virginia colony was not far from his mind when he constructed this passage. Contrasting gently with the "peaceable government" Sandys hopes will characterize English efforts toward metamorphic implantation is a brief passage of Early American folklore devoted to frogs as they herald the annual change of the warmer seasons. Sandys observes, "Froggs . . . now not a little infest *Virginia* in Summer: called *Pohatans* hounds by the *English*, of their continuall yelping" (295). In his dedication to King Charles I, Sandys accounts for any defects found in his book by maintaining that it was "Sprung from the Stocke of the ancient Romanes; but bred in the New World, of the rudenesse whereof it cannot but participate; especially having Warres and Tumults to bring it to light in stead of the Muses" (3).

In the passage above, Sandys comes close to articulating the pattern of *translatio cultus*, at least the classical half of that pattern. Yet, despite Sandys's self-deprecatory pose, his translation in fact suffers few of the slings and arrows of his alleged outrageous fortune. Indeed, as we shall see, such modesty becomes thoroughly conventional among American authors, whose classicism is more than competent. For example, nearly a hundred years later, the colonial Maryland poet Richard Lewis would assert, in the "Dedication" of his translation of the Latin burlesque poem, *Muscipula*, by Edward Holdsworth (a renowned English schoolmaster of the late seventeenth century): "'To raise the Genius,' WE no Time can spare,/ A *bare Subsistence* claims our utmost

Care" (Ruland 1: 29). Lewis's disclaimer aside, somehow he found the "Time" not only to translate *Muscipula* and to pen several original poems (including the justly famous "A Journey from Patapsco in Maryland to Annapolis"), but to craft these very lines in which he alleges that a "bare Subsistence" prevents such an accomplishment.

Sandys's observation that "Warres and Tumults" brought his *Metamorphosis* (Sandys's spelling) "to light in stead of the Muses" suggests the dire circumstances and the anxiety besetting virtually all who relocated in the New World. The wonder is that Sandys got anything done on his translation; that he did so in the face of such odds is a testimony to the indomitable human *aesthetic* spirit. Moreover, Sandys's achievement points to a major premise underlying the whole of this volume. A powerful spirit of aestheticism—that is, an overwhelming motivation to create—pervaded American colonial culture, and this drive has gone largely unrecognized because of the hegemony of the Adamic myth. Far too much attention has been paid, for example, to the literature of the sermon, and especially to Puritan homiletics. This overemphasis has eclipsed other genres, particularly poetry. Even though this discussion centers on Sandys's prose commentary, perhaps consideration of his *Metamorphosis* will draw more attention to poetry. After all, Sandys's prose was provoked, ultimately, by Ovid's Latin poetry.

Another of Sandys's American references strongly suggests a continuity between Peter Martyr and Sandys. In his essay on book VII of the *Metamorphoses*, Sandys notes that he has "read in the histories of the *West Indies* of a ridiculous *Spaniard*, who with much cost and labour, travelled in quest of a fountaine, famous for rendring youth unto age" (340). Of course, Sandys is speaking of Ponce de León.

One of the translated tracts Eden anthologized in *The Historie of Travayle in the West and East Indies* describes de León's "quest" in similar terms. "The writings and Maps of Francisco López de Gómara and Sebastian Cabot" tell of "a fontayne or springe whose water is of vertue to make owlde men younge" (Eden 345). After having become "very ryche," de León discovered Florida in 1512; and, while searching for his fountain of youth, he was "wounded with an arrowe [and] dyed shortely after in the Ilande of Cuba: and so endynge his lyfe, consumed a great parte of the rychesse he had before begotten" (345–46). As Eden's 1555 anthology was issued several times before the publication of Sandys's *Ovid's Metamorphosis Englished, Mytholigiz'd and Represented in Figures* (1632), it is possible—even probable—that "the histories of the *West Indies*" which Sandys consulted were Eden's.[2]

Sandys's ties to the American strand are even stronger than his firsthand observations and his knowledge of promotional and descriptive literature indicate. His older brother, Sir Edwin Sandys, had firm connections with both the Virginia company and the Plymouth group. Edwin's association with the Plymouth "dissenters" prompted his temporary imprisonment in the Tower of London in 1621. Such close ties with Puritanism would have recommended Sandys's *Metamorphosis* to many who formed the Plymouth Plantation and to those who later made up the Massachusetts Bay Colony. Richard Beale Davis, George Sandys's principal biographer, has observed that "Sandys' Ovid . . . [was] to be found in Virginia libraries up to the Revolution" (*Intellectual Life* 3: 1344). Even so, Sandys's commentary on Ovid is perhaps its own greatest recommendation to Christian readers; for it reads like a guidebook on how to accommodate the classical mythos to that of Christianity. As such, this work, like the Christian commentaries on Vergil, would have made Ovid's pagan *Metamorphoses* considerably more attractive to Christian readers and particularly to Puritans.

That Sandys would even want to Christianize the *Metamorphoses* was in his time something of an anomaly. Pearcy, in her *Mediated Muse*, observes, "During the sixteenth century the belief that the *Metamorphoses* were the Bible through a glass, darkly, began to seem old-fashioned, even faintly ridiculous" (62). As early as the 1520s, some scholars even satirized such allegorical readings of the poem. Despite such an anti-allegorical disposition toward Ovid's *Metamorphoses*, Sandys, says Pearcy, transforms "Ovid from a medieval *auctour* whose works might be read as allegories of moral and scriptural truth . . . into a modern author whose myths were as near as mortals after Adam could come to the wisdom of the ancients" (70). Pearcy is correct in asserting that it is Ovid's wisdom which Sandys is particularly determined to pursue; for the frontispiece of Sandys's 1632 edition shows *Sapientia* (wisdom) and *Amore* (Love) holding up the "world" of Sandys's interpretation of the *Metamorphoses*. (Similar "figurings" are seen in fifteen additional elaborate engravings depicting the events of each of Ovid's fifteen books. All sixteen such illustrations precede Sandys's verse couplet translations of Ovid's Latin text.)

In a poem following this full-page engraving, Sandys declares "our Will,/ *Desire*, and *Powres* Irascible, the skill/ Of PALLAS [Pallas Athena, goddess of wisdom] orders; who the *Mind* attires/ With all *Heroick Vertues*." These "*Heroick Vertues*" Sandys maintains are taught in Ovid's "ancient Fables." In Sandys's own words, some of these fables teach "Pietie, Devotion those excite;/ These prompt to Vertue, those from Vice affright" (2). It requires little imagination here to connect Sandys's "Pietie," "Devotion," and "Vertue" to Aeneas's pietas. While Sandys does not cast his *Metamorphosis* (after Sandys's spelling) in terms of the classical epic of deeds and action, it is clear that he intends his readers to think of reading Ovid as a quest for "*Heroick Vertues*" of the mind. Sandys makes good his association of these heroic virtues with Vergil's hero, who is, of course, a man of noble and eloquent mind, as well as a man of deeds and action. Throughout his work, concrete references to Vergil's *Eclogues*, *Georgics*, and especially his *Aeneid* abound. For that matter, Sandys refers to Vergil on practically every other page of his entire prose commentary. Yet in his "empty Page (so left by the oversight of the Printer)," devoted to an enumeration of his sources, Sandys significantly does *not* name Vergil. Sandys's obvious and extensive citation of Vergil suggests that Vergil's works were so widely known that naming him as a source would have been somewhat like naming the Bible. In other words, Sandys's cavalier failure to cite the source he cited most frequently after the Bible indicates that, among the educated of Sandys's day, thorough knowledge of Vergil's texts was tantamount to *donnée*. Such dependence on Vergil, and particularly on the *Aeneid*, reinforces Sandys's calculated effort to view his commentary on Ovid's *Metamorphoses* as an exercise in moral epic.

Admittedly, when Sandys published his 1632 edition, the number of educated American colonists was small, but it would grow over the years. Recall that Davis noted that Sandys's *Metamorphosis* continued to be found in Virginia private libraries until the Revolution. American colonists reading Sandys's commentary within their own context of *translatio cultus* may well have found his highly moral "improvement" of Ovid particularly compatible with their dynamic of relocation in a new, pristine land. There some sort of moral ordering of the social structure was imperative for their survival. Sandys transmogrified Ovid in such a manner that Ovid's exercises in mutability must have proven most seductive to colonists engaged in their own process of transmogrifying the New World. In his treatment of the Proteus passage in Ovid's eighth book, for example, Sandys transforms Ovid's relatively simple portrait of Proteus as a sea god who can change his form at will (independent of divine intervention) into an arresting depiction of "a wise and politique prince; who could temper his passions, and shape his actions according to the variety of times and occasions, in the administration of government."

As the entire *Metamorphoses* is devoted to the philosophical, spiritual, metaphysical, and physical ideas of mutability, Ovid's lack of concentration on Proteus *per se* is understandable. Even so, Sandys clearly wants to ascribe to this symbol of mutability more than the office of change. Indeed, perhaps borrowing from Vergil's fourth *Georgic* the notion that Proteus may serve as a key to essential knowledge (Sandys says his source is Diodorus), Sandys shapes his Proteus into a wholly moral and judicious magistrate capable of "now using clemency, and againe severity . . . rewarding virtue and punishing offences: now proceeding by force like a Lyon; and now like a Fox with subtilty and stratagems." It seems likely that Sandys's counsel arises from his first-hand experience of the Virginia Company's attempt to establish a colony in the New World. Sandys's Proteus figures exhibit those leadership qualities of open-mindedness and fair play which have always appealed to the American mind. His ideal leaders are capable of "high undertakings"—and what greater "undertakings" were there in Sandys's day than colonizing the New World? They also had to "have a versatile witt, that can accommodate themselves to all times and dispositions" (394). As well as any today, these sentiments express the American hope for good government.

Other, less political transformations of Ovid's work surface in Sandys's determination to accommodate the pagan text to a Christian reading. In the first few lines of his verse translation, for example, Sandys (like countless translators of classical authors from the earliest days of Christianity to the present) appropriates Ovid's text to a Christian reading. Rather than Ovid's "Hanc deus et melior litem natura diremit" (Divinity, or, more fittingly, nature, settled this dispute—i.e., of chaos preceding the creation of earth and the heavens), Sandys has: "But God, the better Nature, this decides" (26). In Sandys's rendering, divinity, or God, equals "the better Nature." Thus Ovid's polytheism is transformed into a Christianized monotheism. In his commentary on this same book I, Sandys explains the "fable" of Deucalion's flood in terms of Noah and the Ark: "The Sinnes of men drew on (in which our Poet concurres with *Moses* [i.e., with the Pentateuch, in Sandys's time thought to have been written by Moses]) the generall Deluge." Sandys also seizes this opportunity to make this sweeping observation: "There is no nation so barbarous, no not the savage *Virginians*, but have some notion of so great a ruine [as the flood]" (67).

At another point, Sandys is so diligent in his efforts to Christianize Ovid that he even transmogrifies Jupiter's affair with the youth Ganymede into an instance of relatively innocuous Platonic infatuation. According to Sandys, Ganymede was not the object of Jupiter's amativeness but was "a wise and understanding Soule, uncontaminated with the vices of the flesh, and drawing neerest unto the nature of God." One might suppose that Sandys already has gone too far. But he does not stop even at this juncture. Indeed, Ganymede was seized not out of lust, but because he was by God (not Jupiter) much "beloved, and rapt into heaven (as *Enoch*, or *Eliah* in a fiery charriot)." So the fable of Ganymede is not at all about an overweening passion among the gods, but about the apotheosis of an innocent who also happens to be a paragon of wisdom, a being simply too good for this world. While today one may find this instance of "improvement" upon the pagan myths implausible, even ludicrous, perhaps those of Sandys's century had less difficulty finding it acceptable. In any event, we must admire Sandys's Herculean if misguided effort.

When Sandys embarks on a discussion of the Aeneas myth in response to Ovid's treatment beginning in book XIV, his observations take on a fascinating significance for the idea of the American Aeneas. After making the claim, startling to today's readers, that "*Dido* arrived in *Africa,* two hundred eighty and nine years after the destruction of *Troy;* being supposed to bee the Neece of *Jezabell*" (647), Sandys explicates the fable of the golden bough as an allegory of "our faith and confidence in God, without which there is no entrance into aeternall joyes." To Vergil's hero Aeneas, the golden bough is his means of entering the underworld, where he gains invaluable knowledge about his fate and that of the nation he will found, eternal Rome. Sandys, however, explains that the bough is golden "in regard of the honour and purity of that mettall"; it is hidden "in a wood, because the wisedome thereof is obscured, through so great a diversity of Sects and opinions: Nor can bee found out, if not showne by *Sibyll* [the priestess who guides Aeneas through the underworld]; which is, the will of the Allmighty revealed by his Prophets" (648).

Sandys further Christianizes the Aeneas myth when he states that others besides Vergil maintain that "*Aeneas* was conducted thether [through the underworld] by two white Doves: interpreted by some for Charity and Innocence" (648). These repeated attempts to Christianize the story of Aeneas surely would have made more palatable Sandys's subsequent pronouncements concerning the necessity for "the bond of society." This "bond of society," says Sandys, "gives to every man his owne, suppressing vice, and advancing vertue, the two maine columnes of a Common-wealth, without which it can have no supportance. Besides," Sandys continues, "man is a politicall and sociable creature: they therefore are to bee numbered among beasts who renounce society." Sandys then cites the example of the West-Indians, who are less savage than "*Polyphemus,* who," residing wholly outside the society of men, "feasts himselfe with the flesh of his quests." In Sandys's view, the Native Americans at least "onely eate their enemies, whom they have taken in the warres" (649). Despite Sandys's otherwise consistent advocacy of monarchy, here he appears to be recommending construction of a "Common-wealth" in which human beings, all of whom are "politicall and sociable creature[s]," may, or are even obliged to, participate.

Sandys's efforts to advance "Heroick Vertues," to promote a Christianized Aeneas, to celebrate epic undertakings or "enterpryses" (as Eden "Englishes" Martyr's Latin), and to promulgate sociopolitical moral principles resonate with an unintentional but nonetheless captivating Americanness. All these values eventually would become inseparably intertwined within the American self. Richard Beale Davis's judgment of Sandys's contribution to American life and literature, made some years ago, is perhaps even more applicable at the present moment:

> His stay in Virginia had enabled him to translate the fantasies of an old world while he was surrounded by the marvels of a new, and in the act of translation he brought to a creative focus the parallel interests of literature and colonization. ("America in George Sandys' 'Ovid'" 304)

I have hardly exhausted either Sandys's numerous American references (his several discussions of American flora and fauna, for example) or his "improvements" upon the ancient text. Even so, it now should be clear that Early Americans reading Sandys in terms of their cultural dynamic of *translatio cultus* would have found his commentary closely aligned with their New World adventure, particularly as this adventure continued to demonstrate the possibility of changing or altering Old World institutions and "improving" upon them in the New World.

In the years following Sandys's translation, Massachusetts Bay became a full-fledged colony, though for the most part (until 1676) independent of the Crown. As we have seen, Peter Martyr's *Decades* already had crossed the Atlantic with William Bradford of the Plymouth group. Sandys's 1632 *Ovid's Metamorphosis* surely had found its way into Early American libraries by the 1640s, if not earlier. As Sandys's influence on the development of the heroic couplet in England through Keats is well known, perhaps his *Metamorphosis* exercised some effect on the couplets of such Early American poets as Anne Bradstreet, John Saffin, and Benjamin Tompson.[3] Before examination of these poets, however, I would like to consider briefly several of the second generation of Puritans who composed almanac verse, in order to determine one path along which the classicism gleaned from New World studies made itself manifest.

The first generation of settlers in New England—that is, from about 1620 through about the 1640s—appears to have been somewhat overwhelmed by the Puritan notions of theocracy and by Ramist ideas of the uses of rhetoric. In other words, their aesthetic impulses seem effectively to have been curbed, for the most part, by such severe caveats regarding exercise of the imagination as those levied by William Perkins. As early as 1607, this patriarch of English Puritanism devoted an entire book to condemning the imaginative faculty. There he echoes the Geneva Bible when he declares, "The imaginations of mans heart are evill from his youth." According to Perkins, "Parents, Masters, Tutors, etc. . . . must all joyne hand in hand betime to stop up or at least to lessen this corrupt fountaine" (164–65). Perkins's creative use of his own imagination in the construction of this metaphor (which amounts to an inversion of the Muses' Castalian fount) notwithstanding, he continues by insisting on "the course of naturall Imagination in them [children], which without the speciall grace of God, will bring eternall condemnation both to soule and bodie" (167). Among orthodox Puritans, this attitude toward the primary aesthetic faculty persisted through the theology of Jonathan Edwards.[4]

Another casualty of the Puritan suspicion of the aesthetic faculty, not to make mention of untrammeled literary and artistic expression, was the positive use of classical sources in literary works. While this condition did prevail for a time (recall John Cotton's pronouncement in the "Preface" of the *Bay Psalm Book*, "God's altar needs not our polishings"), these restrictions soon abated—or, more accurately, always remained to some degree in contest. By the late 1640s, the aesthetic spirit in belle lettres had broken through into the public arena, in the unlikely form of almanacs produced by selected (usually graduating) students of Harvard College. As Samuel Eliot Morison has observed, "Thus the Cambridge Almanac became the annual poetry magazine of Harvard College" (*Harvard in the Seventeenth Century* 133). The selections in this poetry magazine often depended rather heavily on classical sources.

Samuel Danforth (1626–1674), orthodox Puritan minister and author of the famous homily *A Brief Recognition of New-Englands Errand into the Wilderness* (1671), also penned the first extant almanac verse. Unlike most other writers of such verse, Danforth published not one or two almanacs, but four, covering the years 1646, 1647, 1648, and 1649. In the verses from the 1647 number, wherein the poet presents a six-line stanza of iambic tetrameter couplets for each month of the year, the entry for September translates a line from Vergil's fourth *Georgic*. In the *Georgic*, this line, "Ignarum fucos pecus a praesepibus arcent," may be literally translated, The bees drive off the idle flock, the drones, from the hives; IV.168. Vergil repeats this line in *Aeneid* I, 435. Danforth's version is: "The idle drones away to drive,/ The little Bees to keep i'th hive" (Meserole 416). Delicate and sonorous as it is, this translation may well have its origins in a grammar school exercise.

In his 1648 almanac verse, Danforth continues to display sophistication in his application of classical sources. Thus, in a stanza devoted to Truth (others treat Justice, Liberty, Unity, Plenty, and so on), he alludes to "Blinde Novio," who denies that any truth that is old can still be true, simply because it is not new (Meserole 49). Probably taken from Horace's *Sermones* (talks), book I, sixth selection, this portrait of the man who will accept knowledge as valid only if it is new strikes an all-too-contemporary chord. Most proponents of present-day technology would have everyone believe, with "Novio" (or Novius in Horace, l. 40), that old knowledge—concerning the classical origins of the American self, say—no longer constitutes knowledge at all. In general, however, Danforth's classicism is overshadowed by his prominent tendency to sermonize, as for example in this couplet from the 1647 verses: "Yet know, one God, one Faith profest/ To be New-Englands interest" (Meserole 415).

Another writer of almanac verse, Samuel Bradstreet, the eldest son of Anne Bradstreet and Gov. Simon Bradstreet (1679–86 and 1689–92), appears to revel in his knowledge of classical mythology in his almanac for 1657. He opens this charming piece with a quotation from Vergil's fourth eclogue: "Aspice venturo laetentur ut omnia saeclo" (52; Behold how all things rejoice in the [golden] age [which] is going to come). Following this compellingly optimistic line, Bradstreet tells the tale (largely of the poet's own concoction) of how Tellus, Roman goddess of the earth, comes to be wooed by Apollo, the sun god, and what consequences this affair has for the coming of summer. As Tellus emerges from "her Lethargee" of winter/spring, "the Titans Herauld spies/ Herward approach; Then 'fore her shrine to bow;/ Who bids her in great Phaebus name to cheer,/ For he [i.e., Phoebus Apollo] was coming, and would soon be heer" (Meserole 427). In Ovid's *Metamorphoses*, the Titan who signals the rise of Apollo, or the sun, is Tethys (see II, 153–60), who also prepares for his setting (see II, 68–69).

"Now rapt with joy" as Apollo approaches, Tellus "on colder couch no longer will . . . lie." In anticipation, she "decks her self by christall glass aloft/ That hangs above her spangled Canopie"; that is, Tellus readies herself, as her earthen image is reflected in the ice-covered "spangled Canopie." As this Canopie begins to melt, "With pearly drops that fall from Limpid stilles/ She [Tellus] dights her too, and then with pleasance smiles." Almost immediately after the earth's thawing begins, "fleet-fire-foming-steeds," Apollo's horses, "from farre appear/ In speedy race the lofty hills to stride." The poet is careful to point out that "none but he [Apollo] can guide" these fiery steeds. As they "Scout the smoaking Plaines," smoking from the intensity of heat, "they draw near/ With burning Carre" (428), or chariot. To this point in the poem, virtually everything Bradstreet describes regarding Apollo, his activity in the heavens, and his flaming horses and chariot is an echo from Ovid's "fable" about Phaeton in *Metamorphoses* (II, 1–400).

The opening lines of the next stanza, however, with their charming archaisms, strongly suggest the influence of Edmund Spenser's calendar poetry. The entire stanza reads as follows:

> To greet his Tellus then he hies apace,
> Whom sprusely deckt he findes i'th verdant gowan
> He whilom sent. Each other doth embrace
> In loving armes, and then they sitten down
> Whilst high-born states, and low Tellurean bands
> Rejoyce to see sage Hymen joyn their hands.

The inevitable result of this fortunate union is that the earth now becomes "deckt" with flowers of all sorts and a new generation of crops arises. These crops Bradstreet describes in homespun imagery: "And buds that erst were green/ Now sucklings at her [Tellus's] milkey papps they been" (428). Whether Ovidian or Spenserian or both, Bradstreet's poem is about a metamorphosis, or renewal, which may be taken to be, as the poet's quotation from Vergil's fourth eclogue suggests, a metaphor for America's role in bringing on a new golden age. Unlike Danforth's verses in the almanacs of 1647 and 1648, Bradstreet's fable of Tellus and Apollo contains not a hint of reference to the Christian mythos. One may conclude that it is quite simply delightful, though pagan.

While the age which resounds through Daniel Russell's almanac poetry for the year 1671 is not precisely golden, it does capture expertly the spirit of classical pastoral. Russell's twelve poems, each on a separate month of the year, tell of nature's mutability. When "The Starry Monarch," the sun, "comes marching up to our North Hemisphere/ . . . his burning Beams, our Frigid Zone/ Doth Metamorphize to a temperate one." The description of the coming of the month of May is particularly charming, "for now," writes Russell, "the Meads abound/ With fragrant Roses, and with Lillies Crown'd." Now all nature affirms the proverb "that *April* Showers/ On *Maia's* Fields do rain down glittering Flowers." Like Sandys above, Russell takes time to observe croaking frogs, whose new presence signals the seasonal metamorphosis: "And now the croaking Crew, late *All a-Mort*,/ By their Night-chantings, their new life report." Like Bradstreet, Russell is enthusiastically preoccupied with renewal. June brings "smiling Fields" who "Strawb'ry Mantles now begin to wear,/ And many Orchards Cherry-cheekt appear" (Miller and Johnson 633). These festive images of nature's plenty are followed in August by pictures of harvest. This is the month when "The Noble Vines with Grapes . . . begin/ To swell with *Bacchus*, which is Barell'd in" (Miller and Johnson 634). Russell's portrait of unabashed harvesting of the fruit of "Noble Vines" for the making of Bacchus's wine certainly denies that the Puritans were too austere for an occasional celebratory lifting of the cup.

In Russell's depiction of the year's metamorphoses, however, the month of September holds even more felicity. Perhaps the most attractive description in this poem is this one of apples finally matured for the taking:

> *Pomona's* Daughters now at age, and dight
> With pleasing Beauty, Lovers do invite
> In multitudes: it's well if they escape
> From each of these, without a cruel Rape.
> (Miller and Johnson 634)

This elaborate pathetic fallacy, in which the goddess of apples yields her harvest to eager "Lovers," seems Spenserian in its exquisiteness and Vergilian in its delicate pastoralism. In its sensuousness and seductiveness, it bespeaks something other than what one thinks of as a typically Puritan attitude.

October, with its chilling winds, jars the poet out of his ideal world and into that of politics and the military. Ostensibly this political and military world is that innocuous, allegorical one of the winds. The reader finds the "*Aeolian* Lords and Commons" (or Aeolus, god of the winds, and his adjuncts and minions) and Boreas, the north wind (their general), gathering into a parliament of sorts. When Russell describes the meeting of this Parliament, however, he appears to be suggesting a commentary upon all such bodies "where it is Voted fit,/ yea and Resolv'd upon, what-ere it cost,/ They'll king it over all, and rule the Rost" (Miller and Johnson 634). The tone of this passage is just acrid enough, and therefore out of keeping with the otherwise felicitous tone of the preceding parts of the poem, that one is invited to think Russell here may be satirizing actions of Charles II's government. As Massachusetts Bay did not become a royal colony until after King Philip's War of 1676, one may conclude that Russell is content not to be subject to royal power. As winter draws nigh, the trees are now "quite bereft:/ The Fruits, those pleasant Fruits, the painted Flowers,/ The Flow'ry Meads, gay Fields, and shady Bowers" (Miller and Johnson 634–35). Russell deplores the loss of the Vergilian pastoral world and portrays Phoebus now "as if with pannick fear . . . In greatest haste, bidding the World good-night" (Miller and Johnson 635). The once "Starry Monarch" has, with the shortening days, relinquished much of his power. Yet, in the hope of renewal signaled by the constant motion of "the Worlds bright Torch," Russell assures his readers that winter cannot long endure.

The only Judaeo-Christian reference within this 1671 entry in the annals of almanac verse comes in its final stanza. Here the poet speaks of the sun's constancy: "Natures Law commands/ That fiery *Phoebus* Charriot never stands,/ Without a Miracle; but that it be,/ Still termed *Certus: semper Mobile*" (Miller and Johnson 635; certain [though] always moving). The reference to a miracle surely is an oblique allusion to Joshua at Gibeon, when, for a time, the sun allegedly stood still (see Joshua 10:12–13). Despite this single Christian reference, the world of Russell's piece, like that of Bradstreet's poem, is overwhelmingly classical. I do not mean to suggest that either Bradstreet or Russell (both were trained to be ministers) ever forgot their commitment to Puritan dogmatics, but I do wish to call attention to the classical revelry which occurs in both poems. In stark contrast to such poems as John Wilson's *Song of Deliverance* or Michael Wigglesworth's *Day of Doom*, so heavily laden with Ramean rhetoric and Calvinist dogma, these poems waft across the pages of seventeenth-century Early American literature, carrying considerable promise of a developing American aesthetic consciousness.

Samuel Eliot Morison has concluded of seventeenth-century Early American almanac verse:

> Thus the classical tradition went hand in hand with conquering Puritanism into the clearings of this vast and savage continent. The glory that was Greece shone down a path that the Roman legions had never traced; and "lightfoot nymphs" [*sic*] played hide-and-seek in the College Yard with homespun Israel, Daniel, and Nathaniel. (*Harvard in the Seventeenth Century* 138)

In this poignantly phrased characterization, redolent of *maladie du pays*, Morison effectively encapsulates the parallel movement of the myths of Adam and Aeneas until the 1670s. Despite efforts to keep them from doing so, the Adamic and the classical modes of discourse traveled beside one another along a course whose progress saw little interruption. Even the Separatist governor of the Plymouth Pilgrims, William Bradford, in his *Of Plymouth Plantation*, either refers respectfully to or quotes approvingly from the works of such classical figures as "that famous Emperor Marcus Aurelius" (18), Rome's Cato (23), "wise Seneca" (61 and 144), and the historian Pliny (145). What has not yet happened to these two modes of discourse is their inevitable blending. Daniel Russell happily presages that blending, however, when he juxtaposes the Christian story of the sun standing still at Joshua's command with the classical notion that Phoebus's chariot is ever in motion.

Classicism shows itself to even greater advantage among those poets whose body of work is more extensive. Anne Bradstreet, Benjamin Tompson, and John Saffin all demonstrate in their poetry a use of classical sources which transcends the limits of ornamentation or aesthetic delight. Each of these writers demonstrates a mature classicism which begins to suggest a blending of the Adamic and classical modes of discourse. Such blending, of course, points the way toward definition of the American self. Because Tompson's handling of epic materials represents the most extensive application of classical sources among these poets, I depart from chronology here, treating Bradstreet and Saffin first and saving Tompson for last.

Among these three poets, only Anne Bradstreet lacked the benefit of training in the Latin grammar schools. Yet her poetry displays much evidence of knowledge of non-Christian, ancient authors. John Harvard Ellis, first editor of her works, concluded of her allusions to Hesiod, Homer, Pliny, Seneca, Vergil and Ovid, among others, that, despite such references, "there is no reason to suppose that she had read their works, either in the originals or in translations." Of her use of Latin quotations, he even wrote that the "few scraps of Latin . . . found scattered through her writings" reflect only what "any one might have picked up without knowing the language" (Bradstreet xliii). I disagree with Ellis's assessment. Bradstreet was surrounded, for a considerable time, by scholarly persons and their libraries. Robert D. Arner has observed that, as the daughter of Thomas Dudley, she "had ready access to the library of the fourth earl of Lincoln at Sempringham where her father . . . served as a steward" (Levernier 190). While a member of the Plymouth colony, she carried on discourse with many well-educated, even university-trained men, any of whom gladly would have loaned the poet their books. Moreover, an examination of Bradstreet's classicism, as demonstrated in her poems, contradicts Ellis's imputation that this poet's use of the ancient, "pagan" authors was casual or amateurish.

The early poem, "An Elegie upon . . . Philip Sydney" (1638), for example, is so cloyed with classical allusions that one is tempted to think the piece an exercise demonstrating, self-consciously, the fruits of Bradstreet's study. Here she follows a catalogue of such classical figures as Achilles, Apollo, Hector, Homer, Melpomene, Scipio, and Thalia with a pair of couplets which capture quite effectively the essence of what Sidney represented to seventeenth-century Englishmen:

> Mars and *Minerva* did in one agree,
> Of Arms and Arts he should a pattern be,
> *Calliope* with *Terpsichore* did sing,
> Of Poesie, and of musick, he was King. (Bradstreet 345)

Implying descent from the Roman gods of war and wisdom, Sidney's careers in "Arms and Arts" establish a pattern to be emulated. The naming, first, of Calliope, muse of epic poetry, and, second, of Terpsichore, muse of choral song and dance, identifies Sidney's artistic attributes as writer of the epic prose romance *Arcadia* (i.e., the "New" *Arcadia*, published first in incomplete form in 1590) and as composer of songs and some sonnets, later set to music, dispersed amid the prose of *Arcadia*.

Bradstreet's later poem, "In Honour of . . . Queen Elizabeth" (1643), again shows a capacity to weave classical elements into the texture of her poetry. Bradstreet opens this memorial panegyric with the assertion that "No *Phoenix* pen" ever can describe effectively Elizabeth's accomplishments (358). The legendary Phoenix, the bird of red and gold plumage who renews itself, usually out of its own ashes, in cycles of five hundred years, served both Christians and pagans as a symbol of resurrection. Lactantius, Christian apologist of the third and early fourth centuries, is believed to be the author of *Carmen de ave phoenice* (Song About the Bird, Phoenix), a Latin poem of 170 elegiacs which adapts the legend of the bird to the Christian mythos. In the later ninth century, this work was expanded to a poem of 677 lines written in Old English. To be sure, such classical authors as Herodotus, Tacitus, and, of course, Ovid (in the *Metamorphoses*) also put pen (i.e., stylus) to paper in retelling the Phoenix legend. These Christian and classical authors probably are the "pens" to which Bradstreet alludes in her poem.

The poet develops the conceit of the Phoenix in a fascinating way in her celebration of Elizabeth I. Following the introduction of the Phoenix image, about a third of the way into the poem, Bradstreet writes, "Come shew me such a *Phoenix* if you can?/ Was ever people better rul'd then hers?/ Was ever land more happy freed from stirrs?" (359). So now Elizabeth herself has become the Phoenix, as a result of her long and successful reign. In addition to comparing Elizabeth to Minerva, an Amazon, and Zenobia, Bradstreet summons up the character of "*Dido* first Foundress of proud Carthage walls/ (Who living consummates her Funeralls),/ A great *Eliza*, but compar'd with ours,/ How vanisheth her glory, wealth and powers" (360).

Given the Phoenix comparison, the reference to Dido is particularly apposite, for, like the Phoenix, Dido perished in the flames of a pyre constructed at her own behest. Unlike Dido, the pagan, however, Elizabeth the Christian queen is, according to Bradstreet, certain to experience resurrection, like the Phoenix. Finally, Elizabeth becomes "a Phoenix Queen, so shall she be,/ Her ashes not reviv'd, more Phoenix she" (361). In other words, as Elizabeth was no pagan, she did not spring from the ashes of her "Funneralls," so to speak; as a Christian, she can expect to be resurrected following purification by flames of the great Armageddon. Upon her death, "She set, she set, like *Titan* in his waves./ No more shall rise or set so glorious sun/ Untill the heavens great revolution" (361). According to the Phoenix legend (as told by Ovid, for example), after the Phoenix has been transformed (that is, reborn), he takes his nest with his "father's" remains and dedicates it to Hyperion or to Titan—both names for the god of the sun (see *Metamorphoses* XV, 393–407). In the passage just quoted, Bradstreet's text, if not the poet herself, provides a clear example of syncretism; the classical Titan, god of the sun (a pun on Son?), blends inextricably with the Christian notion of final judgment, extending the combined classical and Christian interpretation of the Phoenix figure offered in the text.

Use of such a complex classical-Christian figure hardly suggests an amateurish performance or a merely conventional application. Bradstreet's late poem, "Contemplations," displays a similar blending of the Adamic and classical modes. Ostensibly a paean to nature's God, this meditative poem devolves into a lamentation regarding the ravages of time: "O Time the fatal wrack of mortal things/ That draws oblivions curtains over kings" (381). This bleak apostrophe, which opens the final stanza of the poem, is preceded by many charming, spirited images; interestingly, the most positive images Bradstreet invokes in this piece all owe something to classical sources. The poet opens the poem, for example, with this appealing description of dusk, appropriate to the contemplative mood: "Then *Phoebus* wanted but one hour to bed,/ The trees all richly clad, yet void of pride,/ Were gilded o're by his rich golden head" (370). Still celebrating the capacity of "the glistering Sun" to transform nature, Bradstreet, in the lively lines below, conjures up the classical figures of Aurora (or Eos), the Dawn, and Tithonus, her husband, as well as the nineteenth Psalm's "a bridegroom coming out of his chamber, and rejoiceth as a strong man to run a race":

> Thou as a Bridegroom from thy Chamber rushes,
> And as a strong man, joyes to run a race,
> The morn doth usher thee, with smiles and blushes,
> The Earth reflects her glances in thy face. (371)

Later in the poem, Bradstreet echoes this image of nature physically reflecting itself, while the poet mentally carries out her own reflective process, in this image of the denizens of the sea: "You watry folk," first "frisk to tast the air," then dive "Eftsoon to *Neptun's* glassie Hall" (378). The poet's musings upon nature, which she often sees in terms of classical imagery, usually delight her. When these meditations on nature lead her to reflect upon biblical tales or religious doctrine, however, the mood turns dark. Following a stanza in which the poet envies what she assumes to be a song in praise of God superior to her own, this one led by insects of nature (God's art, as Taylor later would say), she muses on the biblical past. Recollections of Adam and Eve and their expulsion from Paradise for their "sin" evoke memories of Cain and Abel, whose unhappy fates were to kill a brother and be his victim. Such sobering thoughts lead Bradstreet to contemplate human beings as fallen creatures, condemned by original sin. Indeed, human guilt "puts all pleasures vain unto eternal flight" (375).

Asking herself whether the earth and its plants and animals will endure the ravages of time, the poet concludes, "Nay, they shall darken, perish, fade and dye,/ And when unmade, so ever shall they lye,/ But man was made for endless immortality" (376). This last thought, lengthened appropriately by the effect of the Alexandrine, seems to bring Bradstreet out of her doldrums; the next stanza is replete with Vergilian pastoralism:

> Under the cooling shadow of a stately Elm
> Close sate I by a goodly Rivers side,
> Where gliding streams the Rocks did overwhelm;
> A lonely place, with pleasures dignifi'd.

At this moment, however, it is not this "bower of bliss" that captures the poet's attention:

> I once that lov'd the shady woods so well,
> Now thought the rivers did the trees excel,
> And if the sun would ever [always] shine, there would I dwell.

Eventually, the poet continues, all waters must travel "to *Thetis* house [a nymph who lived in the sea and was mother of Achilles], where all imbrace and greet" (377). Into this conversation with nature flies "the sweettongu'd Philomel," or the nightingale, whose affecting song causes Bradstreet to wish "me wings with her a while to take my flight" (378).

This Keatsian image contributes a melancholy piquancy to the poem, preparing the reader for yet another morose consideration of that "sinfull creature" (380), the human being. This "sinfull creature" the poet compares to a "Mariner that on smooth waves doth glide,/ Sings merrily, and steers his Barque with ease." Now the poet adds comparison to comparison, for in the very next line she begins a simile which continues for the next five lines:

> As if he had command of wind and tide,
> And now become great Master of the seas;
> But suddenly a storm spoiles all the sport,
> And makes him long for a more quiet port,
> Which 'gainst all adverse winds may serve for fort. (380)

The first line of the succeeding stanza, "So he that saileth in this world of pleasure," marks the conclusion of what is actually an epic simile. Bradstreet's use of an epic simile,[5] a structure definitely derived from classical epic, is truly ironic, especially within this particular context of finding the pleasures of this world to be but vain deceits.

On the one hand, Bradstreet summarily condemns all such pleasures of this world as misguided and not conducive to one's "divine Translation" (380) into the next world. On the other hand, America's first woman poet displays enthusiasm for the pleasures of this world, usually employing classical "fables" to convey that enthusiasm. Despite her disclaimers in "Contemplations" and in the other poems discussed above, she appears to revel in aesthetic pleasures. To be sure, one could argue that Bradstreet's portrayal of how attractive and seductive the world of the perceptions can be and then summoning strength to reject that world is in perfect keeping with the Puritan notion that the life of easeful art is probably not the best kind of life for trials of the spirit. Nevertheless, Bradstreet's rendering of the Adamic mode sounds morose, while her explanation of the secular, aesthetic world of classical discourse looks delectably appealing. The essentially classical world of earthly pleasures seems to occupy the major portion of her attention; in her own words, "Rapt were my senses at this delectable view" (370). The tension between Adam and Aeneas waxes strong in this poet's verse. At least in those poems selected for this discussion, Aeneas often appears to command center stage, even to the point that Bradstreet adapts such a classical form as the epic simile to further her comparatively ineffectual effort to promote the Adamic over the classical.

Classical discourse also dominates much of the poetry of John Saffin (1627–1710), attorney, merchant, and landowner who was born in Exeter, Devonshire, England, but lived in the Massachusetts Bay Colony from the age of seven or eight. Like Bradstreet, Saffin was less formally educated than his contemporaries, the Mathers, Edward Taylor, and Samuel Sewall. Unlike Bradstreet, however, Saffin had the benefit of a grammar school education. His classical grammar school training (under the tutelage of Charles Chauncy, later president of Harvard College) must have remained with this thoroughly secular prototype of the American businessman, for he produced love poems, elegies, and occasional verse, all replete with classical references. While Mrs. Elizabeth Hull, for example, is "Above the Nimphs, in fair and comely feature," a poem to Mrs. Winifret Griffin sees her as one in whom "Fair Venus and Minerva, both combine:/ Resplendently, to make their Graces thine" (Meserole 195).

Madame Senr, "his Vallintine," is to Saffin "The Pallas [Athena] of a Rare Mercurian Braine" (Meserole 205). Saffin's young son Simon, dead from smallpox, possessed a "pregnant witt, quick Genius, [and] parts sublime" which enabled him to be a fine student and to challenge "Pernassus clime/ And Dare Apelles" [a much celebrated, allegedly Greek painter of the fourth century B.C.] to limn his portrait (Meserole 197).

In "To His Excellency Joseph Dudley Eqr. Gover: Etc.," written in 1703 to oppose the governor's removing him from the town council of Boston, Saffin shows his classicism to best advantage. Opening this protest with an invocation to "My humble Muse Sad" (Meserole 202), Saffin maintains that the objections to his removal emanate from the "Vox Populi" (voice of the people). First he issues the governor what is tantamount to a threat—that "he that manageth Affaires of State/ Had need beware, he Don't Precipitate [i.e., provoke unwonted response]." Then Saffin pointedly calls attention to the unfortunate fate of Phaeton:

> You know what Phoebus Said to Phaeton,
> When he would Rule the Chariot of the Sun:
> Me Imitate, the Tracts thy wheeles will guide
> For bear the whip, and doe not over Ride. (Meserole 204)

This crystallization of the "fable" from Ovid (*Metamorphoses* II, 1–400) amounts to a "plea" on Saffin's part that the governor practice *sophrosyne*, or moderation; such counsel is ironic coming from Saffin, who had something of a reputation for getting himself into trouble. As a poet, Saffin nonetheless demonstrates that he is at least as well acquainted with the muse of aesthetics as Anne Bradstreet.

One may be tempted to dismiss Saffin's poems as poetic trifles. When combined with those of Bradstreet and the almanac poets treated earlier, however, they demonstrate amply that, among the Puritan colonists, the aesthetic strain was alive and doing fairly well, despite the restrictions of Ramean rhetoric and church dogmatics (regarding the faculty of the imagination, for example). Second, Saffin's poems suggest that this aesthetic strain derived largely from classical sources. In other words, a pattern begins to emerge, indicating a tension between the more aesthetically inclined myth of Aeneas and the more austere myth of Adam.

Benjamin Tompson—Harvard graduate, physician, and schoolmaster to such notables as Cotton Mather—became known as one of America's first native-born poets. In his poetry, the Adamic and the classical strains interact in such a manner as to indicate that the process of *translatio cultus* has been realized. That achievement points directly to the origins of the American self.

While the following discussion concentrates on Tompson's career as a poet, it is nevertheless necessary to focus for a time on his teaching, in order to determine what this influential man read and perhaps even shared with his students. First we shall examine Tompson's pastoralism. Before we can profitably interpret Tompson's major poems, *New Englands Crisis* and *New-Englands Tears*, however, we need to know something about King Philip's (i.e., Metacomet's) War. The events of that war precipitated these long poems, each of which was printed as a small volume in the year 1676, in Boston and London, respectively. As this schoolmaster's teaching assignments took him to grammar schools in Boston, Roxbury, Charlestown, and Braintree, Tompson probably taught a broad cross-section of the male population of the Massachusetts Bay Colony.

What Tompson may have emphasized to his pupils is indicated in two of his poems, the justly famous "The Grammarians Funeral" (1708) and the much earlier "Upon The Elaborate *Survey* of *New Englands* Passions from the *NATIVES*" (1677). "The Grammarians Funeral," written "upon the DEATH of the Venerable Mr. Ezekiel Chevers, the late and famous School-Master of Boston" (78), employs clever wordplay which captures the academic activities of declining nouns, pronouns, and adjectives, and of conjugating "The *Verbs* irregular," deponent, and regular. For example, on "A doleful Day for *Verbs*" who "look so *moody*," "*Volo* was willing, *Nolo* some-what stout,/ But

Malo rather chose, not to stand out." That is, verbs expressing positive and negative desire found themselves undermined by the less definite, and hence more ambiguous, verb *prefer*. As Tompson's somewhat irreverent, even satirical, elegy continues, Tompson claims that "Next to the Corpse [i.e., Cheever] to make th' attendance even,/ Jove, Mercury, Apollo came from heaven" (79). Significantly, no Christian figures are numbered among those in attendance. Among the authors in the mourning procession are Vergil, Cato, Ovid, and Homer. Tompson concludes that lessons about the grammar and vocabulary of Vergil and Ovid eventually lead to the composition of harmonious Latin meters, for "*Prosodia* gives the measure Word for Word" (80).

These lessons in prosodia demanded that students in the upper forms of the grammar schools imitate the verses they were reading in Latin. Such imitations themselves were, of course, to be construed in Latin. Often the choice of texts for such exercises included selections from Ovid's *Metamorphoses*, Aesop's *Fables*, Horace's *Odes*, and, on occasion, Vergil's *Eclogues*. As none of Vergil's pastorals runs to more than 111 lines, they are of good length to serve as models for a hefty exercise in Latin verse composition. Given that such an activity was expected of students in the grammar schools, one may conclude that the characteristics of the pastoral genre were thoroughly familiar to students coming out of the last form. In addition, many would have attempted to replicate the techniques of the genre. Therefore Tompson's own use of many elements from the pastoral should come as no great surprise, especially as he himself was an instructor and evaluator of students engaged in constructing Latin verses.

In addition to the classical authors named above in our discussion of "The elaborate *Survey* of *New-Englands* Passions" (1677), Tompson lists several authors of New World promotional literature, such as Samuel Purchas, Richard Hakluyt (who published a revised edition of Martyr's *De Orbe Novo* in Paris in 1587), John Smith, José de Acosta (a Spanish historian, poet, and cosmographer who, when in Peru, wrote his most famous work, *A History, Natural and Moral, of the Indies*, trans. 1604), and Peter Martyr. Of these authors who celebrate the New World adventure, Tompson writes, "Here's noveltyes and stile which all out-doe,/ Wrote by exacter hand than ever took/ *Historians Pen* since *Europe* wee forsooke" (123). Note Tompson's enthusiasm for these writers. Such enthusiasm very well may have prompted him to share these works with his students. If he did so, many Early American schoolboys of the Massachusetts Bay area became acquainted with these authors at grammar school. Enthusiasm for such writers as Martyr aside, here we note that Tompson viewed Early Americans as having forsaken Europe.

A strong strain of independence runs throughout Tompson's works. It is likely that he is the author of "A Latin Salutatory Oration of 1662," which

Peter White, editor of his complete works, includes in his edition as "Appendix C" (with a Latin translation). That text's reference to the "honored and thrice illustrious gentlemen," within whose responsibility "administering the Republic" falls (199), then, marks the first time in Tompson's extant writing that he expresses the notion of independence from Britain. In this same tract, the author asserts that, as scholars, those of the college may be called "Athenians" (205). Despite this tract's somewhat witty and even humorous tone, the author here is toying with ideas of definition, suggesting that Early Americans neither thought of themselves as merely displaced citizens of London, nor viewed their system of education as derivative of the English system. To the contrary, this tract, whether by Tompson or not, indicates that some Early Americans were defining their culture in classical terms.

In the later *New Englands Crisis*, printed in Boston in 1676, Tompson speaks on his title page of the "united *Colonyes*" which are "his *Countrey*" (82). In his preface "To the Reader," Tompson declares himself more than willing to do "any Service to my Countrey." Significantly, in the London version, considerably altered from the Boston poem and printed as *New-Englands Tears*, there are no references to united colonies, no "his Countrey," and no "my Countrey." Even the change in title from *New Englands Crisis* to *New-Englands Tears* suggests, by the shift from the direct "Crisis" to the sympathetic "Tears," that Tompson (or his printer in London) wishes not to incur the displeasure of the mother country. In other words, Tompson was perfectly candid with his American readers, who he expected at least would understand his references to "my" country, even if they did not share in this sentiment; he hardly could have expected the English audience to be so tolerant of his independent spirit. Later, in a short poem celebrating his former pupil's work, entitled *Magnalia Christi Americana*, the poet spoke of Cotton Mather's writing as a noble attempt "To raise his Countries Father's Ashes" (161). Such persistent determination to establish independence attests this poet's commitment to a metamorphosis of self and declares a viable condition of *translatio cultus*.

Tompson's evident pastoralism further indicates his commitment to an Early American culture. Eckstein, in the only critical essay on Tompson's pastoralism, holds that this poem's obvious debt to the pastoral tradition, from Theocritus to Vergil to the Renaissance, "suggests a deliberate effort on the part of the poet to adapt his poetry to the latest European literary vogue—the neoclassical imitation and adaptation of the Virgilian pastoral" (113). While I do not discount the possibility that Tompson may wish in this poem to address such a literary fashion, I do not think Tompson's delightful enumeration of Corydon, Damoetas, "Thesiylis" (probably a misprint for Thestylis; see Vergil's second eclogue, ll. 10 and 43), and Daphne, all figures from pastoral tradition, would have required such an external impetus. As a schoolmaster,

Tompson already had sufficient knowledge of pastoral to construct such a performance, with or *without* European models. The fact that his work written before this 1699 piece displays a familiarity with the pastoral genre merely reinforces the preceding conclusion. The early "Latin Salutatory Oration," for example, speaks of "learned country shepherds, having been introduced to the Master's grove" (207). Here the author captures the essence of Vergil's urbane shepherds but places them in the academic relation of master and pupil, entirely appropriate to the occasion (a commencement).

Trying his hand at composing a distich, Tompson writes: "There is many a Maecenas, many a Maro, Flaccus,/ will not be lacking, even *your fields will give you a Virgil*" (emphasis mine; 205). Obviously this writer has a sophisticated grasp of Vergilian pastoral. In an elegy from 1666 on his deceased father, Tompson describes his father's ministry to the youth of Braintree as resembling "Hyblean Bees" who bring homeward their gift of God's grace "Laden with honey" which "They knead . . . into combs upon their knees" (73). Tompson has taken his mellifluous phrase "Hyblaean Bees" directly from Vergil's first eclogue: "Hyblaeis apibus" (54; by Hyblaean bees). This phrase he has blended with Christian ritual in a way that lends aesthetic appeal to the Puritan conversion experience. As the image from Vergil clearly is subordinate to the poet's relation of how the gift of God's grace operates within the convert, the myth of Aeneas serves the Adamic myth.

The reverse is true in the Lord Bellamont "masque." That is, in this pastoral, to which characters in costume gracefully have been added, the classical overwhelms the Adamic. Tompson opens his pastoral section with this Adamic line: "An Eden So long hid you'll quickly See." This image of biblical paradise soon yields to the world of pastoral, however, in the next two lines: "Deep Mines their Riches tender; Gardens Flowers;/ Their Sprawling Vines Stretch out to make you Bowers." This Spenserian bower of bliss (a figure we have seen before) soon develops into a dramatic skit of sorts, in which Corydon, Damoetas, Amaryllis, and Daphne (all figures from Vergil's *Eclogues*) appear, appropriately attired to welcome the arrival of Lord Bellamont, who will serve as governor of New York and all New England, a daunting responsibility. As Tompson puts it, "And not one Face in all this Grand Convent/ But Smiles forth Tokens of their full Content" (158). In his helpful introductory essay, "The Achievement of Benjamin Tompson," Peter White describes the poet's personal role in the ceremony: "Dressed in the costume of Nathaniel Ward's *Simple Cobbler of Aggawam*, Tompson recited a 'rural Bitt' while shepherdesses offered the travelers nectar, flowers, and songs of welcome" (53).

Tompson's use of pastoralism for the creation of charming aesthetic effects aligns him with the almanac poets, Bradstreet, and Saffin, articulating a continuity of the classical mode which stretches from the first generation of Puritans well into the eighteenth century. With these poets we have observed several cases in which the myths of Adam and Aeneas achieve fecund interconnections. In Tompson's two long poems, however, he presents his most dynamic utilization of the myths of Adam and Aeneas. In these texts it is clear that, in Tompson's deft hands, *translatio cultus* has taken place. As already noted, *New Englands Crisis; or, A Brief Narrative, of NEW-ENGLANDS Lamentable Estate at present, compar'd with the former (but few) years of Prosperity*, printed in Boston, resounds with the sentiment of independence.

The events which led Tompson to write *New Englands Crisis* and *New-Englands Tears*, while today understood only vaguely, are amply recounted in Webb's *1676*. According to Webb, the dynamics of a concrete, separate cultural ideology and political system already were in evidence by 1676. In other words, insofar as the present study is concerned, Tompson's *Crisis* and *Tears* describe a *translatio cultus* already in place. As Webb puts it:

> The colonies had first asserted their governmental autonomy in the later 1630s. With varying success, they had defended their political freedom against the English commonwealth and protectorate in the 1650s. For more than a quarter of a century after the execution of Charles I in 1649, however, the major American colonies had mostly governed themselves. (xv)

Then, during the fateful year of 1676, "a concatenation of disasters destroyed the autonomous elites of the American colonies" (xv). These disasters included famine, epidemics, crop failures, and losses of livestock, in addition to the devastating events of Native American resistance to the onslaught of the European invasion of the Atlantic seacoast of North America (i.e., the war with King Philip, or Metacomet, chief sachem of the Algonquin Confederacy).

The fighting of 1676 alone, states Webb, "cost more lives, in proportion to population, than any other war in American history" (xv–xvi). This war—or wars, including Bacon's Revolution, the Algonquin insurgency in New England, and the combined Iroquois and British response—"eliminated so much of the capital invested in colonization by the two founding generations that per-capita income did not achieve 1675 levels again until 1775" (xvi).

Among those engaged in active revolt were blacks and women; virtually all levels of society were subsumed in the conflict. As we saw earlier with those black men who fought in the American Revolution, most of the black men who fought in the wars of 1676 "were returned to slavery, even in instances where they had been promised their freedom as the price of laying down their arms" (6). As for the women who contributed to this Revolution of 1676, they, for example, "organized public opinion against the government" of Sir William Berkeley, governor of the Virginia colony, whom they called "an Indian-lover" (5).

While these wars left the two "disciplined provinces" (xvi; Webb's phrase) of Jamaica and New York (the personal property of James, Duke of York) relatively unscathed, the failure of this revolution against British control left a residual yearning for political and ideological independence from Britain that never was satisfied until the years of the American Revolution after 1776, one hundred years later. The failure of this earlier Revolution of 1676 may be traced, for the most part, to two crucial factors. First, says Webb, "in 1676 even the oldest English colonies were as yet too underdeveloped economically to survive a year without English supplies" (10). Second, Webb continues, "the revolution of 1676 survived only as long as it retained the support of 'the middling sort.' The revolution of 1776 triumphed because it never quite lost their support" (11).

This observation by Webb is absolutely pivotal to an understanding of the radical shift in discourse which occurred after the end of the Revolutionary War. It was largely the perception of the politicians and educational reformers that, if American cultural cohesiveness was to be accomplished, *all* had to appeal to the Adamic mythos of this "middling sort"; hence the Adamic myth was raised up at the expense of the myth of Aeneas. While much more will be said below, in chapter 7, about the events leading to this epistemic mutation, the point I wish to make here is that the lessons of the Revolution of 1676 were not lost sight of in later years.

To return to the events of 1676, Webb concludes that "King Philip's War . . . sapped the physical (and psychic) strength of Puritanism, limited the territorial frontiers of New England, and dramatically reduced the corporate colonies' ability to resist the rising tide of English empire either politically or economically" (412). The sad tale of this war Tompson relates in terms of the classical epic in his two longest poems. Even so, *New Englands Crisis* opens with an Adamic verse jeremiad—a lament admonishing the contemporary generation to emulate the Puritan fathers, as their present unhappy state promises sure destruction because of their backsliding. Tompson's "Prologue" begins with a celebration of the first generation of Puritans, who lived in times when "old Pompion [the pumpkin] was a Saint/ When men far'd hardly[,] yet without complaint." This earlier period was a time when people were content to live "Under thatcht *Hutts* without the cry of *Rent*." The later period, however, saw a gradual shift in attitude, as new members of the society laid claim to the land, motivated by greed, according to Tompson. Then, "Of *Ceres* bounty form'd was many a knack/ Enough to fill *poor Robbins Almanack*," but soon "These golden times (too fortunate to hold)/ Were quickly sin'd away for love of gold." Those of the older generation "had better stomachs to religion/ Than I to capon, turkey-cock or pigeon." Tompson sums up what he sees as a golden age of Puritan austerity in this trenchant couplet: "Although men far'd and lodged very hard/ Yet innocence was better than a Guard" (84).

Tompson exhorts his Boston readers to track "themselves back to their poor beginnings" and thereon "To fear and fare upon their fruits of sinnings" (85). The poet concludes this jeremiad with this ominous couplet: "This is the *Prologue* to thy future woe,/ The *Epilogue* no mortal yet can know" (86).

Despite employing this Adamic form of the jeremiad, Tompson significantly peppers his "Prologue" with classical elements. The allusion to Ceres, goddess of grain, already has been noted. The poet casts another classical allusion into this couplet, comparing New England's backsliding to a stately vessel whose pride is dashed by stormy weather: "Thus the proud Ship after a little turn/ Sinks into *Neptunes* arms to find its Urn" (86). The construction here, "Thus . . . ," borrows the *anaphora,* a structural form from classical rhetoric. This instance is but the second of four such constructions in a sequence. Earlier Tompson six times has repeated the construction, "'Twas ere . . . ." This mingling of the classical with the Adamic is an appropriate preparation for the remainder of the poem, for, as occurs with the elegy on his father and the Lord Bellamont "masque," the rest of *New Englands Crisis* is overwhelmed by the classical mode.

Containing no invocation to the muse (unless we identify "the *Critick* of our years" as God), the poem immediately plunges *in medias res* (into the middle of things). The year is 1675, and hostilities are about to affect the fate of the New England colonies, Tompson's "Countrey." Beginning *in medias res* a poem in which the future of a nation hangs in the balance implicates two telltale characteristics of epic. How these hostilities were precipitated, or rather how Tompson perceived that these hostilities evolved, is indeed of major significance to the future of all America. For Webb maintains that the dramatic decline of the American colonies from "pre-eminence and their long subjection to English empire were a function of their failure to acknowledge the importance, or respect the integrity, of the Amerindians" (411).

Particularly as this tract was widely read, Tompson's own writing of the history of this conflict represents an important cultural rendering of the events which predicted the manner and method of virtually all future dealings of the white people with the Native Americans of North America. Tompson claims first some "feav'rish heat, and *Pagan* spirits," or perhaps "some Romish Agent" or emissary from the Catholic Pope, "hatcht the plot." Then, he toys provocatively with the notions that either "our infant thrivings did invite" (i.e., the colonies' prosperity may have inspired their alleged greed) or the

Native Americans "to our lands pretended right" (i.e., the Native Americans now were making claims on *their* lands). Finally, Tompson concludes that, in any event, "*Indian spirits* need/ No grounds but lust to make a Christian bleed" (86).

At no point in the poem does Tompson concede that the property the Native Americans felt was in contest was in fact their (i.e., the Native Americans') own. Rather Tompson next places in the mouth of the dread King Philip a long speech of twenty-four lines uttered before his "peers" and "Commons," as all were "Kennel'd together," like dogs. This, the only long epic speech given in the poem, opens with these arresting lines: "'My friends, our Fathers were not half so wise/ As we our selves who see with younger eyes." This opening occupies an obverse relationship to "the Prologue"; there the white fathers were wise and the succeeding generations much less so. To say that movements within the two societies, the white and the Native American, were at cross-purposes would be to put it mildly. Tompson's cohorts must look to the past for guidance; yet King Philip, representing contemporary recalcitrance and rebellion against tradition, chooses to overturn that tradition. In Tompson's text, Philip represents the antipodes of acceptable behavior. That is, he is a type of Satan, an anti-Christ. Today's readers may find this sort of blatant rationalization for the white man's greed and wanton behavior ludicrous. In Tompson's day, however, such self-justification was serious business, perhaps absolutely necessary to the theft.

Next Tompson places in Philip's mouth a couplet which is so close to the truth as we see it in the year 2001 that one wonders whether Tompson himself felt pangs of guilt: "Of all our countrey they enjoy the best,/ And quickly they intend to have the rest" (86). All thought that these lines could represent any sort of confession on Tompson's part soon must be set aside; for the remainder of the speech and of the Boston poem appears to be designed to vilify King Philip and to outrage the whites. Philip soon declares, for example, "Now if you'le fight Ile get you english coats,/ And wine to drink out of their Captains throats" (87). However regrettable Tompson's racism is, he is typical of those early settlers who thought of themselves as engaged in the righteous process of forging out of a new continent a new way of life, one wholly representative of their aspirations to establish the seeds of a new country, to build a translation of culture. In accomplishing this cultural imperative, however, Webb concludes:

> New Englanders remained convinced, despite the dreadful lessons of 1676, that the only "reasonable" response to Indian self-assertion was "the utter extirpation" of the aborigines. The mass of Virginians wanted "to ruine and extirpate all Indians in Generall." (411)

While neither forgetting nor condoning this obvious racism, we shall investigate the role played by classical discourse in justifying that destructive racism. Fairly early on in *New Englands Crisis*, Tompson begins to make associations to Vergil's *Aeneid*. For example, in an attempt to trace the trickery of the Native Americans, the poet remarks: "Methinks I see the Trojan-horse burst ope,/ And such rush forth as might with giants cope" (88). Later in the Marlbury episode, he draws an epic comparison between the stealth of the Native Americans and Aeneas's arrival in Carthage, cloaked in a mist so as to be invisible: "Most like Aeneas in his cloak of mist,/ Who undiscover'd move where ere they list" (94).

In this same episode, Tompson's intimate knowledge of Ovid's *Metamorphoses* shines through unmistakably, as he describes a mother's reaction at watching her own child being roasted alive: "Let here the Mother seem a statue turn'd/ At the sad object of her bowels burn'd" (95). In book VI of Ovid's poem, after watching all fourteen of her children die before her, Niobe, moved beyond ordinary human grief, changes into a marble statue. Immediately after the conclusion of the "New Englands Crisis" section, Tompson describes the fates, at the hands of the Native Americans, of such communities as Marlbury, Providence, Rehoboth, etc.

In this collection, one episode indicates in its very title an indebtedness to Vergil. "On A FORTIFICATION At *Boston* begun by Women. *Dux Foemina Facti*" (the leader [Dido] of the exploit [was] a woman) takes its Latin phrase from the *Aeneid* (I, 364). While this inscription may have been inspired in part by the popularity of medals struck with these same words in commemoration of Elizabeth's "defeat" of the Spanish Armada in 1588 (significantly, the London edition of *New-Englands Tears* includes this episode but omits the Latin quotation), I suspect that Tompson may have had another motive.

The role that women played in the Virginia revolution of 1676 was well known throughout the colonies. Webb observes, "Women, servants, and slaves organized and fought the revolution, which was excited by Indian attacks and made articulate by educated English emigrants" (414). To be sure, Tompson was no emigrant but a native-born citizen, and he appears to have had little interest in the plight of servants and slaves. Still, as a highly educated citizen, he may have wanted to record a New England incident of women in rebellion as a rejoinder to the Baconian "news wives" who wrote and talked armed revolt. Many have observed that Tompson's tone in this episode is mock-heroic. The following pair of couplets appear to support this claim:

A tribe of female hands, but manly hearts
Forsake at home their pastry-crust and tarts
To knead the dirt, the samplers down they herle,
Their undulating silks they closely furle. (98)

Yet Tompson is careful to observe that their efforts "draw forth Male stronger hands." While the men complete the fortification, the poet insists that "the beginners well deserve the praise" (99).

New-Englands Tears is much less an epic than a collection or anthology of newsworthy tracts, gathered to elicit among the British citizenry a sympathetic response to the ravages of King Philip's War. Significantly, the long tract entitled "New Englands Crisis," taking up 302 lines of the Boston epic, is entirely omitted from the London anthology. In addition, there is no "Prologue." What is left are all the episodes devoted to explicating the deplorable fates of several villages, to which are added "Sudburies Fate," a short epitaph on the death of Major Simon Willard of the colonial militia, an elegy on the death of John Winthrop (whose reputation was well known in London), and a tract about the death of an important Native American sachem. These parts have been rearranged to create the illusion of continuity. Yet, with the omission of the jeremiad (probably of little interest to the largely Anglican audience of London) and the section which vilifies King Philip (it is doubtful that Charles II would wish to be compared with a Native American "King"), this version loses much of its drama. The additions which have been made to this version, because of their dependence upon classical elements, do have intrinsic interest for the present discussion, however.

The elegy on John Winthrop Jr. (1606–1676), for example, opens with this wholly classical couplet: "Nine Muses, get you all but one to sleep,/ But spare *Melpomene*, with me to weep." Tompson treats this enlightened, secular man—governor of Connecticut for nineteen years and first resident American member of the Royal Society—quite appropriately. At the same time, the poet draws this Adamic comparison, even though he casts it in the form of an epic simile: "As *Moses* took the Law in Clouds and Fire;/ which Vulgars barr'd at distance much admire" (109). After all, Winthrop was a Puritan communicant. The lines describing the death of the "Grand Sachem" display an almost bitter satire as they declare that, for a full description of this chief's "Pedegree," one should be forced to seek out "*Hesiods Theognis*." The Native American chief's men come at the colonial militia "Like *Hydra's* Heads"; even so, Tompson writes, "that Lucifer receives defeat" (113). This poem contains the most directly solicitous lines in the slender volume:

> Least [for Lest] such *Moecaenas's* beyond Sea should,
> Restrain their yearly showrs of Goods and Gold,
> Be pleas'd to know there is an hopeful race,
> Who as you oft have been inform'd have grace. (114)

Despite the mocking tone of the first couplet, the next does seem to encourage the award of assistance.

The "Sudburies Fate" episode, however, offers the most substantial additions of the Aeneas myth. This particular episode calls upon the muse: "Once more run Lacquey Muse the Councel tell/ What sad Defeat our hopeful Band befell." While the phrase "Once more" extends the opening invocation, "Lacquey Muse" may strike some as satirical. In Tompson's century (actually until the early 1800s), however, the word "lacquey" could mean a servant, as well as one who is fawning or obsequious. Perhaps Tompson's intention here is to appear self-deprecatory. In addition, the presence of two invocations in *New-Englands Tears* suggests that Tompson may be trying to appeal to an audience with a more sophisticated reading background. In describing the results of an attack by Native Americans, Tompson pens this affecting couplet: "The Parents Vesture with the purple stain'd/ Of his *Ascanius* by him newly braind." The allusion here to Aeneas's son Ascanius sets the stage for three more allusions to the *Aeneid* which follow immediately:

> *Euryalus* his Soul reaks through the wound,
> Of *Nisus* gasping by upon the ground;
> While the *Rutilian* like enraged bears,
> The Garments with Mens Skins, asunder tears. (112)

No one who has read about the emotionally charged friendship of Vergil's Nisus and Euryalus (IX, 176–449), each of whom sacrifices his life for the other, can read Tompson's lines without being affected by this horrific scene of self-sacrifice. In addition, Tompson's identification of the attacking Native Americans as "Rutilian[s]"—that is Rutulians—certifies that the poet interprets the Native Americans as Rutulians, perhaps led by Turnus as King Philip, and the Early Americans as Trojans preparing to found a new nation, not in Italy but along the Atlantic seacoast of North America. If one adds to *New Englands Crisis* these four new parts—the elegy on Winthrop, the Willard epitaph, "Sudburies Fate," and the "Grand Sachems Death"—one has assembled all the elements essential in a full-fledged epic, though only about 840 lines long. The many references to Vergil's *Aeneid*, combined with those in *New Englands Crisis* (including the Trojan horse, Aeneas and his cloak of mist, and the exploit led by a woman), together suggest that Vergil's text is Tompson's primary model for his experiment in writing the first significantly American epic.[6]

One thing that makes Tompson's extended *New Englands Crisis* significantly American resides in the fact that the poet creates as his "hero" a satanic characterization of King Philip. Hence Tompson brings to center stage the entirely American problem of racism against Native Americans. While the poet is studious to point out positive qualities of such whites as

Major Willard, who manifests "True *Heroic* Martial" virtue (112), Tompson's severely negative portrayal of King Philip causes the characters of all Philip's white victims, for example, to soar toward the realm of sainthood. Such an exaggerated perspective meets precisely what Webb has identified as an absolute cultural imperative "to ruine and extirpate all Indians in Generall," an attitude which has mitigated only somewhat in recent years.

The formal combination of the Adamic jeremiad and the classical epic indicates another significantly American cultural dynamic, the intertwining strands of Adam and Aeneas. These two modes of discourse, each giving force to the other, when used to vilify Native Americans, express dramatically the transplantation of "the action of dwelling in a place."

We may draw a distinction between Tompson's performance and the manner in which the three Almanac poets, Anne Bradstreet, and John Saffin handle their classicism. This distinction has to do with the degree of *translatio cultus* each author represents. To be sure, Bradstreet, Saffin, and the almanac poets do accomplish a transfer of "elegance of design or orderliness" and demonstrate how well the secular, more aesthetically oriented myth of Aeneas can be blended with the more austere Adamic myth. Tompson, however, carries the Adam and Aeneas dialectic forth to such an extent that he actually begins to define his New World culture in terms of the interplay of both discourses. Jim Egan, in *Authorizing Experience*, points out that, for some time, Tompson's "*Crisis* and *Tears* have been misunderstood as confused productions" (107). But when read as attempts to define New England (if not all the Atlantic colonies) as a land remade, in Egan's phrase, "into something entirely new" (109), then these poems can be read as exercises in the quest for American selfhood. The theoretics of Tompson's quest nevertheless come about at the expense of Native American occupants, whose lands are required for the cultural success of the transplanted Europeans.

Of course, one could argue that the very moment Peter Martyr began to articulate the opening up of the New World in terms of the myths of Adam and Aeneas, the metamorphosis of Europeans into Americans was underway. Recall that Aeneas was called Roman before he ever set foot on Italian soil (*Aeneid* VI, 851). George Sandys, in his *Metamorphosis* of 1632, transforms his translation (itself a transformation) into something distinctly American, when he explains Ovid's text in terms of the American (Virginian) environs. Sandys's fusion of the old (European) with the new (North American) is pregnant with implications for what it means to be American. The public ministerial and private poetic careers of Edward Taylor, too, are fertile with such meanings, except that Taylor's work, like Tompson's, exemplifies a transplantation of "the action of dwelling in a place."

2

Edward Taylor's Classicism

Readers of Edward Taylor's poetry seldom have emphasized his classicism. A. Owen Aldridge has observed, for example, that, despite his obvious classical training at Harvard, Taylor "makes no effort to display this classical background in his poetry." From his reading of Taylor's poems, Aldridge concludes that, "out of thousands of lines of verse, one may discover hardly a dozen classical allusions, and these are the most rudimentary" (79). Perhaps Aldridge's overlooking of the sizable number of classical allusions in Taylor's poems alone, not to mention those in the sermons, represents yet another instance of cultural blindness, for I have managed to locate almost eight dozen classical allusions in the Westfield minister's published poems, and nearly two dozen in the sermons collected as *Christographia* and the *Treatise Concerning the Lord's Supper*. The recently published two-volume *Upon the Types of the Old Testament*, a sequence of thirty-six sermons, features well over six dozen classical allusions (this sequence became available to the public only after Aldridge's remarks had appeared). The sum of the classical allusions appearing in Taylor's published poetry and prose comes to about two hundred.[1]

Despite what has just been said, the following examination of Taylor's use of classicism is not based upon quantitative data. As this poet's work draws not merely on classical figures of history and myth but also on classical literary and rhetorical structures, the present evaluation relies upon qualitative criteria. Finally, Taylor's application of the myth of Aeneas in his prose differs markedly from the way this mode of discourse appears in his poetry.

The ways in which Taylor uses the myth of Aeneas in his poetry and in his prose identify a distinctly American cultural pattern of acceptance and denial. This pattern of acceptance and denial contributes substantially to the radical shift in discourse that took place after the American Revolution.

Taylor, of course, wrote quite a while before the Declaration of Independence was signed. I differ with many of Taylor's readers, who hold that he was a somewhat conservative, perhaps even reactionary Puritan. Investigation of his application of knowledge regarding the classical cultures of Greece, Egypt, and Rome reveals that the attitude of Taylor the poet, at least, toward the ancient non-Judaeo-Christian civilizations resembles that of a humanist. In other words, while Taylor the Puritan minister unarguably was a conservative in theological matters, Taylor the poet was much more consciously receptive to classical thought and culture than commonly has been assumed.

To be sure, the ministerial atmosphere in which Taylor was immersed while attending Harvard, between 1668 and 1671, would have discouraged the student from developing a fondness for things classical. In the *Survey of the Summe of Church Discipline* (1648), for example, Thomas Hooker, a seventeenth-century defender of New England Congregationalism, for whose son Taylor composed an elegy (1697), admonished the Puritan clergy not to concern themselves in their writings with pleasing "the niceness of men's palates." He urged them instead to recall that the greatest scholar among the Church Fathers, Jerome, designer of the Latin Vulgate Bible, was severely censured by his contemporaries for producing writings in which he was "Ciceronianus non Christianus" (Miller and Johnson 2: 673).[2] For Puritans, to affect a Ciceronian style was to write ornate prose rather than to adopt the plain style. Among Jerome's contemporaries, as among Taylor's, a Ciceronian was one who showed excessive enthusiasm for pagan culture by alluding repeatedly to its authors. John Calvin, the founder of Calvinism, whose influence upon the New England Puritans was enormous, in the latter part of the sixteenth century had placed restrictions upon the construction of verse in general. In the *Epitome* of the *Institutes of the Christian Religion,* the spiritual cornerstone of the Puritan movement (Taylor owned a copy), Calvin enumerates these restrictions for song or poetry:

> Hinc praeterea plusquam clarum est, neq; Vocem, neq; cantum habere quicquam momenti, nisi ex alto cordis affectu profecta. Quin eius iram aduersus nos provocat, si e summis duntaxat labris & gutture exeunt: quando id est, sacrosancto eius nomine abuti, ac eius maiestatem derisui habere. Vocem & cantum tanquam adminicula orationis commendamus, quatenus purum animi affectum comitantus.

> Moreover there is nothing more clear; it is of no moment at all to have the voice and singing unless they have sprung from deep love of the heart. If such is not the case, they provoke His anger against us, even if, in so far as this matter is concerned, they come forth from the best lips and throat: whatsoever it is, it abuses His holy name and holds His grandeur in derision. We recommend the voice and singing as a support of speech, where accompanying love pure of spirit. (211)

Song was allowed and even invited for prayer, then, but never just for amusement. It was to be executed only by those whose hearts and minds were wholly attuned to contemplation of God.[3] Richard Baxter, one of the seventeenth century's foremost Puritan authorities on meditation, presents a similar view in *The Saints' Everlasting Rest* (1650), a book well known and widely circulated in both England and the colonies. Part 4 of this work treats meditation on heaven, and chapter 7 is titled "Concerning the fittest time and place for this contemplation, and the preparation of the heart unto it." In this same chapter, the one which Taylor probably would have found most compelling for his "Preparatory Meditations," Baxter demands that the meditator "thrust these thoughts [of the world] from the Temple of thy heart, which have the badg of Gods prohibition upon them" (715–16).

One of those worldly pursuits which bore the "badg of Gods prohibition" was carrying on discourse with the classical Muses. For all Puritan writers of the latter half of the seventeenth century, the warnings of these two men, along with Hooker's admonition concerning Ciceronianism, established an atmosphere hostile to the literature of the ancient pagan authors. Thus, when Taylor arrived at Harvard in 1668, he found himself confronted by one of the foremost paradoxes of the day. Classical pagan literature might be studied—in fact, its study was required—but only for knowledge and not for amusement. At the same time, in all matters of faith, divinity students were admonished to focus their attention entirely upon the Holy Scriptures and their Author.[4]

This ideal prescription, as we have seen, was not always followed. Indeed, many poems by the almanac poets, Anne Bradstreet, John Saffin, and Benjamin Tompson (among many other seventeenth-century Early American authors) rely heavily upon the pastoral tradition of Theocritus, while several of the same authors display a more than casual acquaintance with the work of Vergil and Ovid. As we shall soon see, Taylor, too, made ample use of the classical authors and their culture, thereby demonstrating in his work yet another instance of *translatio cultus*.

One indication of Taylor's interest in classical literature was his regard for the golden mean. In his elegy on the death of his first wife, Elizabeth Fitch

(1689), the bereaved husband affectionately recalls Mrs. Taylor's moderation toward her domestics: "Remiss was not, nor yet severe unto/ Her Servants: but i'th' golden mean did goe" (474). *God's Determinations*, an undated poem, celebrates the golden mean twice. "The Outward Man Accused" asks of him who would put on a display of perfection, "When thou was got in such a merry veane/ How far didst thou exceed the golden mean?" (411). A later piece of this series warns that Satan "tempts to bring the soul too low or high . . . To keep on either side the golden mean" (477). Like many Christian humanists through the eighteenth century, Taylor has allied this most prized of classical virtues with his own Christian vision.

A recent study underscores Taylor's regard for the golden mean. Mukhtar Ali Isani in "Edward Taylor and Ovid's *Art of Love*," maintains that, shortly after the turn of the seventeenth century, Taylor translated the Daedalus passage from Ovid's *Ars amatoria*. This passage is often cited as an excellent example of how blatant disregard for *temperantia* (moderation) brings about disaster. A couplet from Taylor's translation captures the essence of the Daedalus myth. While warning his inexperienced son, the brash Icarus, not to fly too close to the sea or the sun, Ovid's Daedalus speaks these poignant lines: "inter utrumque uola; uentos quoque, nate, timeto,/ quoque ferent aurae, uela secunda dato" (Fly between each; you, son, *will* also fear the winds, whithersoever the gentle breezes carry [you], speeding along you *will* set sail; *Ars amatoria*, II, 64–65). Taylor renders this passage as "You fly between both, and take heed of storm/ And let the aire carry thy oares right calme" (Isani 70). The New England poet conveys adequately the solicitous urgency of the father's future imperatives in the phrase "take heed of storm." The "storm" raging here could well be that within the mind of a youth all too often given to intemperate behavior. In 1626, George Sandys had observed of the Daedalus myth, as Ovid treats it in book VIII of *Metamorphoses*, "This fable applaudes the golden Meane, and flight of virtue between the extreames."[5] Ovid treated the Daedalus myth, as a fine example of intemperance, more fully in *Ars* than in the *Metamorphoses*. Taylor's decision to translate and preserve the *Ars* passage,[6] then, underscores the importance he attached to the golden mean.

Some have suggested that Taylor wrote *God's Determinations* as a catechetical tract for circulation among his new communicants. Thus his promotion of the virtue of *sophrosyne* indicates that there was at least one value from classical culture which Taylor wished to convey to his congregation. Certainly such wise counsel would serve any culture at any time. Taylor's humanistic posture here, it may already have become apparent, resembles the balanced behavior characteristic of Vergil's hero Aeneas. This kind of humanism definitely marks Taylor's authoritative attempt to refine or elaborate upon his parishioners' standards of living, one of the characteristics of *translatio cultus*.

What most readily identifies Taylor as a humanistic Puritan is his artful use of classical allusions, touched on above but now to be examined in detail. Often in his poetry and occasionally in his sermons, Taylor alludes to the histories or mythologies of ancient Greece, Egypt, and Rome, indicating broad familiarity with these cultures. To be sure, the Bible treats many aspects of these three pagan cultures. This investigation, however, concerns itself exclusively with those allusions whose origins are *not* biblical. In Taylor's poems and sermons, these classical references function either metaphorically or typologically. In the sermons they sometimes perform a third function not seen in the poems, serving as examples for the instruction of the congregation.

Taylor's metaphorical allusions never simply display erudition, as they sometimes do in lesser writers. Indeed, when his classical allusions act metaphorically, they use "the echoed element as a vehicle for the poetic tenor that it acquires in the new context" (*Princeton Encyclopedia*). Such is the intrinsic response of all better writers who employ allusions. Even so, it should not be surprising to discover proportionately fewer metaphorical classical allusions in Taylor's sermons than in his poems. Taylor the Puritan minister probably would be defensive about the possibility of incurring Jerome's charge: "Ciceronianus non Christianus." But the poet speaking directly to God would have no such fear; surely that omniscient Audience would understand the poet's motives correctly.

For his typological allusions, however, Taylor did not rely on a strictly intrinsic response. As in the biblical typology he employs in his sermons, Taylor took as his guide for employing certain of his classical allusions Samuel Mather's *The Figures or Types of the Old Testament* (1683), a work extremely popular with Calvinistic clergy in New England in the late seventeenth and early eighteenth centuries. Taylor owned and annotated a copy of this collection of sermons on typology. In it, Mather, the uncle of one of Taylor's classmates at Harvard, describes a *type* as "some outward or sensible thing ordained of God under the Old Testament, to represent and hold forth something of Christ in the New" (52). Mather, conservative minister that he was, cautioned against indulging one's imagination regarding the drawing out of types: "It is not safe to make any thing a Type meerly upon our own fansies and imaginations; it is Gods Prerogative to make *Types*" (55).[7] Since Mather confines his discussion of typology to figures of the Bible only, never alluding to non-biblical, classical figures, he probably would not have endorsed Taylor's modification and extension of typing to embrace ancient figures not mentioned in the Bible. Perhaps Mather even would have accused Taylor of being, if not a Ciceronian, at least overly imaginative.

When typological and metaphorical allusions to ancient pagan cultures appear in Taylor's poetry, they embellish his conceits and complement his imagery. In his sermons, such allusions usually teach by recalling to his colonial listeners analogies and illustrations which carry familiar moral implications. Although most of his parishioners would not have been familiar with Greek culture and language, they would have recognized immediately that an allusion to Midas concerned avarice and that a reference to Alexander implied worldly ambition.

Taylor himself was quite familiar with Greek language and civilization. In his *Diary*, written between April 1668, just as he was leaving England for America, and December 1671, when he preached his first sermon at Westfield, Massachusetts, he records that, on the fifty-fifth day of his journey across the Atlantic, he read "the fourth chapter of John in Greek" (*Diary* 12). Taylor knew some Greek before he entered Harvard, then, and so met one of the college's requirements for admission (Morison, *Founding* 333 and 433). Certainly while there he acquired more thorough knowledge of this language and culture. In his personal library, the Westfield minister included at least one Greek grammar, a Greek New Testament, and an edition of Theocritus's *Idylls* (T. H. Johnson, p. 216, item 141; p. 213, items 111 and 112; and p. 214, item 122).[8] Scattered throughout the *Christographia*, a collection of fourteen sermons in which Taylor opposes Solomon Stoddard's opening of the Lord's supper to all (even if they had never experienced conversion), are quotations from the Greek New Testament, together with literal translations. Taylor uses these quotations to justify particular interpretations or points of exegesis.

Taylor opens his seventy-ninth meditation (Second Series) with a stanza in which he names Prometheus, giver of fire to mankind, and Pandora, whose box, when opened, brought strife into the world of men. Since Taylor delivers in this piece one of his most impassioned statements of his intense desire *(eros)* for God (indeed, the text is Cant. 2:16, "My Beloved is mine and I am his"), the elaborate conceit he establishes by using these two allusions piques one's curiosity. The lines of this stanza are:

> Had I Promethius' filching Ferula [fennel]
> Filld with its sacred theft the stoln Fire:
> To animate my Fancy lodg'd in clay,
> Pandora's Box would peps [pelt] the theft with ire.
> But if thy Love, My Lord, shall animate
> My Clay with holy fire, 'twill flame in State. (226)

To be sure, Taylor remarks in the first two lines of the next stanza: "Fables fain'd, Wonders do relate so strange/ That do amuse when heard." Although probably deprecating himself here for having drawn so grand a conceit, he has created a figure of no little significance.

This conceit may be read on several different levels. One is the metaphorical suggestion that Taylor here is casting off the originally pagan convention of invoking the Muses and opting for the Christian practice of calling on God's love for poetic inspiration. Only God's love can animate a "Fancy lodg'd in clay." Although the stated subject of this stanza is, indeed, poetic inspiration, this is not the subject of the entire poem. God's love, freely given, animates, not just his "Fancy lodg'd in clay," but his very body, "My Clay." And with what does God's love animate him? With "holy fire." The larger subject of the poem, then, is not merely poetic inspiration. It is God's love for man and man's desire for (invocation of) that love—the eros-agape motif.

Recognition of the poem's true subject demands that one perceive the metaphorical reading of the initial conceit as inadequate or incomplete. What has Prometheus to do with poetic inspiration, the ostensible subject of the stanza? Indeed, what does Pandora add to the subject? Neither of these allusions is sufficient as a metaphor for poetic inspiration. But they do function well when understood as types, not of poetic inspiration but of man's relationship to God. A fuller examination of the Prometheus-Pandora myth assists this typological reading. Prometheus, against the will of Zeus, stole fire and gave it to man. In retaliation for his crime, Zeus gave man (who was the favorite of Prometheus) woman or Pandora, replete with a box of woes she was instructed not to open. Zeus created Pandora to be innately curious, and so she was—in the wrong place and at the wrong time, of course. She opened the box and released into the world of man all his subsequent travails. It becomes easy to see, then, that Prometheus is a type of Satan, who defied God; and Pandora is a type of Eve, whose curiosity (among other things) caused her to eat of the Tree of Knowledge and then to tempt Adam also to eat, bringing about man's fall from grace.

In a brilliant stroke, Taylor has constructed a succinct, if patriarchal, retelling of man's fall from grace, through classical, not Christian, allusions. At the same time, he has articulated why fallen man must depend upon the love of God to animate his otherwise inanimate (clay) body. For, without God's gift of grace, original sin or the innate depravity which resulted from Eve's theft of the forbidden fruit (resembling man's acceptance of Prometheus's stolen fire) constantly reminds man of his fallen state, his clay lodging. Seeing a Christian allegory in terms of Greek mythology surely must indicate an appreciation of that mythology. Note the remarkable facility with which Taylor has incorporated this Prometheus-Pandora conceit within the Renaissance tradition of employing classical allusions, as well as within the orthodox Christian practice of typology. In addition, the effective blending here of the myths of Adam and Aeneas points up the dialectical tension between these two modes of discourse.

Taylor's instructional references to ancient Greek culture, though less remarkable, provide practical exempla for the writer of sermons. Two among his several Greek exempla are of particular interest: a reference to the Spartan King Leonidas and another to the most famous Greek painter, Apelles.[9] Leonidas, who died with three hundred of his fellow Spartans while defending Thermopylae in 480 B.C., appears in the first sermon of Taylor's *Treatise Concerning the Lord's Supper,* within an illustration of the linguistic precedent for calling the Eucharist a feast. In defense of his translation of the New Testament Greek words *deipnon* (Matt. 23:6, Mark 12:39) and *arisen* as *feast,* Taylor observes, "Leonidas heartened his Spartans by telling them that they at night should feast in Hades" (*Treatise* 12). The reference is apropos, not merely because it illustrates how the Greeks understood the word but particularly because it subtly suggests a classical parallel to the New Testament Last Supper. Although few of Taylor's congregation would be likely to appreciate his effort at accuracy, much less his subtlety, it reflects his reverence for the biblical text. But it also indicates his respect for anecdotes drawn from Greek literature.

Both the sermon in which the allusion to Apelles appears and its accompanying "Preparatory Meditation" (Second Series, 56) contain quite a few classical allusions. Since the sermon, the last of the *Christographia,* argues that man's works are nothing in comparison to the most noble works of Christ on earth, the intermittent appearance of such obviously fabricated ornaments as classical allusions emphasizes Taylor's point that imperfect man can make only abortive attempts to effect excellence. The allusions appear in an anecdote recorded in the life of Apelles, which Taylor applies as an analogy. "When Apelles the painter," writes Taylor, "saw his Servant drawing out the picture of Venus, overlay it with gold, he told him, that he has not drawn out or painted a Beautiful person, but a Rich person" (467).

Since Taylor names Clement of Alexandria in the preceding paragraph and cites him a number of times throughout this sermon, one would expect the minister from Westfield to have derived this anecdote from Clement. The Alexandrine Church Father does indeed relate such an anecdote in the *Paedagogus*, or *Tutor,*[10] with one exception. Instead of Venus, he names Helen as the painting's subject. Perhaps Taylor's memory has lapsed a bit (his translation is a paraphrase of the original), or perhaps he deliberately alters his source, hoping to jog his educated parishioners' memories more effectively by calling up Apelles's most famous painting, the Aphrodite Anadyomene.[11] Whatever the reason for Taylor's liberty with his source, he achieves his intended purpose. For, in his next sentence following the Apelles exemplum, he remarks, "So indeed it is with us: all our pensills in all their draughts attain not to anything of the Excellencies of Christ's operations."

Taylor's Greek allusions suggest a broad familiarity with, and a great appreciation for, this ancient culture's history and mythology. Examination of the Westfield minister's Egyptian allusions affirms that Taylor had considerable interest in ancient Egypt as well. While nonbiblical references to Egypt represent his smallest group of classical allusions, this group does, nonetheless, shed light on Taylor's reading. In the first sermon of *Christographia,* Taylor names Ptolemy Philadelphus (285–46 B.C.), remembered today for his embellishment of the Mouseion, a temple of the Muses in Alexandria, in which were preserved many of the literary manuscripts of the ancient world.[12] Taylor cites this famed king of Egypt, however, not because of his accomplishments in the Mouseion but because of his alleged role in ordering a translation of the Old Testament from Hebrew into what became known as the *Septuagint.*

This example, cited before Taylor's congregation, is not important because of the role it plays in the sermon.[13] Rather, the presence of this allusion in a sermon of 1701 suggests which Ptolemy the poet is citing in a poem of 1705. Taylor's discussion, in a sermon of 1703, of Ptolemy Philadelphus's Pharus, a lighthouse and one of the ancient Wonders of the World, indicates which Ptolemy interests Taylor (*Upon the Types* 724). In the late poem, the sixty-seventh meditation (Second Series), Taylor speaks of "Transparent Silver Bowles with flowers Enfringed/ Sent to the Temple by king Ptolemy" (200). These lines are almost a paraphrase of a description given in the *Letter of Aristeas,* known today to be spurious and included with the Old Testament *Pseudepigrapha.*[14] The *Aristeas* relates that the High Priest Eleazer, having returned to Israel after completing a translation of the Old Testament for inclusion in the Mouseion, wrote a letter thanking Ptolemy for his many gifts, among them "the vessels which you sent, twenty of silver and thirty of gold, the five cups," and other items contributing to "the furnishing of the Temple requirements" (Charlesworth 2.15).

Tracing the source of this allusion, however, does not fully explain its function in the poem. This sixty-seventh meditation invokes a typological interpretation of Malachi 4:2: "But unto you that fear my name shall the Sun of righteousness arise." The first stanza, which contains the Ptolemy allusion, accomplishes a subordinate typology of its own. This is the entire stanza:

> My China Ware on Amber Casket bright
> Filld with Ambrosian Spirits soakt and Bindg'd,
> Made all a Mass of Quicken'd metall right,
> Transparent Silver Bowles with Flowers Enfringd
> Sent to the Temple by King Ptolemy
> Compared thereto are but vile Trumpery. (200)

In this catalogue, the poet's finest wares are juxtaposed to Ptolemy's gifts. Surely both form part of an assemblage worthy of placement in a temple. But what is one to make of "Made all a Mass of Quicken'd metall"? Samuel Mather's *Figures or Types* offers a clue. In one of his later sermons, entitled "The Gospel of the Sea and Lavers in the Temple," he cites the description, in 1 Kings 7:23, of Solomon's constructing, inside his famous temple, "a molten sea, ten cubits from the one brim to the other," as a type of the "sea of glass like unto crystal" in Revelation 4:6 (Samuel Mather 377). Then he maintains that "The main thing aimed at in this typical Sea . . . in the Temple is our Spiritual washing in the Blood of Jesus Christ from Sin and from Uncleanness" (380). At one point in this discussion, Mather observes that some "ingenious" exegetes have taken the "Crystal Sea to be the World and say 'tis compared to . . . Crystal for transparency" (384). Perhaps this passage suggested to Taylor the arresting image of "Transparent Silver Bowles," which in the *Aristeas* remain simply bowls.

Now that the rather obscure referents of this stanza have been identified, the meaning becomes clear. Fabricated objects, such as Ptolemy's gifts, "Ambrosian Spirits," and even Solomon's metallic sea, though they might be the sort of offerings required by the Old Testament Yahweh, are now, since the coming of Christ, mere display. They are worthless when compared to the "Sun of righteousness." At their best, these fine objects serve Taylor and his congregation as types, or shadows, of Christ. In addition, Taylor probably has in mind here severe criticism of the Roman Catholic practice of adorning houses of worship.

Though not in so elaborate or compressed a manner, Taylor's third Egyptian allusion calls on the reputation of yet another ruler, the mythical Egyptian, Sesostris, who supposedly flourished centuries before Alexander's conquest. In one of the *Christographia* sermons, the Westfield minister sets up for his congregation a stark contrast between persons who allow themselves to be suppressed by tyrants, such as the Egyptian Sesostris and the Hebrew Ahab, and those fortunate others who give themselves to God. Taylor relates that Sesostris made captive kings pull his chariot in exchange for a few more days of life. To assume the yoke of God, however, one is not required to put off crown and scepter but only "to leave Sin" (*Christographia* 425). This allusion to Sesostris has particular interest because it suggests what Taylor may have been reading at the time he composed this sermon in August 1703.

Norman S. Grabo, editor of *Christographia*, traces this allusion to the *Bibliotheca* of the Sicilian historian, Diodorus. Taylor does, indeed, take his anecdote about Sesostris from Diodorus (I, ch. 58). The allusions Taylor employs in "Meditation Fifty-Six" (mentioned above), written within a month of the sermon, however, suggest that Diodorus was not the only ancient historian he was reading. In the fifth stanza of a poem written in October 1703, Taylor presents a cluster of six allusions to historical figures of Greece, Rome, and Egypt. All six of these figures—the famed Theater of the

Emperor Titus, Nero's "Golden House," the ingenious war machines of the Greek mathematician and philosopher Archimedes, the Pyramids, the man-made lake of the Egyptian King Moeris, and the labyrinth of the Egyptian ruler Psammetichos—illustrate the poet's notion that the greatest architectural achievements of men merely ape nature. Even nature, who "doth better work than Art," cannot compare with the accomplishments of Christ on earth, says Taylor, for Christ's accomplishments outshone "both works of nature and Art" (181).

In the last sermon from *Christographia* (for which this meditation prepares), Taylor clearly articulates the theme of both poem and homily: "For nothing but the author of nature can actuate nature above the power of Nature" (*Christographia* 448). These six classical allusions, like the Apelles exemplum from this same sermon, represent the best accomplishments of man, "natures Ape." Their presence magnifies the works of God still more and makes evident the intimate relation between sermon and poem.

The stanza in which this cluster of pagan architectural achievements occurs is one of Taylor's richest in classical allusions; it contains three of his seven Egyptian references. The Lake of Meoris and the pyramidal monuments standing in the middle of this lake are described in detail by Diodorus (I, chs. 51 and 52). The Sicilian historian does not, however, describe any labyrinth attributed to a King Psammetichos. At one point, he claims that such a structure was built by a King Mendes or Marrus (I, ch. 89), while at another he says that it was constructed by a King Menas (I, ch. 61).[15] It is Herodotus, the Greek historian, who maintains that the labyrinth was built by a group of twelve Egyptian princes, among whom Psammetichos eventually gained ascendancy. Taylor's attribution of this legendary maze (in reputation superseded only by that of the Cretan King Minos) to Psammetichos suggests that he consulted Herodotus, even though Johnson does not list this book as one of those in Taylor's library. Since Diodorus repeatedly cites Herodotus as his primary authority for the Egyptian material, perhaps Taylor's scholarly curiosity led him to seek out the Sicilian's source. Probably the poet had read Herodotus at Harvard.[16]

The fact that the pyramids, Lake Moeris, and the phrase "Psammitich's Labyrinth" all occur within three lines of one another makes it more probable that Taylor had Herodotus in mind when he made these allusions. For only in Herodotus are the Labyrinth and Lake Moeris discussed successively, and only the Greek historian follows the discussion of these two artificial wonders with a detailed account of the reign of Psammetichos (ca. 670 B.C.). A third piece of evidence supports the claim that Taylor knew at least Herodotus's second book, which is devoted almost entirely to Egyptian civilization. In a late Second Series meditation (1713) on Revelation 22:16, "I am the root and offspring of David," the poet speaks of "Posamnitick's Labyrinth." Taylor here may be drawing on his memory, perhaps even forgetting the poem in which he had made this allusion ten years earlier, where he spelled the ruler's name Psammitick, and hence suggesting that the copy of Herodotus he saw was borrowed. (Since there were no public libraries in New England at the time, people often lent their books.)

While Taylor may have forgotten his spelling, he did not forget his reading. The central task of the poem is to decipher the puzzle posed by the biblical verse. How can Christ be both David's root and his offspring? He calls this riddle a "Labyrinth of Wonders bright" (Stanford, *Poems of Edward Taylor* 288). Logically, so the poet reasons, a root is the cause of an effect, a branch. Having debated with himself other possible solutions, Taylor concludes that even "Posamnitick's Labyrinth now doth appeare/ An Easy thing unto the passage here" (289). Since the image at the opening of Revelation 22 is a river out of whose center rises the Tree of Life (the throne of God), the poet's choice of this allusion is particularly apropos. Herodotus, in the passage giving information about the Labyrinth, Lake Moeris, and Psammetichos, observes that the artificial lake had "two mightie towres of stone [which he earlier calls "Pyramides"] appearing fifty foote above the water, and being as much under. On the toppe of ech towre is a great image wrought of stone, sitting in a chaire of majestie, so that the towres conteyne in height an hundreth paces."[17] These "towres" or thrones of "majestie," like the Tree of Life, rest in the center of the lake. The allusion to Psammetichos's Labyrinth does not function merely as a metaphor; rather, it also embodies one of Taylor's more compressed typologies. In his struggle to solve the riddle of the biblical verse, Taylor has typed the Egyptian allusion (and its associations with its anti-type in Revelation) in a way which reflects his private search for knowledge of man's temporal world.[18]

At the same time, Taylor weaves into his poetic texts elements from the *Letter of Aristeas* and Herodotus's *Hystory*, providing, within the work of this Puritan humanist, two other instances of the tension between the myths of Adam and Aeneas. As in these two cases, all Taylor's other allusions to ancient Egypt occur in essentially positive contexts. In Taylor's day, such a positive attitude toward Egypt signaled quite a departure from the norm. In *Figures or Types*, for example, Samuel Mather defines sin as "the Egypt of the Soul" (155). Mather modifies this view, however, when he remarks that the Egypt which held Israel in bondage, though a type of Rome, represents bondage "chiefly over the bodies," whereas the Church of Rome (Roman Catholicism) enslaves "the Souls of Men" (156). If Samuel Mather is representative of late-seventeenth-century Puritan conservatism, whose theological tenets Taylor supposedly shared, then one would expect Taylor to take a cautious approach toward Egypt. Taylor the poet obviously did not feel bound by Mather's conservatism.

While, in the poems, Taylor's allusions to ancient Greece and Egypt show considerable enthusiasm, his appropriation of ancient Rome's culture goes beyond allusion. Taylor borrows from Rome's pastoralism and from its rhetoric. Moreover, allusions to Roman history and literature occur with some frequency, indicating that Taylor was more familiar with this ancient nonbiblical culture than with Greece or Egypt. In the collection, *Upon the Types of the Old Testament*, for example, Taylor even offers his Westfield congregation quotations from Horace, Ovid, Gellius, and Vergil. These quotations in the public sermons, however, the minister clearly selects to denigrate classical, and especially Roman, sources of information. In one instance, Taylor echoes the hostility of Raleigh's diatribe against the Roman authors for pilfering the Bible for their tracts. In a sermon from 1698, for example, Taylor remarks that the story of Noah and the Ark was "stolen" by Ovid and Horace: "The Poets Ovid, Horace, etc. speake of Deucalions flood in Such a way, as plainly shews it to be Noahs applied to another person, and time. And in many things deformed" (*Types* 644).

In the public sermons, Taylor gives many illustrations of Roman figures from history which serve as exemplars of how one should not behave. In his poetry, however, Taylor shows another, more positive attitude toward things Roman. The pastoral tradition Taylor readily incorporates into his poetry. In a series of four poems from 1704–5, celebrating the sensuous garden imagery of the Song of Solomon, for example, Taylor evokes classical pastoralism in such lines as these:

> Oh that I was the Bird of Paradise!
> Then in thy Nutmeg Garden, Lord, thy Bower
> Celestiall Musick blossom should my voice
> Enchanted with thy gardens aire and flower.
> This Aromatick aire would so enspire
> My ravisht Soule to sing with angells Quire. (193)

These synaesthetic images of a "Bower," the Lord's, wherein "Celestiall Musick" aires resonate with echoes of Vergil's shepherds piping in musical contests. In the same poem, Taylor describes "an Arching bower" which stores nuts "of evry kinde" (194). Two poems away from this one, when describing the fruits of the valley, Taylor refers to "that brave Camphire bower" (197). As the word "bower" does not occur in the Geneva Bible, Taylor's biblical text for reading to his congregation, Taylor very likely has adapted the language of pastoral to his own needs, in yet another blend of the myths of Adam and Aeneas.

Perhaps Taylor's most dramatic incorporation of pastoral elements appears in a late poem, this one also inspired by the Song of Solomon. The first stanza of "Meditation 162" Second Series (from the year 1723) reads like a paraphrase of the opening of Vergil's first eclogue:

> A shadow, Lord, not such as types show here
> Nor such as Titerus his broad Beech made
> In which he with his Oat straw pipe't there
> A Forrest march, such his dark blackish trade.
> But tis a milke white Shadow sparkling bright
> That doth excell all excellent delight. (378)

In the opening of Vergil's first *Eclogue*, one may find the naming of Tityrus who plays on his slender reed while lying under a beech whose shade spreads as the rays of the afternoon sun lengthen. Significantly, Vergil repeats much of this description in his verse epitaph which closes his fourth *Georgic*: "carmina qui lusi pastorum audaxque iuventa,/ Tityre, te patulae cecini sub tegmine fagi" (565–66; I who have written for mere amusement the songs of shepherds and audacious in youth I have sung thee, Tityrus, under the covering of a spreading beech).

Except for the "slender reed," all the elements Taylor names in this passage are present in Vergil's fourth *Georgic*. Yet the Mantuan has added an element not appearing in the earlier passage: "lusi," or I have written songs for mere amusement (see *Oxford Latin Dictionary*). It is this added element which is most pertinent to an explication of Taylor's text. For he, like Vergil, has turned away from writing poetry for amusement alone (though, as we shall see, Taylor did glory in his command of words, much as Vergil did later in his career). In this poem, Taylor sets aside the frivolity of pastoralism so he can enjoy the light paradoxically cast by the shadow of his idea of God. Similarly, Vergil earlier had set aside the writing of pastoral amusements (however often tinctured with poignant realism) that he might pursue the writing of the greatest literary masterpiece of Roman civilization, the *Aeneid*. Taylor's utilization of Vergil here bespeaks the maturity of a sophisticated humanist. Indeed, his striking fusion of the myths of Adam and Aeneas constitutes another brilliant poetic performance.

Apparently Taylor, in his private poetry, recognizes full well the helpful role Latin culture can play, even though his negative application of Roman classicism in his public sermons seems to deny the possibility of such a positive role. This pattern of acceptance and denial, until now only suggested, emerges full force as we turn our attention to Taylor's indebtedness to the classical rhetoric of Rome.

Many, if not all, Early Americanists recognize Taylor's praxis of poetic meditation in his poetry. None that I am aware of, however, traces Taylor's use of the construct linking memory, understanding, and will beyond St. Ignitius Loyola's 1548 *Spiritual Exercises* to its provenance in classical rhetoric. The *meditatio* now must be seen as an exercise of mind originating in the classical rhetorical tradition, one fully available to virtually all poets of the Renaissance. Such recognition should free Early American poetry (and probably also the poetry of other countries which display this mode) from the tyranny of a twentieth-century critical approach which has been excessively loyal to the Christian adaptation of the praxis of *meditatio*.

Of course, scholars of the English Renaissance generally are aware that the tripartite construct of memory, understanding, and will is as old as St. Augustine's contention that memory, understanding, and will reflect the Trinity—God the Father, the Son, and the Holy Ghost. Still, few if any of them speak of the probability that John Donne or George Herbert, for example, may have learned how to carry out the praxis of *meditatio* in their grammar school days.[19] The Early American poets Edward Taylor, Philip Pain, and Nicolas Noyes had access to such ancient texts (often used in the grammar schools) as Pliny's *Panegyricus*, Apuleius's *Florida*, Quintilian's *Institutio oratoria*, and Gellius's *Attic Nights*, all of which (among many others) identify the *meditatio* as a rhetorical exercise.[20] These Early Americans did not need to consult Loyola's Catholic *Exercises* (unlikely, especially given the Puritan hostility toward all things "popish") or Richard Baxter's *The Saints Everlasting Rest* (1650) in order to school themselves in the praxis of *meditatio*. As Louis Martz instructs in his *The Poetry of Meditation* and *The Poem of the Mind: Essays on Poetry, English and American*, the process of meditation governs the structure of many of the poems by Herbert, Donne, Taylor, and even T. S. Eliot and Wallace Stevens, among others. In neither of these books, however, does Martz, working within a Christian and/or Adamic context, seek a classical source for the *meditatio;* this oversight has helped to prevent readers of meditative poems from recognizing that Protestant poets of the Renaissance, in particular, could and probably did learn the praxis of *meditatio* from classical sources.[21]

This apparent lack of familiarity with classical sources, together with the hegemony of the Adamic myth, keeps Early Americanists from grasping the obvious importance of imagination (a faculty essential to the process of *meditatio*) in, for example, structuring Edward Taylor's poetry. Martz leads the way to this unfortunate oversight when, in his foreword to Stanford's edition of *Poems of Edward Taylor*, he quotes lines in which Taylor uses the term *fancy* (during Taylor's era, a synonym for imagination) but then does nothing further with that idea. Scheick, *Will and Word*, appears thoroughly preoccupied with the Puritan notion that "in Adam's Fall/ We sinned all." As a result, he gives an inordinate amount of space to an explication of Taylor's theology and consequently ignores the fact that Taylor cites *fancy* some forty-five times in his published poetry. Surely such repeated application should not go unremarked in an avowed treatment of faculty psychology in Taylor's verse.[22]

Such a cursory treatment of the faculty of imagination is particularly troubling in that, from Aristotle's *De anima* (in Greek; it was another grammar school text) through Pierre de Charron's *De la Sagesse* (1601), imagination was understood to be the mediator between the senses (perception) and the understanding, or reason. As such, according to Aristotle in "On Memory," both the senses and imagination are inseparable from memory: "Thus memory belongs incidentally to the faculty of thought [understanding], and essentially it belongs to the primary faculty of sense perception" (*Complete Works* I, 715). Since "imagination must be a movement resulting from an actual exercise of a power of sense" (*Complete Works* I, 682), it follows that the imaginative faculty "moves" within the memory from sense perception to understanding.[23] To one so given to the process of meditation as was Taylor, fancy or imagination served the memory as the initiator of movement within the mind—that is, as the place of origin for the entire poem. A critical approach to Taylor's poetry based not on the Adamic mode, but on the classical, promises to reveal heretofore unrecognized aesthetic qualities within his canon. Arguably, for example, knowledge of the possibility of an essentially secular origin for Taylor's meditative poems profitably could have informed Gatta, *Gracious Laughter*, driving home more emphatically Gatta's judicious conclusion that "in its best moments Taylor's wit summons up facts of human nature more deeply innate than depravity, reconfirming Aristotle's fitting definition of our kind as the laughing and playing animal" (208).

Rowe, *Saint and Singer*, describes Taylor's use of fancy, though she does not point out the frequency with which Taylor names this faculty. Nor, perhaps because of the overwhelming influence of critics writing from the perspective of the Adamic myth, does Rowe appear prepared to enjoy Taylor's poems for their aesthetic qualities. She does much hard work with the now-published Nebraska manuscript of Taylor's sermons *(TYPES)* and convinces Taylor's readers that we cannot hope to understand his meditative verse fully except in conjunction with each poem's homiletic counterpart. In this admirable book, the author nevertheless presses too hard for a strictly spiritual, sanctifying function for the poems and misses the fervent ecstasy Taylor experiences as he experiments with a wholly human language—wholly inadequate, that is, to express his often passionate conversations with the Deity.

At one point, for example, Rowe writes, "Taylor denigrates the decadent fancy as a product of the sin-wracked sensual life that infects the human vision and voice" (268).[24] Contrary to Rowe's assertion, it is not the faculty of the imagination/fancy per se that Taylor denigrates; rather, he censures *his* fancy repeatedly. In his own words, it is "*my* fancy stagnate" (Stanford, *Poems of Edward Taylor* 175), "*my* dull fancy" (1), "*my* narrow Fancy" (359), and "*my* befogg'd Dark Phancy, Clouded minde" (45) (emphases mine). And even these instances of a negative attitude toward this faculty in himself always address his feelings of inadequacy to the task before him: to carry on a colloquy with the Deity. What honest poet in the position of composing such poetry has not joined Taylor in admitting her or his incapacity to employ language as a bridge between self and Deity? Rowe also does not notice that, in the poems, "fancy" usually appears in the essentially positive context of initiator of the poetic process, while in the sermons "imagination" is called the "efficacy of errors," as is clearly reinforced in the Geneva Bible (Genesis 6:5 and 8:21), whose text his congregation knew quite well.[25] Recall that Taylor refers, in his sermons, to classical personalities, myths, and events as exempla of misconduct but only rarely places in negative contexts the ninety or so classical allusions in the poetry. This tension in Edward Taylor between his public prose and his private verse suggests a primary demonstration of the tension between the myths of Aeneas and Adam—a tension which neither Scheick nor Rowe appears to recognize.

That there is a distinction to be drawn between Taylor's public and private written discourse long has been known. The nature of the differences between these two modes, however, has received less attention. This poet's public and private positions regarding both his classicism and his use of the imaginative faculty very likely can be explained by Emory Elliott's cogent observation that "the mysterious realm of the imagination and passions [was] once considered the special domain of the clergyman" (*Revolutionary Writers* 33). In accord with the colonial American educational system, practically all in Taylor's congregation in Westfield, Massachusetts, had attended the Dame or Petty Schools, in which girls and boys alike were taught to read the Bible in English; few, if any, however, had gone on to the grammar schools (boys only) which were perceived as largely college preparatory. So Taylor could not have expected his congregation to grasp fully the contradiction between the condemnation of the imaginative faculty in Genesis (and in other places in the Geneva Bible) and the Aristotelian promotion of this faculty.

The dialectic of Adam and Aeneas, when applied to Edward Taylor, clarifies the distinctions to be drawn between his public and private positions toward Adamic and classical discourse. While Taylor remains conservatively orthodox in his public, overwhelmingly Adamic discourse, his private, usually classical poetry (as in its adoption of the *meditatio*) reflects the mind of a humanist, albeit a Christian humanist.[26]

These public and private positions establish a pattern of acceptance and denial. That is, Taylor was fond of classicism, to the extent that he weaves into his poetry allusions to classical myths and figures which enrich the texture of his verbal experiments. In addition, his praxis of the *meditatio* displays not merely an awareness that this construct has its origins in classical rhetoric, but a sound subscription to that process of mind as described by ancient rhetoricians. Yet he appears to have chosen not to broadcast this fondness but rather publicly to endorse the better known (that is, known to more people) Adamic mode of discourse. For Taylor, such a move certainly was "safer" during a period when public hysteria led to the Salem witch trials.

Even at a later time, such a position of acceptance and denial, as we shall see, could be politically expedient. Still, Cotton Mather's *Magnalia Christi Americana*, despite its author's protestations to the contrary, promotes public acceptance of the myth of Aeneas.

3

Cotton Mather's Epic in Prose

Contrary to the situation of Edward Taylor, whose classicism has not received much attention, Cotton Mather's evident use of classicism has been pointed out by many scholars, including Sacvan Bercovitch, Jane D. Eberwein, Winton U. Solberg, and Gustaaf Van Cromphout. Solberg, "Cotton Mather: *The Christian Philosopher* and the Classics," for example, notes that, while most agree that *The Christian Philosopher* "is the best example of the way in which Newtonian science was first disseminated in British America" (324), in this work Mather draws on numerous classical sources. Solberg concludes that Mather's intention in this book "was to harmonize religion and the new science, and he skillfully used the literature of classical . . . antiquity in producing one of the most important documents of early American intellectual history" (366).

Gustaaf Van Cromphout in "Cotton Mather as Plutarchan Biographer," cogently argues that Mather's *Magnalia*, in the construction of its many biographies, owes much to Plutarch's *Lives*. He goes on to observe that Mather owes his "concept of biography . . . to the two great traditions regnant in his time, the classical and the Judaeo-Christian" (466). While such assessments of Mather's work are helpful, still one is left with questions. Why would Mather wish to infuse his work with so many classical sources? And what is the nature of his use of classicism?

While further investigation of the classicism of *The Christian Philosopher* may prove productive, especially in light of the Aeneas and Adam dialectic, the most significant text published by Mather surely is his *Magnalia Christi Americana (Great Works of Christ in America)*. Christopher Looby recently has crystallized present-day thinking about *Magnalia,* when he observes that such critics as Sacvan Bercovitch and J. A. Leo Lemay, among others, maintain that this text has "inaugurated . . . a mode of writing that conflates individual experience and national destiny in a celebration of representative American selfhood" (109). As a cultural artifact, then, the importance of *Magnalia* hardly can be exaggerated. Nevertheless, this work's indebtedness to classicism has been insufficiently explored, despite some attempts to do so.

Bercovitch's readings of *Magnalia Christi Americana,* which demonstrate its heavy indebtedness to classical epic, are well known among Early Americanists. In his early article, "New England Epic," Bercovitch ably demonstrates how the prose *Magnalia* makes use of such epic conventions as invoking the muse, beginning *in medias res,* constructing a "collective epic hero" (the New England Theocracy; "New England Epic" 343), and writing in an elevated style about the fate of a nation (Mather's New England). Furthermore, Bercovitch observes that *Magnalia* draws several specific parallels to the *Aeneid;* for example, "in the terms Mather would have preferred," Bercovitch asserts, "the founding of Rome prefigures that of New England and Virgil's poem finds its anti-type in his Church History" (340). Bercovitch was among the first to point out Mather's "implicit mythicizing" in *Magnalia.* Recall from our introduction above that Bercovitch sees Mather's John Winthrop, first colonial governor of Massachusetts Bay, as an American Aeneas.

About half of Bercovitch's "New England Epic" is devoted to a discussion of admittedly broad parallels between *Magnalia* and *Paradise Lost.* Two years before "New England Epic" appeared, however, George F. Sensabaugh concluded in his *Milton in Early America* that, in *Magnalia*, Mather's "three citations from Milton are all but lost," particularly in comparison to his quotations from classical authors. Therefore, remarks Sensabaugh, "to say Mather's adaptations of Milton constitute a substantial debt would force the evidence out of proportion" (41; entire discussion, 38–41). While I do not wish here to debate Milton's influence upon *Magnalia,*[1] I think it more provocative to ask how Mather's prose epic is *unlike* Milton's *Paradise Lost.* Bercovitch, "New England Epic"; Bercovitch, *Puritan Origins;* and Solberg all leave me with two compelling questions: Why would Mather have wished to construct an American Aeneas figure? Even more important, what are the consequences of such a construction?

Before we can attempt to resolve these questions, a few observations about *Magnalia* and Mather's classicism in general are in order. While the fact that many have recognized *Magnalia*'s importance as a cultural artifact may be reason enough to concentrate on this work, two other factors direct our attention to it. First, this work, having been reprinted in 1967 and again in 1979, is more readily available than any of Mather's other texts. Second, this two-volume work exerted formidable influence upon educated American readers in both the eighteenth and the nineteenth centuries. The two reprintings of *Magnalia* in 1820 and 1852 probably were responsible for the influence this work had on both Hawthorne and Melville, among other authors of the American Renaissance. As a repository for the collective Early American cultural past, *Magnalia*'s influence was substantial during the eighteenth century. One can even say, as the investigation below argues, that *Magnalia* embodies a principal, if not *the* principal, documentation of *translatio cultus*, the transplanting and dynamic rearticulation of Old World culture on the American strand.

While *Magnalia* indeed documents *translatio cultus*, it, like Taylor's public sermons and private poetry, also exemplifies the motif of acceptance and denial. In Mather's case, however, this pattern of acceptance and denial appears not to be a matter of wholly conscious choice, while in Taylor's work this pattern operates on a conscious level. Taylor's denial was public; his acceptance, though private, seems to have been fully conscious. Mather, however, repeatedly denounces the myth of Aeneas as pagan, heathenish, erroneous, even an abomination; yet this same Mather so saturates the *Magnalia* with classicism, particularly with borrowings from Vergil's *Aeneid*, that his stubborn denials finally fail to convince. In one of the attempts to construct a cultural history of America, Samuel L. Knapp in 1829 explains Mather's ambiguous attitude toward ancient classical writings in the following manner: "Acquainted with the pure fountains of classical literature, and often refreshed with copious draughts from them, he feared his piety might be questioned by having this generally known" (60). This pattern of fully conscious denial and less than conscious acceptance (a sort of covert acceptance) predicts the manner by which the motif of acceptance and denial will become manifest following the radical shift in discourse wherein Americans accepted the American Way as their own but lost sight of its origins in the character and behavior of Vergil's Aeneas.

Solberg tells us that, in *The Christian Philosopher*, for example, Mather is studious to counter his references to classical sources with illustrations such as that of Theophilus, a second-century Christian who wrote to inform the non-Christian world of "the Christian idea of God and the superiority of the doctrine of Creation over the immoral myths of the Olympian religion" (332). In Mather's "General Introduction" to *Magnalia*, after pages and pages of text heavy with references to and quotations from both Greek and Latin texts written largely by classical historians, the third-generation Puritan minister writes that the reader "must sensibly acknowledge, that the two short Books of *Ecclesiastical History*, written by the Evangelist *Luke* [i.e., the books of Luke and the Acts in the New Testament], hath given us more *glorious Entertainments*, than all these Historians if they were put all together" (96).[2] Then, in the very next paragraph, Mather continues his prior practice of citing events or quoting from Latin and Greek ancient history and mythology. It must be insisted that one does not at any time sense that Mather's disclaimers are insincere. Recall that he admonishes young ministers not to traffic "with muses that are no better than harlots." One is left to conclude, then, that Mather's undeniable, relatively unfettered embrace of classicism must, to some degree at least, be unconscious.

About his own classical training, particularly in grammar school, Mather reveals a great deal in his "Essay on the Memory of my Venerable MASTER: EZEKIEL CHEEVER." As discussed earlier, Mather joined another of his grammar school masters, Benjamin Tompson, in his remembrance of Cheever, although Mather's verse tribute lacks Tompson's irreverence. Making reference to the learning of "*Prosodia*, but with that Design/ Our Masters Name should in our *Verses* shine" (Knight 88), Mather informs us that it was because of Cheever's instruction that he now is able to claim the office of poet. In addition to writing poems, Cheever's pupils had to write themes, all in Latin, of course: "And if we made a *Theme*, 'twas with Regret/ We might not on *his* [Cheever's] Worth show all our Wit" (Knight 88–89). Among the texts Cheever's students came to know were Ovid's *Metamorphoses* (Mather, like Sandys before him, refers to it as Ovid's *Metamorphosis*) and *De tristibus*, Cicero's *De officiis*, and Cato's *Distickes*.

Predictably, Mather has more to say about Vergil than any other classical author. "Our Stately *Virgil* made us but Contrive," writes Mather, "As our *Anchises* to keep *him* Alive" (Knight 88). Parsing Vergil's *Aeneid*, in other words, taught Cheever's students to keep their master alive—for example, in Mather's verses written in Cheever's honor, just as Vergil's own text keeps alive Aeneas's memory of his beloved father Anchises. This same "father" Cheever also taught his "sons" that "Young *Austin*" (Saint Augustine) "wept when he saw *Dido* [Vergil's Queen of Carthage] dead,/ Tho' not a Tear for a *Lost Soul* he had"; for "Our Master would not let us be so vain,/ But us from Virgil did to *David* train" (Knight 90). Thus Mather asserts that Cheever protected his students from becoming overly fond of Vergil's mighty hexameters, as had Saint Augustine—another instance of Mather's habit of disclaiming his fondness for classical authors.

At another point in the poem, Mather is careful to observe that, although Cheever assuredly did teach his young charges Latin grammar, "The *Bible* is the Sacred *Grammar*, where/ The *Rules of speaking well*, contained are" (Knight 90). Once more, albeit perhaps a bit too late, Mather attempts to disclaim any real dependence upon classical authors. While he probably did not take any suggestions from Benjamin Tompson's burlesque of Cheever's teaching methods for his own portrait of their former schoolmaster, Mather probably did borrow a few hints from his first grammar school teacher's *New Englands Crisis* when he composed *Magnalia Christi Americana*. Tompson's work is relatively free of Mather's preoccupation with disclaiming a fondness for classical materials, so he cannot be the source of Mather's disclaimers. As several definite verbal and structural parallels do exist between Tompson's *Crisis* and Mather's *Magnalia*, however, Tompson's earlier work may have served Mather as a sort of model in miniature.

Like Tompson before him, for example, Mather refers several times in his "General Introduction" to "my own country" (Mather, *Cotton Mather* 92, 111 [twice]), by which, of course, he meant New England. Like his predecessor, Mather twice quotes Vergil's phrase "Dux faemina facti" (a woman was the leader of the deed). Vergil uses this phrase in the *Aeneid* to describe how Dido led her people to Carthage to escape the cruelty of the tyrant Pygmalion (I, 364). In the *Magnalia*, Mather first uses this phrase to introduce his discussion of his colony's theological altercation with Anne Hutchinson (VII, ch. 3). Much later in this same book, he employs this phrase a second time, here in an epitaph recapitulating the events which befell Hannah Dustan of the village of Haverhill from March 15 through April 30, 1697. Having recently given birth, Dustan witnessed the death of her newborn child at the hands of attacking natives; she and her nurse, Mary Neff, subsequently were taken prisoner, her husband and seven other children having fled. After enduring many hardships, including rough travel and privation, Dustan and Neff seized the right moment, killed many of their oppressors (taking their scalps), and escaped to the safety of their settlement (*Magnalia* 634–36). Both Mather and Tompson quote the same passage from the *Aeneid* to celebrate "heroic" acts of women against hostile Native Americans.

Mather, like Tompson before him, describes King Philip, or Metacomet, of the 1676 Algonquin revolt, as "Kennell'd with the rest of these horrid salvages" (VII, 561). Tompson's phrasing in *New Englands Crisis* is quite similar; he describes Philip and his band "Kennel'd together all without a summons" (86). A fourth parallel occurs as each writer calls the Native Americans "Myrmidons." This was Homer's term, though Vergil borrowed it some four times to designate the subordinates of Achilles and his father, Peleus; these subjects were gifts to them from Zeus, who transformed them from ants into human beings.

Both Mather and Tompson capitalize on the inhuman origins of the Myrmidons. In *New Englands Crisis*, for example, Tompson depicts a group of Native Americans bedding down after a day of brutal assault upon white settlers:

> Their Myrmidons inclos'd with cleftes of trees
> Are busie like the ants or nimble bees:
> And first they limber poles fix in the ground,
> In figure of the heavens convex . . .
> And under these the Elves do make their nests.
> Rome took more time to grow then twice six hours,
> But half that time will serve for indian bowers. (91)

Tompson's simile, "like the ants or nimble bees," calls up the myth of the Myrmidons' transformation from insects into humans. His description of their temporary domiciles as forming "the heavens convex" (a counterfeit heaven far below the cosmic one, recalling the realm of Milton's fallen angels) furthers his overall effort to establish that the Native Americans embody the anti-Christ; and his calling all Native Americans "Elves" suggests their alignment with demonic forces.[3] The ludicrous comparison of their temporary structures with the Eternal City only further denigrates them.

Mather is less subtle in his use of the Myrmidon allusion. As this reference appears within the context of Mather's explication of the colony's wars with Native Americans, the connection to Tompson's vilification of Native Americans is strengthened. Following yet another grisly depiction of the "savagery" wrought by Native Americans upon white settlers, Mather asks, "Reader, who should be the *father* of these *myrmidons?*" Mather's implication is clear; drawing upon his contemporary readers' awareness that the Myrmidons' origin is not human, Mather suggests (as Tompson, too, had) that these hostile Native Americans surely must derive from some demonic or Satanic source. Thus he justifies, or extends a prior justification of, the white effort to eliminate them. Insofar as the two writers exhibit almost identical attitudes toward appropriation of Vergil's epic poem, the salient point is that both Tompson and Mather interpret the Native Americans, enemies of the colonists, as resembling the enemies of Aeneas and his Trojan followers.

Verbal similarities aside, two substantial structural parallels between Tompson's *Crisis* and Mather's *Magnalia* support the conclusion that Tompson's work served Mather as a model. As was pointed out earlier, Tompson opens his short epic with a ninety-two-line "Prologue" which may be identified as a poetic jeremiad (Tompson 84–86). Certainly Mather's *Magnalia* is acknowledged universally as serving the purpose of the jeremiad, to admonish the author's New England readers of their "declension" (Perry Miller's term) from prior "golden times" (evocative of Vergilian pastoral) of the first generation of Puritan colonists. Indeed, it seems to be central to Mather's purpose in *Magnalia* to raise up an earlier, happier, more confident era to serve his readers as a model of what ought to be.

We must give Tompson credit as the first author to blend the Adamic jeremiad and the classical epic form, thereby establishing a precedent for Mather's own efforts. What Mather's *Magnalia Christi Americana* represents within this context, then, is a fuller, much more expansive attempt to articulate the American self. As we shall see, Mather's prose epic much more successfully enacts the dynamic tension between the Adamic and classical strands of the idea of Americanness.

In the substantial *Columbia Literary History of the United States*, edited by Elliott et al., several critics note in separate essays Mather's indebtedness to the ancient epic tradition. Everett Emerson, in "History and Chronicle," for example, speaks of *Magnalia*'s "epic contours" (53). In "From Cotton Mather to Benjamin Franklin," Kenneth Silverman remarks that Mather's work "lent the Puritan past epic stature" (106). In "The Puritan Vision of the New World," Bercovitch observes that the second and third generations of New Englanders "enshrined their forebears . . . as giants of a golden age, like Vergil's legendary Trojans entering upon the future site of Rome" (39) and then repeats his observation that, in *Magnalia*, Mather hoped to create a "New World epic" which would be greater than Vergil's *Aeneid* (42). From such commentary, it is surprising that Mather's acknowledged debt to the classical tradition, and to Vergil in particular, has not received more attention. I suspect that the hegemony of the Adamic myth has obstructed our efforts.

In any event, the role of the myth of Aeneas in *Magnalia* dramatizes a pivotal moment in the development of American culture; for, when the classical strand of discourse intertwines with the Adamic, what emerges is perhaps the first full articulation of the American self. As detailed treatment of Mather's use of classicism in *Magnalia* easily could occupy the space of an entire volume, the following investigation must of necessity be guided by an effort to select those applications of classical sources which most forcefully indicate the classical origins of the American self.

Mather typically denies his dependence on classical sources, and toward the conclusion of *Magnalia*, he attempts to establish that the ancient, pagan writers appropriated much of their mythology from biblical sources. The eventual victory of the colonists over the Native Americans Mather attributes to "our Lord Jesus Christ . . . who is the great Phoebus, that 'SUN of righteousness'" (VII, 579). During the Renaissance, authors frequently made a pun on sun/Son (of God), and that practice was habitual with Mather, too. The elaborate conceit just mentioned might seem merely one more case of such "elegant" punning. When one looks at this particular passage more closely, however, one finds more at work than elegant punning. For, throughout this fifteenth and final section of chapter 6, Mather has been demonstrating how the ancient Greeks and Romans had, after the manner of Sandys and Raleigh, pilfered the Old Testament for their notions of Apollo and the Python. Accordingly, Apollo becomes a latter-day Joshua and the Python a later manifestation of Og (the giant king of Bashan defeated by Moses; VII, 579). Mather then goes on to offer this trenchant observation: "We have by a true and plain history secured the story of our successes against all the Ogs in this *woody* country from falling under the disguises of mythology" (II, 579). This statement amounts to yet another disclaimer, a defense in anticipation of a possible charge that Mather has depended on classical authors and myths excessively. In fact, at least to a modern reader, he seems not merely to have told the "history" of *New English Israel* (II, 674), but forcefully to have blended the myths of Adam and Aeneas in a syncretization of Phoebus and Jesus. His disclaimer, then, seems too little, too late. If Mather's text is not "true and plain history," then *Magnalia* provides an illustration of the poststructuralist idea that history really is fiction in disguise.

Just what Mather means when he claims to write history (or, more precisely, what an examination of Mather's text proves his history really to be) deserves extended attention, for such consideration can instruct us regarding the aesthetic dimensions of *Magnalia*. That Mather's idea of a "true and plain history" does not correspond exactly to that of many historiographers today is evident from his portrayal of Sir William Phips, colonial governor of Massachusetts Bay from 1692 to 1695. As Silverman cogently observes, "Although *Magnalia* places Phips as a successor in the honored gubernatorial line of William Bradford and John Winthrop, he seems an exemplar not of Governor but of the Self-Made Man" (*Life and Times* 163). Mather could not have been unaware of Phips's questionable conduct during his early treasure-troving years nor of his thumbing his nose at Governor Bradstreet before he (Phips) occupied the same gubernatorial seat. What Mather gives us in "The Life of . . . Phips" is a narrative of panegyric quality—not "true and plain history" as we understand history.

It is, of course, arguable that many other portions of *Magnalia* are narrative. To be sure, today's understanding of history was current during Mather's era. Hobbes, in *Leviathan* (1650), remarks that "The Register of Knowledge of Fact is called History" (pt. I, ch. IX, 40). The word *history* continued to carry its two Latin meanings: tale or narrative; and relation of factual events. For that matter, in Greek, *istoria*, ιστωρια, is first a learning by inquiry and then an accounting of one's inquiries or a narrative of them; hence an *istor*, ιστωρ, is a wise man, one whose knowledge is correct and who serves in the capacity of a judge. Given Mather's extensive and obvious classical background, perhaps it is this last understanding of the concept of historian to which Mather, or his text, subscribes in *Magnalia*. If so,

Mather need not be seen as acting as historiographer at all, but rather as judge of what is best and correct about the American culture as he saw it. Such a perspective encourages us to read *Magnalia* as an exercise in mythopoeia.

The work of Stephen Greenblatt reinforces this emphasis on textuality. Richter points out in his excellent *Critical Tradition*, "The genuine innovation Greenblatt has brought to literary history is implicit in [the] poststructuralist notion that history and literature are equally 'texts'" (954). Using this approach, Mather's *Magnalia Christi Americana*, despite any claims to factual disinterestedness, is not history in an objective sense but may be read more accurately (truthfully or honestly) as a literary text containing tropic strategies adapted from poetic discourse. In his works which treat *Magnalia*, Bercovitch has been arguing in a similar vein for years. Much of the discussion of *Magnalia* here accords with the understanding that this text relies heavily upon adaptations from poetic discourse. I have become convinced that *Magnalia* must be considered one of the few major texts of Early American literature, and this type of reading may broaden aesthetic appreciation of Mather's "literary" achievement, at least in *Magnalia*.

Mather's adaptations of certain classical elements represent his most substantial incorporation of modes from poetic discourse. Some of these substantial adaptations occur at the beginning of Mather's text. Almost everyone writing about *Magnalia* has declared that the work's opening lines, "I write the *Wonders* of the CHRISTIAN RELIGION, flying from the depravations of *Europe*, to the *American Strand*" (89), derive from the first words of Vergil's *Aeneid:* "Arma virumque cano" (Arms and the man I sing). At least one critic, David Shields, disagrees, tracing this passage to the fifth section of George Herbert's "The Church Militant" (D. Shields, "Herbert and Colonial American Poetry" 281–85). I suspect that Mather's source for his opening may be even more general, neither Vergil nor necessarily Herbert. To "write" is not to "sing"; Mather's medium in executing *Magnalia* is decidedly prose (though a few scattered lines of poetry do appear in the work). At least consciously, his emphasis is what he says it is, "the *Wonders*," or the ostensibly miraculous effects, of his faith's transplantation to New England—hardly the tale of a secular man and his valor at arms. I submit that Mather's opening phrasing is so common as not to be traceable definitively to Vergil or anyone else.

In this same brief opening paragraph, Mather's invocation of "the Holy Author," though resembling Milton's invocation to the "Heav'nly Muse" of *Paradise Lost* more than Vergil's four-line invocation in the *Aeneid* (ll. 8–11), definitely follows the conventions of the literary epic. In the third paragraph of the "General Introduction," Mather demonstrates awareness of another epic convention as he proceeds to enumerate "the *Actors*, that have, in a more exemplary manner[,] served" (89) the colonies of New England. As Kenneth Murdock observes, "The manner of introducing both the actors and the causes of action is . . . reminiscent of the epic tradition" (Mather, *Cotton Mather* 372). Both Vergil and Milton, for example, employ this convention early in their epics (i.e., the *Aeneid* and *Paradise Lost*).

Only in the opening of the second section of the "Introduction" does Mather display his first unmistakable borrowing from Vergil's epic, and this instance proves crucial to the entire text of *Magnalia*. Mather writes: "The Reader will doubtless desire to know, what it was that—tot Volvere casus Insignes Pietate Viros, tot adire Labores,/ Impulerit" (impelled men distinguished in devotion [to the Gods, family, and country] to endure so many misfortunes, to encounter so many hardships; *Aeneid* I, 9–11).

Mather's passage is almost exactly like the one in Vergil's epic, where it comprises the major portion of Vergil's four-line invocation and marks the first of many times Vergil names his hero's primary virtue (pietas). The only difference is that Mather has rendered Vergil's phrase "insignem pietate virum" as "insignes pietate viros." That is, Mather has altered the Mantuan's grammatically singular description of Aeneas as a *man* distinguished in pietas to the plural *men* so distinguished. Hence Mather, appropriating the central Roman virtue to the New England adventure, ascribes the virtue of pietas to the first generation of New England settlers. As we shall discover, this occasion is only the first in which Mather celebrates this virtue; at several pivotal moments, Mather continues to alter Vergil's text for his own mythopoeic ends.

On the title page of the first of *Magnalia*'s seven books, for example, Mather has the line: "Tantae Molis erat, pro CHRISTO condere Gentem" (So much labor did it cost to establish a people for Christ). For those who know (including, of course, all Mather's contemporaries who had passed through the sixth form of grammar school), this line is an obvious adaptation of the *Aeneid*, I, 33: "Tantae molis erat Romanam condere gentem" (Of such great effort it was to establish the Roman people). This line is only the last line of a passage which had to hold special import for all early Americans: "multosque per annos/ errabant acti fatis maria omnia circum./ Tantae molis erat Romanam condere gentem" (And so they [Aeneas and his band of men] wandered for many years over all the oceans, driven by destiny. Of such great effort it was to establish the Roman people). No less effort had been expended by Mather's immediate ancestors. Do the seeds of the American cultural imperative, its Manifest Destiny, lie in the example of Vergil's hero, "driven by destiny"? By blending this well-known passage with the idea of the oceanic vicissitudes of the Puritan Fathers, Mather signals the importance of Vergil's epic to his own enterprise. In effect, he syncretizes ancient myth with more recent events and religious convictions. In so doing, he invites his readers to understand *Magnalia* as a conscious exercise in mythopoeia.

This linking of history and the mythic characterizes Mather's practice throughout *Magnalia*. Moreover, it demonstrates his preference for Vergil's *Aeneid* over Homer's two epics. For Vergil in the *Aeneid* frequently points out how a mythic event in his hero's "life" is relevant to the future history and greatness of Rome. Homer's more disinterested, oral-formulaic rendering of the Troy story does not easily permit such historical interpretation. Mather's joining of history and myth thereby underscores his affinity for Vergil's *Aeneid* and reinforces the contention that Mather has modeled his history after Vergil's example.

Indeed, Mather has designed his entire work after the *Aeneid;* the first six books of *Magnalia* are arranged to treat the problems encountered by the Puritans as they fled England and traversed a perilous sea to New England, with a particular focus on how these vicissitudes emboldened the early settlers to develop sufficient character to meet the overwhelming difficulties of their journey, arrival, and adaptation to a new land. This pattern resembles Aeneas's character development in the first six books of the *Aeneid*, to that climactic point in the underworld at which his deceased father Anchises for the first time addresses him by the title "Romane" (Roman; VI, 851). At this moment, Aeneas has become the embodiment of pietas. Now Aeneas is equal to his next, most difficult task, that of supplanting (in books VII–XII) Turnus and his band of "natives" in order to found the civilization of Rome. Like Vergil before him, Mather devotes the remainder of *Magnalia* (all of book VII) to an explication of the Puritans' "battles" to establish the colony. Calling this book *Ecclesiarum Praelia; or, A Book of the Wars of the Lord*, Mather devotes the first five chapters, less than a third of the total length of this book, to "disturbances" to the colony brought on by unfortunate and sometimes hostile encounters with such groups as Antinomians (for example, Ann Hutchinson), Quakers, and impostors posing as ministers.

These chapters establish the tone for the last two-thirds of book VII, which, along with its extended "Appendix," treat in much detail the colony's war with Metacomet (called King Philip by the British), leader of the Algonquin Confederacy. The effect here recalls Vergil's epic, in which book VII and most of book VIII treat mounting hostilities between the Trojans and the people of Latium, with large-scale fighting delayed until book X. Appropriately, Mather entitles the major portion of his book (ch. 6) "Arma Virosque Cano" (Arms and men I sing), adapting Vergil's opening phrase of the *Aeneid*, "Arma virumque cano" (Arms and the man [Aeneas] I sing). That chapter describes the armed conflict with King Philip, whom Benjamin Tompson has already identified as the American Turnus. It is worth observing that Mather peppers the remainder of book VII and its "Appendix" with fifteen additional allusions to Vergil.

Mather's portrayal of Sir William Phips, however, depends upon Vergil's epic for much more than numerous allusions. Phips becomes Mather's fullest Aeneas figure. Eberwein observes that "the close verbal association between pietas, the reverence for tradition associated with Vergil's Aeneas, and New England piety amplifies the reference" of Mather's title for this "episode," "Pietas in Patriam." (Mather's episodic and digressive narration of lives and events contribute two more characteristics of the literary epic.) Eberwein, however, does not identify Phips as an American Aeneas figure, as Bercovitch does John Winthrop. Furthermore, in the *Aeneid* as in *Magnalia*, pietas projects much more than "reverence for tradition"; for that matter, Mather takes great pains, as we shall see, to separate his discussion of pietas in relation to Phips from "New England piety."

Kenneth B. Murdock is hardly the first to criticize Mather for allegedly "tacking on" his lengthy life of Sir William Phips at the end of book II of *Magnalia*. According to Murdock, "Its length was disproportionate to the space given to other governors of Massachusetts" (Mather, *Cotton Mather* 34). Inclusion of this previously published (1698) tract, Murdock maintains, constitutes a serious assault on the aesthetic unity of Mather's already sprawling text. On the contrary, the life of Phips is essential to Mather's mythopoeia. The necessity of this allegedly superfluous life is signaled loudly in its title: "Pietas in Patriam: The Life of His Excellency Sir William Phips, Knt. Late Captain General and Governour . . . of the Massachuset-Bay." Indeed, pietas identifies Vergil's hero. And on Mather's title page for this life (in the 1697 edition of *Pietas in Patriam*, published first in London), Mather prints this line adapted from book XII of the *Aeneid:* "Discite Virtutem ex Hoc, verumque Laborem" (Learn virtue or valor from this man and true toil). In the *Aeneid*, Vergil's hero speaks this line, in the heat of battle against Turnus's band of natives, to his maturing son Ascanius (or Julus). The original line, altered but little by Mather, reads: "'Disce, puer, virtutem ex me verumque laborem'" (435; Learn valor from me, son, and true toil).

Mather draws yet another intimate connection between his hero and Vergil's when he writes of Phips's attention to the complicated affairs of state that they "caused him to take many a tedious Voyage, accompanied sometimes with his *Fidus Achates* and very dear Friend, Kinsman and Neighbour, Colonel *John Philips*" (340). Of course, the phrase "Fidus Achates" refers to Aeneas's ever-faithful friend and confidante, Achates. Continuing this heroic representation, Mather frequently cites Phips's "Heroick Virtue." Unlike most of Mather's other portraits in *Magnalia*, this one paints Phips as primarily a military and political figure and sometimes an adventurer—certainly not a minister of the gospel. At another juncture, Mather describes Phips's escapades salvaging wrecked Spanish galleons, certainly an essential portion of his portrait. For it was as one who recovers Spanish gold that Phips amassed his famous fortune. I bring up this point because Mather cites Peter Martyr's *Decades* as a possible source for one of Phips's searches. Phips knew, says Mather, "particularly, that when the Ship which had Governour *Boadilla* [Francisco de Bobadilla, viceroy of the Spanish West Indies until his death in 1502] aboard, was cast away, there was, as *Peter Martyr* says, an entire Table of *Gold* of *Three Thousand Three Hundred and Ten Pound Weight*" (352).

In Eden's translation of Martyr, this phenomenally rich store of gold is described as "rounde pieces of three hundreth pounde weyght, and one of three thousande, three hundreth and tenne pounde weyght" (Eden 105). Mather appears to have changed but little the phrasing of the translator of the *Decades*. In the passage just cited, Martyr goes on to describe the wreck of the vessel attempting to transport this booty "to the Kynge [Ferdinand of Spain] in that shyppe in the which the governour *Boadilla* was coming home into Spayne, the shyppe with all the men beinge drowned by the way, by reason it was over laden with the weight of golde" (105). That Phips would have consulted Martyr's *Decades* for information regarding Spanish gold that might be salvaged attests the persistent popularity of Martyr's work and suggests that many (not just a few) Early Americans were familiar with Martyr's narration of the New World exploration in terms of the Aeneas myth.

Phips's life, as Mather renders it, gives balance to Mather's epic saga by establishing the importance of the secular man to the survival of the colony. In this portrait, as many already have observed, Mather constructs the prototype of America's self-made entrepreneurial man who also moves within his community as a thoroughly political being. In Mather's own inimitable words:

> The old *Heathen* Virtue of PIETAS IN PATRIAM, or, LOVE TO ONE'S COUNTRY, he turned into *Christian;* and so notably exemplified it, in all the Rest of his *Life*, that it will be an Essential *Thread* which is to be now interwoven into all that remains of his *History*, and his *Character*. (288)

In this portrait of Sir William Phips, Mather gives several clues to his overall construction of *Magnalia:* the syncretizing of Christian and Roman virtue in pietas, his determination to reveal exemplary character through historical events (recall Vergil's identical purpose in the *Aeneid*), and his identification of pietas as central not merely to his portrait of Phips, but to his overall scheme. The lives of John Wilson, William Bradford, Richard Mather, and particularly John Winthrop (Bercovitch's American Aeneas, in his *Puritan Origins* 5, 64, 66) all exemplify devotion to God and family. But

Phips's life, the longest in *Magnalia*, most clearly embodies practical, worldly devotion to *patria* (the fatherland). It matters little that, as Bercovitch states, Mather's "*aim* [italics added] . . . was not to clothe local history in myth" but "to preserve the myth [of the Puritan errand into the American wilderness] from the course of history" ("Puritan Vision," 420). The results of Mather's work, regardless what his purpose was, constitute a splendid example of the tension between the myths of Adam and Aeneas.

How remarkably different are the uses of the *Aeneid* made by Mather in *Magnalia* and by Milton in *Paradise Lost*. For example, Milton *never* alludes to Phoebus, Apollo, Vergil (or Virgil), Maro, or the Mantuan; yet Mather in *Magnalia* calls God Phoebus and cites Vergil by name often. On the one hand, Milton, in *Paradise Lost*, draws less than forty allusions and/or parallels to Vergil's opus and quotes or translates only two passages from Vergil.[4] It should not go unremarked, either, that it is difficult to read more than a pair of lines from *Paradise Lost* without hearing an echo, no matter how faint, of Vergil's mighty hexameters. On the other hand, Mather incorporates in *Magnalia* some one hundred allusions and/or parallels to Vergil. Rather than Milton's mere echoes, all in English, Mather either cites Vergil by name or, more often, adapts actual lines from the *Aeneid* for his own purposes. Milton, in his use of Vergil, then, appears not nearly so self-conscious in his borrowings, whereas Mather seems determined to remind his readers of the connection between *Magnalia* and the great Roman epic.

Conventional wisdom holds that Milton did *not* see the *Aeneid* as a mythic possibility, but rather as a model for imitation (in Dryden's sense of imitation). Hence Milton borrows or adapts the structure of the *Aeneid* for his own objectives of form—not as a mythic presence. Milton clearly gestures toward the *Aeneid* as an accomplishment of the past, one to be respected and even imitated, but not as a living myth. In Mather's *Magnalia*, however, the author's gestures toward Vergil's epic are as toward a living myth. Turnus comes alive again in the Native American resistance to European invasion. John Winthrop and William Phips breathe new life into Vergil's hero Aeneas. These characters from *Magnalia* once again embody the classical virtues; Turnus and Aeneas are, as Milton's fallen angels in rebellion against God are not, living presences—not mere manifestations. In other words, in Milton's characters, any resemblance to Vergil is subsumed within Milton's determination to give his figures theological identity as metaphors for his theodicy.[5] In Mather's work, however, the author's self-conscious shaping of his materials recasts the *Aeneid* as a living mythic presence—an amalgam of the myths of Adam and Aeneas.

When understood in this way, *Magnalia* becomes an effective herald of the transformation of Adam into Aeneas. Despite Mather's protestations to the contrary—his labeling of pietas as a "heathen virtue," for example—what he creates in *Magnalia* is the story of a people motivated as much by classical virtues and examples as by Christian ones. The two myths of Adam and Aeneas become blended so as to yield a description of a people who are not British, not "Heathen," and not even clearly Puritan, but who are American. Moving from this blend, the secular emphasis of the Enlightenment and the dynamic of the Age of Reason combine with the Early American exuberance, first for cultural and later for political and economic independence, to privilege the discourse of Aeneas over that of Adam.

With the appearance of Cotton Mather's *Magnalia Christi Americana*, *translatio cultus*, transplantation of the action of dwelling in a place, has been accomplished. Mather's New England, in his words, has progressed from a "Condition . . . very like that of the *Romans* in the time of *Romulus*, when every Man contented himself with *Two Acres* of Land; and as *Pliny* tells us . . . *It was thought a great Reward for one to receive a Pint of Corn from the People of* Rome, *which Corn they also pounded in Mortars*" (italics are Mather's; Mather, *Cotton Mather* 141). Clearly Mather sees transplantation of Europeans onto the American strand in terms of the Aeneas myth.

In 1702, following the precedent set by Benjamin Tompson in *New Englands Crisis*, it has become feasible, despite Mather's protestations to the contrary, to interpret the American adventure in freedom, not exclusively in terms of the Adamic myth, but in language and figures taken from both the myth of Adam and the myth of Aeneas. While the sweep of Mather's prose epic—with its descriptions of perilous sea voyages, relocation to the West, and emphasis on wandering exiles—far exceeds Tompson's more modest effort in *Crisis*, the necessary ingredient, not present in Tompson, which Mather incorporates into the classical half of the American self is pietas. Just so does Mather invent the American self.

The Adamic myth could and did provide the means to chastise a backsliding people, who appeared satisfied with relatively little. In his fictionalized portrait of Phips, however, Mather ironically celebrates the first full-blown American capitalist. For, while the Adamic myth (at least the New Testament version of that myth) condemns the quest to acquire worldly goods, the myth of Aeneas throws open the door to such gain. It is certainly true that Vergil's Aeneas, *pius* as he was, does not himself represent free enterprise as virtuous. Nonetheless, the historical empire of Augustus (like certain passages of the Old Testament) did promote the possibility of gain for those enterprising enough to seize the opportunity. However witting or unwitting he was, Mather in this portrait not only gives permission for the rise of such figures as Phips, but even encourages their incarnations. It is Mather's peculiar handling of the third element of pietas, loyalty to a homeland in this world, that so indelibly stamps his effort as American.

In this tracing of Early Americans' use of classicism from its first articulations through its guarded applications in such writers as Bradstreet, Tompson, Taylor, and Mather, we have found that, even before a single Englishman set foot on American soil, America had been invented by Peter Martyr, first in terms of Aeneas and then as a blending of Aeneas with Adam. Before George Sandys observed the transmogrification of a portion of the Virginia coast into a British base of operations, he and others had been conditioned by Richard Eden's popular translation of Martyr's *Decades* to view the American adventure as a blend of these two discourses. Sandys, reclining on Virginia's beach while translating a major part of Ovid's *Metamorphoses* (see frontispiece), serves as a compelling and attractive metaphor for what actually was occurring as a result of European intervention in the New World. From around 1500 to the 1620s, both these discourses traveled alongside one another, with the classical slightly privileged over the Adamic, probably as a result of the Renaissance enthusiasm for reclamation of classical knowledge.

Following the arrival of the Puritans, for the next one hundred years Adam and Aeneas continue their journey in tandem, with the Puritans' emphasis on their religious expression occasionally, but not always, valorizing Adam over Aeneas. For example, Puritan efforts in the seventeenth century to separate these two discourses in order to privilege the Judaeo-Christian over and against the classical are reflected in Edward Taylor's public denial of the classical mode as he privately accepts it.

With Benjamin Tompson, despite his opening jeremiad, the tension between these two modes tips decidedly in the direction of Aeneas, as we observe the poet of *New-England Tears* and *Crisis* usually articulating the colonial wars with the Algonquin Confederacy in terms of the *Aeneid*, not the Geneva Bible. For a brief moment, the myth of Aeneas dominates that of Adam, and Tompson's Rutulian Native Americans predict Mather's "Indians" in *Magnalia*. While Tompson displays no anxiety in his promotion of classical figures over Christian ones, Cotton Mather registers a great deal of concern. Born a generation after Taylor, Mather does not manage, even in his public writings, to separate Aeneas from Adam as Taylor does. Strikingly, these two modes become locked in contest; while Mather declares that the Adamic myth rules the classical, the Aeneas myth persistently asserts itself.

This contest for dominance, so evident in Mather's *Magnalia*, serves as a fitting prelude to our discussion in the next part of this book. As we shall see, the myth of Adam, its hegemony already slipping as it interacts with the Aeneas myth in *Magnalia*, swiftly loses ground in Early America as the eighteenth century progresses—so much so that, in fact, Adam effectively becomes Aeneas.

PART II

Adam Becomes Aeneas: 1720–1784

Fig. 1. *The Fishing Lady*, circa 1750. Attributed to Eunice Bourne. Courtesy, Museum of Fine Arts, Boston. Reproduced with permission.

4

Surge for Cultural Independence
The Flourishing of American Classicism

Eighteenth-century America evinced an intriguing time of rapid immigration and internal population growth, when colonial American ingenuity and thought first entered the world arena. Trade and commerce with the American colonies became increasingly valued by Europe. The secular Enlightenment relaxed the rigid grip of New England Puritanism upon an evolving American consciousness. Toward the last quarter of the century, women authors began to assert themselves in print with an increasing boldness. This time of Jonathan Edwards, Benjamin Franklin, Thomas Jefferson, Phillis Wheatley, and George Washington was a time of profound promise of things to come. It was a time when Adam became Aeneas.

This same era was filled with contradictions. Recall the example of Cotton Mather's Sir William Phips, whom the secular myth of Aeneas taught that the New Testament's denial of worldly goods was unsound, perhaps even in error. That is to say, acquisition and wealth not only became celebrated but stood as concrete evidence of moral worth. Whereas the myth of Adam was largely spiritual and theocratic, the myth of Aeneas suggested to writers and thinkers a political, social, and cultural ideology tinctured with a secular spirituality wholly compatible with deism and the Age of Reason. Colonial Americans discovered that, Jonathan Edwards's conservative or even reactionary jeremiads notwithstanding, they could attain a comfortable morality "beyond the holy circle."[1] As we shall see, the life and character of George Washington came to represent for all Americans the dramatic enactment of pietas, the principal virtue of Vergil's Aeneas.

When Mother Britain steadily signaled that she intended to share selfishly in colonial America's growing bounty, she inevitably provoked into resistance her "child's" newly revived economic self-consciousness. Such challenges to British autonomy recalled the events of the "revolution" of 1676, when colonial Americans first tried to overthrow British domination and declare independence. A major part of the revitalized economic system rested upon the institution of slavery, a set of practices *not* borrowed from either the myth of Aeneas or that of Adam.[2] The source of slavery in the modern era is human avarice, though many who practiced it alleged that justification could be found in the history of Rome and/or in the Bible. In any event, the eighteenth-century struggle for economic independence was attended by similar moves toward political self-sufficiency.

Many have explored the political and ideological origins of the American Revolution. Bridenbaugh, *Cities in Revolt;* Nash, *Urban Crucible;* and Jack Greene, *Quest for Power* are but three such explorations. Therefore, little attempt will be made here to emend the conclusions of these investigations. What has not received adequate attention is the colonial American struggle toward cultural independence, particularly as manifested in the literary quest for self-definition. This literary struggle for self-definition grew out of the remarkable creation of a conspicuously American classicism.

British classicism, according to Donald Greene, exhibited an exuberance in the areas of thought, ideas, and creativity. American classicism, too, manifested an exuberance for these, but it particularly embraced declarations of literary independence, an identifiably American pastoral, and a peculiarly American effort to assuage a fear of pastlessness, as was evident in the praxis of the pastoral elegy. Before investigating each of these expressions of American classicism individually, we would do well to survey the colonial American setting out of which they grew.

Background

In a recent full-length video, *American Art and the Metropolitan Museum (1650–1914): Part One*, Vincent Scully speaks of colonial American houses as centers of family ritual and repositories of household gods. Little prompting is needed to draw an analogy here between American settlers and early Romans, as both performed supplicatory rituals to their respective ideas of an intimate deity. Romans and colonial Americans alike sought aid in surviving from a power or force greater than themselves. The Romans made obeisance to the *Lares*, or tutelary house divinities, and to the *Penates*, or gods of the hearth. For those eighteenth-century Americans still subscribing to the Adamic myth (and this group included the overwhelming majority, as it still does today), this activity centered on Judaeo-Christian monotheism. Even the great portion of the intellectual elite often called upon Providence to guide their daily enterprises. One is tempted to conclude, nevertheless, that, while Scully does not state the connection, he has the Roman analogy in mind as he makes this observation.

In the realm of *belles lettres*, such writers as John Adams (1704–1740) and Jane Turell were, during the 1720s and 1730s, composing versions of Horace's odes. Adams was a Harvard graduate of the class of 1721, which also included Ebenezer Turell, who later married Jane. Never completely settled as a minister, Adams turned his efforts toward serving both as a graduate tutor at Harvard and as a frequent contributor to the poetry section of the *New England Weekly Journal*, then under the editorship of Mather Byles. Following Adams's death in 1740, a collection of his verse, *Poems on Several Occasions*, was published five years later in Boston. This collection includes English versions of six of Horace's odes.

Quite imaginative in his rendering of Horace's Latin, Adams appropriately introduces this group of poems by devoting the first of the six to the first ode of book I, Horace's obligatory plea that Maecenas, his patron, praise the Roman poet's efforts. Horace concludes his Latin ode with this exaggerated pledge: "quodsi me lyricus vatibus inseres,/ sublimi feriam sidera vertice" (but if you enroll me among the lyric poets, I will achieve the highest fame [literally, I will strike the stars at the highest summit]). Adams, while matching the Roman's hyperbole, distends the Latin into graceful couplets of iambic tetrameter: "If you the deathless Bays bestow,/ And by Applauses make them grow,/ Towards the Stars, my winged Fame/ Shall fly, and strike the heavenly Frame" (Adams 62).

With Horace's fourth ode of his first book, Adams is even more liberal. Here the Early American poet drops completely the Horatian convention of giving a personal frame of reference by addressing individuals (borrowed from the early Greek lyric) and instead concentrates upon the ode's central emphasis on the great leveling power of death, the equalizer. Whereas Horace admonishes his wealthy friend Sestius that he cannot in death take his fortune with him, Adams mutes the personal address and makes it democratic by proposing that, in Pluto's realms, "Friend, the circling Youth will never crown/ Thy sumptuous Feast" (64). In Adams's version, there are no wealthy patricians, merely a classless society in which all face the same doom. At an earlier point, when discussing how the promise of spring causes one to forget death's certainty too easily, Horace observes that winter's end has arrived when "nec prata canis albicant pruinis" (neither are the fields made white with frost). But for this same line from the Latin, Adams creates this affecting pastoral image: "And now the Fields, in native Beauty drest,/ Are by the Arms of Frost no more carest" (63). Horace says nothing about "native Beauty."

In her imitation of Horace, Jane Turell, too, is concerned to point out "native" characteristics. This wife of Adams's former classmate constructs her poem with even less dependence on Horace's original (or I should say originals). "An Invitation into the Country, in Imitation of Horace" seems to conflate much of the imagery of both Horace's seventeenth ode of book I and the second of his Epodes. This delightful piece opens with an address to Turell's father, Benjamin Colman, a minister of Boston and the subject of Joseph Seccombe's fine pastoral elegy discussed later in this chapter. Even less formal than Adams, Turell evokes the "flowery vales and green retreats" which her own rural Medford promises her father if he visits her, well removed from Boston's "thick smokes and noisy" din. In her "retreat," she exchanges Horace's pears and grapes (in the epode) for "Pomona's bounty" (her own apples). Whereas Horace's grapes yield him satisfying home-prepared wine, Turell asserts, "No wine but what does from my apples flow,/ My frugal house on any can bestow." Actually following quite closely Horace's portrait of the modest wife who goes about her chores of tending her family, milking the cows, and preparing meals, the wife of Jane's poem spreads for table "what is meat and wholesome" and offers "My good fat bacon and our homely bread,/ With which my healthful family is fed." These lines capture so closely the picture of a wholesome, fit, average American family that they might have been written yesterday. A description she gives of her homespun linen, however, returns us to colonial America: "For me no fair Egyptian plies the loom,/ But my fine linen all is made at home" (Evert Duyckinck and George Duyckinck 125).

What is particularly notable about these two poets is the ease with which each adapts the ancient Latin to her or his own world. To these writers, Horace is no alien. Once again we observe colonial Americans enacting *translatio cultus*. Each writer manipulates expressions of her or his classical heritage, yet each produces a recognizably American poem. Turell, of course, merely by her example (along with that of her worthy predecessor, Anne Bradstreet), affirms that women of her time could acquire a fairly sophisticated knowledge of the classics, despite so-called "manly," Puritan objections. Yet it should be pointed out that Turell's father, Reverend Colman, encouraged her learning and that her husband not only encouraged her writing of verse but also was responsible for preserving her poetry. Indeed, immediately after his wife's death in 1735, Ebenezer Turell published in Boston the volume *Reliquiae Turellae, et Lachrymae Paternae*. The book was published again in 1741, this time in London, under the title *Memoirs of the Life and Death of the Pious and Ingenious Mrs. Jane Turell . . . Collected Chiefly from Her Own Manuscripts*. This slender volume also includes a poetic "Epistle to the Rev. Turell, Occasioned by the Death of His Late Virtuous Consort," by John Adams, Ebenezer's Harvard classmate. So, as with Bradstreet, men apparently fostered this young woman poet's work.

As we shall soon see, men were *not*, but women were, the principle agents behind the publication of the poems of a later woman poet named Phillis Wheatley. In her manipulation of classical elements, Wheatley surpasses Turell, Adams, and, for that matter, Anne Bradstreet, all as a result of her struggle to define herself and her world.

Another author who manages classical elements in an intelligent manner is East Apthorp, whose medium was not poetry but the more public sermon. Known by students of colonial America today for his role, however minor, in the pamphlet warfare which came to be called the Apthorp–Mayhew Controversy, Apthorp was a staunch Anglican cleric, born in Boston in 1733 but educated at Jesus College, Cambridge University. His commission to the colonies enlisted him as a member of the Society for the Propagation of the Gospel; rather than serving as an evangelist to Native Americans and African Americans, however, he maintained that his chief role was to advance the general cause of religious tolerance in the colonies. After his ministry began in America, he soon incurred the marked disapproval of most of his parishioners and Congregational colleagues. This fact suggests with what a firm grip the Puritan interpretation of the Adamic myth held the minds of the populace. It is as the voice of tolerance and as an instrument for the advancement of the classical mode of discourse that Apthorp interests us here.

Considering that he spent in America only five years of his adulthood, from 1760 to 1765, Apthorp was able to make a considerable impact on the people of Massachusetts, not merely for his controversial disagreement with the Congregational establishment, but also for his learning and cultivation of the arts. While at Cambridge University, where he took the Chancellor's Prize Medal for achievement in classical scholarship in 1755 and the Members' Latin Dissertation Prizes in 1756 and 1757, Apthorp finally found himself elected a Fellow of his college. His learning and cultivation are clearly evident in his sermon (actually a sort of treatise), *Of Sacred Poetry and Music: A Discourse at Christ Church, Cambridge, at the Opening of the Organ*, published in Boston in 1764. Sounding something like a general apologist for music as applied to the worship service, Apthorp cites the ancients often as esteemed authorities for his argument. At one point, for example, he asserts: "It is well known that in the *Grecian* and *Ionian* cities, music was so much in vogue, that a man was reckoned ill-bred, who could not touch an instrument [for example, the lyre]." He continues, declaring, "All their poetry, especially of the lyric kind, and in the rites of Religion, was accompanied with music: And universally among the ancients, poetry and music were inseparable" (6). At the bottom of the page on which this passage appears, Apthorp cites specific supportive tracts from Pliny and Cicero.

Later in *Of Sacred Poetry and Music*, Apthorp remarks enthusiastically:

> In Isaiah (exclusive of that inspiration, which is above all comparison) we have all the majesty of Homer; in Jeremiah, all the pathos of Euripedes; in Ezekiel, the terrible graces of Aeschylus; and in the short prophecies of Joel, Nahum, and Habakkuk, all the pomp and rapture of Pindar. (11–12)

While arguing that "Religion is the natural source of Poetry," Apthorp vigorously insists, "Poetry is the child of Admiration. Our nobler passions, when strongly excited by wonder and surprize, vent themselves in elevated sentiments and figurative language." Appearing to echo Longinus and Burke on the sublime, he continues, "Invention, Enthusiasm, and Sublimity of stile form the essence of Poetry." Once again seeking reinforcement for his discussion from a classical source, Apthorp quotes from a pair of lines in Horace's *Sermones* (I, 4): "Ingenium cui sit, cui Mens divinior atque os/ Magna sonaturum" (ll. 43–44). In Latin, Horace completes this thought with the clause "des nominis huius honorem"; the entire two lines may be translated as: You may give the honor of that name [i.e., poet] to him for whom there may be the genius, for whom there may be the more divine judgment and a voice which is going to sing great things. The appositeness here between the thought of Apthorp and that of Horace hardly needs the remarking and demonstrates how well Apthorp knows his classical sources. As well Apthorp's use of classical elements in support of his argument for the interdependence of music and poetry bespeaks a cultivated aesthetic sensibility.

In *The Felicity of the Times* (1763), an earlier sermon celebrating the close of the French and Indian War, Apthorp labels the event "an advantageous and honourable Peace" which will hold in check French aggression on the North American continent and particularly curb the threat posed by the French navy. Quoting from both Horace and from Isaiah, this literary aesthete declares:

> *Thy tacklings are loosed, they could not well strengthen their mast, they could not spread the sail: then is the prey of a great spoil divided—Look upon Zion, the city of our solemnities: thine eyes shall see Jerusalem a quiet habitation—for there the glorious LORD will be unto us a place of broad rivers and streams, wherein shall go no hostile galley with oars, neither shall Gallant ship pass thereby.* (11)

Here is illustrated as happy a blending—even a flowing together—of actual texts from the myths of Adam and Aeneas as I have located. One would have to know Horace thoroughly to hear from a recitation exactly where Horace ends and Isaiah begins. To be sure, in the printed version, Apthorp tells us that he takes from Horace's well-known ode on the Ship of State (I, 14, 4–10) the passage beginning "Thy tacklings" and ending "could not spread the sail," while the remainder of the quotation derives from Isaiah 33:20–22.

From the great depth of Apthorp's classicism, as well as from his cultivated aesthetic sensibility, one senses that, had he remained in the colonies, this man would have made many more contributions to the combination of Adam and Aeneas myths in America. As one not particularly given to bouts of public conflict, he left the country in 1765 when he became embroiled in the Apthorp–Mayhew Controversy. He returned to England, where he remained until his death in Cambridge fifty years later, in 1816. Apthorp enjoyed numerous preferments within the Anglican Church, and he participated actively in England's intellectual life. No less a classical scholar than Edward Gibbon said of him, "I sincerely respect the learning, the piety, and the candour of this gentleman."[3] Perhaps Apthorp's lack of enthusiasm for controversy would have forced him to leave America in any case, as the storm of the Revolution gathered force.

While neither Adams, Turell, nor Apthorp was particularly given to controversy, each suggests, in her or his own manner, concrete ways in which the Aeneas myth began to dominate discourse in colonial America after the 1720s or so. These writers, unlike those writing before the 1720s, feel no compunction about expressing themselves in a purely aesthetic manner. After the 1720s, we find John Adams translating or paraphrasing (to adopt Dryden's distinction between metaphrasing, or transliterating; and paraphrasing, or rendering a loose translation) and Jane Turell imitating (what Dryden called making a still freer version of the original) Horace with no apology or attempt to Christianize their sources, whereas Benjamin Tompson feels he must preface his *New Englands Crisis* with a jeremiad of ninety-two lines. We also observe East Apthorp constructing his treatiselike sermons by unobtrusively weaving into his argument authoritative Latin sources and by blending classical and Judaeo-Christian elements and feeling no necessity for explanation; whereas Cotton Mather, who obviously adores classicism, makes denial after denial and, with George Sandys, alleges that the ancients pilfered from the Bible.

Of course there are seventeenth-century exceptions to the rule; the almanac poet, Daniel Russell, for example, composed his lovely Spenserian calendar piece without a single biblical reference. Before the 1720s, however, such instances are few and far between. After the 1720s, the general cultural temper becomes more liberal, permitting greater exercise of aesthetic inclinations.

From the examples of Adams, Turell, and Apthorp (two ministers and a woman of renowned piety), we may judge that even those openly professing the Christian faith no longer counted restraint of their aesthetic sensibilities as necessary for proper observance of that faith.

One additional peculiarity shared by these writers is that their work strongly suggests it has been prompted by the American experience. Adams wants to promote a democratic classless society, while Turell's humble household dramatizes the preparation of wholesome meals and the making of clothing from homespun. Apthorp's insistence on religious tolerance and his secular emphasis on artistic sensibility and on the importance of classical learning predict the atmosphere that led to the Constitutional Convention of 1787.

All these American characteristics—a classless society, an unpretentious home life, and a secular atmosphere of tolerance—are represented in the embroidery panel, *The Fishing Lady*, reproduced in this book (fig. 1). Attributed to Eunice Bourne of Barnstable, Massachusetts, this large panel, over two feet high and over four feet long, dates from about 1750. One of a group of *Fishing Lady* panels, this particular example is featured prominently in Montgomery and Kane, *American Art: 1750–1800, Toward Independence*, in a section entitled "Textiles." The item is criticized for its faulty perspective (252), which, of course, hardly measures up to a Claude Lorraine. Yet the embroidery itself, intentionally or not, makes a strong statement regarding white people's domination of the New World landscape. That is, this panel is clearly anthropocentric—classical. It is pastoral yet domestic. Sheep and dogs gambol on grassy banks, while in the foreground, without ferocity, a pack of yelping hounds pursues a stag. In the tepid, spring air butterflies and birds frolic and swoop.

The panel contains nine birds. The four perched in trees look Oriental in their plumage, and a prominent red bird, if it is supposed to be a North American cardinal, lacks its red crest. Even the white partridge and the pair of "wild" ducks flanking the foreground seem transplanted from Oriental watercolors, imparting a cosmopolitan air. I emphasize the birds not merely to point out a possible Oriental influence (further suggested by the delicacy of line defining the foliage throughout the panel), but particularly to call attention to the last two birds, the only ones in flight. As their swooping wings clearly expose scarlet tips, these birds are North American red-winged blackbirds, not European thrushes, which have reddish feathers under the wings. Therefore this panel must be identified as American and not a counterfeit of an English panel.

Occupying the central area of this large panel are three couples, adult men and women, enjoying the gay ambiance apparently created for their pleasure. Two of the couples have at their feet picnic baskets filled to overflowing with capon and sweetmeats, while the third couple (on the far right) strolls meditatively through this spring delight. If we take the diminutive human figures in the left foreground as children, we have here a portrait of familial bliss, a domestic pastoral scene of plenty. The gentleman standing over a fishing woman, whose line has hooked a plump fish, appears to be wearing the military "blue coat" and sword of the colonial American militia, so the happy people even share in the promise of protection from "marauding" Native Americans.

Four groups of domestic structures stand in the panel's background. After the American manner, only one appears to be made of brick, while the three other groups of farmhouses and barns are made of wood. Perhaps most significantly, among these structures of human design there is no obligatory church—no building with a steeple undeniably signaling a Christian house of worship. What we have in *The Fishing Lady*, then, is a peculiarly American, wholly secular scene showing people who have taken command of the environment, converted it to their own needs and pleasure, and who require no assistance, nor wish any interference, from abroad. In short, this panel represents a self-sufficient, already independent America, enjoying a latter-day version of the classical world's mythical golden age, as described, for example, in Vergil's fourth eclogue.

The popularity of this embroidery panel among Americans of the later 1700s attests its significance as an instrument of cultural self-definition. On a recent tour of Mount Vernon, I discovered in Martha Custis Washington's parlor a version of *The Fishing Lady*, on which, I was told, America's first First Lady was working shortly before her death. Moreover, Ms. Washington's panel clearly was adapted to her own pastoral vision; rather than the scattered wooden buildings and single brick structure, she had placed behind the central fishing lady (Martha?) group several brick buildings arranged in a quadrangular manner, markedly resembling the outlying brick structures one may view from the back door of the Washington mansion.

Poems of Literary Independence

Glimmers of a move toward literary independence begin to surface with some regularity in colonial America during the 1720s, as poet after poet declares separation from Britain and/or Europe. In fact, there are so many examples of such poems that together they constitute an as-yet-unacknowledged genre. This group of poems should not be confused with the "Westward the Course of Empire" poems, which are devoted largely to a realization of the potential of the British Empire in the New World and usually are the products of

Loyalists. I am concerned throughout this section only with poems whose authors make concrete, self-conscious attempts either to diverge from British and/or European literary traditions or to define the idea of Americanness in contradistinction to ideas of what is considered British or European. Attendant upon the more emphatic of these efforts is an anxiety recognizable within any colony's feeling toward the colonizing country, precisely at that moment when what was restive loyalty has changed into a temper of independence. Invariably, the authors of these poetic declarations of literary independence belong to what must be considered an intellectual elite, for they were politicians, moneyed merchants, members of the landed "gentry," and/or persons of influence within their communities who possessed at least the equivalent of a grammar school education.

One such person was Aquila Rose, who flourished as printer, poet, and politician of Philadelphia from about 1719 into the early 1720s. To judge by the commemorative literature provoked by his early death, this man exercised considerable influence over the literary community of Philadelphia; so formidable was his influence that he motivated the earliest statement of literary independence I have found. Since Aquila Rose died on August 22, 1723, at age twenty-eight, and the author in his poem speaks of Rose as if he were still alive, this work must have been written before August 1723. In "An Encomium to Aquila Rose, on His Art in Praising," Joseph Breintnall, a more senior member of the literary coterie which surrounded Rose, penned these startling lines:

> Go on, and find more Candidates for Praise,
> Our infant Country's Reputation raise;
> Doubt not but Strangers far remote will come
> For what they are so much in Want at Home,
> And visit us as ancient *Greece* or *Rome*. (Rose 43)

These lines characterize a mind eager to see his "Country," which Breintnall probably thought of as the colony of Pennsylvania, receive recognition on the world scene. That recognition, Breintnall significantly maintains, should come from his country's literary achievements and not necessarily from its political, economic, or military exploits.

While he does cite both Greece and Rome as glorious precedents to be emulated, the triple rhyme—*come*, *Home*, and *Rome*—gives weight to the Roman example. So exhilarating has been Rose's effect, at least on this author, that it has emboldened him to view his own "Country's Reputation" as not only rivaling that of England but even surpassing it. The spread of this reputation will come so soon that "Strangers far remote" imminently will visit this New World to get the same sort of intellectual sustenance the Old World once sought from the ancient Greeks and Romans.

This kind of thinking often precedes a colony's struggle for political independence, for it signals the acquisition of a cultural identity fully in the process of separating itself from its parent land. In America during the eighteenth-century, this determination to develop an independent identity draws increasingly on the myth of Aeneas and not on the Adamic myth. Indeed, Breintnall makes no mention in this passage of anything resembling Judaeo-Christianity.

The next example of this independence genre presents one of the most aggressive declarations of American literary self-sufficiency published before Ralph Waldo Emerson's famous Phi Beta Kappa address, delivered on August 31, 1837, and known to all serious readers of American letters as *The American Scholar*. Hailing from Boston, this amazing little document is not known nearly as well as Emerson's *Scholar*.

Its author, John Perkins, a Harvard graduate in the class of 1695, was known to his contemporaries for his skill not as a poet, but as a physician. Perkins is the first native-born author of an American literary independence poem. Born at Ipswich on August 28, 1676, Perkins prepared for admission to Harvard at the Ipswich grammar school. After leaving Harvard, Perkins studied medicine, returned to Ipswich to practice for a time, and a few years after his marriage in 1697 seems to have located permanently at Boston, where his wife held some property. This same John Perkins enjoyed the support of Cotton Mather in his promotion of inoculation for smallpox. Little is known of Perkins after 1720 or so, until his death on December 26, 1740, while on a journey to South Carolina to restore his health.

Not much is known, that is, except for his publication on August 4, 1728, in the *New-England Weekly Journal*, of an amazing little poem, "On Reading the *Poem* to His Excellency, by Mr. Byles." Earlier, Mather Byles, literary editor of the *New-England Weekly*, had published (not in the *Weekly* but as a pamphlet) a creditable poem upon the arrival in Boston of Gov. William Burnet.

Perkins's perhaps excessively enthusiastic appreciation of Byles's Burnet piece appeared in print at least one other time, in one of the first volumes which can be called an anthology of American poems. This anthology, *A Collection of Poems by Several Hands*, was published in Boston in 1745 and contains a majority of poems by Mather Byles which did not appear in his *Poems on Several Occasions*, issued in the same year. In the anthology, Perkins's poem is the fourth selection and bears the title, "To ———." For convenience, as Mather Byles certainly is the person to whom the poem is addressed, I refer to it as "To Mather Byles."

"To Mather Byles" compels our attention not because of what it observes about Byles's poetic performance, but because of what this brief poem asserts about New England's literary independence. This work of twenty-four lines, written in iambic pentameter couplets and triplets, opens with these tense lines:

> Long has New-England groan'd beneath the load,
> Of too too just reproaches from abroad,
> Unlearn'd in arts, and barren in their skill,
> How to employ the tender muses quill. (*Collection* 13)

Despite past failings, now the name of the young poet Byles soars "on the radiant wings of fame" (13). Others who might aspire to such achievement, says Perkins, can only "fondly gaze" after Byles's example, for he "Has lost th' attracting world, and shines among the stars" (14). This last line is an alexandrine, surely cast for effect. The image here of winged fame shining among the stars echoes that of Adams's translation of Horace's first ode.

Whether or not Byles deserves such hyperbolic praise is not the key point concerning Perkins's verses. The author clearly directs the young poets of New England to observe Byles's example "With anxious care" (13) so that this example may "Inspire our imitation, as it does our praise" (14). Notice that Perkins zealously recommends that native New-Englanders emulate another native New-Englander—not someone from Old England or Europe. Such aspiration will lead other native poets to proclaim (as Byles already does) loudly and "in harmonious lines" that "*New England's* sons, e'rewhile of barb'rous name" have lately become "A match for *Albion*, or the *Graecian* fame" (14).

Perkins's unabashed objective in this poem is not merely to separate New England's literary accomplishment, but to declare that his country is now the equal of England and even of Greece, whose example has shown the way for letters within Western civilization. It is easy enough today to argue that Perkins's "saying it does not make it so," but again that is to miss the point. Simply put, Perkins insists, in 1728, that a divergence from British and/or European literary tradition has been established, and he appears to be most impatient to assert to the rest of the world this divergence, this new identity.

While not approaching the greater substance of Emerson's *The American Scholar*, "To Mather Byles" deserves brief comparison with the later essay, if only because of its zeal. Written over 110 years after Perkins's verses, Emerson's *Scholar* opens with a complaint resembling Richard Lewis's earlier claim that colonial Americans have no time "'To raise the Genius.'" In Emerson's words, Americans are "a people too busy to give to letters any more . . . [than] simply a friendly sign." Both Emerson and Perkins exaggerate the dearth of exemplary works within their respective literary scenes, each expressing his exasperation in his own way. Perkins notes, for example, accusations that American authors are "Unlearn'd in arts, and barren in their skill," saying that heretofore these have proven all too true. He ignores the work of Anne Bradstreet, Benjamin Tompson, and Cotton Mather. Emerson—choosing not to acknowledge the critically acclaimed writings of Washington Irving and James Fenimore Cooper—maintains that "exertions of mechanical skill . . . [have] postponed expectation of the world" that America would produce first-rate writers. In another close parallel, Perkins declares that now Byles's example will lead the way to literary separation from England and Europe; and Emerson urges that "our day of dependence, our long apprenticeship to the learning of other lands, draws to a close" (McMichael 1: 837). One is left wondering whether Emerson, had he been aware of these earlier attempts to achieve literary independence, would have written precisely the same essay.

The next three proponents of the quest for literary independence return us to Philadelphia. Richard Lewis, Maryland's finest poet of the eighteenth century and author of the first poem in this cluster, seems to have exercised an influence on the other two (Lemay, *Men of Letters* 131–33). Lewis's poem appeared on July 3, 1729, as an anonymous, untitled contribution to the *American Weekly Mercury*. Writing as "a distant Musc" (Lewis at this time lived in the Baltimore area), the poet declares that "Themis at length . . . has ventured o'er/ And Arts can flourish on Columbus Shore" (Lemay 131). If Themis, goddess of laws, justice, and order, now has located in the New World, and specifically in Penn's colony, then it follows that she must have fled Europe, site of her origin. Here Lewis certainly is describing more than a mere translation of studies. Rather, he is speaking of a transmutation of culture. Conditions have become so calm within this peace-loving Quaker colony that the goddess of order and justice feels more comfortable in Pennsylvania than in the Old World.

Later in the poem, Lewis pointedly singles out Greece, Rome, and even Britain as restive in their comparative, historic contests for peace: "Go on brave Souls, out-rival Ancient Greece/ Or Rome, or Britain's Self in Arts of Peace." As these "brave Souls" have succeeded in "Arts of Peace," they now may progress in the aesthetic arts; in Lewis's words, "the sacred Arts" may be learned by "Rural Swains." According to this inspired and inspiring poet, a Delphic oracle has proclaimed that:

> E'er Time has Measured out a hundred Years
> Westward from *Britain* shall *Athens* rise,
> Which soon shall bear away the learned Prize;
> Hence Europe's Sons assistance shall implore,
> And learn from her, as she from them before.
> (Lemay, *Men of Letters* 132)

Echoing Breintnall's earlier zeal, this poem proclaims that a rising Athens, emulating the ancient seat of wisdom, within a century will acquire such substantial learning that the sons of Europe will seek knowledge "on Columbus Shore," as once they turned to the ancients. Lewis's enthusiastic prediction very well could have provoked the next two poems in this Philadelphia cluster.

George Webb, author of the second Philadelphia poem, was a member of Benjamin Franklin's intellectual and literary conclave, known as the Junto. He opens his poem, published in Titan Leeds's almanac for 1730, with these evenly paced couplets:

> Goddess of Numbers, who art wont to Rove
> O'er the gay Landskip, or the smiling Grove,
> Who taughtst me first to sing in humble strains,
> Of murm'ring Fountains, and of Flowery Plains.
> (Silverman, *Poetry* 341)

Webb most likely first was taught "to sing in humble strains" during his grammar school days, when he would have been required to write imitations in Latin of various Latin poets. The imagery Webb conjures up here certainly is that of the eclogue tradition. Webb's reference to his grammar school training back in Gloucester, where he achieved considerable stature as a scholar, recalls Benjamin Tompson's practice of asking his pupils to make Latin imitations of Vergil's *Eclogues*. As we have seen repeatedly, it was not from British examples of pastorals, but rather from their Latin grammar school training, that Americans learned how to cast "humble strains,/ Of murm'ring Fountains, and of Flowery Plains."

The only other pastoral reference in this poem of seventy-two lines occurs about midway through, as Webb describes how, in Pennsylvania, a land far from war or "Lawless Tyrants," "Fearless the Hind pursues his wonted Toil/ And eats the product of his grateful Soil" (Silverman, *Poetry* 352). While this last couplet may owe something to Vergil's *Georgics*, the remainder of the piece concentrates on how calculated to perfection is Penn's colony, as indicated by her "happy Constitution" and "Sweet Liberty." These last two phrases extend the enterprise of literary independence into the arena of politics, suggesting that such concerns as a proper contract for government and the freedom of self-determination were on the rise. Webb nevertheless finds time to prophesy that "hopeful Youth" "Shall Liberal Arts to such Perfection bring,/ Europe shall mourn her ancient Fame declin'd,/ And *Philadelphia* be the *Athens* of Mankind" (351–52).

In "To George Webb" (1731), Jacob Taylor also appears determined to locate in America (which Taylor refers to as the "Western World") the highest of literary achievements. Like Webb classically trained in England, Taylor immigrated to the Friends' colony just before 1700. His "To George Webb" closely resembles Perkins's "To Mather Byles." Both poems maintain, for example, that their subjects will serve their communities as inspiring examples. As Taylor puts it, Webb "will a Thousand generous Youths inspire." Both poems also claim that the Muses now favor New World poets, as they once did those of Greece and Rome. Taylor joins Webb in asserting that, as the poets' art increases in Philadelphia, it declines in Europe. In Taylor's view, Europe's poets must soon "confess declining Days,/ Content with Fame, and so resign the Bays" (Silverman, *Poetry* 370–71). This notion that America's future holds great promise, while Europe will decay, becomes a frequent refrain throughout the remainder of the eighteenth century.

This refrain sounds again in the next literary independence poem we shall examine.[4] In Boston, the year 1761 witnessed an extraordinary publishing event: publication of *Pietas et Gratulatio (Devotion and Gratitude)*, a collection of three poems in Greek, twelve in English, and sixteen in Latin. On the surface, all these poems lament the death of George II and celebrate both the accession of George III and his marriage to Charlotte Sophia.

Because a proper reading of our next poem of literary independence, Francis Bernard's Latin ode in sapphics, is greatly facilitated by a consideration of the contents of the *Pietas* volume and the circumstances of its printing, a brief excursus into the background of this remarkable volume is necessary. This volume is perhaps the single most significant indicator of the level of sophistication achieved by Americans in classical studies during the eighteenth century. As such, its importance to investigation of the Aeneas myth can hardly be exaggerated.

The unusual contents of *Pietas et Gratulatio* were gathered, ironically, at the suggestion of the author of the Latin literary independence poem, Francis Bernard, who had been appointed royal governor of New Jersey in 1758 and governor of Massachusetts in 1760. During the early years of his administration, Bernard enjoyed considerable popularity. After Parliament's Stamp Act legislation, however, he found himself in the unhappy and certainly unpopular position of being responsible for enforcing these intolerable measures.

Bernard's plan for the volume, executed by others, was to hold a contest among faculty and graduates of Harvard College for the best Latin, Greek, and English poems and then to collect those selected into an impressively produced quarto volume, this to be presented to the new king. Several British universities already had presented similar volumes. Isaiah Thomas relates that the three Greek poems were printed from a fount of Greek types or characters presented to Harvard College by one of its early benefactors, Thomas Hollis of London; this gentleman is the same Thomas Hollis whose opposition to British tyranny was well known in the American colonies by way of his extensive correspondence with the activist, patriot, and Congregational minister, Jonathan Mayhew. Hollis's fount of Greek characters never was used except to print the *Pietas* volume, and in 1764 it was "destroyed by the fire that consumed Harvard Hall, one of the college buildings, in which the types and college library were deposited" (Isaiah Thomas 70–71). Both the fount of Greek characters and nearly five thousand volumes from the college library were lost in this disastrous fire; and Francis Bernard was instrumental in raising funds to restore the library's holdings.

The introduction to *Pietas et Gratulatio*, a prose epistle to the new king, is a most curious document. Rather than sounding chords of adulation, this prose letter reads more like a declaration of expectations, even on occasion striking a note of admonition. Such passages as the following may "look" innocuous enough:

> Other Empires have generally been formed by the infringement of the Liberties and the destruction of the Lives of mankind: that, which will owe to your Majesty its firm establishment, will be founded upon the maintenance of the Freedom of the people, the security of their Possessions and the Encrease of their numbers. (vi)

The future tense verbs of this passage, "will owe" and "will be founded," recall the future imperatives Edward Taylor translated from Ovid's Icarus and Dedalus episode in *Ars amatoria*. Interestingly, some of those rulers of empires who have infringed upon mankind's liberties and brought about "the destruction of . . . Lives" are enumerated in detail within one of the English-language poems of *Pietas et Gratulatio;* Alexander the Great and Julius Caesar receive severe censure for their alleged profligacy and overweening ambition (21–22). Then, in the volume's introduction, are not the noble objectives of life, liberty, and the pursuit of happiness implicit in the phrases "the Encrease of their numbers," "the maintenance of the Freedom of the people," and "the security of their Possessions"? In addition, notice that, rather than following the standard practice (for that time) of capitalizing every proper noun, only the key words, "Encrease," "Freedom," and "Possessions," are capitalized, thus emphasizing their importance to the reader—who was to have been the new monarch.

Another passage reveals a similar effort to appear inoffensive and at the same time to recommend a certain mode of behavior with an intense subliminal urgency: "The spirit of Liberty has, for many centuries, distinguished the English Nation: but it has been reserved for your Majesty's Reign that it should be free from that abuse, with which its Enemies have been always ready to charge it" (vii). This passage first ascribes to Britain the distinction of acting as the preserver of "Liberty," but then immediately claims that it is up to George to prevent the former abuses of that "Liberty." What the author of this epistle appears to be doing here is, on the one hand, criticizing the restraints upon freedom imposed by previous monarchs, and, on the other, forestalling the imposition of any new ones, should the new king happen to be contemplating them.

One particularly telling passage insists, "We are persuaded that this Country will become a more interesting Object to Great-Britain, than it has been in the time of any of your predecessors" (xiii). Hence the principal motivation, certainly for this prose epistle if not for the entire project, becomes evident. This author wants to make it known that he will brook little or no interference with the progress of a burgeoning economy. The reference to "Country" rather than to New England may suggest a further concern for colonies outside the New England arena, hinting at a growing sense of commonality in opposition to British domination.

Charles W. Akers, in his biography, *The Divine Politician: Samuel Cooper and the American Revolution in Boston*, observes that Cooper, who contributed two English odes to *Pietas*, had two years earlier preached a sermon on the death of George II, in which he maintained a position quite close to that articulated in the prose epistle. Speaking of this sermon and the *Pietas* volume in the same context, Akers asserts, "By praising English kings for what they were not or were assumed to be, Cooper and his countrymen also established what monarchs must be" (38). While no author of the prose epistle has been ascertained and Akers does not identify Cooper as the author of the letter, I suspect that this politically active, impassioned American patriot, who later baptized the poet Phillis Wheatley, was this tract's principal designer.

Speculation plays no role whatsoever in a final segment of background embracing Bernard's contribution to the literary independence genre. For, in the twenty-ninth selection of the *Pietas* volume, these extraordinary lines appear: "Behold Britannia! in thy favour'd Isle;/ At distance, thou, Columbia! View thy Prince" (92). Publication of this selection (attributed to one of the Boston Olivers) in 1761 marks one of the first uses of the noun *Columbia* (Lewis had earlier used *Columbus*) to identify the Atlantic colonies. The use of this noun confirms that the American colonies by this time were thinking of themselves as a unit, a collective body with common purpose, albeit a loose one. This use of *Columbia* suggests, furthermore, that the phrase "this Country" appearing in the introductory epistle may indeed refer to the American colonies in general.

As for George III's reception of the *Pietas* volume, he appears never to have acknowledged it. It is certain that he did not benefit from its instruction.

Despite an atmosphere charged with intimations of liberty, made possible by Bernard's urging of the project, Bernard's literary independence poem appears in this volume somewhat unexpectedly, given the fact that Bernard's Loyalist leanings (for example, his support of the Stamp Act) eventually contributed to his dismissal as governor in 1769. In 1761, nevertheless, he was given the honor of composing the final poem of *Pietas et Gratulatio*, where his Latin sapphic ode is called simply "Epilogus." In Leo M. Kaiser's superlative anthology, *Early American Latin Verse, 1625–1825: An Anthology*, the editor gives this poem the title, "The Future Glories of the American Muse." Kaiser almost certainly borrows this from Evert A. Duyckinck and George L. Duyckinck, *Cyclopaedia of American Literature*: "Thirty-one [the last entry in *Pietas et Gratulatio*] is the Epilogue . . . prophetic of the future glories of the American muse" (1: 13).

Below the ode is quoted entire and followed immediately by my translation:

XXXI. "Epilogus"

Isis et Camus placide fluentes,
qua novem fastos celebrant sorores,
deferunt vatum pretiosa regi
dona Britanno.
Audit haec flumen, prope Bostonenses
quod Novanglorum studiis dicatas
abluit sedes, eademque sperat
munera ferre.
Obstat huic Phoebus, chorus omnis obstat
virginum; frustra officiosa pensum
tentat insuetum indocilis ferire
plectra juventus.
Attamen, si quid studium placendi,
si valent quidquam pietas fidesque
civica, omnino rudis haud peribit
gratia Musae.
Quin erit tempus, cupidi augurantur
vana ni vates, sua cum Novanglis
grandius quoddam meliusque carmen
chorda sonabit,
dum regit mundum occiduum Britannus,
et suas artes, sua jura terris
dat novis, nullis cohibenda metis
regna capessens;
dum Deus, pendens agitationes
gentium, fluxo moderatur orbi,
passus humanum genus hic perire,
hic renovari. (105–6)
(The Thames [as it flows past Oxford]
and the Cam [as it flows past Cambridge],

flowing gently, where the nine sisters
celebrate [their] festivals, carry the
precious gifts of poets to the British King.
A river near Boston [the Charles],
which washes the temple [i.e., Harvard College]
consecrated to New England's learning,
comes to know this [by hearing] and
aspires to carry similar gifts.
Phoebus [as God of the arts] stands
against it [i.e., this aspiration]; the
entire chorus of Virgins [i.e., the Muses]
stands against it; inexpertly the dutiful,
untaught youth, unaccustomed to the task,
attempts to strike the strings [of the lyre].
Yet, if [there is] any enthusiasm
for giving pleasure, if civic devotion
[i.e., pietas] and faith have any force,
the charm of the uncultivated Muse
[i.e., the American Muse] will by no means perish.
Rather the time will come, unless poets
eager for honor predict the future falsely,
when their string will sound a grander and
a better song, so to speak, within New England,
[even] while Britain still rules the Western world,
and gives her laws and her arts to new lands,
embracing kingdoms contained by no borders; [and]
until God, weighing the pursuits of the
races, has tempered the transitory world,
having allowed the human race to perish here [on earth]
to be renewed there [in heaven]).

Bernard makes a number of important observations in this neatly structured, almost perfect ode—an unusual poetic achievement for a governor in any age. In the first stanza, Bernard establishes that the intellectual centers of Oxford and Cambridge have provided the British poets, who have honored the new king, with the education necessary to qualify them as poets. Bernard states clearly that it is in such repositories of learning that one may expect to discover the dwelling of the Muses, and so he establishes a sort of poetics of preparation for any aspiring bard. New England, too, he points out in the next stanza, enjoys a citadel of learning where aspiring poets strive to make their way. Curiously, Bernard next insists that the Old World Muses not only fail to sanction this new poetry, but actually oppose it! Hence Bernard asserts a radical discontinuity between the literary cultures of Great Britain and America.

I do not mean to suggest any such discontinuity; indeed, I maintain that no discontinuity ever existed. Still, I am aware that this governor's insistence that such discontinuity was in evidence prepares us for the radical shift in discourse which begins to take place almost immediately after the 1783 Treaty of Paris. In other words, Bernard's almost cavalier claim that discontinuity already exists suggests how easily such a thought can come about.

The governor-poet acknowledges that, even without benefit of the Old World Muses, New Englanders still struggle diligently to join the ranks of the best poets. In the fourth and fifth stanzas, Bernard capitulates to the American Muse by holding that the enthusiasm and devotion among New World poets are present within her in such quality and quantity that "the time will come . . . [that] their string will sound a grander and a better song." Particularly arresting here is Bernard's reference to pietas in the fourth stanza. As the title of the collection was *Pietas et Gratulatio* and as Bernard was given the task of stating the final words of the volume, the governor-poet probably felt obligated to use the word. But what is worth scrutiny is not merely *that* he uses the word, but *how* he uses it. It appears in the clause, "si valent quidquam pietas fidesque/ civica," which may be translated as "if civic devotion and faith have any force." So it is clear that, in this instance, Bernard wishes to dissociate devotion from any religious context; by the same token, *faith (fides)* also is separated from a religious meaning. What the governor-poet delineates, then, is the sort of civic pietas that Cotton Mather earlier ascribed to Sir William Phips.

When Bernard's "Epilogus" is seen as a final word, a last commentary, on the contents of the *Pietas* volume, his definition of *pietas* as "civic devotion" assumes greater significance still. In effect, he has defined the concept of the entire work. Such a reading, first of all, removes the concept of pietas from any notion of Puritan piety. Second, despite Bernard's guarded projection of American greatness into the future, this reading aligns *Pietas et Gratulatio* with the political perspective described in the prefatory prose epistle.

The title, "Epilogus," identifies not only the function of epilogue, or concluding tract, but also that classical rhetorical figure of argumentation which "hypothetically supposes that if certain events were to occur then other events would follow" (Myers and Simms 101). This Latin poem, then, self-consciously functions as a peroration, or formal recapitulation, of a volume whose entire purpose perhaps is not at all to express devotion and thanks for a shift in government, but rather to argue that the colonies should be accorded relatively free status. If what Bernard predicts comes to pass (despite his attempt to promote the appearance that American greatness will be postponed, and given the fact that America registers not only an "enthusiasm for giving pleasure" but a "civic devotion and faith" of some force), then the colonies may indeed threaten to resist any British domination and/or tyranny which the new government chooses to impose upon them.

The *Pietas et Gratulatio* volume, avowedly the most sophisticated American poetry composed until this moment in the eighteenth century, thus becomes inextricably caught up in America's struggle for political independence; it becomes art in the service of politics. Bernard's political interpretation of pietas, indisputably taken from the Latin, unmistakably asserts the secular emphasis of the Aeneas myth. The *Pietas* volume therefore becomes in its entirety yet another promoter of classical discourse. What obviously advances this classical discourse as an American version of that discourse is Bernard's claim for the existence of the American Muse, wholly other than the Old World Muse.

Another salient passage in Bernard's fascinating poem occurs in the stanza following the *pietas* clause, this passage also a clause: "cupidi augurantur/ vana ni vates" (unless poets eager for honor predict the future falsely). At this time and place, any poets interested in predicting an era of glorious literary accomplishments in the New World almost surely would have been American poets (with the possible exception of George Berkeley). Thus Bernard must have in mind here other poets who have contributed to the genre to which his own poem belongs. Such a reference within one poem to others of its type makes it obvious that pre–Revolutionary War Americans already had identified the literary independence poem as an American genre.

Two final observations press themselves on this discussion of Francis Bernard. First, the acceptance-and-denial pattern, established by the governor's promotion of pietas and his contradictory claim for a radical discontinuity between Old and New World Muses, becomes something of a norm as Americans attempt a radical cultural separation from Britain and Europe. Such a pattern consists of acceptance of classical values and/or principles and subsequent denial of their origins. Second, Bernard's rather surprising endorsement of American literary independence marks an exception to the rule, for he is the only Loyalist, among the examples given, to do so.

In 1761, Bernard hardly could have guessed that the American colonies soon would become embroiled in a military and political revolt against his king—the ostensible inspiration for the *Pietas* volume. John Trumbull in New Haven, Connecticut, and Philip Freneau and Hugh Henry Brackenridge in Princeton, New Jersey, the next group of literary independence writers, appear to be more hopeful that America will soon be free. As Trumbull's *An Essay on the Use and Advantages of the Fine Arts* and Freneau's and Brackenridge's *A Poem on the Rising Glory of America* are better known than the other poems of this genre, their treatment need not occupy a great deal of space.

Best known to readers of American literature for his satirical poem, *The Progress of Dulness* (1772–73), and the mock epic *M'Fingal* (1782), John Trumbull became a staunch Federalist and leader of a famous literary group, the Connecticut Wits. Trumbull's *Essay on the . . . Fine Arts* was first delivered in September 1770 as a Commencement Address at Yale University, when Trumbull was twenty. The essay was published as a pamphlet soon thereafter. Holding that the liberal arts (here Fine Arts) do not receive enough emphasis within the curricula of American colleges, Trumbull resolves that the "more pure and intellectual pleasures . . . have their source in the Fine Arts, and are more especially found in the elegant entertainments of polite Literature" (4), to which he devotes much of his attention. Throughout the essay, or adapted satura (a classical form, part prose and part poetry), Trumbull repeatedly refers to a fired imagination. For example, he remarks that Shakespeare is "endowed with the most noble extravagance of imagination"—a quality Pope and Dr. Johnson would have found objectionable. At one point, Trumbull even claims that his contemporary authors in Britain "Sacrifice ease and elegance to the affectation of classic correctness, fetter the fancy with rules of method, and damp all the ardour of aspiring invention" (11). Here we have gathered together many of the primary characteristics of romanticism.

Trumbull sounds the chord of unmistakable oneness of purpose among the colonies when he asserts that "*America* [emphasis mine] hath a fair prospect in a few centuries of ruling both in arts and arms" (11). He also certifies America's high level of literacy in this declaration: "Perhaps there is no nation, in which a larger portion of learning is diffused through all ranks of people" (12). This last claim, I am chagrined to say, we can no longer make. Its having been made in 1770, however, suggests why the printed word was such an effective means of motivating the American mind into the spirit of revolt. Recall that Monaghan has established that literacy among women in the American colonies was practically universal. Directly related to this high level of literacy among all Americans is Trumbull's acknowledgment that Americans have produced "many elegant essays," "nor hath Poetry," he continues, "been entirely uncultivated among us" (13). Yet he names not a single American author, not even in addressing a totally American audience.

In the concluding section of *Essay on the . . . Fine Arts*, Trumbull lapses into heroic couplets as he extols the prospect of "Fair Freedom," who predicts that "America shall rise" with great pomp and circumstance to become "The Queen of empires and the Nurse of arms" (14). Unlike any of the other authors within the genre of the literary independence poem, Trumbull maintains that women, too, "the happy land shall grace/ With pow'rs of genius, as with charms of face." As this couplet features the only instance of enjambment in this poem of 112 lines, Trumbull's enthusiasm perhaps leads him to assert that some woman writer will soon "rise and wrest with daring pen,/ The pride of genius from assuming men" (15). Surely these lines contain one of the most impassioned predictions of future female literary greatness ever penned by an American male! While it is probably true that Trumbull did not envision an African American as possessing this "daring pen," Phillis Wheatley nonetheless travels far, as we shall see, toward wresting "The pride of genius from assuming men."

Of Freneau and Brackenridge's *Rising Glory of America*, Kenneth Silverman has written:

> By its encouragement to think of America as not British, more than British, by its rational address, by its projection of the national past beyond the great migrations of the seventeenth century, "The Rising Glory of America" may be said to end the colonial period of verse. (Silverman, *Poetry* 421)

Freneau and Brackenridge join Trumbull and virtually all other poets of the literary independence genre in encouraging Americans to think American, which was simply to think "not British." In delivering *Rising Glory* as a commencement exercise, these two graduating seniors of the New Jersey College (later Princeton University) agree with Trumbull that the American colonies are best thought of as a collective unity. As for Silverman's focus on these poets' concern for America's past, this editor of *Rising Glory* touches on a major concern in the American sense of self—a fear of pastlessness, examined further below in connection with the pastoral elegy.

While *Rising Glory* does contain several pastoral references, it owes much more to the epic. Freneau and Brackenridge obviously are familiar with pastoral, as such phrases as "sylvan settlements," "industrious swain" (430); "flow'ry meads, and groves and gliding streams" populated by "woodnymphs, satyrs, fauns" (433); and "Groves" adorning "their verdant banks" (443) ably attest. These two poets also adopt the pastoral convention of the conversation, in this case among the figures Leander, Acasto, and Eugenio. Eugenio sounds more Italian (in the tradition of Tasso) than Vergilian and Leander, and Acasto are classical sounding enough. Yet we have no singing contest, no protestations from a disappointed lover, and no mention of having come from tending one's flocks of sheep or returning to such charges—all conventional motifs of pastoral.

The subject matter of this poem, America's rise to great distinction among the ranks of the world's nations, is clearly heroic, more akin to the epic. In his "prelude" opening the poem, Leander denies any classical past and, for that matter, even a British past, claiming, like Bernard before him, that out of America will spring "A Theme more new, tho' not less noble" (424). Then Acasto ironically gives an invocation to the Muse: "begin O muse!" He celebrates the achievement of Columbus, who through "Famine and death, the *hero* [emphasis mine] made his way" (424). Freneau and Brackenridge's denial of what is obviously the case—that they are drawing on the classical genre of pastoral and particularly that of the epic—becomes commonplace in American consciousness during the Revolutionary era and thereafter.

These poets continue their emphasis on heroic actions by praising "those heroes so well known," who "peopled all the rest [of the North American Atlantic seaboard] from Canada/ to Georgia's farthest coasts" (430). Recalling the French and Indian War, they lament the loss of "America's own sons," who played the role of "the hapless hero"; indeed, due to this conflict, "full many a hero lay" "'Midst fire and death" (431). Freneau and Brackenridge are determined not to "pass those glorious heroes by, who yet/ Breathe the same air and see the light with us" (432). These two poets are attempting to democratize the notion of epic heroism so that it embraces the ordinary American—not unlike Derek Walcott's contemporary effort, in his book-length epic *Omeros*, to give epic significance to the ordinary lives of Caribbean people. *Rising Glory* draws to a close with the authors' assertion that "patriots fam'd and heroes yet unborn" will surely distinguish America and will merit "the magic sound/ Of song heroic" (441).

With the exception of these last two commencement addresses, all the literary independence poems we have examined appear to have been composed "beyond the holy circle." Nonetheless, Brackenridge, Freneau, and Trumbull, according to Trumbull's *Fine Arts*, are compelled to summon "the great Archangel's call" (16) which promises ultimate joy, while Freneau and Brackenridge describe America's rise in glory as "The blissful prelude to Emanuel's reign" (442). The shift in emphasis in these last two works signals the beginning of a turn away from privileging the myth of Aeneas over that of Adam.

The primary impetus behind this shift in attitude was the gathering storm of rebellion; in Trumbull's words, Fair Freedom's "Heroes mark their glorious way/ Arm'd for the fight." That fight will shortly evolve into the American Revolutionary War. To defeat the British, America required an appeal to the grassroots Adamic myth, not to the mythos of an intellectual elite. Awareness of this requirement gradually dawned even in the thought and writing of such intellectuals as Trumbull, Freneau, and Brackenridge, as is becoming evident in these commencement addresses. Freneau's capitulation to the radical shift in discourse forms an episode within chapter 7 of this volume.

From this examination of the genre of literary independence poems, many common characteristics may be identified. All maintain that America or parts of America will rival Rome, Greece, and Britain; that America or a part of it will become a principal center of learning; and that, except for the final two contributions examined, this new literary accomplishment will proceed from an anthropocentric, secular impulse. Many of these poems are exhortatory in tone, urging others to emulate the example of their American superiors; or they predict authors of great genius to come. As the moment of armed rebellion draws near, poems of this genre manifest the acceptance and denial pattern, whereby their authors appropriate elements of classicism and then deny their origins.

Predicting the rhetoric of the rising rebellion, the poems of this genre speak of a liberating moment in which all the Atlantic colonies will participate. The most dramatic characteristic displayed by each example of this genre is an urgency—even an anxiety—to bring about a palpable separation from the mother country and hence to encourage the discovery of an identity which eventually comes to be called American. What comprises that elusive American identity was first articulated by Cotton Mather in *Magnalia Christi Americana*. By the 1720s however, as this section has suggested, the classical portion of the Adam and Aeneas dialectic was beginning to dominate.

Pastoral: Naive and Subversive

The fact that most poems of the literary independence genre owe a great deal to the tradition of pastoral indicates the pervasiveness of this genre in America during the eighteenth century. Throughout this section, we should remember that colonial American schoolmasters of the grammar schools often assigned their students the task of construing their own Latin versions of eclogues or pastorals, usually with the example of Vergil before them. Until now, it was almost universally held that Early Americans slavishly imitated the allegedly superior British writers of pastoral. While some poets such as Mather Byles do show an intimate acquaintance with British authors of pastoral, not all do so; and several display a sophisticated awareness that this subtle genre may be used to expound gentle and not so gentle social and political critiques of the establishment. Toliver, *Pastoral Forms*, insists that "all worthwhile pastoral" exploits "the potential contrasts between a golden age and the normative world," yielding a "dialectical, tensive structure" (5). This "dialectical, tensive structure" usually manifests itself as an outgrowth of, or even a commentary upon, the social and intellectual milieu in which the author finds herself or himself. These "commentaries" ordinarily remain gentle entertainments, projecting an urbane elegance into the midst of an ideal rural landscape.

The revisionist work of Annabel Patterson instructs us that "what people think of Vergil's *Eclogues* is a key to their own cultural assumptions, especially as those are organized by the concept of the artist/intellectual" (163). As the brevity of the *Eclogues* "made them a natural exercise for elementary education in the classics," Patterson observes, "they entered the European consciousness at a formative stage" (164). So the British and people of the Continent who enjoyed the benefit of a grammar school education were introduced to the pastoral genre in much the same way as the Early Americans. Patterson maintains that Europeans of the Renaissance and eighteenth century understood pastoral's "dialectical, tensive structure," as characterized, on the one hand, by the idyllic, Theocritean simplicity of shepherds' singing contests and love songs; and, on the other, by Vergil's exploration of a kind of realism which embraced "the consequences of civil war, problems of land ownership, and the relationship of writers to rulers." These two sides of the dialectic formed, in the minds of those Europeans who adapted eclogues to their own needs, "a metaphorical system by which they could allude to the power structures of their own society, describe their own poetics, and determine their own cultural stance" (168).

Early American writers used the pastoral mode to express their own "cultural assumptions," and they also addressed the power structures of their pre–Revolutionary War times and even constructed their own poetics within this same mode. These uses already have been suggested in connection with the literary independence poems. Patterson's insightful delineation of the properties of pastoral within the European praxis of the genre offers fruitful means of considering the American praxis. Still, as we shall see, another description of the American pastoral, one that breaks the mode into the naïve and the subversive, serves the present purpose.

Many Early American pastorals—those by Mather Byles, for example—are concerned with little beyond providing pleasant entertainments; these we may best refer to as *naive* pastorals, those whose texts appear to be content with their contemporary social order or are not designed to make cultural commentary. Others, however, elaborate harsh critiques of a sociopolitical world which the author wishes to hold up for scrutiny. George Puttenham, Elizabethan author of the immensely popular rhetoric handbook, *The Arte of English Poesie* (1589), understood the pastoral's potential for subversion when he wrote that the "eclogue" was devised to enable the poet "under the vaile of homely persons and in rude speeches to insinuate and glaunce at greater matters, and such as perchance had not bene safe to have beene disclosed in any other sort."

We may guess what Puttenham meant by his notion of the safe and the unsafe, and so apply Puttenham to the demands of Early American authors choosing to employ the subversive pastoral. The sixteenth-century rhetorician suggests that the pastoral may serve as a mask, enabling authors to utter what others less concerned about personal safety may assert in satire or straightforward social commentary. According to Puttenham, Vergil in his own "*Egloques*" treats "by figure matters of greater importance then the loves of *Titirus* and *Corydon*," for Puttenham holds that these poems "containe and enforme morall discipline, for the amendment of mans behaviour" (167).

One type of Early American pastoral, then, is naive. Often it is the product of an author who does not need or choose to adopt a mask, either because he or she does not wish to comment on social and/or political concerns; or because the societal foibles exposed are relatively minor; or because, if the author desires to engage in full-scale censure of the society's perceived failings, he or she selects satire or some less self-effacing genre.

A second type of Early American pastoral, the subversive pastoral, is the subtle product of an author who wishes to, or must, adopt a mask in order to make her or his critique of societal ills known in print. This author is motivated by an intense desire to alter unacceptable or inappropriate behavior.

The concept of naive and subversive pastorals proves helpful and clarifying for an examination of the practice of this genre among Early Americans and perhaps even among later American authors. At the same time, such an understanding of the pastoral mode helps to define a distinctly American classicism.

Both Marx, *Machine in the Garden*, and Lewis P. Simpson, *Dispossessed Garden*, treat versions of the naive pastoral. Both point out how a future golden age is contrasted with the normal, everyday world of nature and human life. Such an opposition accommodates well with Adamic notions of a heavenly paradise opposed to the world of the flesh. Neither of these two authors, however, emphasizes that the myth of the golden age promised a paradisiacal existence *in the real, secular world* of women and men; that is, the classical myth projected a golden world which somehow would transform the present age into a more perfect version of this wholly secular world. Such a transformation is proposed, for example, in Eunice Bourne's elaborate embroidery panel, *The Fishing Lady*. To those Early Americans who subscribed to the secular Enlightenment, this promise of transformation stood within the realm of possibility and to some appeared not so incredibly remote, simply because its success depended, not on a dream of a life not of this world, but on the observable, measurable accomplishments of human beings. Many of the authors of the literary independence genre theorized, for example, that America someday would supersede the military, political, and artistic achievements of Great Britain and Europe, much as Vergil had prophesied that the great Pax Romana would enable the Romans to supersede the accomplishments of any culture before Rome.

The following discussion of American pastoral during the eighteenth century is, for the most part, chronological. No attempt has been made to be comprehensive; any such undertaking would require an entire volume. While such a book-length study would be desirable, the intent here is to compare the naïve pastoral with the subversive pastoral. This exercise ascertains that both these pastoral forms, when they fall into American hands, display uniquely American qualities. While not ignoring connections to British pastoral of the period, this treatment affirms a more intimate relationship between classical pastoral and that of eighteenth-century America.

By contrast, we shall see that the poet-minister Thomas Cradock of Maryland directly imitated all but one of Vergil's ten eclogues, casting each of his nine poems as a satire. While these nine satires do borrow from the pastoral, they convey an unmistakable tone of ridicule and antagonism, disqualifying them as of the pastoral mode. Some writers, such as Robert Beverley and Jean de Crèvecoeur, took pastoral elements that are confined largely to the medium of poetry and adapted them to the medium of prose, much as Cotton Mather before them had appropriated many epic characteristics to his prose *Magnalia Christi Americana*. Many later writers, from Cooper to Melville and beyond, also would adapt the epic to prose. It seems that American writers, perhaps more than authors from other lands, prefer to adapt classicism to prose. In any event, this examination reveals that Americans were largely responding to their American experience as they constructed American pastorals.

The treatment of pastoral as naïve can prove problematical. For example, when talking about Beverley's *History and Present State of Virginia* (1705), Marx insists that Beverley "leaves us with a sense of unresolved conflict" (86) which runs counter to "the ideal reconciliation of nature and art which had been depicted by writers of pastoral since Virgil's time" (87). I am not convinced either that Vergil intends to accomplish an "ideal reconciliation" between art and nature, or that his eclogues bring about such a reconciliation, as Marx seems to imply. While they may aspire toward such a goal, his eclogues do not achieve it. Indeed, in the fifth eclogue, Daphnis dies and is lamented and even deified, but on earth he remains dead. Vergil himself leaves the eclogues behind for the genres of the georgic and the epic, suggesting by his career that he has achieved no reconciliation through his explorations in the pastoral mode. Beverley leaves us with an unresolved conflict, because he, like Vergil before him, seeks to take advantage of the pastoral's potential to treat "by figure matters of greater importance then the loves of *Titirus* and *Corydon*." Indeed, as we shall soon learn, Beverley's

History explores pastoral's capacity for subversion. The fact that Beverley received a grammar school education, very likely at Beverley Grammar School in Yorkshire, indicates that this author was thoroughly familiar with Vergil and his eclogues. In addition, two references to Peter Martyr's *De Orbe Novo Decades* in Beverley's *History* (137 and 229) suggest that Martyr's *Decades* remained a respectable source of knowledge about the New World into the eighteenth century and that Martyr's comparison of Columbus and his sailors to Aeneas and his band of men continued to be read.

Beverley's *History*, written by 1703 but not published until 1705, reveals the author's familiarity with classicism; indeed, the book contains two classical allusions for every reference to the Bible or to Christianity. Such expressions as "Olympick Games" (98), "Mercury's Wand" (188), "Furies in the Shape of Old Women" (202) and "Water of Lethe" (207) reflect Beverley's grammar school training. Significantly, besides referring to Christian and Muslim ("as Mahomet promis'd in his Paradise," 299) ideas of paradise, Beverley also cites the classical construct of a happy afterlife retreat to "Elizium" (202, twice).

This undeniable knowledge of cultures outside North America is distracting in an author who, like Beverley, was posing as a Native American. In his "Preface," Beverley pledges not to "pretend to be exact in my Language" and hopes that "the Plainness of my Dress" will give the reader "the kinder Impressions of my Honesty" (9). So we see Beverley self-consciously donning the humble mask of someone with rude speech, or at least trying to strike such a pose. In fact, Beverley begins to drop this pose when, in a chapter describing Native American towns, buildings, and fortifications, he states, "A Grass-plot under the covert of a shady Tree . . . is as pleasant and refreshing to *them* [italics added], as a Down Bed and fine *Holland* Sheets are to *us* [italics added]" (177). Just a few pages later, he denies his Native American identity when he declares, "I don't pretend to have div'd into all the mysteries of the *Indian* Religion, nor have I had such opportunities of learning them, as Father *Henepin* and Baron *Lahontan* had, by living much among the *Indians*" (195).

Despite Beverley's failure to maintain his mask, we must acknowledge his attempt. In addition, despite his avowed purpose of providing "a tolerable Entertainment" (11), the principal aspiration of an author of naïve pastoral, Beverley writes in dedicating his *History* to Robert Harley, then speaker of the House of Commons, that the distance of the colonies from England "makes 'em liable to be ill used by Men, that over-act Her Sacred Authority, and under-act Her Vertues" (6).

One way in which some Virginians over-acted and under-acted—that is, moved beyond the bounds of "morall discipline"—was in their poor treatment of Native Americans. While Leo Marx and Lewis Simpson both amply point out Beverley's use of naïve pastoral elements, neither emphasizes the fact that the Native American golden age began to be sullied soon after the arrival of the white man. When the Europeans arrived in the New World, for example, "Paradice it self seem'd to be there, in its first Native Lustre" (16). Beverley paints a picture of the Native Americans which anticipates Rousseau's Noble Savage. Not only did the indigenous peoples of the New World appear to the Europeans "to retain the Virgin Purity and Plenty of the first Creation," as well as "their Primitive Innocence," says Beverley, but "they seem'd not debauch'd nor corrupted with those Pomps and Vanities, which had depraved and inslaved the Rest of Mankind" (17).

These "fallen" Europeans "found the *Indians* . . . very fair and courteous at first, till they got more knowledge of the English" (24). In his conclusion to the third book of four in *The History*, this one devoted entirely to Native Americans, Beverley, having long since dropped his "Indian" persona, now insists that Native Americans "have lost their Felicity, as well as their Innocence." Despite the fact that Beverley's "Indian" seems contemptuous of Native American cookery and what he perceives to be their "superstitious" religions, he is reluctant to say that Virginia has been improved by the white man:

> I shall in the next place [i.e., book IV] proceed to treat of Virginia,
> as it is now improv'd, (I should rather say alter'd,) by the English. (233)

While one critic has found Beverley's sympathy for Native Americans to be "a passive emotion" (in Bercovitch, *Cambridge History* 102), such commentary as Beverley gives strikes me as encouraging "the amendment of man's behaviour." The fact that Beverley has dropped his "Indian" pose and, in effect, come forward as a white man and a member of a landed gentry only adds force to his critique of the whites' interference in Native American affairs. Clearly he hopes to correct, not to antagonize. Beverley dons a mask, even if only temporarily; provides information which asserts a need for moral revision; wants to ameliorate the present corrupting influence of the whites' behavior; and adopts a tone of corrective exhortation. In all these ways, he casts his pastoral in the subversive mode. Moreover, *The History* represents one of the earliest attempts to defend Native Americans.

Not at all concerned with mending social ills is Mather Byles's "Belinda: A Pastoral," published in his *Poems on Several Occasions* (1744) but appearing first on September 21, 1730, in the *New England Weekly Journal*, a Boston newspaper of which Byles was literary editor. In this delightful example of naive pastoral, Byles is concerned exclusively with conveying the injured sentiments of the jilted lover, Strephon.

Given Byles's well-known enthusiasm for the work of Alexander Pope,[5] one may expect to hear numerous echoes in this piece of Pope's *Rape of the Lock*, a mock-heroic poem which owes much to pastoral tradition. Indeed, Byles calls Strephon's would-be lover Belinda, the same name as the heroine of Pope's *Rape*. In an earlier poem from 1725, Byles alludes to Belinda, this time in a context which clearly nods to Pope's *Rape*.[6] This brief poem of twenty-six lines (as against seventy-eight in "Belinda") is addressed "To a Young Lady: Written with a Silver Pen, Presented by Her to the Author," and depicts its author as smitten with love and eager to sing in hyperbole. The following couplet provides an apt illustration: "Where e'er you point the Lightning of your Eyes,/ Victim's fall thick, and Fate resistless flies" (*Poems on Several* 96). Pope, in a description of his Belinda's early morning toilet which closes the first canto (of five), observes, "And keener Lightnings quicken in her Eyes."

While the remainder of Byles's brief poem fairly blazes with additional echoes of Pope's phrasing in *Rape*, "Belinda: A Pastoral" more closely resembles Vergilian eclogues than it does Pope. Such expressions as "shady forests form a soft retreat," "deck the surrounding bow'rs," "whisper o'er the meads," and "O snatch me to some gentle seat" are all but literal translations from Vergil's *Eclogues*. For that matter, Byles's "Belinda" actually reads somewhat like an imitation (in Dryden's sense) of the second eclogue, which is a complaint of the shepherd, Corydon, against the unsympathetic and unattainable "O crudelis Alexi" (*Eclogue* 2, l. 6; O cruel Alexis.). To be sure, Byles has changed Alexis, an ephebe, into the female Belinda, though the gists of the two poems remain aligned. In addition, Byles has made another, more appealing alteration; rather than have the jilted lover "montibus et silvis studio iactabat inani" (l. 5; broadcast [his] useless pursuit [i.e., the making of verses] to the hills and woods), as does Vergil's Corydon, Byles has Strephon sing his complaint to "all th' admiring swains" (l. 26), who "curs'd his [Strephon's] rival, and BELINDA blam'd" (l. 27). Byles, who has been called Pope's most loyal imitator in the American colonies, here has bypassed his English "superior" and sought the example of the classical world's most excellent practitioner of pastoral.

Byles's modus operandi here travels the same path followed by such authorities of pastoral as France's Rene Rapin and England's Pope. In other words, all—American and Europeans alike—return to the classical tradition to derive their forms (though one could argue convincingly that Pope himself found Rapin more authoritative than Vergil; for Pope, in his many pastorals, appears to be unaware of any subversive mode). This pattern of seeking out original classical sources, rather than aping the productions of allegedly superior British models, we have observed several times and will see again in this discussion and in our treatment of the American pastoral elegy.

Richard Lewis, the Maryland poet, moves a step or so beyond Byles in his rendering of the pastoral tradition, in the excellent "Journey from Patapsco" (Mar. 1732). Here he clearly appropriates pastoral to the American environment. In one of the great nature poems of the eighteenth century in America, Lewis describes what he experienced on a trip from "Patapsco in Maryland to Annapolis, April 4, 1730," in the middle of spring. Particularly arresting is the unique way Lewis incorporates elements of pastoral. After depicting a field of wheat ripening "with cheerful green," Lewis paints this affecting scene:

> Safe in yon Cottage dwells the *Monarch Swain*,
> His Subject Flocks, close grazing, hide the Plain;
> For him they live; and die t'uphold his Reign. (Pearce 612)

This triplet, a rhyme pattern which Lewis uses with some frequency, combines the pastoral notion of shepherds and their flocks with a strong sense of American individual independence. (Few of Vergil's or Theocritus's shepherds can be observed to tend real sheep.) That Lewis's Swain is a monarch of his own domain is not in America a contradiction, because there each man at that time reasonably could hope to become ruler over his own tract of land.

Extending this scene of domestic pastoral, Lewis describes the Swain's sons at daily chores, as well as his several fruit trees, such as "The *Peach*, the *Plum*, the *Apple*," the "lowly *Quince*," and the "lofty *Cherry Trees*." Together the trees of this orchard exude "Evolving Odours [which] fill the ambient Air,/ The *Birds* delighted to the Grove repair:/ On ev'ry Tree behold a tuneful Throng,/ The Vocal Vallies echo to their Song" (613). Since we know that Lewis is determined to picture a rustic scene he actually observed, his use of the pastoral idiom, in combination with descriptions of the natural environment altered by an American farmer, represents an attempt to "own" pastoral for America. In other words, throughout the poem Lewis appears, as in these two passages, to be consciously interweaving elements from the pastoral tradition with characteristics of the colonial American landscape for the purpose of creating an American pastoralism.

Another poet concerned with constructing an American pastoralism is William Livingston (1723–1790), statesman of New York and the first governor of the state of New Jersey. At least he was concerned to do so in 1747, when he published his long pastoral poem, *Philosophic Solitude*, which saw some thirteen printings before 1800. So popular a pastoral by one of the principal advocates of separation of church and state at the United States Constitutional Convention of 1787 deserves extended treatment. Many have pointed out *Philosophic Solitude*'s indebtedness to "The Choice" (1700), by the British poet and Anglican churchman John Pomfret. The following discussion establishes that this poem owes more to the pastoral tradition of Vergil and Theocritus than it does to Pomfret, and that both Livingston and Pomfret, of course, derive from Horace their notion of country joy as opposed to city drudgery.

The retreat to the country, away from the noise and hurly-burly of the city, is as old as Horace and Rome, if not older. Horace devotes one of his odes (I, 17) and the second of his epodes to country joys removed from city life. While the ode sings of the country's horn of plenty, the epode, in the voice of Alsius, celebrates rural simplicity and ease of life. Both Pomfret and Livingston speak, in terms directly paralleling Horace, of rural bounty and the simple life. In addition, the frugality Pomfret insists upon in "The Choice" recaptures sentiments expressed in Horace's poems on contentment (2, 16 and 3, 16). As Horace observes, "quanto quisque sibi plura negaverit,/ ab dis plura feret" (3, 16, ll. 21–22; the more each [person] denies to himself, the more he bears away from the gods). Pomfret wishes to retire to a "Competent Estate,/ That I might Live Genteely, but not Great," where "A frugal Plenty shou'd my Table spread,/ With healthy, not luxurious Dishes, fed" (791). Livingston's retreat is more opulent than either Horace or Pomfret recommends, and the difference signals his embrace of Vergilian pastoral.

Indeed, the sort of retreat Livingston describes resembles pastoral's golden age realized. Unlike Pomfret, who wishes to locate "Near some fair Town" (791), Livingston wants to reside "From noise remote . . ./ Far from the painted belle, and white-glov'd beau,/ The lawless masquerade, and midnight show." For he seeks to be:

> Full in the centre of some shady grove,
> By nature form'd for solitude and love;
> On banks array'd with ever-blooming flowers,
> Near beauteous landscapes, or by roseate bowers. (Smith, *American Poems* 154)

The solitude Livingston hopes to find is wholly within the realm of ideal pastoral. In his own words, Livingston would have "Me to sequester'd scenes" guided by the Muses:

> To mossy banks, edg'd round with op'ning flowers,
> Elysian fields and amaranthine bowers,
> To ambrosial founts, and sleep-inspiring rills,
> To herbage's vales, gay lawns, and sunny hills. (155)

This picture once again conjures up Eunice Bourne's *The Fishing Lady*. While Livingston pointedly desires to construct for himself a recreation of Vergil's golden age, Pomfret borrows little from pastoral for his "private Seat," save what modicum there is of pastoral in these lines:

> A little Garden, grateful to the Eye,
> And a cool Rivulet run Murmuring by:
> On whose delicious Banks a stately Row
> Of shady Lymes, or Sycamores, shou'd grow. (791)

One has to stretch the imagination, even in this passage, to see even a particle of pastoral.

While Livingston's debt to pastoral is considerable, he, like Lewis, tries to "own" pastoral for America. For in his bower of bliss, "all the beauties of the circling year,/ In native ornamental pride appear" (156); here also are "cool grots, perfum'd with native flow'rs" (158). One wishes Livingston's "native" descriptions were less pastoral and more natural, more like those of Lewis. No poet of nature, Livingston nonetheless in this poem sounds a distinctively American note, a note unlike Pomfret. While the English poet prefers friends "Loyal and Pious . . . to *Caesar* true" (791) (that is, loyal to the monarch), Livingston would have a political friend who, as an advocate, would stand:

> Before the Roman bar, while Rome was free,
> Nor bow'd to Caesar's throne the servile knee,
> Immortal Tulley [Cicero] plead the patriot cause,
> While ev'ry tongue resounded his applause. (158)

Whereas Pomfret wishes to have friends who support the monarchy, Livingston, himself an attorney, clearly requires friends whose behavior emulates "the patriot cause" of such a citizen and advocate as Cicero, who opposed attempts to replace the Republic of Rome with a dictator or dictators and eventually was beheaded. Livingston's opposition to monarchical government, and his promotion of a republican one, may account for much of the popularity in America of *Philosophic Solitude*.

Like Pomfret, Livingston mentions Horace first and then Vergil. The parallel stops there. Pomfret names "*Horace* and *Virgil*, in whose Mighty Lines,/ Immortal Wit, and solid Learning shines [*sic*]," immediately after remarking, "At th' End of which [his row of shade trees] a silent Study plac'd,/ Shou'd be with all the Noblest Authors grac'd" (791). In quite a different context, Livingston refers to Horace and Vergil as if contemplation "Amid sequester'd bowers, near gliding streams" naturally prompts such thought, for "Such was the seat where courtly Horace sung,/ And his bold harp immortal Maro [i.e., Vergil] strung" (158). In Livingston, Vergil already receives preferential treatment. While Pomfret continues his delineation of "Noblest Authors" for only a dozen more lines, Livingston, when he finally does get around to discussing how he plans "to improve the intellectual mind" in his blissful bower, devotes some five pages to how "Reading should be to contemplation join'd" (166).

In this revealing discussion, not only does Livingston name Vergil first, but he does not name Horace at all. Nor does he name any other Roman or Greek poet. Indeed, "Virgil, as prince," so Livingston declares, "shou'd wear the laurel'd crown,/ And other bards pay homage to his throne" (166). The poet enthusiastically characterizes Vergil's *Eclogues* in this smooth, flowing couplet: "How do our ravish'd spirits melt away,/ When in his song Sicilian shepherds play!" On the heels of this soothing, warm description come long portraits of Dido and Aeneas, resplendent in martial glory. While Dido "shines in awful majesty" wearing a quiver made of gold, "stern Aeneas thunders thro' the field!" "His helmet flashes, and his arms resound!" Those poets who "Should next compose the venerable" hierarchy include "The far-fam'd bards that grac'd Britannia's isle" (167). As might be expected, Milton comes first, followed by "tuneful Pope," "great Dryden" (169), and "gentle Watts" (170). Livingston remembers Dryden exclusively as translator of Vergil's *Aeneid,* hence providing the opportunity for still another celebration of Aeneas, "the Trojan prince" and "god-like man!" (169). Livingston so celebrates Vergil and his hero that one is tempted to conclude that he would use his bower of bliss to contemplate, above all else, Vergil's *Aeneid*.

In the *Aeneid* (VIII, 670), Vergil places Cato, Caesar's most substantial opponent and Rome's most ardent symbol of pietas, in Elysia "dantem iura" (giving laws) to those who have shown the greatest pietas. Almost as if recalling this, Livingston describes Cato as:

> The unconquerable sage whom virtue fir'd,
> And from the tyrant's lawless rage retir'd,
> When victor Caesar freed unhappy Rome
> From Pompey's chains, to substitute his own. (171)

The Early American poet here underscores his preference for a republican government and his disdain for Caesar's dictatorship/monarchy. Of greater importance, however, is Livingston's celebration of Cato as "fir'd" by the virtue of pietas, a usage emphasizing the Early American fondness for this virtue, especially during the eighteenth century. No such celebration (or even naming) of Cato occurs in Pomfret.

While both Pomfret and Livingston close their poems with considerations of a satisfactory death (their retreats provide each with an appropriate ambiance), they disagree as to the desirability of a wife. Whereas Pomfret, a confirmed bachelor, would "have no Wife" (792), Livingston, who married two years before *Philosophic Solitude* was published, would "By love directed . . . choose a wife/ To improve my bliss, and ease the load of life" (171). Significantly, Horace's Alsius, in the epode on joys of the country life, remarks, from a patriarchal perspective, "pudica mulier in partem iuvet/ domum atque dulces liberos" (2, 39–40; a virtuous woman may be of use, in her office, to home and sweet children). So both Horace (if grudgingly) and Livingston recommend the company of a wife in their blissful rural retreats.

A comparison of Pomfret's "The Choice" and Livingston's *Philosophic Solitude*, then, ascertains that, while Livingston obviously was familiar with Pomfret's poem, he disagrees with his predecessor more than he imitates him. Most arrestingly, their politics are diametrically opposed. Pomfret embraces the monarchy, while Livingston, at the early age of twenty-four, unabashedly demands a government by representation. Surely Livingston did not calculate that his poem would have many readers in the British Isles, for, already in 1747, he is in open rebellion against the mother country.

Both poets delineate their politics—their most important differences—through a reference to Caesar. In the case of Pomfret, the only other readily observable classicism in his poem occurs in the casual naming of Horace and Vergil (touched on above), as well as allusions to "Sharp *Juvenal*" and to "am'rous *Ovid*" (791). Livingston's poem, in contrast, is cloyed with classicism, particularly with pastoralism. Even when, for example, Livingston calls Jove "fictious" (158), he is quick to describe the rising of the sun in the formulaic rhetoric of epic: "Behold, the rosy-finger'd morning dawn,/ In saffron rob'd and blusing o'er the lawn!" (159). Throughout a long meditative passage on Nature's God, Livingston peppers such pastoral phrases as "tune the hallow'd lyre" (161), "ev'ry grove prov'd vocal to my song," "sportive echoes" (162), "in lone grots, for contemplation made" (165), "th' embow'ring groves," and "roseate bow'rs" (166). Near the end of the poem, Livingston syncretizes the myths of Adam and Aeneas: "Mild as the saint whose errors are forgiv'n,/ Calm as a vestal, and composed as heaven" (175). Livingston's own "Calm" here, in his description of a "pudica mulier" (virtuous woman) in terms of Rome's vestal virgins and Puritanism's doctrine that those sanctified in God's grace are absolved of sin, results in an effective blending which recalls Cotton Mather's acceptance and denial motif.

Despite Livingston's determination to depict "the great Father of mankind . . . drest" in "downy fleece" (165), what he achieves is a poem promoting pastoralism and pietas, celebrating the myth of Aeneas, and devaluing the Adamic myth. Livingston rejects Pomfret—that is, rebels against most of the British poet's values. He embraces pastoral and the Aeneas myth, as is signaled by his pastoral rhetoric, his lengthy appreciations of Vergil, and his celebration of

Cato. He even bypasses Pomfret for several of Pomfret's sentiments in "The Choice," and instead returns to the classical source, Horace. In *Philosophic Solitude*, Livingston clearly is concerned with carving out his own idiom, and that idiom is most concentratedly classical, not British, in origin.

What identifies Livingston's effort as a peculiarly American one is most observable in his politics, which are, according to his own testimony, intimately aligned with Roman republicanism. Livingston's pastoralism is not, finally, subversive, because he adopts no mask and does not concern himself particularly with effecting a change in people's behavior. He does, however, grasp the "dialectical tensive structure" of pastoral, and he exploits the genre as an opportunity to separate himself from the British and thereby to define his own cultural position. His naïveté persists only because of the unapologetic candor with which he advocates his position.

Given the open manner in which Livingston advances the myth of Aeneas in *Philosophic Solitude*, we perhaps should be surprised to learn that he became an early advocate of doing away with classical studies in the public schools—though we are given a clue to this attitude by his acceptance and denial of classicism. Howard Mumford Jones, *O Strange New World*, quotes from Livingston's polemical essays on colonial American educational theory, articulating this apparently incongruous but very American stance:

> Livingston, though he denied that Latin and Greek were essentially "useful as preparatory to real and substantial knowledge," inconsistently called upon the testimony of Plato, Aristotle, Lycurgus, and other "ancient politicians" to show that "the Education of Youth" was the principal "Duty of the Magistrate" rather than a duty of the church. (245)

Such a stance, however contradictory, predicts the position of facile acceptance and denial held by so many among the intelligentsia during the radical shift in discourse which occurred after 1783 (see ch. 7 below).

While he did not live long enough to participate in the radical shift, Thomas Cradock (1718–1770), our next adapter of Vergilian eclogue, writes in neither the naïve nor the subversive mode. Rather, Cradock chooses to make outright satires of his "imitations" of nine of Vergil's ten eclogues, creating a species of antipastoral. About Cradock's *Maryland Eclogues in Imitation of Virgil's*, Cradock's editor, David Curtis Skaggs, has written that these nine poems (Cradock does not imitate Vergil's seventh eclogue) "constitute a burlesque of the pastoral myth" (Skaggs 65). Skaggs ably describes the gist of Cradock's *Maryland Eclogues* when he observes, "Cradock exploded the pastoral myth in his eclogues." Rather than sustain Vergil's notion of a golden age, in Cradock's pen, "Maryland became the wilderness scene of greed, immorality, and conflict" (65). Cradock assuredly is concerned to alter behavior which he, as a conservative Anglican minister who ever "remained a Briton" (88), found unacceptable. Still, he himself identifies his imitations as satires, for he opens the Argument of his fourth eclogue, for example, with this candid statement: "The Satyr here is on those of the Clery [clergy]" (106).

Even though his tone clearly is satirical and his disposition antipastoral—that is, even though Cradock composes neither naïve nor subversive pastorals—Cradock's "imitations" are of considerable interest; for they erect a wall of opposition to the domination of the myth of Aeneas. To be sure, such religious movements as the Great Awakening arose to counter the advancing Aeneas myth. These movements were not so successful until after 1800 and after the radical shift in discourse was accomplished. Nathan O. Hatch has called this post-1800 period in the history of American religious consciousness the era of the democratization of American Christianity (for more on this provocative notion, see ch. 7).

Cradock, in Maryland in the 1740s and 1750s, prefaces his satirical sixth eclogue with this lament: I "am sorry to say some very great men make the important Truths of our holy Religion the daily Subjects of the[ir] wanton Raillery!" This sort of challenge to the "holy circle" never would have been uttered in Edward Taylor's world—nor even in that of Cotton Mather. Thomas Cradock nonetheless felt threatened enough to devote his entire sixth eclogue, bearing little resemblance to Vergil's own sixth eclogue, to a portrait of a schoolmaster, Celsus by name, who taught his students such principles as "the whole *Bible's* a notorious Cheat,/ A Maintenance for lazy Priests to get" (181). It is perhaps no accident that the name Celsus also identifies the first great polemical adversary of Christianity, with whom the Church Father, Origen, carried on a written debate (circa 177 A.D.).

In his first and fourth eclogues, Cradock has a great deal more to say on the subject of priests, who are less than committed men of the cloth. Thus Cradock suggests, unwittingly perhaps, that Celsus's criticisms may be justified. Celsus finally asserts, "Religion was the Child of Pow'r,/ To keep poor ign'rant Man from knowing more."

At this juncture, Cradock opens the door to a brief consideration of colonial politics of the time, for he maintains that such assaults on the "Pow'r" of the church lead people to "Libel your G[od], your Country and your King" (182). Here Cradock's angry sarcasm prompts him to declare the British Way and, again unwittingly, place it over and against the American Way of pietas, or devotion to God, family, and country. Whereas Cradock's frustration suggests just how forcefully the American Way was beginning to assert itself—that is, how aggressively the movement toward American self-sufficiency was advancing—the poet underscores Skaggs's conclusion that "Cradock's

America was part of a wider British empire, not an emerging community in its own right" (Skaggs 88). Such a reading helps to explain why Cradock writes neither naïve nor subversive pastoral. As a staunch advocate of the monarchy, and therefore of British rule, Cradock, feeling only contempt for the growing spirit of rebellion, had no need to don a mask, for he had no fear for his safety. Thus he could adopt the genre of satire with impunity.

Cradock has Celsus outline his "pernicious" scheme in a harangue which he concludes by claiming that he, apparently like others residing beyond the holy circle, tells his students that "No Heav'n, no Hell will be hereafter seen,/ But we shall be, as tho' we had never been" (182). Cradock footnotes this section of the poem, explaining, "This is really the Doctrine *they* [emphasis mine] teach"; thus one is to take Celsus as representative of those deists and alleged atheists, those "*very* great men," who concern Cradock so deeply. Cradock's enlightened Celsus, with his notion that priests withheld knowledge from the poor and ignorant, predicts that, after the radical shift in discourse, those same poor and ignorant will hold ministers and priests accountable for their hoarding of knowledge. This Celsus figure did not represent even a few actual deists, however, since practically every one of them was a thinking, moral human being who wanted improved living conditions for all colonial Americans. Benjamin Franklin, for example, wanted schools that would shape useful and dutiful American citizens, and even as notorious a deist as Tom Paine (thought by most to be an atheist) clearly states in his *Age of Reason* that he hopes for a happy life beyond this earthly one. In other words, Cradock regrettably typifies conservative supporters, or reinforcers, of the Adamic myth who unkindly refuse to allow that those who seek an alternative to dogmatic religion can be as moral and righteous as they themselves.

Considerably more subtle and less aggressive than Cradock's satires in the effort to reform human behavior are the *Letters* and *Sketches* of J. Hector St. John (formerly Michel-Guillaume-Jean) de Crèvecoeur. The works of this Franco-American intellectual and noted diplomat are well known to readers of American literature and require little introduction. Selections taken from his *Letters from an American Farmer*, particularly, and from his *Sketches of Eighteenth-Century America* find their way into standard college-level anthologies of American literature. Readers of Crèvecoeur describe these works in terms as diverse as history, fable, travelogue, and sly satire. These writings also contain evidence for the presence of subversive pastoral.

Crèvecoeur, in dedicating his *Letters* to (Guillaume) the Abbe Raynal, historian, *Encyclopediste*, and abolitionist, whose enthusiasm for the future glory of America was conditional, the author claims to be "an humble American planter, a simple cultivator of the earth" (37). In fact, he had been classically educated by the Jesuits at the College du Mont in Caen, France. Perhaps Crèvecoeur adopts this mask because, when the manuscript version was completed (probably some years before 1778, when he and the manuscript were seized by the British), he wanted to appear to be as neutral as possible, despite what then were Tory leanings. The book was published in 1782.

"Ant-Hill Town," the second chapter of *Sketches* (comprised of portions of the original manuscripts of the *Letters* which were omitted and not published until the twentieth century), is almost a textbook example of subversive pastoral. This relatively short chapter opens as the narrator sits "under one of the most enchanting groves of Virginia." While this bower of bliss is admittedly "the work of art," it has been "executed with so much simplicity as greatly to resemble that of nature." The narrator's "verdant temple" possesses "such luxuriancy" that its foliage refuses "all admittance to the rays of the sun." "'Tis a grove of Tempe" (241), he exclaims. The Tempe to which Crèvecoeur refers is a valley in Greece famed in ancient times for its "wild" beauty. The contradiction here between art and wildness signals the duplicity of Crèveceour's subversive mode; much as he would have his readers believe him "an humble . . . cultivator" when he is not, so he would have them think art can create wildness, although art is not wild. This second element of duplicity is, however, a declared one, and readers are given full knowledge of it, suggesting the playfulness of his tone, which never ridicules or becomes sarcastic.

When the narrator claims, therefore, to have located in "this sylvan bower," affording him a cool, calm, and "placid retreat" wherein "feelings of [pleasure] [*sic*] and ease encompass [him] all around," we should be but mildly surprised when this locus of bliss is invaded by other characteristics of that same environment "where the grain is gathered by slaves and where their daily toils absorb the very idea of joys" (242). Reflection reveals that this idyllic scene has been drained of all joy by the institution of slavery. The bleakness of this vignette predicts and prepares for the greater (from Crèvecoeur's perspective) indictment that the author levies against the myth of American industriousness. Today we would argue, of course, that human beings can perpetrate no greater crime upon others than to enslave them. Crèvecoeur's world was quite different, however, and it sanctioned the despised institution.

In his bower, Crèvecoeur's narrator soon observes the "never-ceasing industry" of bees, labeling them "industrious citizens" committed to "that excellent government which pervades their habitations" (244). Subsequently, he draws from his "country" experience the observation that: "'Tis in the country alone that you can follow this rotation of objects which feeds contemplation, which delights, improves, and often assuages the pains of an afflicted mind" (245).

The narrator appears to be on the verge of depression. A bit later, on this same foray, within his "sylvan bower" he discovers a colony of ants, who impress him mightily as "so fair a monument of industry" (247). Several days later, he returns to his country retreat and notices "within a few rods" of the ant colony he had found earlier, a much larger colony of larger ants. Concluding that the two communities, who show no signs of conflict, must feed "on different things," he judges that no cause exists "that could influence their little passions and produce those sanguinary commotions so frequent among mankind" (248).

In his conclusion to this letter, the narrator apologizes to his learned English correspondent, calling this letter's contents the relation of a "trifling incident not worth its passage over the Atlantic." He insists, nonetheless, that this letter does in fact convey accurately how he feels. "Indeed, had I my choice," concludes the narrator of "Ant-Hill Town," "I'd much rather amuse myself with these objects of instinctive economy, knowledge, and *industry* [emphasis mine] than to wade over fields of battle strewn with the carcasses of friends and foes, the victims of so many phantoms" (249).

The enthusiastic promoter of "that restless industry which is the principal characteristic of these colonies" (44), as the narrator's minister puts it in the "Introduction" to *Letters*, by this time has become disillusioned with American industriousness. In the famous third letter, "What Is an American?" for example, Crèvecoeur uses the words "industry" or "industrious" over twenty times, emphasizing again and again that all that is required of a successful American citizen is that he be industrious. Even so, one of the principal causes of the American Revolution was that same American industry which caused Britain and America to feed on the same things, the products of American industry. Whereas Crèvecoeur's bees and ants lead lives of harmony, in his vision, only humans employ their "industry" to foment chaos, making people the victims "of so many phantoms" of disharmonious greed and ambition.

In other words, what Crèvecoeur's narrator appears to conclude in "Ant-Hill Town" is that America's former promise of and potential for greatness, so evident in its strength of industry, now has been sullied by the Revolutionary War. Whereas the industry of bees and ants represents a type of absolute harmony, that American industry which Crèvecoeur's narrator invoked earlier with the force of religious conviction has proven an unreliable phantom. Crèvecoeur's disillusionment here almost labels him a Tory, but the guise of subversive pastoral enables him to express his profound disappointment and still affect neutrality.

This same subversive posture continues in his last entry of the *Letters*. Entitled "Distresses of a Frontier Man," this letter finds Crèvecoeur's narrator now forced, by the onslaught of the Revolution, to contemplate splitting up his family. The autobiographical nature of this letter makes reading it almost painful. Native Americans, however, receive sympathetic treatment, echoing Beverley's earlier sympathy, discussed above. By contrast with both patriots and the British, Native Americans are, in the narrator's view, "without temples, without priests, without kings and without laws. . . . in many respects superior to us" (215). Of course, every nation of Native Americans has, and always has had, its priests or holy persons, its "kings" or leaders, and its laws.

Crèvecoeur's reference here to priests signals the first of two final observations regarding the *Letters* and their relationship to American classicism. Despite the opposition of such clergy as Jonathan Edwards, George Whitefield, and Charles Chauncy, Crèvecoeur's narrator is moved to state, in the popular "What Is an American?" tract, that in America all religious "sects are mixed, as well as all nations; thus religious indifference is imperceptibly disseminated from one end of the continent to the other, which is at present one of the strongest characteristics of the Americans" (*Letters* 76). Although Crèvecoeur's own deistic position undoubtedly colors this point of view, the author draws a portrait here of the religious scene in the colonies that is consistent both with Eunice Bourne's *Fishing Lady* and with the argument that, during the period of American classicism, the discourse of the American Aeneas dominated. Such recognition, however, should not lead to the interpretation that the period of American classicism was one without morality or a sense of moral direction and purpose. Recall that Aeneas was a man of profound commitment to pietas, or devotion to the gods, the family, and the country.

At another pivotal juncture within the *Letters*, this one also located in the "What Is an American?" tract, Crèvecoeur's narrator James articulates precisely the tenets of pietas. It is no accident that this articulation comes at the conclusion of the American portrait. Into the mouth of "our great parent" (surely William Penn) Crèvecoeur places these summary words: that newcomers to the Pennsylvania colony should "carefully educate thy children, teach them gratitude to God and reverence to that government, that philanthropic government which has collected here so many men and made them happy" (90). Such an education, in which children learn "gratitude to God" and devotion to government or to patria, most assuredly bespeaks the exemplary devotion of parents to family and in fact delineates the American Way—devotion to God, Mother, and country.

That Crèvecoeur, a deist and no Christian, should draw this secular prescription for moral behavior should allay most doubts as to whether the myth of Aeneas encompassed a powerful commitment to moral principles. Moreover, this articulation of pietas should help convince the skeptical that, in America in the late 1770s, secular, classical values were preferred to those of the Adamic myth. Indeed, many scholars have pointed to the American patriotic penchant, just preceding and during the Revolutionary War years, for what today usually is referred to as "civil religion." Catherine L. Albanese's *Sons of the Fathers: The Civil Religion of the American Revolution*, is but one such study.

As well, this conclusion presenting a sort of subliminal celebration of the American Way on the heels of a panegyric of American industriousness probably accounts for the great popularity of this third letter, which appears with stubborn regularity in texts of American literature—despite Crèvecoeur's later sinister analysis of the American character. In one of the more compelling recent studies of American letters, Grantland S. Rice in *Transformation of Authorship in America*, points out Crèvecoeur's contradictory and distressing analysis in the later *Letters*, and expresses great surprise that Crèvecoeur's "collection of essays . . . [has] become instantiated as the ur-text of American exceptionalism." I am not convinced that the *Letters* in fact constitute a principal locus of American exceptionalism (by itself, "What Is an American?" surely does). Nor do I agree with Rice that the reason for the *Letters*' immense popularity "seems to lie within the assumptions and fallacies of republican print culture" (116), as many more dynamics were at work following the American Revolution and leading to the definition of the American self.

My own view is that "What Is an American?" appeals to American readers on an instinctual level, for it taps into the American unconscious at its most basic. This letter, without sounding in the least bit classical but still rendering an honest, candid assessment, encapsulates what most Americans think of when they approach the task of self-definition. This is not to deny Crèvecoeur's later, more troubling estimation of the American character. It has been suggested that anthologists may not be familiar with the remainder of *Letters* or, for that matter, with the entirety of *Sketches*. Frankly, I doubt that those who do know these other texts find them especially disturbing. After all, most Americans are adept at accepting and then denying.

While Crèvecoeur's subversive pastoral exudes poignancy, the subversive pastoral created by Phillis Wheatley enacts a powerful, spectacular performance. The mystery here is that it took over 210 years to learn to recognize the subversive mode in this author. To be sure, that Wheatley is a woman and an African American has militated against giving her poetry and prose a fair assessment, but these characteristics hardly are the only ones which hinder judicious evaluation. Many readers of her work refuse to let go of the old double canard: first, that she writes in the "detested" mode of neoclassicism, with its heroic couplets and poetic diction; and, second, that she is merely a derivative imitator of Alexander Pope. Of course, the first of these factors recently has been demonstrated irrevocably to have been absolutely without foundation; the many guides for proper reading of literary works cast in the neoclassic mode are now so widely accepted that no rehearsal of their tenets is required here. The second canard, that Wheatley writes like a slave to Pope, continues to damage her reputation. All four of these factors—her sex, her race, her neoclassicism, and her alleged lack of originality—have combined through the years to relegate Wheatley's poetry to marginal status.

The very nature of Wheatley's poetic mission, motivated in large part by her African heritage,[7] differs radically from that of Pope. Whereas the British master of sound wrote pastorals in the manner of René Rapin's rural, naive simplicity, he was free, when he wished to criticize the foibles or mores of his contemporaries, to choose the unmasked genre of satire. This direct means of criticism was unavailable to a woman author who, at the time her *Poems on Various Subjects, Religious and Moral* was published in 1773, also labored under the disadvantage of being a slave. She therefore adopts the mask of subversion, at least in those poems composed before October 18, 1773, the approximate date of her manumission.

This strategy enabled Phillis Wheatley sometimes to register severe censure, particularly of the institution of slavery, under the guise of being an innocuous purveyor of the status quo. This practice predicts such fictional characters as Charles Waddell Chesnutt's Uncle Julius McAdoo and Langston Hughes's Jesse B. Semple, who manage to get the upper hand over their white adversaries by wearing an innocuous mask that hides tough cleverness and subtlety. Thus Wheatley's intelligent application of a subversive mode, principally within her verse though occasionally in her letters, should surprise no one.

The primary poetic modes available to Wheatley throughout her relatively brief career were those of the pastoral, the elegy, the lyric, and the epic. Indeed, Wheatley not only writes in all four of these modes, but often she mixes elements from them in the same poem. "On Imagination," for example, contains the lyric "I," "me," and "my"; pastoral images of flourishing fields and warm water murmuring over sandy banks; the elegiac intensity of anagnorisis, or revelation; and the epic sweep of taking in a great expanse. While her epic praxis is treated below in chapter 6, the following discussion explores her application of the subversive pastoral. Although this investigation ascertains that Wheatley does not imitate Alexander Pope, more significantly it suggests a reading of her work which releases it from heretofore limiting and biased interpretations.

The famous portrait which serves as frontispiece to the 1773 *Poems* itself makes a subversive—even a rebellious—statement. In the opening poem of this collection, she declares, "Here I sit, and mourn a grov'ling mind" (11). The frontispiece, however, depicts her sitting, aggressively and not at all humbly, before a writing desk on which may be seen paper with writing on it; holding a pen; and striking a contemplative pose—obviously promising still more writing to come. Although it is true that some African Americans in New England at this time were allowed to learn to read and write, by no means did all African Americans enjoy that privilege. Recall that Wheatley's first attempt to publish a volume of poems, in Boston in 1772, met with no success, having been rejected for racist reasons.[8] Wheatley's portrait, obviously celebrating both her race and her womanhood, self-consciously contradicts her mask of humility, in a manner paralleling the sophisticated urbanity of Vergil's shepherds. The alert reader, then, should expect the voice in Wheatley's poetry not to be tepid.

The author of the "Preface" to Wheatley's *Poems on Various Subjects*—probably Archibald Bell, her London printer—claims that "she had no Intention ever to have published" (iv) these poems. However, it was well known by many of her American readers, at least, that in fact she had tried to obtain enough subscribers to publish a volume in Boston the preceding year. This "Preface," however inadvertently, contributes to the establishment of Wheatley's mask. While it may have been the fashion of the day to register such a disclaimer, this published statement contradicts real circumstance and signals the construction of a mask, one most likely designed to increase the sales of her volume. In any event, the volume apparently did well in London, for at least nine reviews appeared there between September 1773, when the volume appeared, and the end of the year. It should not go unremarked that, in the important letter to David Wooster of October 18, 1773, in which she announces her manumission, she writes that John Wheatley, her master, gave "me my freedom" "at the desire of my friends in England" (170). So it is clear that her pen served her well in the struggle for freedom. In other words, her mask aided her with great effectiveness.

"To Maecenas," which opens *Poems*, begins in the world of pastoral, for its first couplet reads: "Maecenas, you, beneath the myrtle shade,/ Read o'er what poets sung, and shepherds play'd" (9). The suggestion to open with a paean to Maecenas, now universal symbol of the loyal patron, hails from Horace's dedicatory poem which introduces book I of his *Odes;* but the shade of the myrtle tree and shepherds piping on oaten reeds belong to Vergil's *Eclogues*.

This poem appropriately presents the major subject matter of the volume. Wheatley's aspiration to work within the genre of the epic, for example, she indicates in four lines describing Patroclus's plea to Achilles that he be allowed to aid the Greeks while wearing Achilles's armor (see Pope's *Iliad*, opening lines of book XVI). Depicting the African Terence as "happier" and herself as "less happy" (11) because his pen brought him freedom while hers has yet to do so, she introduces both her individual struggle for freedom and, by implication, the general topic of freedom. While extolling the virtues of "great Maecenas!" Wheatley vows to sing the praises of the deity "from whom those virtues sprung" (11), thereby focusing on virtuous behavior and on her idea of God, the two subjects named in her title, the "Moral" and the "Religious."

In her frequent references to the Muses and in citing Helicon and Parnassus, the poet expresses her concerted interest in poetic afflatus and its role in her poetics. In addition, she points out that "*Phoebus* reigns above the starry train" and that "bright *Aurora* purples o'er the main," introducing her preoccupation with solar imagery. The fact that Wheatley establishes the atmosphere of pastoral first, before treating any other subject, specifies the importance of this mode to her undertaking. "To Maecenas" states not only that its author harbors "a grov'ling mind," but also that she is unable to "raise the song" whose "fault'ring music dies upon my tongue" (11). Yet this piece constitutes an extraordinary performance, one in which she self-consciously demonstrates her power over words.

Indeed, she appears to be determined to give precisely such a demonstration when she first offers a verbal depiction of Homer's awe-inspiring "Celestial Gods": "As the thunder shakes the heav'nly plains,/ A deep felt horror thrills through all my veins." Next, wishing to achieve in words an opposite effect, she trades the fast-paced mono- and disyllabic words of the example above for the slower, more deliberate, liquid "r's" and "l's" of the following couplet: "When gentler strains demand thy graceful song,/ The length'ning line moves languishing along." In the next stanza, despite this illustration of her power to choose sounds which "must seem an *Eccho* to the *Sense*" (Pope, *Essay on Criticism* l. 365), she expresses an ardent desire to emulate Homer and Vergil: "O could I rival thine and Virgil's page,/ Or claim the Muses with the Mantuan Sage"—no meager ambition. For, if she could bring her verse to such high achievement, "Then should my song in bolder notes arise,/ And all my numbers pleasingly surprize" (10).

Following this implicit challenge to Wheatley herself to rise to the level of greatness, she asks, "why this partial grace,/ To one alone of *Afric's* sable race" (11). In other words, unaware of African authors other than the Latin playwright Terence (who, it is thought, was born in Carthage and perhaps belonged to an African nation), Wheatley wonders why, until now, there have been no other African writers besides Terence. For now, she tells Maecenas, "Thy virtues . . . shall be sung" in *her* poetry. The humble disclaimers regarding her inadequacies mask the ambition of an intelligent poet who, composing at the height of her abilities,[9] is emboldened to "snatch a laurel from thine [i.e., her patron's] honour'd head" (12). Part of what Wheatley means here becomes obvious when we understand that the laurel symbolizes Apollo (god of the arts), poetic inspiration, and victory.

Poetic inspiration is, nonetheless, not all Wheatley is about in the triplet which contains the "laurel" passage; in full, this triplet sounds as follows:

> While blooming wreaths around thy temples spread,
> I'll snatch a laurel from thine honour'd head,
> While you indulgent smile upon the deed. (12)

As these lines comprise the only triplet in this poem of couplets, we may assume that the poet intends (certainly the text "intends") to focus attention on the content of these lines. Of course, among poets of the classical world, to achieve the laurel meant to attain poetic maturity, to "arrive" as a poet. For Wheatley to claim that she will "*snatch* a laurel [emphasis mine]" indicates that she recognizes the uncertain reception awaiting her poetic efforts among white readers. I do not mean to suggest that Wheatley is uncertain; indeed, she is so certain that publication of her *Poems* in 1773 will announce her competence to the world that she is emboldened to record that announcement in her own words and in her volume's first poem. Note, nevertheless, that she, unlike other (probably white) poets, must "snatch" her laurel rather than simply seize or take it. While the good white poet enjoys the opulence of "blooming wreaths" spreading unchecked "around thy temples," she, the good black poet and a slave, finds herself relegated to a position of such impoverished dependence that she is forced either to be silent—which for this aggressive voice will not do; she never seriously considers silence as an alternative—or to "snatch" her place as a poetic voice. The surreptitiousness denoted by the verb *snatch* forcefully extends Wheatley's subversive voice. So bold does she become, in fact, that, after proclaiming her theft, she proceeds to "instruct" her patron-readers to "smile upon the deed" indulgently. Only the apparent harmlessness of her mask of humility empowers her to "get away with" envisioning such aggression. At the same time, resituating her poetic voice within the mode of subversive pastoral reveals the integrity of her rebellion.

An arresting parallel to the triplet just cited occurs in the poetry of Mather Byles, nephew of Cotton Mather and a Congregational minister who enjoyed considerable popularity as a poet and journalist during the first half of the eighteenth century. According to one source, Byles well may have served Wheatley as both Latin tutor and advisor in her composition of poems; certainly her *Poems on Various Subjects, Religious and Moral* (1773) was modeled upon Byles's *Poems on Several Occasions* (1744). In "Written in Milton's *Paradise Lost*," Byles longs to possess "the tuneful Arts/ Of lofty Verse" manifested by Milton's sublime lines, in somewhat the same spirit as

Wheatley hopes to emulate Homer and Vergil. "Thus with ambitious Hand," continues Byles, "I'd boldly snatch/ A spreading Branch from his immortal Laurels" (25). Byles pursues this vain desire throughout the next 150 lines, until he finally concedes that he is unequal to the task: "But, O my Muse, shake off these idle Dreams,/ Imaginary Trances! vain Illusions!" In Byles's own judgment, Milton's "mighty Numbers tow'r above thy Sight,/ Mock thy low Musick, and elude thy Strains" (34).

Here, as in Wheatley's triplet, are nature's spreading plants, the action of snatching a laurel, and, of course, the ambition of an aspiring poet. Of much greater significance, however, are the marked differences between "teacher" and "student." Byles casts his desire to snatch a laurel in the subjunctive mood, as a condition contrary to fact, whereas Wheatley significantly expresses her action of seizing the laurel in the declarative mood. That is, although Byles is content with wishing, Wheatley declares that she *will* accomplish the deed. Byles probably uses the conditional mood because, as he himself states, he is unequal to an achievement such as Milton's. Wheatley, on the other hand, does not compare herself to Milton—nor, in the context of the laurel, to Homer or Vergil, whom she has named earlier in the poem. Rather, she will seize the badge of her poetic maturity from one who dispenses patronage—certainly a more realistic aspiration, signaling Wheatley's deeper commitment to the vocation of author. While Byles went on to pursue the ministry, eventually giving up the writing of poetry altogether, Wheatley continued throughout her life to attempt to make a living from the products of her pen.

Byles has nothing in his poem even resembling the sly comment, "While you indulgent smile upon the deed." Clearly Wheatley fully intends to have her laurel and, in addition, to take that prize while her white supporters (and perhaps even her white detractors) look on, despite the racial and sexist prejudices of her time. Wheatley—unlike her white male "teacher" and example, who because of his race and gender had a much better chance to succeed than she—informs all her readers, white and black, male and female, that she will succeed as an author, despite all the odds against her. Certainly her determination merits the adjective *heroic*. Her white male predecessor's attitude is one of playful subservience toward *his* predecessor, whom Byles recognizes as his superior. Wheatley, in converting Byles's conditional utterance into one of willful declaration, underlines his lack of commitment to his vocation as a poet and thereby subverts his play, in effect rebelling against it, all the while maintaining her posture of subtle subversion.

In this poem, one of her most self-reflexive (the pronoun "I" in the objective, possessive, and nominative cases appears fifteen times), Wheatley constructs a world which appears nonthreatening to her predominantly white audience, but she undermines that construction by asserting that she fully intends to write superior poetry which will "snatch" a victory for her within the world of subversive pastoral. Few will guess what she really hopes to do—indeed, perhaps none at all. But *she* knows.

With a benign mask firmly in place, Wheatley proceeds in subsequent poems to delineate the characteristics of virtue, to exhort young Harvard students to lay aside sin, and to praise King George III's repeal of the Stamp Act. In "To the King's Most Excellent Majesty. 1768," Wheatley closes with these two diverting couplets:

> Great God, direct, and guard him from on high
> And from his head let ev'ry evil fly!
> And may each clime with equal gladness see
> A monarch's smile can set his subjects free! (17)

These lines suggest another message, beyond mere praise. If every evil flies from the mind of George, then it follows that every one of his subjects—perhaps even African Americans—should enjoy freedom.

This pattern of donning a mask and uttering harmless, acceptable generalities serves Wheatley again in the very next poem, the controversial "On Being Brought from Africa to America." She begins with four lines of supplicatory, subservient-sounding gratitude for being introduced to Christianity, much in the manner of Jupiter Hammon, an African American poet who was Wheatley's contemporary but had less skill and daring. Suddenly and radically, Wheatley shifts tone. No longer in the least bit supplicatory, as Hammon always remained, she adopts an accusatory tone. Without any transition, she declares, "Some view our sable race with scornful eye,/ 'Their colour is a diabolic die.'" This last line, appearing in quotation marks, she records as if it were an actual comment she overheard. The couplet which follows and which concludes this eight-line lyric, however, constitutes nothing less than an unmitigated command: "Remember, *Christians*, *Negros* [*sic*], black as Cain,/ May be refin'd, and join th' angelic train" (18). Her mask, once again, has empowered her to castigate all malicious, hypocritical whites who would harm her or her black brothers and sisters. In Wheatley's last extant letter to the British philanthropist, John Thornton, the author expresses a similar sentiment when she observes, "The world is a severe schoolmaster, for its frowns are less dang'rous than its smiles and flatteries" (183). Obviously, Wheatley was too intelligent to be fooled by white duplicity.

Wheatley frequently employs the voice of pastoral throughout her poetry. Even one of her elegies begins by establishing a locus conventional in pastoral: "Where contemplation finds her sacred spring" (53). Perhaps affecting an attitude of philosophic contemplation, the poet invokes Parnassus, home of the Muses, in this line.

"An Hymn to the Morning," probably a paean to the memory of Wheatley's mother in Africa whom she recalled to her white captors as "pouring out water at his [the sun's] rising," celebrates "bright Aurora." As the day passes and the sun rises in the sky, "Ye shady groves, your verdant gloom display/ To shield your poet from the burning day" (56). This sun (or Apollo, god of poetry) awakens "the sacred lyre" of the poet's creativity, evoking within her "The bow'rs, the gales, the variegated skies/ In all their pleasures" (57). Perhaps these are memories of her native Gambia that she adapts to the rhetoric of pastoral.

This same pastoral strain dominates the "new world" she constructs in what is her most important single poem, "On Imagination." Wheatley's power over words, in the service of her forceful imagination, enables her to depict the flourishing of gay scenes with smiling fields, even "Though *Winter* frowns to *Fancy's* raptur'd eyes." Indeed, the poet's imagination can "break . . . [the] iron bands" of "The frozen deeps" "And bid their waters murmur o'er the sands." Of course, to a slave, the image of "iron bands" breaking cannot be accidental. Recall her allusion to Terence, who broke his "iron bands" by means of the power of his pen. In Wheatley's new world, moreover, she pictures with the force of myth a paradisiacal golden age:

> Fair *Flora* may resume her fragrant reign,
> And with her flow'ry riches deck the plain;
> *Sylvanus* may diffuse his honours round,
> And all the forest may with leaves be crown'd;
> Show'rs may descend, and dews their gems disclose,
> And nectar sparkle on the blooming rose. (66–67)

With these references to the Roman deities Flora, goddess of flowers; and Sylvanus, god of forests and shepherds, Wheatley has constructed an almost wholly pagan, classical world, through which may glimmer recollection, once again, of her native Gambia.

If Wheatley is such a staunch, conservative Christian, filled to the brim with a never-questioning piety, as such critics as J. Saunders Redding claim,[10] then why do no biblical figures populate her ideal paradise? Earlier in this same poem, Wheatley speaks of "Soaring through air to find the bright abode,/ Th' empyreal palace of the thund'ring God" (66). If this "God" is Jehovah and not Jove, then, once again, why does she not place in her ideal world Joshua, Moses, Elijah, or Job? Rather than biblical characters, we find Flora and Sylvanus from the classical hierarchy of deities. This practice of celebrating a wholly pagan construction, untempered by references to Judaeo-Christian figures, characterizes the products of her poetic maturity—such poems as "Niobe in Distress," "An Hymn to the Morning," "An Hymn to the Evening," "To

Maecenas," "To a Gentleman of the Navy," "Phillis's Reply to the Answer," "To His Excellency General Washington," and "Liberty and Peace."

Even though she continued to sound the note of orthodoxy in her letters to her intimate friend, the committed Christian, Obour Tanner, and in elegies on such Christian subjects as the Reverend John Moorhead and David Wooster, Wheatley appears to have mitigated her former orthodoxy, at least after 1772, embracing the myth of Aeneas as an indication of her Enlightenment theology.[11] Her emotional late 1783 elegy on the death of Samuel Cooper, for example, portrays the pastor who baptized her. Cooper had a reputation for being one of the most liberal ministers of the day and a leader of the movement that became Unitarianism. Wheatley recalls him as a man of public affairs who dealt enthusiastically with the American Revolution, with the Boston order of Masons, and with the poet herself, whom Cooper often encouraged to write. One must search for the only line, in this elegy of fifty-two lines, which identifies Cooper's function as minister: "Thy Church laments her faithfull Pastor fled" (224; I quote from Wheatley's manuscript version).

One need not search long, however, for the classical world of pastoral in "On Imagination." The line in which Sylvanus appears, for example, probably owes something to Vergil's tenth eclogue. For that matter, Wheatley's "Sylvanus may diffuse his honors round" well may be a translation of Vergil's "venit et agresti capitis Silvanus honore" (l. 24; even Sylvanus came with the rustic honor [or distinction] on his head [i.e., wearing a floral chaplet]). As Wheatley's familiarity with Horace already has been demonstrated, she also may have in mind here the following passage from the second epode: "pater/ Silvane, tutor finium" (ll. 21–22; father Sylvanus, guardian of borders).

Is not Wheatley staking out her own boundaries in this poem? Is she not carving out her own property, the property of her imagination, in a realm beyond the ravages of slavery? Indeed, her poetic realm possesses no iron bands; nor is it, finally, limited even by boundaries. Of course, the boundaries over which Sylvanus rules are those separating civilization from the uncultivated, boundless wilds of the forests and plains; that is, he guards his own realm, the unsullied forests, from the threat of civilization. It can be no accident that Wheatley fixes upon this particular figure from classical myth, for Sylvanus symbolizes release from any and all "iron bands." Wheatley has constructed here a new world, one which empowers her to "amaze th' unbounded soul" (66). In her own phrasing, "Such is thy [the imagination's] power" (67).

Attendant upon the abandon symbolized by Sylvanus is that associated with the goddess Flora. Indeed, in the most popular classical handbook of the day, William King's *An Historical Account of the Heathen Gods and Heroes*

(1710), the author writes that "Flora was a Courtezan, who got a great Sum of Money by her immodest Practices." Her celebrations "came to that Excess of Indecency," according to King, that they became characterized "by Persons appearing naked" (193). Such juxtaposition of Flora and Sylvanus cannot be accidental, because both represent the throwing aside of convention and restraint. What at first looks harmless enough, upon closer examination challenges even the sexual mores of Wheatley's time. One does not recognize the intensity of this subversion of her white oppressors' sociopolitical practices, however, until one has recovered the rhetoric of her subversive pastoral. After all, are not all politics based upon a "border" of one kind or another?

In addition to transporting her into the realm of a golden age pastoral, free from the strictures of a slaveholding civilization, Wheatley's imagination enables her to depict, once again, her mother's dawn:

> From *Tithon's* bed now might *Aurora* rise,
> Her cheeks all glowing with celestial dies,
> While a pure stream of light o'erflows the skies.

The triplet rhyme here, the only one in the entire poem, calls attention to the importance of this image to the poet. As is usually the case in her poetry, the beauty of the dawn soon is followed by the regal image of the sun: "The monarch of the day *I* might behold,/ And all the mountains tipt with radiant gold" (67). I underline the first person pronoun to signal the self-reflexive character of this poem. Using the first person singular pronoun six times, Wheatley clearly intends in this lyric to describe the power of imagination as it functions within her own mind. The images of waters murmuring over sands, flowers decking the plain, and forests in full foliage resonate with the pastoral recollection of her native Gambia.

Wheatley describes Gambia in a later poem, "Phillis's Reply to the Answer," composed as the third installment in a series. The first, "To a Gentleman of the Navy," was by Wheatley; and the second, "The Answer," was written as a response to the first by a man named Rockfort, or Rockford. All three works appeared in the *Royal American Magazine* of Boston between late October and early December 1774. "Rockfort," in "The Answer," described a visit to the west coast of Africa, recalling a place "Where cheerful phoebus [*sic*] makes all nature gay;/ Where sweet refreshing breezes gently fan;/ The flow'ry path, the ever verdent [*sic*] lawn,/ The artless grottoes, and the soft retreats" (142). Whether or not this description actually depicts the torrid zones of equatorial, coastal West Africa, it does describe the world of classical pastoral. Nevertheless, "The Answer" offers a "fair description," in Wheatley's words, of "artless grottos" not made by human hands and "the sylvan shade." The poem prompts "pleasing Gambia on my soul" to return. That memory Wheatley evokes in the following passage:

> With native grace in spring's luxuriant reign,
> Smiles the gay mead, and Eden blooms again,
> The various bower, the tuneful flowing stream,
> The soft retreats, the lovers golden dream,
> Her soil spontaneous, yields exhaustless stores;
> For Phoebus revels on her verdant shores. (144)

The combination of the myths of Adam and Aeneas, clearly seen here, we have come to recognize as commonplace in this period of American classicism. It is surprising, however, in the poetry of one who so persistently has been considered an orthodox Christian, to observe the myth of Aeneas dominating that of Adam. The allusion to "Eden" here remains only a casual reference. The impetus to prefer pastoral's "golden dream" perhaps derives from the fact that the classical world so closely approximates Wheatley's recollection of her homeland.

In her 1773 *Poems*, Wheatley uses the harmlessness of her pastoral mask to celebrate the paintings of an African American artist. Mather Byles, the poet and Congregational minister after whose *Poems on Several Occasions* (1745) Wheatley is thought to have designed her own volume,[12] places a poem to an artist named Pictorio toward the end of his volume. In a similar position, Wheatley arranges a poem dedicated to an African artist named Scipio Moorehead, slave of the Reverend John Moorhead (upon whose death Wheatley wrote an elegy mentioned earlier). Like Scipio, the poet is a slave at the time she chooses to depict in words Scipio's "shades of time." In "To S. M. a Young *African* Painter, on Seeing His Works," Wheatley unabashedly informs the world that African Americans can produce paintings, just as whites can. Signaling her own debt to Vergil's eclogues, she describes one of Scipio's paintings as if it rendered on canvas the first half of Vergil's eighth eclogue: "No more to tell of *Damon's* tender sighs,/ Or rising radiance of *Aurora's* eyes" (115). As Damon, a disappointed lover in Vergil's eighth eclogue, begins to sing in plaintive strains, he opens his section of the poem by referring to the rising of the dawn. In the poem immediately after "To S. M. a Young *African* Painter, on Seeing His Works," Wheatley calls herself "the *Afric* muse" (117). While Byles before her had told of Pictorio's portraits of classical subjects, Wheatley subversively insists that, just as a slave can rival a white man's poetic output, a slave also can challenge a white painter's sophistication.

Wheatley concludes her volume[13] with a poem, "A Farewell to America. To Mrs. S.W.," which, like the volume's first poem, opens with images drawn from pastoral. In a tribute to her mistress Susanna, Wheatley bids "Adieu, *New England's* smiling meads,/ Adieu, the flow'ry plain" (119). In this poem, the poet also alludes to the Greek goddess of youth, Hebe, who to her may have stood for good health. In classical thought, Hebe also represented one who could free people from chains and bondage; in this capacity, her rituals were characterized by unrestrained celebrations. As in the book's very first poem, Wheatley again suggests—subversively, of course—that her real object is freedom. Hence she effectively draws a complete circle, ending where she began: advancing the cause of freedom.

One can only guess who suggested the inflammatory title of this final poem when it appeared in Boston just after Wheatley's departure for London on May 8, 1773. Perhaps she herself proposed this politically charged title of one printed version: "To the Empire of America Beneath the Western Hemisphere. Farewell to America" (219). It is known that she both toned down some of the poems in her London volume and omitted several of her political pieces celebrating colonial rebellion. Still, in the diction of this title, which appeared with a longer version of the poem on May 10, 1773, in the *Massachusetts Gazette and Boston Post-Boy,* she anticipates the tone which she applies to George Washington, whom she later exalts in this electrifying couplet: "A crown, a mansion, and a throne that shine,/ With gold unfading, WASHINGTON! be thine" (146).

Wheatley's last known poem, "An Elegy on Leaving ———," is heavily laden with pastoralism. Such phrases as "ye friendly bow'rs," "each sequester'd seat," and "The groves, from noon-tide rays a kind retreat"—all from the first four-line stanza—place the temper of this piece firmly in the pastoral realm. With fourteen uses of the first person singular pronoun (in all three cases), this poem also is one of her most self-reflexive. Yet, at the same time, this piece is one of her bleakest. Wheatley appears to wish to bid the entire world of poetic creativity adieu: "No more my hand shall wake the warbling lyre" (156). Written only months before her death in abject poverty, Wheatley here may well have penned her own elegy. Despite the bleakness of the line just quoted, she rallies in the last stanza, bidding: "But come sweet Hope, from thy divine retreat" (157). Significantly, this profoundly meditative and introspective poem, in which she deplores "those pleasing hours . . . ever flown" and the "scenes of transport" now retired "from my thoughts" (156), contains not a whit of Christianity. Even her consolation comes from "calm Content" like that evoked by Horace. In only twenty-eight lines, Wheatley constructs a wholly classical lament which finally can only be labeled pastoral elegy.

In contrast to Wheatley's usual application of the pastoral mode, and despite this poem's heavy dependence upon that mode, "An Elegy on Leaving ———" carries no obvious hint of subversion. This poem nevertheless is significant for an investigation of Wheatley's use of the pastoral mode because it presents yet another rejection of the Christianity of her white oppressors. Here, in the last moments in which she exercises her poetic powers, she seeks consolation not in the promise of a Christian heaven or an anticipated entry into Paradise, but in the golden rays of her African sun. Given the fact that she so often celebrates the soothing warmth of the sun, contrasting it with the less hospitable Boston skies, which often are overcast and chilling, it should come as no surprise that she longs for "pleasing Gambia" as her poetic powers wane. As the tone of this fine poem approaches that of prayer, its publication seems almost to go against the desire of the author. In other words, here we seem almost to intrude upon the author's privacy, as we do when we read the poetic meditations of Edward Taylor. As in "On Imagination," here Wheatley's celebration of classical pastoral resonates with her African heritage. In its rejection of the Christianity of white people, "An Elegy on Leaving ———," after all, enacts a final example of subversion. Thus the poem links her oeuvre with that of Baraka, Malcolm X, and other African Americans who have sought their ideas of God outside a Christian context. By putting on a mask of harmlessness and by manipulating the conventions of pastoral, Phillis Wheatley has woven into her poetry the narrative and the example of a courageous and intelligent soul who ever refuses to accept "things as they are" and who struggles constantly to be free.

While several of the pastoral elegies examined in the following section are as thoroughly classical as those we have examined above, many unmistakably commingle the myths of Adam and Aeneas. Wheatley, more readily than any other American classicist, carries out Patterson's construction of "a metaphorical system." Within the parameters of this "system," she critiques both British interference with American affairs and the American institution of slavery. Moreover, she shapes a poetics of the mask, hence prefiguring later African American protest figures in fiction, such as Chesnutt's Uncle Julius and Hughes's Semple. In sum, she establishes a position in relation to her "adoptive" American culture—the position of an oppressed but vigilant and rebellious minority—which would be reflected in African American letters throughout the nineteenth century and the first half of the twentieth.

The Pastoral Elegy: An American Genre

While Wheatley draws on the Adamic myth more frequently in the remainder of her eighteen elegies, in "An Elegy on Leaving" she represents the "flip side" of Eunice Bourne's *Fishing Lady*. Rather than celebrating Bourne's happy scene of pastoral bliss, this elegy laments the loss of that bliss. Both works reside wholly in the context of classical pastoral. In her elegy, "On the Death of Dr. Samuel Marshall 1771," too, Wheatley limns a classical lament, one in which Marshall, as an "immortal shade," looks back upon those he has left behind "from *Olympus*' height." Instead of referring to the deceased physician as a "setting sun," as in elegies on George Whitefield and Samuel Cooper, she calls Marshall *Apollo*, god of the sun and the arts. As one of these arts was that of healing, the reference to Apollo is completely apposite to her earlier reference to Marshall as "*Aesculapius*" (86–87), one of the sons of Apollo and the god of medicine.

Other Wheatley elegies (e.g., "To a Gentleman and Lady on the Death of Avis, Aged one Year," 84–85) portray the realm of death in distinctly chthonic terms; rather than going to a Christian heaven or hell, the departed descends into an underworld populated by shades and divided into a Tartarus of punishment and an Elysium of reward. Such sallies into the classical afterlife are infrequent in Wheatley's elegies, which more often subscribe to Adamic notions of an afterlife. Even so, "An Elegy on Leaving ———," with its numerous references to images and figures from pastoral tradition, easily fits within the genre of the pastoral elegy. In that genre, the poet-shepherd of pastoral tradition forsakes "crowds and noise" for a "sequester'd seat" to which, "wrapt in thought," the poet-shepherd has "strayd'd," either alone as here (and in Milton's *Lycidas*) or accompanied by a second shepherd. In this seclusion, the protagonist contemplates the death of some other shepherd, often another poet, under the aegis of poetic inspiration, usually represented by one or another of the nine Muses. In the present case, Wheatley's line, "There first my bosom felt poetic flame," obviates the obligatory reference to the Muse in this pastoral elegy in which the poet ponders her own departure from the world of pocsy: "No more my hand shall wake the warbling lyre" (156).

Unlike Wheatley, who in her poetic oeuvres sometimes but not always (e.g., in her "Goliath of Gath") keeps separate the worlds of Adam and Aeneas, many other American practitioners of the pastoral elegy often unabashedly blend the myths of Adam and Aeneas. Eleven of the seventeen pastoral elegies I have identified (many others doubtless will be found) feature a clear combination of these two modes of discourse. Six (Wheatley's "Elegy on Leaving" among them), however, remain strictly classical in form and content. Three of these seventeen poems have been discussed by others who have noted their heavy debt to classicism; and two of these same three have been identified as pastoral elegies. The other fourteen poems have not, to my knowledge, been identified as pastoral elegies or as owing a debt to classicism.

George F. Sensabaugh and Leon Howard, for example, have identified Thomas Godfrey's "To the Memory of General Wolfe" as a pastoral elegy; and Silverman in *Colonial American Poetry*, calls James Sterling's "A Pastoral to His Excellency George Thomas" a pastoral elegy (328). At the same time, many have pointed out the excellent qualities, classical and otherwise, of Urian Oakes's "An Elegie Upon . . . Thomas Shepard," though none has gone so far as to identify this poem as a pastoral elegy. What I propose, then, is that we examine salient representatives of this group of poems, as members of a literary genre whose existence in Early America before 1800 heretofore has received scant notice.

Lament characterizes much of the form and content of the pastoral elegy. It is instructive to return to Puttenham's *Arte of English Poesie* regarding the Renaissance perspective on this genre. Puttenham maintains that, in the lament, "the Poet . . . play[s] also the Phisitian, and not only by applying a medicine to the ordinary sickness of mankind, but by making the very greef it selfe (in part) cure of the disease" (172–73). The author of pastoral elegies, then, is a physician helping to heal the grief of those suffering the loss of a loved one.

In other words, pastoral elegies and funeral elegies (whose numbers in Early America are legion) preserve the memory of the departed as they attempt to reclaim for the living something of what has been lost. Taken as a collective whole, these poems enact an attempt on the part of eighteenth-century Americans to trace their culture and minimize the loss of their past. The vital importance to all Americans that we be able to own our past is signaled by Leslie Berlowitz in her "Introduction" to the collection of essays, *America in Theory*. There she observes that Americans of today "fear that they have had no past, no patriarchal traditions or customs in the European sense, no feelings of permanent rootedness and stability." While the radical shift in discourse (see ch. 7 below) is largely responsible for "this 'fear' of pastlessness" (Berlowitz ix), Early American poets of pastoral elegies and funeral elegies were self-consciously engaged with the task of preserving the past. As we soon shall understand, that past which authors of pastoral elegies wished to preserve was a distinctly American past, demonstrating once again the phenomenon of *translatio cultus*. The predominantly Adamic nature of the Puritan funeral elegy identifies this genre as inappropriate for close scrutiny in this investigation of the classical origins of the American self; the investigation that follows concentrates on the classical dimensions of the pastoral elegy, though it will be discovered that several Early American pastoral elegists make peculiarly American use of the Puritan funeral elegy in constructing their pastoral elegies.

Six of the seventeen pastoral elegies identified may be called strictly classical, showing no connection to either the Puritan funeral elegy or the Adamic myth. Of the remaining eleven, four allow the classical mode of discourse to dominate but do admit several characteristics of the Adamic mode, displaying particular links to the Puritan funeral elegy. The other seven signify effective blends of the myths of Adam and Aeneas, with their clear, balanced combination of elements from the classical pastoral elegy and the Puritan funeral elegy.

While all seventeen of these pastoral elegies manifest characteristics which identify them as American, all attest the dominance of the myth of Aeneas, if only by virtue of their genre. They also share another characteristic. Despite the popularity of the pastoral elegy in England, particularly following publication of Milton's *Lycidas*, not one of the seventeen derives its form from Milton's pastoral elegy. This observation is especially surprising when one recalls Milton's immense popularity in Great Britain *and in the American colonies* after the turn into the eighteenth century.

Perhaps that perceived popularity has led two scholars of Milton's reputation in America to conclude that Thomas Godfrey (the young American author of the *Prince of Parthia*, the first tragedy written by an American and subsequently performed) took *Lycidas* as a model in composing his poem "To the Memory of General Wolfe." Leon Howard, in his pioneering "The Influence of Milton on Colonial American Poetry" (1936), maintains that Thomas Godfrey's pastoral elegy "is modeled on Milton's poem rather closely but not slavishly" (77). As evidence for his contention, he quotes the pair of couplets which close Godfrey's poem. Writing thirty years later, George Sensabaugh, in *Milton in Early America*, declares that Godfrey's poem "echoed *Lycidas* a number of times." Then he quotes the last couplet of the poem, which Sensabaugh says "brings to mind the last lines of *Lycidas*" (70–71).

Godfrey's concluding couplet, "So sung the Swains, 'til Phoebus' radiant light,/ Chac'd to her azure bed the Queen of Night," indeed may owe something to the last lines of *Lycidas*, "At last he [i.e., the "uncouth Swain"] rose, and twitch'd his Mantle blew:/ To morrow to fresh Woods, and Pastures new" (ll. 192–93; see Patrides 11). While both Milton and Godfrey have in mind here the traditional pastoral "fear" of night, notice that Godfrey's couplet clearly describes the coming of the day, while Milton's refers to the influence upon the swain of the night's arrival, postponing pastoral concerns until the renewal promised by "To morrow." Interestingly, neither Sensabaugh nor Howard identifies any further parallels. The simple truth seems to be that no other substantial parallels between Godfrey and Milton may be traced in this poem. As was the case with Cotton Mather's *Magnalia Christi Americana* and Milton's *Paradise Lost*, the differences between Godfrey's "To the Memory of General Wolfe" and Milton's *Lycidas* prove more instructive than the likenesses.

As a young man, Thomas Godfrey, a native-born Philadelphian, came under the influence of William Smith, provost of Philadelphia College (later the University of Pennsylvania), who encouraged the young man's literary inclinations by publishing several of his early poems in his *American Magazine and Monthly Chronicle for the British Colonies*. Also through Smith's influence, the young Godfrey obtained a lieutenant's commission in the Pennsylvania militia, apparently engaging in the expedition against Fort Duquesne in the French and

Indian War. Led by the British Brig. Gen. John Forbes, this expedition included the young George Washington, who served on the general's staff.

In "Epistle to a Friend, from Fort Henry," a poem written approximately a year before "To the Memory of General Wolfe," Godfrey commemorates the death of George Augustus Howe, third Viscount Howe and older brother of Richard Howe and William Howe, who served, respectively, as admiral and general for the British during the American Revolution. "Epistle to a Friend, from Fort Henry," with its references to "fears," "terror," and "the fatal field, all drench'd in gore" (21) reads as if it were a study for the later pastoral elegy on Wolfe. Colonel Howe, killed at Trout Brook, Lake George, New York, in a skirmish with the French (1758), merits "a British tear" in this poem, whose muse has fled "fierce war's alarms" to seek "where peace invites with softer charms" (20).

In "To the Memory of General Wolfe," we again find the muse absent. In this strictly classical pastoral elegy, we encounter a population of swains named "Lysidas" (after Vergil's spelling, not Milton's "Lycidas"), Damaetas, Menalcas, Alexis, and Codrus—all conventional names within the pastorals of Vergil and Theocritus. Among these names, only that of Damaetas appears in *Lycidas;* whereas, in Milton, Damaetas appears as a Cambridge don, Godfrey makes of Damaetas one of the two shepherds whose dialogue comprises the majority of the poem. Of course, *Lycidas* is not a dialogue but rather, as Milton says, a monody. Although fully 99 of the 109 lines which make up Godfrey's poem are devoted to the dialogue between Damaetas and Lysidas, the poem opens with a third person speaker; the final two lines, quoted above, conclude in the voice of this same speaker, hence completing the pattern. Milton opens *Lycidas* with his lyric first person "I com to pluck your Berries harsh and crude," rendering somewhat problematical his refusal to allow his lyric "I" to conclude the poem. Instead, Milton employs as a conclusion an Italianate ottawa rima verse, spoken by a third person narrator.

Godfrey's framing of his dramatic dialogue with the device of a third person narrator certainly simplifies his poem, but, more to the point, this technique enacts the completion of a narrative pattern not occurring either in Milton's *Lycidas* or in Vergil's *Eclogues*. It appears, then, that Godfrey has set out to construct his own pastoral elegy, in imitation of no one. At other strategic moments, this Early American poet's pastoral elegy does, nevertheless, often resemble, not Milton's *Lycidas* but Vergil's *Eclogues*, demonstrating how fine a student of Vergil Godfrey could be. At the same time that Godfrey draws resemblances here to Vergil's *Eclogues*, he clearly constructs no mere "imitation" but composes an original, if thoroughly classical, poem.

As noted above, Godfrey comes to the composition of "To the Memory of General Wolfe" after having written "Epistle to a Friend, from Fort Henry." In the earlier piece, Godfrey identifies the problem of treating the subject of war within the ostensibly incompatible genre of pastoral. Surely the obvious choice of genre to describe a warrior fallen in battle would be the epic; Godfrey passes over this genre, however, perhaps because of time constraints or simply because he knows pastoral so much better. In any event, Godfrey, his muse having flown "fierce war's alarms" to seek instead "where peace invites with softer charms," determines to describe the "darksome forests," "terror," and "gloomy way" of war. This project calls up "no enchanting prospects." The dark wilderness of war Godfrey paints includes "the ravaged cot . . . Whose owner fell beneath the savage hand" of Native Americans fighting for the French, and "the fatal field, all drench'd in gore." All these images, of course, form the antithesis of warm pastoral illuminated by the hopeful light of sunny meads and flowery plains. Yet Godfrey is studious to draw a sharp contrast between the destruction of war within "some hostile land" and "the rich fields, with Ceres' blessings stored," which "Grieve for their slaughter'd or their absent lord" (21). Godfrey here self-consciously inverts the world of pastoral, thereby making his condemnation of war all the more painful.

Godfrey elaborates upon this pattern of inverted, antithetical pastoral in "To the Memory of General Wolfe." For example, he omits any invocation to the Muse and begins this poem in darkness: "Set was the Sun" (first line). What light exists in this realm opposed to day emanates from the "fainter lustre" of "pallid Cynthia" (i.e., the moon). Following this opening, third-person description of "Old dusky Night," Damaetas begins the dialogue between himself and Lysidas with the question: "Why rests, my Lysidas, beneath this shade?" As Damaetas's subsequent discourse makes clear, the "shade" he alludes to does not derive from a bright sun. Quite the contrary, Damaetas's shade conjures up "pale ghosts" and "troops of elves in ev'ry glade." The military suggestion of "troops" evokes the threat to Wolfe's own troops, now that death has taken him. Godfrey's allusion to elves recalls Benjamin Tompson's identification of Native Americans as elves in *New Englands Crisis*, thereby suggesting that the troops of elves Godfrey refers to actually are hostile Native Americans. For Godfrey, the shade cast by the "pallid" luster of the moon brings to mind fear and danger. The poet may take this notion from Vergil's insistence, at the conclusion of the tenth eclogue, that "solet esse gravis cantantibus umbra" (l. 75; the evening shade is wonted to be perilous to [those] singing—i.e., to shepherd singers of pastoral). Notice that Damaetas asks why Lysidas reclines "beneath *this* shade [emphasis added]," rather than beneath the shade cast by a warm sun. Indeed, the demonstrative *this* sets up a dichotomy between the shade of night and the shade of day, underscoring how this poem embraces inverted pastoral.

Godfrey's dark opening appropriately prepares for the attitude of mourning he hopes to capture. Moreover, beginning this pastoral elegy in the surreal land of "the Queen of Night," where "horror shadows all the deepning groves," the poet invites the reader to view this memorial to a slain military commander, fallen in the heat of battle, as a symbol of the deadly horrors of war. For that matter, the remainder of the poem perhaps may be interpreted best in terms of symbol. The several tigers, wolves, and boars in Godfrey's poem—all conventions of traditional pastoral—become symbols of the enemies of Britain. For example, the deceased General Wolfe, here given the mellifluous name *Amintor* (a Greek word meaning defender), had served as champion against "the fierce Tiger or the foaming Boar." As traditional pastorals never are populated by members of "the savage race" or by "Savage Tyrants," this poem's lament that, with Wolfe's loss, "now unaw'd the Savage Tyrants tread/ The silent grove" firmly anchors Godfrey's poem in America. For surely these "Savage Tyrants" symbolize those Native Americans hostile to the British. Today, of course, we may deplore Godfrey's failure to observe, first and foremost, that Native Americans were *not* savages in any intelligent anthropological sense; and, second, that many Native Americans fought with the British. Thus Godfrey's poem becomes yet another installment in the saga of white vilification of Native Americans.

Godfrey punctuates his highly artificial world of surrealistic pastoral with other less inflammatory but nonetheless realistic touches. The uncomfortable nights of the soldier on maneuvers, for example, Godfrey describes as follows: "Sickning dews and damps around my [Damaetas is speaking] head/ With falling stars, their baleful influence shed." Godfrey also seizes this opportunity to celebrate Wolfe's well-known heroism. Damaetas's declaration that Wolfe "with gallant pride/ First clomb the cliff, or rush'd into the tide" recalls Wolfe's two most heroic gestures during the famous Siege of Quebec, which took place in early fall of 1759. Wolfe's clever harassment of the French by ordering his men to sail up and downstream with the tide, according to Samuel Eliot Morison, forced "Bougainville's soldiers to march and countermarch to the point of exhaustion" (*Oxford History* 167). In addition, Wolfe scaled the cliffs to the Plains of Abraham, which had seemed impregnable, catching the French off guard and leading to victory first at Quebec and then in the entire French and Indian War. While it is true that Wolfe sacrificed his own life during this offensive, he certainly earned for himself Godfrey's epithet "brave Amintor," which the poet repeats four times. More important, Wolfe gained a permanent place in textbooks of military strategy.

In the phrase "'Ere parting day," Godfrey nods toward the first line of Thomas Gray's "Elegy Written in a Country Churchyard." This probably is more than a mere attempt to honor Gray's famous poem. Morison records that Gray's "Elegy" was a favorite of Wolfe's and that, on the morning of the day when Wolfe died (September 13, 1759), the major general recited Gray's

"Elegy in a Country Churchyard" to a young midshipman, solemnly pronouncing the famous line that his own fate presently would illustrate: "The paths of glory lead but to the grave" (168). Within the highly stylized world of pastoral, Godfrey manages to weave details linked specifically to his subject.

Perhaps an attempt to glorify his subject inspired Godfrey's use of "old Arcos" as a device to prophesy Wolfe's demise. *Arcos*, a Greek word meaning leader, and *Amintor* are both taken from the *Iliad*, a fact that clarifies Old Arcos's connection to the heroic figure of General Wolfe, or Amintor. Godfrey has Damaetas announce the coming of "Old Arcos" in the only triple rhyme in the poem:

> Two moons are wasted since beneath this shade
> As to our Shepherds on my reed I play'd,
> With weary steps old *Arcos* hither stray'd.

Then he adds:

> Thus spoke the Sire, "Here sorrow soon shall reign,
> No longer joy shall dwell upon the plain,
> Corroding care shall banish peaceful rest,
> And pain and anguish seize on ev'ry breast."

Damaetas reacts to this prophecy with typically human skepticism:

> I laugh'd in gayety to hear the Sire
> Speak what I thought his dotage did inspire.
> But now I know what caus'd his mighty dread,
> The first of Shepherds, brave *Amintor's* dead. (32)

This last line, with slight variations, recurs throughout the poem four other times, serving as a refrain, a technique common within pastoral and one employed by several Early American pastoral elegists.

Old Arcos himself may derive at least in part from Vergil's sixth eclogue. Here the bibulous Silenus reveals, despite his inebriated state, that he is possessed of considerable wisdom and even oracular ability. Silenus originated in Greece as head of the older satyrs, but in Roman myth he was often viewed as the equivalent of Sylvanus (see above). Horace's identification of Sylvanus as "pater/Silvane" (father Sylvanus; see above) strengthens the Roman association between Silenus and Sylvanus as figures of wisdom. Both these figures have a close affinity with folklore's Old Man of the Forest, well known for his wisdom and his gift of prophecy. While there is, to be sure, no Old Man of the Forest in Milton's *Lycidas*, his presence in Godfrey's "To the Memory of General Wolfe" lends his subject dignity and even mystery.

Another definitely classical borrowing, which Godfrey adapts to good advantage and which is absent from Milton's pastoral elegy, is the device of the singing contest, here actually a digression, in which two shepherds compete using their abilities as poets, hoping to win a prize. Godfrey's Lysidas points out that Damaetas earlier had "Fix'd in attention all the listning throng" upon the death of Menalcas. Although Menalcas is a name frequently used to denominate shepherds in pastoral, this Menalcas to whom Godfrey refers well may be Colonel Howe of his earlier "Epistle to a Friend." If so, we reasonably can identify Damaetas as Godfrey himself. In any event, Damaetas returns the compliment to Lysidas, pointing out that he too has shown no mean musical ability by winning a few contests of his own. Damaetas suggests, in good democratic spirit, that, instead of competing against each other, both shepherds pool their abilities in a collaborative effort to commemorate their recent loss of "brave Amintor." While one may be tempted to make much of this "good democratic spirit," the truth is that, in Vergil's eclogue on Daphnis (the fifth), which sets the principal paradigm for all subsequent pastoral elegies, the two shepherds, whose dialogue composes that poem, so praise each other's musical prowess that they too decide not to contest but instead to lament the departed Daphnis in complementary strains.

While our investigation of Godfrey's pastoral elegy has revealed many adaptations from classical sources, especially Vergil's eclogues, perhaps the most thoroughly internalized classical element Godfrey displays in this poem is discernible in its action. As with Vergil's first eclogue, time governs this poem's entire movement, which begins not in the afternoon as in Vergil, and ends not as in Vergil's poem upon the arrival of evening, but after sunset, concluding with "Phoebus' radiant light" of the next day. Godfrey dramatizes this movement through time in a subtle manner. Damaetas first agrees, for example, to remain until Cynthia's "sable noon," or midnight; but Lysidas later proposes that they descant " 'til early morn's return."

"To the Memory of General Wolfe," then, is no imitation of Milton. Neither does the poem slavishly borrow from its obvious classical sources. Rather, what Godfrey has constructed is a highly sophisticated pastoral elegy, one which unabashedly inverts the pastoral certainty of the light of day for what Godfrey deems the more appropriate, albeit disconcerting, uncertainty of the night—an atmosphere compatible with Godfrey's protest against the destructiveness of war.

We must emphasize that, although contemporary readers may find unfortunate Godfrey's references to "Savage Tyrants," these labels identify this piece as having come from an American pen. The several pastoral elegies treated below all betray their Americanness, too, although in vastly different ways.

While returning to Urian Oakes's "An Elegie Upon . . . Thomas Shepard" (1677) at first may seem a bit disjunctive, this poem's close ties to the form of pastoral elegy have not received adequate investigation; only at this juncture has the fullest context for such an investigation been established. Reading this poem, perhaps the finest single poetic performance composed in America during the seventeenth century, within the terms of the Aeneas myth reveals that Oakes's "Elegie" both subtly blends the myths of Adam and Aeneas and celebrates Roman pietas in relation to an Early American subject. These two heretofore unrecognized characteristics of Oakes's poem demonstrate how thoroughly *translatio cultus* has taken hold twenty-five years before publication of Cotton Mather's *Magnalia*. Despite the early date, Oakes's "Elegie" declares that the tension between the Adamic and the classical modes of discourse was dynamically in place even before Mather's codification of the American self (as a balanced combination of Adam and Aeneas). The poem also shows that the paradigm for those pastoral elegies which effectively blend the myths of Adam and Aeneas was established long before the pastoral elegy became a genre popular in Early America.

To be sure, there is nothing new in the observation that "Elegie" owes much to the ancient classical tradition. It is, however, new to identify this poem as a pastoral elegy. And it is new to argue that this poem owes a considerable debt to another genre whose origins reside within classical rhetoric—that of the poetic meditation. Commentators upon "Elegie" have pointed out the poem's resemblance to a Puritan sermon, to a meditation, and even to a pastoral lament. William J. Scheick, for example, speaks of "Elegie" "as if it were a sermon in verse" ("Standing" 301) and notes that Oakes depicts Shepard "as the communal soul [will]" of Charlestown, the locale of his parish, "primarily by means of images pertaining to meditation" (303). Scheick maintains that Oakes's poem deals with reason (or understanding) and will (soul or heart), two faculties the mind engages in the process of meditation, but this critic says nothing about either imagination (or fancy) or memory, two additional mental faculties employed in the meditative process. Oakes deals with both imagination and memory in "Elegie." Moreover, Scheick fails to identify meditation as having its origins in classical rhetoric (see discussion in ch. 2); unquestionably Oakes's extensive knowledge of classicism would have acquainted him with the process of *meditatio*.

Oakes draws upon this knowledge when he self-consciously states his uncertainty as a poet: "Oh! that I were a Poet now in grain!" He continues by remarking that, if he were such a poet, he would "invocate the muses all" to "lend their flowing Vein . . . to grace dear Shepard's Funeral!" Indeed, with their aid, he would "paint our griefs, and succours borrow/ From Art and Fancy, to limn out our sorrow!" (Meserole 209). These last two lines of the first stanza of the "Elegie" properly enumerate precisely the first step of the meditative process, in which one focuses upon an image of the subject or upon one closely associated with the subject—that is, fastens upon a locus (via *ars memorativa*). The mental faculty which enables this imaging process to take place is "Fancy." What Oakes proceeds to do next in "Elegie" is to carry out precisely the process he so carefully ascribes to the "Poet." Oakes himself, "Poet" or not, has drawn or limned out in this poem many images of Shepard, his "Honoured BROTHER," employing exceptional "Art" or craft in doing so.

One way in which Oakes demonstrates his "Art" as a poet occurs in stanza 8, where he rejects the idea of using the "Spices, Odours, [and] curious Arts" of Egypt "to embalm the Name/ Of such a Worthy" person as Shepard has proven himself to be. If "men speak their hearts," says Oakes, they will conclude that Shepard "merits an Immortal Fame" (210–11). In the second line of Oakes's five-stanza introduction, "To the Reader," Oakes exclaims, "Behold here, what passion can do!" (208). As Oakes certainly is speaking his own heart when he writes this poem, "Elegie" becomes a testimony of that "Immortal Fame"; Oakes's verses themselves, therefore, become a memorial to Shepard. "Elegie" attests that Shepard has, by his good works, "rear'd himself a Monument" (211). In recording Shepard's memory—and recall that memory is a necessary component of the meditative poem—Oakes's poem, merely by its existence, mitigates the Early American fear of pastlessness.

While it is true that Oakes claims to have derived his general form for "Elegie" from David's powerful lament, delivered upon the deaths of Jonathan and Saul (II Sam. 1:19–27), he has not derived these assessments of image making; the operation of the fancy, or imagination; or the essential function served by memory from the "Sovereign, Sacred Poet," "our guide." These elements, which clearly address the self-conscious act of poetic composition (along with, for that matter, the operations of the understanding and the will), rather originate in the praxis of meditation, a classical form. Perhaps Oakes's failure to acknowledge his debt to the *meditatio* indicates how commonplace this method was at the time. A more likely explanation, however, is that here Oakes displays yet another example of the acceptance and denial motif. To call attention to the essentially classical methodology employed in the composition of this poem well might have put off many among his audience, particularly those steeped almost exclusively in the tenets of Adamic discourse. Claiming David as his "guide," however, would have put off no one; in fact, the net effect of claiming that he seeks guidance from David's famous lament in creating his poem is to strike a poignant balance in the tension between the two modes of discourse which govern the form and content of "Elegie." Without the several references to the biblical lament, this poem would lack much of the pastoralism necessary to make it structurally a pastoral elegy. The fine essay, Hahn, "Urian Oakes's *Elegie*," calls attention to the pastoralism implicit within David's lament by observing that "the allusions to David and Jonathan . . . suggest the traditional pastoral lament of the shepherd for his consort" (172).

Taking this "suggestion" one step further, we may say that David's role as singing shepherd contributes to "Elegie" by suffusing it with pastoralism. For example, when Oakes speaks of how "dear Jonathan fell" (208) and in the next stanza follows this allusion with the phrase "Now Shepard's faln" (209), he consciously echoes the arresting line from David's lament, "How are the mighty fallen," repeated three times within the biblical lament. This biblical line probably resounded within the recollections of all among Oakes's audience.[14] Several other references Oakes makes to "Jonathan's Fall" or to how the community's "Pillar's faln" also reverberate as refrains throughout the poem.

While these allusions to David's lament for Jonathan and Saul establish a portion of this poem's content, they do not give it its form. The structure of this poem derives instead from Oakes's clever combination of all parts of the Puritan funeral elegy with salient elements of the classical pastoral elegy. Hahn is studious to point out the presence of the Puritan elegy's exhortation and the last two of the portrait's (or biography's) characteristics—sanctification, as evidenced by the deceased's good works; and glorification, or treatment of the deceased's joyous reception into heavenly reward. Hahn, however, does not mention Oakes's treatment of Shepard's vocation or conversion, the first element of portrait. It would be superfluous to rehearse those elements that Oakes adapts from the Puritan elegy and which are treated by Hahn. Thus the ensuing discussion deals only with that portion of the Puritan elegy which Hahn fails to examine. Hahn carefully enumerates Oakes's use of the classical elements of *paronomasia*, or punning; *anaphora*, or repetition in rapid succession of the initial phrasing of a clause; and *asyndeton*, or omission of conjunctions. Although Hahn takes up two more classical components of pastoral elegy, the procession of mourners and invocation of the Muses, more needs to be said regarding Oakes's superlative incorporation of these elements. In addition to treating vocation, then, the following portion of our investigation examines Oakes's use of the procession of mourners and the invocation of the muses, before launching into consideration of Oakes's ascription of pietas to his subject.

While not particularly obvious, as little appears to be about this excellent poem, Oakes presents acknowledgement of Shepard's conversion or vocation in the concluding couplet of the twenty-seventh stanza: "A double portion of his Fathers spirit/ Did this (his Eldest) Son, through Grace, inherit" (215). Echoing Elisha's request for "a double portion of thy spirit" from Elijah (II Kings 2:9), these lines very cleverly and succinctly declare that Shepard has received his calling both from his spiritual Father through the gift of His Grace and from his biological father through inheritance. All portions of the Puritan funeral elegy—the three components of portrait or biography and the exhortation—hence are evident in "Elegie"; so we see that the Adamic myth contributes a rich portion of this poem's content.

Beyond these biblical contributions, classicism helps to shape this poem. While Hahn comes closer than anyone else to drawing this conclusion, cultural blindness perhaps keeps him from seeing a procession of mourners long before stanzas 40–44. Hahn says, "In this division of the poem, Oakes introduces the formal procession of grievers (stanzas 40–44)" (175). In fact, Oakes "introduces" his grievers in stanza 21: "not a few of different persuasions/ From this great Worthy, do now truly grieve/ I' th' Mourning croud, and joyn their Lamentations" (213). Hahn judiciously observes that "divine poetical inspiration is classical" and that Oakes takes some time to assume the traditional pose of modesty in the beginning of the poem. Yet such acknowledgment does not lead Hahn to explicate the real problem Oakes confronts head on in his "Elegie"—the problem of form. As Oakes's struggle to settle upon a form occupies the poem's first fourteen stanzas (including the five stanzas comprising "To the Reader"), and as the poet's analysis of his own struggle revolves largely about his ostensible rejection of the classical invocation of the Muses, the poet's complex struggle deserves to be understood.

Oakes indicates his problem in the first stanza, where he appears to reject the auspices of the classical Muses; for "here"—that is, in these very lines—the intensity of his passionate grief has "forc'd a verse, without *Apollo*'s leave/ And whether th' Learned Sistters would or no." The concluding couplet of this stanza states the problem: "My Griefs can hardly speak: my sobbing Muse/ In broken terms our sad bereavement rues." Although his grief "can hardly speak," of course it does give utterance, under the aegis of Oakes's "sobbing Muse." While his "Muse" as yet may speak without permission of the gods of the arts, Apollo and the nine Muses, speak it does. The utterance, by Oakes's own testimony, derives from the classical idea of a Muse as the source of poetic inspiration. Note also that Oakes already assumes the office of serving the community, for it is "*our* [my emphasis] sad bereavement" which Oakes will attempt to record. As he will speak for the community of grievers, he must choose a language or a mode of rhetoric with which they will feel comfortable in their grief. That Oakes selects the rhetoric of Adam may seem, by this juncture in our analysis, inevitable.

Given Oakes's considerable reputation as a classical scholar and his recent appointment as president of Harvard College, his "politically correct" selection of the Adamic mode of discourse attests the acumen of an astute politician and diplomat. This pattern, of publicly denying the tenets of the myth of Aeneas so that one may speak instead the language of the people (i.e., the language of Adam), becomes endemic upon the American strand, particularly after the radical shift in discourse; and its most frequent public advocates were and remain politicians. Oakes's "Elegie" dramatizes a remarkably early example of this politically charged strain of the acceptance and denial motif. As we have already seen in the case of Cotton Mather, Oakes's deep-seated classicism prevails, despite his public rejection of that mode. In his public rejection of any artificiality, Oakes goes so far as to impugn even the use of "numbers, measures, feet." To confine "sorrows and complaints" in this way "Is not to let [them] loose, but fetter [them]." In the next stanza, Oakes moves from what he calls "the learned World's" restriction of grief to measured verse and then to a consideration of the poet's role as composer of the community's dirges. His "softer heart" enables him to receive "great impressions," which "He wisely doth perform [as] his mourning part/ In Verse, lest grief should time and measure miss." Indeed, wisdom teaches that the expression of grief well may be addressed most satisfyingly through the healing balm of time, measured in the duration of the poet's lament. In this same measured time—i.e., in Oakes's lament—the pain of grief then should become somewhat diffused. Behind the poem, however, lies the man Oakes, not a theoretical construct of "the Poet"; and this man himself mourns Shepard's loss. Indeed, Oakes's own grief so overwhelms him that he must concede pain "unmeasurable"—that is, pain not measurable as lines of verse.

Then Oakes remonstrates with himself as he recalls the simple, open-faced eloquence of David's lament for Jonathan, his beloved friend, and Saul. If what Oakes says is true—that grief cannot be measured out in verse—then how is it that the plaintive passion of David's unadorned lines still speaks so clearly and movingly to us today? The verse lament must have its place and must represent a legitimate expression of his own and his community's grief. Oakes makes it plain, however, that, on the surface at least, he will brook no "trifling Poets Use"; indeed, "Th' Imperious Law of Custome we deride" (208). In adopting the first person plural inclusive pronoun "we," Oakes signals again his public function.

What is the origin of the "Imperious Law of Custome"? Let us, the readers of the present, invest the effort required to unravel the meaning of this curious phrase. In the next line, Oakes states unabashedly, "We have Diviner Warrant to produce,/ The Soveraign, Sacred Poet is our guide" (209). Note that Oakes repeats the inclusive plural pronoun twice, in the nominative "we" and in the possessive "our." In the phrase "Diviner Warrant" at least two positions may be retrieved. First, use of the comparative "Diviner" certainly claims for Judaeo-Christianity a religious superiority over classical paganism. Second, Oakes's classicism demands that he acknowledge that divine poetic inspiration resides within the office of the Muses, whose dispensation is only less divine than that of covenanted Christianity.

From this apparent rejection of the inspirational role of the Muses, Oakes proceeds, in the first nine stanzas of the "Elegie" proper, to explicate again his rejection of the entire classical mode, especially the role played by the Muses. Like Cotton Mather, the man protests too much!

> Oh! that I were a Poet now in grain!
> How would I invocate the Muses all
> To design their presence, lend their flowing Vein,
> And help to grace dear *Shepard*'s Funeral!

So begins the "Elegie" proper. Oakes's first line is of particular interest, as it reiterates the modesty expressed in the first line of "To the Reader": "Reader I am no Poet." In addition, his phrase "in grain" is, within the context of the classical pastoral elegy, somewhat arresting. As already observed, in conjuring up David's example, Oakes strengthens this poem's otherwise weak pastoralism. On its surface, of course, the phrase denotes pure, simple, genuine, and thorough. With David's role as shepherd singer to his flocks setting the tone, however, the phrase "in grain" perhaps connotes Ceres's corn, suggesting a Roman setting. As well, *grain* as a verb can mean to paint in imitation of fine woods (reproducing their grains with painting techniques) or marbles.

The first line of the couplet which concludes this stanza is: "How would I paint our griefs." The meaning of the verb *grain*, along with Oakes's penchant for punning (I would say serious, not frivolous, punning), invites us to see Oakes's desire to be a poet, pure and simple, in classical terms and not so precisely in terms of an exclusively biblical David. For if Oakes were a Poet in the classical sense, he would call up all nine of the "Learned Sistters," not his "sobbing Muse" alone. Such an "Imperious Law of Custome" would empower Oakes to appreciate properly this most significant loss of Thomas Shepard. Indeed, as the elegist remarks in the next stanza, "Here is a subject for the loftiest Verse/ That ever waited on the bravest Hearse." Especially given Milton's example in *Lycidas*, this "loftiest Verse" to which Oakes refers must be that of the pastoral elegy. Clearly, then, Oakes knows that casting his grief in the concrete form of the pastoral elegy, derived from the classical tradition or the "Imperious Law of custome," will lend his memorialization dignity and "grace."

Despite Oakes's acknowledgment of the value and appropriateness of the classical mode, he again superficially seems to discard "The celebrated Sisters," declaring that "*We* [emphasis mine] need no *Mourning Womens* Elegy/ No forc'd, affected, artificial Tone" (210). Oakes is a classical scholar speaking to a public sector that neither requires nor wishes any instruction in the classical mode. In returning to denial here, the poet implies that, in his difficult task of limning out this statement of grief, he does require the empowerment which the classical mode can impart (and indeed already has imparted). Continuing to deny the allegedly "affected, artificial Tone" of the pastoral elegy, Oakes disavows "Poetick Raptures," "Daring *Hyperboles*," and "Exube'rant Fancies" of "feign'd Elogies" fashioned after the "forc'd," insincere classical mode. That mode he already has identified, however, as pure and simple, genuine and thorough, surely sufficient to any poet's quill. The problem here becomes how to construct "A Monument" to one of the "Immensest Treasures" ever known, by using the classical mode while seeming not to do so.

The truth is that Oakes's poem already has become cloyed with elaborate "Poetick Raptures," "Daring *Hyperboles*," and "Exube'rant Fancies." Oakes's dilemma is one that already is becoming a typically American problem—how to absorb instruction from the great classical past while appearing not to have done so. Fascinatingly, it has taken him no less than fourteen stanzas (in a poem of fifty-seven) to establish his acceptance and denial. Within these fourteen stanzas, he has praised the classical mode, and more specifically the pastoral elegy; invoked the Muses (how could any idea so repeatedly examined fail to linger a bit?); invested his elegy with pastoralism; subordinated the process of the *meditatio* to his main enterprise; and elaborately expressed his grief at Shepard's loss. All these accomplishments, except for the meditative process, enumerate components of the pastoral elegy. Whether his contemporary audience permits it or not, Oakes has cast his expression of grief in the mode of the classical pastoral elegy.

As undeniable signal of his adopted mode, he repeats the name Shepard twenty times throughout the poem's fifty-seven stanzas, in such phrases as "our Shepard," "dear Shepard," and "good Shepard." While it is of course customary for an elegist to name her or his subject a time or two, often (as in Godfrey's elegy on Wolfe) giving the subject a pseudonym from classical pastoral, here these repeated namings, in combination with identifying adjectives, resound with the force of both epithet and refrain, the first owing something to classical epic and the second to yet another characteristic of pastoral elegy. Obviously, in "Elegie," the repeated sounding of "Shepard" evokes David as shepherd singer, as well as Shepard's own function as pastor to his flock of parishioners. Simply put, repetition of Shepard's name itself connotes the essence of pastoralism, requiring little to no embellishment on this score.

Having established that the form of "Elegie" is that of the pastoral elegy, we now are in a position to consider Oakes's ascription of pietas to his subject. Hahn dissects Oakes's catalogue of Shepard's virtues, depicting, says Hahn, "the paragon of Puritan virtue" (174). Curiously, Hahn does not mention Oakes's extensive discussion of Shepard's devotion to duty, or pietas. Perhaps, if one reads "Elegie" from the perspective of the Adamic myth, Oakes's discussion of pietas as duty may appear mundane, unremarkable, or even commonplace. However, given Oakes's careful delineation of this virtue, which takes up the better part of nearly five stanzas, it must have been important to him. As early as the thirteenth stanza, Oakes calls the living Shepard "a Loan/ Of Heaven," implying Shepard's close connection with the deity, beyond that of an ordinary minister of the gospel. We are hardly surprised, then, when the poet declares that Shepard "was Heav'ens Favourite,/ On whom the God of all Grace did command,/ And show'r down Blessings with a lib'eral hand" (215). In stanza 27, Oakes describes the closeness between Shepard's father and the deceased, a son whose life appeared devoted "to do him [the father] right" (215).

Although these spiritual descriptions are strongly redolent of Christianity, they also bespeak classical pietas. Thus we see how easily both modes of discourse unobtrusively can be superimposed one upon the other. Shepard's elegist even goes so far as to state his subject's attitude toward politics: "Thoughtful and Active for the common good:/ And yet his own place wisely understood." Oakes then articulates the three parts of pietas: the devotion of a son to his father (echoing Aeneas's unfailing dutifulness to his father Anchises); of a "Pious," blessed minister to his God (Aeneas also was the favored of heaven); and of a participant in the democratic political process. Next Oakes observes, "Nothing could make him stray from Duty." So impressed is Shepard's elegist by his devotion to duty (Oakes even repeats this noun twice more) that he is moved to remark: "'twas God that took him thus,/ To give him great Reward, and punish us" (216).

This occasion is not the first on which Oakes rebukes those whom Shepard has left behind; as early as stanza 14, the poet intimates that Shepard's passing presages ill tidings: "So are we all amazed at this blow [Shepard's death],/ Sadly portending some approaching woe" (212). Both these warnings direct the listeners' attention toward the poem's conclusion; the first four of the poem's last six stanzas comprise an exhortatory jeremiad. It is Shepard's devotion to duty that provokes Oakes's unabashed declaration that some dire punishment now awaits his loss. Consequently, the myths of Adam and Aeneas interplay here in a most productive way. The community has suffered the loss of Oakes's pietas, modified from its classical source only by the Christianization of devotion to the gods, now to God. This loss most audibly signals the onslaught of punishment for the community's "Cursed sins!" (219).

In Urian Oakes's "Elegie Upon . . . Thomas Shepard," classicism and Adam work hand in glove to enable Oakes to shape his essentially classical lament. David and Vergil, pietas and jeremiad, blend to create an almost seamless, American structure.

At 342 lines, Oakes's "Elegie" is only the second longest of the seventeen pastoral elegies comprising this American genre. Joseph Green's "An Eclogue Sacred to the Memory of . . . Jonathan Mayhew" (1766), running to 376 lines, surely is the longest. Composed nearly one hundred years after Oakes's "Elegie," Green's contribution to this genre exhibits none of the self-conscious denial that troubles Oakes. Indeed, unabashedly present in Green's title is the identifying "Eclogue," certainly a reference to Vergil's ten *Eclogues*.

Two other Boston authors employ this identifier in their titles. Joseph Seccombe, author of what well may be the first formal American defense of pursuing the pleasures of the sporting life, *Business and Diversion . . . in the Fishing Season* (1743), is also the author of a pastoral elegy which he titles "On the Death of the Reverend Benjamin Colman, D.D. An Eclogue" (1747).

Jeremy Belknap, renowned for his classicism and one of the founders of the Massachusetts Historical Society, published a pastoral elegy sixteen years later, entitled more directly, "An Eclogue Occasioned by the Death of the Reverend Alexander Cumming." Belknap candidly concludes his "Argument," which immediately precedes the poem, by declaring, "The eclogue is formed partly on the Plan of Virgil's Daphnis." Belknap's manner of expression here suggests that he fully expects his audience to know that Vergil's fifth eclogue, which establishes the paradigm for the genre of pastoral elegy, is his "Daphnis."

By the time Joseph Green writes his "Eclogue Sacred to the Memory of the Rev. Dr. Jonathan Mayhew," then, he is writing within a tradition of Boston pastoral elegies. As our discussion of Green's contribution to the genre unfolds, we shall discover other points of contiguity among these three poems. Green, however, refers particularly to Belknap's "Eclogue" on Cumming.

All three Boston pastoral elegies open with a thorough prose "Argument" or summary of the poem's action, a practice unique among these seventeen American pastoral elegies.[15] In addition, all three employ the device of a natural disaster to prompt recognition of each of the three deaths. Seccombe brings his two shepherds together at the cottage of an old shepherdess, Pastorella, where they all have assembled to escape a storm and where Pastorella tells of Colman's passing. In Belknap's opus, when a tree is shattered by lightning, Florio is provoked to tell Albinus of Cumming's death. Green's Dulcius reveals Mayhew's loss to Fidelio after coming across a withered vine blackened by lightning.

Seccombe employs heroic couplets, but Belknap and Green choose blank verse. Seccombe quotes no famous authors (though his Pastorella evokes Spenser's *Faerie Queene* VI, ix, 4–12), but both Green and Belknap do. Thus the two later authors appear to owe less and less to Seccombe's example. Unquestionably, however, Green's debt to Belknap is sizable. Belknap opens his "Eclogue" with a quotation from Milton's *Paradise Lost:* "Sweet is the Breath of Morn" (in the first line of Belknap's poem, taken from *Paradise Lost,* IV, 641). Like Milton, both Green and Belknap allude to the singing of birds as they celebrate the rising of the new day, a typical pastoral motif, but note that Belknap does not quote *Lycidas*. Perhaps taking from Belknap the idea of citing readily recognizable literary works, Green quotes twice from Alexander Pope's *Essay on Man*. Wishing to expand upon his depiction of a delectable "landskip" (landscape), Green quotes Pope's "To look thro' nature up to nature's God" (l. 52 in Green; *Essay on Man* epistle 4, l. 332, where the line reads "But looks thro' Nature, up to Nature's God"). Green quotes again from the *Essay* when he underscores his argument that God may be perceived in nature: "The state of Nature, is the reign of God" (l. 69 in Green; *Essay on Man* epistle 3, l. 148).

A last and more substantial structural parallel between Green and Belknap is that both make use of a closing prayer. For the prayer, Belknap shifts from blank verse to five stanzas of six lines each. In each stanza, the first two and the fourth and fifth lines are in iambic tetrameter and the third and fourth are in iambic trimeter, with a rhyme scheme of aabccb. Green opts for a simpler scheme of twelve stanzas of fairly regular iambic tetrameter lines, rhyming ab ab. Both authors appear to be attempting to echo the hymn stanza.

In addition to these structural parallels in the pastoral elegies of Belknap and Green, there are still weightier similarities of phrasing. At the beginning of Belknap's "Eclogue," for example, the shepherd Albinus remarks that the newly rising sun "Invites me, from my downy Couch to rise" (l. 4). Early in Green's poem, his swain Dulcius asserts that Aurora "Invites me now to leave my down of ease" (l. 13). While Belknap speaks of an angel's "Emanatione of . . . Heav'nly Light," Green describes the "emanation" of a joyful heart. Moreover, Green almost certainly has paraphrased "thrills my deep sunk heart" (l. 152) from Belknap's "thrills my inmost Soul!" (l. 66).

What these numerous parallels demonstrate loudly and clearly is that these three Boston composers of pastoral elegies were concerned to discover to themselves their own voice, distinctive and original. To be sure these poets draw more parallels of structure (all three) and phrasing (Belknap and Green) from each other than from any other source with the possible exception of Vergil. And interestingly enough, one final parallel shared by all, Seccombe, Belknap, and Green, is that each displays a happy blend of the myths of Adam and Aeneas.

As space does not permit demonstration of the manner by which all three combine the myths of Adam and Aeneas, examination of the most sophisticated of these, the pastoral elegy by Green, should serve our purpose. The two modes of discourse, the Adamic and the classical, are already evident in Green's title, "An Eclogue Sacred to the Memory of the Rev. Dr. Jonathan Mayhew." Indeed, the word "Eclogue" announces the poem's form as Vergilian, while "Sacred" and "Rev." bespeak Mayhew's office as Christian shepherd to his flock. "Memory," of course, attests the overall motive for constructing this poem—to preserve that piece of the community which was Mayhew.

The author of this poem, Joseph Green, was a wealthy Boston merchant and former distiller, this last vocation having earned him the inelegant nickname, "Stiller Josey." Among such contemporaries as Mather Byles, Thomas Hutchinson, James Bowdoin Jr., and John Adams (the future United States president), Green perhaps was best known among the literati for his humorous, often satirical verse. Thus the serious turn of mind which characterizes his "Eclogue" on Mayhew perhaps came as a surprise to the Boston public.

The austerity of his subject, Jonathan Mayhew, may explain Green's change of pace. John Adams later would list Mayhew, along with James Otis, Oxenbridge Thacher, Samuel Adams, and John Hancock, as one of the most influential voices leading others toward the American Revolution. Alan Heimert has called Mayhew "the first American to challenge articulately . . . 'the tyranny of the majority'" (Heimert 575). Indeed, as early as 1748, Mayhew declared publicly, "Were number the mark of truth and right, religion itself would be a perfect *Proteus*, sometimes one thing, and sometimes another, according to the opinion that happens to prevail in the world" (Heimert 576). In his *Discourse Concerning Unlimited Submission*, delivered as a sermon and published in 1750, some ten years before the admonitory "Dedication" to *Pietas et Gratulatio*, Mayhew suggests that monarchs can sometimes prove to be unreliable Protean figures as he boldly urges that "if our King . . . turns tyrant, and makes his subjects his prey to devour and to destroy, instead of his charge to defend and cherish, we are bound to throw off our allegiance to him, and to resist" (29–30).

If Mayhew had lived, surely later he would have proven himself a voice to rival that of Tom Paine in provoking American patriotism against British oppression. It is one of the cruel ironies of history, which perhaps only a revolution can conjure, that the man who penned such a heartfelt memorial to Mayhew later should become a Loyalist.

In his "Eclogue" on Mayhew, Joseph Green nevertheless displays an unmistakable sincerity in the feelings he expresses toward his subject, although he manages virtually to ignore Mayhew's enormous influence upon the politics of the day. Concentrating rather upon Mayhew's extensive reputation for advancing "The light of reason and the depth of thought," about his subject's political activity Green remarks only that Mayhew used "Those gifts of heaven, which he for public good/ Employ'd" (ll. 211–13). The absence of a more substantial assessment of Mayhew's many contributions to the political arena may predict Green's later Loyalism.

Green's happy blend of the myths of Adam and Aeneas, however, indicates that, in 1766, this pastoral elegist was participating fully in the process of American *translatio cultus*. Into the mouths of what are unmistakably classical shepherds, Green places such turns of phrase as "Christian fortitude" (l. 183), "Stamp'd with the seal of Christian charity" (l. 249) and "praises of angelic choirs" (l. 256).

Green's shepherd Dulcius, whose name derives from the Latin for *sweet*, opens this poem with a paean to the arrival of morning, which inspires him to seek his bower of contemplation. Here, "wrapt in thought," as Wheatley would later phrase it, "Amidst this pleasing scene" of "blooming nature's face," Dulcius discovers that "time most friendly to the learned nine." Thus he unobtrusively invokes the Muses. His time spent alone, "in search for things which raise the noble soul," soon is interrupted by his close friend and fellow swain, Fidelio (faithful one, recalling Aeneas's "fidus Achates," or faithful friend Achates). This interruption is a most pleasant one, for Fidelio joins Dulcius to share "the fruitful gains/ Of learning's treasures." These are afforded by Dulcius's contemplative bower, "sequestered from the cares of life!" or more simply phrased by Wheatley, Dulcius and Fidelio have retreated to "friendly bow'rs" to discover "sequester'd seat[s]" far from "crowds and noise" (Green ll. 21, 22, 16, 19, 30–31, and 29; Wheatley ll. 12 and 8).

In this richly pastoral ambiance, Dulcius and Fidelio enter into an intellectual discussion of how remarkably the works of nature bespeak a divine creator. Then they consider God's "grand creation of the human race," whose members He has endowed with "an immortal soul . . . With light of reason, and the power of sense" (ll. 72, 73–74). The mood darkens, however, as this celebration of God's creation of man and nature gives way to a digression on the transitoriness of "sublunary things" (l. 126). Fidelio incisively observes:

> Just so is man! Whole seeds of life are sown
> In nature's secret womb, from whence he springs
> A worm of crumbling dust, and breathes a while
> Within this mortal air. (ll. 98–101)

The metaphor wherein is depicted human lives as first "sown/ In nature's secret womb" endows Green's poem with a memorable image of the feminine principle as a universal archetype of all human creation.

As this sort of intellectual interplay is uncharacteristic of the pastoral, its function here may be to serve as a tribute to Mayhew, who had a reputation for holding in contempt any argument not grounded in sound, analytical logic. This digression concerning the uncertainties of this life on earth soon gives way to the revelation of "A late most sad afflicting breach of heaven" (l. 130), the death of Mayhew. The several transitions here—from a celebration of nature to disputation concerning divine creativity, to God's creation of man, to life's uncertainty, and finally to acknowledgment of Mayhew's death—move with unbroken ease. This performance depends upon Green's individual artistry, not any precedent American or classical.

Dulcius's reaction to Fidelio's declaration of Mayhew's passing, however, does indicate a knowledge of classical tradition. Vergil's Menalcas expresses intense desire to share Mopsus's grief that Daphnis has been "Exstinctum . . . crudeli funere" (extinguished by a cruel death; *Eclogues* V, 20). Similarly, Green's Dulcius urges Fidelio to accept him "as partner in your grief" (l. 137). This gesture of Dulcius toward Fidelio also recalls Thomas Godfrey's Lysidas and Damaetas, who decide to mourn the loss of Amintor (General Wolfe) in concert. For a brief time, Dulcius appears to be inconsolable concerning Mayhew's loss, expressing the typical Renaissance display of grief. Fidelio attempts to mitigate his sorrow by reminding Dulcius that "'tis God who doth what seemth best" (l. 155).

Fidelio's lapse here into the style of the King James Bible signals a shift away from classical discourse toward that of Adam. Fidelio soon commences a lengthy (fifty-two line) portrait of the deceased. He observes that Mayhew "did form his youthful mind/ Upon religion's plan to serve his God" (ll. 190–91). Then Fidelio enlarges upon Mayhew's vocation, or calling to the faith, noting how "with care/ Religion's early plant he wise manur'd" (ll. 196–97). Fidelio next delineates Mayhew's sanctification, as evidenced by the deceased's good works. The swain describes how, after having become "Pleas'd with his tenets," the West Church congregation "did him invite/ To be their guide and pastor during life" (ll. 206–7). While shepherd to the West Church flock, Mayhew "shone/ Distinguish'd in the noble powers of sense,/ The light of reason and the depth of thought" (ll. 209–11). So well respected did the young minister become, not merely in New England but also in Britain, that "the learn'd tribe . . . conferr'd/ Their public honour" upon him. This almost certainly is a reference to Mayhew's receipt of an honorary doctorate from the University of Aberdeen in 1750, in recognition of publication of his *Seven Sermons upon the Following Subjects* (1749).

Dulcius continues to narrate Mayhew's good works, declaring, "No more, the hopeless orphan can receive/ The generous bounties of his liberal heart,/ Stamp'd with the seal of Christian charity" (ll. 247–49). Significantly, Fidelio traces a distinctly Christian version of the operation of Death, as he is supposed to have visited the now "sainted" Mayhew: "Proud to obey th' Almighty's grand behests,/ Death came and entered into Mayhew's walls,/ There, he of late his embassy discharg'd" (ll. 274–76). Three times Fidelio and Dulcius depict the deceased as having been received into heavenly reward, demonstrating Mayhew's end in glorification. Thus, the late West Church minister has gained "the happy shore" (l. 242), has "wafted joyous to the realms of peace" (l. 287), and has attained "that state of Paradise,/ Which blooms forever in eternal joys" (ll. 302–3).

Right in the middle of these demonstrations of Mayhew's "certain" ascent into a Christian heaven, however, Fidelio inserts a classical element, the procession of mourners: "Mourn, O bereaved flock! Yet grateful own/ Your due submission to the powers of Heaven" (ll. 290–91). Then Dulcius recites the long concluding prayer encouraging the living to emulate Mayhew's example. This prayer completes the final stage of the Puritan funeral elegy, the exhortation. The closing prayer maintains that the success of Mayhew's example assures the living that a life lived after the manner of the deceased will bring them, too, to heavenly paradise. Such assurance prompts them to join with the heavenly hosts in celebrating the Deity:

> With angels, seraphs, saints above,
> May we thy glorious praise display;
> And sing of the redeeming love,
> Through the revolves of endless day. (ll. 373–76)

Without blinking an eye, Joseph Green, in "An Eclogue Sacred to the Memory of . . . Jonathan Mayhew," has achieved a harmonious combination of the myths of Adam and Aeneas. Here we have no diatribe against the Muses, as in Oakes. Instead, Green's pastoral elegy is cast self-consciously in the mold of the classical eclogue (on Daphnis), and the poem's transformation into a full expression of the Puritan funeral elegy is accomplished with no break in the form. Fidelio and Dulcius, two urbane shepherds, simply narrate the elements of portrait, including its three subdivisions of vocation (calling to the faith), sanctification (evidence of good works), and glorification (receipt into heavenly reward). Then they deliver an exhortation to the living to put off mourning and concentrate on earning for themselves a reward comparable to that of the deceased. In his pastoral elegy, Green appears to be totally unaware of even the possibility of an incompatibility between his essentially classical form and his largely Adamic content.

This comfortable combination of these two modes of discourse suggests, erroneously of course, that in 1766 no tension at all existed between the myths of Adam and Aeneas. In Green's text, one mode seems to harbor no suspicion of the other; Adam and Aeneas appear happily balanced. In an age when Adam has become Aeneas, such a valorization is to be expected. This universal compatibility was illusory, however.

In 1737, an elegy appeared which is remarkable for little other than its forthright condemnation of the pastoral elegy. "An Elegy on the Much Lamented Death of Sarah Wanton" was published as a broadside, probably for wide distribution, in Newport, Rhode Island. Rather than invoking the classical Muses, this (unknown) author calls upon "Ye Powers divine!" asking them to "assist my flowing Quill,/ And in the same, pure hallow'd lays instill." Lest someone fail to grasp what caused this poet's "Grief [to] excite," he soon clarifies the matter beyond any doubt. In this undertaking, he says,

> Let no poetic Heathenish Jargon stile;
> In artful strains, the Author's mind begile.
> But touch'd with Truth's pure essence, form'd by Jove,
> (The boundless Ocean, of seraphick Love.)
> He may with ease, perform a Task so great.

The obvious acceptance and denial manifested in the allusion to God as Jove notwithstanding, this poet pointedly intends not to cast his memorial in the classical mode.

Another poet penned another elegy on Jonathan Mayhew, using this as an occasion to object to the form of the pastoral elegy. Benjamin Church, a prolific and well known poet, political activist, and sometime Loyalist (eventually he was convicted of treason for selling information to the British), earlier had contributed a pastoral elegy on the death of George II to the famous *Pietas et Gratulatio* (1761). By the time of Mayhew's death, however, Church appears to have been loathe to use the classical form to memorialize the minister of West Church. In the fifth stanza of his "Elegy on the Death of the Reverend Jonathan Mayhew," he states:

> Great is the Task, and glorious is the End,
> When the chaste Muse in Virtue's Cause engage;
> Tis her's [*sic*] to patronize, protect, defend,
> And hold th' *Exemplars* to a distant Age. (Church ll. 17–20)

While Church could have been rejecting his earlier tribute to the British monarch in order to embrace the more recent antimonarchical attitude of patriot Boston, he perhaps wished to distance himself from Joseph Green's pastoral elegy and thereby speak to a wider, Adamic audience. Whatever his reasons, this political gadfly and currier of popular favor undoubtedly had in mind feathering his own nest. Still, note how articulate he is in describing the elegist as one who must "hold th' *Exemplars* to a distant Age." In this sense, Church shares his objective with all other Early American authors of elegies and pastoral elegies; all hope to assuage a fear of pastlessness through their individual "monuments."

Those poets writing in the classical tradition, however, appear to be particularly motivated to encode their memorials in the most permanent form available. For example, John Norton II, who introduced the classical lament into Early American poetry with his "A Funeral Elogy Upon . . . Anne Bradstreet" (1672), appeals to that culture, which in his time was perceived as changeless and eternal, thereby asserting that his subject is changeless and eternal:

> Let not her happy memory e're lack
> Its worth in Fames eternal Almanack,
> Which more shall read, but straight their loss deplore,
> And blame their Fates they were not born before. (Meserole 462)

The fact that this fine elegy contains not a wit of Christianity and does not even present a consolation (a common, expected practice in the classical elegy and one particularly compatible with Christianity) must have struck Norton's contemporaries as somewhat shocking. Nevertheless, "Elogy," with its invocation to the Muses, frequent classical allusions (but no biblical ones), mentioning of "every Laurel, every Myrtel" (462), and pathetic fallacies (all the "heavens seem to express/ The worlds great lose [*sic*]" (461), is thoroughly classical in form and content. The urge is strong, therefore, to label this poem a pastoral elegy. Such a label finally is untenable, however, for this poem contains not a single pastoral reference to sequestered bowers, gay meads, singing shepherds, or other such pastoral codes.

Urian Oakes obviously agrees with Norton that his subject deserves to be remembered within the form of classicism's perceived eternality, for he records in his "Elegie" that Thomas Shepard "merits an Immortal Fame" (Meserole 211). Oakes then proceeds to weave that "Fame" into a tapestry whose threads are both Adamic and classical. With just these two examples, only one of which is arguably a pastoral elegy, and even though Oakes's poem prefigures Cotton Mather's mixture of the myths of Adam and Aeneas in his *Magnalia Christi Americana*, it is clear that the pastoral elegy has not yet been shaped into an American genre. For that, we must await the exuberance of American independence-thinking in the eighteenth century and that century's relaxation of Puritan hostility toward classical paganism. Precisely at the moment that the genre of the literary independence poem is becoming established, and during the period when the Early American naïve and subversive pastoral begins to take shape, the American pastoral elegy starts to come into its own.

With its publication in 1723, Aquila Rose's *Poems on Several Occasions*, which includes several poems not by Rose but about him, became arguably the first anthology of American poetry. This volume contains three pastoral elegies, one that blends the myths of Adam and Aeneas and two more that remain strictly classical. The first, entitled "On the Death of his Friend's much-lov'd Child," is by Rose himself. While it is overwhelmingly classical in form, it does contain a few unmistakable Christian allusions. The second, by Elias Bockett, "To the Memory of Aquila Rose," is strictly classical.

A third poem, also strictly classical, is remarkable in that it was composed by a woman. This excellent poem's title is simply "On the Death of Aquila Rose, by a Young Woman." The poem is arranged into five four-line stanzas of iambic pentameter rhyming ab ab; each stanza is trailed by an iambic pentameter couplet whose second line serves as a refrain for the first four quatrains. The second line of the final stanza's couplet exchanges the distinctly American, descriptive "While faded Laurel Schuylkil Rocks adorn" for the (last) line's resolve to meet other mourners "around Aquila's Urn," where all may "the dear Bard in brightest Numbers mourn" (Rose 55–56).

The poem opens with a highly personalized attack on Fame, whose "rude, uncertain Sound" now can "no more give a vocal wound/ As this sad Truth, Aquila Rose is dead" (55). Every paragon of ability and parts has his or her enemies, but Rose, it is pleasant to see, also had a defender. This woman defender knew well the elements of the pastoral elegy. After her necessary expression of grief, she declares, "Now, no, no more, ye shady Hills and bow'rs,/ Shall your droop'd Heads rejoice to hear those Lays/ That flow'd so sweetly from those lofty Pow'rs/ So near aliy'd [*sic*] to the Orphean Bays" (55). This quatrain is not as simple as it may at first appear, for, in the first two lines, the poet accomplishes a rendering of pastoral pathetic fallacy. The very "shady Hills and bow'rs" of typical pastoral fully participate in mourning Rose's loss. Moreover, the close comparison of Rose as poet-shepherd to "those lofty Pow'rs" allied so intimately with the musical force of an Orpheus obviates the necessary invocation of the Muse. The very subject in this quatrain, in fact, is Rose's poetic capacity for responding to the inspiration of creativity. (Wheatley's later pastoral elegy also avoids a formal invocation.) In a succeeding quatrain, this persona even goes so far as to claim that Rose has composed the music formerly played by "Ye Shepherds," whose pipes now are "mute" (56).

At thirty lines, this poem is comparable in length to Phillis Wheatley's "An Elegy on Leaving," which has twenty-eight lines. Still another link between the two poems is that these pastoral elegies appear at the beginning of America's adventure in classicism and near its conclusion. Hence the entire period of the flourishing of American classicism is embraced by the sophisticated literary productions of two women! Indeed, the woman author plays a significant role during this period, as we are beginning to understand.

That such men and women as Thomas Godfrey, Joseph Green, the anonymous author of "On the Death of Aquila Rose, by a Young Woman," and Phillis Wheatley should select the genre of the pastoral elegy to express their grief is truly surprising, particularly if one holds that, culturally, Early America was merely a satellite of the allegedly superior London. In the "Preface" to his *The Pastoral Elegy: An Anthology*, Thomas Perrin Harrison states flatly, "Pastoral elegy as a literary type free of satiric or romantic bias ends with Milton's *Lycidas*" (v). Harrison's pronouncement perhaps should be revised, first, to include Pope's "Winter, the Fourth Pastoral or Daphne" (1709); and, second, to emend the negative imputation conveyed by the phrase "romantic bias." On the whole, though, we must concede the overall wisdom of Harrison's statement. Certainly by the 1720s in England, the pastoral elegy was an essentially dead genre, not to be revived until Shelley's *Adonais* (1821).

In the American colonies, however, poets between 1720 and 1790 seized upon the composition of pastoral elegies with enthusiasm, producing at least seventeen examples.[16] To claim that the genre was popular during this period in America is no exaggeration. As we have seen, the authors of these poems do not seek out British examples for instruction to give shape to their individual productions. Rather, they draw on their own grammar school training or private tutoring to recall the examples of Vergil and perhaps even Theocritus. This journey back to classical precedent, however, does not lead them to produce vapid imitations of the ancients. Remarkably and unexpectedly, these poets freely adapt their pastoral elegies to their own literary ambiance, often gesturing toward other American examples of the genre, referring to their own local geography or specific social or cultural events, and displaying a definite energy in experimentation. Just as none of these pastoral elegists slavishly imitates models from the British or the ancients, none slavishly imitates another American poet. In addition, all these poets exhibit a concern to capture an American past for Americans. These practices confirm that these creators of American pastoral elegies assuredly are American writers.

An American Classicism

Heretofore, the universal approach among students of American culture has been to treat that culture which existed in America before July 4, 1776, that allegedly miraculous moment of transubstantiation, as derivative of Europe and especially of Britain. This investigation, however, has examined example after example demonstrating that Early Americans were committed to cultural independence long before 1776. It has become necessary to assert that a distinctly American classicism dominated Early American thought and action during the period 1720–90.

This American classicism perhaps may best be delineated according to eight basic criteria, the first seven immediately evident and the last requiring more "teasing out." From the examination of American classicism to this point, enough evidence has been adduced to conclude that Early Americans closely consulted classical sources in order to construct their own versions of pastoral or pastoral elegy.[17] American authors did not go to British sources, at least not to solve their problems of form. We have discovered, contrary to expectation, that American writers borrowed more from other Americans than from the British. Such a decisive determination to be reliant upon American resources logically led to a healthy, energetic experimentation; not only were American writers unafraid to depart from classical paradigms, but they eagerly displayed such departures, giving their productions the stamp of individuality and originality.

Certainly one concrete way to achieve this individuality, one way for American authors particularly to distinguish themselves from British or European authors, is to incorporate into their works elements of local or regional geography and society. These five measures begin to distinguish American classicism: a reliance upon classical sources; a determination *not* to seek out British (or European) sources in matters of form (which is not at all to suggest that these authors do not *know* British and Continental literary works); a definite tendency toward self-referentiality; a hearty, energetic commitment to experimentation; and a conscious attempt to invest their work with an American ambiance.

Taken together, these five characteristics point directly toward a sixth characteristic: a candid resolve to discover to themselves and to their culture an identity. This identity at first may be simply *not to be British*, but Pennsylvanian, New Englander, New Yorker, or Virginian, though this identity moves steadily toward becoming American.

In the struggle toward achieving that American identity, American authors promote six principal genres. The first three (in addition to the largely Adamic elegy) are the literary independence poem, the naïve and subversive pastoral, and the pastoral elegy; all three have received treatment in this book. I have argued that, in Early American hands, these genres have been transformed into Early American genres. The other three genres—the epic to be taken up in chapter 7, the satire, and the ubiquitous American pamphlet—also demonstrate, in American hands, a plasticity of form which constitutes the seventh characteristic of American classicism: the conscious construction and appropriation of literary forms for American cultural imperatives.

From Ebenezer Cook's *Sotweed Factor* to Timothy Dwight's *Triumph of Infidelity*, eighteenth-century American writers expressed themselves often, freely, and eagerly in the genre of satire; this genre has received extensive treatment in other places—for example, in Granger, *Political Satire*. The situation of the American pamphlet is similar. In two magisterial works, *Ideological Origins of the American Revolution* and *Pamphlets of the American Revolution*, Bailyn gives what has seemed an all but definitive analysis of this genre. In light of our present recovery of American classicism, however, both genres—satire and the pamphlet—should be reexamined. To do so here would burden this recuperation of the American self's classical half unnecessarily. The following brief observations are offered to encourage extensive treatment of satire and the pamphlet in other places.

The fact that John Trumbull makes numerous references to Vergil's *Aeneid* in his mock-heroic *M'Fingal*, for example, may be more than incidental. *M'Fingal* was the most popular poem of the American Revolutionary era (a time when poetry itself was popular), enjoying numerous printings. About the obvious classicism in this poem, Richard M. Gummere remarks, "The frequent Greek and Latin allusions become purely exhibitional" (149).

Such failure to take seriously American writers' use of classicism is all too common, as we have seen. Take, for example, the case of Cotton Mather's *Magnalia Christi Americana*. It has been demonstrated that this author's application of classicism was absolutely crucial to the shape of his text and to the construction of the American self. At one point in the third canto of *M'Fingal*, for example, the disparaged Scottish-American Tory M'Fingal is challenged to single combat, much after the manner of several heroes of classical epic. Lest Trumbull's audience should miss the source of his burlesque, the poet adds a footnote: "The learned reader will readily observe the allusions in this scene to the single combats of Paris and Menelaus in Homer, Aeneas and Turnus in Virgil, and Michael and Satan in Milton" (note to l. 362). When this note (not to mention the scene) is read within the context of the tension between the myths of Adam and Aeneas, the interplay of Milton's *Paradise Lost*, the *Iliad*, the *Aeneid*, and *M'Fingal* provides a rich illustration of this period's valorization of the myth of Aeneas.

With regard to the omnipresent American pamphlet of this period (1720–90), Bailyn, without demonstration, asserts that the pamphleteers' admittedly "elaborate display of classical authors" may "have been dragged in as 'window dressing with which to ornament a page or a speech and to increase the weight of an argument,' for classical quotation, as Dr. Johnson said, was 'the *parole* of literary men all over the world'" (*Ideological Origins* 24). Such a broad generalization now requires proof.

Bailyn's quotation from Johnson, while erudite, signals the problem. As classicism in general was on the wane in Britain (the great Doctor despised the artificiality of the pastoral mode, an attitude that led him to find fault with, for example, Milton's *Lycidas*) but on the rise in America, this immortal British literary dictator cannot speak for Americans. Surely this chapter demonstrates that many (but not all) American writers of this period in fact had their own voice and that that voice should be heard. Perhaps American satirists and pamphleteers have woven classicism into the texture of their productions with far greater consequence than that of mere "window dressing."

During the eighteenth century, while British classicism, sometimes called neoclassicism, was lapsing steadily into a state of decline, to yield eventually to Romanticism, American classicism, surprisingly, was flourishing. One of the clearest indications of this flourishing constitutes our eighth and final measure of American classicism: the eighteenth century's valorization of pietas.

As early as Urian Oakes's "Elegie Upon . . . Thomas Shepard," we have observed the promotion of this, Aeneas's primary virtue, in all three of its manifestations—devotion to God, family, and country. Cotton Mather later codifies this virtue in relation to his mythic American self, a blend of Adam and Aeneas. Many authors of eighteenth-century America continue to promote this "ideal" blend, though more valorize Aeneas over Adam as the century travels "beyond the holy circle." In his *Philosophic Solitude*, for example, William Livingston enthusiastically promotes pietas in the figure of Rome's Cato; this poem was one of the most popular in the colonies before the Revolution, going through at least thirteen printings by 1800. Francis Bernard, initially a popular governor of Massachusetts, self-consciously singled out the civic portion of pietas as a worthy indicator of American virtue. Later, Jean de Crèvecoeur restored pietas to its triune integrity.

As we are about to see in the next chapter, it was in the character of George Washington that pietas received its most celebrated and dramatic expression. Indeed, Washington, it is no exaggeration to say, became *the* American Aeneas! Yet, during this same period in Britain (1720–90), Vergil's pietas underwent such erosion as to become the subject of satire. To be sure, Dryden, in the introduction to his justly famous 1697 translation of the *Aeneid*, defines pietas as comprehending "not only Devotion to the Gods, but Filial Love and tender Affection to Relations of all sorts." As this heroic virtue of pietas identifies Aeneas, it extends to "Care of his people; Courage and Conduct in the Wars; Gratitude to those who had oblig'd him; and Justice in general to Mankind" (V, 286). Despite this full definition, James D. Garrison, in his fascinating *Pietas from Vergil to Dryden*, demonstrates that, when Dryden penned this definition, the British poet did so in an age which already had become "less than congenial for the writing of an epic poem" (1). Garrison subsequently makes clear that, after Christianity's appropriation of the term to *piety*, "the word that had proclaimed the epic heroism of Aeneas becomes increasingly vulnerable to irony" (3). For that matter, "the English piety eventually surrenders its claim on political discourse and retreats to the domain of private religious experience" (3–4).

What happens to the concept of pietas in Britain, then, is that the temper of "the word's literary history" curves away "from epic and toward satire, from an aristocratic to a middle- and finally lower-class social environment, from the public to the private domain" (5). Just the opposite occurs in the American colonies, where the word and its associated meaning undergo valorization.

In Britain, not only does the virtue of pietas decline during the eighteenth century; but also, as the genre of the epic yields to that of satire, the reputation of the *Aeneid*'s author, particularly as a great moralist, deteriorates. In *Augustus Caesar in "Augustan" England: The Decline of a Classical Norm*, Howard D. Weinbrot makes clear that the appellation "Augustan," as descriptive of English letters written after the Glorious Revolution, does not accurately reflect that period's generally negative attitude toward Augustus Caesar, whom historians and writers alike judged to have been a tyrant. Weinbrot notes, for example, "Virgil and his epic lost esteem and influence because of their association with Augustus; as seventeenth-century royalism waned, so did admiration for that royalist poem" (128). In his "Conclusion," Weinbrot states, "Horatian satire [not so severe as Juvenalian] and Virgilian epic dramatically lose force and credibility as the century progresses" (233).

In the American colonies at mid-century, however, William Livingston calls Vergil the "prince" of poets who "shou'd wear the laurel'd crown,/ And other bards pay homage to his throne," (166). And, on the eve of the Revolution, Phillis Wheatley aspires to rival "*Virgil's* page" and to "claim the *Muses* with the *Mantuan* Sage [i.e., Vergil]" (10). To be sure, not all among the American patriot, intellectual elite so revered Vergil and his epic, but most obviously did. Americans steeling themselves for armed rebellion similarly made Addison's *Cato* an extremely popular play, prompting George Washington to demand that it be performed twice at Valley Forge during the spring following the devastatingly harsh winter of 1777–78. As we soon shall discover, this entire play may be interpreted as an explication and exaltation of Vergil's pietas.

That pietas comes to be perceived enthusiastically owes a great deal to the general, greater regard for piety emanating from the strong contingency of the Adamic myth on the American strand. Indeed, with the forces of resistance to the rise of classicism manifested by the Great Awakening and, as we have observed, by opposition to the pastoral elegy, the myth of Adam does in fact remain in place, ever challenging the hegemony of the myth of Aeneas. In the case of the valorization of pietas, nevertheless, Adamic discourse does not quarrel with the primacy of devotion to the gods/God promoted by this classical concept. Instead, advocates of Adamic discourse find pietas/piety to be intimately compatible, on all three registers of this construct. While worship of God after one's chosen path has ever remained a central issue since the times of the Puritan fathers, the sanctity of the family, particularly on the peripheries of the frontier, and allegiance to the common good of the colony isolated from any other acceptable manner of existence complete the triune integrity of pietas. As we shall see in the next chapter, the construct of pietas helped to lend cohesiveness to Revolutionary ideology and became a poignant indicator distinguishing the culture of the American colonies from that of Great Britain. The easy accommodation of pietas to Adamic discourse effectively blurred the difference between the classical and the biblical modes, showing how conducive to *translatio cultus* was the interplay between Adam and Aeneas.

The pattern now has become clear. While Britain was involved with a denigration of classical values and forms, Americans were investing major creative efforts toward privileging classical discourse. Indeed, Americans were demonstrating in *belles lettres* a reliance on classical sources, leading them *not* to depend on British examples of creativity or form. Surprisingly, Americans authors sought each other's example and consequently displayed an eagerness to experiment and to ground their literary productions in a firmly American ambiance, all as part of a campaign to discover an identity separate from that of Britain or Europe. When expressing that new identity, Americans flexed their intellectual and creative muscles by declaring their literary independence in poem after poem, by developing their own versions of the pastoral and particularly the subversive pastoral, and by expiating a fear of pastlessness through the construction of pastoral elegies.

In no sense does the praxis of the pastoral elegy in America represent an attempt to revitalize or reconstruct a dying British genre. Rather, during the eighteenth century in America, this genre's products offer what is perhaps the clearest illustration of the tension between the myths of Adam and Aeneas. Eleven of the seventeen known pastoral elegies mingle some elements of Christianity, such as references to Christ and to the Christian heaven and hell, with allusions to numerous other biblical persons and events—all after the standard practice in Britain and on the Continent, whereby the pagan myths are made "safe" for a Christian audience. Seven of this same group of poems exhibit balanced blends of the Puritan funeral elegy and classicism. All seventeen, nevertheless, by virtue of their genre, lean decidedly toward classicism.

A palpably recognizable current of the American Adam remained implacably in place, however. It was represented by the Great Awakening evangelicalism of George Whitefield (the Voice of the Great Awakening) and the more moderate efforts of Jonathan Edwards to restore the Calvinistic orthodoxy of the Puritan fathers. In addition, classicism's secular

By His HONOUR

SPENCER PHIPS, Eſq;

Lieutenant-Governour and Commander in Chief, in and over His Majeſty's Province of the *Maſſachuſetts-Bay* in *New-England.*

A PROCLAMATION.

WHEREAS the Tribe of *Penobſcot* Indians have repeatedly in a perfidious Manner acted contrary to their ſolemn Submiſſion unto His Majeſty long ſince made and frequently renewed;

I have therefore, at the Deſire of the Houſe of Repreſentatives, with the Advice of His Majeſty's Council, thought fit to iſſue this Proclamation, and to declare the Penobſcot **Tribe of Indians to be Enemies, Rebels and Traitors to His Majeſty King** *GEORGE* the Second: **And I do hereby require His Majeſty's Subjects of this Province to embrace all Opportunities of purſuing, captivating, killing and deſtroying all and every of the aforeſaid Indians.**

AND WHEREAS the General Court of this Province have voted that a Bounty or Incouragement be granted and allowed to be paid out of the Publick Treaſury, to the marching Forces that ſhall have been employed for the Defence of the *Eaſtern* and *Weſtern* Frontiers, from the *Firſt* to the *Twenty-fifth* of this Inſtant *November*;

I have thought fit to publiſh the ſame; and I do hereby Promiſe, That there ſhall be paid out of the Province-Treaſury to all and any of the ſaid Forces, over and above their Bounty upon Inliſtment, their Wages and Subſiſtence, the Premiums or Bounty following, viz.

For every Male *Penobſcot* Indian above the Age of Twelve Years, that ſhall be taken within the Time aforeſaid and brought to *Boſton, Fifty Pounds.*

For every Scalp of a Male *Penobſcot* Indian above the Age aforeſaid, brought in as Evidence of their being killed as aforeſaid, *Forty Pounds.*

For every Female *Penobſcot* Indian taken and brought in as aforeſaid, and for every Male Indian Priſoner under the Age of Twelve Years, taken and brought in as aforeſaid, *Twenty-five Pounds.*

For every Scalp of ſuch Female Indian or Male Indian under the Age of Twelve Years, that ſhall be killed and brought in as Evidence of their being killed as aforeſaid, *Twenty Pounds.*

Given at the Council-Chamber in *Boſton*, this Third Day of *November* 1755, and in the Twenty-ninth Year of the Reign of our Sovereign Lord *GEORGE* the Second, by the Grace of GOD of *Great-Britain, France* and *Ireland*, KING, Defender of the Faith, *&c.*

By His Honour's Command,
J. Willard, Secr.

S. Phips.

GOD Save the KING.

BOSTON. Printed by *John Draper*, Printer to His Honour the Lieutenant-Governour and Council. 1755.

Fig. 2. The Penobscot Broadside, 1755. Given to the author by Richard Hamilton, governor of the Penobscot Nation.

pull away from the "holy circle" elicited an inevitable reaction, as Benjamin Church and the author of the Sarah Wanton elegy registered objections to the pastoral elegy.

The myth of Aeneas, as the praxis of the pastoral and pastoral elegy suggests, nonetheless, assumed a position of dominance during this period. The eighth measure of American classicism, the promotion of pietas as a principal virtue, ascended to the highest place among American virtues—yet another indication of this dominance. Now, with all of the eight criteria describing American classicism established—reliance on classical sources, bypassing British examples, dependence on American ingenuity as a primary resource leading to the construction of an American tradition, the courage to experiment, embracing of the American milieu, determination to discover a unique identity, construction of distinguishably American genres, and a valorization of pietas—Adam had become Aeneas, at least among a majority of the intellectual elite, the same elite that later would construct the United States Constitution.

The contentment that, according to Eunice Bourne's *Fishing Lady*, was promised by the raising up of America's classical age did not, in fact, materialize. For the golden age pastoral paradise Bourne claims for America at mid-century is tainted, most glaringly by the hated institution of slavery and by colonial policy against Native Americans. About slavery and American pastoral, Lewis Simpson has pointed out that southerners tried to adapt slavery to pastoral. If the tawny-faced, diminutive male figure just below the male and female couple occupying the left portion of Bourne's *Fishing Lady* is in fact a mulatto slave, then Bourne's own Barnstable, Massachusetts, was tainted by the hated institution. Certainly Boston was corrupted by it, as the poet Wheatley attests. Wheatley, in a strategy the converse of that employed by Simpson's southerners, appropriates pastoral in an effort to subvert the whites' practice of slavery. Her struggle, that of a minority speaking against the oppression of an insensitive, tyrannical majority, identifies her voice as distinctly American.

As Wheatley's subversive pastoral represents the voice of protest for African Americans, Robert Beverley's subversive pastoral challenges poignantly the white man's interference with Native Americans. A text which more glaringly exposes the negative attitude of whites toward Native Americans is Spencer Phips's "Proclamation" against "the Tribe of *Penobscot* Indians." Dated 1755, just five years after the creation of Bourne's *Fishing Lady*, this broadside makes plain the white colonists' utter contempt for the people of the Penobscot nation, even offering a reward of twenty pounds "For every Scalp of such Female Indian or Male Indian *under* the Age of Twelve Years" (emphasis mine; see fig. 2). The *Fishing Lady* declares not a hint of such a formidable problem as that indicated by Phips's "Proclamation." And yet these two illustrations suggest the fullness of the American experience; the *Fishing Lady* promises the vision of a wholly secular golden age pastoral, while the "Proclamation" states the harsh, insufferable reality.

Many years before the Revolution, then, *translatio cultus* had become encoded within the American self. The hope for a human-centered, golden, pastoral, heavenly Eden had fastened itself upon the American consciousness. Out of that same largely classical way of thought and action had evolved already a subversive methodology for dealing with oppression brought on by the majority. That majority, whose mode of discourse generally is the province of an intellectual elite, had cast aside the European version of classicism to embrace its own American classicism. Now all that remained of the struggle to create a cohesive American self was George Washington's dynamic enactment of the Vergilian Moment.

Fig. 3. The Apotheosis of George Washington. Capitol Rotunda, Washington, D.C., completed by Constantino Brumidi in 1865. In the center, George Washington is seated in majesty. On his right is the Goddess of Liberty and on his left is a winged figure, symbolic of Victory and Fame, sounding a trumpet. Surrounding Washington are thirteen maidens, symbolizing the original States, holding a banner emblazoned with the motto "E Pluribus Unum." The border comprises six allegorical groupings. Below Washington is War, with Freedom holding a shield and accompanied by the Eagle. Continuing clockwise, Art and Sciences are represented by Minerva, Goddess of Wisdom, teaching Benjamin Franklin, Robert Fulton, and Samuel F. B. Morse. Marine, personified by Neptune, is accompanied by Venus. Commerce is represented by Mercury, who holds in his hand a bag of gold as he turns toward Robert Morris, financier of the American Revolution. Mechanics is symbolized by Vulcan. Agriculture is represented by Ceres with a cornucopia. America, wearing a red liberty cape, turns over to Ceres a team of horses pulling a reaper. Flora gathers flowers and Pomona bears a basket of fruit.

5

George Washington and the Vergilian Moment

William Alfred Bryan opens the preface to his *George Washington in American Literature* with an observation which, in these debunking days, may sound excessive. "Until Lincoln appeared as challenger for the title of foremost American hero," Bryan declares, "George Washington had no rival for that title" (vii). While I am not concerned with bolstering or adding to Washington's heroic image, I intend to analyze the role that image played in defining the *American* character, as distinct from the Continental or the British. And the simple truth is that, to an overwhelming majority of Americans during the Revolution and for decades beyond, Washington was the heroic symbol Bryan describes. The principal means by which he embodied that symbolic, heroic image was his abiding, personal investment in the cause of virtue. As James T. Flexner, one of Washington's more recent biographers, phrases it, Washington above all else was "a man who, through the storms of personal temperament and outside circumstance, labored to keep *virtue* his guiding star [emphasis mine]" (*GW: Forge* 4:9).

For that matter, Americans, like Europeans somewhat earlier, appeared to be preoccupied with the notion of virtue, on a grand scale. In the *Blackwell Encyclopedia of the American Revolution*, James T. Kloppenberg, in an essay entitled simply "Virtue," explores this concept within American revolutionary thought. He begins the piece by remarking, "Virtue was ubiquitous in eighteenth-century American discourse" (*Blackwell* 688). Yet few hazard a delineation of this concept, virtue. Neither Flexner nor Kloppenberg does. One who does attempt to describe virtue in connection with Washington is Marcus Cunliffe, in his highly readable biographical treatment, *George Washington: Man and Monument*. In an especially provocative section entitled "The Classical Code," Cunliffe states, "Both the man and the legend are classical or, more specifically, Roman, in shape" (151). He cites Washington's widely known regard for Joseph Addison's *Cato* (1713) and enumerates various Roman virtues, as in the following passage: "And *virtus* [which Cunliffe correctly defines as *courage*] was one of the famous Roman virtues (and, in practice, a Virginian one). *Gravitas*, *pietas*, *simplicitas*, *integritas* and *gloria* were other valued Roman qualities" (152). *Gravitas* Cunliffe later defines as "seriousness," *simplicitas* as "lucidity," and, most curiously, *pietas* as "regard for discipline and authority" (153).

While the Roman concept of pietas incorporates discipline and authority, Dryden's definition of this most vital of Roman virtues comes much closer to the mark: "Not only Devotion to the Gods, but Filial Love and tender Affection to Relations of all sorts" (V, 286). Dryden finds that the definition of *pietas* supplied by Jean de Segrais in the introduction to his version of the *Aeneid* (the first significant French version) ably extends his own understanding. Translating literally from Segrais, Dryden writes that "Piety alone comprehends the whole Duty of Man towards the Gods; towards his Country, and towards Relations." Dryden then studiously records Segrais's holding that pietas includes "even Valour it self, with all other Qualities which are good" (V, 288). During the Revolution, Washington praised the "Roman Valour" of his men. Cunliffe's cataloguing of so many virtues (six in all) and his inadequate definition of pietas perhaps confuses more than it clarifies Washington's Roman character. He is careful, nonetheless, to emphasize the importance of duty to Washington: "Duty. Here is another Roman clue to Washington: duty seen as a cluster of obligations." Attempting to clarify what he means by "obligations," Cunliffe asserts, "These are not individual but *social* [*sic*] necessities" (153). In the preceding chapter, we learned from Urian Oakes's elegy on Thomas Shepard that "duty" is a synonym for pietas; we also saw that Oakes interpreted *duty* in terms of the tripartite structure of pietas: devotion to God, country, and family.

In his interpretation of duty, Cunliffe may have in mind Cicero's *De officiis* (*On Duties*, 46–43 B.C.), widely studied in American classical grammar schools as a text of proper civic behavior. This work vilifies Caesar as the tyrannical enslaver of Rome (destroyer of the Republic), while Cato Uticensis is valorized as a noble republican. However, Cunliffe does not say in his text that he is drawing on Cicero. Of more importance to our consideration of the developing American cultural consciousness, moreover, is Cicero's earlier, famous definition of duty in terms of pietas: "Pietas, per quam sanguine coniunctis patriaeque benevolum officium et diligens tribuitur cultus" (Duty [is that] by means of which benevolent respect and careful treatment are shown to those related by blood and to the fatherland; *De inventione*, ca. 86 B.C.). In later, philosophical works, such as *De natura deorum*, Cicero always delineated the tripartite structure of pietas, reserving first place for reverence to the gods. Because Cunliffe fails to make this essential connection between duty and pietas, he confuses the issue by defining *pietas* unsatisfactorily as "regard for discipline and authority." Presumably Cunliffe does not understand *pietas* in terms of Vergil's *Aeneid*, or as Americans did while classicism flourished in the eighteenth century. At least his text does not demonstrate such an understanding.

The primary subject of this chapter is an analysis of this elusive concept, *virtue*, particularly as it defines the character and influence of George Washington. As few, if any, of today's scholars writing about this man and his culture adequately interpret this concept, we must make an effort here to create a working definition. Jerrold E. Seigel admonishes that the meanings of the word *virtue* are "potentially as various as the bases on which men [and women] value their acts" (4: 476). According to Seigel, Niccolo Machiavelli's theories regarding the concept were by far the most influential during the Renaissance. Machiavelli, Seigel maintains, stressed the active principle of *virtu* to such a degree that the "sense of virtue as what is morally right has been forced out." This understanding of the term leads Machiavelli to conclude in *Lettere* that "each man has his fortune founded on his style of action." Therefore, Seigel continues, it may be said that "a man's fortune thus depended first of all, on himself, on his personal style" (4: 480).

All those who attempt to describe George Washington agree that his "personal style" most clearly enabled him to rise above all others during his lifetime. So the Machiavellian use of the term proves instructive in a preliminary examination of Washington's relation to virtue. In addition, it was Machiavelli's view that, while individuals cannot rearrange themselves to fit the times, those men are happiest whose dispositions fit the necessary conditions of any given time and place. This notion helps to validate Flexner's argument that Washington was the indispensable person whose style and disposition fully and happily accorded with the necessities of his place and time. The majority of Washington's public embodiment of virtue derived not from his military achievement, but rather from his public service during peacetime. Thus his focus upon virtue as "his guiding star" finally departs from Machiavelli's persistent association of *virtu* with "military prowess." We must, therefore, look elsewhere for an adequate description of virtue in the Washingtonian sense.

In his discussion of post-Machiavellian virtue, Seigel observes that "attitudes toward virtue have continued to be shaped by changing circumstances, and especially by the pressures on conduct and action which derive from the political situation in the widest sense" (4: 483). The political situation in the colonies while American classicism flourished was one in which an intellectual elite held power (not even the grassroots Great Awakening achieved ascendancy). Nevertheless, the Adamic mode of discourse never could be discounted, as is attested, for example, by the young Benjamin Franklin's retraction of the blatant deism (approaching pantheism) he had expressed in *A Dissertation on Liberty and Necessity, Pleasure and Pain* (1725). What was needed, therefore, was a concept of virtue which would bridge both modes of discourse, the Adamic and the classical. As noted in the preceding chapter, the virtue which slides easily from one mode of discourse to the other is Vergil's pietas. This same pietas gained steadily in esteem among Americans from Mather's *Magnalia Christi Americana* until the end of the century, while in Britain during the same period this virtue underwent devalorization. The American promotion of pietas, then, became a convenient means of distinguishing American virtue from British.

So pervasive in America was preoccupation with what Francis Bernard phrased, as early as 1761, "pietas fidesque civica" (civic devotion and faith) that religious, political, and philosophical attitudes became inseparably intertwined, creating what Sydney E. Ahlstrom has called a "Republican Religion" (1: 445). Because this blend of religious, political, and philosophical attitudes embraces the evolution of Washington's career, and because he himself eventually became the undeniable living cynosure of this "Republican Religion," the setting of this phenomenon merits detailed consideration. Because Addison's *Cato*, Washington's and America's favorite drama, defines pietas so thoroughly that the play's subject may arguably be said to be explanation of this concept rather than the final hours in the life of the title character, this play warrants extensive treatment as Addison's American play. As well, examination of the textbooks of America's public schools following the ratification of the Constitution reveals that the virtue of pietas continued to be raised up as the American Way and that Washington was consistently promoted as the epitome of that Way.

A final consideration regarding pietas and Washington's role in promoting this virtue demonstrates that J. G. A. Pocock's suggestion that the Machiavellian moment, as transplanted in America, characterizes the American Revolutionary spirit proves to be inadequate. As already pointed out, Washington's personal style of leadership derives only in part from the Machiavellian emphasis on military prowess, wherein military prowess is the equivalent of virtue. Simply put, Pocock's insistence on Machiavelli's *virtu* does not describe Washington's embodiment of devotion to God, to country and to family; indeed, this American virtue transcends Pocock's realms of property and corruption, the two principal causes which provoke military expression. As we shall discover, in America the confrontation of pietas, not virtu, with corruption or with tyrannical Great Britain, constitutes, not the Machiavellian moment, but the Vergilian moment.

Political, Religious, and Philosophical Setting

> Without having recourse to Solon, Lycurgus, Aristotle or Plato, amongst the ancients; or Hume, Harrington, More and Machiavel, Burgh and Vatel [*sic*], amongst the moderns, [one may] prove that men are attached to that which is agreeable to them; that fire is a good servant but a bad master; that it is comfortable and useful on the hearth; but that it is neither agreeable to warm your hands, nor convenient to roast an egg, at an house in flames. (3)

So begins a pamphlet published in 1786 in "New-York" entitled *Honesty Shewed to be True Policy; OR, A General Impost Considered and Defended* by "A Plain Politician," written in defense of a tax designed to defray the expenses of the members of Congress. The catalogue of authors named by this "Plain Politician" reads like a pantheon of political theorists, each of whom would be found "comfortable and useful on the hearth" of any thinking American of the Revolutionary War era. Solon, the Athenian statesman, used verse to proclaim such governmental reforms as the repeal of all Draconian laws (not dealing with homicide). It is claimed that Lycurgus, Sparta's legendary legislator, founded Sparta's "eunomian" (well-ordered) constitution, resulting in systematic social and military orders. Both Plato and Aristotle, in their political philosophies, held that the state should promulgate the cause of virtuous behavior. The name of Cicero is conspicuous here by its absence; we have seen (in ch. 3) that his *De officiis*, a description of the virtuous political person, was a common textbook in the Latin grammar schools of colonial America from their seventeenth-century beginnings. When the omnipresence of Cicero's political thought within the American colonies is coupled with the "Plain Politician's" omission, one is reminded of George Sandys's failure to name Vergil as one of the sources from which he sought assistance in the composition of his commentaries on each of the fifteen books of Ovid's *Metamorphoses*. So pervasive was Sandys's use of Vergil (naming or citing him on practically every other page) that including him seems simply to have slipped Sandys's mind. Our "Plain Politician" probably was as familiar with Cicero (and Vergil as well) as Sandys was with Vergil.

Cicero's attitude toward virtue, and particularly toward pietas, certainly is worth pointing out. In such works as *De inventione*, *De republica*, and *De officiis*, Cicero almost always used the word *pietas* to refer to duty to one's family and to one's country. In *Pietas from Vergil to Dryden*, James D. Garrison observes, for example, "The *pietas* of Cicero's *Republic* is more than right thinking: it is a public virtue identified with the ethos of the ruling class" (10–11). This usage is much in keeping with Mather's application of *pietas* to Sir William Phips in *Magnalia Christi Americana* and with Francis Bernard's "pietas fidesque civica," or civic devotion and faith. After 45 B.C., however, Cicero usually applied *pietas* first and foremost to the gods, although devotion to family and country were retained. Hence Cicero's full career displays indisputable familiarity with the triune integrity of pietas—a career about which the author of *Honesty Shewed* probably would have been informed.

Let us turn now to the "moderns" listed by the author of this pamphlet. Hume was known to Americans largely for his three-volume *History of England*. Contrary to most of the other authors named by the "Plain Politician," Hume holds that interest in the self, and not virtue or reason, is the principal motivating force behind human action. James Madison, particularly, was influenced by Hume's insistence on politics as a science proving that government must derive from the natural inclinations of human beings. James Harrington's *The Commonwealth of Oceana* (1656) advanced the teaching, among many others, that the stability of a commonwealth turned on the ownership of some three-quarters of the land by its citizens (defined during the Revolutionary era in America as white males). Harrington's "agrarian law" appears to have been accepted almost literally by Noah Webster, whose contribution to the shaping of the American character, as we shall see, was determinative. In a tract from the period of the Constitution, he wrote, "*Virtue*, patriotism, or love of country, never was and never will be, till men's natures are changed, a fixed permanent principle and support of government." Rather, for "Virtue" (and note here how he defines this concept in terms of pietas, as we have seen Cotton Mather and Francis Bernard do), Webster would substitute "an equality of property" which would be accompanied by "a necessity of alienation, constantly operating to destroy combinations of powerful families." For, according to Webster, virtue as "an equality of property" constitutes "the very *soul of* a republic" (quoted in Pocock 534).

The "More" to whom our "Plain Politician" refers may be Sir Thomas More, author of *Utopia*. In his version of an ideal political arrangement, More presents a view diametrically opposite that of Harrington; indeed, in

More's *Utopia,* private property does not exist. Given that the pamphlet's subject is taxation, however, a more likely identification of the "Plain Politician's" More is one Maurice Moore, American patriot and author of the pamphlet, *The Justice and Policy of Taxing the American Colonies* (1765), in which he vigorously opposed the Stamp Act on the grounds that the colonies had no representation in Parliament. Moore's brother was James Moore, a Son of Liberty who led the colonists in the pivotal victory at Moores Creek Bridge (February 1776). Maurice Moore's son, Alfred Moore, was appointed to the United States Supreme Court by John Adams. Perhaps it was Maurice Moore's sometimes fickle political conduct which provoked our "Plain Politician" to couple Moore with Machiavelli in the phrase "More and Machiavel"; Moore was known as a person of ambition and ability. In any case, the naming of Machiavelli in this highly public context clearly demonstrates that the Italian political theorist and his work were known to the intellectual elite of the Revolutionary era.[1] His theory of virtue, seen largely as "military prowess," would have been familiar to many.

The last two "moderns" whom the "Plain Politician" chooses to name are James Burgh, British schoolmaster, moralist, and political theorist; and Emmerick de Vattel, a Swiss jurist and political theorist (or synthesizer). Both insist on the necessary role of virtue within the ideal republic. According to Bernard Bailyn, Burgh's *Britain's Remembrances; or, The Danger Not Over* (1746) represents the most "sustained and intense attack on the corruption of Augustan England" (86). So popular did *Britain's Remembrances* become in America that Franklin reprinted it in Philadelphia in 1747, another printer issued it there in 1748, and a Boston printer published it again in 1759. This work, along with Burgh's three-volume *Political Disquisitions* of 1774, gave much fuel to the American argument that morality had decayed in Britain but was restored in America. Vattel, in his *The Law of Nations* (1758), advanced a view of virtue which emphasized the notion that natural rights and duties among the citizenry of a given state emanate from the so-called laws of nature.

As when we observed the "Plain Politician's" omission of Cicero, now we see him omit the names of the two most influential political theorists in eighteenth-century America, John Locke and Charles Louis de Secondat, the Baron de Montesquieu. On the subject of virtue, Locke is clear. In the second of his *Two Treatises of Government,* he addresses the issue of pietas per se:

> And though that *Honour* and *Respect,* and all that which the *Latins* called *Piety,* which they indispensibly owe to their Parents and their Life times, and in all Estates, with all that Support and

> Defence [which] is due to them, gives the Father no Power of Governing, i.e. making Laws and enacting Penalties on his Children; Though by all this he has no Dominion over the Property or Actions of his Son. (316)

Here Locke rejects the idea of pietas, as irrelevant to his argument against the divine right theory of monarchy and for constitutional government based upon natural rights. Garrison analyzes this passage in the following manner: Locke suggests "here that a political understanding of pietas is at best an anachronism that cannot be revived by Restoration nostalgia for the ideals of Roman civilization" (Garrison 16). Yet colonial Americans were opposed to Locke's denigration of pietas and instead were much concerned with reviving this concept, derived from "the ideals of Roman civilization." They employed the idea of pietas to construct their own version of a republican government—one not British or Continental.

In *The Spirit of the Laws* (1748), Montesquieu, however, advances a definition of virtue which is much in line with Cotton Mather's delineation of pietas as applied to Sir William Phips; it also accords well with Francis Bernard's phrase "pietas fidesque civica," or civic devotion and faith. Following the time-worn tradition, stemming from the ancient Greek political theorists, that each class of citizenry generates its own character, Montesquieu maintains that "virtue" is "necessary in a popular government" (22). This "virtue" he defines as "a most simple thing"; indeed, "it is a love of the republic." "The love of our country," Montesquieu continues, "is conducive to a purity of morals, and the latter is again conducive to the former." Concerning who among the persons of a republic are more likely to avoid corruption, Montesquieu observes, "When the common people adopt good maxims, they adhere to them more steadily than those whom we call gentlemen. It is very rarely that corruption commences with the former; nay, they frequently derive from their imperfect light a stronger attachment to the established laws and customs" (40).[2]

While the phrase "their imperfect light" appears to nod gently toward Plato's "Allegory of the Cave," the general sentiment expressed in this passage comes strikingly close to Augustus Caesar's understanding of the character of the common people, or plebeians. Such an understanding probably motivated Augustus Caesar to preserve Vergil's *Aeneid* from the flames, to which the dying poet had consigned it. Vergil had performed books IV and VI for the Emperor and his wife Livia. Subsequently Augustus Caesar used the epic as a tool for promulgating the virtue of pietas, especially among the common folk.

It is puzzling to find that Franz Neumann, author of the excellent introduction to what many consider the definitive English language edition of *The*

Spirit of the Laws, asserts that Montesquieu's principle of virtue is "more the Machiavellian virtue than Christian virtues" (xli). While Montesquieu's definition may echo Machiavelli more than Christianity, it definitely owes a still greater debt to the political thought of Greece and Rome. In any case, Montesquieu's treatment of virtue aligns his thought with that of the American colonists more clearly than that of Locke, at least as concerns the issue of virtue as pietas. In his magisterial *The Enlightenment in America*, Henry F. May declares that, among the delegates of the Constitutional Convention of 1787, "The political writer most often mentioned was not Locke but Montesquieu, the great patron of historical relativism" (98).

In this same book, May holds that his thesis "is not about the Enlightenment *and* religion, but rather about the Enlightenment *as* religion" (xiii). One of the desiderata of this Enlightenment religion, according to May, was "to revive the virtue and greatness of republican Rome" (164). As we have already seen, this Roman virtue was, of course, pietas. In keeping with our consideration here of the political, philosophical, and religious context of George Washington's career, we observe that the "Plain Politician" who authored *Honesty Shewed* repeatedly insists that government must be conducted only by "the wisest and most virtuous men" (4 et passim).

The paragon of such virtue, of course, was Washington. Of Washington's role, not merely as a paragon of virtue/pietas, but also as an embodiment of Americanness, Catherine Albanese writes in *Sons of the Fathers*, "Despite minority opposition to him as commander-in-chief and as president, almost overnight, Washington became a living 'tribal' totem for an emerging nation-state" (144). Albanese goes on to conclude:

> During his very lifetime, the printed record revealed that the story of George Washington, father and founder of his country, fitted a paradigm which had much in common with the composite portrait of the great religious leaders of other cultures who, like him, had been divine men. (145)

That the Revolutionary era in America was characterized by such a religious consciousness was recognized even abroad during the same period. Edmund Burke observed trenchantly in his *Second Speech*, "The religion most prevalent in our northern colonies is a refinement of the principles of resistance: it is the dissidence of dissent, and the protestantism of the Protestant religion" (453). It was not merely as a paragon of love of country, however, that Washington qualified as high priest of May's Enlightenment religion, Albanese's civil religion, Ahlstrom's "Republican Religion," or what I shall call America's faith of rebellion. Despite Washington's known proclivity for deism, to the common people, and even to many members of the intellectual elite of the early nineteenth century, Washington epitomized the pious believer and the best family values. For, in addition to a spirit of political self-determination, Americans—all Americans—asserted their "natural" right to choice of religious expression and promoted the family as an autonomous unit, free of class or social restrictions.

To be sure, the thought of all those "ancients" and "moderns" listed by our "Plain Politician" played a vital role in shaping the religious, political, and philosophical dimensions of America's faith of rebellion. But it was the promotion of pietas, perhaps more than any other single factor, which most clearly differentiated America from Britain and the Continent. The blending of devotion to God, family, and country constituted the fullest expression of America's faith of rebellion. Joseph Addison's *Cato* helped to restore the triune integrity of pietas, emphasized by both Vergil in the *Aeneid* and Cotton Mather in *Magnalia Christi Americana*. In restoring pietas, the American adventure in freedom represents the revitalization of Rome's republican spirit.

Cato: Addison's American Play

Other than Vergil's *Aeneid*, surely the most definitive treatment of pietas available during the eighteenth century in England and America, was the tragedy of *Cato* (1713), by Joseph Addison, author of the famous *Spectator* essays on the imagination. While this play was one of the most popular plays in eighteenth-century England, *Cato* certainly was *the* single most popular play during this same period in Early America. Because this play constitutes an English-language presentation and promulgation of the virtue of pietas, requiring no knowledge of classical languages or cultures, *Cato* served as a primary vehicle for disseminating pietas to those Early Americans unfamiliar with Vergil's *Aeneid*—that is, to those schooled exclusively in the tenets of the Adamic myth.

Cato, or salient selections from *Cato*, proved immensely popular in nineteenth-century American schoolbooks, so that Addison's play continued as a primary means of promoting pietas among the American people. *Cato* demands our attention because of its popularity in eighteenth-century America, its promotion of pietas to an English-language public, and its persistent popularity in American schoolbooks of the nineteenth century. Moreover, *Cato* very likely was George Washington's favorite piece of literature, and American writers subsequently identified Washington with *Cato* and pietas.

The general eighteenth-century denigration of pietas in England probably accounts for the failure of British critics from then until the present to recognize this play as an analysis and celebration of the Vergilian virtue.[3] In "The Meaning of Addison's Cato," perhaps the best essay on Addison's play,

M. M. Kelsall states, "That part of the play with which Cato is principally concerned is little more than an exposition of what the term '*Roman* virtue' meant to Addison" (156). Good, as far as it goes! While Kelsall is careful to praise Cato for his "goodness" (156) and for his advocacy of "public spirit" (158), he never gets around to explicating Cato as the supreme symbol of pietas, or devotion to the gods, family, and country. American scholarship on Addison's play in the twentieth century ignored any connection to pietas, although this lack of awareness most likely reflected the hegemony of the Adamic myth. In the eighteenth century in America, however, the pietas connection was not ignored; rather, it was celebrated.

As practically everyone writing about *Cato* has observed, the play was universally popular during the eighteenth century on both sides of the Atlantic. In Great Britain, the sentiments expressed in *Cato* appear to have been embraced by both Tories and Whigs; the details of this British fondness for the play need not concern us here. In America, however, we encounter a different history, one which helps to explain how the American Way (God, Mother, and Country) came into being. As for Washington's association with *Cato*, Garry Wills in *Cincinnatus* prefaces each of thirteen chapters of this highly readable work concerning Washington's rise to power with a salient quotation from Addison's play. According to Wills, Washington knew *Cato* "intimately" and "cited [it] often" (134). In a chapter on Washington's role in the evolving United States, Wills maintains that Washington's "obvious moral paradigm is [the play's] title character" (135). Indeed, Washington's "life verged on legend, even as he lived it, because he had models he was trying to live up to" (xxiv). Certainly the model of Cato's stoic embodiment of Roman republican pietas informed the acts of Washington's career which, Wills asserts, "seemed to revive the ancient republic that men were yearning for" (xxvi).

In the admirable essay, "Addison's *Cato* in the Colonies," Litto maintains that, after the Stamp Act controversy of the mid-1760s, interest in *Cato* among colonial Americans shifted from that of "pre-Revolutionary classic to instrument of rebellion" (442). Actually, the use of *Cato* as an "instrument of rebellion" in the colonies dates from a much earlier time. Bernard Bailyn, for example, documents instances in which the play was used as a tool of political polemics at least as early as 1732.[4] The poet and statesman, William Livingston, included an encomium to Cato in his immensely popular *Philosophic Solitude* (1747):

> The unconquerable sage [Cato] whom virtue fir'd,
> And from the tyrant's lawless rage retir'd,
> When victor Caesar freed unhappy Rome
> From Pompey's chains, to substitute his own. (171)

Earlier in this same poem, Livingston expressed his decided preference for Cicero's republicanism over any sort of monarchy; for Cicero pled "the patriot cause" "Before the Roman bar, while Rome was free,/ Nor bow'd to Caesar's throne the servile knee" (158).

In addition, Mather Byles, the most prolific eighteenth-century American poet before Phillis Wheatley and Philip Freneau, speaks of Cato as a figure of "Majesty" in his poem about painting, "To *Pictorio*, on the Sight of His Pictures" (*Poems on Several*, 1745, 91). In a poem attributed to Byles, published in *A Collection of Poems by Several Hands* (1744), one of America's first anthologies of poetry, the author devotes the entire poem to the romantic love interests of *Cato*. "Written in the blank Leaf of Mr. Addison's *Cato:* Given to a Lady," celebrates, as paragons of modesty and charm, two women: Marcia, daughter of Cato and beloved by Juba; and Lucia, daughter of Lucius and beloved by Portius. The opening line of this blank-verse poem, "Go, gentle volume, teach the fair to love" (45), along with its title, reveals at least two details about *Cato* in America. Contrary to today's perception of the play as romantically cold, then it was viewed as an exemplum for courtship; it also was thought to be a suitable gift to a woman during the courting ritual. Concerning *Cato*'s reputation in Early America, these illustrations suggest that this play was not merely a source of political inspiration. Instead, it influenced society on several levels.

Litto records that Benjamin Franklin printed forty-eight copies of the play in August 1743, at the request of William Parks, printer of the first Virginia paper, the *Virginia Gazette*, established in Williamsburg in 1736. Parks also was a bookseller and printer of books in his own right.[5] Very likely, it was by way of Parks that the Washington and Fairfax families became acquainted with *Cato*. For, in 1758, Washington, then aged only twenty-six, wrote to Sally Fairfax, wife of his best friend, George William Fairfax, "I should think my time more agreable [*sic*] spent believe me, in playing a part in Cato, with the Company you mention, and myself doubly happy in being the Juba to such a Marcia, as you must make" (*Writings* 2: 293). The situation Washington proposes here is very likely one with which he was familiar at first hand; for he, like most literate Early Americans, probably had participated in an evening's entertainment in which each member of "the Company" took a role in the reading of some play. Obviously *Cato* was just such a play.

Litto speculates that Franklin's printing of *Cato* for Parks is evidence that "such private printings [of *Cato*] were probably frequent" (435). We know of at least two public printings of *Cato* before the mid-1760s. Given the fact that British works issued by British presses usually held a monopoly on sales in the colonies during this period and that Early American presses usually printed works by American authors, any American printings of works available from British presses certainly indicate remarkable interest on the part of American readers. Moreover, by the 1760s, *Cato* had been performed virtually up and down the Atlantic seacoast. On September 10, 1736, for example, when Washington was a boy of only four, the students of the College of William and Mary performed *Cato*, this fact recorded by William Parks's own *Virginia Gazette*.[6]

Beginning with one public printing in 1767, however, American printers issued *Cato* at least seven additional times before 1801. This fact indicates an even greater American interest in the play *after* the Stamp Act controversy and suggests, as Litto asserts, that it became a tool of rebellion.[7] It is easy to conclude then that Addison's play fascinated American readers and audiences. Yet we are left with the question "Why were American readers and audiences so fascinated by *Cato*?" Why does Patrick Henry, for example, echo Cato's words, "It is not now a time to talk of aught/ But chains, or conquest; liberty, or death" (Addison, *Cato* II.iv.79–80), in his impassioned declaration, "I know not what course others may take, but, as for me, give me liberty, or give me death!" (Bartlett 465)? Nathan Hale, who very likely had been teaching *Cato* to a "morning class of young ladies" from the New London community, chose to say, immediately before being hanged by the British as a spy, "I only regret that I have but one life to lose for my country" (Bartlett 484). These words clearly resemble those spoken by Cato as this paragon of Roman republicanism greets the corpse of his son Marcus: "What pity is it/ that we can die but once to serve our country!" (IV.iv.81–82)?[8]

It is easy to conclude that Addison's play fascinated American readers and audiences. Yet we are left with the question, "Why were American readers and audiences so fascinated by *Cato*?" Only a close examination of the play can answer this question. But before we can meaningfully examine the play itself, we must know something of its creator.

Joseph Addison, one of the great men of letters of his time, was born on May 1, 1672, into the household of Lancelot Addison. Addison's father was distinguished as a staunch Anglican who opposed the Puritan Interregnum. The son became more liberal than the father—some said practically a pagan, as he grew to embrace such classical values as Vergil's pietas. While an undergraduate at Queen's College, Oxford, he so distinguished himself as a classical scholar that he later was made a Demy at Magdalen College; still later, after taking his master of arts degree in 1693, he published several neo-Latin poems which helped him to secure a fellowship, which he held from 1698 to 1711. In his earliest surviving prose piece of criticism, "Dissertation on the Worthier Roman Poets" (1692), Addison identified Vergil as the greatest among all poets of any time or language. In his *Joseph*

Addison, Otten claims that Addison wished "to be a modern Vergil, the poet who sings the nation's greatness and the greatness of men who lead her in peace and war" (29).

Certainly his highly successful play, *Cato: A Tragedy*, reveals his devotion to Rome's greatest epic poet. According to conventional wisdom, Addison already had completed the first four acts of *Cato* during his 1700–1704 Grand Tour of the Continent. Kelsall records that Addison, after first suggesting to John Hughes, a fellow member of the Kit-Kat Club, poet, and contributor of essays to the *Spectator* and the *Guardian*, that he complete the tragedy, carried out that office himself sometime in 1712, at the urging of Hughes. In a brief dedicatory poem, used among several others to introduce printed versions of *Cato*, Hughes reveals his intimate familiarity with Addison's play. The following passage from this poem, quoted in the 1767 Boston edition of the play, displays Hughes's full grasp of Addison's undertaking:

> Tho' *Cato* shines in Virgil's Epic song,
> Prescribing laws among th' *Elisian* throng:
> Tho' *Lucan's* verse exalted by his name,
> O'er Gods themselves has rais'd the hero's fame;
> The *Roman* stage did ne'er his image see,
> Drawn at full length; a task reserved for thee. (Addison 3)

Hughes here signals two of the most influential portraits of Cato hailing from the ancient world. Indeed, other than Plutarch's portrait in his *Lives*, the two authors named by Hughes (Lucan and Vergil) give the most memorable interpretations of the life of Cato Uticensis. While Lucan devotes the greater part of book IX of his *De bello civili* (65 A.D.; "on the civil war," or *Pharsalia*, as it came to be known) to praise of Cato, it is Vergil's brief tribute to Cato in the *Aeneid* which is most famous. Aeneas had a great shield, fashioned by Vulcan, god of the hearth and husband of Venus (Aeneas's mother), and designed for Aeneas's military campaign against Turnus and his allies. At the center of that shield stood the figure of Cato, giving laws in the shadowy afterlife to those whose earthly lives exemplified pietas. In Vergil's own words: here Vulcan adds, among others residing in the Underworld, "secretosque pios, his dantem iura Catonem" (VIII, 670; the 'pius' [that is, those displaying pietas], set apart [from all others] and Cato giving laws to them). If Aeneas is "hic pietate prior" (XI, 292), or the one (who is) first in pietas, and if Cato is prophesied to be the one who, in the afterlife, gives laws to those already known for their pietas, then surely Cato of Utica was viewed by subsequent generations as the human epitome of Vergil's hero. Even Dante in *La Commedia* later would assign to Cato the venerable position (among pagans, second only to Vergil) of sitting at the entrance to Purgatory, judging who was worthy of entry upon the path leading toward heavenly bliss (*Purgatorio*, Canto I). All these celebrations of Cato's character were well known to both Addison and his colleagues, and to the American colonists, because they comprised a significant part of the tradition of classical and Renaissance learning which helped to shape European civilization.

Yet another indication that Addison found pietas of primary importance may be traced in his two *Spectator* essays on "Chevy-Chase," a fifteenth-century ballad. These prose pieces appeared on May 21 and 25, 1711—within a year or so after Addison completed *Cato*. In the first of these essays, Addison observes, "The greatest modern critics have laid it down as a rule, that an heroic poem should be founded upon some important precept of morality, adapted to the constitution of the country in which the poet writes" (115). Then he proceeds to suggest uncanny parallels between the ballad's English and Scotch warriors and those of the *Aeneid*. Even though Addison never uses the word *pietas* in either essay, the "precept of morality" that he delineates in them certainly is devotion to country, family, and the gods. One of the principal motives for the composition of epics, Addison continues, "hath been to celebrate persons and actions which do honour to their country" (116). These persons and actions Addison then finds in abundance in both the *Aeneid* and the ballad.

In the second *Spectator* essay, Addison extols the "behaviour of those women who had lost their husbands" in the battle described in the ballad, showing the intimacy of family. In the earlier essay, Addison identifies in the ballad parallels to Aeneas's fatherly reaction to the death of Lausus, slain by Aeneas when the son came to the rescue of his father, the impious Mezentius. The infamous impiety of Mezentius, of course, contrasts with Aeneas's own pietas—not the Christianized *piety*. Indeed, the Dryden translation which Addison uses in these two essays refers repeatedly to "the pious prince" Aeneas (117 and 122). As quotations from the Latin text emphasize Aeneas's reverence for the gods, the ballad's quotations underscore the Christian piety of the English and the Scotch. In this manner, Addison subtly argues that the ballad and the *Aeneid* promote the same "precept of morality." In reference to his premise that this moral precept should be "adapted to the constitution of the country in which the poet writes," Addison in these two essays strongly suggests that he would prefer to be able to discover among his countrymen the primary virtue of pietas. As so much of *Cato* deals with what may be called the structure of pietas, one is tempted to view the play's presentation as similar to that of the essays—i.e., as yet another attempt to ascribe pietas to the constitution of his own countrymen. Perhaps because Britain's system of government is based upon the concept of a limited monarchy, which participates measurably in Machiavelli's promotion of virtu as "military prowess"; because of the eighteenth century's general denigration of pietas; and because of the growing association in Britain of pietas almost exclusively with Christian piety, pietas does not become the British "precept of morality," even though this virtue is embraced by Early Americans.

The structure of pietas in *Cato* becomes evident in the very first speech of the play. Portius, eldest son of Cato, tells Marcus, Cato's second son, that this particular dawn heralds a most important day, one "big with the fate/ of Cato and of Rome." "Our father's death," Portius continues, "Would fill up all the guilt of civil war,/ And close the scene of blood." Besides ironically predicting Cato's death—he will make the unhappy discovery which he then must announce—Portius's lines allude to issues of country, in the expression, "the fate . . . of Rome"; and issues of family, as the two brothers discuss their father's fate. Portius, in a somewhat expository fashion, summarizes the status of the civil war: "Already Caesar/ Has ravaged more than half the globe, and sees/ Mankind grown thin by his destructive sword" (I.i.3–8). As Cato and his followers constitute the remnant of Pompey's forces which Caesar has not yet overcome, Cato's death, Portius feels, probably would stop the bloodshed. Thus the son places the onus of peace squarely on the shoulders of Cato. For the first time in the play, both the major dramatic conflict and the source of Cato's tragic dilemma are articulated. It is now up to Cato, who has fought unsuccessfully to preserve the Roman Republic, to concede defeat and capitulate to the dictatorship of Caesar. For the implacable republican, giving in to Caesar is too costly a defeat; indeed, Cato would rather be dead than live to see the Republic destroyed.

While the dramatic conflict revolves about the Republic's destruction and how that destruction affects Cato, Portius's opening speech appears to be calculated as well to introduce the triune integrity of pietas. For Portius closes his brief speech with this exclamation: "Ye gods, what havoc does ambition make/ Among your works!" (I.i.1). Because this outburst makes careful reference to "your works" (that is, to the earthly creations of the "gods"), this expression is much more than a simple oath. To be sure, this exclamation does state the remaining part of pietas and thereby introduces the final element in the concept's triadic structure. But these words operate on at least two additional levels. The reference to "your works," for example, Cato himself will echo in his famous speech on Platonic immortality which opens the fifth act. There he will declare: "If there's a pow'r above us,/ (And that there is all nature cries aloud/ Through all her works) he must delight in virtue" (V.i.15–17). And we can safely conclude that this reference to "virtue" in the singular is to pietas. In any event, Portius's exclamation also serves as an invocation, merely one of many debts this play owes to classical epic, and particularly to Vergil's *Aeneid*.

On the surface, then, Portius's speech which opens the play appears to be serviceable enough dramatically. Close examination, however, reveals that these lines do much more than present the central conflict. They also subtly introduce the triune structure of pietas, predict Cato's famous speech on Platonic immortality (a speech frequently included in American readers of the nineteenth century), and indicate the play's debts to the epic. In Portius's next speech, after Marcus announces his hope that "Some hidden thunder in the stores of heaven" will avenge Caesar's tyranny, we see another example of borrowing from epic. This instance significantly comes from Vergil's *Aeneid* (I.i.22). In reference to Caesar's greatness, which Marcus says Caesar owes "to his country's ruin" (I.i.24), Portius proudly observes:

> Believe me, Marcus, 'tis an impious greatness,
> And mixed with too much horror to be envied:
> How does the luster of our father's actions,
> Through the dark cloud of ills that cover him,
> Break out, and burn with more triumphant brightness!
> His sufferings shine and spread a glory round him. (I.i.25–30)

Here Addison skillfully conflates two borrowings from the *Aeneid*, both highlighting Cato's association with the gods. By calling Caesar's greatness "impious," Addison sets up an antipodal relationship between Cato, who most definitely is pious, and Caesar, viewed as an infidel of sorts. Addison's source here very likely is the impious Mezentius, to whom he already has alluded in his *Spectator* essays on the "Chevy-Chase" ballad. In the *Aeneid*, as in the later play, Mezentius represents the absolute antithesis of Aeneas, who is first in pietas. In the *Aeneid*, again as in the play, this impious character thumbs his nose at the gods as he pursues a destructive course motivated by selfish ambition.

Addison's description of Cato's "triumphant brightness," which breaks out of "the dark cloud" and burns, "spreading a glory round him," surely owes much to Vergil's description, in book I of the *Aeneid*, of how Aeneas, having been enveloped in a protective cloud as he and his faithful friend Achates walk through the streets of Dido's Carthage, suddenly "restitit . . . claraque in luce refulsit,/ os umerosque deo similis" (broke forth [from the cloud] and gleamed brightly in the clear light, similar to a god [with respect to his] face and shoulders; ll. 588–89). In both the play and the epic, Cato and Aeneas diametrically oppose impiety and, because of their close association with the gods, are much favored by them (indeed, Cato later declares, "The gods take care of Cato"; II.ii.61). In fact, both figures are depicted as "super" human beings with nimbuslike auras.

In the play's second scene, Portius tells old Sempronius, a Roman senator who soon will be revealed as a traitor to Cato, that his father "has this morning called together/ To this poor hall his little Roman senate,/ (The leavings of Pharsalia) to consult/ If yet he can oppose the mighty torrent/ That bears down Rome, and all her gods before it" (I.ii.11–15). Caesar, leader of "the mighty torrent," is seen as the destroyer of the most exalted portion of pietas, devotion to the gods. Beyond the repeated crime of Caesar's impiety, however, Addison in these lines alludes to Vergil's portrait of Cato giving laws to the good in Elysium, as depicted on Aeneas's shield. Here Cato is carrying out similar duties, as he assembles his good, loyal followers (with the significant exception of Sempronius). Again Cato's piety toward the gods is emphasized through the text's association with the *Aeneid*.

Perhaps the play's most famous scene is that between Juba and Syphax. Juba, Numidian prince and constant follower of Cato, defines "A Roman soul" for Syphax, a Numidian general and, unbeknownst to Juba, fellow traitor with Sempronius. "A Roman Soul," begins Juba, focuses upon the highest virtues, in order:

> To civilize the rude unpolished world,
> And lay it under the restraint of laws;
> To make man mild, and sociable to man;
> To cultivate the wild licentious savage
> With wisdom, discipline, and lib'ral arts;
> Th' embellishments of life. Virtues like these,
> Make human nature shine, reform the soul,
> And break our fierce barbarians into men. (I.ii.30–38)

As many have pointed out, the first five lines of this passage paraphrase lines 851–53 of book VI of the *Aeneid:* "tu regere imperio populos, Romane, memento/ (hae tibi erunt artes) pacique imponere morem,/ parcere subiectis et debellare superbos" (You *will* [future imperative] remember, Roman, to rule the people [or nation] with masterful sway [those will be your skills], and to establish law with peace, to spare the vanquished and to crush the haughty).

Addison's words, within an American context, clearly and provocatively articulate (even more forcefully than Vergil's Latin) what later would be referred to as the doctrine of Manifest Destiny. These lines also predict all later imperialistic policy within American thought. Perhaps more disturbing, from the standpoint of the early twenty-first century, are the expressions (not in the Latin but in Addison's phraseology) "wild licentious savage" and "break our fierce barbarians into men." Thinking like this resulted in deplorable documents such as that of Spencer Phips regarding the Penobscot people (see fig. 2) and even today permits the relegation to second-class citizenship of persons somehow deemed unacceptable. In Addison's time, this mode of thought led directly toward that energetic Enlightenment attitude which "gave permission" to Europeans to presume that they were the superiors of all non-Europeans; indeed, non-Europeans became seen as "fierce barbarians" who required instruction from their superiors. Only after being instructed could non-Europeans hope to "break . . . into men"—that is, merit identification as human beings, rather than as members of a subhuman species. Such thinking empowered Europeans to launch extensive, devastating military/cultural campaigns to dominate the globe.

No one can doubt that these lines advocate, for their own time, passionate commitment to country. This same scene evokes, too, the other components of pietas. In response to Syphax's bitter attack upon Cato's character, Juba answers that Cato is "Great and majestic [even] in his griefs." "Heavens, with what strength, what steadiness of mind," Juba declares, "He triumphs in the midst of all his sufferings!/ How does he rise against a load of woes,/ And thank the gods that throw the weight upon him!" (ll. 78–82). These lines are perfectly sincere and in fact describe the relationship Cato has with the gods. For, when this paragon of pietas confronts the corpse of his son Marcus, his first words are "Thanks to the gods! my boy has done his duty" (IV.iv.70).

The great value of the family comes to the fore when Syphax urges Juba to "Abandon Cato." Juba exclaims, "Syphax, I should be more than twice an orphan/ By such a loss" (ll. 94–96). Syphax, whose task is to dissuade Juba from his loyalty to Cato, calls up the unhappy memory of Juba's own recently departed father by relating the old man's last words:

> The good old king, at parting, wrung my hand,
> (His eyes brim full of tears) then sighing cried,
> "Prithee be careful of my son!"—His grief
> Swelled up so high he could not utter more. (ll. 111–14)

Even though these words are spoken by a traitor, their auditor is as yet unaware of any treachery. Indeed, Juba reacts most affectingly: "Alas, thy story melts away my soul./ That best of fathers! how shall I discharge/ The gratitude and duty, which I owe him!" (ll. 115–17). The parallel here between the duty and gratitude Cato later accepts from his son Marcus and the duty and gratitude Juba appears ready to offer cannot be accidental. Juba, it appears, would make a fine son for Cato![9]

In addition to convincing his audience that Juba is worthy to inherit Cato's mantle of pietas, Addison gives his audience a bonus of sorts in this scene, which concludes with a portrait of Marcia as a female exemplar of pietas. Perhaps because of this portrait, and the stirring characterization by Juba of a Roman, Noah Webster, at the end of the century, selected this scene for inclusion in his *An American Selection of Lessons in Reading and*

Speaking (1785; with some *forty* more editions before 1801). When challenged by Syphax regarding his love for Cato's daughter Marcia, Juba retorts that, even though Marcia's beauty may fade, "Beauty soon grows familiar to the lover" (145). He has no doubt that Marcia's virtue will endure. "Cato's soul," asserts the lover, "shines out in every thing she acts or speaks" (151–52).

In the following scene, we easily become convinced of the truth of Juba's assertion, for Marcia expresses an almost perfect pietas as she comments on Juba's enthusiasm for Cato's cause:

> My prayers and wishes always shall attend
> The friends of Rome, the glorious cause of virtue,
> And men approved of by the gods and Cato. (V.v.15–17)

Marcia utters piety toward the gods in her first phrase and in her endorsement of "men approved of by the gods and Cato." Her filial duty toward her father gleams in every syllable. Most dramatic, however, is her equation of the pursuit of virtue with Rome itself in the appositive, "the glorious cause of virtue." In Marcia's thinking, republican Rome is, or should be, the secular embodiment of pietas. Knowledge of *Cato,* we are beginning to understand, makes particularly poignant the many comparisons Early Americans were fond of drawing between ancient Rome and the newly formed United States. An example is Phillis Wheatley's "And new born Rome shall give Britannia law."

Significantly, the first act of *Cato* closes with a six-line epic simile, yet another concrete connection between the play and the classical epic:

> So the pure limpid stream, when foul with stains
> Of rushing torrents and descending rains,
> Works itself clear, and as it runs, refines;
> Till by degrees the floating mirror shines,
> Reflects each flower that on the border grows,
> And a new heaven in its fair bosom shows. (vi.82–87)

Robert Otten has remarked of this passage that "Cato, himself, is always the 'floating mirrour'" (150). The possible comparisons hardly stop here, however; for the phrase "rushing torrents" echoes Portius's citation of "the mighty torrent/ That bears down Rome, and all her gods before it" (I.ii.14–15). Clearly, then, the implication is that the "pure limpid stream" of Roman republicanism has been made "foul with stains" of Caesar's "impious [impure] greatness." The "floating mirror," then, is indeed "Cato, himself," but only insofar as his example, which we observe in action for the remainder of the play, becomes part of the reflections cast by each of his disciples, including Portius, Juba, and Marcia, who survive him; for they alone will remain to realize the hope of a return to republican Rome. Augustus's seizing power as emperor and Britain's failure to embrace pietas as its national virtue insured that neither Rome nor Britain would fulfill Addison's aspiration. The American colonies, however, did adopt pietas as their national virtue. That is, "the flower that on the border grows" took root, flourished, and blossomed among the Atlantic colonies.

The first act closes without having provided even a glimpse of Cato, the title character. Yet we feel we know much about him, and we have been encouraged to hold him in highest regard. Toward accomplishing this objective, Addison has marshaled many forces, from history, political theory, the genre of the epic, and particularly Vergil's *Aeneid*. We are not to be disappointed, for in Cato's entrance and first words shine "the floating mirror" of pietas. Lucius, a senator loyal to Cato and the father of Lucia, prepares for Cato's arrival by invoking the gods, "May all the guardian gods of Rome direct him!" (II.i.6). This invocation immediately is followed by Cato's address to his senators, which he begins: "Fathers, we once again are met in council./ Caesar's approach has summoned us together,/ And Rome attends her fate from our resolves" (ll. 7–9). His address sounds the chord of filial piety, and his focus upon the problem of "Caesar's approach" signals what is at stake here for the country. From the very first moment we set eyes on Cato, he exudes pietas.

When pressed by Julius Caesar's emissary, Decius, to yield to Caesar's newly acquired authority as dictator, for example, Cato speaks as a personification of pietas. Decius scornfully plays upon Cato's insistence that his "life is grafted on the fate of Rome" (II.ii.7), demanding, "What is a Roman, that is Caesar's foe?" Cato unhesitatingly responds, "Greater than Caesar; he's a friend to virtue" (l. 41).

Later, in the third act, after the treachery has been discovered, Cato labels the times those of "an impious, bold, offending world," one in which, nevertheless, proper punishment of the offenders (death without torture) serves as an act of piety: "When by just vengeance guilty mortals perish,/ The gods behold their punishment with pleasure,/ And lay th' uplifted thunderbolt aside" (III.v.66 and 68–70). These sentiments cannot have been far from General Washington's mind when he found it necessary to punish desertion with swift finality.

Cato continues by declaring, "Meanwhile we'll [Cato and those loyal to him] sacrifice to liberty," for in doing so they will counter Caesar's impiety and will "piously transmit it [liberty] to your children." Then in the attitude of prayer, Cato continues, "Do thou, great liberty, inspire our souls,/ And make our lives in thy possession happy,/ or our deaths glorious in thy just defence" (III.v.72 and 78–81). Only liberty makes possible the full expression of pietas, then; only the liberty of Republican Rome can insure the happy praxis of devotion to one's gods, family, and country.

While Addison's *Cato* surely is not the sole source of such sentiments, this position came to be all but universally held among American patriots of the Revolutionary War era, provoking such customs as gathering around a designated Liberty Tree to dispute any British infringement upon American freedoms. Any number of pamphlets, broadsides, and poems in celebration of the goddess Liberty voiced these convictions. Cato's "sacrifice to liberty" addressed the American disposition to freedom with increasing force as the century progressed. The central point, however, is that Cato speaks of this "sacrifice to liberty" in terms of pietas. In Cato's view, what is at stake is the unhappy fate of the Roman Republic at the hands of the enemy of pietas, Julius Caesar. He insists unbendingly that his fellow republicans teach their children reverence for this dying mode of government, always with pious observance. Preservation of the Republic, then, in Cato's mind becomes the means by which both the gods and the family may be preserved intact. Precisely this manner of thinking led to the American faith of rebellion.

As Cato's own fate draws nigh, he becomes increasingly preoccupied with the notion of an afterlife. First he reassures his surviving son, Portius, that he (Cato) thinks he (Portius) was "ever good and dutiful" (V.ii.25), that Portius has lived a life exemplary of pietas. Next Cato looks inward and says, "The righteous gods, whom I have sought to please,/ Will succor Cato, and preserve his children" (V.ii.27–28). His last speech of the play also displays this resolute faith in some sort of immortality, this resolve having come about as a result of an earlier monologue, which opens the fifth act and focuses on the soul's immortality. Having just inflicted upon himself the fatal blow, Cato delivers this speech, calling his son to him and expressing concern for the welfare of those friends whom he has urged to escape Caesar's capture: "Portius come near me—are my friends embarked?/ Can any thing be thought of for their service?" (V.iv.80–81).

Finding that his faithful friend, Lucius (Achates), has yet to leave, he exclaims, "O Lucius, art thou here?—Thou art too good!—/ Let this our friendship live between our children" (V.iv.83–84). Having sealed the bond between Portius and Lucia, Lucius's daughter, Cato moves on to Juba and Marcia. He gives permission for the match by recognizing Juba's consummate pietas; to Cato, even though Juba is a Numidian prince, "Whoe'er is brave and virtuous is a Roman" (91). Significantly, in this line, Addison calls up both the old Roman meaning of *virtus* in the adjective *brave;* and pietas, of course, in "virtuous" and in his ascription of Roman identity to Juba. Upon the "vain world," he pronounces the judgment that it has become the "abode of guilt and sorrow"—this phrase redolent of Christianity. The gods, the family, and the country all are present as Cato finally settles upon "ye pow'rs that search/ The heart of man and weigh his inmost thoughts" (V.iv.93 and 96–97). Lucius speaks the eulogy over Cato's body:

> There fled the greatest soul that ever warmed
> A Roman breast. O Cato! O my friend!
> Thy will shall be religiously observed. (V.iv.100–102)

Given the liturgical tone of these lines, it is easy to understand how such emphasis on the religious element of pietas, which pervades the play, could only promote the American faith of rebellion.

Another less obvious auxiliary means of promoting pietas, at least in an American public schooled exclusively in the Adamic myth, is Addison's subtle manipulation of Judaeo-Christian, biblical elements. We have heard Cato identify the secular world as an "abode of guilt and sorrow." Next, in Lucius's eulogy, the phrase, "Thy will shall be . . . ," echoes the language of the Lord's Prayer, "Thy will be done." In the fourth scene of act 4, at the climax of the play, the corpse of Cato's son Marcus signals the play's swift conclusion. Cato cries out over his son's body: "How is the toil of fate, the work of ages,/ The Roman empire fall'n!" (IV.iv.103–4). The expression "How is . . . The Roman empire fall'n" clearly echoes David's lament over Jonathan and Saul: "How are the mighty fallen" (II Sam. 1:19–27). In addition, the rhythm of the equivalent phrases, "the toil of fate, the work of ages,/ The Roman empire," captures the parallelism characteristic of Hebrew poetry.

Another subtle biblical reference occurs in Cato's famous monologue on the immortality of the soul. Cato first observes that, if "a pow'r above us" exists, "he must delight in virtue" (certainly a powerful recommendation of pietas). This comment is followed by one concerning a secular subsistence: "This world was made for Caesar" (V.i.17 and 19). While this statement certainly prepares us for Cato's closing observation that the secular world is "th' abode of guilt and sorrow," more significantly, "This world was made for Caesar" paraphrases Jesus of Nazareth's "Render therefore unto Caesar the things which are Caesar's; and unto God the things that are God's" (Matt. 22:21).

Such biblical echoes surely made this play's powerful classicism more palatable to an American public largely ignorant of classical discourse. The technique here parallels that of Urian Oakes in his pastoral elegy on Thomas Shepard, as well as suggesting that of Cotton Mather in *Magnalia*. Addison, however, like Green in his pastoral elegy on Jonathan Mayhew, makes no apology for blending Adamic and classical modes of discourse.

Having placed Addison's *Cato* in an eighteenth-century American context, we now are prepared to investigate the role that others—that is,

American patriot writers—assigned to this play. As Garry Wills has suggested, the primary role of Cato would be given to Gen. George Washington. Washington himself was well informed regarding pietas, Aeneas, and Cato. He understood how integral these elements were to the task of establishing American identity. As early as 1760, soon after his marriage to Martha Custis, Washington purchased for the centerpiece of his fireplace mantle, "A Groupe of Aeneas carrying his Father out of Troy, with four statues, *viz.* his Father Anchises, his wife Creusa and his son, Ascanius, neatly finisht and bronzed with copper" (Washington, *Writings* 2: 334, n. 6).

This "Groupe of Aeneas" symbolizes what is perhaps the most poignant representation of pietas in the entire *Aeneid*. On his back, Aeneas carries his father, to whom he has entrusted replicas of the Penates and Lares. Aeneas holds the hand of his young son Julus and is flanked by his wife Creusa. As Aeneas departs from the ashes of Troy with his family and his household gods, moreover, he fixes his gaze on the prospects for a new country, which is to become Rome. The choice of this "Groupe" signals Washington's high regard for Vergil's epic hero, as well as Addison's *Cato*. It declares undeniably Washington's knowledge of pietas and his capacity to "read" Addison's play not merely as a paean to the goddess Liberty, but as a celebration of pietas.

Most biographers of George Washington agree with Flexner's judgment that Washington never pursued "any deep study of the classics since he knew no Latin and would, had it been possible, have known less Greek" (*GW: Forge* 241). Yet Cunliffe maintains that Washington's "adolescent notebooks which have survived show that he learned some elementary Latin" (*George Washington* 25). Flexner notes that Washington "attended a school (probably after his father's death)," a fact "made clear by a letter George Mason wrote him in 1756 which referred to a Sergeant Piper as 'my neighbor and your old schoolfellow'" (*GW: Forge* 24). At the death of his father, Washington was already eleven years old. Most biographical studies of Washington hold that the future first president attended school at intervals from the age of seven until he was about fifteen. It was customary for young boys to attend a Petty school (at which only reading in the English Bible and some writing were taught) during their early years. Thus it is very unlikely that Washington still would have been attending a Petty school at age eleven. A youth who had mastered the curriculum of the Petty school typically moved on to a private tutor or a Latin grammar school (where such skills as surveying sometimes were taught). It is likely, then, that Washington first learned about Vergil's Aeneas from his own study of the *Aeneid* in Latin. His later reverence for Aeneas (indicated by the mantlepiece sculpture) and for the virtue of pietas support the conclusion that Washington did know Latin, at least during his adolescent years. Perhaps he was never particularly proficient in Latin; or perhaps in later years he did not have the time, or even the desire, to keep up his knowledge of Latin. In any event, Washington did not earn John Adams's highly influential indictment: "That Washington was not a scholar was certain. That he was too illiterate, unread, unlearned for his station and reputation is equally past dispute" (qtd. in Cunliffe, *George Washington* 25).

Carroll and Meacham, in *The Library at Mount Vernon*, write that Washington "knew elementary Latin" and quote a Latin inscription of Washington's own composition from 1745, when Washington was thirteen (11–12). Interestingly, this inscription appears in a Latin translation of Homer; probably this translation was one of Washington's grammar school texts. To be sure, the majority of titles in Washington's library are practical guides to proper care of horses and other farm animals and books on gardening. Sprinkled throughout these, however, are works of poetry (by such authors as Freneau, Wheatley, and Burns), novels, essays, some plays (several by Shakespeare and, of course, Addison's *Cato*), and several travel books.

Of particular note are the many volumes devoted to classical learning. Among the inventory Augustine Washington, George's father, left on his death on April 12, 1743 (George was only eleven, remember), were three volumes of Vergil, one probably the *Eclogues* and the *Georgics* and the other two the *Aeneid*, as well as "Sundry [other] . . . Latin books" (148). From George's earliest years, then, he had access to classical materials, those most intimately connected to the Aeneas myth. Among other related titles were *Caesar's Commentaries*, Seneca's *Dialogues* and *Moral Epistles*. and Sulla's *Memoirs*. In his 1997 biography of Washington, Willard S. Randall points out that Washington knew and appreciated Seneca's *Moral Epistles* from his early youth. On the ancient world, Washington had Gibbon's *Rise and Fall of the Roman Empire*, a history of ancient Greece, other histories of Rome, multiple copies of Pope's *Iliad* and *Odyssey*, and two copies of William King's *An Historical Account of the Heathen Gods and Heroes*, a popular handbook of classical mythology, probably known by Wheatley.

Carroll and Meacham report that Washington, when in residence at Mount Vernon, usually rose at 4 A.M. and went to the library, where he engaged in correspondence and study for some three hours. In the evening, he returned to the library, spending two additional hours there. Given such a regimen, it is no surprise that Carroll and Meacham conclude, "No room in the mansion is more intimately associated with Washington's life at Mount Vernon than the library" (28).

Washington's career was embraced almost entirely by American classicism. He was ever mindful that, compared to other members of the intellectual elite, he was relatively uneducated. Given that the discourse of this elite body was largely classical, surely Washington applied a significant portion of the five hours a day he spent in the Mount Vernon library to a cultivation of classical knowledge. In light of the evidence presented above, it is almost shocking to find, in a 1988 biography of Washington, this somewhat derisive statement, "To his later chagrin, he never was introduced to the mysteries of Latin or other classical languages" (Ferling 5). As well as calling into question the time-honored notion that he knew no Latin, Washington's choice of a "Groupe" featuring Aeneas merges at some later point with his vision of a new country, to become the United States of America.

Washington was a student of pietas, a fact that helps to explain his interest in having *Cato* performed at Valley Forge on May 11, 1778. This play represented not merely a paean to Liberty, but, for the uninitiated, a virtual guidebook for the assimilation of pietas within American consciousness. In other words, common sense dictates that the idea of liberty, in and of itself, is not a definite stimulus to rebellion. Values—the values of religious commitment, the sanctity of the family, and the necessity for a form of government whose sole function is to insure the unencumbered expression of religious and family values—can constitute a definition of liberty. The preservation (or possession) of such liberty can be seen as worth fighting and even dying for. Such a play as *Cato*, with its intensely religious emphasis, unabashedly promulgates America's faith of rebellion. If Washington were to be identified as the *Cato* of the drama, then it followed that he must become the high priest of this faith of rebellion.

I am not trying to suggest that Washington himself went so far as to "make" himself America's high priest of freedom. While he did wish to define, as vividly as possible, exactly what was at stake for Americans in their struggle for freedom, he left to others the task of shaping the leader of this faith of rebellion. One poet who contributed to this construction was the gifted Annis Boudinot Stockton. In the piece "Addressed to GENERAL WASHINGTON in the year 1777, after the battles of Trenton and Princeton" [*sic*], Stockton compares her subject with Aeneas:

> —Not good Aeneas who his father bore,
> And all his household gods from ruin'd Troy,
> Was more the founder of the Latian realm,
> Than thou the basis of this mighty fabric
> [the new United States],
> Now rising to my view, of arms, of arts;
> The seat of glory in the western world.
> —For thee awaits the patriots shining crown;
> The laurel blooms in blest elysian groves,
> That twin'd by angel hands shall grace thy brow. (Mulford 140)

Recall that Wheatley earlier gave Washington a crown, and particularly note that Stockton is careful to describe all three elements of pietas in meniton-ing Aeneas' father (family), his household gods (the gods), and his role as "founder of the Latian realm" (country). Moreover, Stockton does not miss an opportunity to bring Cato into this exercise in panegyric; for Washington is "high rais'd" (140) even above Rome's noblest republican. Stockton's recent editor, Carla Mulford, postulates that "this poem . . . was perhaps sent to Washington . . . early in 1779" (207). Mulford's assertion is made the more plausible by the knowledge that Stockton and Washington had carried on an extended correspondence following the end of the war during which Stockton sent Washington several more poetic encomia.

Another American writer who helped to shape the image of Washington as high priest of America's faith of rebellion was Jonathan Mitchell Sewall, descendant of Samuel Sewall, the diarist and correspondent of Edward Taylor. Bryan in *George Washington in American Literature*, notes the fame of Sewall's Revolutionary War ballad, "War and Washington" (132), cites sev-eral others of Sewall's adulatory poems about Washington (145, n. 69), and quotes several lines from Sewall's "Epilogue," "which he wrote," observes Bryan, "for a production of Addison's *Cato* in Portsmouth, New Hampshire, in 1778" (144).

More recently, Furtwangler in "Cato at Valley Forge," points out that Sewall wrote "a new epilogue" for the 1778 Portsmouth, New Hampshire, performance, in which "Sewall made the inevitable identification" of Wash-ington with Cato. Then Furtwangler quotes from Sewall's epilogue these salient lines:

> Did Rome's brave senate nobly strive t' oppose
> The mighty torrent of domestic foes?
> And boldly arm the virtuous few, and dare
> The desp'rate perils of unequal war?
> Our senate too, the same bold deed has done,
> And for a Cato, arm'd a Washington. (46–47)

Note the use, in the second line here, of Portius's phrase, "the mighty tor-rent." Portius referred to Caesar's destruction of Roman republicanism, a connection that Furtwangler fails to make. While Bryan cites as his source Sewall's *Miscellaneous Poems* (1801), Furtwangler takes his lines from Sewall's "Epilogue" in the Dunlap Society's *Occasional Addresses* (1890). Neither of these scholars asks the obvious question: Was Sewall's "Epilogue" used in American printings of *Cato* subsequent to 1778?

The answer to this question is surprising and indicates that the Ameri-can public welcomed Sewall's identification of Washington as America's

Cato. Thus the printing history of *Cato* in America after 1778 warrants close attention. To be sure, Washington was identified with numerous classical figures (though seldom with any of the Caesars). For example, Henry Knox's Society of the Cincinnati identified him with Cincinnatus (two centuries before Garry Wills, *Cincinnatus*). Still, the association with Cato appears to have been Washington's most sustained classical identification.[10] And Sewall's "Epilogue" apparently contributed significantly to fostering this identity. Even before the Portsmouth performance of *Cato*, Sewall's "Epilogue" had appeared in print, separate from the play. Entitled "A New Epilogue to Cato" and followed by the phrase "Spoken at a late Performance of that Tragedy," this printing of the poem in a large, brief pamphlet has no date. Housed at the American Antiquarian Society (AAS) of Worcester, Massachusetts, the pamphlet follows the poem with a "newsy" prose piece called "From a late Irish Paper," which has no news after 1776. Thus the American Antiquarian Society has assigned this printing the date of 1777.[11] Given this earlier date, it is entirely possible that the "Epilogue" was known to Washington and his men and that Sewall's poem served as "Epilogue" in the Valley Forge performance of *Cato* on May 11, 1778.

In any case, of the five American printings of Addison's *Cato* from 1779 to 1793, four of them replace the British Dr. Garth's "Epilogue," which offers a commentary on the play's romances, with Sewall's "A New Epilogue." Another significant alteration common to each of these four American printings occurs in Alexander Pope's "Prologue," written for the occasion of Addison's permiere and which followed all British printings of the play and most American printings before 1776. For Pope's line, "And calls forth Roman drops from British eyes" (519), these editions have "And calls forth *Roman* Drops from Freemen's Eyes" (*Cato*, 1779, 1782, 1787, and 1793). All four of these editions replace Garth's "Epilogue" with Sewall's and drop the last ten lines of Pope's "Prologue," which begin "Britains attend" (520). One easily may conclude that these four editions effectively Americanize *Cato*.[12]

While all printed versions of "A New Epilogue" contain variations, one in particular captures our attention. The 1777 version, the earliest apparently printed for broad circulation, contains a rousing, five-line conclusion, obviously designed to encourage enlistment, which none of the other versions includes:

> Rouse up, for shame! Your Brethren slain in War,
> Or groaning now in ignominious bondage,
> Point at their wounds, and chains, and cry aloud
> To BATTLE!—WASHINGTON impatient mourns
> His scanty legions, and demands your aid!

Other portions of the poem are at least as energetically charged. These following lines crystallize the conscious effort of Americans, in Garry Wills's words, "to revive the ancient republic that men were yearning for":

> BRITANNIA's trying sins—and virtues both,
> Perhaps once mark'd the Vandal and the Goth.
> And what now gleams with dawning ray, at home,
> Once blaz'd, in full-orb'd majesty, at ROME!
> (Qtd. from the 1777 version)

Another passage contains an endorsement of Washington even more enthusiastic than we saw in the couplet: "Our senate too, the same bold deed has done,/ And for a Cato, arm'd a Washington!" Here, however, the impassioned poet declares: "In Caesar's days, had such a daring mind" as that of Hannibal, "With Washington's serenity been join'd,/ The Tyrant [Caesar] then had bled—great Cato liv'd,/ And Rome, in all her majesty, surviv'd!" (1777 version). Clearly, Sewall is constructing a superhuman hero, not unlike Addison's Cato. As Garry Wills says of Mason Locke Weems's immensely popular biographical portrait, *Life of Washington* (1800), Sewall "was not recording events, but fashioning an icon" (37).

To an American patriot audience already disposed to find almost exclusively negative notions about the British, Addison's Americanized *Cato* served as an effective—even a seductive—advocate of both anti-British sentiment and what fast were coming to be viewed as distinctively American values. Specifically, these American values would become affirmed by the freedom to enjoy the expression of pietas to the fullest. By now this meant appropriating the virtue not of Vergil's hero Aeneas, but of Addison's English-speaking Cato, personified by America's own George Washington. Indeed, America's Cato was not going to suffer defeat, requiring a sort of noble suicide; according to Sewall and those who helped promulgate the Americanized *Cato*, Washington was certain to triumph over the "British Caesar" (from Sewall's "Epilogue") and bring about a glorious rebirth of Republican Rome. In this manner, *Cato*, as Addison's American play, substantially helped to make it easy for Americans both to *accept* pietas as the American Way, and *deny* that devotion to God, Mother, and Country had origins in classical sources. *Cato* serves as a principal mediator, then, of what now must be called the American Way. Addison's play, Americanized, constituted a nonthreatening, popular, ordinary person's articulation of what certainly is a noble virtue for any culture to take possession of and to maintain. Washington's role as high priest of pietas—known in America as the American Way—simply insured, for an unstable culture during an unstable time, that this virtue would become an ideal toward which his country would aspire.

WASHINGTON AND PIETAS AFTER THE REVOLUTION

The story of Washington and his association with pietas after the Revolution indicates that many Americans, and particularly certain powerful educators, recognized that the appropriated or rearticulated pietas, dramatizing the last act of *translatio cultus*, must remain an identifying characteristic of American culture. Members of the intelligentsia probably reached this decision because they, like Washington, had observed how easily an emphasis on pious devotion to God (the gods), the first rank within the triadic structure of pietas, answered the obvious needs of a general population schooled largely in the myth of Adam. In other words, that societal institution which had promulgated America's faith of rebellion now must be redefined and reoriented in terms of commitment to the product of that faith—the United States of America. Trust in "Providence," which both Washington and Franklin were fond of invoking, was, within the Enlightenment cultures of Voltaire and Gibbon, often denigrated; and, in England and on the Continent, the institutions of family and religion as often were subordinated to the ambitions of empire. Advocacy of God, Mother, and Country, however, suited precisely the necessity that American culture distinguish itself from European cultures.

Given this perceived necessity, pietas, if it was to be embraced by all Americans, had to be severed, insofar as was possible, from its largely secular origins in Vergil's *Aeneid*. The perfect vehicle for disseminating this adapted, now American, virtue was Addison's Americanized play, *Cato*. Campaigns were launched to insure preservation of, and reverence toward, God, Mother, and Country.

Perhaps the first, and certainly the loudest, of these campaigners was Noah Webster. For example, in the "Preface" of his *An American Selection of Lessons in Reading and Speaking* (1789), Webster bluntly states that his purpose is to compel his readers: "to refine and establish our language, to facilitate the acquisition of grammatical knowledge and [to] diffuse the principles of virtue and patriotism." Issued forty times before 1801, *An American Selection* usually was published with a portrait of Washington as frontispiece.

This sort of American educational theorizing certainly was not the exclusive province of Webster. Benjamin Rush, abolitionist, signer of the Declaration of Independence, and physician-founder of the University of Pennsylvania School of Medicine, for example, insists in his "Thoughts Upon the Mode of Education Proper in a Republic" (1786), highly regarded in its time, that the youth (boys) of America must be made to be prejudiced in favor of the American Way of education, as "our strongest prejudices in favor of our country are formed in the first one and twenty years of our lives"

(*Essays on Education* 9). Given such a mandate, continues Rush, "our schools of learning, by producing one general and uniform system of education, will render the mass of the people more homogeneous and thereby fit them more easily for uniform and peaceable government" (10). Rush's tone sounds a somewhat dissonant chord, one that approaches alarm concerning the general lack of order after the end of the Revolution and before the ratification of the Constitution.

In any event, the sentiments expressed here by Rush and Webster became the principles ruling the American system of public education from the late 1780s to the end of the nineteenth century. In today's political discourse, it is a commonplace assumption that the body in power in any culture arranges to perpetuate those values it finds most palatable. Michel Foucault, for example, notes in "L'ordre du discours" that "every educational system is a political means of maintaining or of modifying the appropriation of discourse, with the knowledge and the powers it carries with it" (227). Based upon the texts we have already cited, it is clear that America's newly structured educational system—which would denigrate the traditional classical curriculum in order to valorize what were perceived to be American heroes, American language (a la Webster), and, of course, American thought—was the result of a conscious, calculated plan of action. That plan was "a political means of maintaining or of modifying the appropriation of discourse." This newly appropriated discourse, at least on the surface, consisted almost entirely of tenets of the Adamic myth. The manner and means by which Adam was raised up over Aeneas comprises the subject of chapter 7 of this book.

The title of Webster's reader, significantly, begins with the words *An American Selection*, signaling his conscious motivation. Despite his title, Webster includes among his "American selections" some excerpts from Shakespeare and other British authors, Joseph Addison among them. The selection Webster makes from *Cato*, as noted earlier, is the dialogue between Juba and Syphax, wherein Juba defines a Roman soul, presents the three elements of pietas, and describes Marcia, later to become Juba's betrothed, as a feminine exemplar of pietas. This same selection from *Cato* Webster retains in all forty of the editions of his reader which appeared before 1801. Whether Webster intended it or not, his inclusion of the Juba-Syphax dialogue in *An American Selection* helped to preserve the presence of classical discourse within American public discourse. This dialogue between Juba and Syphax always appears in close proximity to some prose portrait of Washington or some selection from Washington's published speeches. During this same period, one of the editions of the Americanized *Cato*, printed by the famous Isaiah Thomas, was targeted specifically for use in American schools; indeed, on the title page of this edition of 1787, called

"The *Second* Worcester edition" (the first, also printed at Worcester, came out in 1782), is the inscription, "Now published to aid ELOCUTION in the SCHOOLS of the UNITED STATES."

Obviously, the importance of *Cato* to the newly forming American educational system was advanced consciously. Thousands used Webster's *An American Selection* reader, and one known American edition of the play *Cato* was printed expressly for school use. George Washington was known universally as the American Cato, and Addison's play offered a definition of freedom in terms of pietas. This generally positive attitude toward endorsement of *Cato* continued to be promoted well into the nineteenth century.

Addison himself seems to have been appropriated as an honorary American. One striking indication of this popular adoption is the number of printings of Addison's *Works*. In Great Britain, thirteen printings of his *Works* appeared during the nineteenth century, while twenty-two such printings came out in America during the same period; the earliest was published at least by 1811 (a perhaps earlier printing has no date). So it would seem that American interest in Addison during the nineteenth century exceeded that of his own countrymen by a considerable margin.

American interest in republican Rome remained high, though largely in American English texts. The series of history books for children produced by Samuel G. Goodrich, under the pseudonym Peter Parley, proved immensely popular; indeed, their popularity, along with the favorable reception of his other works, such as his series on universal geography, made Goodrich a wealthy man. His best-selling *Parley's Universal History* in two volumes (1838; largely authored by Nathaniel Hawthorne), for example, maintains that, before the death of the Republic, "the Roman people had loved liberty" (1: 282); but that, after Caesar's rise to power, "most of the Romans had now lost the noble spirit which had animated their forefathers" (1: 285). Concerning Washington's survival of General Braddock's defeat during the French and Indian War, this same *Universal History* predictably remarks, "It seems as if he were preserved to be the savior of his country" (2: 259). Another Peter Parley bestseller, the one-volume reference work, *Popular Biography* (1832), with Washington's portrait in the center of the title page, is particularly laudatory in its brief article on Cato Uticensis, holding that his death by suicide "deprived liberty of one of its most ardent friends" (162). Parley's biographical entry on Washington approaches idolatry, claiming for him "great powers of mind," citing "his high sense of duty," and asserting that "history furnishes no parallel to the character of Washington." This portrait closes with this adulatory description: "He stands on an unapproached eminence; distinguished almost beyond humanity for self command, intrepidity, soundness of judgment, rectitude of purpose, and deep ever-active piety" (506).

Setting aside our present-day knowledge of Washington's deism, the attitudes expressed in the Peter Parley books serve as an accurate barometer of the times regarding both republican Rome and Washington. Goodrich, in his *Fourth Reader, For the Use of Schools*, for example, has in "Lesson 103. Religion in the People necessary to good Government," a collection of excerpts from Washington's "Farewell Address" of September 19, 1796. The fact that Goodrich does not identify the source of Washington's remarks suggests that he expects his audience to be so familiar with the "Farewell Address" that no identification is required. This lesson opens: "Of all the dispositions and habits, which lead to political prosperity, religion and morality are indispensable supports" (275). The passage echoes Montesquieu, in *Spirit of the Laws*, on the structure of a republican government. To be sure, both Washington and Montesquieu "echo" the classical thought of such republicans as Cicero and Cato. Washington subsequently observes, in Goodrich's excerpt, "It is substantially true that virtue or morality is a necessary spring of popular government." Speaking of the American adventure in freedom as an experiment, Washington here concludes the "Lesson" by inquiring, "Can it be, that Providence has not connected the permanent felicity of a nation with its virtue?" (276). Given the findings of this chapter, we can safely assume that, by "virtue," Washington has in mind the American Way. These passages all appear in a textbook used in the American public school system, thus bowing to Webster's insistence that American textbooks be devoted to the diffusion of "the principles of virtue and patriotism."

Perhaps surprisingly, texts for schools written in American English were not the exclusive purveyors of Washington as symbol of pietas. Indeed, early in the nineteenth century, at least three editions of a *Latin* biography of Washington, *Georgii Washingtonii Vita*, appeared, "for the use of schools" (viii), each apparently prepared to advance "the principles of virtue and patriotism." The author of this full-length prose study, Francis Glass (1790–1824), was a frontier schoolmaster of Warren County, Ohio. J. N. Reynolds, a former student of Glass, edited the book and published its first edition, perhaps in 1834.[13] In his preface to Glass's *Vita*, Reynolds remarks that, although this work could be used in American universities, the many American English notes seem to have been prepared "for the benefit, principally, of the younger class of readers" (xv). Charles Anthon, perhaps America's best-known classicist during the nineteenth century, asserted, in an 1835 letter to Reynolds, "I cannot help thinking that it will make a very good schoolbook" (225).

No less an American author than Edgar Allan Poe wrote a laudatory review of the 1835 Harper edition of *Vita* for the *Southern Literary Messenger*, then under his editorship. Poe notes in this review of December 1835 that at first he thought the "announcement of this *rara avis*" (Glass, *Georgii*

Washingtonii Vita 243) a hoax but now has come to believe it authentic. Poe's praise of Glass's achievement is most enthusiastic. At one point in the review, he exclaims, "In truth, he was a man after our own heart, and, were we not Alexander, we should have luxuriated in being Glass" (244). These sentiments clearly echo those of the poet who, in "To Helen," wrote "home/ To the glory that was Greece/ And the grandeur that was Rome."

The *Vita* was issued by Harper and Brothers of New York at least three times, in 1835, 1836, and 1842, after which the plates are said to have been destroyed by fire. Like Webster's *An American Selection* and Peter Parley's *Popular Biography*, Glass's *Vita* was published with a portrait of Washington. One of those endorsing the *Vita*, Philip Lindsley, president of the University of Nashville (now the George Peabody College for Teachers), stated, "I have recommended it [the *Vita*] in the newspapers as an excellent textbook for the classical school and academy; and I believe our teachers are about to introduce it accordingly." Lindsley even goes so far as to say, "I will cheerfully do all in my power to extend its circulation in this part of the country" (247).

Given such enthusiastic endorsements and the fact that the *Vita* was printed at least three and possibly four times, we can conclude that Glass's Latin prose biography of Washington was quite popular, at least among the classical academies. Of course, the number of classical schools, in proportion to the population, was greatly reduced from 1800, as the more practical, American-style academies and schools of Rush and Webster proliferated. The persistence of several classical academies into the mid-nineteenth century, nevertheless, helped to insure that the myth of Aeneas persisted as well. And the contribution of Glass's *Washingtonii . . . Vita* to the preservation of classical discourse was substantial.

In a chapter of the *Vita* which emphasizes Washington's character, for example, Glass says of Washington, "Maritus pius, amicus sincerus, dominus benignus, pauperibus succurrere proclivis erat" (He was a devoted husband, a sincere friend, a generous lord, inclined to come to the help of the poor; ll. 14–15 and p. 179). Although the use of the adjective "pius" may, in the context of our consideration of Washington's association with pietas, give us momentary pause, we are not surprised by this respectful assessment of Washington's domestic character. At the bottom of this page, however, Glass's note does arrest our attention. Here he explains that "the adjective *pius* implies, what we usually call affectionate, dutiful, especially towards God, our parents, country, and relatives. It is the epithet by which Virgil invariably designates his hero" (179n.). Lest his readers miss the point, Glass candidly identifies George Washington as the American Aeneas! Throughout the book, Glass refers repeatedly to Vergil, often quoting him and comparing the Latin poet's language or phrasing to his own, in order to clarify his choice of vocabulary. For example, he defines *virtute* (or *virtus* in the nominative) as "'courage,' valor, or military prowess; rarely to be taken in a *moral sense*, in this work" (57, n. 3). To be sure, this delineation of *virtus* closely resembles Machiavelli's *virtu*. *Officium*, however, Glass calls "'moral duty'" (57, n. 4), suggesting that he has an intimate acquaintance with Cicero's *De officiis*. As we saw in the beginning section of this chapter, *officium* is a synonym for pietas. Glass appears to be well aware of this issue and clearly intends for his readers to see Washington as an exemplar of pietas. Still, we must keep in mind that this blatant ascription of the pietas of Vergil's Aeneas to Washington appears in a Latin text designed for advanced students of the ancient language, and not the masses.

While Glass's contribution to promoting Washington as a purveyor of pietas was substantial in the classroom of classical studies, this contribution was not limited to that venue. Indeed, Glass's *Vita* appears to have been translated almost immediately into French, for American students of this modern language. It was translated as *Vie de Washington* by A. N. Girault, formerly of the United States Navy and at the time a pedagogue of French. In the "Preface to the Fourth Edition," dated December 1850, Girault asserts that the standard textbooks of French, "having been written expressly for the youth of France, cannot possess the same attractions for those of this country" that a French version of Glass's *Vita* can offer. The book's publishers, Henry Perkins and Company of Philadelphia, amplify Girault's claim in an address "To Teachers and Students of the French Language," serving the *Vie* as a postscript:

> The Life of Washington would not only furnish the necessary exercise in acquiring the language, but also impress upon their [the students'] minds many facts connected with the history of our *own* country, and with the 'Father of our Country,' of which none of them should be ignorant. (322)

I should add that this last quotation is taken from the twenty-fourth printing of the *Vie*, dated 1850; the book includes a French translation of the Declaration of Independence. Unquestionably, then, Glass's Latin prose *Vita* enjoyed much broader dissemination than he could have imagined; his portrait of Washington as a latter-day Aeneas undoubtedly reached a wide number of the better educated Americans during the middle years of the nineteenth century. Even so, the texts of Glass and Girault obviously did not influence the public at large.

Such texts as those by Webster and Goodrich did address the American public. Their promulgation of pietas was less obvious, of course. Even so, the primary vehicle for the propagation of pietas to the American public during the nineteenth and even the early twentieth centuries was the series of "Eclectic" readers by William Holmes McGuffey (1800–1873). McGuffey, like Noah Webster, was one of the most influential educators in the history of the United States. Largely self-educated, McGuffey rose to become a member of the faculty of Miami University of Ohio, president first of Cincinnati College and then of Ohio University, and finally, for twenty-eight years, holder of the independent chair of mental and moral philosophy at the University of Virginia at Charlottesville. His Eclectic Series of readers began appearing in 1836, with the sixth and final reader of the series coming out in 1857. McGuffey's Series became the standard readers throughout most of country, selling over 125 million copies. New editions of the readers appeared as late as the 1920s, and they still were in use in the Wisconsin school system (at Twin Lakes) in the early 1960s.

McGuffey initiates his program to promote pietas in the *Eclectic Second Reader*. In his portrait of "The Diligent Scholar" (lesson 24), for example, he is careful to insist that "virtue and piety dwell in his heart" (56). For the diligent scholar "has neglected no duty." As a consequence, "happy are the parents of such a son!" (57). Later, in lessons 67 and 68, in a "Story about George Washington," McGuffey treats the character of the nation's first president in a two-part anecdote from Washington's childhood.

This portrait, which recalls "Parson" Weems's *History of the Life, Death, Virtues, and Exploits of George Washington* (1800), tells how George's father planted cabbage seeds in an outline of his son's full name, "George Washington." When the boy later came upon his name spelled by cabbages in a garden, he felt amazement and wonder. Father and son converse for several pages, as the father turns the young boy's amazement at his father's capacity to control and shape a small part of nature toward a reverence for the Author of the entire universe. As George's father says, "God formed all" (184). This incident, McGuffey maintains, caused George never to doubt "that there is a God, the author and proprietor of all things" (185). This clever argument for the existence of God "by design" subtly explicates all three parts of pietas: belief in God, evident throughout the story; respect for parents, suggested by the regard the son shows for the father (this relationship recalls the intense feeling between Aeneas and his father Anchises); and love of country, provoked by this affecting tale from the early life of the man who was to become father of his country.

The Eclectic Third Reader introduces Joseph Addison as the pious author of a paraphrase of Psalm 19 (161). *The Eclectic Fourth Reader*, however, contains three of Addison's essays. Interestingly, these essays do not address the issue of pietas. Several other essays do most poignantly address devotion to God, Mother, and Country. These "essays," or selections from speeches, are by

Daniel Webster, well known as the "Silver-tongued Orator" and senator from Massachusetts; and Wendell Phillips, lifelong associate of the abolitionist leader, William Lloyd Garrison, and an orator of considerable reputation in his own right. In lesson 19, "Washington's Birthday," Webster emphasizes Washington's incomparable "love of country," calls him a "true lover of the virtue of patriotism" (68), and cites "the bright model of Washington's example" (69). The "Evils of Dismemberment," another lesson by Webster, this one on the necessity of preserving the Union, defines all three elements of pietas, all in relation to Washington. Webster calls up family (in his reference to "the people") and religion in the following sentiments: "Let us trust to the virtue and the intelligence of the people, to the efficacy of religious obligation. Let us trust to the influence of Washington's example." Certainly Country comes to the surface in these weighty words: "May the disciples of Washington then see, as we now see, the flag of the Union floating on the top of the capitol" (237).

Wendell Phillips, in "America," initially recalls the mythological Troy and the historical Athens, ending with an impassioned recommendation of pietas. Opening this "essay" with the line, "I appeal to History!" Phillips hails the early examples of Priam's Troy and Demosthenes's Athens, then laments that now—that is, in Phillips's time—both are ruled by the Ottoman Turks. "Who shall say, then, contemplating the past, that England, proud and potent as she appears, may not, one day, be what Athens is, and the young America yet soar to be what Athens was!" (McGuffey 213–14). The parallel here between the sentiments of the eighteenth-century poems of literary independence and those of Phillips is striking. Recall that George Webb, in an almanac for 1730, claimed that Philadelphia soon would "be the Athens of Mankind." In 1728, John Perkins was just as certain that "*New England's* sons, e'erwhile of barb'rous name," were now becoming "A match for *Albion*, or the *Graecian* fame." Phillips presents these aspirations during that same period which saw the publication of Emerson's *The American Scholar* (delivered at Harvard on August 31, 1837).

In the next several lines, Phillips invokes the name of "WASHINGTON" and remarks, "The boon of Providence to the human race, his fame is eternity, and his residence creation." After this stirring assignment of divinity to Washington, Phillips asserts, "In the production of Washington, it does really appear as if Nature was endeavoring to improve upon herself, and that all the virtues of the ancient world were but so many studies preparatory to the patriot of the new" (McGuffey 214). In addition to reminding us of the collection of Roman virtues that Cunliffe assigns to Washington, Phillips's rhetoric echoes these lines from Sewall's "Epilogue to Cato": "In Caesar's days had such a daring mind/ With Washington's serenity been join'd/ The tyrant then had bled, great Cato liv'd,/ And Rome in all her majesty surviv'd." Of course, the majesty which Sewall longs for is that of republican Rome. Both Sewall and Phillips make a point of asserting that Washington constitutes not an imitation of Cato or of Roman virtues, but an improvement upon both. As an embodiment of Roman virtue, Washington assumes not the mantle of Cato, the historical figure, then, but the mantle of Aeneas, Vergil's ideal hero. Having evoked God in Washington's divinity and Country in his patriotism, Phillips cites Washington's fealty to Family, noting that he resigned the "crown" of the presidency because he "preferred the retirement of domestic life" (McGuffey 215).

A final exhortation to adopt pietas appears in the final lesson of McGuffey's *Fourth Reader*, another lesson entitled "America." This "America," however, is the "National Hymn" (as it was then called), set to music in *Mason's Sacred Harp*, which McGuffey advertises as "a new collection of hymn tunes, sacred songs and anthems." Of course, I am referring to "My Country 'Tis of Thee," whose last stanza urges the practice of pietas:

> Our fathers' God! to thee,
> Author of liberty!
> To thee we sing;
> Long may our land be bright,
> With freedom's holy light,
> Protect us by thy might,
> Great God, our King! (422)

In terms resembling the rhetoric of Addison's *Cato*, God, Father, and Country resonate throughout this stanza, in such phrases as "Our fathers' God," "Author of liberty," "our land," and "Great God, our King!" The Revolutionary War's faith of rebellion sounds in the phrase "freedom's holy light." To be sure, this stanza—indeed, the entire song—emphasizes the Deity, but so does each of McGuffey's readers.

McGuffey's *Fifth Reader* continues to endorse pietas, in such "Lessons" as William Ellery Channing's "Religion the Only Basis of Society," reinforcing earlier lessons concerning Washington's attitude toward religion in a republic; and Donald Grant Mitchell's "A Home Scene," which celebrates the family. Even so, this text does not particularly promote Washington as symbol of pietas, nor does it make any mention of Addison. It is probable that this *Fifth Reader* was compiled by McGuffey's brother, Alexander Hamilton McGuffey.

William Holmes McGuffey himself compiled the *Sixth Reader* (1857), which renews the pattern of integrating Addison and employing Washington as symbol of pietas. Including Addison's essay, "Discontent, an Allegory," the *Sixth Reader* prefaces this lesson 81 with a brief prose portrait of Addison, in which the British author is called author of the famous *Cato*, a "brilliant essayist and poet" who was "genial and loveable; his moral character was above reproach" (295). Whether or not this assessment is accurate is beside the point here, for Addison himself is promoted as a moral exemplar, an individual of apparently limitless creativity.

Toward the end of the *Sixth Reader*, this adulatory portrait of Addison is continued, in an appreciation of him by William Makepeace Thackeray. Here Thackeray appears disposed to make of Addison a sort of secular priest of religious consciousness. Thackeray concludes this affectionate portrait by declaring that Addison's was "a life prosperous and beautiful—a calm death—an immense fame and affection afterwards for his happy and spotless name" (438). McGuffey follows this nomination of Addison for sainthood with a speech from *Cato* on immortality of the soul (V.i.1–31). In this excerpt, Cato defines pietas—as he does in practically all his speeches in the play. As we saw earlier, this speech declares, "This world was made for Caesar," Cato echoing Jesus's pronouncement, "Render therefore unto Caesar the things which are Caesar's; and unto God the things that are God's" (Matt. 22:21). Despite the obvious Platonism of this speech, an audience of American schoolchildren, trained not in the tenets of Plato but in the rhetoric of the King James Bible, could be expected to hear the New Testament in this line and so find Cato almost Christian in his hope for immortality. At the same time, the American Way is endorsed.

This lesson on the immortality of the soul McGuffey follows with two "essays" on Washington. Jared Sparks's "Character of Washington" speaks of our first president as a symbol of pietas, employing such statements as "He uniformly ascribed his successes to the beneficent agency of the Supreme Being." Certainly accurate here, Sparks was the scholar who first took on the monumental task of assembling and editing the entirety of Washington's papers. Sparks also calls Washington, the man he knew so well, "charitable and humane," "liberal to the poor, and kind to those in distress," and "a tender and affectionate" husband and patriarch (442). These words echo Glass's *Vita* almost exactly. Finally, Sparks emphasizes Washington's great "love of his country," which was, Sparks insists, "invested with the sacred obligation of a duty" (443). So we observe all parts of pietas firmly extolled.

Gen. Henry Lee's "Eulogy on Washington" is no less a portrait of pietas. He utters his famous assessment: "First in war, first in peace, and first in the hearts of his countrymen, he was second to none in humble and endearing scenes of private life." Having affirmed Washington's devotion to his country and to his family, Lee comments on his spiritual prowess: "Pious, just, humane, temperate, sincere, uniform, dignified, and commanding, his example was edifying to all around him, as were the effects of that example lasting" (445).

Obviously McGuffey intends that those "effects" of Washington's pietas will remain "lasting" on the character of American schoolchildren.

Despite the comments above, McGuffey's Eclectic School Series can and should be read as almost wholly devoted to the advancement of the Adamic myth; one might even go so far as to describe its treatment of the Adamic myth as decidedly biased in the direction of New Testament Christianity. While it has not suited our purposes here to demonstrate the undeniable presence of the Adamic myth in McGuffey's readers, we nevertheless have observed that the myth of Aeneas, stripped almost completely of its secular, classical origins, in fact persists, though clad in Washingtonian dress. Unwittingly, in his peculiar recommendation of pietas, McGuffey displays a clear case of acceptance and denial. Unquestionably, devotion to God, Mother, and Country characterizes the American character at its innermost core; yet the "American Hymn," in particular, shows that no classical reference is necessary to establish either the origins of the American Way or its definition. One only need recall the example of Addison's Cato or, especially, Washington.

Such vehicles as Addison's *Cato*, Webster's *An American Selection*, Benjamin Rush's educational theoretics, Samuel G. Goodrich's numerous best-selling children's books, Francis Glass's *Georgii Washingtonii Vita*, and William Holmes McGuffey's Eclectic School Series all actively saw to it that the vision of George Washington as the American Aeneas would be maintained after the Revolutionary War. Perhaps the central motive for the construction and preservation of this icon, in the words of Garry Wills, *Cincinnatus*, had to do with Washington as "the embodiment of stability within a revolution, speaking for fixed things in a period of flux" (xxi). After the Revolution, Washington continued to serve this stabilizing function. Perhaps more important, in post-Revolutionary times, his example defined both the American character and the American ideal. Surely Washington, as the American Aeneas, always represented both the "thing itself" (the physical realization of pietas) and the promise that all should strive to achieve.

Vergilian Moment versus Machiavellian Moment

Patriot Americans such as Jonathan Mitchell Sewall and Wendell Phillips argued that Washington's character and virtues represented an improvement upon the character of Cato and the virtues of Rome. Nor did American culture slavishly imitate that of ancient republican Rome. In the American struggle toward cultural identity, the task of "New-born Rome" was not to duplicate the past but to improve upon it. The checks and balances of a neo-Harringtonian bicameral Congress, for example, signaled the construction of a dynamic and improved Roman republicanism, as did the creation of a judiciary which could check excesses of Congress, the Executive, or even of the People. Whether or not such improvements actually have been realized is not the issue here; the crucial point is that this ideal (a dynamic and improved Roman republicanism) appears to have animated not only American society and politics, but also the behavior of America's indispensable leader, George Washington. I am not trying to suggest that this classical mode of discourse, manifested here in Cato and in Vergilian pietas, ever at any time operated to the exclusion of any other influence. The myth of Aeneas, however, did exercise a formidable and even a determinative influence—an influence that has been obscured by the hegemonic Adamic myth. So strong was the endorsement of this improved and dynamic Roman republicanism, as demonstrated in the character and actions of Washington (as these were portrayed within American schoolbooks from Webster through McGuffey), that the influence of classicism upon Early America is virtually incontestable.

At the same time, certain other subordinate principles, or subordinate premises, must be admitted to our understanding of the dynamics of this cultural process, and these are equally incontestable. We must recall, for example, that American classicism, which shaped the career of George Washington and indeed the course of eighteenth-century America, was imbued with the notion of independence long before the 1760s, often identified as the decade when the first glimmerings of independence arose. In the attempt to revive the Roman republic, all who looked back on Cicero's and Cato's Rome realized full well that the old Rome could not, and in fact must not, be imitated. Rather, it had to be re-visioned in terms of peculiarly American necessities. At the same time, America's intellectual elite was shaping new-born Rome. Of this elite, those who were politically aware knew that the major imperative was to involve *all* patriot Americans in the American bid for freedom. The mode of discourse available to all Americans was the myth of Adam; therefore, the Adamic myth must be valorized. The faith of rebellion, which sustained the Revolution and marked the beginning of the rise of Adamic discourse in American thought and action (because this faith of rebellion was defined in terms of liberty and pietas/God), would not, in and of itself, nourish America after the war. Following the Revolution, all Americans needed, urgently, to define themselves as not European and particularly as not British. A process of acceptance and denial—accepting certain classical values, especially pietas as the American Way; and then immediately denying that these values had any classical origins—would instill cultural cohesiveness.

From the early 1720s (the period of Trenchard and Gordon's *Cato's Letters*, which indicted the British aristocracy and monarchy as corrupt), this determination to separate the idea of "Americanness" from that of "Britishness" reflected a conviction that both British society and British government were corrupt. The learned, often fascinating, and highly influential work by J. G. A. Pocock, *Machiavellian Moment*, maintains that "modern and effective government had transplanted to America the dread of modernity itself, of which the threat to virtue by corruption was the contemporary ideological expression" (509). Pocock's argument is persuasive and even seductive in its subtlety. The moment of Machiavellianism which Pocock describes occurs at that point in time, after the beginning of the Renaissance, when a people (any people of the West) confronted the idea of republican government; this confrontation provoked an attempt by those in power to bring about a renewal of virtue, or (to adopt Pocock's Italian) a *rinnovazione*. When—not if—this attempt to enact a *rinnovazione* inevitably encountered corruption, then the Machiavellian moment occurred.

While the major portion of Pocock's study explores "how Machiavelli and his contemporaries pursued the intimations of these words," *virtue* and *corruption* (viii), *The Machiavellian Moment* concludes by focusing on how these ideas of virtue and corruption become transplanted to America. This transplantation comes about, Pocock maintains, by way of James Harrington's "synthesis of civic humanist thought with English political and social awareness, and of Machiavelli's theory of arms with a common-law understanding of the importance of freehold property" (Pocock viii). Pocock is studious to point out that the Puritan jeremiad—

> that most American of all rhetorical modes—was merged with the language of classical republican theory to the point where one can almost speak of an apocalyptic Machiavellism; and this too heightened the tendency to see that moment at which corruption threatened America as one of unique and universal crisis. (513)

I do not quarrel with the general premises of Pocock's argument. Certainly, as we saw in the pamphlet by the "Plain Politician," Americans were thoroughly familiar with the thought of both Machiavelli and Harrington. Even so, acknowledging the dominance of classical discourse during America's Revolutionary era calls into question the precise function, during this period, of the Puritan jeremiad, a clear indication of Adamic discourse. Moreover, our consideration of Washington's role in promoting not Machiavellian virtu but Vergilian pietas demands that Pocock's analysis of the applicability of Florentine thought, or even of British republican thought, to the American Revolutionary era be refined and finally modified. The remainder of this chapter, therefore, is devoted to the thesis that what was transplanted to America was not a "dread of modernity" but a rejection of it. This rejection resulted from the conscious choice of the virtue of pietas over Machiavellian virtu, and the equally conscious identification of corruption as the interference of a society and a political system perceived by Americans to be morally decadent.

Pocock holds that the problem is the "presentation" or appearance "of the republic and the citizen's participation in it," or how citizens define themselves in relation to the newly constructed republic (or the republic in process of construction); and the "'moment' is defined as that in which they [the citizens] confronted the problem grown crucial" (vii–viii). If these things are so, for Americans, becoming Americans, then, the problem more specifically is to define themselves in terms of what they are (or what their republic in process is) *not* to be. Such a definition had been evolving in America at least from the 1720s (perhaps even from the 1670s, the era of King Philip's War), and the moment for Americans must be defined as that in which patriot Americans confronted corruption and their destiny in the Revolutionary War. With reference to *Cato*, what is *not* American is Caesar or any hint of a dictator or monarch. What *is* American is, first, Cato, the reluctant leader who ever responds to what he perceives to be his duty; and, second, the republican mode of government, which stands or falls on the basis of its representatives' virtue. In "Honesty Shewed to be True Policy" for example, the "Plain Politician" many times called for the selection of delegates to Congress from among only "the most virtuous men."

According to Washington and other patriot Americans, the corruption against which they marshaled their efforts was manifested by British interference in American affairs. The British failure to accept Americans as equals led to a presumption of superiority that inevitably fostered British exploitation of American resources in human beings (e.g., the use and abuse of the American militia during the French and Indian War[14]), goods, and property. This problem of British interference devolved into the question of how to counter or terminate that interference. When military opposition finally seemed the only acceptable solution, this opposition effort demanded a simple, clearly focused motivation. Thus a faith of rebellion was "preached" by such "evangels" as Tom Paine, Patrick Henry, and Josiah Quincy. In this effort, the figure of Washington quickly assumed the central position as icon. During the war, and especially immediately after the winning of the war, the "problem grown crucial" was the definition of the American self, in order to establish cultural cohesiveness. This process, too, was one of negation—a process of defining what American culture was not. Certainly America was not European and not British. America, therefore, must be a republic, but it must not have a monarch, with all the attendant baggage of a nobility and preferments.

Alan Rogers asserts in *Empire and Liberty* that it "was common knowledge that British society consisted of three social orders, of which each would be best served by a different form of government: royalty, whose natural form of government was monarchy; the nobility, whose natural form was aristocracy; [and] the commons or people, whose form was democracy." Rogers concludes, "This 'mixed constitution' created a framework that insured stability and the preservation of the rights of all men" (14–15). America, nevertheless, exhibited "only two socioconstitutional elements—the Crown and the people" (15).

By the end of the Revolution, of course, the people had become the People. Moreover, out of the first Congress of the Colonies, or Continental Congress, ironically called by the Crown in Albany, New York, in 1754, something new and distinctly American emerged. "The new constitution," known as the Albany Plan of Union, "had to be ratified by the people," observes Rogers (15–16). Rogers explains what he means by this observation when he proposes that "the very fact that the delegates decided to send the new constitution to the lower houses of assembly implies they believed the people had the right to construct a government" (16). So, as early as 1754, colonial Americans were well on their way to becoming the People.

Unless the mode of government were to be altered in some drastic, unforeseen manner, the concept of the People, in whom the power of government at least ostensibly lay, must continue to be nurtured; that is, the republican form of government, which already was being endorsed by the people and which was recognized as distinctly not British, must continue to foster an illusion of democracy, or equality for all. It follows, then, that the reins of government ultimately must reside in the hands of the People. Because it is not practical for all the People to participate in the conduct of the affairs of so large a state as the United States of America, only a representative government will serve the needs of all the People. The key distinction here between what was American and what was not lies in America's concept of the People. For the People, the mode of universal discourse was the Adamic myth, but the exercise of power actually lay in the hands of an intellectual elite which in a way "replaced" both European/British royalty and nobility, and whose mode of discourse was the myth of Aeneas, or classicism. This delineation of the American interpretation of government does not match the situation of government in Europe, and this palpable difference signals the problem with insisting upon a formative transfer to America of the characteristics which describe the Machiavellian moment in Europe and Great Britain.

Early on in *The Machiavellian Moment*, Pocock defines virtue, quite properly within a European context, in terms of Greek *arete* and Latin *virtus*. While he does not see *virtus* in relation to its original meaning of courage, he interprets both *arete*, or nobility of mind and action (as in Homer's Achilles), and *virtus* as "first, the power by which an individual or group acted effectively in a civic context; next, the essential property which made a personality or element what it was; [and] third, the moral goodness which made a man in city or cosmos what he ought to be" (37). Undoubtedly civic virtue long has been celebrated in colonial America, even as early as Urian Oakes's portrait of Thomas Shepard. But, as we have seen, this civic virtue was extolled as an element of pietas, not of Machiavelli's virtue. Moreover, the largely secular applications of the term *virtue*, as offered by Pocock, fail to address, in an American context, the issues of family or God, both of which were of vital concern to Addison's Cato, to Washington, and to the developing American self. For that matter, Americans came to define Liberty itself according to the capacity to realize the values of religion, family, and patriotism. Consequently, the term *virtu* is inappropriate, or at the very least inadequate, to describe American preoccupation with the concept of virtue.

In a discussion entitled "The Americanization of Virtue," Pocock asserts that, as the Revolution drew nigh, Great Britain became perceived as a body which threatened "corruption emanating from a source now alien, on which Americans had formerly believed themselves securely dependent" (507). Early in the eighteenth century, poetic declarations of literary independence became so frequent in the colonies that the literary independence poem emerged as a genre. That genre allowed Americans to begin to define themselves as separate from, and not dependent upon, Britain. This attitude of independence carried over into the areas of politics and economics, as pamphlets criticizing British policy toward the colonies began to appear, and as booksellers such as William Parks printed their own editions of *Cato*. The illustrations given here could be multiplied many times over. After the beginning of the eighteenth century, then, American colonists were no longer "securely dependent" on British sociopolitical or literary sources.

Later in the "Americanization of Virtue" section, Pocock correctly declares: "The crucial revision was that of the concept of the people." But then he errs in asserting, "Instead of being differentiated into diversely qualified and functioning groups, the people [after the Revolution] was left in so monistic a condition that it mattered little what characteristics it was thought of as possessing" (517). Yet, as we have seen, to such members of the intelligentsia as Benjamin Franklin, Samuel Goodrich, Benjamin Rush, Noah Webster, and William McGuffey, it mattered a great deal what the People thought, simply because all knew that thought could and would be translated into action.

Immediately after the Revolution, for example, Benjamin Rush called for a uniform system of education, founded on virtue, which would "render the mass of the people more homogeneous and thereby fit them more easily for uniform and peaceable government." While the concept of the People may have been a monistic one, the nature of that monism appears to have come under the control of an emerging American system of education. This system of education was shaped in large part by an acceptance of the power of pietas as the American Way, such that the gods, family, and country easily became transformed in American schoolbooks into God, Mother, and Country.

What sort of mechanism enabled or empowered this monistic concept of the People? Only a devalorization of the myth of Aeneas and a raising up of the myth of Adam can account fully for this cultural phenomenon. The details and intricacies of this dynamic radical shift in discourse comprise the entirety of chapter 7 below, so here let us observe only that this radical shift resulted from the self-conscious calculations of America's intellectual elite and that this radical shift was understood by that same group as absolutely necessary to achieve something akin to cultural cohesion.

Even if, as Pocock believes, "the people were an undifferentiated mass, possessed of infinitely diverse qualities" (517), that mass could become united as a single body by the versatile virtue, pietas. As has been demonstrated, pietas can identify civic virtue as residing in a totally secular domain, while at the same time it points to the transcendent realm of the idea of God. So when Pocock insists, "Virtue can develop only in time, but is always threatened with corruption by time" (527), he does not describe the operation of pietas. Rather, he characterizes the operation of Machiavellian virtu. If the primary virtue to which Americans subscribe is pietas and not the European virtu, then it follows that Americans must be taught the value of the American Way. This triadic structure is vulnerable to the corruption of time only in its elements of country and family, both of which are confined to the realm of time. Each individual's idea of God, however, resides in the relative world of time only insofar as that individual addresses her or his idea of God in some form of orison or contemplation. The idea of God, nevertheless, finally does not exist fully in the relative, but rather resides in some sort of Boethian sempiternity. Pietas modified by Adamicism, then, constitutes a peculiarly American institution, one that *can* move both within and outside time; that is, this institution is both secular and sempiternal. This institution accounts for the strength of the American self, which approaches an almost mystical quality. This self made possible the transition from the faith of rebellion to cultural cohesiveness and the "faith" of the American Way.

Pocock's attractive Italian word, *rinnovazione*, a renewal of virtue, also proves inappropriate to capture the process which shaped the republican virtue of America. Discovering this term, used in the Aristotelian sense of "the primacy of spirit and form over matter," in the letters of Savonarola as early as 1494 (107), Pocock points out that its use later in the work of Machiavelli became associated with the world of materiality. The Latin, *renovatio,* from which *rinnovazione* derives, has two denotative meanings: "the act or process of renewing" and "the renewal of a debt, i.e., with interest added to principal and amounting to compound interest" *(Oxford Latin Dictionary).* In the sense in which Pocock applies *rinnovazione* to the European development of republican thought, this term carries precisely the meaning both he and Machiavelli require of it. Because of this term's intimate association with materiality, the American renewal of virtue—wherein the idea of virtue must, at least for a time, de-emphasize the corrupting influence of commerce as evidenced by British decadence—demands a different and more exact term. In order to establish a degree of distance from Pocock's (and Machiavelli's) emphasis on the material world, we need an expression which captures the notion of a restoration of virtue but which also embraces the desire to improve upon that renewal. The Latin *instauratio emendata,* an improved or corrected renewal or restoration, serves our purposes well. Because it lacks any commercial connotations, this phrase addresses the American emphasis upon virtue as pietas; indeed, explicit within the American modification of this virtue by the Adamic myth, in which the gods have become subsumed in the idea of God, is a restoration which has undergone its own "correction." In addition, efforts to ascribe the virtue of pietas to an improved Roman republic are described precisely in the phrase *instauratio emendata,* an improved restoration.

Now we can meaningfully delineate the idea of an American self in terms of a blending of the myths of Adam and Aeneas. Avoiding Cotton Mather's sense of a divided loyalty (divided between his religious commitment to Christianity and his obvious delight in classical learning), the combination of Adam and Aeneas, as determined by the political and social imperatives of America's Revolutionary times, yields an American self and an idea of American government, both of whose origins are largely classical. Almost overnight, however, their classical origins are denied by the immediate promotion of the Adamic myth. This promotion was the conscious calculation of an American intelligentsia that understood that the concept of the People demanded an appeal to the universal Adamic discourse, in preference to the Vergilian discourse, the province of that same intelligentsia. In 1783, as peace with Great Britain was imminent, George Washington issued his famous "Circular Address to the Governors of the Thirteen States." Leading the way toward this necessary acceptance and denial pattern, he alerted the country that "the moment to establish or ruin" the "national Character [of The People] forever" had arrived (*George Washington: A Collection* 241).

While insisting that the newly formed United States of America must, in order to secure the regard of foreign nations, affirm to the world "our united Character as an Empire" (243), Washington closes his "Address" with the "earnest prayer":

> that God would have you and the State over which you preside, in his holy protection, that he would incline the hearts of the Citizens to cultivate a spirit of subordination and obedience to Government, to entertain a brotherly affection and love for one another, for their fellow Citizens of the United States at large, and particularly for their brethren who have served in the Field. (249)

Washington here speaks the language of the People. With the recovery of Vergilian discourse, we readily recognize that devotion to the gods now becomes "that God" in whose "holy protection" Washington would leave the states of the new nation, that devotion to country Washington rearticulates as "subordination and obedience to Government" displayed in "the hearts of the Citizens," and that devotion to family he urges as "a brotherly affection and love for one another" by all "Citizens of the United States at large," establishing a motivation for viewing the entire nation as a communal family. All these attitudes are calculated to promulgate cultural cohesion on a national scale and in terms of Vergil's (and Cato's) pietas. Washington says nothing here that is incompatible with the universal mode of discourse, the People's Adamic myth. At this juncture, the renewal of pietas, "corrected" for an American public schooled in the myth of Adam, has been instituted; and the national character has been articulated, not as a Machiavellian *rinnovazione*, but as a Vergilian *instauratio emendata*.

In its availability to all persons, what Washington advances here is reminiscent of democracy and is even egalitarian. Washington recommends his revision of Vergilian pietas as the national "Character" of all Americans, irrespective of social class. Pietas offered as an *instauratio emendata*, or an "improved" and corrected restoration of virtue, therefore, helps to promote the desired democratic spirit.

This democratic spirit, fostered by Washington's revisionist pietas (to become, of course, the American Way), collides with Pocock's judgment that American thought stumbled into the modern world "in a pre-modern and pre-industrial form," having "never taken the shape of a rigorous Hegelian or Marxian commitment to a dialectic of historical conflict" (549). According to Pocock, "American metahistory has remained the rhetoric of a spatial escape and return, and has never been that of a dialectical process" (550).

Recovery of the Adam and Aeneas dialectic, which is neither Marxist nor finally Hegelian, enables students of American history to recognize that, contrary to Pocock's claims, America has been and continues to be responsive to the dynamics of a rigorous paradeictic (model used as argument) which does not, as Marxist thought does, address politics as the class struggle. In "Theory and the American Founding," John Patrick Diggins, reading de Tocqueville's *Democracy in America*, states this problematical situation succinctly when he writes:

> Having skipped the feudal stage of history, Americans were "born free." With no real aristocracy to denigrate labor and resist the "virtuous materialism" of an emergent capitalism, Americans enjoyed "equality of condition," and they identified wealth not with privilege but with work and natural right. [Recall de Crèvecoeur's earlier emphasis on "industry."] Once property is seen as compatible with democracy, all expectations of class warfare become the fallacy of pure theory and hence . . . [none of] Marx's hopes will come to pass in America. (21)

Diggins advises, as does Tocqueville, that, in order to understand America, "one must shift attention from its political institutions to its beliefs, sentiments, mores, and 'habits of the heart'" (21). Such an understanding motivates Washington's recommendation in 1783 that the governors of the thirteen states concentrate immediately on shaping the American "Character" in terms of a revised pietas which provides a vivid demonstration of Diggins's analysis.

Even if one believes that the absence of a class struggle in America may well be illusory, one must acknowledge that all Americans, to a greater or less degree, subscribe to the concept of "We the People." Thereby, at the very least, they consent to the "illusion" of equality. Therefore, the idea of the American self is not readily conducive to the Marxist notion of politics as class struggle, because it resists incorporation into Marxist conceptions of economics and dialectical materialism. Contrary to Pocock's view that "American metahistory has remained the rhetoric of a spatial escape and return, and has never been that of a dialectical process," American metahistory has not depended solely upon a Jeremiah Johnson–style escape into an ever-expanding wilderness, only to return again to "civilization" as that encroaching "civilization" tames that wilderness. Indeed, American metahistory has *always* been determined by the dynamics of the Adam and Aeneas dialectic. Expansion, while it was feasible, was useful, but it was not determinative of the American self. Men such as Washington and other members of the American Revolutionary intelligentsia self-consciously founded the American self, not in terms of the carefully crafted class structure of Britain and the Continent, but in terms of a subtle combination of the Adam and Aeneas dialectic.

This combination utilized the strong supports of each strand in the dialectic—the Adamic, transcendental belief in deity became blended with the spiritual, enately familial, and the sociopolitical agencies of triadic pietas. The result was an American self that would take sustenance from its moral and religious dimension first, before it would exercise its political awareness.

In his "Farewell Address," delivered at the conclusion of his eight-year presidency, Washington admonished his countrymen that the preservation of the Constitution, with its built-in mechanisms for change, must remain "sacredly obligatory upon all" (*Writings* 518). Thus Washington ascribed religious proportions to the concept of Americanness. The president also declared, "'Tis substantially true, that virtue or morality is a necessary spring of popular government" (521). Herein Washington incorporates into American consciousness the American Way, or pietas revised, as the American national moral identity. Why? Because, as Washington continues, "Religion and morality are [the] . . . firmest props of the duties of Men and citizens" (521). Just as earlier Washington (and many others) had encouraged the faith of rebellion, Washington here transforms that faith of rebellion into the perdurable faith of the American.

Of course, Washington embodied the cynosure of this new, identifying "faith," whose origins are largely classical. Only after a reclamation of the myth of Aeneas, so thoroughly obscured by the hegemonic Adamic myth, does the heavily classical American self begin to reemerge. Pocock, who was unaware of the classical origins of the American self, is not to be faulted for arguing that the American republic was "a concept derived from Renaissance humanism," which "was the true heir of the covenant and the dread of corruption, the true heir of the jeremiad" (545). Reclamation of the American Aeneas enables us to understand that, while the American idea of a republic does owe a debt to "Renaissance humanism," American republicanism also owes much (perhaps more) to Roman republicanism as taught by Cicero, Cato, Vergil, and Addison—not Roman republicanism filtered through Renaissance humanism. Of course, Puritan covenantal ideas of a secular existence, and the ominous admonishment contained in the rhetoric of Puritan jeremiads, both play determinative roles in the evolution of the American self. But so does the myth of Aeneas play a determinative role in that evolution.

While Pocock "stresses Machiavelli at the expense of Locke" (545), the interpretation advanced here stresses Vergil at the expense of Machiavelli. In his concluding section of *The Machiavellian Moment*, Pocock holds that the foundation of the American republic "was not seen in terms of a simple return to nature," certainly a position with which this book has no quarrel. Rather, Pocock interprets this foundation "as constituting an ambivalent and contradictory moment within a dialectic of virtue and corruption" (545). Virtue Pocock understands as a "complex" deriving from a "diversity of social forces" (497). Corruption he sees as "the confusions and alienations of the moral identity" brought on, particularly in Britain, by a government committed to progress, in which some were enriched but others impoverished by this same government, such an effect being seen "as a necessary evil in a world of specialization and class struggle" (503). When this dialectic is examined in light of the myth of Aeneas, however, virtue is no complex emerging from diversity, but simply the triadic structure of pietas. And, while Pocock's interpretation of the Industrial Age describes undeniable effects on American society and culture, corruption becomes defined most immediately as decadent British society and government. What takes place in America, therefore, when virtue confronts corruption, or when, during the Revolutionary era, pietas as the American Way confronts British decadence, enacts not the Machiavellian, but the Vergilian moment.

America does indeed suffer her day with an idea of progress wherein a few become enriched while countless others are plagued by poverty, inevitably bringing about "confusions and alienations of the moral identity." But are not these conditions, to a greater or less extent, donnée within any industrialized culture? Despite the fact that the United States has become a highly industrialized country, American culture does not see itself, first and foremost, in the terms upon which Pocock insists. During the crisis of identity—that is, during that period in which the problem of identity became crucial—Americans put on classical identity but at the same time denied the origins of that identity, in order to subscribe to a mode of discourse common to all citizens. This mode of discourse was modified by pietas. Thus, when Pocock concludes that "American self-consciousness originated and acquired its terminology . . . within the humanist and neo-Harringtonian vocabularies employed by the English-speaking cultures of the North Atlantic" (546), he is only partially correct. For, in America's avowed determination to be not British and not Continental, the culture adopted an interpretation of virtue, an improved pietas, which was in disrepute in Britain during the eighteenth century. The culture then blended this virtue with the newly reemerging Adamic myth, in order to create an American self which was self-consciously unique in the modern world. Of course, not all Americans were aware of the dynamics giving rise to this American self, part Adamic and part classical. All Americans did accept this definition as vitally American, however. And most definitely the epitome of that new, American self resided in the example, and recommendations of George Washington, the fulfillment of the Vergilian moment.

6

The American Epic Writ Large
The Example of Phillis Wheatley

THE EVENTS WHICH SURROUND, PREDICT, AND ENACT THE VERGILIAN MOMENT GIVE RISE TO THE PREOCCUPATION WITH THE LITERARY GENRE of the epic in the era of the American Revolution. The major attempts in this genre include Timothy Dwight's *The Conquest of Canaan* (1785), Joel Barlow's *The Vision of Columbus* (1787) and its extensive revision twenty years later as *The Columbiad*, John Trumbull's *M'Fingal* (a mock epic; 1775, revised and enlarged in 1782), and Phillis Wheatley's entire oeuvre, which constitutes an intertextual epic.

The appearance of John P. McWilliams's *American Epic: Transforming a Genre* greatly facilitates our present investigation. His treatments of the works by Dwight, Barlow, and Trumbull are thorough and most helpful, as is his insistence that epic not be confined to those forms found in poetry. Rather, we must recognize that American authors have opened this genre to include such prose works as Cotton Mather's *Magnalia Christi Americana* and Herman Melville's *Moby Dick*.

When read in light of the Adam and Aeneas dialectic, however, *The American Epic* requires some emendation. *M'Fingal* has been touched on in chapter 4, and the importance of Barlow's *Vision* and *Columbiad* for the radical shift in discourse necessitates delaying consideration of these two works until chapter 7. Dwight's *Conquest*, however, may be commented upon profitably here, as a means of establishing the context for an examination of Wheatley's experiment with this genre. Her experiment wholly escaped McWilliams's attention; indeed, his failure to identify Wheatley's use of this genre urges a full investigation of the epic within her work.

Let us first reexamine Dwight's venture into the epic genre. McWilliams does not recognize, for example, the operation of pietas in Dwight's biblical epic, *Conquest of Canaan*. In a post-Constitutional essay, Dwight promoted an improved, Washingtonian pietas, thus demonstrating his knowledge of, and preference for, this virtue. Nathan O. Hatch asserts, "In Dwight's mind the classical definition of virtue was bankrupt even before the premature demise of those republics which embodied it" (*Sacred* 106). Dwight insists, however, that pietas should typify the American character. In *The True Means of Establishing Public Happiness*, printed in New Haven in 1795, during the throes of the radical shift, Dwight proposed a national virtue for America "which embraces piety to God, Good-will to mankind, and the effectual Government of ourselves" (13). To be sure, Dwight wanted readers to believe that he derived these three pillars of virtue from "that enlarged and Evangelical sense." Thus he participated in the wider effort to denigrate all things classical (a manifestation of the radical shift spearheaded by the redoubtable Noah Webster).

Despite this effort, we easily ferret out the tripartite structure of Vergil's pietas, Christianized after the manner of Washington in his major address to the people (discussed in ch. 5 above). Dwight's reference to "Piety" would look Christian enough, were it not used in conjunction with "Piety to God," "Good-will to mankind," and the "effectual Government of ourselves." These last three phrases recall devotion to the gods, to family and friends, and to country. Given that Dwight's subscription to an "improved" pietas was offered little more than ten years after the appearance of Washington's "Circular to the States" and following America's treaty of peace with Great Britain, we fairly may ask not *whether* Dwight's modified pietas was woven within the text of the earlier *Conquest of Canaan*, but *how* it was so woven.

If Kenneth Silverman is correct that Joshua, the hero of *Conquest of Canaan*, is the combined figure, Joshua/Washington (I for one have no reason to doubt it),[1] then we should not be surprised to hear this manifestation of America's faith of rebellion countering the Tory position of Hanniel (Joshua/Washington's adversary in establishing the parameters of rebellion) with these impassioned words:

By friendship's ties, religion's bonds combin'd,
By birth united, and by interest join'd;
In the same view our every wish conspires,
One spirit actuates, and one genius fires;
Plain, generous manners, vigorous limbs confess,
And vigorous minds to freedom ardent press. (Dwight, *Conquest* 28)

As in the passage from Dwight's *True Means*, the phrases "friendship's ties," "By birth united," "religion's bonds combin'd," and "vigorous minds to freedom ardent press" bespeak Vergil's pietas, in the modified form of *instauratio emendata:* devotion to family and friends, to God, and to country, in that order. Despite Dwight's claims throughout *The Conquest* that his inspiration is the Judaeo-Christian Jehovah, he opens the epic with the classical convention of the invocation, though here he invokes the divine Almighty. He also gives his leading characters long speeches. Moreover, speaking in the voice of his hero, Joshua/Washington, he states that the objectives of the Israelite/American cause are "To found an empire and to rule a world" (Dwight, *Conquest* 27). As the words "empire" and "world" do not appear in Joshua ("empire" occurs only once in the KJV, in Esther 1:20; "world" is not used until 1 Sam. 2:8), one may surmise that the motives of the biblical Joshua were not, particularly, to establish an empire nor to rule a cosmic world. These aspirations do accord well, of course, with the imperialistic strain within American consciousness. In short, Dwight has constructed his *Conquest of Canaan* in terms of the interplay of the myths of Aeneas and Adam, even though he would have his readers think that he summons up only the myth of Adam.

We are led to the next, more significant emendation of McWilliams, *American Epic*, by its failure to examine the potential for viewing all efforts to compose the so-called "great American Revolutionary era epic" collectively as a single American epic writ large. Because proper demonstration of a great "intertextual" American epic requires the space of an entire book, the present investigation is limited to consideration of the work of a single author, Phillis Wheatley.

I select this author because of her importance to the definition of the American adventure in freedom and because McWilliams's brief treatment of her is, to say the least, unfair. Regrettably, from the moment of her death, the treatment accorded Wheatley typically has been unfair and inadequate. An investigation of her preoccupation with the epic genre helps to advance the women's part and to articulate the role played by African Americans in the construction of the American Republic. Moreover, Wheatley's preoccupation with the epic takes on the characteristics of intertextuality, making her work a good illustration of the intertextual process by which, together, all Early American epics constitute the "American Epic writ large."

In his introduction, McWilliams remarks, "Nor is this book's middle-aged male author so wholly resistant to change that he would have excluded American epic literature by or about women had he found it." McWilliams subsequently clarifies his position: "I have found no American instances of women writing epic poems, of men writing epic poems about women heros [*sic*], or of women writing novels that are meant to recall the heroic tradition we think of as epic" (10). Ironically, McWilliams quotes from Wheatley's "To Maecenas," the opening poem of her *Poems on Various Subjects, Religious and Moral* (1773); but he concludes that she "laments that her muse lacks not only the poetic fire, but an appropriately heroic subject" (17). As we have seen in the chapter on American classicism, however, Wheatley's self-deprecatory stance in this poem contributes mightily to the creation of her subversive pastoralism.

Another critic, Sandra M. Gilbert, in "The American Sexual Politics of Walt Whitman and Emily Dickinson," claims that "there are in the Anglo-American canon no successful pre-twentieth-century epics . . . composed by women" (143), failing to make any mention of Wheatley.

Gilbert is quite simply mistaken (whatever "successful" may mean), and McWilliams has not looked far enough. In the poem McWilliams cites, Wheatley sardonically laments her inability to create an epic and then, after a fourteen-line demonstration of her capacity to capture Homer's elevated dignity and power to move his audience, proclaims that both Homer and Vergil have inspired her by their examples:

> O could I rival thine [Homer's] and Virgil's page,
> Or claim the Muses with the *Mantuan* Sage;
> Soon the same beauties should my mind adorn,
> And the same ardors in my soul should burn. (10)

Rather than denying an ability to work within the epic genre, Wheatley effectively proves to any careful reader that she is quite familiar with this genre and can capture its grandeur. Early in "To Maecenas," then, she declares her intention to work with the epic genre.

If he had read just a few pages beyond "To Maecenas," McWilliams would have come across "Goliath of Gath," the first of Wheatley's two *epyllia*, or short epics.[2] In that poem he would have found an eight-line invocation to the Muse, long speeches, a theme in which the fate of a nation hangs in the balance, machinery of the gods (here Christianized; e.g., a cherub sent to Goliath from God), an epic simile, and epic epithets—certainly enough characteristics of the epic to establish that this author is not merely aware of epic conventions but in fact has chosen to work within them. None of these conventions can be located in I Samuel 17, the poet's biblical source. Wheatley's later "Niobe in Distress for Her Children Slain by Apollo, from

Ovid's Metamorphoses, book VI, and from a View of the Painting of Mr. *Richard Wilson*" exhibits the same characteristics, transforming this "non-epic" episode from the *Metamorphoses* into a short epyllion, or epic. These poems are 222 and 212 lines long, respectively, making these by far the longest poems in her extant oeuvre.

"Goliath," a rendering of the David and the giant pericope, may have been suggested to Wheatley by Mather Byles's poem, "Goliah's Defeat: In the Manner of Lucan." Byles's mention of Lucan may have suggested to the younger poet the possibility of treating the story of David and Goliath in epic style, although Byles's poem is only seventy-eight lines long and, true to Lucan, is replete with exaggerated language, bordering on bombast, and wholly lacks an invocation to the Muse and the machinery of the gods.

In "Goliath of Gath," Wheatley solicits inspiration for "my high design" in an eight-line invocation to the "tuneful nine." She promises that her high design will include "dreadful scenes and toils of war"; consequently she seeks, in addition to the support of the Muses, the assistance of "Ye martial powers" (31). Though such an invocation does not occur in the biblical version, of course, it does resemble Vergil's opening of the *Aeneid*. After this elaborate invocation, which establishes a pattern of heightened diction and tone, we have a brief description of the Philistine and Israelite armies, followed by a longer, "epic-like" depiction of the armor of "the monster" ("champion" in I Sam. 17). The biblical version includes this last epic characteristic, one of the rare instances in the Bible in which a description of armor occurs.

In this poem, Wheatley also employs the Homeric convention of conceiving many names for a single character, each of which extends the character's identity. Goliath is given such ominous epithets as "the monster" (31ff.), "a mighty warrior" (31), "enormous chief" (32), "the giant-chief" (33), and "Philistia's son" (37). David benignly is called "Jesse's son" (33), "Jesse's youngest hope" (34), "The wond'rous hero" (34), "shepherd brother" (35), and simply "the young hero" (35). Another epic characteristic which appears in "Goliath" is long speeches. Both the giant and David make two speeches, each of ten to fourteen lines; and a cherub (one of the Christian machines), in a speech of nineteen lines, warns Goliath about his pride. All these speeches are rather long for such a short piece.

Wheatley intensifies the drama of the well-known confrontation between the heavily armored giant and the "beardless boy" (37) armed with only a sling, by making two interpolations. The first is a thirty-line description of the visitation by a "radiant cherub" to the defiant Goliath, in which the cherub warns that the giant's defiance of Jehovah foretells his doom. The cherub begins, "Rebellious wretch! audacious worm!" (37), then asserts that Goliath's pride provokes "the judge of all the gods" (37),[3] and concludes, "Goliath say, shall grace to him be shown,/ Who dares heav'ns monarch and insults his throne?" (38). This first interpolation alters the biblical version in three ways. First, it strongly parallels the use of the machines of the gods, the messengers Mercury and Isis, in the *Iliad*. Second, it contributes to an atmosphere of foreboding and dramatic irony. Finally, the cherub's suggestion that Goliath is a rebel "Who dares heav'ns monarch" establishes an unmistakable analogy between "the monster" and Milton's Satan after the fall from heaven.

The second addition the poet makes to the narrative is only six lines long. But the brevity of this interpolation increases the feeling of impending doom for Goliath and Philistia, both of whom the lines predict will be punished for their misguided faith in the false Dagon and for their aggression against the people of the true God Jehovah. She also seizes this opportunity to use the epic formula "th' ensanguin'd plain" in the line, "'Tis thine to perish on th' ensanguined plain" (40).

Wheatley's "Goliath of Gath" radically alters I Samuel 17. Placed within the context of the two books of Samuel (a single book until the Bible of Felix Pratensis in 1517–18 passed down the division now considered traditional), the story of David and the giant marks a clear justification of David's prowess and cunning as a youth preparing to rule the peoples of Israel. Within Wheatley's subversive poetics, however, her rendering of an obvious underdog's victory over an apparently invincible enemy, through use of a small amount of strength cunningly and precisely focused, assumes greater significance. If David's intelligent and skillful defense of his country is viewed in terms of the united colonies' defense against British aggression, then David becomes an American colonial. Goliath, as a manifestation of British oppression, symbolizes evil transgression against God's law, wherein the "law" clearly upholds the sovereignty of the united colonies.

Taking this subversive reading one step further, David becomes symbolic of slaves in revolt, trying to uphold God's law, which teaches "Christians" that "Negros, black as *Cain*/ May be refin'd and join th' angelic train" (18). Philistia hence symbolizes oppressors of black people, whether British or American. Consistent with the central subject of all her poetry and prose, the struggle for freedom, Wheatley writes in "Goliath" that David "Freedom in *Israel* [an oppressed people] for his house shall gain" (34).

A third subversive reading understands young David as a rebel against both the Philistine Goliath and the adult world, for he "shows up" the Israelite army with his intelligence and skill. The parallel here is to Wheatley herself, defeating oppression with her pen. Here in "Goliath of Gath," Wheatley effectively though subversively snatches a laurel from the "honour'd head" of her white readers, while they "indulgent smile upon the deed" (12).

In "Niobe in Distress," Niobe rebels against divinity itself, as she claims to be more worthy of worship, because she is more fertile, than Latona, mother of the twins, Apollo and Phoebe (sun and moon). This work contains the same epic properties that distinguish "Goliath," with three differences. No elaborate description of armor appears here; appropriately, classical machines replace Christian ones; and the poet abandons the practice of employing several different names for her characters. It is a mistake to dismiss "Niobe" as merely an "academic" exercise, however. Much like "Goliath," this epyllion represents another, even more sophisticated argument for freedom of the oppressed.

The invocation of "Niobe in Distress" is ten lines long and repeats the first person singular pronoun twice, in the objective and possessive cases. In "Goliath," the poet used this same pronoun in the possessive case twice and in the nominative once. Such self-reflection suggests that these epyllia have considerable personal significance for this poet. When she calls upon the Muse in "Niobe in Distress," she asks that she not be allowed to "sue in vain,/ Tho' last and meanest of the rhyming train!" Here she dons a mask of innocuous self-deprecation, for she is going to attempt something new, something not in Ovid but in Wheatley's own calculation. "O guide my pen in lofty strains to show/ The *Phrygian* queen," the poet declares, "all beautiful in woe" (101).

Note that the first two lines of the invocation, and of the poem, begin conventionally enough, seeming to do obeisance to the patriarchal power structure by giving first place to "APOLLO'S wrath to man." In the last line of this lengthy invocation, however, Wheatley slips in the determination to picture Niobe, who provokes Apollo's anger, as "all beautiful in woe." Thus it becomes clear that the poet's sympathies lie with Niobe, who usually in commentaries on this Ovidian episode, is cast in the role of antagonist.

The majority of late Renaissance commentaries—which should have been readily available to Wheatley in the libraries of Byles (who inherited Cotton Mather's huge library) and many others—interpreted this episode from Ovid as a fable against pride, one in which Niobe is condemned to suffer because of that "sin" of pride. George Sandys, for example, in the popular commentary that accompanies his translations of the fifteen books of the *Metamorphoses*, asserts that Niobe's behavior proceeds from a "contempt both of God and man, and an insolent forgetfulness of humane instability" (293). Writing at the middle of the seventeenth century and less than twenty years after Sandys, Alexander Ross, Anglican minister and author of numerous books in English and Latin, says in his *Mystagogus Poeticus; or, The Muses' Interpreter* (1647) that Niobe represents "pride, insolence, and contempt of God himself" (181). King, *Heathen Gods and Heroes*, observes, "She having bore a great many children, being seven Sons and seven Daughters, was so vain and rash as to prefer her self to Latona" (102). All concur that vanity motivated Niobe to challenge Latona's authority as a deity; but King, significantly, does not censure Niobe for impiety.

Several contemporary critics of Wheatley comment insightfully on "Niobe in Distress." Emily Stipes Watts, for example, notes that Wheatley treats Niobe less harshly than Ovid; indeed, "Wheatley depicts Niobe as a proud and beautiful woman who has dared to challenge the gods" (38), suggesting that Wheatley's conception of Niobe is heroic. While David Grimsted thinks that this epyllion represents Wheatley's "antislavery stance" (358), Lucy K. Hayden states that Wheatley surpasses Ovid "in displaying Niobe's anguished grief over their [i.e., her seven sons'] deaths as well as those of her seven daughters and her husband's suicide" (442). I have no quarrel with any of these assessments except that none carries the Niobe episode far enough. The poet, by means of her subversive style, points the way to a fuller reading of the poem. A clue to that subversion is encoded in Wheatley's title, "Niobe in Distress." Sondra O'Neale, *Jupiter Hammon*, notes that, during the Revolutionary War era and after, "distress" was a term describing the condition of the slave (202). So Niobe's "distress" identifies her situation as one of enslavement to a tyrannical oppressor.

We may presume that Niobe represents subversion or rebellion; that a central issue of the poem is fertility; and that Wheatley's sympathies clearly reside with Niobe, who, like Wheatley, suffers the tyranny of slavery. Latona, far less fertile than Niobe, and her vindictive children, Apollo and Diana, then, represent the racist white oppressors who would hold in check those potentially more productive than they. The emphasis on fertility need not be confined to procreation. Instead, fertility may be read as a metaphor for creativity. The poem's central focus shifts away from Niobe to the poet, who may have to suffer for writing her poems—those children who challenge white domination of her and her black brothers and sisters. In a lengthy twenty-four line interpolation, or addition, of lines not appearing in Ovid, Wheatley speaks of Niobe's children in these glowing terms: "Seven sprightly sons the royal bed adorn,/ Seven daughters beauteous as the op'ning morn." This couplet she follows with a four-line epic simile:

> As when *Aurora* fills the ravish'd sight,
> And decks the orient realms with rosy light
> From their bright eyes the living splendors play,
> Nor can beholders bear the flashing ray. (102)

If indeed these "children" are her poems, a suggestion which is strengthened by the affectionate comparison to her mother's beloved dawn, then Wheatley, by suggesting that they occupy a status equal to that of the gods (for only the eyes of deities flash light celestial and refined), subversively claims that her poems equal in artistry any produced by white folks.

In the couplet which closes this interpolation, Wheatley writes, "Thy love [i.e., Niobe's] too vehement hastens to destroy/ Each blooming maid, and each celestial boy" (103). Thus she subversively warns herself not to become too open about her zeal to be free. She must not be blatant in her protests against slavery, but instead must maintain, for now, her subversive posture. When the white oppressors hold practically all the power and all the physical means to enforce restraint, then the oppressed must balance their inevitable rebellion with subtle intelligence. Wheatley, of course, knows that, if her subversion becomes apparent, she will very likely be denied her medium of power—published words.

The idea that Wheatley, in this poem, is carrying out her own private rebellion against oppression is reinforced by a subsequent passage. At the dramatic moment when the goddess Latona (or the white spokesperson of oppression) reacts to Niobe's boast of equality, and perhaps even superiority, Latona charges that Niobe has instilled within her fellow Thebans "rebellious fires." In addition, Latona herself has become enraged by Niobe's tongue, which, in giving utterance, "rebels." Latona's son Apollo follows his mother's lead by pledging to "scourge" Niobe's "rebel mind" (106).

Significantly, in this passage Ovid makes no reference to rebellion or subversion; rather, in Latona's complaint, he stresses Niobe's impiety toward divinity. The emphasis upon rebelliousness, therefore, is wholly Wheatley's invention. Here Wheatley's language is clearly that of subversion, in keeping with her subversive pastoral style. In fact, within the context of patriot America's growing dissatisfaction with British interference in American affairs, this portrayal of rebels who rebel only to be scourged (by the oppressive British) for their rebellious thinking captures the rhetoric of America before the Revolutionary War.

Interpreted as an allegory of Wheatley's subversive poetics, "Niobe in Distress" may be seen as this poet's apologia for not using her poetry, written before her manumission on or before October 18, 1773, more actively to rebel against her white oppressors. Wheatley died some five years before her hope of freedom for *all* Americans, regardless of race, was dashed by the ratification of a Constitution which labeled a black man only three-fifths of a white man. Given the time and place in which she wrote, to attack the white establishment openly, while still a slave, would have been to risk losing her ability to exercise her power within the medium of words. And for Wheatley, losing the opportunity to express herself in print would have been to fail in her battle against oppression, which she had chosen to fight by employing her strategy of subversive poetics.

Wheatley continues to fight her battle for freedom, then, in both her epyllia. Like Joseph Green and George Washington, among others, this writer unhesitatingly commingles Christian and classical elements within her discourse. In addition in "Goliath of Gath," she refers to the Sun as Phoebus, and she describes David's leaving behind his shepherd's duties to meet Goliath in what are definitely images from classical pastoral: "He left the folds, he left the flow'ry meads./ And soft recesses of the sylvan shades" (33). In her intertextual epic, Wheatley continues this congenial blend of the classical with the Christian without any interruption.

In the term *intertextuality*, I have in mind the excellent definition in Michael Awkward's *Inspiriting Influences: Tradition, Revision, and Afro-American Women's Novels*, here slightly modified for the epic. Although Wheatley certainly is no novelist, she has served as an inspiriting influence among African Americans. Awkward delineates *intertextuality* as "a paradigmatic system of explicit or implied repetition of, or allusion to, signs, codes, or figures within a cultural form" (5). Here the "paradigmatic system" conforms to that "cultural form" which we usually term the epic. As with McWilliams's treatment of the epic in *American Epic*, this investigation does not confine itself to poetry, but discovers an occasional interplay of epic characteristics between Wheatley's prose and poetry, therefore embracing her entire extant oeuvre.

Epics, first of all, contain heroes of either gender who embody national ideals. Second, usually they are written in the early stage of a nation's move toward a unique cultural consciousness. Third, they have as their subject some major struggle which symbolizes the principal value of the nation. Wheatley's venture into the epic form exhibits all three of these characteristics. Furthermore, Wheatley develops a central figure of heroic proportions (whether Washington or Niobe), whose character always manifests a compulsion to be free; finally the hero of Wheatley's intertextual epic is neither Washington nor Niobe but the poet herself, as she represents the predicament of the oppressed human being ever struggling to be free. As a figure of the oppressed seeking liberation, Wheatley as poet-hero of her intertextual epic imprints herself upon the inchoate United States, as a representation of this country's struggle to achieve liberation from colonial domination.

After Wheatley's formal manumission sometime between late August and October 18, 1773, her need to adopt a carefully crafted subversive strategy in her freedom struggle abated. Now she could become more direct in her liberation discourse. For example, in her famous letter of February 11, 1774, to Samson Occom (himself a Native American victim of oppression), Wheatley writes, "In every human Breast, God has implanted a Principle, which we call Love of Freedom; it is impatient of Oppression, and pants for Deliverance" (177). These noble words speak for *all* human beings. Here she establishes clearly that *no* human being is glad to be oppressed; quite the contrary, "we" profoundly resent any oppression, with an impatience that mounts inevitably into rebellion. For only through such rebellion can "Deliverance" be achieved.

Wheatley continues her liberation discourse by declaring: "And by Leave of our Modern Egyptians I will assert, that the same Principle lives in us." Note her use of the first person plural pronouns "our" and "us." Although Wheatley has received formal manumission and theoretically has enjoyed that freedom for several months, she does not exclude herself from the freedom struggle for her black brothers and sisters. She pleads to be granted equal status in the struggle of *all* human beings to be free, concluding with this poignant indictment of her white oppressors: "How well the Cry for Liberty, and the reverse Disposition for the Exercise of oppressive Power over others agree,—I humbly think it does not require the Penetration of a Philosopher to determine" (177). No naive, consensual follower here! Wheatley speaks her mind with biting clarity and candor.

The language in which Wheatley casts this statement reveals clearly that she grasps the duplicity of those whites who all too often "view our sable race with scornful eye" and who "Exercise . . . oppressive Power over others." Particularly arresting about this last passage, written during the fanfare for colonial American opposition to British oppression, is that Wheatley ferrets out in-house oppression on the part of her racist American enslavers. As "the cry for Liberty" becomes ever more strident, Wheatley challenges those white American patriots in positions of power to demand universal freedom for *all* those suffering oppression.

I cannot resist pointing out that the plea Wheatley utters in 1774 just as well could be made at the present moment, when the civil rights movement of the 1960s has failed to realize its full promise. Recognition that Wheatley's statement about liberation for *all* human beings is addressed to a Native American sweeps into the arena of the *American Aeneas* a definite, multicultural perspective. Furthermore, this eighteenth-century Boston poet's plea resonates today with a force at least as strong as that registered over two hundred years ago.

Wheatley hoped that America's freedom struggle might include freedom for blacks and for Native Americans, as well as for whites. This hope is heard loudly and clearly in "To His Excellency General Washington," in which the poet speaks of "freedom's cause" and "The land of freedom's heaven-defended race!" (145–46). Note that "freedom's cause" has become the province of a "heaven-defended race," not of heaven-defended races. Wheatley's meaning is obvious: in a world where even "Negros, black as Cain,/ May be refin'd, and join th' angelic train" (18), the notion of multiple races is no longer relevant. Indeed, the freedom struggle this poet describes has no racial overtones but is the struggle of all Americans—i.e., of all the oppressed.

While Wheatley already has announced in "To Maecenas," the opening piece of *Poems* (1773), that freedom is to be her major subject, her personification of freedom as the goddess Liberty is not developed fully until "To . . . Washington." Wheatley composed this poem in Providence, Rhode Island (Boston at the time was occupied by the British), completing it by October 26, 1775. The poem begins with this enthusiastic couplet: "Celestial choir! enthron'd in realms of light,/ Columbia's scenes of glorious toils I write" (145). Significantly, the poet locates the first action of her poem in the heavens, which are filled with light. We are soon to learn that an important source of this light emanates from the goddess:

> While freedom's course her anxious breast alarms,
> She flashes dreadful in refulgent arms.
> See mother earth her offspring's fate bemoan,
> And nations gaze at scenes before unknown!
> See the bright beams of heaven's revolving light
> Involved in sorrows and veil of night!
> The goddess comes, she moves divinely fair,
> Olive and laurel bind her golden hair. (145)

Keeping the subject of the poem clearly before her, the poet subordinates freedom to its cause, the inevitable victory of American patriotism over British colonial rule. The line, "And nations gaze at scenes before unknown," captures the cosmic sweep of epic as the poet declares America's revolt to be the first successful rebellion against colonialism. The "bright beams of heaven's light" are "Involved in sorrows and veil of night" only because Washington and his armies have not yet seized the laurel of certain victory.[4]

The remainder of Wheatley's Lady Liberty personification very likely owes a debt to Milton's depiction of Mirth in the opening lines of "L'Allegro." While Milton begins his portrait of Mirth with the line, "But come thou Goddess fair and free" (68), Wheatley describes Liberty as follows: "The goddess comes, she moves divinely fair." The persona of Milton's poem insists that Mirth "in thy right hand lead with thee,/ The Mountain Nymph, sweet Liberty" (69). Perhaps Milton's Mountain Nymph serves as the model for Wheatley's Liberty. In any event, her figure of Liberty recalls Milton's Mirth, or Euphrosyne, in other instances, too. In another poem from the next year, Wheatley uses the phrase "Columbia's Joy" (147); surely this joy must be freedom. King, *Heathen Gods*, associates Euphrosyne "with true Joy and Comfort" (141). Wheatley, in her portrait of Liberty, refers to "Unnumber'd charms and recent graces." Moreover, in the poem "Liberty and Peace," she repeats her Lady Liberty figure and refers to "every Grace her sovereign Step attends" (154). Both these allusions may have their origins in "L'Allegro," for

Milton himself states that Euphrosyne's parents were Bacchus and Venus, whose children were "at [the same] birth" Euphrosyne and "two sister Graces more" (69; her other sisters were Thalia and Aglaia).

Although one easily can explain the olive and laurel which bind the hair of Wheatley's Liberty as the olive of peace[5] and the laurel of victory, where does she get Liberty's golden hair? Wheatley's detractors have alleged that she imparts to Liberty telltale signs of white womanhood because she is trying to "write white"—that is, she is selling out her black brothers and sisters to white oppression. I submit that this "golden hair" image owes nothing to white folks and instead may be traced to this poet's passion for light imagery, particularly that associated with her mother's dawn (see ch. 4). In "L'Allegro," Milton proposes an alternative myth of his own making, in which Aurora and Zephyr are the parents of Mirth. Wheatley's Liberty likely owes little to this alternative myth, other than a suggestion that Aurora is a mother figure. While Milton's Aurora surely would have reinforced her construction of Liberty, Wheatley did not require Milton to elicit her mother's dawn, which she conflates with Milton's Mirth to shape her Lady Liberty.

How does Wheatley accomplish this conflation? Recall that "To . . . Washington" opens "in realms of light." William King records that Aurora was, by Astreas (one of her husbands), "Mother to the Stars" (33–34). As Liberty "flashes dreadful in refulgent arms," the stars seem to dim, much as the coming of the dawn dims our capacity to see the stars. The nations can now "gaze at scenes before unknown!" precisely because "the bright beams of heaven's revolving light" hail the coming of the morn. As the poet says, "the goddess comes, she moves divinely fair." Given "the bright beams" resulting from a light that revolves in the heavens, Liberty herself then becomes the source of those bright beams, as she "moves divinely," suggesting the motion of a heavenly body. If Liberty is a manifestation of Wheatley's beloved Aurora, then the possibility that her (Liberty's) hair could be anything but golden is remote indeed.

Picturing Aurora with hair of gold derives from a long tradition. In the *Metamorphoses*, for example, Ovid calls her the golden goddess (VII, 703), as does Vergil in the *Aeneid* (VII, 26). During the Renaissance, both Ariosto and Tasso depict Aurora with golden hair. In the epic, *Orlando Furioso*, Ariosto at one point gives this variation on the formulaic rising of the dawn: "when the golden-haired Sun set forth from Tithonus' splendid hall and routed the dark shades of night" (VIII, 86). Here the Sun is surely Aurora, since Tithonus was one of her husbands. At a later point, Ariosto gives yet another variation on this epic formula: "Fair Aurora had (much to jealous Tithonus' rage) just spread her golden tresses to the Sun, who remained half-hidden still, half-revealed" (XI, 32). In his epic, *Jerusalem Delivered*, Tasso, in the famous Edward Fairfax translation of 1600, renders his own variation upon this epic formula, in these sonorous lines: "The purple morning left her crimson bed,/ And don'd her robe of pure vermilion hue;/ Her amber locks she crown'd with roses red" (III, 1–3). So Wheatley's Aurora inevitably must be given "golden hair."

That Wheatley sees Lady Liberty as a conflation of Milton's "Goddess fair and free" and her own mother's dawn gives her icon a distinctive stamp. In addition, she capitalizes upon the historical truth that America's liberation struggle holds implications for the entire world. As she puts it so well, "Fix'd are the eyes of nations on the scales,/ For in their hopes Columbia's arm prevails" (146). Indeed, America's adventure in freedom heralded a new dawn in world politics. By the time she composes "Liberty and Peace," Wheatley turns prediction into reality when she declares, "LO! Freedom comes. Th' prescient Muse foretold,/ All Eyes th' accomplish'd Prophecy behold" (154). Now that the Treaty of Paris (September 1783) has awarded political sovereignty to the United States, America's promise can be realized. Or so Wheatley hoped. For one who placed so much hope in America's liberation struggle, to have seen that hope defeated by the United States Constitution of 1789 surely would have been unbearable.

Nevertheless, attempting to represent the enthusiasm and dreams of the moment, Wheatley proclaims in "Liberty and Peace": "And new-born *Rome* shall give *Britannia* Law" (154). Here Wheatley adapts part of a line from Vergil's *Aeneid*. Vexed by Aeneas's dallying with Dido, Jupiter sends Mercury, his messenger, to warn Aeneas that he was to be about the business of founding Rome and, as a consequence, dispatching laws to the entire world (IV, 231; "ac totum sub leges mitteret orbem"; and bring the entire world under [his] laws). The myth of Aeneas sounds prominently in Wheatley's intertextual epic, its theme being the struggle for liberation and a projected teleology in emulation of the Roman example.

Wheatley, however, is no easy republican. Indeed, she asserts, "A crown, a mansion, and a throne that shine,/ With gold unfading, WASHINGTON! be thine" (146). A recent television biography of Washington, based on James T. Flexner's four-volume *George Washington*, employed this very line to inform the general that a monarchist movement was afoot to declare him king, a notion that disturbed Washington deeply (see *Collected Works* 305–6). In her monarchist position, Wheatley predicts those who later would pursue an imperialist policy within American politics.

While Wheatley's politics were somewhat imperialistic, perhaps reflecting her aristocratic African heritage,[6] she always was very much an advocate of liberation from British domination. She continues to celebrate that liberation struggle in "On the Capture of General Lee." Although much has been made of the fact that Gen. Charles Lee aspired to supplant Washington as commander-in-chief, Wheatley did not know this when she addressed this poem to James Bowdoin, a signer of Wheatley's letter of attestation and founder of Bowdoin College. What is of importance about this poem are its demonstrable epic qualities. In language decidedly elevated in tone and diction, Wheatley presents Lee as having been betrayed into the enemy's hands. He, moreover, comports himself with heroic dignity and valor. After suffering the ridicule of a long speech spoken by the leader of "the British camp," Lee responds in a speech of his own of twenty-seven and one-half lines. Accusing the British leader of "arrogance of tongue!/ And wild ambition" which is "ever prone to wrong!" (147), Lee brazenly asserts:

> "For plunder you, and we for freedom fight.
> Her cause divine with generous ardor fires,
> And every bosom glows as she inspires!" (148)

Employing an effective chiasmus in "For plunder you, and we for freedom fight," Wheatley displays both her familiarity with classical rhetoric and her ability to give her hero a lengthy speech, replicating a common convention of the epic. If Lee is heroic, in Wheatley's conception in this poem, then his heroism merely points to a hero greater than he. For Lee challenges his adversaries to

> "Find in your train of boasted heroes, one
> To match the praise of Godlike Washington.
> Thrice happy Chief! in whom the virtues join,
> And heaven-taught prudence speaks the man divine." (148)

This eloquent tongue-lashing strikes "Amazement" in the "warrior-train,/ And doubt of conquest, on the hostile plain" (148). Appropriate to the epic genre, Wheatley here creates an episode which, by means of its energetic language and dramatic heroism, conveys the power and grandeur of epic. Indeed, Washington is to Lee no mere man, but one of Homer's or Vergil's demigods, a latter-day Achilles or Aeneas.

In an elegy on the death of Maj. Gen. David Wooster, Wheatley sings the praises of another hero who, according to the author herself, "fell a martyr in the Cause of Freedom" (186). In a twenty-line speech, the poet has the dying Wooster utter a moving and powerful prayer that God may "lead Columbia thro' the toils of war" (149). Unexpectedly, perhaps, but nonetheless dramatically, Wheatley places in the general's final words a plea that victory in this martial contest will extend the prize of freedom to "Afric's blameless race":

> "But how, presumptuous shall we hope to find
> Divine acceptance with th' Almighty mind—
> While yet (O deed Ungenerous!) they disgrace
> And hold in bondage Afric's blameless race?
> Let Virtue reign—And thou accord our prayers
> Be victory ours, and generous freedom theirs." (149–50)

So "The hero pray'd," concludes Wheatley.

In this last poem, echoing her position in the famous letter to Samson Occom, Wheatley expresses her anxiety that the American struggle for freedom in the end may not include freedom for *all* Americans. Her determination that it must, I reiterate, addresses pressing needs in America today. As Wheatley's epic vision unfolds, we understand how applicable that vision is to us at the beginning of the American Republic's third century.

The agents who Wheatley hopes will help to bring about the reality of freedom for all Americans invariably are composites of the myths of Adam and Aeneas. Wooster, for example, in his heroic sacrifice manifested a "mind/ Where martial flames, and Christian virtues join'd" (149). In her 1773 *Poems*, the poet is more explicit as she describes "The warrior's bosom in the fields of fight." In such a warrior, properly motivated to defend the right cause, "Lo! here the Christian, and the hero join/ With mutual grace to form the man divine." Wheatley's hero is always "to virtue true." To insist, as Wheatley does, that her heroes be divine (recall "Godlike Washington") is not to be particularly true to Christian dogma. Indeed, there are no heroes per se in the New Testament, and the word *hero* is not used in either the Geneva or the King James Bibles. Her hero is one in whom "valour kindles" and "*virtue* lies" (72). Although Wheatley's hero Wooster does manifest "Christian virtues," when her idea of the hero arises within the context of "man divine," both "valour" and "virtue" assume an unmistakably classical imputation.

As Wheatley assigns her heroic figures a classical origin, their virtue becomes a feminized pietas *instauratio emendata*, in the tradition of Addison's Marcia. Like the *Death* paintings by John Singleton Copley and Benjamin West, depicting General Wolfe and General Montgomery, respectively, Wheatley's Wooster assumes the attitude of one slain in battle, as "Inly serene the expiring hero lies . . . (while heav'nward roll his swimming eyes)." Then he speaks his twenty-line epic speech, delivered as an orison, in which he not only pleads for the freedom of "Afric's blameless race," but also expresses the passionate desire that "fair freedom" will keep American citizens "ever Virtuous, brave and free" (149). Here the American struggle for freedom, the grand theme of Wheatley's intertextual epic, merges with her insistence on virtuous behavior. In her paean to Washington, Wheatley notes that the general is "Fam'd for thy valour, for thy virtues more." Thus she establishes Washington's reputation for virtuous behavior. She concludes this panegyric by exhorting the general to "Proceed . . . with virtue on thy side" (146), so separating American behavior from that of the British, which she considers less than virtuous.

The poet already has announced her concern for virtuous behavior in the title of her 1773 volume, *Poems on Various Subjects, Religious and Moral*. In "To Maecenas," Wheatley declares: "Thy virtues, great *Maecenas!*, shall be sung/ In praise of him, from whom those virtues sprung" (11). These lines signal to her "audience" that, in addition to exploring the modes of pastoral and epic, treating her own and humanity's freedom struggle, asserting her right to recognition as a mature artist, and using solar imagery as her principal metaphor, she intends to investigate both the moral implications of virtuous behavior and the ultimate source of that behavior—i.e., her idea of God. Wheatley's aspirations here capture the cosmic sweep of epic. Consistent with epic, she states her preoccupation with the primary element of pietas, devotion to her idea of God. Her very next poem, "On Virtue," applies her treatment of virtue to herself, as this poem opens with these candid words: "Thou bright jewel in my aim I strive/ To comprehend thee."

In this early poem from 1766, the poet admits that the concept as yet eludes her: "Thine own words declare/ Wisdom is higher than a fool can reach." Nevertheless, she depends on her perception of virtue for guidance: "Attend me, *Virtue*, thro' my youthful years!/ O leave me not to the false joys of time!/ But guide my steps to endless life and bliss" (13). The Adamic notion of a post-physical, spiritual paradise evoked by the last line demonstrates how effectively Wheatley blends the classical with the Adamic. While noting that virtue leads "celestial *Chastity* along," Wheatley declares that "*Greatness*, or *Goodness*," most properly identifies virtue. Ever the ambitious poet, she implores virtue to "Teach me a better strain, a nobler lay,/ O thou, enthron'd with Cherubs in the realms of day!" (14). Concluding this piece with an alexandrine (for Wheatley a striking departure from the regularity of iambic pentameter),[7] she seizes the opportunity to express her fondness for solar imagery. Thus she ends the poem with the characteristic phrase, "in the realms of day!"

The description of virtue given by Wheatley in this poem agrees well with the general Enlightenment understanding of this concept. Carol Blum, in her article, "Virtue," in *The Blackwell Companion to the Enlightenment*, points out that virtue signified "a Thomastic sense of good moral function in accord with God's will," as well as "chastity mainly, although not exclusively, female" and "the enjoyment of a reputation for moral worth" (543). In "On Virtue" and throughout *Poems*, Wheatley clearly endorses chastity and the determination to achieve a "reputation for moral worth" by doing good. In

"On Recollection," for example, after lamenting the power of recollection to recall the follies of the past, the poet asks virtue to "exert thy pow'r, and change the scene;/ Be thine employ to guide my future days,/ And mine to pay the tribute of my praise" (64).

Recall that Addison's *Cato* may be interpreted as an explication of pietas. In it, Juba, the young African prince of Numidia, describes Marcia, Cato's daughter, in language which predicts Wheatley's: "The virtuous Marcia . . . [who] improves her charms/ With inward greatness, unaffected wisdom,/ And sanctity of manners" (525). However suspiciously patriarchal this "softened" version of pietas may sound to a present-day audience, Addison unapologetically states that, for his own century, "Cato's soul/ Shines out in every thing she acts or speaks"; indeed, Marcia is one who, "with becoming grace[,]/ Soften[s] the rigor of her father's virtues" (525).

Just so, Wheatley appears eager to appropriate virtuous behavior to herself and so to establish herself, though not in any immodest, arrogant, or even self-conscious way, as a heroic figure and even as the hero of her own intertextual epic. Like Marcia before her, she celebrates virtuous behavior in significant male figures about her, in terms of the triune structure of pietas. For example, in Marcia's very first speech in *Cato*, she declares, "My prayers and wishes always shall attend/ The friends of Rome, the glorious cause of virtue,/ And men approved of by the gods and Cato" (525). Cato's devotion to the gods, to country, and to family and friends resonates here in the noble spirit of his daughter, who serves as a reflection of himself. More to the point, in these words Marcia assumes the office of one who exhorts and promulgates the virtue of pietas—an office also occupied by Phillis Wheatley.

In the 1773 *Poems*, that the poet assumes this office—to promote what becomes, for her as for Washington, an improved pietas—is indicated primarily in her elegies. In many of her eighteen extant elegies, as she recollects and celebrates the worthy lives of deceased subject after deceased subject, she emphasizes preserving the institution of the family. Such poems as "On Friendship" and particularly her letters to Obour Tanner (Wheatley's African American "soul mate," according to William H. Robinson) demonstrate her commitment to venerating friends. In the elegies she also pursues her preoccupation with her idea of God. In "On the Death of the Rev. Dr. Sewall, 1769," for example, she notes that "Great God" is "incomprehensible, unknown/ By sense" (20). In her 131-line poem, "Thoughts on the Works of Providence," she explores the nature of the Deity. As we have come to expect, Wheatley determines that "*Wisdom*, which attends Jehovah's ways,/ Shines most conspicuous in the solar rays" (44).

Wheatley does articulate a patriotic attitude in the 1773 *Poems*, and particularly in "To the King's Most Excellent Majesty. 1768," in which she extols the repeal of the Stamp Act. Understandably, however, her celebration of American independence is not evident in the volume published in London. The poem, "A Farewell to America. To Mrs. S. W.," sounds innocuous in the *Poems*. But, when published on May 10, 1773, in the *Massachusetts Gazette* and *Boston Post-Boy*, the work bore this grand title: "To the Empire of America, Beneath the Western Hemisphere. Farewell to America. To Mrs. S. W." (219). The more provocative title bespeaks Wheatley's monarchist, but nonetheless American, patriotism. In poems such as those on Washington, Lee, and Wooster, and especially in "Liberty and Peace," Wheatley rivals Philip Freneau for the title "Poet of the American Revolution." Obviously, Wheatley subscribes to the evolving American Way—i.e., to devotion to God, to family and friends, and to country. And as unconscious hero of her own intertextual epic, one promoting the virtue of an improved pietas, Wheatley as poet/persona embodies a feminine type of Aeneas. For, as Marcia exhorts the African Prince Juba to "Go on, and prosper in the paths of honor" (Addison, *Cato* IV.iii.541), Wheatley as national epic poet urges George Washington to "Proceed, great chief, with virtue on thy side" (149).

Wheatley's emphasis upon the woman's part is extended by her practice of invoking the Muse or Muses. In "To Maecenas," the poet invokes Maecenas himself, famed patron of poets during the golden age of Latin literature. She implores him to "grant, *Maecenas*, thy paternal rays,/ Hear me propitious and defend my lays" (12). This invocation of a male figure is a rarity within Wheatley's extant oeuvre. Indeed, she states clearly in this piece that the source of poetic inspiration resides within the female Muses, for she observes that "The *Nine* [have] inspire[d]" Vergil's "heav'nly numbers" (10) and that "Terence all the choir [the nine Muses] inspir'd" (11). However, when we understand that her Maecenas is her collective audience, we readily grasp why she makes such a solicitation. She knows full well that the purchasing power for her poems rests largely in the hands of white males.

In the eight- to ten-line invocations in her two epyllia and "Thoughts on the Works of Providence," Wheatley presents a detailed analysis of the Muse's role. The invocation in "Goliath of Gath" suggests that the poet assumes that the biblical author of I Samuel 17 had the same source of inspiration that she now summons:

> Ye martial pow'rs, and all ye tuneful nine,
> Inspire my song, and aid my high design.
> . . .
> You best remember, and you best can sing
> The acts of heroes to the vocal string:
> Resume the lays with which your sacred lyre,
> Did then the poet and the sage inspire. (31)

As her task is to retell the confrontation between young David and the giant, Wheatley apparently thinks the nine Muses alone are insufficient to assist her "high design." At least at this early stage in her poetic career, she thinks she must call upon the masculine spirits of battle as she prepares to write of war's "dreadful scenes and toils" (31)—and as she pursues the "high design" of epic. As she names this poem (or a version of it) in her Boston "Proposals" of February 29, 1772, we can assume that "Goliath" is earlier than "To Maecenas," "Thoughts," the hymns to "Morning" and "Evening," and "Niobe in Distress." These latter poems all figure in the 1773 volume, are not named in the "Proposals," and contain elaborate invocations. Except for the obligatory nod in "Maecenas" discussed above, this reference in "Goliath" to male principles as necessary agents of inspiration is the only reference Wheatley makes to male figures as sources of inspiration.

As Wheatley matures as poet, she appears to gain more confidence in the female principle; for in "Thoughts," not named in the 1772 "Proposals" and almost certainly composed after, the poet calls upon the "Celestial muse." At first encounter this reference seems to connote Judaeo-Christianity as she declares: "Celestial muse, my arduous flight sustain,/ And raise my mind to a seraphic strain" (43). The later "To a Gentleman of the Navy," published on October 30, 1774, however, Wheatley opens with the exclamation, "Celestial muse!" After speaking of her two friends, officers of the navy and, in Wheatley's words, "two chiefs of matchless grace," in epic and exaggerated terms who could have forestalled the destruction of Troy, she declares: "Calliope, half gracious to my prayer,/ Grants but the half and scatters half in air" (140). Obviously in this case the Celestial muse is Calliope, muse of epic poetry. So the "Celestial muse" of "Thoughts" may indeed be this same Calliope. Another factor which lends credence to this conclusion is the fact that, in "Isaiah lxiii.1-8.," a poem on an avowedly Judaeo-Christian subject, Wheatley invokes the "heav'nly muse" (after Milton?), not the "Celestial muse."

Just two poems before "Isaiah," in the first of the two companion poems, "An Hymn to the Morning" and "An Hymn to the Evening," the poet seeks aid from "ye ever honour'd nine." Subsequently she calls upon "Calliope [to] awake the sacred lyre,/ While thy fair sisters fan the pleasing fire" (56). As Calliope is the only one among the Muses whom Wheatley names in her extant poetry, she plainly gives priority to this Muse's inspiration of epic discourse. It follows, then, that the identity of the "tuneful goddess," the "Muse!" upon whom Wheatley calls in the ten-line invocation opening "Niobe in Distress," her second epyllion, must be Calliope. The "Celestial choir!" which opens "To . . . General Washington," must be the nine Muses. Note that this poem, like "An Hymn to the Morning," moves from all the Muses to simply "Muse!" several lines later (145). We can conclude that the poet, once again, must have Calliope in mind to provide inspiration for the cause of the goddess Freedom: "How pour her armies through a thousand gates." Wheatley elaborates upon this image with a six-line epic simile:

> As when Eolus heaven's fair face deforms,
> Enwrapp'd in tempest and a night of storms;
> Astonish'd ocean feels the wild uproar,
> The refluent surges beat the sounding shore;
> Or thick as leaves in Autumn's golden reign,
> Such, and so many, moves the warrior's train. (145)

In "On the Capture of General Lee," Wheatley again names the "Celestial muse!" (146), or Calliope, as she relates General Lee's "Hero's fate" while a captive of the British. "On the Death of General Wooster" also summons inspiration from "the Muse," or Calliope, in order to relate the noble death of another casualty of the Revolution, whose "Country's Cause . . . ever fir'd his mind" (149). The muse of "Liberty and Peace," although not named, may nonetheless be deduced. Calling her "Th' prescient Muse" whose prediction of an American victory in the struggle for independence at last has been realized, Wheatley quotes a line and a half from "To . . . General Washington." As the Muse in the poem about Washington is Calliope, then that same Muse, whose prediction proves accurate, must be the inspiration for "Liberty and Peace." All these references to Calliope contribute substantially to the fiber of Wheatley's intertextual epic. Moreover, that Wheatley enlists the aid of the principal female figure among the Muses bespeaks an admirable determination to write in the epic mode.

An investigation of Wheatley's epic hymns, a form strictly classical in origin but widely adapted by Renaissance poets from Spenser to Milton, demonstrates more powerfully her portrayal of the feminine principle. According to Francis C. Blessington, epic hymns may be defined as lyrics of praise that celebrate "a moment of solemn relief from the inexorable action related in the narrative, and dramatic structures [of epic], a moment without [outside] the movement of narrative time, an escape into an ideal world." These epic hymns, Blessington continues, provide "a pause in the action in order to acknowledge the ideal toward which the epic struggles" (472–73). This form's appearance in Wheatley's poetry suggests how sophisticated and learned a student of the epic mode she was.

Among her several epic hymns or paeans to various deities, only one, the "Ode to Neptune," centers on a male principle. Even in this instance, the poet invokes Neptune, god of the seas, for the purpose of securing safe passage from Boston to London for a female friend. This paean to the god of seas serves the *apeuktic* function of epic hymn, in which the poet prays ("The

Pow'r propitious hears the lay") that nothing untoward befall "Mrs. W" in her journey: "Be still, O tyrant of the main;/ Nor let thy brow contracted frowns betray,/ While my Susannah [not Wheatley herself] skims the wat'ry way." "Ode to Neptune" also pleads for a period of serenity, during which the sun may shed "benign his ray,/ And double radiance" may deck "the face of day" (76). A peaceful sea may reflect a second sun and hence a "double radiance." This plea for tranquillity, and a subsequent depiction of the quietude that may result if that tranquillity is granted, afford a temporary respite from Wheatley's subversive struggle for her own freedom in *Poems* and from America's nascent freedom fight, the central theme in her intertextual epic.

This epic hymn's emphasis upon one woman's desired safety points toward the power of the female principle, explicated by Wheatley in other epic hymns: "An Hymn to the Morning," "On Imagination," "On Recollection," "On Virtue," and the Freedom as goddess section in "To . . . General Washington." Only the last poem postdates Wheatley's manumission. As a paean delivered in subversive praise for a collective woman/goddess in rebellion against oppression, a portion of "Niobe in Distress" also serves the function of an epic hymn. Wheatley construes these epic hymns as powerful representations of: woman in nature, in "An Hymn to the Morning"; woman in art, in "On Imagination" and "On Recollection"; woman in society, in "On Virtue"; and woman in politics, in "Niobe in Distress" and "To . . . General Washington."

"An Hymn to the Morning" begins with a four-line invocation to "ye ever honour'd nine," an unusual concentration in a poem of only twenty lines. As the first phrase of the poem asks the Muses to "Attend my lays," we may conclude that the poet employs this four-line invocation to serve both this poem and its companion, "An Hymn to the Evening," a poem of eighteen lines which has no separate invocation. In this purely classical, *klytic* (invoking the presence of the goddess) hymn, Wheatley finds it insufficient merely to invoke the nine Muses; for, in line 13, the enraptured poet addresses by name Calliope, the Muse whose specific office is to inspire epic poetry. "*Calliope* awake the sacred lyre," the poet insists, "While thy fair sisters fan the pleasing fire" (ll. 13–14). "Morning" enables Wheatley and/or her reader to pause, creating a respite amid her several elegies—that is, her poems on pivotal occasions marking significant moments in the American freedom struggle, such as repeal of the Stamp Act by George III, a monarch whose "smile can set his subjects free!" (17). Pausing here also allows rest from the making of subversive records of her personal battle for freedom, such as "Goliath of Gath."

Celebration of her beloved dawn, or Aurora, evokes the memory of Wheatley's mother and perhaps gives the poet an opportunity to recall a freer time in her own life. The only hint of her African heritage suggested in this purely classical form comes in this couplet: "The bow'rs, the gales, the variegated skies/ In all their pleasures in my bosom rise" (57). "All their pleasures in my bosom rise" predicts her gesture toward her homeland in "Phillis's Reply to the Answer," in which she enthusiastically declares, "Charm'd with thy painting [verbal descriptions of the western coast of Africa], how my bosom burns!/ And pleasing Gambia on my soul returns" (144). In "Morning," we encounter references to "bow'rs," "gales" (here understood as gentle, warm breezes), and "variegated skies" (this last phrase resembling the epic formulas used to call up the dawn). All these phrases sound like the vocabulary of pastoral. Thus, in "Morning," the evocation of Wheatley's African heritage can be identified only by way of a later reference in another poem, underscoring the intertextual nature of Wheatley's opus, even if not consciously constructed.

Whether or not Wheatley, in "Morning," conjures up a recollection of her African homeland, she does pause to capture that moment in nature when first light frees all from the gloom of night. This moment the poet heralds with the apostrophe, "*Aurora* hail." She follows it with "and all the thousands dies,/ which deck thy progress through the vaulted skies." It is significant that she punctuates the conclusion of this couplet with a colon, for what follows immediately is a depiction of what the senses of sight, sound, and touch absorb during that moment when light bursts upon nature. Her purpose here seems to be to portray the spontaneity of this synaesthetic moment. First "the morn awakes, and wide extends her rays," stimulating the sense of sight. Then "On ev'ry leaf the gentle zephyr plays," arousing the sense of hearing, as the leaves "play" while the "gentle zephyr" moves them along.

This warm breeze must be experienced through the persona's sense of touch; how else could the speaker know that the breeze is both gentle and warm? "Harmonious lays the feather'd race resume," the poet continues, again calling up the senses of sound and sight, as the persona responds first to the sounds of the birds and then to their identity. We know she sees them, because without that experience the next line would be impossible to construe: "Dart the bright eye, and shake the painted plume" (56). The persona can know that the bird's eye "darts" only because she has taken in the expanding rays of the dawn, as reflected in the eye of the bird. Birds shake their feathers, of course, as part of their daily waking routine. The fact that the persona has chosen to call the feathers "plumes" suggests one of Eunice Bourne's exotic birds in *The Fishing Lady* or, even more likely, the memory of some particularly colorful species of African fowl. That this close description is drawn from nature does not lessen Wheatley's capacity to intimate the power of the female principle's participation in the affairs of nature; after all, it is Aurora, goddess of the dawn, who has made this scene possible.

So moved is the poet by her evocation of Aurora that she summons up the muse of epic poetry, Calliope, another powerful female force—this one able, if she chooses, to awaken in the poet "the sacred lyre" of epic discourse. This relaxed moment within her intertextual epic permits her, without conscious calculation, to make her intertextual invocation to the epic muse. In keeping with her subversive methodology, this plea to "awake the sacred lyre" occurs in an apparently innocuous celebration of the dawn. Again Wheatley has snatched her laurel while her white readers "indulgent smile upon the deed." Note that the conspiracy here has been brought about by women, with the poet plainly in control of all parts—Aurora, Calliope, and her eight sisters. Again the action points toward Wheatley as heroine of her own epic struggle to be free. One is tempted to conclude that Wheatley is fully conscious of the conspiracy.

This pause captured in "Morning" results in a declaration of the dimensions of Wheatley's poetic adventure and eases her readers into an explication of her own theory of poetics. This theory she presents in "On Recollection" and "On Imagination," both located at the center of *Poems*, suggesting that they comprise the centerpiece of her volume. Within these two poems, this poet delineates how memory and imagination empower her poetic production. At the same time, Wheatley depicts these two abstractions as goddesses, Memory and Imagination. Thus each poem becomes a hybrid—an epic hymn used as a metaphorical arena for explicating her poetics. That she chooses the epic hymn for her theoretical declaration reminds us of her subversive strategy. To deal with oppression and to accuse oppressors, she employs a genre favored by Renaissance authors preoccupied with classical tradition. Once more, her predominantly white readers "indulgent smile upon the deed."

"On Recollection" and "On Imagination," as stated, invoke the presence of Memory and Imagination, fulfilling the klytic designation of the epic hymn. In addition, each poem-as-hymn primarily serves the *mythic* function of "relating a story about the god" (Blessington 471). Here the poet introduces her readers to her idea of the principal attributes of each goddess. As mother of the nine Muses and therefore a fecund female principle, Memory possesses "immortal pow'r" which enables the poet's mind to retain "The ample treasure of her secret stores." Wheatley holds that "in her [i.e., in Memory's or Mneme's] pomp of images display'd," this faculty "To the high-raptur'd poet gives her aid,/ Through the unbounded regions of the mind,/ Diffusing light celestial and refin'd" (62). The office of memory, then, is to present to the mind of the enraptured poet, moved to engage the creative process, a range of images virtually without limit. The mind temporarily is freed from the vicissitudes of the real world. Even so, Wheatley clearly insists upon a moral function for memory when she asserts that Mneme diffuses "light celestial and refin'd," or purified. The poet's memory enlightens her mind, clarifying the significance of the "pomp of images display'd."

This insistence upon memory's moral function, invoking the "Moral" in the title of her *Poems*, leads the poet next to explore immoral behavior. As Mneme "paints the actions done/ By ev'ry tribe beneath the rolling sun" (63), memory has blessed "ev'ry virtue" and "Has vice condemn'd." While recall of virtue's achievements conjures sounds "Sweeter than music to the ravish'd ear" (predicting Keats's "unheard melodies"), rehearsal of deeds carried out by "the race/ Who scorn her warnings and despise her grace" unveils "each horrid crime." Reading this passage subversively, the phrase "horrid crime" likely refers to slavery.

This adverse memory provokes Mneme to deliver a "cup of wormwood" to some unspecified receiver. Having herself suffered under the yoke of slavery for many years, surely Wheatley is qualified to receive this cup of bitterness. We should note, though, that the poet identifies "*each* [my emphasis] horrid crime" and thus multiplies the possible victims many times over. Accordingly, "Days, years" have been "misspent," bringing about "a hell of woe!" This "hell of woe" is not Wheatley's, however; for, in an earlier version, "Recollection, to Miss A—— M——" (March 1772), the poet renders this line: "The time mis-spent augments their hell of woes" (213). *Their* clearly refers to [the white] *race* four lines earlier. The later revision, in which the poet has removed the pronoun "their," causes the line to become more ambiguous, bespeaking a refinement of Wheatley's subversive style. Perhaps her more direct identification in the version of March 1772 indicates her reaction to Boston's rejection of her first proposal for a volume issued on February 29, 1772.

In any event, memory has brought starkly to the surface "the worst tortures that our souls can know." The use of the collective pronoun *our* arrests our attention; while it may identify the poet and her black brothers and sisters, this collective *our* definitely includes the perpetrators of "each horrid crime." Assuredly their victims have endured and still do endure "the worst tortures"; but, as Wheatley's text clearly points an accusing finger at "the race" that causes these horrid crimes, these "worst tortures" extend to those who have brought the slaves from Africa to America, to those who sold them as chattel, and to those who have purchased them.

When she next states that "eighteen years," her age at the composition of this poem, "have run their destin'd course," the reader who does not read carefully may easily conclude that she is talking about herself. If she is identifying herself as the culpable party, then her readers are left to wonder exactly what her horrid crimes were. Unless she has in mind the horrors she sustained during the terrifying Middle Passage (tortures for which she bore no guilt), Wheatley's own "hell of woe" surely came at the end of her life, when she herself declined, as she watched her three children die, all because of starvation and neglect—conditions for which she also bore no guilt. Thus, when she subsequently refers to the "follies" which passed during "that period," she probably recalls not her own "follies" but those of others. According to the *Oxford English Dictionary*, *folly*, or, more particularly, *follies*, is used in the Miles Coverdale and the King James Bibles as a synonym for *sins* or *crimes*; given Wheatley's fondness for the King James Bible, we may conclude that she understands *follies* as the crimes of slavery.

These follies, which have passed "Unnotic'd" (perhaps "suppressed" would be closer to the sad truth), she now observes "writ in brass" (63). The phrase "writ in brass" closely resembles Shakespeare's "Men's evil manners live in brass" (*Henry VIII* IV.ii.45), a resemblance fully in keeping with Wheatley's usage. Immediately following recollection of these evil deeds, the poet says, "Sure 'tis mine to be asham'd, and mourn." Superficially, she appears again to be implicating herself as an agent of past "follies." Recalling her subversive praxis, along with the serious definition of *follies*, we find here no harmless exercise in self-recrimination. Rather, what prompts her to be "asham'd" is her status as a slave (not to mention the shame of all those enslaved); she mourns, and as well feels shame, because, in the Middle Passage, she lost her African parents and perhaps relatives or protectors.

Abruptly, the next stanza shifts away from the preceding unhappy recollection, with the apostrophe, "O Virtue." This phrase introduces a four-line *euktic* hymn, in which the poet solicits Virtue as a goddess who perhaps can intervene on her behalf, and not merely by assuaging her grief. Rather, "smiling in immortal green" (the color of Dante's Hope), she perhaps can "change the scene" radically by bringing about Wheatley's freedom. If Virtue does ameliorate the poet's predicament by serving as "guide" to her "future days," then Wheatley, as poet and ultimately as heroine of her own intertextual epic, vows "to pay the tribute of [her] praise." Having thus composed a hymn within a hymn (the larger one on Memory and the smaller, enclosed one on Virtue), Wheatley has created a unique structure, demonstrating her originality. But she has accomplished more.

If Virtue can nullify future instances of "the worst tortures," Wheatley, as exemplary heroine of her intertextual epic, can point the direction toward release for all oppressed people. Recollection and Virtue work in conjunction, then, to state the problem—that is, the universal struggle against oppression, this struggle embracing both the growing colonial resistance to British authority and the poet's own campaign to secure freedom for herself and all those enslaved. The dual virtues also warn oppressors of the inevitable consequences of continued oppression. Indeed, the remainder of "On Recollection" delivers the dire admonition that "The wretch" who provokes "the vengeance of the skies" (divine punishment) by prolonging "the worst tortures" finally will awake "in horror and surprize," only to howl "in anguish" and repent "too late." That man is "thrice blest," however, "who, in her [Memory's] sacred shrine,/ Feels himself shelter'd from the wrath divine!" (64). This latter attitude describes the classical obeisance appropriate toward the gods.

This epic hymn, "On Recollection," which incorporates the short hymn on Virtue, explains to attentive readers what is at stake in Wheatley's intertextual epic. Assuredly, the poet employs recollection to conjure up an "ample treasure" of entertaining images and strains "Sweeter than music." Memory permits her to explore all regions of her mind, "unbounded"; but neither intellectual honesty nor commitment to her central subject—freedom, implied by her use of the participle "unbounded"—will permit her to ignore freedom's enemy, oppression. What ensues in this poem is one of Wheatley's most penetrating investigations into the very nature of human oppression. That she casts this investigation in classical terms suggests her growing frustration with the ineffectiveness of Christian and/or biblical appeals concerning slavery.

Nor do Christian and/or biblical appeals inform her next poem, "On Imagination." Again Wheatley couches her theoretics in terms classical, perhaps reflecting her continued frustration with the Christian churches' failure to address the slavery issue. As the "imperial queen" of the mind, "Imagination" projects a powerful vitality (65), whose control extends even to the mighty recollection. The poet extols this faculty, challenging, "Who can sing thy force?" (66). Then, as in "To Maecenas," where she proves her capacity to handle epic discourse, she proceeds to demonstrate the force that, in her hands, imagination can exert. For Wheatley, Imagination is a decidedly feminine principle, as is Imagination's subordinate, Fancy. Together these two entities empower the poet to create a new world of idyllic pastoral by acting upon the body of "images display'd" by recollection. For a time this pastoral world releases the slave from oppression.[8]

Wheatley's construction of an ideal pastoral world appears to fulfill the classical hymn's directive to transport the reader into a moment outside "narrative time, an escape into an ideal world." As we saw in discussing this poem in chapter 4, however, her pastoral accomplishes more than idealistic transport. For this ideal world contains the figures Flora and Sylvanus. Flora's most recognized identity is as goddess of flowers, and Sylvanus's is as God of boundaries. These identities do not approach the application Wheatley makes with her subversive praxis, though. As we saw earlier, Flora from ancient times was a prostitute, and Sylvanus symbolizes wilderness beyond boundaries. With this pair in her ideal world, Wheatley frees her soul and challenges the status quo. She seeks to break the "iron bands" of slavery and enjoy "flow'ry riches" and sparkling roses bejeweled with nectar, in stark contrast with the barren cold of Boston's "northern tempests" (68).

Wheatley's ideal world calls her subversive tactics into play once more, this time in relation to her white enslavers. William King's *Heathen Gods and Heroes* (1710) was the most popular handbook of classical mythology from the time of its publication until the appearance of John Lempriere, *Classical Dictionary* (1788). According to King, Flora was married to Zephyrus, god of the West Wind. The marriage forms a link to the earlier line, "We on thy [Imagination's] pinions can surpass the wind." In Wheatley's hands, the "force" of Imagination's wings can exceed the power of the wind and "leave the rolling universe behind." Note the poet's use of the pronoun *we*, which first appears in the poem's first line, in the phrase "we see." Wheatley challenges all her readers to observe the results of "my attempts" (her poems) and to acknowledge her "triumph" in relating this daring analysis of imagination in "my song." We, her audience, may participate in her quest for the sublime vantage point, but this song, this effort, remains hers and not ours. For she is the creator who sings of an imagination so powerful that its wings can carry all beyond the realm of the wind, placing her readers mentally in such a position that "there in one view we grasp the mighty whole." Thus we experience a superlative moment in the aesthetic quest for the sublime.

Lest her readers forget that this enabling force originates within her own mind, the poet asserts that, under her control, imagination can "with new worlds amaze th' unbounded soul." In "On Recollection," she ranges "Through the unbounded regions of the mind"—a process that eventually leads her to indict slavery and its practitioners. Now this "new world" unbinds the soul, functioning as a locus for release. Of course, the white folks, the majority of her readers, are not bound, at least not in the manner in which she and her fellow slaves are bound.

This unbounded new world that Wheatley has created may look harmless enough, but it has been generated by a power which exceeds that of Flora's husband. Flora herself, we have learned, is much more than the goddess of flowers. King tells us that Juno requested her aid in finding a means to conceive a child without sexual union. Flora helpfully directed her attention to a certain flower, whose odor allowed her to conceive Mars, "God of Battels" (154). When we find that in some traditions Sylvanus, too, was a son of Mars, encountering these two deities in Wheatley's new world looks neither harmless nor accidental. Wheatley clearly is fighting a battle of ideas whose weapons are words. With these military associations, the poet here presses hard the bounds of her subversive praxis by issuing an implicit threat.

"Winter" is the entity who "frowns to *Fancy's* raptur'd eyes" and therefore is to be overcome. This entity may be taken to be Boston's white people who refused to support the poet's first proposal for a book and who endorse the institution of slavery. Wheatley's battle for freedom, then, assumes two fronts. The first is total rejection of servility, through a temporary escape into an ideal world of unrestrained abandon. Upon closer scrutiny, we discover that this so-called ideal world contains symbols which not only suggest movement outside the boundaries of societal order but whose menacing military alignment severely admonishes.

Wheatley's second front, this one perhaps less menacing, represents an effort toward *rapprochement*. She signals this strategy in the line, "Sylvanus may diffuse his honours round." Recall that, in the preceding poem, "On Recollection," Mneme has the power to fly "Through the unbounded regions of the mind," as Imagination and Fancy do here. Memory also has the capacity for "Diffusing light celestial and refin'd." Perhaps, then, part of the "honours" Sylvanus diffuses is light—the light of knowledge. Can Wheatley be hoping or even expecting that her conscientious readers will grasp her message? She certainly expects all readers to recognize the power of her imagination in the creation of such a new world; for, immediately following this construction of a new world, she declares, "Such is thy pow'r . . . O thou the leader of the mental train." If, as she maintains, the products of this faculty "are wrought" "In full perfection," then surely slavery cannot exist in her ideal structures. As an oppressed poet nevertheless exercising her own agency,[9] she wishes to bring enlightenment to all oppressors. If she is successful in doing so, their dark night of oppression cannot and must not long persist, for such persistence could provoke military response. Just so, Wheatley indicates her determination to sing the moral song proclaiming that all must be free.

The next few lines appear to celebrate the sublime, or the enthusiastic, passions; however, they include much more than a celebration of the sublime. Describing Imagination, "the imperial queen," Wheatley writes, "Before thy throne the subject-passions bow,/ Of subject-passions sov'reign ruler Thou." Why are the passions subject? Given the "imperial" office of this goddess as ruler of mental faculties, Imagination's dominion over the passions certainly is credible. But are we equally certain that these "passions" connote only sublime feelings? A glance at one of the texts of Alexander Pope gives us a clue. Wheatley's familiarity with Pope is almost proverbial, yet gestures toward this poet are not particularly common in her work. Even so, we should not be surprised to encounter such a gesture. Pope's "Epistle to Bathhurst" is devoted entirely to a consideration of the consequences of a passion for riches; such a passion can become so intense that it amounts to avarice. As Pope puts it so well, "The ruling Passion, be it what it will,/

The ruling Passion conquers Reason still" (182, ll. 155–56). By the time Wheatley writes "On Imagination," in her poetics imagination has become the equivalent of reason, for Imagination is "the leader of the mental train." In this position, Wheatley anticipates Wordsworth's "Imagination . . . [is] Reason in her most exalted mood" (Stillinger 360).[10] If by "passions" Wheatley is attempting to call up cases of avarice in addition to her obvious reference to the sublime, then each expression of passion must also indicate one of slavery; for surely slavery is the handmaiden of avarice. Departing from Pope's example, Wheatley clearly states that the passions she calls up are "subject" to the rule of her imagination. So, rather than endure oppressive "woes, a painful endless train" (*Poems* 152), this poet's "imperial queen" (note the association of "imperial" to political power) has only to command and "joy rushes on the heart." At least for the duration of this poetic moment, then, the poet accomplishes the abolition of avarice/slavery.

Having reclaimed her ideal world, "Fancy," Imagination's subordinate, now directs Imagination's attention to the dawn that belongs to the poet's mother: "now might Aurora rise . . . While a pure stream of light o'erflows the skies." Before, this pure light pointed toward knowledge gained by Wheatley's careful readers. If it does so here as well, then we follow as she personalizes her struggle for freedom: "The monarch of the day I might behold" (67). As readers of her intertextual epic, we participate in her predicament as unintentional heroine.

And we learn how powerful is her compulsion to be free. At the very moment when she "might" linger long in this, a second ideal world, Wheatley reports with regret that "*Winter* austere forbids me to aspire." This strong line sounds the end of her celebration and analysis of the power of Imagination, the imperial queen. Now a return of the gelid cold, associated with the poet's white oppressors (not to be taken as all Boston's whites), brings us up short. They would, if they could, "forbid" Wheatley both to exercise her creative capacity and to publish her work, for such abilities indicate that Africans are not inferior and so undercut a major justification for slavery.

Perhaps the most poignant forbidden behavior Wheatley must renounce is that of aspiration. Cruel Winter puts an end to her "Soaring through air to find the bright abode" (66); and "northern tempests," or individual occasions of oppressive torment, "damp the rising fire" of her creative anima. These freezing storms "chill the tides of *Fancy's* flowing sea." Fancy's first surge produced the new world of Flora and Sylvanus; her second created the pure light of her mother's dawn. Twice Wheatley has demonstrated the staying power of her "imperial queen," the goddess Imagination. Yet now she brings to a close "my song," because, she states, her song is "unequal." In fact, the words "unequal lay" are the last two of the poem. Readers initially may think the poet means that her "lay" cannot indefinitely sustain a mythical world. Given her subversive praxis, however, more is at work here. The word *unequal*, especially when used by a slave, captures our attention; if her song is not equal, then it follows that its singer also is not equal. This question of equality resides in the socioeconomic politics of the real world. How would her white audience have reacted if the poet had claimed that her song was an "equal" one?

Wheatley's accomplishment in this poem amounts to a verbal assault upon her oppressors. In the mouth of her imperial queen, she has placed a narrative of outrage against the despised institution. However, she holds out an olive branch of sorts, when she suggests that proper enlightenment of white enslavers may bring about the abolition of oppression. If release from oppression is not forthcoming, then Wheatley retains another weapon—her pen, her poems. "On Imagination," in particular, drives home the threat of her pen (recalling her contemplative pose, pen in hand, in the frontispiece to her 1773 *Poems*). So powerful is the performance of her goddess Imagination that this poem hurls an epic curse, after the fashion of Polyphemus, who, at the end of book IX of *The Odyssey*, pronounces a curse upon Odysseus. The typical epic curse, according to Stephen Greenblatt, is "uttered from a position of powerlessness, but also in the expectation that powerlessness will not endure forever" (xv). This description certainly applies to Wheatley's predicament.

While not quite exerting the force of an epic curse, Wheatley's "On Virtue" powerfully illustrates her continuing preoccupation with epic hymns. Cast in the role of "Auspicious queen," the goddess Virtue joins the pantheon of Wheatley's formidable goddesses. Wheatley even underscores Virtue's forcefulness in "On Recollection," as Virtue "exert[s] thy pow'r" (64) in the interpretation of Memory's "pomp of images." Like "On Recollection" and "On Imagination," this epic hymn, while invoking the presence of the goddess, moves toward the mythic function in its description of this goddess's office. Indeed, in Wheatley's conception, imploring Virtue's attendance upon her assures that the goddess will not abandon her "to the false joys of time!" but instead will "guide my steps to endless life and bliss" (13). In accord with Blessington's insistence that the epic hymn promotes "an escape into an ideal world," into "a moment without [outside] the movement of narrative time," Wheatley fulfills this function of epic hymn once again in "On Virtue."

In viewing virtuous behavior as a guide toward "endless life and bliss," Wheatley asserts that "the ideal toward which the epic struggles" accords with her objective of securing release from cruel oppression. In the tradition of *Cato's* Marcia, Wheatley extols virtuous behavior as part of the dynamic evolution of America's sense of a cultural self, separate from that of Britain and the Continent. The rebellion this poet registers in her epic hymns to Niobe (in "Niobe in Distress") and to Freedom (in "To . . . Washington") carries over into her politics. Two of the more substantial statements concerning her politics appear in these hybrid works. While "Niobe in Distress" is an epyllion and "To . . . Washington" a panegyric, both contain sections which serve the klytic function of the epic hymn. The poet's paean to the goddess Freedom, in the praise poem on Washington, has been discussed above; here we only need add that the four-line tribute emphasizes the light emanating from the goddess:

> The goddess comes, she moves divinely fair,
> Olive and laurel bind her golden hair:
> Wherever shines this native of the skies,
> Unnumber'd charms and recent graces rise. (145)

Wheatley echoes this depiction in "Liberty and Peace," where Freedom appears as "the bright Progeny of Heaven" who "spread[s] her golden Ray . . . To every Realm" (156).

Wheatley claims this same radiance for her characterization of Niobe, which differs radically from that of Ovid. In Ovid, Niobe does not appear "all beautiful in woe," yet she is so described twice in Wheatley's epyllion (101 and 110). Unlike Ovid, Sandys, or William King, Wheatley, in a twenty-four line interpolation, makes Niobe a goddess. In this lengthy interpolation, the poet carefully points out that Niobe's father was "Tantalus divine" and that *his* father was "Dodonean Jove." She also calls attention to the fact that Niobe's maternal grandfather was "*Atlas*, who with mighty pains/ Th' ethereal axis on his neck sustains." Atlas has strong and unmistakable connections to Africa, a detail that cannot have been lost on Wheatley. The poet takes care also to observe that "Her spouse, *Amphion*, who from *Jove* too springs,/ Divinely taught to sweep the sounding strings" (102). These genealogical attributions of divinity bring to Wheatley's Niobe a great dignity wholly absent in Ovid's; the emphasis in her interpolation rests upon Niobe's divinity. She and her equally divine husband produce children who seem to inherit a part of their parents' divinity, though sadly not their immortality.

Niobe's seven sons and seven daughters nevertheless shine as bright and "beauteous as the op'ning morn." Their brilliance Wheatley further elaborates in a four-line epic simile emphasizing that they give off light:

> As when *Aurora* fills the ravish'd sight,
> And decks the orient realms with rosy light
> From their bright eyes the living splendors play,
> Nor can beholders bear the flashing ray.

Even though Niobe's fourteen children appear to compete with Wheatley's beloved dawn in brilliance, "Wherever, *Niobe*, thou turn'st thine eyes,/ New beauties kindle, and new joys arise!" (102). This description of Niobe's divine power parallels Wheatley's depiction of Freedom: "Wherever shines this native of the skies,/ Unnumber'd charms and recent graces rise." Of "the imperial queen," Imagination, she says, "At thy command joy rushes on the heart." This half-woman, half-divine character symbolizes rebellion against an oppressive tyranny. That Wheatley (in "Niobe in Distress") assigns her so many divine attributes clarifies both Wheatley's narrative of the American colonial struggle for freedom and her personal struggle to be free. Rather than transforming Niobe into cold marble, as Ovid does, Wheatley insists, by ending her poem with Niobe utterly untransformed, that her Niobe remains the immortal goddess described earlier, in the lengthy interpolation. Indeed, Wheatley presses the case for Niobe's divinity to such a degree that we almost become persuaded that Niobe is the equal of Latona, mother of Apollo and Phoebe. She does not deserve the punishment she receives, despite her "love too vehement" (103). Indeed, Niobe's "Love too vehement" merely masks "Love of Freedom," which "is impatient of Oppression and pants for Deliverance."

These powerful female figures, thinly masked as goddesses, move decisively, if not always successfully, in the arenas of nature, art, society, and politics. In these examples, Wheatley invites her readers to see women, irrespective of race, as formidable players in world affairs. She uses the form of the epic hymn to register objections to oppressive practices and to assert the power of women, even when they may, as in the case of Niobe, be forced into the role of rebellious underdog. Niobe remains "all beautiful in woe," admonishing the current power structure that her struggle has not abated; it has not been, nor will it be, forgotten. In "Liberty and Peace" (composed well after her manumission, when her need to employ the subversive mode had begun to diminish), Wheatley celebrates Freedom, declaring that now "On *Albion's* Head the curse to Tyrants [has come] due." Then she recommends:

> Now sheathe the Sword that bade the Brave atone
> With guiltless Blood for Madness not their own,
> Sent from th' Enjoyment of their native Shore
> Ill-fated—never to behold her more! (155)

At first glance, one may suppose that the poet is attempting to describe the British, French, and German soldiers sent to fight and die in a strange land.

These lines also capture the plight of African Americans, men such as Crispus Attucks, about whose martyrdom Wheatley almost certainly speaks in the "On the Affray in King Street, on the Evening of the 5th of March," a work that has not survived. Other than the Boston Massacre on March 5,

1770, what major event is known to have occurred on this day of the month during Wheatley's lifetime? Samuel Eliot Morison describes this event as follows: "On the evening of the 5th, a group which John Adams described as 'Negroes and mulattos, Irish teagues and outlandish jack-tars' began pelting with snowballs a redcoat who was standing sentry-go at the customs house on King (now State) Street" (*Oxford History* 200). The *Oxford English Dictionary* notes that, during Wheatley's century, *affray* designated "a breach of the peace, caused by fighting or riot in a public place." In this poem, the poet surely spoke of Adams's multicultural and very American mix of men. This event, involving black men and occurring only a few feet from the Wheatley mansion on the corner of King Street and Mackerel Lane, could not have escaped Wheatley's attention. From the Revolution's very beginning, then, this poet was aware of the sacrifice African American men were making for freedom's cause. She certainly was aware, too, that African American men in large numbers continued to give their lives for the same cause throughout the Revolutionary era.

The phrases "for Madness not their own" and "guiltless Blood" seem better applied to the predicament of Africans caught up in the chaotic conflict of a continent not their own, a conflict in which they are "guiltless." The language of the line, "Sent from th' Enjoyment of their native Shore," resembles the line, "snatch'd from *Afric's* fancy'd happy seat," in "To the . . . Earl of Dartmouth" (*Poems* 74). For, as she states in "Phillis's Reply," in Wheatley's mind the "sportive fancy" conjures up recollections of "pleasing Gambia," a land of "native grace in spring's luxuriant reign" where "Smiles the gay mead, and Eden blooms again" (144). In "On Imagination," Wheatley's Imagination, the "imperial queen," recreates this same paradisical world—a land where "fields may flourish, and gay scenes arise," a "fancy'd happy seat" in her native Africa recalled by her and her black brothers and sisters, far from "Madness not their own." If "new-born *Rome* shall give *Britannia* Law," then, "As from the East," Wheatley declares in yet another epic simile, "th' illustrious King of Day,/ With rising Radiance drives the Shades [of oppression] away,/ so Freedom comes array'd with charms divine,/ And in her Train Commerce and Plenty shine." Surely this new "Commerce and Plenty," about which the poet speaks, will encourage "The generous Spirit that *Columbia* fires" (155) to grant all African Americans their freedom.

Wheatley still hoped, as late as 1784, that America's epic freedom struggle would summon up a "generous Spirit" on behalf of all African Americans. Recall her earlier Wooster elegy, in which the dying general, another martyr to the freedom fight, pleads that the newly forming country, Columbia/ America, will extend "generous freedom" to "Afric's blameless race." Even at the beginning of the twenty-first century, of course, Wheatley's dream of freedom for all Americans—including women, blacks, and Native Americans—has yet to be realized fully. Nonetheless, this first African American to publish a book exemplified in her work a substantial—indeed, a heroic—determination to see America's promise of freedom made good for all Americans, not just white American males.

In drawing the parameters of this freedom struggle, Wheatley employs the most exalted literary discourse available to her, that of the epic. While carrying out the grand design of "Liberty and Peace," she invokes the muse of epic, Calliope. She constructs epic hymns, all but one of which celebrate powerful women figures in nature, art, society, and politics. She writes two poems of some length which self-consciously manipulate concrete elements of epic—her short epics, or epyllia, "Goliath of Gath" and "Niobe in Distress." Both these poems contain heroic figures of great strength who defy patriarchal hegemonies.

So pervasive in this poet's work is her preoccupation with epic discourse that, unconsciously, she weaves an intertextual epic throughout her oeuvre. In constructing this intertextual epic, she draws upon Vergil, Homer, and Milton, as well as upon her own African heritage. Moreover, as we have seen is characteristic of American literature and culture generally, she often commingles elements of the myths of Adam and Aeneas. Not only does she vividly endorse a Washingtonian pietas in this intertextual epic, but she also elaborates a feminized version of this pietas, after the tradition of Marcia in Addison's *Cato*. Again and again she reiterates the epic theme of America's freedom struggle—a struggle which someday must deliver freedom to all Americans, regardless of race, gender, or creed.[11]

One final point remains regarding Wheatley's voice, raised on behalf of women. While she may have required the "approval" of "the most respectable characters in *Boston*" (*Collected Works* 7), all white males, to authenticate her authorship, she was encouraged to write largely by women. Her mistress, Susanna Wheatley, promoted her as a talented author to Selina Hastings, Countess of Huntingdon; Hastings later backed the publication of the *Poems*, after the Boston patriarchy had rejected a version of it. It is likely that the poet was taught to read English by Mary Wheatley, daughter of Susanna and several years Phillis's senior. Wheatley sought emotional support from her black soul mate, Obour Tanner, as is obvious in her many letters to Obour. In short, if Phillis Wheatley succeeded in becoming one of the world's famed authors, her accomplishment was assisted substantially by an *interracial* community of women! How could she not use the power of her pen to advance the cause of women?

Phillis Wheatley utilized epic discourse; that issue is no longer in contention. Nor should doubt remain that her application of epic discourse proves her an artist of considerable intellect and sophistication. Yet Nina Baym in "Mercy Otis Warren's Gendered Melodrama of Revolution," opens with this stark pronouncement: "Among the many Massachusetts intellectuals who wrote to support the patriot cause before and during the American Revolution, Mercy Otis Warren (1728–1814) was the only woman" (531). While one might have expected to see the name of Abigail Adams inscribed in the log of Revolutionary era intellectuals, surely Wheatley's substantial contribution to intellectual discourse of this period no longer can be ignored. If such critics as McWilliams, Gilbert, and Baym do not ignore Wheatley altogether, they do not take her seriously, for they have not really "read" her works.

The lack of serious attention to this minority author regrettably typifies the hegemonic attitude predominant among academics; traditionally that attitude has marginalized minorities in American culture. Wheatley's poems and prose demonstrate that she has mastered the two principal modes of discourse which govern American culture, the Adamic and the classical. Not only has she mastered both modes of discourse, but also, in deftly and cogently manipulating them, she constructs a distinctly American discourse which moves from necessary subversion to direct expectation. After more than two hundred years of relative neglect and misappropriation, the minority discourse of this gifted author still cries out for serious attention. In the spirit of James Madison's determination to protect the minority voices within American culture, Wheatley's creative discourse demands to be heard, alongside that of Timothy Dwight, John Trumbull, and Joel Barlow.

PART III

AENEAS BECOMES ADAM: 1784 TO THE PRESENT

7

THE RADICAL SHIFT IN DISCOURSE

JOEL BARLOW MARKEDLY ALTERED HIS ATTITUDE TOWARD EPIC DISCOURSE BETWEEN THE WRITING OF HIS *VISION OF COLUMBUS* (1787) AND HIS *Columbiad* (1807). At least the attitude displayed in the "Introduction" to *Vision* differs significantly from that in the "Preface" to *Columbiad*. In *Vision*'s "Dedication" to Louis XVI, Barlow celebrates the French king for "raising an infant empire, in a few years, to a degree of importance, which several ages were scarcely thought sufficient to produce" (104). In order best to represent the rise of the "infant empire" (the newly formed United States of America), Barlow avows that, "at first," he "formed an idea of attempting a regular Epic Poem," which suggests that he had a high regard for the classical epic genre. Reflection taught him, however, that "the most brilliant subjects incident to such a plan would arise from the consequences of [Columbus's] discovery" of America and therefore would receive the most plausible representation "in vision" (121). Hence the *Vision of Columbus* became a narrative revealed to Columbus while he was imprisoned. This narrative consisted of a succession of events occurring in the "land of transport" (126) where "fair Freedom seeks her kindred skies"—the shape of this narrative assumed the structure of a vision.

The structure of this vision significantly resembles that of book VI of the *Aeneid*, in which Anchises, Aeneas's deceased father, contributes to his "omnis curae casusque levamen" (III, 709; alleviation of every anxiety and misfortune), by granting him a vision of Rome's future glories. It is no exaggeration to say that Anchises's revelation to Aeneas provides the prototype for all subsequent such visions of future glory. Prominent among these are those composed by Francis Bernard in the "Epilogus" of *Pietas et Gratulatio*, and by Philip Freneau and Hugh Henry Brackenridge in their "Rising Glory of America." In addition, there is a close connection between Barlow's Isabella, who has served Columbus so long as his "gentle guardian" and now has become "thou dear departed shade" (127), and Vergil's Anchises, who acts toward Aeneas in a similar (albeit more intimate) manner.

Barlow employs "a radiant seraph" (128) to bring to Columbus, "the great Discoverer" (142), the vision of glory. The seraph promises Columbus that he is about to behold

> Far happier realms their future charms unfold,
> In nobler pomp another Pisgah rise,
> Beneath whose foot thine own Canaan lies;
> There, rapt in vision, hail the distant clime,
> And taste the blessings of remotest time. (130)

On the one hand, Columbus, like Moses, will view the "promised land" of America. On the other, like Aeneas, he will be given the vision of grand events to come. Barlow deftly blends the myths of Adam and Aeneas.

The "Preface" to *The Columbiad*, however, makes evident a radical change in Barlow's "public" stance toward his classical predecessors who worked in the epic genre. Addressing "The classical reader" (375), Barlow again defends his decision not to adopt the "regular epic form" for his poem, maintaining that "The attempt . . . must have diminished and *debased* [emphasis mine] a series of actions which really were great in themselves and could not be disfigured without losing their interest" (376). Soon Barlow submits that "the real design of the poem, should be beneficial to society." According to Barlow, however, the works of Homer have had just the opposite effect. As Barlow puts it, "They have unhappily done more harm than good."

Barlow continues his assault on Homer's *Iliad* and *Odyssey* with one of the most hostile denunciations of a classical author this researcher has encountered. While Homer may have been a genius, eliciting from Barlow a "veneration . . . equal to that of his most idolatrous readers," Barlow's "reflections on the history of human errors have forced upon" this poet "the opinion that his existence has really proved one of the signal misfortunes of mankind" (379). Nor does Barlow limit his assault to Homer; he takes on Vergil as well, finding the *Aeneid*'s morality "nearly as pernicious as that of the works of Homer" (379–80). Barlow even goes on to remark, "The real design of his poem was to increase the veneration of the people for a master, whoever he might be, and to encourage like Homer the great system of military depredation" (380).

Interestingly enough, despite his disclaimer regarding the classical epic discourse of Homer and Vergil, Barlow places on his *Columbiad* title page a famous stanza devoted to Columbus, from Tasso's *Jerusalem Delivered.* In this stanza, given below in the contemporary Ralph Nash translation, Tasso suggests his own epic's debt to the classics:

> You, Columbus, will spread your fortunate sails so far toward an unknown pole that Fame (that has a thousand eyes and a thousand wings) will scarcely follow with her eyes your flight. Let her sing of Alcides and Bacchus, and of you let it be enough that she only give some hint for your posterity: for that little will give you a lasting memorial most worthy of Poetry and History. (327)

Barlow picks up on Tasso's allusion to Hercules (Alcides), maintaining that the epic heroism explicit in carrying out his twelve labors would have given Homer a moral dignity wholly absent in his emphasis on the exploits of Achilles and Odysseus (significantly, Barlow does not mention Bacchus). Placing this quotation beneath the title of his own "epic," however, definitely locates *The Columbiad* within a long European tradition of epics. Certainly Tasso's knowledge and use of Vergil's *Aeneid* are beyond question.

That Barlow himself read Vergil is obvious from *The Columbiad*'s opening couplet: "I sing the Mariner who first unfurl'd/ An eastern banner o'er the western world" (413). This echoing of the first lines of the *Aeneid* ("Arma virumque cano, Trojae qui primus ab oris/ Italiam fato profugus Lavinaque venit/ litora"; Arms and the man I sing, the first who came from the regions of Troy, exiled by fate, to Italy and the Lavinian shores) is not so immediately present in the earlier *Vision of Columbus* which begins "Long had the Sage, the first who dared to brave/ The unknown dangers of the western wave" (125).

The later *Columbiad* contains an eight-line invocation, although Barlow invokes the inspiration of "Almighty Freedom"—"no miracle, no Muse but thee" (414). The epic convention of invocation is wholly lacking in the earlier *Vision*. Rather than the Christian seraph of *Vision*, the *Columbiad* invokes Hesper, bearer of the vision to Columbus and a classical designation for the evening star, according to Barlow's own note at the bottom of the page. Barlow also points out in this same note that, "Considering Hesper as the guardian genius, and Columbus as the discoverer of the western continent, [the United States] may derive its name, in poetical language, from either of theirs indifferently, and be called Hesperia or Columbia" (420 and 420n.).

Barlow omits from the *Columbiad* any Adamic references to "the Saviour [who] bleeds" and to "blood-stain'd steps [which] lead upwards to a throne" (129), both present in the opening lines of *Vision*. Thus, despite the hostile attitude toward Homer and Vergil expressed in the "Preface" to *The Columbiad*, the work's author displays a much greater loyalty to classical particulars in the later poem than in the earlier one. The net effect is that his *Columbiad* looks remarkably more Roman and/or Vergilian than *A Vision*.

In the later poem, however, Barlow condemns the martial emphasis of Homer's and Vergil's epics. The American patriot poet holds that "the aspiring genius of the age" will brook no more images of Olympian deities and their internecine warfare; no more, in Barlow's conception, shall "Titans groan beneath the rending ground." Indeed, Barlow insists that "No more" will the military exploits of the epic hero "madden up the mind,/ To crush, to conquer and enslave mankind,/ To build on ruin'd realms the shrine of fame,/ And load his [mankind's] numbers with a tyrant's name" (762–63).

In Barlow we can discern the operation of the acceptance and denial paradigm. Like Edward Taylor and Cotton Mather, both of whom publicly denied their obvious classicism, Barlow publicly censures classical morality, disavows the ancient epic form, but then exhibits in the text of *Columbiad* a more pronounced dependence upon epic form than he had shown earlier in *Vision*.

In the epic's "Postscript," Barlow observes that he has adopted many American principles of orthography (actually following Noah Webster's lead in promoting these "Americanized" innovations). Thus, he eliminated the *u* in *labor* and *honor,* and spelled *though* simply *tho*. Barlow subsequently names Webster, about whose work with an "Americanized" (Webster's coinage) spelling he asserts, "Our language will be much indebted [to Webster] for its purity and regularity" (856).

By 1807, Webster had already become the major player in bringing about a radical shift in discourse, whereby all things classical became debased and all things Adamic were valorized. Thus Barlow's reference here to Webster is particularly striking. Barlow's shift in attitude from veneration (one of Barlow's favorite words) for the great authors of classical epic to abject condemnation of the morality of Homer's and Vergil's epics is a clear example of the radical shift in discourse. As we have observed with Barlow, this radical shift is attended, perhaps inexorably, by a somewhat grudging acceptance of concrete classical particulars.

DYNAMICS OF THE RADICAL SHIFT

The twenty-year period between *Vision* and the *Columbiad* is roughly the time period (give or take five years on either end) in which the radical shift occurred. As we indicated above in the "Introduction," the paradeictic of the Foucauldian epistemic mutation accounts for this radical shift in discourse—that is, it entailed a demonstrably conscious attempt to denigrate the classical mode and valorize the Adamic. Foucault's "L'ordre du discours" provides a set of cultural determiners to chart this radical shift. According to this paradeictic, certain *external controls* coalesce, after the Treaty of Paris (1783), to reject all things British and to prohibit positive expression of what quickly came to be called Old World values. These external controls, motivated largely by political factors, soon began to establish procedures for making *internal rules* of discourse (recalling Foucault's definition of this concept). These rules debased the myth of Aeneas, now perceived as *not* American, and self-consciously raised up the Adamic myth, thought to embody the hard-fought and now realized objectives of the errand into the wilderness. With this Adamic mode of discourse ineradicably planted and in the process of being cultivated, *access to the knowledge* of the debased myth of Aeneas could be regulated—that is, the Aeneas myth could be deprecated in favor of the more palatable Adamic myth.

How, more precisely, did this politically motivated radical shift come about? As David Simpson argues convincingly in *Politics of American English*, "We should not underestimate the extent of the schism that the process of independence introduced into American minds about their residual allegiance, if any, to things British, whether cultural, economic, or simply emotional" (46). While a major manifestation of this schism assuredly has been the promotion of the myth of Adam over that of Aeneas, the first indication of this promotion originated not (as one may expect) in the discourse of Calvinistic Protestantism, but in that of education. This "indication" (ironically and again not as one may expect) hailed from England and not from the American colonies. John Locke's *Some Thoughts Concerning Education* (1693), a substantial work which has exercised major influence on theories of education from the moment of its publication to the present day, was among the first to advocate the usefulness of studying English grammar in preference to, and even in lieu of, Latin. Although Locke maintains that Latin is "absolutely necessary to a Gentleman" (193), he posits that the young Latin scholar, "Ten to one," abhors his Latin studies "for the ill usage it procur[es] him" (194). Particularly in the era of Louis Quatorze, French had become the international language of commerce. In Locke's own words, Latin was a language "long since dead everywhere" (204). Actually, Locke was a bit premature in pronouncing Latin dead as an international language, at least for intellectuals. Locke counsels parents, in choosing a master or tutor, above all to be "certain, it should be one, who thinks *Latin* and *Language* the least part of Education" (210). Instead, they should select an instructor who places the building of moral character uppermost among his (or her) objectives.

Despite his generally negative assessment of Latin studies, when Locke comes to a consideration of history, he asserts that, "by a gradual Progress from the plainest and easiest Historians, [the student] may at last come to read the most difficult and sublime of the Latin Authors, such as are *Tully* [Cicero], *Virgil*, and *Horace*" (220). Following an enthusiastic endorsement of Cicero's *De officiis* as a paradigm of civil law, Locke advances this peroration: "A Vertuous and well behaved young Man, that is well versed in the *General Part of the Civil-Law* [or *De Jure Naturae et Gentium*, by Samuel F. von Pufendorf, written in Latin in 1672 and not "Englished" until 1703], . . . understands *Latin* well, and can write a good hand, one may turn loose into the World, with great assurance, that he will find Imployment and Esteem every where [*sic*]" (221). The less essential Greek studies Locke commends to "the Education of a profess'd Scholar" (233–34) and not to that of a gentleman.

It is important to note that, in his treatment of the study of Latin and Greek, Locke does not denigrate either classical thought or the ancient authors; his object is to improve the praxis of pedagogy. Within the British sphere, Locke's educational theories eventually became subsumed within a two-class system of education. The working classes came to be taught no Latin, only the more practical English grammar, along with equally utilitarian skills-training. The upper (gentleman) class retained the less utilitarian classical curriculum.

Undoubtedly it was Locke's penchant for practicality which attracted Benjamin Franklin to *Some Thoughts Concerning Education* in 1749, while he was composing his *Proposals Relating to the Education of Youth in Pensilvania* [*sic*].[1] Quoting extensively from Locke's much expanded posthumous "fifth" 1705 edition of *Some Thoughts* (really his fourth real revision; Locke died in 1704), Franklin is careful to quote Locke's unequivocal pronouncement: "I am not here speaking against Greek and Latin. I think Latin at least ought to be well understood by every Gentleman" (*Papers* 3: 409). In his own text, Franklin articulates a similar position, insisting that the Academy he is proposing must offer a curriculum such that "none that have an ardent Desire to learn [Latin, Greek, French, German, and/or Spanish] should be refused" (415).

Regarding his attitude toward the ancient languages in particular, Franklin is perhaps better remembered today for his fourth and seventh

"Silence Dogood" essays, which frequently are anthologized in current college and university textbooks of American literature. In both these "Dogood" tracts, the youthful Franklin ridicules what he—writing in 1722, while apprenticed at his brother's *New England Courant*—views as a pretentiousness in the learning of some Harvard scholars and in many of the elegies published at this time. Masquerading as a widow named Silence Dogood, the young author maintains that both students and elegists often complete a discourse or a line with some impressive-sounding Latin phrase, whether apt or not. In these early works, Franklin echoes Locke, who, in *Some Thoughts*, also expresses impatience with pedants. As Locke candidly puts it,

> what can be more ridiculous, than to mix the rich and handsome Thoughts and Sayings of others with a deal of poor Stuff of his own; which is thereby the more exposed, and has no other grace in it, nor will otherwise recommend the Speaker, than a threadbare, russet Coat would, that was set off with large Parches of Scarlet, and glittering Brocard [archaic for Brocade]. (209–10)

Like Locke, however, Franklin never denigrates either classical authors or their thought. Just a glance through his own *Autobiography* and his far-ranging and voluminous writings reveals Franklin's substantial knowledge of, and reliance upon, apt Latin passages and phrases.

Franklin's *Idea of the English School* sets forth a more closely reasoned and practical alternative to the traditional Latin curriculum of the grammar schools and colleges of his day than the earlier *Some Thoughts*. Writing early in 1751, this effort aimed to persuade the public and especially his fellow trustees on the board of the Philadelphia Academy to adopt a proposed English School rather than a proposed Latin and Greek School. Franklin organized the English School's curriculum into six progressive classes, designed to inculcate within each scholar "a solid Foundation of Virtue and Piety" (*Papers* 4: 106). While the entire curriculum would employ only the English language in speech and writing, "the best Translations of Homer, Virgil and Horace," as well as other classical authors, were to be integrated within the sixth form or class. Following this program, scholars would emerge from the English School "tho' unacquainted with any antient [*sic*] or foreign Tongue, . . . Masters of their own, which is of more immediate and general Use" (4: 106). Franklin pointedly observes:

> the Time usually spent in acquiring those Languages, often without Success, being here employ'd in laying such a Foundation of Knowledge and Ability, as properly improv'd, may qualify them to pass thro' and execute the several Offices of civil Life, with Advantage and Reputation to themselves and Country. (4: 108)

Both the sentiment and the phrasing set forth by Franklin in this passage are repeated in later years by such educational reformers as Anthony Benezet, Benjamin Rush, and Noah Webster. While these later reformers enjoyed no little success in their efforts (which were often abetted by Franklin), Franklin in the early 1750s found that a majority of the trustees of the academy were not in sympathy with his English School; hence, the final version of the Philadelphia Academy's plan provided for a rector of the academy (head of the Latin and Greek School), paid him twice as much salary as the English master, and gave him immediate responsibility for only half as many students as those allotted the English master (see *Papers* 3: 424–25). This outcome caused Franklin considerable disappointment. The road to his English School was to be an arduous one, but the eventual victory would be decisive for American culture.

After Franklin's failure to establish an ascendant English School curriculum in the public sector, the next step in promoting the Adamic myth came from England. Robert Lowth's immensely popular and influential *A Short Introduction to English Grammar* was published in London in 1762. Of those grammars which predate Lowth's, Colyer Meriwether, the early-twentieth-century historian of colonial American education, remarks, "All of these yielded very submissively in popularity to Lowth" (150).

In the "Preface" to his *Grammar*, the British Lowth forcefully states his position regarding the teaching of English grammar *before* Latin grammar in the grammar schools:

> if children were first taught the common principles of grammar, by some short and clear system of English Grammar, which happily by its simplicity and facility, is perhaps fitter than that of any other language for such a purpose; they would have some notion of what they were going about, when they should enter into the Latin Grammar; and would hardly be engaged so many years, as they now are, in that most irksome and difficult part of literature, with so much labour of memory, and with so little assistance to the understanding. (x)

While Lowth's *Grammar* probably did not see an American edition until a Philadelphia printing in 1775, the fact that several more American printings did occur later suggests its use in the colonies well before 1775.

Surely the renowned Philadelphia schoolmaster Anthony Benezet (1713–1784) was familiar with Lowth's *Grammar*, Locke's *Some Thoughts Concerning Education*, and Franklin's writings on educational theory. In (or about) 1778, in *Some Necessary Remarks on the Education of Youth*, Benezet recommended that

> no latin [*sic*] be attempted to be taught [in the standard grammar schools], unless a School should be erected solely for that purpose: "The teaching that language, in an English School, infallibly consuming more of the masters time, than can be spared from his other business; and the few Latin-Scholars must be very indifferently attended." (6)

Earlier in his teaching career, in the 1750s, this Quaker son of Huguenot parents had set up schools for young women in which, according to Benezet's chief biographer, George S. Brookes, "The curriculum was not limited to the mere rudiments, but provided also an elementary knowledge of Latin and French" (40). Perhaps it was the education Benezet enjoyed during his youth, while his family remained in London for sixteen years before migrating to America, which recommended to him this approach. In any event, at least by the late 1770s, he had fallen away from teaching Latin, opting instead for the more utilitarian approach urged by the Friends and by Franklin.

In a letter to Robert Pleasants written in October 1780, for example, Benezet echoes the attitude of Lowth's passage quoted above. Here the most popular of Quaker schoolmasters complains that many authors of English grammars pattern their methodology after Latin grammars, thereby bringing "great discouragement and perplexity to the Learner" (Brookes 351). In an effort to remedy this difficulty, Benezet designed his own twelve-page guide, "An Essay Towards the Most Easy Introduction to the Knowledge of the English Grammar." This he appended to the third edition (1782) of his *The Pennsylvania Spelling-Book; or, Youth's Friendly Instructor and Monitor.* It is somewhat ironic to observe that, in this rejoinder to English grammars which he thought leaned too heavily on Latin grammars, he cites "the Latin Accidence" as an authoritative paradigm (1) and refers to English objective and possessive cases as accusative and genitive cases, after the fashion of Latin grammars (8–9).

Still, Benezet's letter to Pleasants reveals an attitude far different from that of the British Lowth. Lowth's grammar of English clearly was composed as an advanced introductory handbook for the study of the English language, or even as a thorough, pre-Latin introduction to language study in general (Lowth refers often to his notion of "Universal Grammar"). Lowth's *Grammar* was used in some American colleges.[2] Benezet, in contrast, declares in his letter that he wants to render a study of the classical languages obsolete: "I also much desire to see such a knowledge of the English Language taught in our Schools, as to make the use of the learned Languages unnecessary" (351). His rationale for dropping the classical languages is his conviction, apparently reached experientially in his long tenure (some forty years) as a schoolmaster, that such study "has a natural tendency to wed to the world, and beget an enmity to the cross" (351). Such censure of the ancient authors (and of course their culture) marks a radical departure from Locke, Franklin, Lowth, and the British educational system.[3] However, it also suggests that classicism has been internalized so deeply by generations of students that this well-known educational theorist feared its decisive influence.

Benezet is even more forceful in another letter written in 1783 to John Pemberton. Because of Benezet's powerful influence on Benjamin Rush, a leading "warrior" in the "war" on classical studies in America, the passage is worth quoting entire:

> I might add the prodigious hurt done by those romantic and mad notions of heroism etc. which are early implanted in the tender minds from the use of those Heathen Authors Ovid, Virgil, Homer etc. which they are generally taught in, which nourishes the spirit of War in Youth and in other respects is so diametrically opposite to our Christian Testimony; but to this it would probably be answered that such authors might be avoided, but this would not answer my concern which is *absolutely to avoid our Youth spending their time in classical studies*, the chief tendency of which is, to find the corrupt passions of the Human heart. (italics added; Benezet in Brookes 389–90)

A prominent critic of classicism in America, Meyer Reinhold cites much of this passage from Benezet, but he ignores Benezet's earlier inclusion of Latin within his school. In his "Vergil in the American Experience from Colonial Times to 1882" (1882 is the year after the nineteenth centenary of Vergil's death), Reinhold intends to demonstrate that the attitude toward Vergil in the American colonies and early republic was universally hostile. But Benezet's fear attests the Mantuan's wide influence, whether for good or ill, on the Early American mind. Reinhold also fails to make the connection between the ancient authors' celebration of the glory of warfare and Benezet's abhorrence of war (he became a Quaker by the 1770's).

Here Reinhold makes a concerted effort to show "that the *Aeneid* was not as popular in America in the seventeenth, eighteenth, and nineteenth centuries as the *Iliad* (known mostly from Pope's version)" (Reinhold 227). In fact, Pope's *Iliad* was unavailable to Early Americans until after 1720 and so has no bearing on attitudes toward Vergil obtaining in the seventeenth and the first quarter of the eighteenth centuries.

Reinhold's essay on Vergil in America has several other problems as well. The essay is uninformed concerning both the genre of the pastoral elegy and the poetic statements of literary independence outlined above. Nor does it mention the pastoral, a genre extremely popular in eighteenth-century America. Discussing Cotton Mather's *Magnalia Christi Americana*, Reinhold observes that Mather quotes often from Vergil and opens the saga after the opening of the *Aeneid*. Then Reinhold concludes that this "analogy is not carried out systematically by Mather" (Reinhold 229–30). Yet the treatment of *Magnalia* in the present book demonstrates that this epic saga indeed does follow Vergil "systematically."

Reinhold calls Philip Freneau "America's first important poet," ignoring Anne Bradstreet and Edward Taylor (both demonstrably classicists), Mather Byles, and Phillis Wheatley (who before the Revolution was much better known than any of the poets named). Then the author identifies Vergil as "one of the principal literary influences" (Reinhold 234) on Freneau's poetry. But he ignores the fact that Freneau later, during the radical shift in discourse and subsequent denigration of the Aeneas myth, penned the vituperative poem, "Epistle to a Student of Dead Languages" (1795), in which the poet condemns the pursuit of "some antique gibberish to attain" when "all ancient sense (that's worth review)/ Glows in translation, fresh and new" (Freneau, ed. Clark 398).

At another point in the essay, Reinhold states that Timothy Dwight, in his *Conquest of Canaan* (1785), was "the first American to write in the epic genre" (Reinhold 236). As the present volume shows, however, Benjamin Tompson's *New Englands Crisis* and *Tears* (1676) make ample use of epic elements. Cotton Mather's 1702 *Magnalia* should be considered an epic in prose. And let us not forget Phillis Wheatley's intertextual epic and her two epyllia of 1773 ("Goliath of Gath" and "Niobe in Distress," from *Poems on Various Subjects, Religious and Moral;* see J. C. Shields, "Phillis Wheatley's Use of Classicism" 97–111 and ch. 7 above).[4]

Most of the evidence Reinhold adduces for the alleged lack of Vergil's influence (and all demonstrations of a hostile reaction to Vergil, even during the nineteenth century, map a kind of "anxiety of influence") comes from tracts written *after* 1780—that is, from periods during and after the radical shift. Hence his evidence actually adds force to my argument in this book. Given all these difficulties with Reinhold's essay, his following observation should provoke little surprise:

> Such potentially transportable themes as the birth of a new nation in a new land, the wandering of a divinely guided people, the struggle between the settlers and the native people, the

> transplantation of culture—these did not, in general, leave their mark on American thought and literature. (227)

I suspect that Reinhold, like many before him, has fallen victim to the hegemony of the Adamic myth. If one is convinced at the outset that a decisive classical influence cannot be discovered, that prophecy is likely to be fulfilled.

But to return to the dynamics which first constituted that hegemony to which Reinhold has fallen victim, education in Great Britain was reinforcing its two-class structure at the moment the American attitude toward public education inexorably shifted toward Benezet's radical position. Following Benezet's death in 1784, his fellow Philadelphian, Benjamin Rush, along with the younger Connecticut Yankee, Noah Webster, took up the American war against the teaching of Latin and Greek in the public schools. During the 1770s, Rush wrote of Benezet that he "is held in veneration in these parts and deserves to be spread throughout the world" (*Letters* 1: 76).

With the signing of the Treaty of Paris on September 3, 1783, the new American Republic almost immediately demanded an identity, and that identity must contain not even a hint of anything British—or, for that matter, European. The key words in this partial description of the shift in discourse are *suggest* and *look*. While this radical shift occurred, it was not final or irreversible. Nor was it totally isolated from, or entirely unmotivated by, some strands of British thought. Nor were all in America anti-British; Noah Webster, particularly before 1800, often lamented that, while America "is independent in government," it remains "totally dependent [on Britain] in manners, which are the basis of government" (*Fugitiv* 84). In 1789, Webster bristles with indignation when he observes that "an astonishing respect for the arts and literature of their parent country, and a blind imitation of its manners, are still prevalent among the Americans" (qtd. in Simpson 65). Despite Webster's forceful rhetoric, he—even he—could not avoid acknowledging Britain as America's "parent country"; some measure of influence logically and inevitably follows such an admission of origin.

Ironically, the best illustration of British influence comes from Webster. For example, the powerful influence exerted upon Webster's thought by the pioneering British linguist John Horne Tooke, *Diversions of Purley*, is detailed in David Simpson's *Politics of American English* (81–90). Tooke's insistence upon an Anglo-Saxon (rather than a Latin) origin for the basic syntactical structure of the English language especially appealed to Webster because, according to Simpson, stressing such a provenance spoke out "for the linguistic (and wider) authority of the common man against the learned class and, perhaps, their patrons, [were] now cast as the usurpers of the rights of freeborn Englishmen" (83). Of course, such a position argued against a classical (Latinate) curriculum in the schools.

Along parallel lines, recall Weinbrot's demonstration that, during the eighteenth century, Great Britain harbored a growing hostility toward classical thought and culture, particularly Vergil. If Weinbrot is correct (and his argument is most convincing), the evident popularity of epic and satire in America just prior to and during the American Revolution cannot be read as simple, servile, colonial imitation of outworn, outmoded literary practices of the mother country (as the "political judgments on the mutations of literary history" approach would have it). Instead, it may be seen as part of the natural maturation of a distinctly American classicism, beginning as early as the 1720s and predicted by the pastoral elegies and statements of literary independence from Britain.

Another invigorating way of "reading" the popularity of satire and epic in America in this period reinforces the idea that Americans did not slavishly imitate Britain. In Britain, the "force and credibility" of classical satire and epic declined as sentiment grew for limiting the power and influence of the monarchy and developing a more parliamentary form of government. At the same time, in America, prior to the firm establishment of a republican government, satire provided an easily accessible mode for criticizing an ungrateful parent (Britain). Epic, with its loose structure and grand design, could define a grand purpose for the American adventure in freedom, and at the same time hold up a mirror to reflect a myriad of virtuous possibilities for a new state combining highly diverse (European) origins.

Britain's denigration of pietas (by which this Roman virtue is watered down to become "piety," and usually a mendacious piety at that) during the very period when Early Americans decide to valorize this virtue certainly lends support to Weinbrot's position that, as the eighteenth century wore on, Britain devalued classical thought and culture. Still more to the point, Weinbrot's disclosure lends great force to the argument offered here: that Early Americans celebrated classicism at the same time the British were becoming disenchanted with this mode of discourse. With regard to Webster's campaign (many other "soldiers" joined him) against the teaching of the classics in American public schools, it is useful to note that a substantial strain of hostility toward classical thought and culture obtained in Britain at precisely the moment when it proved most helpful for Webster, providing him with voices of authority (Lowth and Tooke) upon which to draw. Perhaps because classicism was so thoroughly embedded in the British class system and cultural ideology, no radical shift occurred in Britain. There, hostility toward the ancients merged with a general rejection of neoclassicism in preference for the evolving romantic mode—although, in their works, none of the British Romantics denied his or her classical training. Indeed, classical allusions and exempla abound in the works of Austen,

Wordsworth, Coleridge, Keats, Byron (the favorite poet of his youth was Pope, and he preferred heroic couplets), and the Shelleys.

At least on the surface, developments in America did not confront an embedded class structure perpetuated by a bipartite educational system *and* by economics. Nor was the American shift in discourse burdened by an intense and implacable loyalty to a timeworn tradition. In fact, so vehemently opposed to Great Britain was the newly formed United States that apparently it was willing to sacrifice its own American classicism to separate itself from Britain.

Simply put, American classicism, practiced largely by the intellectual elite, looked suspect to a society supposedly being founded to celebrate egalitarianism. Thus, in 1795, Freneau, the "former" classicist, attacks the imposition of "some antique gibberish" upon schoolboys when, according to him, "All ancient sense (that's worth review)/ Glows in translation, fresh and new" (Clarke 398). Royall Tyler, the sophisticated attorney and Harvard graduate, in his immensely popular play, *The Contrast* (1787), mercilessly satirizes British pretensions to learning and raises up as paragons of *American* virtue the families Van Rough and Manly.

Even earlier, almost precisely at the moment of the Treaty of Paris, such intellectuals as Benjamin Rush and Noah Webster, publicly at least, cast aside their own classical backgrounds and pushed mightily for an *American* educational system bereft of classical studies. In other words, none of these individuals ever forgot his own classical background, and American Classicism never completely died out. Instead, it gradually merged with, and even at times prefigured, American Romanticism. Nevertheless, each person cited above sounded an egalitarian chord—because it was the politic thing to do! In consequence, the classical mode of education—obviously *not* designed to prepare skilled workers for a budding industrial democracy, since not everyone can plead or speak with the voice of learned authority—quickly was perceived by such men as Rush and Webster as the most vulnerable manifestation of "decadent" Britain and the Continent. At this juncture it was convenient, of course, to forget the earlier Puritan establishment of Latin grammar schools, apparently for universal male education; after all, were they not initially built for Puritans by Puritans?

The elevation of the Adamic myth over the Aeneas myth is even more complex than we have discovered to this point. Recall the Dame or Petty schools which always were in place from the first days of settlement in New England (and later established throughout the other English colonies). Each of these schools taught how to read in English, which universally meant, until around the 1720s, how to read first the Geneva Bible and thereafter the King James version of the Bible. At this very early stage in the progress of young students, almost always boys *and* girls, it was the Adamic myth which formed the universally held ideology. The *New England Primer* was the basic text; from very late in the seventeenth century (circa 1687) until the early 1800s, this text, with its celebration of "In Adam's fall/ We sinned all," was basic to the American Dame schools.[5] Monaghan, "Literacy Instruction and Gender in Colonial New England," concludes that, "from the earliest days of settlement, . . . and throughout the colonial period, the colonists expected that all children ought to be able to read, no matter how low their station or how poor their circumstances" (30).

With the Adamic myth already ubiquitous and with so many tenets of the Aeneas myth clearly paralleling Adamic ones (the founding of a new nation in the wilderness, the errand impelled by divine injunction, the displacement of "natives" already in residence, and the subsequent establishment of a new, dominant culture), it was not particularly difficult for Rush and Webster to read the signs of the times. All indicators spoke loudly in favor of the more democratic (by virtue of its universal availability) Adamic mode of discourse, rather than the undemocratic (because available only to a primarily male elite educated in Latin grammar schools or tutored privately) Vergilian mode. Despite their elevation of the Adamic mode, however, neither Rush nor Webster appears ever to have forgotten his classical studies. Both were educated in Latin grammar schools; Rush took a degree from the College of New Jersey (now Princeton), and Webster graduated from Yale. In his letters, Rush quotes *often* (sometimes inaccurately, as if from memory) from the classical authors and appears to have been particularly fond of Vergil. According to Harry Warfel, Webster mastered his Latin lessons so well "that in his old age he could write Latin letters to his favorite grand-daughter" (36). Based on this last observation, Noah Webster's own granddaughter could read his Latin, and it is highly probable that she wrote back in a similar Latin. Even some women, then, possessed considerable knowledge of Latin during and after the radical shift. As well, it is quite possible that the Early American intellectuals and poets Annis Boudinot Stockton and Elizabeth Graeme Ferguson, both of whom spent their youths in Philadelphia, attended Anthony Benezet's early Latin and French academy (both Benezet and Stockton were descendents of Huguenots). Recall how extensive was the classical knowledge of the African American intellectual and poet, Phillis Wheatley of Boston, whose career spanned the Revolutionary era. Still, notwithstanding Webster's obvious acceptance and denial of the myth of Aeneas, he and others persevered in their assault upon classical studies.

With Benezet's democratic, socially leveling, and strongly Adamic example lighting their path, first Benjamin Rush and then Noah Webster made war upon the classical curriculum which dominated the American public school system before 1784.[6] Each man waged this war despite his own classical background and obvious personal fondness for classical studies. For example, Rush, in "Thoughts Upon the Mode of Education Proper in a Republic" (1785; the title heralds a distinctly American system), with a nod to diplomacy, offers "testimony against the common practice of attempting to teach boys [no mention of girls] the learned languages . . . too early in life." This last phrase he clarifies with the next statement: "The first twelve years of life are barely sufficient to instruct a boy in reading, writing and arithmetic." Rush's scheme, as Benezet before him had recommended, is to take the classical languages out of the grammar school and reinforce the teaching of English grammar. Essentially the Dame school curriculum is to be extended into the grammar schools. For, as Rush continues, "Too much pains cannot be taken to teach our youth to read and write [this last skill usually *not* taught in the Dame schools] our American language with propriety and elegance" (Rudolph 18).

In a 1789 letter to John Adams, Rush is more direct when he asks this rhetorical question: "Who are guilty of the greatest absurdity—the Chinese who press the feet into deformity by small shoes, or the Europeans and Americans who press the brain into obliquity by Greek and Latin?" (*Letters* 524). In this same letter, Rush makes a curious admission. In claiming that only reading Lowth's *Introduction* and Hume's *History of England* taught him "any knowledge of style or language" (his classical studies having contributed not a particle), he asserts that he owes whatever stylistic sophistication he may have to "having nearly forgotten the Greek and suspended for many years the delight with which I once read the Roman poets and historians" (524). Despite his democratic views, Rush's earlier delight manifests itself repeatedly, as he peppers his correspondence with classical references.

Whatever favorable memories he may harbor of his personal study of the classics, Rush declares emphatically in this same letter to John Adams, "I expect to prevail in the United States in my attempt to bring the dead languages into disrepute, for my next attack upon them shall be addressed to our American ladies" (524). Then Rush proceeds to articulate most forcefully and candidly his determination to raise the Adamic myth above the Vergilian mode:

> If the years spent in teaching boys the Greek and Roman mythology were spent in teaching them Jewish antiquities and the connection between the types and prophecies of the Old Testament with the events of the New, don't you think we should have less infidelity and of course less immorality and bad government in the world? (525)

In this statement we find the archetype of later extremist fundamentalism, as well as an implicit assertion of American cultural superiority; both positions are dangerous extremes. The notion of a legally enforced system of Judaeo-Christian education flies in the face of the United States Constitution's guarantee of religious freedom. Rush and Adams were to carry on this debate, in which Adams always asserted the intrinsic value of a classical education (a background shared by the two correspondents), until Rush's death in 1813. It is to their credit that, throughout the course of their correspondence, neither lost his sense of humor on this issue.

A priceless example of the good humor between Adams and Rush occurs in an exchange of letters during October 1810. Several months earlier, Rush, as professor of medicine at the newly consolidated University of Pennsylvania School of Medicine, had introduced to the medical world his "Tranquillizer," a chair designed to restrain maniacal patients. In a letter of October 2, Rush had quipped, "Were every Greek and Latin book (the New Testament excepted) consumed in a bonfire, the world would be the wiser and better for it" (*Letters* 2: 1067). Adams replied on October 13, opining that only a period of confinement in Rush's own "Tranquillizer" would relieve him of his "Fanaticism against Greek and Latin" (2: 1073, n. 1). Binger, a recent biographer of Rush, affirms the physician's penchant toward fanaticism: "There can be no doubt of his idealistic, if not Messianic, concern with the spreading of republican education" (168). Later Binger declares flatly that "education without religion [the Christian religion] was anathema to him [Rush]" (170). Apparently Rush never subscribed to the Constitution's first amendment. Neither did his younger colleague, Noah Webster.

While Rush made a substantial contribution to the war on the Aeneas myth, his effort cannot rival that of Noah Webster to that war. Webster penned not only educational theories but also immensely popular textbooks which embodied his anticlassical theories. These texts largely schooled the first generation of Americans born in the newly created United States. As a student at Yale during the mid-1770s, the young Webster may have heard his tutor, Timothy Dwight, hint that classical studies were expendable, even at the college level. Describing the atmosphere at Yale then, Harry Warfel observes that Dwight took it upon himself to continue "the work he and John Trumbull had begun in 1771 to liberalize the curriculum and substitute English composition and the study of English literature for a portion of the work in ancient languages" (24). Moreover, whatever pedagogical theories Webster was honing in his own mind could only have received reinforcement from the notions of Benezet and Rush, which were gaining in popularity at the time.

Webster met Rush in person as early as February 1786, during a lecture tour Webster took to promulgate his rapidly developing ideas regarding the steps America must take toward nationalization. In Warfel's words, "With Dr. Rush he formed a lasting friendship, their conversation on 'harmony of taste' proving them to have many similar ideas on education and nationalism" (136). Webster's fervor in his self-anointed task of addressing education for the new republic may be observed from this powerful outburst in "On the Education of Youth in America": "The education of youth [is] an employment of more consequence than making laws and preaching the gospel, because it lays the foundation on which both law and gospel rest for success" (*Fugitiv* 18). In this essay, which appeared serially in Webster's own *American Magazine* of New York during 1787 and 1788, Webster identifies the first error of the contemporary American educational system as "a too general attention to the dead languages, with a neglect of our own." Then, to justify this shift in emphasis, he offers the old saw that "the most valuable of [the Greek and Roman authors] have English translations, which, if they do not contain all the elegance, communicate all the ideas of the originals" (45). Anyone who has read *Beowulf* or the *Aeneid* in the original and then compared original with translation (any translation) knows full well that much more than "elegance" is lost in translation. To ward off this sort of attack, Webster allows: "But suppose there is some advantage to be derived from an acquaintance with the dead languages, will this compensate for the loss of five or perhaps seven years [traditional time frames within the Latin grammar schools] of valuable time? Life is short . . . and every hour should be employed to good purposes" (46). Here we hear again the appeal to "good" practicality and economic utility, sounded earlier by Franklin and Benezet. In fairness to Webster, he does not, as Benezet and Rush do, deprecate the ancient authors for their allegedly immoral example. Rather, Webster's scheme, much like Rush's, was to expand the study of the English language (via writing and reading) from the Dame schools into the grammar schools; for, Webster maintains, "the high estimation in which the learned languages have been held has discouraged a due attention to our own" (48).

Some, like John Adams, raised objections to the plan of Rush and Webster. For example, Samuel Knox, a Maryland Presbyterian minister who also enjoyed a respectable reputation as an educator, in an essay entitled "Essay on Education" (1799), lamented "the impropriety of excluding the study of the Latin and Greek languages from a system of liberal and polite education" (Rudolph 302). Knox pleads that, if parents would exercise better discipline over their children's instruction, making them learn the rudiments of Latin grammar at an earlier age, "there could not be so much objection made as there commonly is against the acquisition of the Greek and Latin classics" (303). To be sure, in *Some Thoughts*, Locke had suggested that a scholar's mother might serve as a tutor "and make him read the Evangelists [Gospels] in *Latin* to her" (211). The impracticality of Knox's recommendation (e.g., parents' lack of preparation to serve in such specialized capacities) aside, objections to the republican education plan were made, and resistance was registered.

In the public sector, such resistance was ignored, as the more immediately egalitarian, anticlassical, Adamic position gained ground. For example, no less formidable a figure than Benjamin Franklin joined Webster in his quest to expand English studies, eliminate classical studies, and so enlarge the possibilities for more "useful" pursuits. In the private sector, however, the energies of resistance manifested themselves in a continuation of such institutions as the Boston Latin School and other Latin grammar schools. These now became independent schools. Not until the second half of the twentieth century did the intellectual elite in America surrender its youthful training in Latin and Greek, since these languages were required for admission to the most prestigious colleges and universities. Nevertheless, as external controls designed to denigrate classical studies in the public sector became firmly entrenched by the late 1780s, procedures quickly were established for constructing internal rules of discourse. That is, since the public generally agreed with the anti-British, anticlassical approach to a more "useful" system of *American* (and Adamic) education, the system, at least in the public sector, became altered in accord with Webster's theories and recommendations. Davidson, in *Revolution and the Word*, articulates the attitude toward education held by both Webster and Rush: "Each educator saw public schooling not just as a way of disseminating knowledge but also as a way of perpetrating the status quo and fostering loyalty to a federal government" (64).

One method of "perpetrating the status quo" was to shift the mode of discourse—i.e., to change the language. In other words, as the language of instruction changed in Webster's texts, so did the language of politics; as David Simpson puts it, "Webster is both the most important and the most complex figure in the national language argument" (48–49).

Immensely influential in effecting this shift in language was Webster's revision of *The New-England Primer*. Here he tones down the harsher dictates of Calvinism. For "In Adam's Fall/ We sinned all," he substitutes "A Was an Apple-pie made by the cook"—certainly an improvement in the eyes of such non-Christians as Franklin and Washington. Adam is hardly forgotten, however, as Webster includes in his thirty-six-page version a commentary on the Lord's Prayer, the Shorter Catechism, other distinctly Christian prayers, and a dialogue of "Some Short and Easy Questions." The first two of these "short and easy" questions read: "Q. Who made you? A. God. Q. Who redeem'd you? A. Jesus Christ."[7] This text, taken together with several readers and Webster's three-part *Grammatical Institute of the English Language*, played, in the apt words of Harry Warfel, "so formative a part in the development of a unified American culture and national spirit, that it is difficult to overrate their contribution" (92).

The influence of his own texts, loose copyright laws during the early days of the Republic, and the financial success of Webster's textbooks encouraged a plethora of pirated editions and imitative, allegedly original versions, all of which merely extended the influence of Webster's Adamic educational methodology. Webster's influence was so pervasive precisely because, as David Simpson astutely concludes, "the medium of persuasion for Webster's generation was the printed word" (55).[8] At this time, the Founding Fathers were striving to insure, in their construction of the Constitution, the possibility of a distinctly American expression of Vergil's pietas—i.e., the American Way. This expression marked the zenith of the classical origins of the American self.[9] At the same time, however, internal rules of discourse were becoming codified which would result in the unabashed promotion of the Adamic myth over that of Aeneas. The moment that most effectively dramatizes the codification of internal rules for Adamic discourse is the reception of the Constitution by the People.

Recently this miraculous phenomenon has been analyzed intelligently (and entertainingly) by E. L. Doctorow in "A Citizen Reads the Constitution," which serves as "Epilogue" to *America in Theory*, the fascinating collection of essays mentioned above edited by Leslie Berlowitz, Denis Donoghue, and Louis Menand. Doctorow argues that "the ordaining voice of the Constitution is scriptural, but in resolutely keeping the authority for its dominion in the public consent, it presents itself as the sacred text of secular humanism" (287). This well-known author of *Ragtime* and many other novels then deplores that he was not taught this perspective much earlier: "I wish Mrs. Brundage had told me that back in Wade Junior High School. I wish Jerry Falwell's and Jimmy Swaggart's and Pat Robertson's teachers had taught them that back in their junior high schools" (287–88). Next Doctorow vividly describes the reception of this "sacred text" by the People:

> Every major city had its ship of state rolling through the streets, pulled by teams of horses—a carpentered ship on wheels rolling around the corners and down the avenues in full sail, and perhaps with a crew of boys in sailor uniforms. It was called, inevitably, the Constitution or Federalism or Union. Companies of militia would precede it, the music of fifes and drums surround it, and children run after it, laughing at the surreal delight. (288)

Finally he levies this wholly accurate observation: "From the very beginning it [the Constitution] took on a symbolic character that its writers, worried always that they might never get it ratified, could not have foreseen" (289).

Doctorow's analysis is, for the most part, on target; yet something is missing. This something is an awareness of the tremendous tension, at this moment in the evolution of the American self, between the classical and Adamic portions of that self. For the question—and it is the crucial question—left unanswered by Doctorow's junior high anecdote is: Why was America after the radical shift not taught that the Constitution "presents itself as the sacred text of secular humanism"?

The answer, put most simply, is that the radical shift, in which Adam is valorized and Aeneas becomes almost totally discredited, achieved a huge popular success and continues to hold sway even today. The Constitution embodies the efforts of a group thoroughly schooled in the pietas of the Aeneas myth, even though the members of this same group were fully cognizant of the Adamic myth (both Washington and Franklin, for example, were fond of calling upon Providence). Even so, this text was received by the People, the overwhelming majority of whom were schooled exclusively in the Adamic mode, in much the same way legend says the Greek-speaking, Jewish population under Ptolemy Philadelphus received the *Septuaginta*—as the inspired word of holy scripture. Virtually all literate persons in America in 1789 were schooled in the tenets of the Adamic myth. Moreover, what most urgently was required in America after the Revolution was a sense of unity and cohesiveness. And, as Thomas Bender has cogently observed of the cultural tendencies of America during this period, "The ideal of concord and sameness underlay religion as well as democracy" (55). As a result of these three factors, it was almost inevitable that the People would receive the Constitution as an extension of their common biblical text.[10]

The Founding Fathers doubtless were surprised by the reception accorded the Constitution. First, to them it never was a "sacred" text but only the hard-earned results of their mental and physical effort and anguish. Second, it was embraced extremely enthusiastically by the People. To the People, the Constitution became not "the sacred text of secular humanism," but an extension of the sacred text of the nonsecular, biblical myth of Adam. And this reception occurred almost overnight! The impact of the ecstatic, vocal embrace of this document as a cultural determinant cannot be exaggerated. While the Constitution itself, as the product of an intellectual elite, represents the last grand, public statement of the Aeneas myth, its jubilant adoption by the People symbolizes perhaps the single most powerful assertion of the Adamic myth in the history of our country. Indeed, according to Robert A. Ferguson, not only were the People sharing "in the act of writing" the Constitution "through the related act of ratification" (*Cambridge History* 487), but they were energetically and irreversibly defining themselves to themselves.

In *Voicing America,* Christopher Looby clarifies this assertion. Looby's position is that interpretations of the Early Republic's literary works have tended to ignore the significance of orality in our country's establishment. His own reading of this orality is based on his premise that, "since [the United States'] legitimacy was explicitly grounded in an appeal to rational interest, not visceral passion—voice [*sic*] embodied a certain legitimating charisma that print could not" (4). While I would question an alleged lack of passion during this or any era of American history, I shall move on to address Looby's analysis of how the voicing of America does or does not manifest itself. Later in his study, Looby takes to task James Wilson, one of the first Supreme Court justices, signer of the Declaration of Independence, and delegate to the Constitutional Convention, for claiming in one of his decisions in 1793 that "natural persons . . . spoke it [the United States] into existence" (20). Looby asserts that "Wilson hallucinates the creative utterance proceeding from the natural voices of embodied persons" (21).

Looby's text is not informed by *America in Theory,* Doctorow's "Epilogue," or, to be precise, by the manner in which the People embraced the Constitution. Therefore one should not be surprised that Looby misses something that Wilson may have had in mind when he wrote of "natural persons" who "spoke" the United States into being. Wilson was a resident of Philadelphia, and Doctorow notes, "Of all the ratification processions, Philadelphia's was the grandest" (Berlowitz et al. 288). Wilson himself, then, witnessed these "natural persons" whose reveling voices effectively merged with the text of the Constitution. Wilson's "natural persons" speaking America into existence were no hallucination, but his clear recollection of enthusiastic gestures made by real people in the process of appropriating the Constitution as an embodied extension of their own Adamic myth.

This formative, voiced gesturing toward the new nation's defining document wrought a self-conscious transformation of the People into Americans. Surely the events of this defining moment in the evolving American self represent the most emphatic voicing of America. Moreover, they enact the single most resounding pronouncement of acceptance and denial, as the People (not the intellectual elite) seized upon their Adamic definition of themselves, while denying that the text of this document was wholly the construction of an intellectual elite subscribing to the Aeneas myth.

The character of this reception by the People surely was not lost on the politicians. How easy it must have been to convert the way of Aeneas into the American Way, how seductively tempting to allow the People to believe that the three precious principles comprising the rock upon which our way of life is built—religious liberty (devotion to God), decent family life (devotion to mother, or family), and a strong, dependable defense within which citizens may participate openly in the process of government (devotion to patria, or country)—are merely extensions of the Adamic myth.

This pattern of denial and acceptance helps to clarify further why American citizens were not taught that the Constitution was "the sacred text of secular humanism." For the sake of political expediency, the classical origins of the American self were denied in order to accept the People's misconception that American origins were largely Adamic. The Founding Fathers did not think the text sacred, and from the beginning the People appropriated it as an extension of their understanding of American righteousness. The intellectual elite, the primary political figures of this earlier time, were pleased, even eager, to deny the unpopular classicism and to accept the now popular Adamic revisionism for the sake of ratification and national cohesion. As Cynthia S. Jordan phrases it, "The Revolutionary generation had so obviously come to understand the link between language and authority, language and power—specifically the power to reshape reality according to ideology by renaming the world according to their own image of it" (497). So Aeneas became Adam and remains so even today. This denial of access to the myth of Aeneas was brought about by a curiously unwitting collusion between educators such as Rush and Webster, who saw to it that classical studies were, for the most part, marginalized in the public schools; and politicians such as Washington and Jefferson, who, at least in public, assented to the popular Adamic ideology. That collusion insured that, for a majority of Americans, all notions of Americanness would reside in Adamic revisionism and not in the now detested British/Continental classicism.

Some Consequences of the Radical Shift

The motive behind this radical shift in discourse is obvious, and it is arguable that the shift itself was necessary. Otherwise, how could an illusion of American unity, perceived by all thinking persons then as absolutely essential to the success of the American adventure in freedom, have been accomplished so effectively? Appeal to a mythic construct common to everyone—the myth of Adam, revised according to the sacred text of the Constitution—seemed essential. Even so, the price paid for denying the classical origins of the American self has been high. At a minimum, it has kept us unaware of an essential influence shaping what it means to be American—in government, in society, in literature, and in the other arts. In addition, Americans' denial of their classical origins has played a key role in what Leslie Berlowitz has termed a "'fear' of pastlessness" (*America in Theory* ix).

Anti-intellectualism has been exacerbated as a result of the denial of classicism. To be sure, anti-intellectualism is inevitable in any culture. In the United States, however, celebration of vertical, Adamic virtues at the expense of horizontal, secular, classical values promotes suspicion of ideas and/or theoretical constructs, especially when such constructs are derived from a substantive, decidedly undogmatic, scholarly grasp of ancient literature and culture. According to the "wisdom" of many present-day politicians (and this attitude was prevalent as early as Washington's presidency), for example, persons advocating innovative, theoretical approaches to problem-solving and dealing with societal ills are popularly touted as "left-wingers" and are most definitely perceived as unpatriotic.

A fourth loss brought on by a divestment of America's classical origins has been particularly costly to the field of American Studies. As Jonathan Culler put it recently, "American studies has not had the influence on other disciplines that one might expect and has produced an interdisciplinary subfield rather than a reorganization of knowledge."[11] Suppression of America's classical origins, beginning with the radical shift in discourse, has "muddled" American cultural consciousness. This confusion may be understood best, perhaps, in terms of a pattern of acceptance and denial vividly observable in the People's reception of the Constitution and even in the realm of the law. For example, Stanley N. Katz has traced how Americans in the late eighteenth century were "confronted with the apparent contradiction of a commitment to [British] common-law values and procedures" accompanied by "a rejection of things British . . . by anti-British rhetoric and common-law reality" (*Colonial British America* 476).

The pattern of denying a specifically classical heritage while accepting it occurs much earlier—indeed, as early as the private literary and public ministerial careers of Edward Taylor and Cotton Mather. This dual pattern always suggests an attitude of intellectual elitism (such an attitude *not* to be perceived as somehow "evil"). In accepting or embracing the faculty of imagination as necessary to meditation and then denying its positive function, Taylor in his public sermons presents a paradigm of acceptance and denial. Whether or not others followed his example (unlikely, since his meditations did not begin to appear in print until 1937) is of minor import; the point is that there, in a literate, thinking seventeenth-century American, the pattern obtains. Taylor attempted to avoid dealing with the duality in his thought and praxis by issuing the injunction that his private poetic meditations not be printed.[12]

In *Magnalia* and much later in *Manuductio ad Ministerium* (1726), Cotton Mather tries to address the considerable contribution made to *Magnalia* by classical literature and thought, and especially by the *Aeneid*, by denying that contribution. Subsequently such figures as Anthony Benezet, Benjamin Rush, Noah Webster, and Philip Freneau—all thoroughly trained in the ancient classics, as were Taylor and Mather—reject the Aeneas myth by urging a drastic reduction of the classical curriculum in what were to become known as distinctly American schools. At the same time, they themselves (with the possible exception of Benezet) embodied the benefits of classical training.

As Foucault declares, "Every educational system is a political means of maintaining or of modifying the appropriation of discourse, with the knowledge and the powers it carries with it" ("L'ordre" 227). After the Revolution, the intellectual elite quickly saw that one means to bring about a consolidation of power (i.e., to restore order to a somewhat chaotic American confederacy) was summarily to raise up the revised, somewhat secularized (through the Constitution's this-world orientation) Adamic myth over the Aeneas myth. This operation would suffuse American consciousness with a sort of "quick-fix" mentality. The confusion which followed, and which persists to the present day, never really has been dealt with. "Quick-fix" became a permanent feature of American consciousness. Denying the classical origins of the American self became so pervasive that Americans generally (but not totally) lost sight of what already had been accepted as integral to Americanness—the American Way. (This is not the only manifestation of America's indebtedness to classical thought and culture, of course.) In endeavoring so determinedly to establish absolute difference, Americans accomplished not the difference they sought, but rather a Derridean fusion of difference and deference. While the intense anxiety of the struggle toward American self-identity demanded that something substantial of the Old World past be discarded (namely, the vulnerable Aeneas myth), inevitably some trace would persist. The theories of Derrida and Foucault cross at this juncture, for, as Foucault cautions:

> Nothing would be more false than to see in the analysis of discursive formations an attempt at totalitarian periodization, whereby from a certain moment and for a certain time, everyone would think in the same way, in spite of surface differences, say the same thing, through a polymorphous vocabulary, and produce a sort of great discourse that one could travel over in any direction. (*Archaeology* 148)

If the radical shift had been totally successful in bringing about an absolute shift in discourse (an impossibility, according to Derrida and Foucault), then the "menace" of decadent classicism would not have persisted. Such statements as the following, made by Edward E. Hale (1822–1909), strongly suggest that it must have been rare to remember classical studies in a positive light: "The classical men made us hate Latin and Greek" (qtd. in Graff 19).

Hostility toward classical studies, common during the nineteenth century and even commoner today, probably originated in the radical shift. George A. Kennedy, one of the foremost classicists today, trenchantly observes of classical studies in the era after the radical shift and through most of the nineteenth century: "The United States was a new country, with new needs, some observers claimed; it was best to give instruction in the mother tongue, not in the dead languages of the Old World, and to concentrate on vocational training" (qtd. in Reinhold, afterword by George A. Kennedy 326–27). Much to the chagrin of all classicists, the products of this revisionist educational system were epitomized by such men as Andrew Jackson. Whereas the first generation of leaders universally had been trained in classical languages and literatures, these new leaders "were largely indifferent to the classics and some regarded such study as a positive wrong: elitist, aristocratic, decadent" (Reinhold 327).

As we shall discover later in this chapter, the substantial cultural grid of the Aeneas myth persisted long after the radical shift had taken its toll. Still, by the mid-nineteenth century, the myth of Aeneas had become so debased that Thomas Robbins, editor of the third American edition of Cotton Mather's *Magnalia Christi Americana,* could declare, "The world looks with amazement on a great Country, united in one territory, more extensive than Rome, a great population in rapid increase, all looking for Salvation in the name of the DIVINE NAZARENE" (Mather, *Great Works of Christ* viii). The irony unwittingly expressed by Robbins when he compares his allegedly completely Christianized "great Country" to Rome hardly requires remarking. So blinded has Robbins become by the privileging of the Adamic myth that he can make this comparison to Rome in his "Preface" to the very text which first fully articulates the combined Adamic and classical American self. The blindness persists; recently (November 1992) the governor of Mississippi claimed that "all America is a Christian nation." Robbins's interpretation of the American self could have been made only after the myth of Aeneas had become so devalued that it no longer served to balance the Adamic myth. Surely it is obvious, now more than ever, that America cannot long survive, much less flourish, in the absence of the tempering balance of the secular half of the American self.

Contrary to what one might expect from this survey of dreary attitudes, Americans after the era of the radical shift did not reject all learning outright. Davidson, *Revolution and the Word,* whose very title ("the Word") attests the rise of the Adamic myth in the new Republic, observes that this era saw a proliferation of self-improvement books which "encouraged self-reliance, free thinking, inductive reasoning, and a questioning of principles and authority" (69). Davidson reveals that novels, almost all addressing in some substantial way an urgent necessity for education (sans classical studies), were "often targeted specifically for children, women, or a new and relatively untutored readership, not for the intellectual elite" (70). As for the early American novel itself, Davidson concludes that, "as a genre, [it] tended to proclaim a socially egalitarian message" (73). It is not worth debating whether such a message recorded contemporary conditions accurately (i.e., whether egalitarianism actually obtained). Davidson expertly captures the *illusion* of popular equality and unity promised in the American political arena by the "word" of the Constitution and in the spiritual realm by the "word" of the New Testament. Both these cultural grids derived from the ascendancy of the Adamic myth.

Another cultural consequence of the elevation of the Adamic myth occurs in what Nathan O. Hatch calls *The Democratization of American Christianity.* As the power of the People increased dramatically following ratification of the Constitution, "the issue of the well-being of ordinary people became," according to Hatch, "central to the definition of being American, public opinion came to assume normative significance, and leaders could not survive who would not, to use Patrick Henry's phrase, 'bow with utmost deference to the majesty of the people'" (6).

Hatch maintains that it was "America's nonrestrictive environment" which enabled the People to shape "the culture after their own priorities rather than the priorities outlined by gentlemen such as the framers of the Constitution" (9). As we have observed, however, another cultural dynamic contributed to privileging the priorities of the common people over those of the cultural elite—the valorization of the Adamic myth. Hatch points out that, during the three or so decades after the American Revolution, "the passion for equality . . . equaled the passionate rejection of the past. Rather than looking backward and clinging to an older moral economy, insurgent religious leaders espoused convictions that were essentially modern and individualistic" (14). According to Hatch, a pronounced result of this "rejection of the past" was a rejection of the authority of an educated clergy, provoking "a violent anticlericalism, a flaunting of conventional religious deportment, a disdain for the wrangling of theologians, an assault on tradition, and an assertion that common people were more sensitive than elites to the ways of the divine" (22). Hatch speaks of this cultural phenomenon in language uncannily similar to that I use to describe the radical shift:

> This vast transformation, this shift away from the Enlightenment and classical republicanism toward vulgar democracy and materialistic individualism in a matter of decades, was the real American Revolution. For many Americans the cultural crisis was [as] severe as any in American history[,] and they fought strenuously over the fundamentals of their own revolution in the midst of profound changes in economic, social, and political life. (*Democratization* 23)

Despite the remarkable contiguities of perception between Hatch's delineation of America's religious democratization movement and this book's description of the Adam and Aeneas dialectic, Hatch attributes the democratization of American Christianity to "a structural looseness of American society in the next generation" after the Revolution and the advent of numerous "populist religious leaders," "from many unexpected quarters" (46).

Hatch's delineation is accurate and admirable. What it lacks is an investigation of the nature of this "structural looseness." To be sure, such cultural critics and leaders as Webster, Washington, Rush, and Jefferson were keenly aware of the potential for chaos in the land. These same elitists, educational theorists, and politicians were equally aware of conflict between the Adamic and the classical modes of discourse. Those in power saw denigration of the classical mode as a necessary sacrifice on the altar of cultural cohesion. Independence had rendered the faith of rebellion no longer tenable, so the religious consciousness of the People required a new focal point. Recall that Washington, in his famous "Circular" to the States, prescribed replacing the faith of rebellion with faith in America, or the American Way. This faith in America, in its Adamicized substitution of the gods with God, accommodated the People's reliance upon the Adamic myth. Thus a democratized, and democratizing, Christianity, subscribed to by a majority at this time, quickly merged with the newly shaped, culturally cohesive faith in America.

One politician who understood the political value of promoting the Adamic myth was John Adams, second president of the United States. In his *Diary*, Adams observes:

> One great Advantage of the Christian Religion is that it brings the great Principle of the Law of Nature and Nations, Love

> your Neighbor as yourself, and do to others as you would that others should do to you—to the Knowledge, Belief and Veneration of the whole People. Children, Servants, Women and Men are all Professors in the science of public as well as private Morality. No other Institution for Education, no kind of political Discipline, could diffuse this kind of necessary Information, so universally among all Ranks and Descriptions of Citizens. The Duties and Rights of the Man and the Citizen are thus taught from early Infancy to every Creature. (Ahlstrom 1: 444)

To Adams, that fact that the Adamic myth was available to virtually everyone made this mode of discourse the most useful (because universal and pacifying) means of disseminating the principles of "political Discipline."

Hatch makes numerous points that bolster our treatment of the Adam and Aeneas dialectic. He is careful to note, for example, that "these populist forms of Christianity so prevalent in America are wholly foreign to European and British Christians: the gospel music, colloquial preaching, unrefined preachers, aggressive communication, unsanctioned institutions, dynamic growth, and recently overt political mobilization" (*Democratization* 218–19). In fact, the cultural dynamic which permitted the establishment of these non-European and non-British religious phenomena is the valorization of Adam over and against Aeneas. In Europe and Great Britain, no such valorization ever occurred, and most of these areas retain cultural confidence in the separation of an elite aristocracy from a working class.

Thomas Jefferson aided and abetted the development of this distinctly American cultural characteristic, while seeming not to. As president of the United States, he espoused the egalitarian, Adamic ideology. By 1814, however, he could observe in a letter to Peter Carr: "The mass of our citizens may be divided into two classes—the laboring and the learned. The laboring will need the first grade of education [that of the English language and Adamic curriculum] to qualify them for their pursuits and duties; the learned will need it as a foundation for further acquirements" (19: 213). Note that, although Jefferson makes a clear distinction between the laboring class and the better educated, higher class (a schema paralleling the British system), both classes are to receive heavy doses of the Adamic myth. So, even as Jefferson acknowledges the continuation of the pre-Revolutionary and Revolutionary War intellectual elite, he is predisposed to bolster the Adamic side of the American self, at some cost to the classical portion of that same self. Thus he, too, displays a somewhat mitigated pattern of acceptance and denial.

As the Adamic myth continued to be valorized and the Aeneas myth denigrated, inevitably the two became confounded. This confounding is evident in Samuel Lorenzo Knapp's *American Cultural History: 1607–1829* (1829), the first book-length attempt to delineate the progress of American culture. Knapp was born in 1783 in Newburyport, Massachusetts, and received his formal education at Phillips Exeter Academy and Dartmouth College, both bastions of the "old" classical curriculum. Thus the author of America's first cultural history was clearly, therefore, a product of the era after the radical shift—i.e., the period when the classical origins of the American self were being actively obscured by the promotion of Adamic origins. Yet he enjoyed a classical education. It therefore is instructive to examine Knapp's description (as close as he comes to definition) of what makes up American culture.

Proceeding from the premise that "the end depends on the beginning—*Finis origine pendet*" (36), Knapp (Latin phrasing notwithstanding) declares, "Nothing but a thinly scattered race of rude men stood in their [i.e., the early settlers'] way to the founding of an empire larger than the world had ever seen" (37). Having limned this hopelessly naïve, unkind portrait of Native Americans, Knapp's anticipation of "the founding of an empire" suggests that his next step will be to depict, in the words of Phillis Wheatley, "new-born *Rome*" (1784; 154). Instead, Knapp drops the classical association to empire and proceeds to paint this arresting picture:

> Every thing, in America, was to be begun, and every thing seemed to depend [note the association here to the Latin *pendet* quoted above (without attribution) from Manilius's *Astronomica* 4.16] on themselves; with the happy difference, however, between us and those in paradise, for our safety and happiness were to depend [again] upon eating freely of the tree of knowledge, which was forbidden to him who first sprang from the dust of the earth. (Knapp 37)

Despite his deeply Latinate syntax, Knapp asserts a view that American beginnings derived wholly from an Adamic paradise (more hopeless naiveté). In his enthusiasm, however, he portrays Adam as one who "sprang from the dust" not with assistance from God, but unaided, via a sort of pristine American self-reliance. "Here was offered," Knapp continues, "the opportunity to cultivate the mind without the trammels and fetters which embarrass and bind those born in aged and decaying communities" (37). One can be certain that a major manifestation of those "trammels and fetters" was the baggage of a classical education. So the question how it was that Knapp cultivated his own mind becomes more or less not worth asking.

In consideration of the beginnings of American politics, Knapp maintains:

> The political compact was to be formed and altered as the covenanters could agree; for there was no other lawgiver than their own understandings; no *Solons* but their own wisdom, no *Lycurguses* but the severe discussions of their own judgments. (37–38)

Knapp almost seems to want his readers to believe that the American social contract, like Adam, "sprang from the dust," and that location on the American strand is the only criterion necessary for the exercise of wise judgment. This portrait of alleged early American consciousness contrasts starkly with Cotton Mather's calling John Winthrop in *Magnalia* an even greater lawgiver than the patient Lycurgus (213).

Knapp caps off his grossly romanticized picture of incipient American consciousness by declaring, "Thus stripped of every shackle, they began their work of founding an empire" (38). Today, of course, we are problematically aware of this earlier period's cruel practice of slavery, suppression of women, and progressive destruction of Native American civilization. Holding these issues in abeyance, one still is struck by Knapp's consistently failed attempts to disclaim any European or Western contribution to the American consciousness. Knapp demands that America be so novel that he seems almost to allow the Adamic self to merge into the American self. What Knapp's portrait of American beginnings displays, finally, is such intense anxiety concerning influence that his obviously patriotic effort becomes a ludicrous, unintentional exercise in self-parody.

Despite Knapp's classical background, the author of America's first cultural history manifests the pattern of acceptance and denial. His attitude toward classicism, as expressed in *American Cultural History*, has become at best ambivalent. It may well be that, as an individual, Knapp possessed a more positive attitude toward classicism. In his "Preface," he states that his chief intention in writing this work is to place it "readily within the reach of all classes of youth in our country . . . a single volume of common size, in a cheap edition." He goes on to observe, significantly: "The elements of learning have been simplified, and thousands of children have been beguiled along the pathway of knowledge, who never could have been driven onward" (4).[13] Clearly Knapp intended his volume to be used as a textbook in the public schools. Given this intention, Knapp's ambivalence may be attributed in part to his effort to reach a wide array of readers who did not share Knapp's classical training.

Opposition to the Radical Shift

While we have encountered intimations of the acceptance and denial motif in the work of Edward Taylor and Cotton Mather, among others, the acceptance and denial pattern did not settle into the American consciousness until after the radical shift began. A felicitous, public blending of the myths of Adam and Aeneas had characterized American classicism from Aquila Rose to George Washington. When this happy blend yielded to the denigration of all things British and classical, the general population failed to recognize the role played by the classical mode of discourse in shaping the American self, and a palpable anxiety of resistance to this radical shift in cultural consciousness arose.

Early on, the sentiment was confusion, as Knapp so clearly exemplifies. Later, certain elements within the intellectual elite registered open protest against the loss of classical discourse. While these voices of protest were not strong enough to stem the tide of change, they deserve acknowledgment, if only because they demonstrate how powerful the radical shift was.

One who objected strenuously to the radical change in the American public school system (i.e., to the projected loss of classical studies) was Samuel Knox, the Maryland Presbyterian clergyman and educator mentioned above. In an address to state legislators that prefaces his *Essay on Education* (written 1797, published 1799), Knox called attention to the marginalization of classical studies in America's public schools: "Some are found to have taken up the opinion that the acquisition of the Greek and Latin languages, the minutiae of their grammars, and a well-formed taste for the beauties of the ancient classical writers has a tendency to damp natural genius, pervert its powers, and misapply its attention" (283). Knox cites as an example one of the many anticlassical tracts by Benjamin Rush, ally of Anthony Benezet and Noah Webster.

In the text of his *Essay*, Knox encourages the study of Latin and Greek, as a stimulus to the mind and for the wealth of learning such study provides. This educator and minister maintains that it is "only from the study of these and other languages that the improvement of our own language can be promoted" (302). In his public system of education, Knox would include large selections from Caesar, Horace, Livy, Sallust, Tacitus, Theocritus (in Greek), and, of course, Vergil. While he is not specific about works by other authors young scholars should pursue, he is specific about both Vergil and Theocritus. He prescribes Theocritus's *Idylls* and Vergil's *Bucolics* (or *Eclogues*) for the purpose of composing poetic imitations, and he insists on close analysis of Vergil's *Georgics* and the *Aeneid* (338–42). At the same moment Knox is constructing his ideal educational system with the old

Latin grammar schools clearly in mind, he finds it necessary to observe that "much objection" is being made in the land "against the acquisition of the Greek and Latin classics" (303).

In an essay entitled "The Friend, No. IV," published in June 1789, Timothy Dwight offers the sort of objection to tradition that elicited Knox's response. Dwight holds that, while the works of Aristotle, Homer, and Vergil should not be ignored by aspiring American authors of pastoral and epic, "nature ought to be consulted in preference to Aristotle; and other approved writers, as well as Homer and Virgil, Sophocles and Theocritus." "On this plan," Dwight continues:

> the wings of genius would be no longer clipped, and its flight, taking the natural direction, and using the natural strength of opinion, would be free and elevated; on this plan, the writer who produced pleasing selections of images and sentiments from the widely extended and endlessly diversified paradise of nature, would be assured of regaling the taste of his readers. ("The Friend, No. IV" 567)

In this approach, generally hostile to tradition when employed in the service of imaginative literature, Dwight maintains that writers, in America, should employ "the perpetually variegated rovings of imagination." As America is now "disjointed from the customs and systems of Europe" and is engaged in "commencing a new system of science and politics," a new "independence of mind will be assumed by us to induce us to shake off these rusty shackles" of past authority and "examine things on the plan of nature and evidence, and laugh at the grey-bearded decisions of doting authority" (567).

This essentially romantic attitude, which leads Dwight to recommend an empirical reliance upon nature, promotes the use of imagination and disdains authority, much as we have seen Phillis Wheatley do in her subversive practices. Dwight, however, as a white male academic and citizen of the new Republic, writes under no disadvantage requiring a subversive posture. He openly joins the war upon the authority of the ancients. In doing so, he repeats an earlier and less successful attempt he made to defy ancient tradition—by writing an epic allegedly not classical, *The Conquest of Canaan*. Of course, Dwight and his allies (Rush, Webster, etc.) succeeded in their overall campaign to denigrate classical studies in America, despite the efforts of Samuel Knox and his allies to conserve the study of Latin and Greek. Although the Boston Latin School has endured to the present day, serious study of classical languages and culture has been relegated to marginal status. Even so, before 1850 at least two more offensives were launched to halt the devaluation of ancient languages.

The first of these offensives occurs after 1800, during the Age of Jacksonian Democracy—no small surprise, since that age particularly advanced an egalitarian, leveling movement on behalf of the common man. Curiously enough, Francis Glass, author of the Latin *Georgii Washingtonii Vita (A Life of George Washington)*, signals that the myth of Aeneas has lost its power, when he translates a passage of his own Latin prose:

> Making use of common sense, he [Washington] could better perform all the (civil) offices, to which his countrymen unanimously called him, than if, tinctured with more polished learning, he would shake the American populace (by his eccentricities) with laughter, by aiming at things obviously repugnant to common sense. (*Georgii* 180)

Here, in a nutshell, Glass (unwittingly, of course) declares that the successful American politician no longer will admit to any pretensions to learning, at least not in her or his self-presentations before the People. Ironically supporting the radical shift by labeling uncommon learning a blot upon one's character, Glass reinforces the Adamsonian portrait of Washington as a non-intellectual—this effort deep within one of the most formidable instruments ever offered up in opposition to the loss of Aeneas.

Glass's confusion may have been caused in part by one Thomas S. Grimke, called "the leading anti-classicist of the Jacksonian era." Like Anthony Benezet before him, Grimke, in pamphlet after vituperative pamphlet, opposed classical studies largely on the basis of their alleged anti-Christian biases (Miles 272). Those who rose up to laud Glass's Latin prose biography of Washington did so within the context of opposition to the radical shift. Edgar A. Poe, editor of the *Southern Literary Messenger,* reviewed Glass's undertaking glowingly in 1835, reporting that Glass's work "has already done wonders in the cause of the classics." Poe continues:

> we are false prophets if it do not ultimately prove the means of stirring up to a new life and a regenerated energy that love of the learned tongues which is the surest protection of our own vernacular language from impurity, but which we are grieved to see is in a languishing and dying condition in the land. (*Georgii* 243)

John Quincy Adams, sixth president of the United States, followed right behind Poe in his enthusiastic attempt to preserve study of the classical languages and cultures. Writing in the same month and in praise of Glass's *Vita,* Adams laments:

> The fashion of the present day is to depreciate the study of the dead languages, even of the Latin; and the youth of our country

> are told, that instead of turning over with the nocturnal and diurnal hand the Greek exemplars, and their faithful followers of the golden age of Rome, they are to form their principles of taste and eloquence, and poetry from modern writers and orators in their own vernacular language. (*Georgii* 246)

As for the notion much promulgated throughout the land, that translations provide adequate substitutes for the original Latin or Greek, Adams issues this reproach:

> If all the young men of our country could be taught to read and understand your *Life of Washington*, and then to read a page of Livy, Sallust, or Tacitus, and afterward endure a translation, it would be time to burn up all the classics. I should be sorry to lose them, and therefore hope your *Life of Washington* may be extensively read. (*Georgii* 247)

Notwithstanding Adams's patriarchal, sexist identification, "all the young men of our country," his tone here (particularly in such phrases as "time to burn up all the classics" and "should be sorry to lose them") strikes a desperate chord, as if the battle to maintain the dignity of classical studies were about to be lost. In 1843, Andrew Preston Peabody, Unitarian minister and later professor of Christian morals at Harvard, sums up the character of the second, and regrettably the last, major offensive conducted in resistance to the radical shift by affirming, "The controversy has become a real and an earnest one. War to the death has been declared and waged against classical culture" (Miles 264). As Thomas Robbins suggested ten years later, in asserting that all America seeks salvation "in the name of the DIVINE NAZARENE," the war against classical studies seemed utterly victorious. Such was hardly the case.

Conclusion
Persistence of the Myth of Aeneas

Despite all efforts to eliminate classical studies, they persisted. The myth of Aeneas persisted, too, though it occupied a somewhat marginal status. When one lifts the scales from one's eyes—that is, when the investigator of American culture after the radical shift in discourse sets aside the hegemony of the Adamic myth—glimmerings of the Aeneas myth shine forth from many quarters. Among the plantation gentry of the antebellum South, for example, Aeneas loomed large. One senses that a Latin Horace or Vergil was never far from the grasp of Margaret Mitchell's Ashley Wilkes.[14]

Perhaps less obviously, the cultural grid of the American Aeneas may be traced in the work of the major authors of the American Renaissance (this term now more apropos than ever before): Ralph Waldo Emerson, Henry David Thoreau, Walt Whitman, Nathaniel Hawthorne, and Herman Melville. Space does not permit a thorough investigation of the roles played by the Aeneas myth in the works of these authors; such an undertaking, eventually to include less well-known authors (male and female, white, black and brown), would consume several volumes. It is sufficient here to establish the existence of this classical cultural grid in these authors.

Nor can the woman's part in bringing about the establishment of the American cultural self be ignored; indeed, her role has been determinative. Brief indication of the importance of the classical mode to Emerson, Thoreau, and Whitman serves our present necessity, which includes a demonstration of how women came to bear major responsibility for disseminating the American Way (pietas modified) to all Americans. Because the classical mode of discourse is so readily discernible in the work of Hawthorne and Melville, and because the interplay of the myths of Adam and Aeneas in their work so clearly exhibits the problematical legacy of this cultural dynamic for the American self, I devote an entire chapter to analysis of the Adam and Aeneas dialectic, first in Hawthorne's "Egotism; or, The Bosom Serpent" and "My Kinsman, Major Molineaux," and then in Melville's *Billy Budd*.

Unlike Samuel Knapp, who, in his *American Cultural History*, was attempting to reach the popular mind, Emerson, Thoreau, Whitman, Hawthorne, and Melville usually seem disposed to attract an audience comprised of *persons-thinking* (to adapt Emerson's phrasing). Emerson's testimony that Aristophanes, among other ancient authors, is "full of American history," recently has led Richard Poirier to declare that Emerson intends "less to disown the Old [World] than to rediscover its true origins otherwise obscured within encrustations of acquired culture." For, as Poirier contends, the only constructive and recreative way for persons-thinking to proceed is to "Get rid of culture, get rid of literature, but only after they have taught us how to reach again the sources of both, which are within us" (45–46).

It is clear that the pattern of acceptance in Emerson yields an intellectual maturity characterized by conscious assimilation. In his journals, which are filled with classical allusions, quotations, and commentary on the ancient authors, Emerson articulates such thoughts as these, for example, on Homer and the Greek tragedians: "In this great empty continent of ours stretching enormous almost from pole to pole with thousands of long rivers and thousands of ranges of mountains, the rare scholar who under a farmhouse roof reads Homer & the Tragedies adorns the land" (8: 292).

Anyone who has glanced at Thoreau's chapter on "Reading" in *Walden* knows how enthusiastically the younger man shared Emerson's devotion to Homer and Greek tragedy. This enthusiasm for Homer and the Greek authors in general, rather than the eighteenth century's delight in Vergil and Latin authors, can be attributed at least partly to the nineteenth century's scholarly rediscovery (largely by way of German philology) of Greek literature, especially Homer's *Iliad* and *Odyssey*. As for negative attitudes toward the classical authors, a disposition which Thoreau regretfully acknowledges does exist, the author of *Walden* asserts, "They only talk of forgetting them who never knew them. It will be soon enough to forget them when we have the learning and the genius which will enable us to attend to and appreciate them" (1546). The parallel here to Poirier hardly needs remarking.

A less formally educated Walt Whitman[15] expresses a similar point of view in "Starting from Paumanok," in *Leaves of Grass:*

> Dead poets, philosophs [for philosophes], priests,
> Martyrs, artists, inventors, governments long since,
> Language-shapers on other shores,
> Nations once powerful, now reduced, withdrawn, or desolate,
> I dare not proceed till I respectfully credit what you have left
> wafted hither,
> I have perused it, own it is admissable, (moving awhile among it,)
> Think nothing can ever be greater, nothing can ever deserve
> more than it deserves,
> Regarding it all intently a long while, then dismissing it,
> I stand in my place with my own day here. (Whitman 17–18)

Like Emerson and Thoreau before him, Whitman embraces all thought available to him, including the classical, "left wafted hither," not to ridicule that thought or to label it not American, but to absorb it, adapt it, and make it his. In so doing, he brings all knowledge to himself only so he can sing the song of the United States—so he can utter the astronomical motion, the centripetal and centrifugal pulling and hauling of the words and ideas of others, absorbed into himself in order to bring forth "Song of Myself."

These powerful statements affirming the essential importance of ancient Western thought and literature to Emerson, Thoreau, and Whitman closely parallel similar declarations made by Hawthorne and Melville, as will soon become apparent. Unlike Knapp, whose objective was to reach the broad public, these authors were attempting not to produce a commodity but to create art. Hence their attitude toward the ancients was more candid and less ambivalent. As Robert D. Richardson's *Myth and Literature*, points out, however, a virtual barrage of newly discovered mythologies—from

Macpherson's Ossianic poems and Paul Mallet's *Eddas* to Anquetil-Duperron's *Zend-Avesta* and Charles Wilkins's *Bhagvat-Geeta*—presented to the world of the literary, recreative imagination a variety of alternatives to the myths of both Adam and Aeneas.[16] Surely all these competing mythologies would have distracted writers of the American Renaissance from the dialectic of the myths of Adam and Aeneas.

To a limited degree, such was the case. There is, in addition, a time factor to be considered. Knapp was removed from the radical shift by only a single generation. He was taught by many who could recall at first hand the heyday of the American Aeneas, and very likely he received some of this cultural information from those instructors. Unlike Knapp, such later authors as Emerson, Thoreau, Whitman, Hawthorne, and Melville were removed from the shift by almost two generations. It stood to reason that, the longer it was since the radical shift, and the longer the Adamic mode had held dominion over the classical mode, the less likely it was that, even within the intellectual elite, successive generations would have intimate, dynamic recall of the classical mode. These three factors—the privileging of the Adamic myth at the expense of the Aeneas myth, the influx of many newly discovered alternative mythologies, and the probable effects of the passage of time—made it increasingly likely that a muted, watered-down version of the American Aeneas would be transmitted to most American writers of the nineteenth century.

There is no question that the general population of early-nineteenth-century America wholeheartedly bought into the acceptance and denial pattern regarding the nation's classical heritage. Contrary to conventional wisdom, though, serious writers of this period (and after) did *not* accept the Adamic myth. To be sure, the manifestations of their continued allegiance to the Vergilian mode have been muted to some degree by the radical shift, competing mythologies, and the ravages of time. Still, an awareness of the American Aeneas, and even a dynamic, if revisionist, expression thereof, may be discerned in the works of serious American writers of the nineteenth century. On the whole, American Studies scholars of the present century (most twentieth-century writers of creative American literature significantly excepted) also have capitulated to the Adamic myth. As a result, the effort to draw out or reclaim an American classical discourse entails an archaeology of sorts. The following discussion amounts to a demonstration of that methodology.

Perhaps the first and most substantial query guiding such an archaeology is: Why is it that such writers as Emerson in *The American Scholar* and Melville in "Hawthorne and His Mosses" felt the need to enact a second, self-conscious declaration of literary independence? It seems that the first abortive efforts of Webb, Perkins, Adams (the poet, not the president), Jacob Taylor, and John Trumbull to carry out this office were not merely ignored by Emerson and Melville (and others); rather, they were largely unknown to them. That is to say, these first efforts to establish a distinctly American literary mode, independent of Britain and the Continent, were abortive, first, because of the determinative effects of the radical shift; and, second, because an energetic and thriving romanticism, for the most part hailing from (like it or not) British and Continental influences, generally denigrated the neoclassical mode in which American writers of the eighteenth century cast their (poetic, especially) productions. Thus, writers of America's classical period struck writers of the American Renaissance as quaint or even "antique."

Despite the laudable efforts of the Duyckinck brothers in their two-volume *Cyclopaedia of American Literature* to bring to the attention of nineteenth-century Americans the work of such eighteenth-century Americans as John Adams (1705–1740), Joseph Green, Mather Byles, and even Phillis Wheatley, Evert and George reproduced only one of the literary independence poems, F. Bernard's "Epilogus." Except for Bernard's "Epilogus" and Trumbull's "Essay on the . . . Fine Arts" in America, these early efforts to declare literary independence were largely localized statements made within, and for the sake of, individual colonial regions. As such, they themselves attest a lack of national identity. While Bernard's "Epilogus" and Trumbull's "Essay" may be considered self-conscious attempts to sound a national chord, even these efforts to assert independence became subsumed within the all-encompassing struggle for military and political independence. A way of summing up this process is to declare that American classicism became quite simply another instrument to be used in the quest for American independence.

For whatever reasons, these earlier documents of literary independence *never* were reclaimed after the radical shift; nor was any attempt made either to acknowledge or to appreciate the possibility of a distinctly American literature cast in the classical mode. Hence a second process of asserting American literary independence became inevitable. That this was so illustrates how very effective were the efforts of Webster, Rush, and others in unwittingly bringing about a general but covert feeling of cultural confusion and loss. The age of Emerson, Thoreau, Hawthorne, Melville, and Whitman was called "the American Renaissance" by F. O. Matthiessen. Actually the term, "American Renaissance," comes from late nineteenth-century American literary histories. What never has been effectively argued heretofore is that, given the particulars of the first attempt to declare and to practice an American literary independence, the term "American Renaissance" now gains in validity. The writings of these authors in fact enact a rebirth of a literary response to the idea of Americanness. More to the point, however, the reincorporation or "revision" of the American Aeneas within the nineteenth century's literary response to the idea of Americanness, despite the radical shift in discourse, constitutes a dynamic reassertion of America's cultural indebtedness to classical thought and letters.

During this time of spirited endeavors to delineate the American self, one Mrs. A. J. Graves eloquently articulates the woman's part in the struggle for cultural identity. Graves was one of the most popular authors of the nineteenth-century's conduct books for women. Her *Woman in America: Being an Examination into the Moral and Intellectual Condition of American Female Society* appeared in 1843. In the following year, she published the nostalgic *Girlhood and Womanhood; or, Sketches of My Schoolmates*. Her use of the word *moral* in the subtitle of *Woman in America* recalls Phillis Wheatley's *Poems on Various Subjects, Religious and Moral*. Graves underlines her connection to Wheatley and to Addison's Marcia in this arresting passage from the prefatory material in *Woman in America:* "Woman's empire is *Home*; and, by adding spirituality to its happiness, dignity to its dominion, and power to its influences, it becomes the best security for *individual integrity*, and the surest safeguard for national *virtue*" (i).

Here, feminized, are the tenets of Washington's modified pietas. For what Graves reconstructs in these several phrases is a microcosmic, mirror image (much as Marcia is a mirror image of her father Cato) of the American Way. The woman's home is interpreted as an "empire," just as the American sociopolitical system was viewed as an empire (recall Wheatley's "To the Empire of America Beneath the Western Hemisphere"). Clearly, a primary office of woman within her "empire" is to attend to the spiritual nourishment of children and perhaps even her husband. Note the forcefulness of Graves's "adding . . . *power* [emphasis mine] to its influences." Of course, the "Home" is itself representative of family and friends. Finally, we learn that the woman's dominion provides "the surest safeguard for national virtue"; to put this last responsibility of woman another way, it devolves upon her to instruct those in her charge in the best paths of social interaction, to guide her charges' civic development, and to ensure that all enter the arena of sociopolitical discourse trained in this same "*national virtue*"—that is, pietas *instauratio emendata*.

We find no explicit classical reference in this passage or elsewhere in Graves's *Woman in America*. However, we are by now well prepared to recognize the origins of this acceptance and denial so characteristic of the American self. Like Marcia and Wheatley before her, Graves binds to woman the responsibility of exhorting her male counterpart to embody and enact proper pietas. Ironically, Noah Webster assigns this office to women as early as 1787–88, when he first published his widely distributed essay, "On the Education of Youth in America" (the title echoes essays by Franklin and Benezet, discussed above). This work came out in six installments, in Webster's own *American Magazine*, and was reprinted at least four times before 1800. In several pages devoted to the education of women, Webster declares:

> The women in America (to their honor it is mentioned) are not generally above the care of educating their own children. Their own education should therefore enable them to implant in the tender mind such sentiments of virtue, propriety, and dignity as are suited to the freedom of our governments. (68)

As with Graves, the three elements of a Washingtonian pietas are implicit here. The idea of the Christian deity resonates throughout any educational schema Webster offers; the institution of family he promotes in the phrase "the care of educating their own children"; good American citizenship he advances in the phrase "suited to the freedom of our governments." Webster underscores the woman's role in the development of good citizenship later, when he asserts that "another powerful reason" female education "should be particularly guarded" is women's "influence in controlling the manners of a nation" (69). Webster closes his description of the woman's role in the education of American youth by observing "real honor and permanent esteem are always secured by those who preside over their own families with dignity" (71).

Webster's emphasis on security and dignity is echoed by Graves, in her phrases "adding dignity to its dominion" and "the best security of *individual integrity*." In the third part of his immensely popular *Grammatical Institute of the English Language* (12th ed., 1796), Webster cites Marcia in Addison's *Cato* as an exemplar of the virtue of modesty (249). This evocation of Marcia also recalls Cato's daughter as a mirror of her father's pietas. As we have learned that Webster's influence on the McGuffey readers was decisive, here we see that his language and thought describing (some may insist on "prescribing") the woman's role in educating America's youth thoroughly informs Graves's preface to *Woman in America*.

As the life and thought of Noah Webster dominated events which brought about the radical shift in discourse, this author of education theories and textbooks and America's best-known lexicographer has earned the last word concerning the valorization of Adam over Aeneas. Regardless of the consequences of the radical shift—a fear of pastlessness, America's macabre celebration of anti-intellectualism, confusion concerning what constitutes an American, and the privileging of Adamic discourse—Webster's determinative role in causing the radical shift cannot be ignored. Webster certainly was among the first to recognize that military victory did not bring an end to the American Revolution. In an essay entitled "Remarks on the Manners, Government, and Debt of the United States" (1787), Webster observes, over two hundred years before Hatch's pronouncement that the democratization of American Christianity "was the real American Revolution":

> A fundamental mistake of the Americans has been, that they considered the revolution as completed, when it was but just begun. Having raised the pillars of the building, they ceased to exert themselves, and seemed to forget that the whole superstructure was then to be erected. (*Fugitiv* 84)

This superstructure was composed largely of the Adamic myth, valorized over and against the Aeneas myth.

8

The Persistence of the American Aeneas in Hawthorne

Part of the nineteenth-century literary response to the idea of Americanness, despite the radical shift, was a dynamic reassertion of America's cultural indebtedness to classical thought and letters. During a spirited time of renewed endeavors to delineate the American self, Hawthorne first and Melville later displayed in their work a powerful reassertion of the American Aeneas. These two authors were hardly the only ones to do so.

Robert Richardson in *Myth and Literature in the American Renaissance*, contends that Nathaniel Hawthorne's attitude toward Latin and Greek literatures resembles "something anticlassic" (172). Richardson even says that, finally, Hawthorne "is clearly opposed to whatever is classical" (173).[1] Investigation of "My Kinsman, Major Molineaux," perhaps Hawthorne's most challenging tale, proves that its author's knowledge of and admiration for Vergil's *Aeneid*, and especially for its hero's journey through the underworld, determined how Hawthorne constructed this tale. Richardson's contention, then, is incredible.

Checking into Hawthorne's educational background should have led Richardson toward a different conclusion. Long before he wrote "My Kinsman," Hawthorne acquired an intimate familiarity with Vergil's epic in its original Latin. Hawthorne was soundly educated in ancient classical works, first by tutors at Salem while he prepared for entrance to college and later through the thoroughly classical curriculum at Bowdoin. While the young Hawthorne's tutorial studies would have emphasized parsing most of Vergil's *Eclogues*, *Georgics*, and the *Aeneid*, and committing to memory lengthy passages from each, his chief biographer, Arlin Turner, points out that, during his four years at Bowdoin, the fledgling author "gave little attention to other studies than ancient languages and biblical and classical literatures." Henry Wordsworth Longfellow, continues Turner, "has been cited as speaking of the 'graceful and poetic translations' Hawthorne gave from the Latin authors" (*Biography* 39). As for Hawthorne's subsequent attitude toward his college days, Turner writes, "It was not his habit to disparage the country college he attended or to call his four years wasted" (43).

Others have ignored Hawthorne's thorough and apparently welcome happy classical training. In searching for the source of his "Egotism; or, The Bosom Serpent," for example, scholars have looked no farther back in time than Spenser's *Faerie Queene*. Perhaps the most substantive investigation[2] is Sargent Bush Jr.'s "Bosom Serpents before Hawthorne: The Origins of a Symbol." Bush reconstructs admirably an early-nineteenth-century milieu in which newspapers reported allegedly "actual" ingestion of snakes by several humans, any or all of which Hawthorne may have viewed. At one point Bush asserts, "The full notion of a snake's residing in the human heart does not derive from the Bible" (197).[3] Bush is correct, of course; in the biblical myth of Eden, the serpent does not physically enter the body. Bush finds the origin of such vivid imagery in the homilies and treatises of English and American Puritan ministers, such as Cotton Mather, Increase Mather, and Thomas Hooker. His conclusion remains, however, that the oldest source of Hawthorne's "lasting literary symbol for the insidious and corrupting effect of sin on the soul of man" (199), outside the obvious one in Genesis, is the *Faerie Queene*.

Given Hawthorne's extensive knowledge of Latin, Bush and others might have searched for a serpent's physical invasion of the body of a human being in classical sources, including Vergil's *Aeneid*. In books VII–XII, Aeneas must fight Turnus and the Latins for possession of the territories surrounding the site of what would become Rome. Juno, up to her old tricks in attempting to thwart at every turn progress toward founding the Roman Empire, observes that the Trojans and Italians appear to be on the brink of forming an alliance. She determines to incite the Latins and Rutulians, whose chief is Turnus, to hostility against the Trojans. Juno accomplishes her objective by enlisting the aid of the Fury Alecto. First Alecto, in the form of a snake, possesses Amata, queen of Latinus, the Latin King; then she appears before Turnus in the guise of an old priestess, who informs him that Aeneas is about to take as his bride

Lavinia, daughter of Latinus and Amata. Unbeknownst to Latinus, Amata has promised Lavinia's hand in marriage to Turnus. Finally, Alecto contrives a situation which prompts Julus (or Ascanius), Aeneas's son, to kill a valuable pet of Latinus's household, provoking further hostilities against the Trojans. Alecto, Juno's agent in vengeance, is successful, of course, in bringing about war between the Italians (Etruscans) and the Trojans.

In the *Aeneid*, the Fury Alecto, replete with head full of sprouting snakes, shifts the initially friendly attitude of the Italians to one of intense hostility; that is, Alecto changes the thinking of the Italians concerning the Trojans. Vergil employs the narrative constructs of supernatural machines as metaphors for what are, finally, shifts in mental perspective. One may ask, as Hawthorne's narrator does many times, whether a shift in mental attitude is brought about by physical or mental means; in epic and story, however, the results are the same—the minds of certain principal characters are altered. The Italians declare war on Aeneas and his band, and Elliston changes from contented husband to jealous malcontent.

It is the picture Vergil paints of Alecto invading the bosom of the unsuspecting Queen Amata in the shape of a serpent, however, which most closely approximates Hawthorne's "Bosom Serpent." Thoroughly macabre is Vergil's portrait: "huic dea caeruleis unum de crinibus anguem/ conicit, in que sinum praecordia ad intima subdit,/ quo furibunda domum monstro permisceat omnem (VII, 346–48; the goddess hurls from her black hair one [among the many] serpent[s] on her [i.e., Amata], and places [it] within the innermost part of her heart, so that, having become maddened by it, the queen may throw the whole household into confusion). Then the vengeance-seeking Fury reveals her hideous modus operandi: "ille inter vestis et levia pectora lapsus/ volvitur attactu nullo fallitque furentem,/ vipeream inspirans animam" (VII, 349–51; the thing, gliding between her clothing and smooth breasts, turns itself round about and arrives by touching the frenzied woman insignificantly, breathing into her soul its poisonous breath). While it is true that Hawthorne's serpent "gnaws" Elliston almost constantly, and Vergil's serpent invades the body "by touching [it] . . . insignificantly," both poet and short-story writer use the serpent as a metaphor to indicate radical shifts in demeanor and behavior. Vergil's stark portrayal of a physical invasion is a source Sargent Bush correctly asserts "does not derive from the Bible," though Bush manages to locate his nonbiblical, physical invasion sources only as early as the seventeenth and early eighteenth centuries.

Most curiously overlooked by those seeking Hawthorne's source for this tale is the fact that most editions of Spenser's *Faerie Queene* published between 1900 and 1970, a year before Bush's article appeared, gloss the crucial Spenser passage (III, xi, 1) as having been derived from Vergil's *Aeneid*, book VII.[4] The ultimate source of Hawthorne's serpent metaphor in Vergil seems so obvious that one is left bewildered by previous failures to make the classical connection. Perhaps Richardson's idea that Hawthorne held a negative attitude toward most things classical was a belief common among many, if not most, concerned with tracing Hawthorne's sources and the uses he made of them.

Few if any commentators on "My Kinsman, Major Molineaux" have named a classical source for this provocative tale, though several have proposed Dante's *La Commedia* as a possible source.[5] Like "Egotism; or, The Bosom Serpent," both Hawthorne's "Kinsman" and Dante's *Commedia* have their roots in Vergil's *Aeneid*. Why scholars have not gone to Vergil as the obvious source for both works remains puzzling.

Hawthorne's composition of "My Kinsman" owes considerably more to the *Aeneid* than does "Egotism." Indeed, this entire story constitutes a response to the journey of Vergil's hero, Aeneas, to the underworld (book VI). Hawthorne actually inverts Aeneas's fateful journey, turning Vergil's narrative inside out. Moreover, Hawthorne is studious to promote the Roman virtue of pietas, or devotion to the gods (God in a Judaeo-Christian context), to the family, and to the country. While Vergil's hero Aeneas most faithfully and consistently manifests this virtue in the *Aeneid*, Hawthorne's apparent hero Robin in "My Kinsman" represents a perversion of this virtue.

The action of "My Kinsman, Major Molineaux," which first appeared in 1831, begins in Massachusetts Bay of the 1730s. The story's hero, Robin, whose very name is emblematic of beginnings, is nearly eighteen years old. Robin seeks to leave the protective confines of his rural home and strike out on his own in the "city," where he hopes to elicit the aid of a kinsman. To break with his innocent, youthful past, Robin must cross a river by means of a ferry. Should he later return to the secure home of his past, he will have been changed irrevocably—innocence lost cannot be regained. The story of Adam and Eve becoming unparadised (to echo one of Milton's early titles for *Paradise Lost*) is an obvious parallel here. In the Genesis tale, however, there is no river crossing. The structural device of a river crossing into a world from which there is no return comes from classical myth.

One possible source for the ferry/ferryman motif, of course, is Vergil's *Aeneid*. In book VI, the hero Aeneas must cross the River Styx into Hades in order to learn the purpose of his existence—to make possible the founding of the Roman Empire. To achieve enlightenment, ironically within a realm in which the dreamy half-light of the underworld replaces the clear light of day, Aeneas must pay a fee to the dreaded ferryman, Charon. Unlike the dead souls who surround him, awaiting an opportunity to cross, Aeneas "pays" not with money but with the famed golden bough, the key to future knowledge. Thus Aeneas crosses the Styx: "Occupat Aeneas aditum custode sepulto/ evaditque celer ripam inremeabilis undae" (VI, 424–25; Having buried [in sleep] the guardian [Cerberus], Aeneas seized the entrance [to the Underworld] and swiftly left behind the bank of [that] water from which there is no return).

As in the *Aeneid,* Robin crosses a river, obtaining "his conveyance at that unusual hour [near nine o'clock in the evening] by the promise of an extra fare" (Hawthorne, "Kinsman" 3). This crossing brings him into a dimly lit, somewhat surreal domain in which he experiences many revelations, not the least of which is the unwelcome knowledge that his kinsman is a despised agent of the British crown. As Robin finds him in the disgraceful (hellish) state of having been tarred and feathered, he will prove not to be any help to Robin as he tries to establish himself in this New England "city."

Standard interpretations of "My Kinsman" read this work largely as a product of the myth of the American Adam, seeing Robin's plight as an allegory for loss of innocence. If we recognize the persistence of the Vergilian myth, even if only on the level of a deep-seated structural grid (which, once reclaimed, does not necessarily lead to an *aporia,* or impasse), we obtain quite another reading. Though much has been made of Robin as a sort of latter-day Adam who loses Paradise after being rather rudely initiated into adulthood,[6] he can be viewed as an Aeneas figure who crosses the Styx in order to become enlightened. In that case, the emphasis shifts—away from his loss of innocence and toward the nature of his enlightenment, or, as proves to be the case, toward Robin's blindness. As Aeneas seeks his father Anchises as his final guide, the one who will introduce him to Rome's future glory and grandeur, Robin seeks out his kinsman as a guide to life in the city. While Aeneas receives a fulfilling vision of pagan beatitude, Robin, who allows several other unsavory characters to substitute as guides, summarily rejects his kinsman, once he discovers that the major has fallen from his position of power. Within the parameters of the Aeneas myth, rejection of family constitutes a perversion of pietas, the Roman virtue of devotion to the gods, family, and country, so pervasive in Vergil's *Aeneid.* This instance is only one among several other erosions of the classical mode in this tale.

In preparation for his journey, Aeneas first seeks the religious counsel of the Sibyl who resides at Avernus, the entrance to the Underworld. Aeneas does as the Sibyl instructs, plucks the golden bough, and sets off on his journey, accompanied by both the Sibyl and his loyal friend Achates. Unlike those of Aeneas, Robin's preparations are limited to assembling what he supposes is acceptable dress, some money (a few coins and some paper bills), and a trusty cudgel (this last recalls a knight's lance, presumably to bash the heads of would-be challengers). While Robin searches constantly for a reliable guide, he never finds one. When Aeneas, the Sibyl, and Achates reach the Styx, they "pay" with the holy object, the golden bough. This golden bough signals yet another contrast between epic and tale. For Robin "pays" with money and must, because of the late hour (or the ferryman's greed), give an extra fare. The bough symbolizes royal power, inestimable value (it is gold as well as a living branch), and regeneration (when plucked, another "simili frondescit virga metalo" [l. 144; branch sprouts with the same metal]). Robin's money (both coinage and paper), however, fulfills only a temporary need and then has no further value; certainly it has no intrinsic power to regenerate—no life.

As for Robin's club, "a heavy cudgel formed of an oak sapling, and retaining a part of the hardened root" (4), this weapon mimics Aeneas's golden bough, plucked from a holm-oak (or ilex [l. 209]). Though called an oak, the holm-oak is not a true one, but a Mediterranean evergreen. While Aeneas uses the golden bough as a protective instrument for obtaining his passage to knowledge, Robin displays his oaken club as a threat to those he thinks may show hostility toward him. E. H. Miller in "Playful Art" sees this cudgel as a phallic symbol which Robin brandishes periodically "to prove to himself and to his elders his rights to manhood" (149). So interpreted, Robin's dead piece of oak contrasts the more with Aeneas's eternally regenerative, precious green-golden bough. What more powerful phallic symbol than Aeneas's (phallogocentric) golden bough has the classical world produced? Robin carries about his sterile bludgeon, presenting a less than friendly posture to all whom the young man encounters in the city. Thus this instrument prevents the acquisition of knowledge. So perceived, this dead cudgel is the antithesis of Aeneas's golden bough, in illustrating still another perversion of the Aeneas myth. Hawthorne names this oak club five times in "My Kinsman"; the last two namings find Robin acting upon the hostility his posture threatens. Confronting the grotesque man of the red and black countenance for the second of three times, Robin uses the cudgel to block his passage. Insisting that the man (ghoul?) inform him of the whereabouts of his kinsman's home, Robin "flourish[es] his cudgel, and then thrust[s] its larger end close to the man's muffled face" (10). The red/black man refuses to be intimidated, however, and returns hostility for hostility.

Whereas Aeneas undergoes several harrowing experiences but eventually does reach Elysium, the underworld abode of heroes and the good, as well as the site of his revelation regarding Rome's future glory and grandeur, poor Robin endures many unpleasant experiences but never finds his Elysium. Aeneas meets Dido, his former lover during his days in Carthage. Christian commentators of the Renaissance predictably viewed the Queen of Carthage as a whore who temporarily detains Aeneas on his journey to found Rome. Recent commentary, however, is more sympathetic, pointing out that, when Aeneas confronts her in the underworld, she turns and walks away, having said nothing. Aeneas is left to blame himself for her plight. Emphasizing the details of this scene, as rendered by Vergil, discloses that Aeneas is *not* perfect and therefore is the more vulnerable and, of course, the more human. Robin also encounters a whore, and appearances are later confirmed. Turning down a street whose houses are not so well built as those on the previous avenue, Robin discerns, just inside an open door, "a strip of scarlet petticoat" (8). The owner of this "scarlet petticoat" (a detail that Hawthorne repeats five times, as he did with the cudgel), Robin soon learns, is also the possessor of "bright eyes" whose "sly freedom . . . triumphed over those [eyes] of Robin." Before the end of the tale, he recalls her "seductive tones" (14). Robin encounters this "lady of the scarlet petticoat" once more (16), when she passes by the youth, having joined in the fracas stimulated by Major Molineaux's tarred and feathered body.

The noise created by this grotesque celebration at the expense of the unfortunate Molineaux resembles the terrible groans and sounds of lashes Aeneas hears coming from the forbidden region known as Tartarus, realm of those being punished for crimes above ground. The narrator of "My Kinsman" describes this noise as "the antipodes of music" which "came onwards with increasing din" (15). When Aeneas first hears these sounds of chaos, he "Constitit . . . strepitumque exteritus hausit" (l. 559; stands fast and, terrified, he drinks in the din). When Aeneas inquires of the Sibyl what were the crimes of the tortured souls who emit this horrible noise, she tells him that she has never crossed into Tartarus and can convey to him only what Hecate, goddess of magic and witches, has told her, because "nulti fas casto sceleratum insistere" (l. 563; no one with a pure divine will [can] stand on the unholy threshold). In a move indicating a further perversion of the Aeneas myth, Robin nevertheless finds the approaching unholy din appealing: "'Surely some prodigious merry-making is going on,' exclaimed he. 'I have laughed very little since I left home . . . and should be sorry to lose an opportunity. Shall we step round the corner by that darkish house, and take our share of the fun?'" (41). Unlike the Sibyl and Aeneas, who both possess souls or hearts purified by divine will, Robin, with his impure soul, ventures into Tartarus.

Earlier in the confrontation with "the lady of the scarlet petticoat," the "shrewd youth" (a phrase repeated so often and in varying constructions as to warrant further investigation), Robin steps "nearly to the threshold" (9) of the young prostitute's domicile, but he does not cross it. Perhaps like another of Hawthorne's protagonists, Young Goodman Brown, who eventually does yield to "crossing the threshold" (65), Robin's "Faith kept [him] back a while" (66). After his first meeting with the prostitute and before he finds the din of the "frenzied merriment" (17) so attractive, Robin peers into a church, an experience which unexpectedly "made Robin's heart shiver with a sensation of loneliness stronger than he had ever felt in the remotest depths of his native woods" (12). Robin, like Young Goodman Brown, appears to be losing his faith. Thus he becomes eligible to cross over into Hades's Tartarus, the region of lost souls.

While Aeneas goes on to receive the blessed vision of empire, Robin lacks any such positive vision. His "companion" at the end of the tale refuses, when asked, to show Robin "the way to the ferry," symbolically suggesting that it is impossible for him to go back home. Unlike Aeneas, who can and does return to the upper world, Robin, unable to make the return journey because he is no longer pure of spirit, remains in the hellish metropolis. The ostensibly kind friend offers the young man this alternative: "As you are a shrewd youth, you may rise in the world without the help of your kinsman, Major Molineaux" (17). Here the tale concludes. Robin certainly does not refuse at least to try to succeed without his kinsman. Robin then appears to symbolize the new beginning in the American colonies—that is, the colonial struggle to throw off British restraints and interference and assert the distinctly American right to exercise free choice and self-reliance.

Given this line of reasoning, Major Molineaux should symbolize the rejected, detested British dominion. But does the old, defeated man actually symbolize Britain—a rejected, immoral, decadent, despotic overlord? Or is Robin in fact a perverse Aeneas?

Before we can answer these queries satisfactorily, we must deal with this repeated epithet, "shrewd youth." Interlaced with numerous uses of *shrewd* and its variants is a series of expressions calling attention to Robin's need for a guide. The pattern moves in a rather deliberate manner. Within two and a half pages, *shrewd* (5) is succeeded three times by the term *guide* ("guide," 5; "guided," 5; "guide," 7), undermining Robin's assertion of his shrewdness; real sagacity does not so urgently need guidance. The second use of *shrewd*, as "shrewdness" (7), is followed forty lines later by a fourth expression, "the necessary guidance" (8); this aid, of course, is denied Robin. The third appearance of *shrewd* (8), occurring only fifteen lines after "the necessary guidance," is followed a page later by the fifth use of *guide* (9). The fourth *shrewd* (10) comes only nine lines below the fifth use of *guide*, while the fifth *shrewd*, as "shrewdly" (11) appears a page later. *Guide* (13) occurs a sixth time, two pages later, when the supposedly "kind" man encounters Robin outside the church edifice, saying, "'Can I be of service to you in any way?'" (13) Finally Robin obtains the guidance he thinks he needs, only to be followed twenty lines later by the sixth *shrewd* (13). A seventh *shrewd* comes a page later, and the next and seventh *guide*, evident in Robin's request that the "kind" man "show me the way to the ferry" (17), occurs very near the story's end. Just eleven lines later, and in the tale's concluding declarative, the eighth and final *shrewd* appears.

The contiguity of *shrewd* and its variants, to *guide* and its variants sets up an interactive pattern which effectively turns the narration of Vergil's heroic Aeneas and his guides (the Sybil and Anchises) inside out. Whereas Aeneas is appropriately humbled by his search for enlightenment in the darkness of the underworld, always relying on guides equal to the task, Robin proudly proclaims that he is intellectually competent, although he constantly claims to be almost desperately in need of a guide or guides to direct him to his Kinsman, the Major, who presumably will serve as his ultimate guide to success in an urban setting.

David Leverenz, who also thinks Robin is much less than pure, judiciously calls attention to the *Oxford English Dictionary*'s many definitions of the attributive *shrewd*, particularly the first definition of the word as *evil* or *wicked* (*Manhood* 235–36).[7] This critic, however, fails to connect *shrewd* and *guide*. James McIntosh, a recent editor of this and other Hawthorne tales, glosses the first appearance of the word *shrewd* with this note: "In Shakespeare's *Midsummer Night's Dream*, 2.1, Puck is identified as 'that shrewd and knavish sprite/ Call'd Robin Goodfellow'" (5n. 7). Shakespeare's comedy likely influenced Hawthorne's construction of Robin. But do this gloss and Leverenz's *Oxford English Dictionary* definition lead to Leverenz's conclusion that Robin is actually, and insidiously, one of a group of "upwardly mobile young men [who] are really devils in training" (*Manhood* 233)? While Robin later may earn the identity of a knave, is it not simply too early to judge him so at this first appearance of the word? At this juncture one goes too far to claim that Robin is evil, because Robin is just now acquiring his reputation and he has not yet rejected the Major.

At the first use of *shrewd*, the reader sees Robin as the brunt of some joke whose humor depends upon knowledge to which Robin has not been made privy. Thus Robin, or rather his predicament, elicits a measure of sympathy. As the action of the tale unfolds, Robin himself actually becomes comic, as his alleged—one may almost say protested—"shrewdness" continues to serve him ill. Quite soon the reader expects the appearance of this word *shrewd* and its variants to pronounce Robin *not* shrewd. When the woman of the "scarlet petticoat" accosts him the first time, for example, Robin affably calls her "pretty mistress," since he knows "nothing to the contrary" (8). Nor is he aware of the irony implicit in the epithet *mistress*. Robin's behavior earlier in the story consistently bespeaks innocence more than depravity, even as the conduct of all about him signals duplicity and concealment. Indeed, Robin "was a good youth . . . so he resisted [the] temptation" (10) prompted by the woman of the "scarlet petticoat."

Later in the tale, just after he has met the "kind" man, Robin tells him that he has "the name of being a shrewd youth" (13). By this time, Robin has encountered a number of the town's citizens and is indeed in the process of acquiring a reputation, one that reflects his not being in on the calamitous joke—that his kinsman has fallen into disrepute (an ironic play on *reputation*). Perhaps because of Robin's youth and lack of experience and knowledge, the townspeople judge him to be corruptible—susceptible to temptation. Certainly, at the moment when Robin refused to rise to the defense of the Major, one may say that Robin has succumbed to temptation and has joined the "fiends [townspeople] that throng in mockery." In other words, when, in the tale's last two lines, the so-called "kind" man pronounces Robin "a shrewd youth," we are justified in thinking that Robin has become a knave.

As the tale evolves, Robin has gained a reputation (for susceptibility) and frequently become the object of derisive laughter. He also has a penchant for seeking "amusement" in the midst of a serious situation. Outside the church, for example, Robin looks "elsewhere for amusement" (11); he believes the sounds of "wild and confused laughter" to be "some prodigious merrymaking" (14). Given these three traits, one becomes inclined to view Robin as a character in some grotesque comedy, though perhaps not the comedy McIntosh suggests. Closer to the spirit of Hawthorne's "shrill voices of mirth or terror" (15) is the comment in *The Merry Wives of Windsor* about Mistress Ford: "She enlargeth her mirth so farre that there is shrewd [malicious] construction made of her" (II.ii.222–24). For Robin's reputation, doubtless known to the "kind" man, surely is the result of a malicious construction. When Robin yields to the temptation offered by the townspeople's "convulsive merriment" (17) and joins the din, he confirms his susceptibility to being drawn into a grotesque comedy, so that his reputation now in fact describes a malicious knave (and *The Merry Wives* has its Robin, too.)

In stark, perverse contrast to Robin's failure to find the correct guides and his subsequent plunge into evil, in effect discovering only more darkness in darkness, Vergil's Aeneas makes the correct choices with the help of sanctioned assistance and does receive enlightenment. Unlike Aeneas, who by the time he receives his beatific vision has learned proper devotion to gods, family, and country, Robin finds no solace, but only fear, in peering into the church (God), rejects his kinsman (family) and rebels against his country when he joins in the rebel revelry. Rather than being transformed into the heroic founder of an empire, Robin "converts" to a position absolutely antithetical to Vergil's pietas.

So where do we look for heroic behavior in "My Kinsman, Major Molineaux"? Indeed, does the tale have a hero? Or has Hawthorne created in Robin what may be one of the West's first antiheroes? For a character resembling the heroic, we must turn to the Major. Describing the elaborate assembly gathered to escort the "dethroned" Molineaux from the town, Hawthorne writes, "On they went, in counterfeited pomp, in senseless uproar, in frenzied merriment, trampling all on an old man's heart" (17). This picture of colonists strutting along, manifesting false pomp "in senseless uproar"—that is, without sense, reason, or logic—all at the expense of "an old man's heart," is grotesque rather than expressive of joyous, righteous jubilation. Something is amiss in this picture. It is possible to see this hideous surrealism as merely a projection of Robin's imagination—part of his visionary, dreamlike initiation into adulthood, with its repugnant vicissitudes. Such an interpretation, however, omits the unforgettable image, "trampling all on an old man's heart."

The conflict between heart and head is a frequent one in Hawthorne (and in Melville). Whenever head begins to assume ascendancy over heart in Hawthorne (e.g., in "Ethan Brand"), disaster is imminent. Ordinarily the Adamic myth, usually residing in the heart, promises ultimate verticality or heavenly reward for all believers, whereas the myth of Aeneas, usually residing in the head, promises secular horizontality, or collective control over the world here and now, as manifested in empire. Yet Hawthorne, or at least the narrator of this tale, makes the representations of the Adamic myth look foolish, in Robin's case, and grotesque or even monstrous in the case of the colonists. Molineaux, however, is described by the narrator as having "a steady soul." Even so, "steady as it was, his enemies had found means to shake it." Note that the old man does not lose that soul, despite having experienced "the foul disgrace of a head grown gray in honor" (16). Robin's kinsman has become the victim of perverse practitioners of the Adamic myth.

"My Kinsman," then, may be read as a perverse variation on the theme of head and heart, one in which the narrator comes down on the side of Molineaux, symbol of the Aeneas myth but given a heart. Robin fails to budge in defense of his kinsman, instead clinging to a stone post while the unholy pageantry streams past him (17). He and the colonists together may be seen as symbols of the Adamic mode perverted; at the tale's conclusion, they remain bereft of hearts and totally focused on rebellion.

In "My Kinsman, Major Molineaux," the tension between the myths of Adam and Aeneas manifests itself in an elaborate perversion of both these modes of discourse. Robin perverts the pious example of Aeneas; he and the colonists also pervert the Adamic mode. Clearly Robin is neither Aeneas nor Adam. Rather, it is Molineaux who emerges with the positive qualities of both Aeneas and Adam. Hawthorne demonstrates in this tale that he can respond aesthetically to two modes of discourse, the Adamic and the Vergilian or classical, at one and the same moment.

The dialectic of Adam and Aeneas is not the only dialectic which obtains in this tale. There is at least one other, signaled by Robin's "companion," the "kind" man with whom he strikes up an acquaintance near the tale's conclusion. Even a cautious reader may be seduced by the affability of this "companion," until he declares, "May not a man have several voices, Robin, as well as two complexions?" (14). The problem posed here for the naive young man is to distinguish between the way things appear and the way they are—i.e., between dissembling and reality. As many have held,[8] the difference between illusion (or outright delusion) and reality is central to this tale—or so it would seem.

The fact that the Adam-Aeneas dialectic embraces the entire world of "My Kinsman" invites a radically new reading of this tale. This new reading derives from the interplay that inevitably occurs between these two interconnecting modes of the dialectic, resulting in a third mode of discourse. This new mode one is tempted to call "Hawthornesque," were it not for the fact that it also appears in Melville, particularly, and to lesser degrees in Emerson, Thoreau, and Whitman, among others. It may more simply be called a "re-vision" of the Aeneas-Adam dialectic. And it functions in "My Kinsman," as elsewhere, on different levels of awareness. Hawthorne's characters, for example, are unaware that their world is encompassed by the Adam-Aeneas dialectic, though the townspeople are fully aware that they are hiding the truth from Robin as to the whereabouts of his kinsman. All characters, with the significant exception of Molineaux, appear to be motivated by conformity, thirst for power, and greed.

Robin ventures to the unknown world of the city because he is told that his older brother is to inherit the farm (through primogeniture). The townsfolk appear to be prompted to action by more than simple anti-British politics. It is a lamentable commonplace that, in the real world, greed and self-aggrandizement often abuse politics. For example, the house with the Gothic window is the finest mansion in the town; Robin (probably accurately) judges that it once belonged to his kinsman. By the tale's conclusion, this house is occupied by an old gentleman with a tapping cane (a play on the biblical Cain; the new occupant of the house has betrayed his "brother" Molineaux out of jealousy). As the red/black man appears "like war personified," it is plausible to think of him as some sort of military general, connected to the new occupant of the mansion. In their jealous bid for power and wealth, the red/black man and the old gentleman now residing in the mansion with the Gothic window exploit the "temporary inflammation of the popular mind" (3), capitalizing upon the conformity of the masses, who readily join in the revelry "like fiends that throng in mockery around some dead potentate" (17).

Recall that, in the first paragraph of the tale, the narrator remarks, "The people looked with most jealous scrutiny to the exercise of power which did not emanate from themselves" (3). Robin loses his ties with a sustaining spirituality, stoops to cowardly conformity when he refuses to rise to the aid of his kinsman, and apparently capitulates to the "carrot" of rising "in the world without the help" of his kinsman. He becomes, in short, merely another soldier in the crowd—a blind conformist to be used or controlled (recall his temptation by the prostitute) by those more subtle and more ambitious than he. When one remembers the narrator's observation in the first paragraph, however, that "The inferior members of the court party, in times of high political excitement, led scarcely a more desirable life" (3), one can hold little enthusiastic hope that even Robin's temporal fortunes will wax propitious.

Outside the bounded awareness of this tale's characters, Hawthorne's narrator looms large, casting the entire tale in carefully chosen words and images which utilize in a most dynamic way the myths of Adam and Aeneas to comment on his characters' actions. Robin crosses the Styx, for example, *not* into a classical Hades wherein dead shades may find reward as well as punishment, but into a Dantesque/Miltonic Inferno peopled by grotesque, hostile ghouls, all of whom exist in a state of rebellion against an apparently benevolent master. Given this reading, the red/black man becomes a kind of Lucifer, leading his host of fallen angels in a full-scale revolt against their master Molineaux, a surrogate deity. If Robin converts to their cause, as the tale leads its readers to think probable, then the proponents of the Adamic myth perverted have won another convert to their rebellion. Robin will have traded the possibility of true enlightenment for the appearance of convivial, fulfilling fellowship with those in a state of rebellion—this fellowship actually promising for him inexorable moral degradation and spiritual blindness. Molineaux, would-be benefactor rendered powerless, takes with him, out of the colony, the last vestige of a heart. Herein lies the horror of Hawthorne's tale; for, in contrast with Milton's *Paradise Lost*, in which rebellion proves unsuccessful, in Hawthorne's tale the rebellion is all too successful. In "My Kinsman," the Adamic crown of morality has been traded for that of cruel, evil rebellion—Hawthorne's unpardonable sin.

It is worth the remarking that, in this new reading, the rebels of Hawthorne's story—Robin and all the townsfolk save Molineaux—represent an inversion of "the distinction between secular and sacred revolution" made by Sacvan Bercovitch in *American Jeremiad* (133). Unexpectedly, this body of colonists does not enact "The Revolution fulfilled [as] the divine will" but rather rebellion as "a primal act of disobedience, as Lucifer's was." The Tory Molineaux, also unexpectedly, becomes symbolic of the "Revolutionaries [who] were agents of the predetermined course of progress" (134).

The old man, Major Molineaux, then, symbolizes Aeneas and is the one who also has a heart. This fact constitutes a strong, positive reassertion of Aeneas's famous piety. Robin, in rejecting Molineaux, rejects his family; and, in embracing unholy revelry at the expense of his kinsman, rejects religion as well. Molineaux/Aeneas, however, remains true to these two elements of pietas, family and religion. As well, the old man's loyalty to Britain, to *patria*, remains constant; it is for this loyalty that he suffers tarring and feathering and the loss of his colonial fortune. Robin is unwilling to endure any such risk. The old man, in his actions, then, embodies all three elements of pietas. Robin, however, in moving against his kinsman, joins the rebellion which dramatizes Hawthorne's unpardonable sin. The youth, by surrendering his allegiance to a renegade regime whose motives for revolt are, according to the text of this tale, power, greed, and comfortable conformity—and *not* the noble, virtuous motives of securing the blessings of life, liberty, and property—perverts not one or two, but all three, elements of pietas.

The narrator's emphasis on "steady soul," on his "majestic . . . agony," and, above all, on the "old man's heart" bespeaks a Christ-like figure, a significant component of the Adamic myth. In stark contrast with Robin, who trades the enobling Aristotelian emotions of "pity and terror" (the catharsis of the *Poetics*) for the "bewildering excitement" (16) of the crowd's unholy merriment (enacting still another perversion of classical discourse), Molineaux achieves stature as symbol of the best of both the Adamic and the classical modes. When so perceived, Molineaux's "foul disgrace" and "overwhelming humiliation" (16) transform into a syncretized Adam-Aeneas.

Recognizing the Aeneas and Adam dialectic as fully operational within "My Kinsman, Major Molineaux" has an enabling and intensifying effect upon the possibilities for meaning this text may yield. This tale may be read profitably as Hawthorne's severe critique of that aspect of colonial rebellion which, when it sacrifices family, religion, and country for power, greed and feeble conformity, perverts the best of human values, and indeed perverts the entire American quest for economic, religious, and political freedom. It is Molineaux, an Adam-Aeneas figure, who emerges as a salubrious moral symbol in this tale. Accordingly, the notion that Hawthorne harbored an anticlassical mental attitude pales all the further into incredibility. The Aeneas myth obviously enriches this tale, confirming that the classical mode of discourse is alive and well in Hawthorne's thought. ▩

9

The Persistence of the American Aeneas in Melville

The hegemony of the Adamic myth has exerted a blinding effect as well on readings of Herman Melville's *Billy Budd, Sailor (An Inside Narrative)*. Perceived by many to be one of Melville's most enigmatic texts, the majority of those writing about *Billy Budd*, from F. O. Matthiessen and Lawrence Thompson to James E. Miller Jr. and William B. Dillingham, approach a reading of this short novel either as Melville's final affirmation of commitment to some sort of modified Adamic Christianity or, quite the contrary, as a restive perhaps even vituperative attack upon this religious mode.[1] Yet none of these critics gives anything but passing acknowledgment to the extensive classicism this work evidences. Most Melville scholars have held, for that matter, that Melville's use of classicism in the body of his work reflects little more than a conscious attempt to ornament his poems and prose. Gail H. Coffler, the scholar who has done more with Melville's classicism than any other, insists, however, that "exegesis of [*Billy Budd*] depends, to a great extent, upon interpretation of an intricate pattern of classical allusions" (ix).[2]

Given the emphasis placed in this book upon authors' educational backgrounds, one must ask what is known about Melville's formal education, especially his classical training. According to William H. Gilman, Melville spent four or more years in elementary schooling in New York City. Upon his family's relocation in Albany, he entered the Albany Academy, where he "studied no Latin during his first year." In the second year, Gilman continues, "he probably got through only the elementary [Latin] grammar and reader." Throughout his discussion, Gilman repeatedly cites efforts by local academies to provide their young scholars with opportunities to acquire a practical education, at the expense of the older classical curriculum (51–72).

After the death of Melville's father, still feeling "the need of education, however, and about the time he went in [business] with Gansevoort [his older brother] he entered the Albany Classical School" (71). Gilman further observes that, of course, this academy included courses in classical studies and English; as well, he points out that Melville's interests seem to have shifted away from a merchantile course (the young Herman had earlier even won an award for ciphering) toward a more literary one. According to a letter from his schoolmaster of this time, he distinguished himself at the Albany Classical School "in the writing of 'themes' or 'compositions,' and fond of doing it, while the great majority of pupils dreaded it as a task, and would shirk it if they could" (72). Curiously missing from this schoolmaster's letter is the word *English* to identify these writings; perhaps these compositions were written in Latin, as was always the practice during study of Latin before the twentieth century. Hershel Parker, one of Melville's most recent biographers, notes that, on September 1, 1836, "Herman was readmitted to the Albany Academy after five years' absence, and enrolled in the Latin course" (107). After yet another family financial reversal, however, Herman was forced to withdraw from the Albany Academy by March first of the following year.

If the young Melville acquired at least two more years of Latin studies at the Albany Classical Academy, we may safely conclude that he had some four years of Latin studies under his belt when he began his brief tenure at Lansingburgh Academy[3] in the winter of 1838 and spring of 1839. Although his avowed purpose in attending this academy was to acquire the practical skills of engineering and surveying, Herman could have taken still more Latin; during this period he was only a year or so away from his first venture into serious writing (resulting in "Fragments from a Writing Desk"). This budding writer, attending an academy which "boasted an extensive library" (Robertson-Lorant 67), just may have wanted to hone his classical expertise. In any event, the acquisition of four or more years of Latin would have left an indelible mark on any evolving young writer. Moreover, Herman considered himself "scholar" enough that, when a position in surveying and engineering failed to materialize, he did not hesitate to assume the vocation of schoolmaster on two separate occasions. According to Gilman's descriptions of these schools,[4] it is doubtful that either school would have required its master to give instruction in Latin. Still, a credential demonstrating some expertise in classical studies would have helped Melville secure these positions.

Let us now turn from speculation about Melville's early classical training, thorough as it must have been, to the facts about his reading from the time of the composition of *Typee* (late 1845–46) through the remainder of his long career. Dryden's translation of Vergil's complete opus was highly popular and widely available during and before this time. By at least March 1849, Melville owned Dryden's translation of the *Aeneid;* at this time he purchased the thirty-seven volumes of Harper's Family Classical Library.[5] In addition, Merrell R. Davis in *Melville's Mardi* establishes that Melville consulted Charles Anthon's compendious *A Classical Dictionary* (also a source for Hawthorne's *Wonder-Book* and *Tanglewood Tales*) for "the names Mardi and Media to designate the islands of a fictitious archipelago and their ruler" (77). Actually, Melville consulted Anthon more extensively than Davis indicates.[6]

To be sure, a writer of Melville's acumen would easily have been able to locate any classical source he wished to see and use. It is from the texts written by Melville, however, that one may adduce most clearly this author's use of the discourse of the American Aeneas. Like Edward Taylor, Cotton Mather, and Nathaniel Hawthorne, Melville, too, can, in the words of David Simpson, "respond to more than one discourse at a time" ("Return to 'History'" 733). The discussion below will demonstrate that, in *Billy Budd,* the heretofore unacknowledged American Aeneas persists in dialectical tension with the generally acknowledged American Adam. In the dialectic between Adam and Aeneas lies a great portion of the artistry of this superb short novel. That dialectic also contains Melville's crystallized idea of what it means to be American—or, more precisely, the promise that being American holds.

Melville suggests the discourse of the American Aeneas in the very first paragraph of *Billy Budd,* even before he introduces the Adamic discourse. While practically everyone writing about *Billy Budd* has noted the phrase "like Aldebaran among the lesser lights of his constellation" (43), none has pointed out the association of this simile with the hero of Vergil's epic, Aeneas. In "Comet, Stars, and Cynosure: *Billy Budd* in a Symbolist Context," for example, Reinhard H. Friederich points out the significance of Budd's unmistakable association with the principal star of the constellation Taurus (the Bull). Even before the reader actually sees Budd, he has been characterized as an "Aldebaran-like prototype." This association enables Budd to carry throughout the novel the lustre of "a brilliant star which gives off radiance to others" (264). In addition to Friederich's citation of the obvious connection to Taurus the Bull, which the present treatment will not ignore, this second sign of the zodiac is subject to the rule of Venus. This goddess, of course, is Aeneas's mother, which suggests a tenuous connection between Melville's Budd and Vergil's hero.

As early as *Mardi* (1849), Melville cites Aeneas, himself an ancient sailor and navigator, in intimate association with Taurus. As Taji and his compatriots bid adieu to Dominora (England; Melville's earlier name for the *Bellipotent* had been *Indomitable*), they catch sight of King Bello (the parallel to *Bellipotent* is obvious) sallying forth on a finely appointed vessel. Subsequently, *Mardi*'s narrator draws this arresting parallel: "And when Aeneas wandered West, and discovered the pleasant land of Latium, it was in the fine craft *Bis Taurus* that he sailed" (481). As Vergil does not name Aeneas's ship(s) in the *Aeneid*, "Bis Taurus" may well be Melville's own invention. But why should Melville wish to give the hero's ship such a name, unless he were thoroughly familiar with astronomy and astrology? And what sailor of Melville's intellect would not carry with him a sophisticated knowledge of the heavens? *Mardi* proffers a further clue to the title *Bis Taurus*. Several pages before the Aeneas/Taurus reference, we find this exclamatory apostrophe: "Here's to thee . . . , old Aldebaran! who ever poise your wine-red, fiery spheres on high!" (431). The plural *spheres* indicates that Melville is aware that Aldebaran is a binary star,[7] hence the Latin attributive *bis* (which, in combination with another word, means *double*) for Taurus. One can readily see that Aldebaran, Taurus, and Aeneas all are juxtaposed, appropriately, in *Mardi*. Given the plethora of scholarly identifications of Mardian echoes in *Billy Budd*, it is plausible to suppose that Melville retained these associations when he penned the phrase "like Aldebaran among the lesser lights of his constellation."

A single association between Budd and Aeneas is, nevertheless, insufficient to interpret the "welkin-eyed" sailor as an Aeneas figure. A second, unmistakable association of Budd to Aeneas occurs not far from the first, in the third paragraph of chapter 2.[8] Here, concerning Budd's uncertain origins, Melville speculates that there was "*above all*, something in the mobile expression, and every chance attitude and movement, something suggestive of a mother eminently favored by Love and the Graces" (51; [emphasis added]). Love is, of course, Venus,[9] ruler of the sign Taurus and goddess of beauty—hence the many identifications of Budd as "beauty" and Apollo (another deity associated with beauty in art). Venus, as just noted, is the mother of Aeneas. Not once but twice, then, Melville draws pointed associations between Budd and Vergil's hero, identifying Budd as an Aeneas figure. Actually these two, Budd and Aeneas, may be viewed as brothers. Melville introduces for Budd several other classical parallels—to a "young Alexander" (44); to a "heroic strong man, Hercules," created by a "Greek sculptor" (51); and to a "young Achilles," a student of the old Dansker's Chiron (71). These parallels merely reinforce Budd's classical origins—except for one crucial factor.

Each of these associations emphasizes youthfulness. Melville compares Budd to an adolescent Alexander in the process of "curbing the fiery Bucephalus"—an act, take note, not yet completed. (Recall that Bucephalus was aptly named bull-headed.) According to Melville, the demigod Hercules is portrayed by the sculptor with "that humane look of reposeful good nature" on his face; he is no fierce, invincible latter-day Titan.[10] This image extends Melville's earlier depiction of Budd as cast "in a form" characterized by "strength and beauty" (44). Budd's strength predicts this allusion to Hercules and his beauty the one to Venus. The comparison of Budd and the Dansker to a developing Achilles and an "old sea Chiron," most directly reveals Budd's lack of finish, of mature polish. Chiron was the wisest of the centaurs and was entrusted with the education of Jason, Hercules, and Achilles. These indications of Budd's unfinished form allude to the incomplete form of the novel itself; as Melville puts it toward the novel's conclusion, "Truth uncompromisingly told will always have its ragged edges; hence the conclusion of such a narration is apt to be less finished than an architectural finial" (128). In addition, these classical parallels signal Budd's function as a symbol of honesty, good nature, and truth as yet uninitiated into the realm of the diabolical.

While this discussion takes the Adamic discourse in *Billy Budd* as a *donnée*, it is worthy of note that the Adamic myth appears *after* introduction of the Aeneas myth. Whereas Melville presents the Aldebaran bridge between Budd and Aeneas in the center of the novel's first paragraph, he introduces the Adamic discourse in the first third of his second paragraph, when he portrays a black Budd cynosure who "must needs have been a native African of the unadulterated blood of Ham" (43). Much later in the novel, Melville describes Budd upon the eve of his execution as "in all respects stand[ing] nearer to unadulterate Nature" (120). As Ham was a son of Noah and hence was born long after the Fall of Adam and Eve, Ham's descendants can hardly have been "unadulterate" in the strict sense; yet Melville here, as in most of his long works, incorporates as many "Representatives of the Human Race" (43) as possible. Billy Budd is to be understood, then, as symbolizing the "unadulterate" nature of humanity, regardless of race. As symbol of both Adam and Aeneas, however, he partakes of the potential good "nature" of both the Adamic and the classical modes of discourse.

This "good nature" is perhaps too good (or too unfinished) for the sort of world into which Melville, its creator, casts it. From the outset, Budd appears destined for sacrifice. Before the novel's second paragraph concludes, Melville names a second bull, following Aldebaran's association with the constellation of Taurus. Probably recalling an actual statue of a Mesopotamian bull seen during his tour of the Levant in January 1857, he writes that "the Assyrian priests doubtless showed [pride] for their grand sculptured Bull when the faithful prostrated themselves" (44). This "grand sculptured Bull" is but an artist's representation of the bull of ancient sacrifice. His ritual was celebrated to insure continued fertility, both of the land, which produces crops and sustains the farm animals, and of human beings, who survive on the "fruits" of the land. Joseph Campbell describes the significance of this ritual: "Through his death, which is no death, he is giving life to the creatures of the earth" (57).

While this depiction of the bull's sacrificial function is indeed pregnant with associations to Budd's "apparent" apotheosis at the novel's conclusion, it also suggests another connection to Venus as ruler of the bull's sign of the zodiac and as mother of Aeneas (perhaps of Budd as well). She serves, then, as universal genetrix. Campbell goes so far as to suggest that Venus-Aphrodite (a later manifestation of Gaea, Mother Earth) may be identified as a Mother-of-God figure, in both classical and Christian traditions (42–43). Seen from this perspective, the two modes of discourse, those of Adam and Aeneas, may be observed to merge, making Budd an even more powerful, primal avatar—an Aeneas/Adam. This reading is reinforced when one acknowledges the long Old Testament tradition of bull sacrifice as a means of expiating sins.[11]

The most striking image which suggests Budd and the Bull are interconnected, however, follows that of young Alexander (another classical cynosure figure) taming his bull-headed steed Becephalus and appears as an exclamatory summary utterance of the Aldebaran cynosures: "A superb figure, tossed up as by the horns of Taurus against the thunderous sky, cheerily hallooing to the strenuous file along the spar" (44). This image not only evokes the primeval bull-in-the-ring ritual, present from the dawn of Western civilization; it also points directly to the novel's conclusion. The ritual slaying of the bull in the ring, according to Campbell, symbolizes "the plane of juncture of earth and heaven, the goddess and the god, who appear to be two but are in being one." The ritual itself, then, may be seen as "a reconstruction of the primal undifferentiated state" wherein the female earth (Gaea, or Venus genetrix as a later manifestation) and the male heaven (Zeus, thunderous king of the gods and the heavens) are not yet become separated—this condition resembling, says Campbell, Adam and Eve before they are cast out of Paradise (57). This "undifferentiated state" is richly suggestive of the androgyny many have seen in Budd's infrequently described feminine attributes.

The fact that Melville portrays Budd's "superb figure" as "cheerily hallooing to the strenuous file along the spar" just after enduring a surely lethal toss upon the bull's horns, moreover, predicts Budd's generous, almost cheerfully melodic outburst, "'God bless Captain Vere!'" immediately before his (Budd's) execution. In addition, this fecund image appears to focus not upon the brilliance of the Taurean constellation, but rather upon those gathered in "strenuous file along the spar"—that is, upon the sailors as "Representatives of the Human Race." After all, Melville's target in this novel seems to be "an average man of the world [whose] constant rubbing with it blunts that finer spiritual insight indispensable to the understanding of the essential in certain exceptional characters, whether evil ones or good" (75). These primeval, Taurean images suggest a moment in the evolution of civilization when Adam had not yet become self-consciously "the Adamic" nor Aeneas "the classical." These images, then, call up within the human breast "what remains primeval in our formalized humanity" (115).

The bull is not the only animal association by which Melville characterizes Budd; he also compares him to a goldfinch (45), to "animals" in general (49), to a loyal, steadfast St. Bernard (52), to "a dog of generous breed" (107), and finally to "a singing bird" (123). The references to "animals," and to dogs specifically, make Budd's "novice magnanimity" more credible (85). This magnanimity helps the young man avoid fear as he approaches his execution and enables him to utter the unexpected "God bless Captain Vere!" (123). It is this same magnanimity of spirit which "providentially covers all at last," Lethe-like, with "holy oblivion" (115). Captain Vere, then, becomes Budd's Abraham who carries out what he, in his limited vision and limited faith, fully believes he must do; and for Budd, as Vere's Isaac, guiltless victim or sacrifice.

The bird comparisons are even more arresting. Like the sacrificial imagery, they close the circle—balance the structure—of the novel as a whole. The goldfinch itself, within Christian art, is a sort of "saviour-bird" or "symbol of the Passion of Christ."[12] This bird's early association with Budd seems to suggest another connection to the Adamic myth. As such, it is a more complex comparison, for Melville uses it to illustrate Budd's entrapment by his fate. Indeed, objecting to his impressment by Lieutenant Ratcliffe of the *Bellipotent* "would have been as idle as the protest of a goldfinch popped into a cage" (45).

Having placed this bird in a distinctly Christian context, Budd as a goldfinch figure is most obviously interpreted, perhaps, as Christ entrapped in his "blessed theanthropy." The god-man's human side resists its fate (e.g., in Gethsemane), which is sacrifice on the cross. Yet Budd never at any moment resists his fate. Rather, "like the animals . . . he was, without knowing it, practically a fatalist" (49). Such a characterization, in which Budd appears wholly resigned to his lot in life, whatever that may prove to be, comes closer to the Greek idea of *moira*, one's portion in life. This idea of destiny is linked to the epic heroes of Homer and for them functions as a source of consolation, rather than as a road to enlightenment. In this sense, one scholar observes, "one's share is above all else death; as such *moira* may be either a fact of nature, a special destiny, an outcome of divine anger [e.g., Artemis delays Agamemnon's ships at Aulis] or of divine decree" ("Fate" in *The Oxford Classical Dictionary*).[13] For Budd, *moira* is a fact of nature; that is, he will surely suffer death, not because of divine wrath or decree but because his radically good nature condemns him to serve as an unresisting sacrifice for a world which may not deserve his sacrifice.

Worthiness of sacrifice, however, is not the issue here. The consequence of his sacrifice and the potential that others may put on elements of his radically good nature govern the effects of the death of this novel's central figure; for Budd's final benediction is "delivered in the clear melody of a singing bird on the point of launching from the twig" (123). Melville's own commitment to the pursuit of Truth prevents him, in his imperfect, human state, from finding It; Budd is poised as if *about* to embrace discovery. Yet the reader at this very point makes her or his own crucial discovery: Budd's spirit (recall the goldfinch) is about to be freed from its cage. While the Greek idea of *moira* does not address the idea of death's result in such exalted terms (dead souls persist as shades, mere shadows of the substantive life on earth), certainly the Christian myth does. Neither here nor elsewhere in his opus does Melville project an Augustinian City of God, but he does hint that death brings happy release from life's vicissitudes. In the fine "Epilogue" of *Clarel*, for example, Melville writes that, if one remains true to the elemental dictates of the heart, "Emerge thou mayst from the last whelming sea,/ And prove that death but routs life into victory" (523). Emphasis ought be placed here on Melville's use of the conditional "mayst"; ever true to himself and his art, Melville, sounding a distinctly modern note, again refuses to capitulate to dogma. In any event, here we see elements from both discourses, Adamic and classical, merge.

Why is it that elemental good must be sacrificed? Why indeed if not as an inexorable consequence of encounter with elemental evil? This elemental evil Melville ascribes to violet-eyed Claggart. Perhaps because, along with Vere, Claggart joins Budd as one of this novel's exceptional natures, Claggart parallels Budd in several ways. As Budd is compared to a Greek sculpture of Hercules (and later to "a statue of young Adam before the Fall"; 94), Claggart possesses "features all except the chin cleanly cut as those on a Greek medallion" (64). As a finely wrought representation, he, not unlike Budd, may be seen as an idealization of what he represents—"a depravity according to nature" (75). That his pallor is "tinged with a faint shade of amber akin to the hue of timetinted marbles of old" suggests yet another comparison to Greek sculpture; within the context of *moira*, as described above, this persistent comparison identifies him, like Budd, as fated by his nature to enact his portion.

Also like Budd, "nothing was known of his former life" (64–65). The temper of the speculation concerning Claggart's origins, however, is vastly different from that which characterizes Budd's. Whereas Budd's origins are spoken of in terms of nobility, Claggart's are shrouded in mystery intimating infamy. Claggart is talked of as possibly a swindler or a debtor. Budd, however, is compared to Greek and Roman epic heroes; indeed, "noble descent was as evident in him as in a blood horse" (52). This comparison to a thoroughbred emphasizes that he is close to the earth. Budd's elemental closeness to the Earth-Mother aligns him with the sort of figure Mircea Eliade calls a *terrae filius* (son of the earth). Think of Oedipus, Romulus and Remus, even Moses. Though abandoned, a *terrae filius* is "protected by nature" and perhaps becomes "a hero, king or saint" (249). "The appearance of such a ['primeval'] child," Eliade continues, "coincides with a moment in the dawn of things: the creation of the cosmos, the creation of a new world, of a new epoch of history." When such orphaned children are protected and saved from death, Eliade maintains, "the Earth-Mother (or the Water-Mother) is dedicating it to a tremendous destiny which a common mortal could never attain" (250). Those who hold that, as Melville drafted and redrafted his manuscripts of this novel, his focus shifted from Budd to Claggart to Vere[14] have not grasped the significance of Melville's *terrae filius*.

Claggart is the antithesis of Eliade's son of the earth. This difference is indicated in another paradoxically shared similarity: both Budd and Claggart have musical voices. Whereas Budd's voice is melodic and cheerful, Claggart's is seductive and deceptive. Budd completely misses the ironic undertone of Claggart's "low musical voice" as he chants, "'Handsomely done, my lad! and handsome is as handsome did it, too!'" (72), after Budd spills some soup across the path of the approaching master-at-arms. Both Budd and Claggart are the bearers of an inner light: "Not the less was [Budd's face] lit, like [Claggart's], from within, though from a different source. The bonfire in [Budd's] heart made luminous the rose-tan in his cheek" (77). Claggart's luminosity, somewhat like that of Vere, emanates not from the heart but from the less bright intellect.

All these bases of comparison actually serve as touchstones helping us distinguish how remarkably different are Claggart and Budd. In no way are these two more different than in their traits of elemental evil and elemental good. It is in depicting Claggart's evil nature that classical discourse comes, for a time, to the forefront. While calling Claggart "the direct reverse of a saint!" (74) and maintaining that "Coke and Blackstone [renowned British attorneys] hardly shed so much light into obscure spiritual places as the Hebrew prophets" (75), Melville nonetheless concludes that Claggart's elemental evil may be defined best by consulting a classical source. This definition he takes from Plato: "Natural Depravity: a depravity according to nature." Upon giving this definition, Melville immediately notes that, while it may savor of Calvinism, Plato's definition (or one "attributed to him") "by no means involves Calvin's dogma as to total mankind" (75).

Why, we do well to ask, does Melville move beyond biblical and Judaeo-Christian religious sources? The brief dialogue Melville presents between himself and "an honest scholar" of long ago serves as a sort of preface to the definition from Plato and signals a possible explanation. Within this exchange, the honest scholar declares, "I am the adherent of no organized religion, much less of any philosophy built into a system" (74). Melville claims that it is the unpopularity of "Holy Writ," doubtless a by-product of the skepticism characterizing the *fin de siècle*, which motivates his determination not to "define and denominate" (75) Claggart's elemental nature in biblical terms. This author seldom, if ever, has yielded to popular injunctions in his prior career, so this explanation is neither reliable nor to the point. Claggart was one "in whom was the mania of an evil nature, not engendered by vicious training or corrupting books or licentious living, but born with him and innate" (76).

Claggart, then, is evil not because he has rebelled against God in the Judaeo-Christian sense, but because he himself is evil by nature. Regardless of how terrifying and devastating his character ultimately may prove to be, society remains relatively unaware of this man's mad pursuit of the destruction of the very fabric, or heart, of humanity. As Melville puts it, "Civilization, especially if of the austerer sort, is auspicious to it" (75). A disciplined society, such as that which Vere insists must obtain on his vessel, fails to see beyond Claggart's calculated attention to the details of decorum. It is not overturning the *rules* of society, the mere glue holding it together, that most compellingly motivates Claggart; indeed, he, like Vere, is an enforcer of the rules, or the exterior trappings which enable human interaction to take place. But he, unlike Vere, determinedly *uses* these exterior trappings to penetrate to the very heart of human kind. In other words, Claggart must endeavor to preserve the facade of order and continuity so that he may manipulate society's rules, hence merely using them as tools to achieve his ultimate objective—the utter destruction of the human heart. Such men are, as Melville says, "madmen"; in his portrait of Claggart Melville prophesies Hitler.

Claggart is totally unlike the common man, wholly Other. Why? Because he cannot be redeemed! Unlike ordinary men, the Claggarts of this world do not act as they do because they have turned away from the good. If they had, the possibility would remain open that somehow they might be motivated to reverse their direction. Rather, they are, from the very outset, in dogged pursuit of their given, natural, course, which is ever to oppose, gainsay, destroy the good. Melville turns to a classical source, then, because Christianity, in particular, does not deal with the unredeemable.[15] Christianity is simply inadequate to handle or to explain elemental good, which cannot knowingly do evil, and elemental evil, which cannot knowingly do good. Melville, however, does not completely reject Christianity. He keeps returning to that phrase from Holy Writ, "the mystery of iniquity" (II Thess. 2:7), for at least the biblical text acknowledges that evil does have its mystery. In order to explain the existence of a Claggart, upon whose actions (which always are finally motivated by "the hidden nature" within) "the point of the present story turn[s]" (76), Melville must consult both discourses, the Adamic and the classical. Once again the two modes join.

Melville appears determined to dramatize the inadequacy of the Adamic mode alone to delineate Claggart, in particular, when he further distinguishes Budd's form (which always partakes of the "heroic") from that of Claggart (which personifies a monstrous "Envy"). As Melville insists, however, "Claggart's was no vulgar form of the passion." Claggart's envy clearly is *not* identifiable as "that streak of apprehensive jealousy that marred Saul's visage perturbedly brooding on the comely young David"; rather, "Claggart's envy struck deeper" (77–78). Melville follows this statement of the inadequacy of the Adamic mode to sound the dissonant chord of a Claggart by adding that the master-at-arms had "no power to annul the elemental evil in him, though readily enough he could hide it." He could apprehend "the good" easily enough, but he was "powerless to be it." As in the classical idea of *moira*, Claggart is, finally, "like the scorpion for which the Creator alone is responsible," only able to "act out to the end the part [or portion] allotted it" (78).

In the next chapter Melville continues to underscore his attempt to depict "Passion, and passion in its profoundest." Indeed, these two forms, Budd and Claggart (and later Vere) do not demand "a palatial stage whereon to play" their parts. Rather, their "profound passion is enacted" "Down among the groundlings, among the beggars and rakers of the garbage" (78). Here Melville consciously opts *not* to cast his novel in the form of the drama, for he wishes to shape tragic life, not tragic drama. The Aristotelian insistence that tragedy portray not merely a noble character, but one of the noble class, is inadequate to his purpose. Nor is the demand that the play depict a finished resolution ("an architectural finial" of sorts) compatible with Melville's aesthetic of a slightly unfinished form. Yet "the form of Billy Budd was heroic," and that of Claggart functions as Budd's antipode. Melville attempts to depict the confrontation of absolute good and evil—in effect, articulating a theodicy; his style compares Budd to demigods and Claggart to their opposite. Several factors, taken together, suggest the somewhat looser structure of the epic: Melville's elevated subject matter and style, his determination to see the events unfolding on board the *Bellipotent* as a microcosm of civilization at large, his resolution to cast Budd in the heroic mold, and his rejection of the dramatic form as too confining. Like Cotton Mather in his *Magnalia Christi Americana,* Melville adapts for *Billy Budd* the form of an epic in prose. Precedents exist in Melville's own work for this adaptation; both *Mardi* and *Moby Dick* arguably are prose epics. Melville even names *Magnalia* in his "The Apple-Tree Table or Original Spiritual Manifestations" (1856), in which he speaks of "the mouldy old book . . . Cotton Mather's *Magnalia*."[16]

In his resolve that his hero be heroic, not because of his class but because of his nature, Melville modifies this structural manifestation of Vergilian discourse, giving it a leveling effect. That is, in his preference for the life teeming in the pit of Shakespeare's Globe Theater, say, the author projects a classless realm which flies in the face of Britain's strict allegiance to its class system and hints at this author's American identity. Even though the setting of this novel is a British, and not an American, man-of-war vessel, the central figures on board act on the basis not of class, but of individual inner nature. Such nature clearly extends well beyond the external limitations of any formal class system. Indeed, the superior forms of humanity, Melville suggests, are—for good or ill—the movers and shakers of civilization, regardless of their assigned class or possible origin in the pit. Melville's rejection of class constraints upon the actions of certain superior natures asserts a leveling effect that recalls the American democratic ideal, so heavily dependent upon the tenets of Adamic discourse. This democratic ideal projects an America in which the individual, any individual, who has "the right stuff" (*Billy Budd* 95, not Tom Wolfe!) can attain superiority. It is this ideal of the Adamic mode which at this juncture blends with classical discourse to create, as was observed of Hawthorne in "My Kinsman, Major Molineaux," a third mode of discourse, the distinctly American.

Melville's empathic and even protective demeanor toward ordinary sailors (readers of *Redburn* know that such men are not "ordinary" in the usual sense) expands his leveling and Americanizing effect. Their identification as "Representatives of the Human Race" already has been remarked. Almost exactly halfway through *Billy Budd,* Melville declares, as if with a sense of pride, "The sailor is frankness, the landsman is finesse" (86). This distinction advances in a succinct way the assertion that sailors, for the most part, are good, honest folk, while those on land all too often are dissembling confidence types who play "a barren game hardly worth that poor candle burnt out in playing it" (87). These "landsmen" recall the confidence tradition which recurs in much of Melville's oeuvre. During Budd's trial, Vere refers to those noncommissioned crewmen as "the people" (112). Later Melville as narrator asserts that "the people of a great warship [are] in one respect like villagers, taking microscopic note of every outward movement or non-movement going on" (116). As close observers paying particular attention to detail, the sailors parallel the mental action of the readers of Melville's text. Thus the author draws his audience all the more intensely into his book. Melville's belief that sailors are an honest lot and his pronouncement that they are universal representatives of mankind (despite his lack of faith in landsmen) suggest that Melville wishes all human beings would try to emulate sailors' generally honest behavior. Of course, Billy Budd is a sailor, the best of a set of already worthy human representatives.

On the page following the reference to "the people," Melville describes Vere's announcement to the sailors the results of the drumhead court. The audience manifests "a dumbness like that of a seated congregation of believers in hell listening to the clergyman's announcement of his Calvinistic text" (117). Superficially, this simile may seem to be the somewhat bemused observation of a cultured despiser of religion, to paraphrase Schleiermacher. However, it connects Melville's text to the homilies of a Cotton Mather or a Richard Mather, serving as a bridge to the past. In addition, it links the masses of people (and these people assuredly are Americans) firmly to the Adamic myth. Significantly, this same group venerates the spar from which Budd was hanged "as a piece of the Cross" (131), reinforcing the sailors' alignment with Adamic discourse. Rather than subjecting the entire novel to the constraints of Adamic discourse, this late emphasis upon an important component of that mode underscores the tension within that dialectic, which defines what it means to be American. Recall that Budd, whose death provokes an Adamic response *among the bluejackets*, embodies *both* modes of discourse.

More substantially than Claggart, "Starry Vere" points to the classical mode of discourse as complementing the mode represented by the bluejackets. To be sure, the last exceptional character aboard Melville's microcosmic ship is that vessel's captain, the Honorable Edward Fairfax Vere. Practically all those writing about this character observe the similarity between the name *Vere* and Latin *verum*, or truth. This name also appears to echo *vir*, Latin for *man*.[17] *Ver* itself may be applied figuratively or poetically to a youth; and the captain's name can be interpreted as related to *vis*, whose plural is *vires*, force or violence. One could extend this clever name-tracing business *ad absurdum*. Particularly arresting, however, are the possible applications to Vere's character of *ver*, youth; and *vires*, violence or force. For Vere fails, at the moment he condemns Budd (or the good), to grasp "Truth" in its fullness. Instead he chooses to remain loyal to the violence and force of war. In affirming his loyalty to the destructiveness of war, the captain renounces his learning, sophistication, and apparent wisdom for an ignoble, immature endeavor.

Harry Levin concludes that the behavior of both Budd and Vere declares that "manhood, on joining the navy, submits itself to the King's law"

(196). Levin, however, has overlooked Melville's thought regarding men and war, as expressed in *Battle-Pieces* (1866). In two of the best poems from this collection of responses to the Civil War, for example, Melville is explicit. "Shiloh, A Requiem" exclaims parenthetically, "What like a bullet can undeceive!" And "The March into Virginia" minces no words when its persona makes this stinging assessment: "All wars are boyish, and are fought by boys" (*Poems* 41 and 10).

Is it not war which, directly or indirectly, results in the deaths of Claggart, Budd and later of Vere? And a later war brings down even Lord Nelson, that epitome of British naval excellence and heroism. As Melville portrays each of the exceptional natures on board the *Bellipotent*, one senses that war, fully sanctioned by civilization, contrives conditions which make it possible for men like Claggart to seize power and sentence excellent "natures" to futile deaths. Surely one of the primary thrusts of *Billy Budd* is to call into question the value of the devotion of so many exceptional natures to such destructive undertakings.

As for Vere's apparent wisdom and learning, Melville has much to say. While Vere earns "the appellation 'Starry Vere,'" linking him immediately to another star cynosure, Budd, Melville states bluntly that, "whatever his sterling qualities[, he] was without *any* [emphasis added] brilliant ones" (61). Of Vere's use of recondite classical allusions, which aligns him with the Aeneas myth, Melville observes, "He seemed unmindful of the circumstance that to his bluff company such remote allusions, however pertinent they might really be, were altogether alien to men whose reading was mainly confined to the journals" (63). In an earlier version of this portion of the novel, Melville identified precisely what sort of allusions Vere was likely to make: "Some allusion to Plutarch, say, or Livy" (315). While many Melville scholars see in this portrait Melville's own hidden self (admittedly, the compulsion to do so is strong), within the context of the novel this element of Vere's character suggests an unwillingness to empathize with others and even a contempt for his colleagues' lack of erudition.

Melville continues this portrait by observing that Vere's "honesty" prescribed in him a directness resembling "that of a migratory fowl that in its flight never heeds when it crosses a frontier" (63). The bird simile establishes a link to Budd's goldfinch, a second parallel to Budd. Vere's "migratory fowl" is already in flight, however, suggesting much greater mobility than Budd's caged goldfinch. At the same time, the failure to note the crossing of a boundary predicts Vere's hasty assessment, "Fated boy," (99), uttered when Budd has just killed Claggart. Both his knowledge of antiquity ("He had a marked leaning toward everything intellectual. He loved books"; 62) and his faith in *moira* align Vere with classical discourse. Still, that alignment does not give him a capacity to grasp fully a being as novel as Billy Budd. For example, when Lieutenant Ratcliffe tells him of Budd's standing salute from the cutter to the "old Rights-of-Man" (49), Vere understands it, as Ratcliffe had, "mistakenly . . . as a satiric sally" (95). Vere, who at times manifests "a queer streak of the pedantic" (63), clearly is intelligent; but just as clearly he does not have an intellect "which drops down into the universe like a plummet" (*Portable Melville* 405).

It is very likely that Vere's classical bent, along with the undeniable tension occasioned by the recent Nore mutiny, prompts Vere to opt for rule by military democracy, "founded on the rude basis of a barbarous horde, submitting, for their common interest, to the dominion of one chieftain."[18] While the human representatives aboard the *Bellipotent* may not be characterized exactly as a "barbarous horde," recall that Budd the sailor and paradigm of natural good is identified by Melville as "a sort of upright barbarian" (52). Again, "a barbarian Billy radically was" (120). Certainly all the men aboard this vessel submit, if not without some grumbling misgivings, to the authority of Captain Vere. Whether such submission is ultimately "for their common good" appears to be a central problem within this novel. Nevertheless, even the chaplain, a "minister of the Prince of Peace serving in the host of the God of War—Mars" (122; another blending of the myths of Adam and Aeneas), horrifyingly "lends the sanction of the religion of the meek to that which practically is the abrogation of everything but brute Force" (122). Melville's calculated use of the adverb "practically" ominously echoes Vere's earlier statement, during the trial, that Budd's killing of Claggart was "a case practical, and under martial law practically to be dealt with" (110).

Melville counters Charles Mitchell's charge that "Vere becomes a Claggart by killing Billy" (115), by pointing out, unequivocally, that "the essential right and wrong involved in the matter, the clearer that might be, so much the worse for the responsibility of a loyal sea commander, inasmuch as he was not authorized to determine the matter on that primitive basis" (103). If not on a "primitive basis," one in accordance with the harmonious portion of nature, then on what? Vere must act, if he is to remain loyal to his commission, according to the dictates of the god of war, Mars. How is it, then, that Vere has come to be so devoted to duty to country, perhaps above the other two elements of pietas, devotion to God (the gods) and family? Merton Sealts suggests a clue in this assessment of Vere: "Along with Melville's Jack Gentian, another patrician figure with a background of military service, Vere too might well be called 'an old-fashioned Roman,' not only in his patriotism and devotion to duty but also in his regard for established principles and values that have come down to him from the past" ("Innocence" 415). While Sealts's assessment is unassailable, an examination of Melville's portraits of John (or "Jack") Gentian, in light of the Aeneas myth, bears more fruit regarding Vere's characterization.

Written late in Melville's career, the first and second of three "Jack Gentian Sketches" contain several classical allusions, in such phrases as the "Chinese Achilles," "fate working through force" (in reference to the Civil War), and "Knights of the Golden Fleece." Gentian quotes a portion of an imitation of Horace (perhaps by Melville himself) and articulates several Latin maxims, such as *sic transit* and *tempus fugit*. On one occasion, Melville has Gentian state, about two deceased friends, "In pace, in pace—*Requiescant*." In giving this maxim, Melville recalls enough of his grammar-school Latin to make his verb correctly plural. Melville describes Gentian as "an oldfashioned Roman in [his] patriotism" who would "consign to oblivion the fact that [his] countrymen, claiming the van of Adam's alleged advance, were but yesterday plunged in patricidal strife" (*Short Works* 406). Gentian is seen, then, as an American Roman whose country gives lip service to the notion of a highly evolved Adamic discourse, pledging peace and equality but delivering war and inequality in a Civil War fought primarily over the issue of slavery. As Sealts suggests, this picture of Gentian resembles Melville's portrait of Vere. Note that the discourses of both Adam and Aeneas blend artfully in the Gentian portrait. Whereas Gentian is avowedly an American, however, Vere is British, at least on the surface. Both are military men, staunch patriots and supporters of order at any cost. In his behavior, each communicates a deep respect—even reverence—for the past, often calling it up in conversation. Finally, while both explicitly note the contradiction between ideal and reality (between preachment and praxis), both as officers are practical enforcers and guardians of established order and/or the status quo.

These close parallels between Gentian and Vere help to unmask Vere as a representative (type) of Americanness. Vere's Americanness nevertheless strongly sounds the chord of classical discourse, and he allows his intense loyalty to patria, now become virtually synonymous with war, to throw his pietas out of balance. In other words, Vere has subordinated the other two measures of pietas, God and family, to the present enterprise of war. So powerful is his commitment to war that he allows Mars to become his god and Budd, his surrogate family, to become a sacrifice on the altar of Mars. That the price of such loyalty is indeed high becomes evident in his lack of composure after Claggart's death, so obvious to the ship's surgeon that he questions Vere's sanity: "Was he unhinged?" (102). During the trial, Vere attempts to justify his behavior and faith in the god Mars by insisting on the exigencies of practicality. After Budd's hanging, he justifies them by pulling out of his classical background, of all things, the Orpheus myth. One of the principal myths of artistic creativity, the Orpheus myth had been useful to Vere on other occasions when the constraints on order needed to be intensified. In other words, Vere is so dedicated to the god of war that he even uses the order of rhythm which characterizes music as an instrument to compel obedience to his god, Mars. The description Melville gives of Vere's application of the Orpheus myth serves as an effective commentary on this man with "a mind resolute to surmount difficulties even if against primitive instincts strong as the wind and the sea" (109). For surely this myth of the greatest of musicians, one whose music could move even inanimate objects such as rocks and trees, as well as soothe the savage beast, sings the powerful tale of man's most primitive or primal (not in the sense of backward) responsiveness to rhythm and aural beauty.

Yet Vere values the Orpheus myth because it represents, in his own words, "forms, measured forms [which] are everything; and that is the import couched in the story of Orpheus with his lyre spellbinding the wild denizens of the wood" (128). So, following Budd's execution, "The band on the quarter-deck played a sacred air." This playing of sacred music immediately after Budd's hanging, ostensibly for the crime of murder, many may find inappropriate and even grotesque. But Melville makes it evident that the music and the chaplain's "customary morning service" here both are "subserving the discipline and purposes of war" (128). Clearly, then, Vere uses both music and religion as instruments of the god of war, not out of villainy but because of an all-consuming resolution to carry out the will of his great god Mars. While this explanation does not make of Vere a Claggart, neither does it make it right that Vere perverts music, symbol of creativity. If "measured forms are everything" to Vere, this exceptional man who nonetheless is "without any brilliant" qualities, fails utterly to grasp the creative quality of art. In fact, he is predisposed to such a failure and therefore also predisposed, however regrettably, to give his allegiance to the antipode of creativity, patently destructive war. Thus Vere fails to grasp Budd's significance as a *terrae filius*.

In this sense Vere falsifies the Orpheus myth—not because Melville as narrator has construed a false Orpheus, but because something within Vere's flawed nature sounds a false music.[19] Music played only as a series of measured forms is not music, not art, but is at best the mere illusion of art. And what room is there for art amid the destructiveness of war? Another way of articulating the notion that music without feeling is not music is to recall Vere's words as he imposes his will (what he perceives to be the will of Mars) on the drumhead court: "Let not warm hearts betray heads that should be cool" (111). To Vere, then, and by his own testimony, the choice of heart over head, of feeling over cool, measured intellect, constitutes a betrayal of that to which Vere wholly subscribes. One would do well to bear in mind Melville's poignant observation that Vere is "a true military officer [who] is in one particular like a true monk. Not with more of self-abnegation will the latter keep his vows of monastic obedience than the former his vows of allegiance to martial duty" (104). A monk retreats to an environment stripped of everything not designed specifically to assist him in expressing complete devotion to his idea of the deity. In a similar manner Vere retreats to his "monastery," the *Bellipotent* ("powerful in war"), where he may yield himself to full expression of his own idea of god, Mars. This comparison becomes more significant when one recalls that, in identifying Claggart as a being beyond redemption, Melville already has indicated that the Adamic myth alone is insufficient for his purposes, and Vere's alignment is with the Aeneas myth, equally insufficient alone. This monk comparison is to an outworn, outmoded religious perspective; hence the military officer also is outmoded and superfluous in a world which someday may realize the potential of the Adam and Aeneas dialectic. Because Vere has resigned "what remains primeval in [his] formalized humanity" to the god Mars and because he has surrendered his own heart for the cause of war, Vere fails at this moment to yield to the essential goodness symbolized by Billy Budd. That he does so not out of villainy, but because Claggart does and he does *not* possess "a depravity according to nature," Vere's failure is truly horrifying. Why? Because such a failure inexorably leads to elimination of the good. Vere does not realize "that finer spiritual insight indispensable to the understanding of the essential in certain exceptional characters, whether evil ones or good," until the later moment of his own death. Melville records that, upon Vere's death, "he was heard to murmur . . . 'Billy Budd, Billy Budd.'" And he (Melville) is careful to add, "These were not the accents of remorse."

If not of remorse, then of what? In the poem "Shiloh," in *Battle Pieces*, Melville asserts, "What like a bullet can undeceive!" Vere dies from the lingering effects of "a musket ball from a porthole of the enemy's main cabin" (129). Surely Vere himself is undeceived! Upon his death, Vere experiences *anagnorisis;* in his moment of revelation, he receives the ecstatic vision of Budd as the good. As Abbie Findlay Potts puts it in her classic *The Elegiac Mode*, "The first *anagnorisis* or discovery" of the earliest elegies "was of the worth and daring of the human spirit" (43). According to Potts, "The characteristic drive of elegiac meditation [is] toward always better things—better men, better states, better hypotheses, truer truth" (44–45). If Merton Sealts is correct that, among several qualifiers which may be attributed to *Billy Budd*, "one might add the further adjective 'elegiac'" ("Innocence" 417), then the interpretation of Vere as one who achieves discovery becomes the more plausible. Vere dies, then, not as Joyce Sparer Adler maintains, "on the heels of his sacrifice of Billy to Mars" as "Melville's Judgment upon him for his denial of God" (177), but as a manifestation of one who has discovered "truer truth." At one point in her fine analysis of the clarity of the elegiac form, which in origin, of course, is an entirely classical form, Potts asserts, "The aim of elegiac composition is the refinement of human understanding in a series of revelations about the nature of human life and human destiny" (73). Surely few would deny that Melville's career as author represents an almost constant attempt to probe the secrets of truth. In *Billy Budd*, he presents a horrifying demonstration of how a well-motivated man like Vere can be misdirected by a fallen world (one fallen not merely in the Puritan or Calvinistic sense) and, in consequence, become a tool in the destruction of the good symbolized by Budd. According to his own declaration, Melville hopes, by this example, to admonish and/or to teach "an average man of the world" to grasp "the essential in certain exceptional characters, whether evil ones or good" and to avoid failing to do so because of blunted spiritual insight.

Vere fails to grasp Budd's essential goodness because, in his stubborn, religious loyalty to the god Mars (a loyalty equivalent to that pledged to a religious dogma), his pietas is out of balance. Recall that, in Homeric Greece, the supreme virtue was *arete* (nobility of mind and action on the battlefield), symbolized by Achilles. Later, during a time of relative peace, classical Greece elevated the virtue of *sophrosyne* (moderation, balance, and sanity in all things); *sophrosyne*, or *temperantia* in Latin, became the supreme virtue of the Pax Romana begun by Augustus and predicted by Vergil in book VI of the *Aeneid*. In *Billy Budd*, Melville also appears to be promoting *sophrosyne*. That is, his characters have three options. Either they cannot, because of their depraved nature (as in the case of Claggart), act except to oppose the good, thus thwarting all virtue. Or alternatively, they err by subordinating two aspects of pietas to a third, as Vere advances devotion to patria at the expense of proper devotion to the gods and to family. This stubborn resolve almost costs Vere his sanity. Or finally, because of a lack of knowledge, a character may fall victim to the misguided actions of a Vere and a Claggart, as Billy Budd does.

What is missing in all three of Melville's exceptional characters is an adequate sense of proportion or balance. While Claggart's innate depravity and Vere's misplaced loyalty have been touched upon, Budd's lack of knowledge has yet to be explored. Budd's role in the novel begins the book, provokes the other two exceptional "natures" into action, and closes the novel. Therefore it is appropriate to focus on that role in concluding this discussion of *Billy Budd*. While the form of Billy Budd, and of *Billy Budd* as well, may be heroic or epic, the tone of the events following Budd's death, concentrating almost entirely on the effects of that death, is, as Sealts has suggested, elegiac. Here epic and elegy merge, as Melville proves himself an "authentic elegist," one who, in the words of Potts, "is preoccupied . . . with his diagnosis of whatever is dead or sterile, or bloated, disproportionate, corrupt, death-dealing" (95). Foremost among the problems Melville diagnoses as plaguing modern civilization are war, with its corrupting, death-dealing imbalances, and the sterility of religious dogma, the problem particularly symbolized in the character of Billy Budd.

Melville embeds in his portrait of Budd more than mere diagnosis, for Budd's inchoate, unfinished nature points the way toward solution. Milton R. Stern asserts that *Billy Budd* demonstrates that, for Melville, "the possibility of change or hope . . . [is] entirely gone now" ("Melville, Society, and Language" 465) and attests "Melville's final certainty about the unregenerate nature of humanity" (467). On the contrary, *Billy Budd, Sailor* displays hope and suggests humanity's capacity to regenerate itself. This hope for regeneration resides within the exceptional good nature of Billy Budd, a *terrae filius*.

If Budd's advent "coincides with a moment in the dawn of things: the creation of the cosmos, the creation of a new world, of a new epoch of history," then Melville's novel symbolizes the possibility of some sort of new world or epoch. Budd's pristine innocence does not serve him well; it does not enable him to survive, proving that knowledge is necessary for survival in a world this side of paradise. Budd does feel devotion to country (he vehemently opposes even the idea of mutiny); to an essential, undogmatic goodness (or godliness); and to the "family" of society aboard ship, whether *The Rights of Man* or the *Bellipotent*. Pietas is alive and well in him, albeit without benefit of sophistication. Budd's very nature is generous or capacious and at the same time undeveloped, unfinished. He is an "upright barbarian" (52) "who in the nude might have posed for a statue of young Adam before the Fall" (94).

This image symbolizes the best the Adamic and classical discourses have to offer. Melville here has blended both discourses by projecting onto each what is impossible in one alone but probable in a fusion of both. That is, a nude statue of Adam can offer only iconographic (if not, from a Calvinistic perspective, pornographic) representation, posing the challenge of a graven image to supremacy of Jehovah. Similarly, for classical art, a figure from Hebrew mythology can manifest only incongruity of thought and even of subject. Yet Melville's blending of both into a single image adds force to each and symbolizes a powerful third mode—not classical, not Adamic, but American. The first two discourses, if not all three, agree that humanity, in a broad sense, lives in a real, fallen world in which evil exists, and that an individual inevitably encounters evil at some point.

Budd strikes and kills Claggart not merely because of Budd's flaw (an inclination toward stuttering), but also because of his lack of sophistication. His limited experience and lack of "intuitive knowledge of the bad" disarm him at the crucial moment when the embodiment of natural depravity, Claggart, confronts him. The innate generosity which accompanies Budd's lack of sophistication nevertheless invests him with the capacity for understanding when, just prior to his death, he intones the unforgettable refrain, "God bless Captain Vere!" despite knowing that it was "all sham" (132). That is, Budd accepts fully his role as sacrifice; and his death is a "death, which is no death," at least symbolically.

To be sure, when "Billy ascended," when "in ascending [he] took the full rose of the dawn" (124), he literally experienced "the running of me [him] up!" (132), not because of some miraculous, transcendent apotheosis but because this procedure identifies the manner of execution aboard ship during the era of this novel. Certainly, one must grant that the language Melville uses to describe this event is heavily laden with transcendent symbolism: "The East was shot through with a soft glory *as* of the fleece of the Lamb of God seen in mystical vision, and simultaneously therewith, watched by the wedged *mass* of upturned faces, Billy ascended." Emphasis has been added to the words *as* and *mass* to draw attention, first, to the fact that the suggestion of Christian ascension is offered as a figure of speech; and, second, to the collective impact of this suggestion on all present.

To those present—even to Vere, who postpones recognition until the ecstatic moment of his death—Budd's death is, as Joyce Sparer Adler puts it, "a good death" (174), one which in Melville's earlier version represents the appearance of "the full shekinah . . . of that grand dawn" (412). Perhaps the strong associations of this Judaeo-Christian concept of God's appearance in His full glory (before Moses as a cloud, in Exodus 33:7–11, for example; or as the transfigured Christ, in Luke 9:32–35) prompted Melville to replace this phrase with "the full rose of the dawn" (124), which is less identifiably Judaeo-Christian. Actually, this latter phrase duplicates epic formula. In any event, it is evident that Melville is struggling here to draw on the transcendent significance of symbol—a process ably explored in the last century throughout the works of Paul Tillich, to cite only one author. The transcendent symbolism Melville suggests here is, then, decidedly not dogmatic. Recall that Budd's "sailor way of taking clerical discourse" (121), offered him by "the minister of Christ though receiving his stipend from Mars" (120), discloses the young foretopman as one who, "though on the confines of death," never could be converted to any dogma (121).

This failure of the ship's chaplain to proselytize Budd defines more deliberately the significance of the latter's noble barbarism than it does any lack of intellect; for Melville earlier makes clear his respect for "the honest scholar" who declared, "I am the adherent of no organized religion, much less of any philosophy built into a system" (74). Such a position accords with Melville's own, as demonstrated throughout his career; he often struggled to probe the meaning of all religions coming within his purview. One case in point is his long fascination with Zoroastrianism's light/dark dualism, particularly as articulated in Pierre Bayle's substantial *An Historical and Critical Dictionary* (English translation, 5 vols., 1734–38). Melville never found any dogma, whether religious, political ,or philosophical, that satisfied him. This same attitude he thought he had discovered in the author of *Mosses from an Old Manse*, when, in mid-1850, he celebrated "that lasting temper of all true, candid men—a seeker, not a finder yet" (*Portable Melville* 416).

William B. Dillingham judiciously points out that Melville pasted the timeless maxim, "Keep true to the dreams of thy youth," to the underside of "the inclined plane" of the small portable desk on which the author composed his last work (*Later Novels* 365). Dillingham is also correct in holding that *Billy Budd* represents Melville's "final portrayal of a man," Edward Vere, "who failed to know and to be true to himself" (366). Indeed, this novel offers to an unappreciative audience the learned product of "a writer whom few know" (114). *Billy Budd* is Melville's gift of a lifetime's wisdom acquired by a committed soul who ever aspired to construct the grand edifice but was honest and brave enough to admit that "grand ones, true ones, ever leave the copestone to posterity. God keep me from ever completing anything" (*Moby Dick* 127–28). As in his youth, Melville renews his pledge always to be a seeker, never a finder. As earlier, his resolve in *Billy Budd* is to leave his last work an unfinished "architectural finial"; to do so is to represent truth honestly—to return to the dreams of his youth.

A lifetime of probing into the mysteries of iniquity taught Melville profound disappointment, as again and again the American promise fell short of realization—in the institution of slavery, in the ignominious Civil War, and in the failure of even exceptional natures to enact justice. In the novel's final emphasis on memory, embodied in the concluding elegiac ballad, "Billy in the Darbies," Melville shows that, as Joyce Sparer Adler observes, "Billy does have power. Though impotent to save himself, he has power to invoke the future. His death, illuminating the nature of the world represented by the *Bellipotent*, will quicken the imagination of the crew [of mankind]" (174). The chains that hold Billy Budd in bondage, that prevent him from realizing the promise of true American identity, were placed upon him by dogmatic beliefs held by Vere and his civilization. This cultural blindness leads to a horrifying failure to ferret out and to recognize a seductive, ignoble madman, one "depraved by nature." Such wisdom causes *Billy Budd* to be uncannily prophetic of events in the twentieth century, predicting such megalomaniacs as Hitler and Stalin. In Melville's view, then, women and men of this or any century risk their very lives and the future of civilization whenever they give up doubt for certainty. To yield doubt, questioning, for an absolute, any absolute—religious, political, ideological—is to stop thinking, to grow fallow and stale, to be unrealized.

Melville knew that American character was not Adamic, nor was it classical. It resided, and continues to live, in the tension obtaining between the two. This tension is always in a state of flux, ever promising change and renewal. In this sense, Melville's aesthetic of an unfinished form merges with the idea of what it means to be American. Herein lies the value, the promise, of the Adam and Aeneas dialectic insured by the United States Constitution. So long as the tension between the secular horizontality of classical discourse and the spiritual verticality of Adamic discourse remain in a state of tension, each will stand watch over the other, ever holding up to the world the promise of the best that is American. Melville's *Billy Budd, Sailor* attests the promise, but not yet the reality, of American identity.

Having thoroughly internalized the tenets of the Aeneas myth, as well as those of the Adamic, both Melville and Hawthorne demonstrate in their work the persistence of the Aeneas myth. Hawthorne deftly blends both myths, classical and biblical, in "My Kinsman, Major Molineaux," constructing an incisive critique of Americanness. Contrary to the position of current critics, Hawthorne probably did not seek out Spenser as a source for Elliston's interior serpent in "The Bosom Serpent," but merely recalled Vergil. Certainly Melville's detailed knowledge of classical culture and literature, particularly Vergil's *Aeneid*, informs and profoundly shapes *Billy Budd*. Yet the power of classical knowledge in shaping the works of these authors has gone relatively unremarked. The shaping power of classical discourse in American literature and American culture before 1800 also has received scant attention. This failure to acknowledge either the tension between the discourses of Adam and Aeneas or, particularly, the presence of the classical half of the American self has been astonishingly stubborn. One must conclude that America's classical origins have been, and remain, besieged. ▩

Conclusion

America's Classical Origins Besieged

Despite the declared war on classical languages and literatures, the American Aeneas tradition figures powerfully within the work of Nathaniel Hawthorne and Herman Melville, as it does in the work of virtually every writer of the American Renaissance. In other words, despite concerted attempts by such notables as Noah Webster and Benjamin Rush to denigrate classical discourse and advance Adamic discourse, to "convert" Aeneas into Adam, Aeneas persisted.

The nature of this persistence, moreover, defines the American self. Adam alone does not characterize the American self. Indeed, that self may be defined most fully in terms of the interplay of these two strands, Adam *and* Aeneas. Yet the American Adam wields such power in American discourse that a sixteen-year odyssey has been required to recover this interplay. This study is the fruit of that journey.

As the subsequent explication makes clear, recovery of the Aeneas strain has become a matter of urgency. Surrounded by hostile forces, literally hounded out of history, the myth of Aeneas is, at the present time, virtually unknown to the American people. Several factors presently work to constrain that recovery. One is the marginalization of American literature written before 1800, a trend largely responsible for the unfounded anxiety that America has no past it can call its own. Another is a thoroughgoing, seemingly implacable anti-intellectualism. In the final analysis, then, it is not merely the American Aeneas which is besieged, or which has become the target of distress, but the American self, this distress having come about as an inevitable consequence of a lost awareness that one half of that self is classical. Only when Americans have recovered the whole American self can we deal honestly with determining who and what our culture is, or should be, about.

Not all commentators on American culture have failed to see the classical half of the American self. For example, in a letter to Amy Lowell, quoted by Leo Marx in *The Machine and the Garden*, D. H. Lawrence appears to recognize the classical half exclusively:

> Have you still got hummingbirds, as in Crèvecoeur? I liked Crèvecoeur's "Letters of an American Farmer," *so* much. And how splendid Herman Melville's "Moby Dick" is, & Dana's "Two Years before the Mast." But your classic American literature, I find to my surprise, is *older* than our English. The tree did not become new, which was transplanted. It only ran more swiftly into age, impersonal, non-human almost. But how good these books are! Is the *English* tree in America almost dead? By the literature I think it is. (Marx 73)

Lawrence, in using the attributive "classic," most immediately wishes to convey that America's achievement in literature, as represented by the work of Crèvecoeur, Melville, and Dana, is of lasting significance, worth, and maturity. In addition, this use of "classic" connotes the cultures and literatures of ancient Rome and Greece. Especially within the context of the classical half of the American self, "classic" points to the possibility of a deeper assessment of American culture. In using literature to "read" culture, Lawrence finds "classic American literature" to be "*older* than our English," so much so that the implantation of the English tree in American soil grew "more swiftly into age," becoming "impersonal, non-human almost."

This impersonality of a tradition which appears to have roots thrusting so far into the past as no longer to be easily recognized as human connotes the "cold pastoral" of classicism, perhaps one of Marx's reasons for using this quotation. Lawrence is directly on target here, suggesting that America's classicism is more conservative than that of Britain. During the time when British interest in the pastoral elegy had been exhausted, when the pastoral itself began to irritate Samuel Johnson (who deprecated Milton's *Lycidas* in his *Lives of the Poets*), and when the British increasingly associated pietas with sanctimoniousness, Early Americans were composing sophisticated pastoral elegies based not on British authors but on classical ones, were writing pastoral poems as serious social commentaries and as a means of subversion, and were elevating the notion of pietas to the extent that this virtue became rearticulated as the American Way. In asking whether the "*English* tree in America [is] almost dead?" and concluding that, "By the literature, I think it is," Lawrence "reads" only the classical half of the American self. At the same time, he recognizes that American culture (to judge by its literature) has achieved solid maturity.

In citing Crèvecoeur, Melville, and Dana, Lawrence points to other aspects of America's classical origins. While he recollects Crèvecoeur's tenth letter, "On Snakes; and on the Hummingbird," he does not mention that Crèvecoeur, in the last paragraph of the third letter, the famous "What Is an American?" invests the American character with pietas. In the mouth of the Pennsylvania colony's founder, William Penn, Crèvecoeur places this description of the "immunities of a freeman." He must "carefully educate thy children, teach them gratitude to God and reverence to that government, that philanthropic government, which has collected here so many men and made them happy" (*Letters* 90).

In this description of America's literature as "classic" juxtaposed alongside two American sea novels, the passage plays upon the origin of this word in the Latin *classis*, meaning a fleet at sea including the troops in it. The word classis can, however, also connote the whole body of citizens called to arms or simply an army, or in a tropological sense an indication of the lowest rank of citizens. Whether consciously or not, Lawrence has selected the attributive here which more accurately describes the American situation than can the related word, "classical," which comes from the Latin *classicus*, meaning of or belonging to a class and by transferral coming to identify the first or highest class of Roman citizens. While calling up the associations classic carries with the Latin culture and language, at the same time this word enlists a broad, more inclusive category which comes closer to evoking American images of the common, ordinary citizen. In short, the word classic with its inclusive, leveling associations sounds more democratic than the aristocratic classical. (The *O.E.D.* does not carry these derivations to this extent.)

Lawrence in this passage has managed to ascribe to the American people a democratic classicism, demonstrating his extraordinary capacity for "reading" the American self correctly. We must remember, however, that Lawrence was an extremely knowledgeable outsider and viewed the American self from that more objective perspective.

Americans themselves, at the end of the eighteenth century, saw construction begin on their national capitol, cast in an architectural style decidedly classical. At the same time, they were becoming blinded to the classical origins of their own character. During this early period, it was wholly acceptable, perhaps even necessary, to "look" classical, as in the architecture of the District of Columbia, for "looking" classical sowed the principle of order in the land. At the same moment, it became a cultural imperative that the People definitely not "be," or "seem to be," classical. As the first generation of Americans came away from the revised, anticlassical public school system, even *looking* classical would soon become suspect. But by that time, in the District of Columbia's architecture the classical style had been established irreversibly. Thus this architecture constitutes yet another illustration of the pattern of cultural acceptance and denial which is so characteristically American.

The British Lawrence could recognize America's classicism, but Americans themselves, with surprising consistency, have refused to see, much less accept, what even an outsider can identify. In America, amid the hurly-burly of today's intense, complex, and often divisive multicultural condition, many sing the anthem of a return to "simpler," good old American values—without knowing what those values really were. Yet, more often than not, the chorus urging this "return" repeats the refrain of dogmatic, fundamentalist, Judaeo-Christian rules and regulations. America's intellectual elite seldom will join such a chorus. So we appear to be burdened with a return to a center which simply cannot hold. For, persisting at the center of the American self is not the Adamic mode alone, but the dialectic of Adam and Aeneas. Once Americans have reclaimed the wealth of their classical selfhood, perhaps we can discover a center which can stand fast.

Three factors in particular have resulted in our inability to perceive the American self as a whole. First is a failure to claim as a distinctly American property Peter Martyr's myth of the golden age. This failure has prevented recognition that America was invented first in terms of the Aeneas myth. Second, the failure to recognize that America's classical origins bespeak a most usable American past has been largely responsible for a sweeping marginalization of Early American literature. Third, the construction of the radical shift in discourse, and subsequent generations' failure to detect it, together signal the utter success of many of our country's founders in bringing about this shift. All ramifications attending recovery of the Aeneas myth and its dynamic interaction with the Adamic myth arise out of these three principal factors.

Regarding the phenomenon of the radical shift, we do not need a rehearsal of the mechanisms which brought it about; what we require now is a consideration of the possible consequences occurring from restoration of the American Aeneas, ending cultural blindness. I have written this study as an aggressive provocateur, a deliberate instigator of debate and reevaluation of America's cultural origins, committed to the principle that such constructive controversy can lead to a better understanding of how America can "work" or how it can not "work." In the ensuing discussion, therefore, I deal with some lingering questions in relation to Martyr's golden age myth, try to suggest how ignorance of America's thoroughly usable past has dictated the marginalization of Early American literature, and grapple with some of the consequences which may or should result from restoration of cultural sight, that is, from a lifting of the siege besetting the American Aeneas.

Peter Martyr's Golden Age Myth

This delineation of the origins of the American self began not in New England, as so many others have, but oddly, perhaps to some, in Spain with an Italian's interpretation of Columbus's first encounter with the New World; this encounter Peter Martyr told in largely classical terms. These terms this Italian historian, who was an acquaintance of Columbus and who, as chaplain, served the court of King Ferdinand II of Aragon and Queen Isabella I of Castile, derived from drawing parallels between Columbus's exploration and the wanderings of Vergil's Aeneas. While it is known that Gaspar Perez de Villagra's *History of New Mexico* (1610) owes much of its structure to the *Aeneid* and that this work therefore represents a definite and powerful continuity of a tradition established first by Martyr, I move next not to de Villagra but to Richard Eden's immensely popular 1555 English translation of Martyr's Latin *Decades* because this investigation is concerned with the classical origins of the American self as they developed within the tradition of the American English language and culture. Europe saw, in one way or another, New World exploration in classical terms, as well as Adamic, because all of Europe's intelligentsia knew and carried on discourse in Latin. I suspect that the cultural debt of Latin America to the ancient classical world has been considerably underestimated, as has America's. For many see this indebtedness to be merely a literary one, as Harry Levin remarks in *The Myth of the Golden Age in the Renaissance*. Calling the golden age myth "essentially a literary subject," Levin observes that during the renaissance "there were few men of letters in whose works we could not find some sort of allusion to it" (xvii). Peter Martyr's *Decades*, widely known in Latin and in its many translations but virtually universally known among the literate English in Eden's translation, also makes much of this golden age myth—this usage probably prompted by Martyr's having first explained Columbus's arrival on the isle of Hispanola, "as when Eneas arrived in Italy" (66); indeed, the famous author of the *Aeneid*, Vergil, had also written the almost as famous buccolics or pastorals, known as the *Eclogues*, on which the pastoral tradition in Europe and America is largely based.

Levin writes that nothing the Europeans "had previously experienced could have prepared them for their initial view of the Amerindians." The sight of an *apparently* uncivilized people, preferring minimal dress (doubtless because of the Caribbean heat), so Levin maintains, moved these first European explorers to bring the classical golden age myth "into play, almost as if it had been touched off by a reflex action" (60). Just as likely, Peter Martyr's intimate knowledge of the *Aeneid* induced the Italian chaplain to the Spanish court to interpret Columbus's journey to the land in the west in the imagery of Vergil's consummate seaman, Aeneas. While Martyr's explication of the European encounter with the New World was assuredly natural for him, given the renaissance preoccupation with ancient classicism, the latter-day notion that Martyr's "reflex action" was so ordinary that that action can not have led to anything other than a literary response does not necessarily follow.

Can it be that late-nineteenth- and twentieth-century scholars have construed this renaissance response to the New World adventure to have been just so natural and so commonplace, leading them to look casually upon classical elements wherever they appear in writing by or about America from 1500 to the present, and causing them to have become blinded to the possibility that what these earlier writers were actually accomplishing was nothing less than the invention of America? So much window dressing and/or so many displays of erudition, as such scholars as Kenneth Murdock and Bernard Bailyn have held of Early Americans' use of classicism, in fact, attest how profoundly deep lie the classical roots of the American self. In his descriptive, though timely *The Founders and the Classics: Greece, Rome, and the American Enlightenment*, Carl J. Richard has recently taken great pains to refute directly such claims levied by Murdock and Bailyn; supplying "a large portion of the founders' intellectual tools," Richard contends that "the classics exerted a formative influence upon the founders," whom Richard defines as "prominent late eighteenth- and early nineteenth-century American leaders, excluding loyalists" (vii and 7–8).

When Urian Oakes subtly reconstructs the life of the beloved pastor, Thomas Shepherd, as a subject for pastoral elegy and then invests him with the virtue of pietas, he is rearticulating ancient classicism in terms he finds appropriate to the American strand. When Cotton Mather appropriates the classical epic, specifically Vergil's *Aeneid*, as a model for his prose *Magnalia Christi Americana* and in the process most studiously ascribes to the American self the virtue of pietas, he too is constructing the American self as a subtle yet dynamic blend of the myths of Adam and Aeneas.

The signs of this construction persist during the remainder of the eighteenth century as authors, both women and men, compose pastorals, pastoral elegies, and epics, all placing on their works a distinctly American stamp and all displaying, by the same token, an attempt to rearticulate elements from the ancient classical world by defining and shaping the idea of Americanness as a combination of Adam and Aeneas. Eunice Bourne's *Fishing Lady* becomes emblematic of this self-definition whereby transplanted Europeans metamorphosize into Americans. Depicting Martyr's golden age myth but replacing Native Americans with these metamorphosized colonial Americans, Bourne's embroidery may be described in the same words Martyr used to tell of Native Americans. In the second book of the first *Decade*, Martyr writes in Eden's translation, "The inhabitantes of these Ilandes have byn ever soo used to live at libertie, in playe and pastyme," just as Bourne's Early Americans stroll through idyllic groves and sit by the side of pools bearing succulent fish ready for the hook.

In stark contrast, however, Martyr's "simple sowles," satisfied with "a fewe clothes" become supplanted by men and women sporting the latest styles, in short wearing many clothes, perhaps too many for the best comfort in Bourne's warm pastoral landscape. Like Martyr, nevertheless, Bourne's "simple sowles" appear content and not to require "the use of pestiferous monye." Indeed, "they seeme to lyve in that goulden worlde of the which owlde wryters speake so much: wherein men lyved simplye and innocentlye without inforcement of lawes, without quarrelinge Iudges and libelles, contente onely to satisfie nature, without further vexation for knowelege of thinges to come." As well, Bourne's pastoral displays no indication of a Judaeo-Christian church, thrusting her version of American colonial pastoral still closer to Vergil's classical vision, one which also parallels Martyr's "goulden worlde."

Reflecting upon Bourne's representation of pastoral within eighteenth-century America soon leads one to query how precisely it is that these figures can continue to don all their finery. In the real world, replication of such an idyllic scene costs in time, effort and money; so "pestiferous monye" does insinuate itself into this pastoral world of calm content. The golden world described by Martyr also erodes as the *Decades*' author muses: "And surely if they [the Native Americans] had receaved owre religion, I wolde thinke their life moste happye of all men" (70–71). The implication here is that only benefit of conversion to Christianity can lead to true happiness. Martyr of course does not move on to acknowledge that all Native Americans had and have their own religion which most now as then prefer to keep.

While Bourne's ideal classical paradise is soon to become flanked by Spencer Phips's "Proclamation" or advertisement for the seizure of Penobscot scalps, Martyr's "goulden worlde" almost immediately becomes blackened by what David E. Stannard calls "the most massive act of genocide in the history of the world" (x). In his recent *American Holocaust: The Conquest of the New*

World, Stannard projects that, as early as the end of the sixteenth century, of the 100,000,000 to 120,000,000 Native inhabitants before Columbus's arrival, "somewhere between 60,000,000 and 80,000,000 natives from those lands [colonized by the Spanish and Portuguese: the Indies, Mexico, Central and South America] were dead." Still more horrible is Stannard's next statement: "Even then, the carnage was not over" (95). Surely Phips's broadside suggests how the carnage extended into succeeding centuries.

Just so was Martyr's golden age description of the New World blasted beyond sensible conception. Martyr's golden age fable and its subsequent devastation at the hands of invading Europeans, nevertheless, loudly herald the condition that all present-day states of North and South America have been founded upon an imperialistic, Eurocentric perception of cultural supremacy. These invaders so devastated the Native populations that no significant Native American presence challenged the appropriation of their own oppressed discourse by these same invaders, now become citizens of colonial regimes. What Edward Said has described in numerous sites within his published writings is true of the countries of the Americas, that is, that the oppressors of a people often, after that people's defeat, assume the fable or story of the oppressed. For as we have seen, the mantle of Peter Martyr's golden age Native Americans came into the possession of Bourne's Early Americans. Later in this same century we have observed that colonists becoming independent citizens of the newly formed United States adopt the English language and the English common law tradition and promptly begin to deny their British sources (e.g., Noah Webster's insistence upon an American English).

The myth of Aeneas provides no little authority for this acceptance and denial maneuver when we recall that Juno convinces Jupiter to promise her that the Latins will not be forced to give up their language after Aeneas's conquest. As in the *Aeneid*'s last book, then, wherein Aeneas and his band become metamorphosized into Latins or Romans, Washington and his revolutionaries retain the language, which was already in place, as metamorphosized United States' citizens. In other words, such Europeans as Peter Martyr first invented America in terms of the golden age/classical mythos, then proceeded in fact to destroy that idyllic world by means of their own avarice. Subsequently the New World's new possessors denied any such destruction by assuming the trappings of that same golden age/classical mythos. So we come to understand that this acceptance and denial methodology has been built into the American mythos from the first moments of America's invention.

The result of this kind of appropriation leads not at all to the fulfillment of Martyr's "goulden worlde" but to a reality ever dogged by its unacknowledged motives, those of greed and more greed, but somewhat appeased by the vestiges of that idyllic classical world reappropriated after the radical shift in discourse as the Adamic paradise of neverending possibility. This faith in the possibility for some kind of pastoral, golden age paradise is perhaps the strongest pillar of the American self; indeed, the notion of change, the possibility for metamorphosis, is built into our Constitution. Like it or not, this peculiar manner by which Americans have appropriated or rearticulated Martyr's golden world identifies this version of the myth as a distinctly American property.

Marginalization of American Literature before 1800 and a Usable Past

What if Americans began to lift the siege that has hidden the classical half of the American self? Would an acknowledged golden age/classical mode of discourse, albeit a tarnished one, register as any less an American property? Would exposure of the general denial of America's classical origins lead to a healthier, richer, more usable past?

Time after time, the preceding discussion has exposed as exaggerated or false charges that Early Americans slavishly imitated British models. The body of literature recovered by the Adam and Aeneas paradeictic is simply too large to label accidental, and too consistent in its return to classical models to dismiss as merely the product of an occasional brush with the Aeneas myth. In other words, most Early American authors treated herein sought to be Americans by means of their pens. Their literary works represent their dynamic efforts to separate themselves from the imperial British. This urge toward self-sufficiency moved them to rework or rearticulate the two grand mythic strands of the West, the myths of Adam and Aeneas, in such a way that what emerged no longer was British or Continental but distinctively American. Surely such measured, conscious efforts should not be relegated to marginal status. Yet precisely this fate has been shared by virtually all American authors who died before 1800.

Early American literature's marginal status in literary anthologies has been addressed by others, such as Raymond F. Dolle and R. C. DeProspo, whose work is particularly meritorious. Not as much has been done with literary histories covering this field. Before we investigate the literary histories, however, a few observations must be made regarding how editors of literary anthologies handle the specific issue of classicism in Early American literature.

Lest any should doubt that Early American literature occupies a marginal status and that this marginalization is zealously maintained, consider the following example. Most current college anthologies quote from Cotton Mather's important "Introduction" to *Magnalia Christi Americana,* but all omit section 2 of the "Introduction," in which, as noted in chapter 4, Mather ascribes the virtue of Vergil's pietas to all living on the American strand. Mather accomplishes this ascription in no meager or summary fashion; rather, in the following manner he quotes lines from the *Aeneid:*

> The Reader will doubtless desire to know, what it was that
>
> —tot Volvere casus
> Insignes Pietate Viros, tot adire Labores,
> Impulerit
>
> (impelled men distinguished in devotion [to the gods, to the family and to the country] to endure so many misfortunes, to encounter so many hardships) (25)

The Latin of this passage, which comprises the major portion of Vergil's four-line invocation in which the poet names his hero's primary virtue, Mather slightly rewrites, so that Vergil's "insignem pietate virum" becomes the Puritan writer's "insignes pietate viros." Vergil's singular nouns Mather makes plural. In this way he invests the first generation of New England settlers and their progeny with the virtue of pietas, appropriating the central Roman virtue to the New England adventurers.

This passage, which present-day editors who quote from the "Introduction" all omit, is a pivotal element within *Magnalia* and arguably was of major importance in establishing the American self. Yet few, if any, undergraduate students will ever see this passage or come to grasp its significance.

This illustration is only one among countless similar instances which could be cited. In short, the style of handling classical material in American literature is either to omit it altogether, as in the case just given, or to treat that material as trivial. Never is such material acknowledged as important or even essential to the text. Undergraduates are thus taught that classicism contributes little of significance in American texts, when in fact it often makes substantial commentary upon the American self.

While several writers of recent literary histories do mention classicism within Early American literature, all denigrate its recurring presence. Richard Ruland and Malcolm Bradbury are only the least condescending of recent historians when they observe, "The promise of a golden age that would replace European decay and monarchical institutions and call forth its own heroic epic was to obsess the eighteenth century on both sides of the Atlantic." Describing the nascent spirit of nationalism in America during the early to middle 1770s, they remark, "The index of the golden age was a balanced progress, and so in incorporating the neoclassical ideal, the poets of America began to interpret the colonies in the language of heroic and pastoral epic."

They contend that "secular epic [not really an epic but a long narrative poem] gets off to a decidedly shaky start in Roger Wolcott's 1500-line *Brief Account of the Agency of the Honourable John Winthrop* (1725)." Both ignore the work of Benjamin Tompson and forget Cotton Mather's contribution to the American epic.[1] Then they conclude hastily with a quip: "Rarely were the Muses summoned as frequently across treacherous waters as now, but they remained curiously English Muses and apparently loath to travel" (48–49). Most significantly, these historians quote but little from Early American texts.

In the usually reliable *Benet's Reader's Encyclopedia of American Literature* (1991), Hayden Carruth and George Perkins assert in their essay "Poetry: Before 1960" that classicism "broke upon America . . . certainly not before 1745 when *Poems on Several Occasions* by John Adams (not the future President) appeared." Carruth and Perkins then claim that "these contained a trace of classical delicacy and regularity." Our examination of Adams's classicism in chapter 4 has demonstrated that this poet displayed considerable sophistication, for example, in his English-language versions of six odes from Horace. Without quoting a line of poetry, these authors finalize their judgment upon Early American use of classical elements by declaring, "Classicism was never more than a password to the *haut ton*, sincerely as it may have been imitated on occasion" (858). Surely the discussion in part 2 of this book proves beyond doubt that classicism served Early American authors from about 1720 to 1784 as much more than high fashion. In fact, we have observed that classicism determined American thought and action in this period.

Without quoting a line of poetry from the era of Edward Taylor to that of the Connecticut Wits, Albert Gelpi, writing a historical survey of American poetry history for the highly influential *The New Princeton Encyclopedia of Poetry and Poetics* (1993), polishes off American classicism in this brief comment: "Whatever the political differences with the mother country, the models for eighteenth-century poetry were unashamedly English: the neoclassicism of Pope and Swift, the pastoralism of Thompson and Gray, the hymnology of Watts" (48). While each of these British authors named was well known to most literate Americans of the eighteenth century, I take particular exception to this historian's claim that "the models for eighteenth-century poetry were unashamedly English." The first objection one might well raise to Gelpi's curt dismissal is to the implication that Americans, then as perhaps now, have something for which they should be ashamed regarding an alleged subservience to British literary models.

Indeed, the predicament of marginalization itself casts its dreary pall over Early American literature. If, as I have argued throughout this work, the models for a great deal of the poetry written by Americans were in fact not British, then much of the agency which has besieged this body of letters must begin to relax. I have never tried to maintain that British literature and culture had *no* effect whatsoever upon the colonization of the Atlantic communities. To be certain, such a position, were it seriously held, could only prove as ludicrous as it would be preposterous. Pastoral elegies which do not follow British models were, nevertheless, composed, as well as were identifiably American pastorals, both subversive and naive, epics and literary independence poems—most of these works shaped by a conscious attempt to demonstrate a palpable independence from British models. How could such an effort not have been motivated by "political differences"—these differences having arisen over a long course of disaffection from the Mother country's perceived abuse of her "child"?

As Phillis Wheatley put it in the poem "America" (1768), the fledgling country

> . . . grew up daily virtuous as he grew
> Fearing his Strength which she undoubted knew
> She laid some taxes on her darling son
> And would have laid another act there on
> Amend your manners I'll the taxes remove
> Was said with seeming Sympathy and Love. (134)

At the tender age of fifteen, this highly political poet already has learned the lesson of dissembling governments which treat a colony with "seeming Sympathy." While the ultimate model for Wheatley's couplets here well may have been Pope, it does not necessarily follow that this poet became a derivative imitator of the British poet's sonorous lines. As I have demonstrated in "Phillis Wheatley and Mather Byles: A Study in Literary Relationship," there are many more contiguities of phrasing and vocabulary between Wheatley and the poems of Byles (a much older Congregational minister and part-time poet of Boston) than between Wheatley and Pope, Milton, Thomson, or even the King James Bible. This same article concludes that Wheatley designed her *Poems on Various Subjects, Religious and Moral* (1773) after Byles's *Poems on Several Occasions* (1744), thereby describing yet another example of Early American authors' tendencies toward self-referentiality and their determination *not* to seek out British sources.

In chapters 4 and 6, we observed that Wheatley's sophisticated rearticulation of classical materials reveals an artist whose particular stance against oppression reflects her experience as a slave. Yet Ruland and Bradbury remark of her that, while she quickly learned "the prevailing conventions of Augustan verse," these conventions "scarcely allowed of any private voice or any expression of her own condition." They also assert that her "work is primarily a display of the complex web of classical allusions and elegant circumlocutions she had mastered" (69). Unlike other historians who take the trouble to mention

Wheatley, Ruland and Bradbury at least quote from her work. They misstep, however, when they claim that Wheatley, unaware of the irony she allegedly conjures, uses "golden-haired Muses" in "Liberty and Peace" to "celebrate a freedom that goes unquestioned by the author's own situation" (70). These two imply that Wheatley is hopelessly insipid, when in fact this subtle poet renders the goddess Freedom in terms of the golden-haired dawn of Wheatley's own mother. Wheatley does not confuse the Muse with her golden-haired Freedom/Aurora; nor is this impeccable classicist confused in her application of classical materials. Ruland and Bradbury are hardly the first who have failed to take the trouble to read this excellent poet closely enough to discover that the idea of freedom is the central subject of her entire oeuvre. Once we recover the secular, classical half of the American self, we find that Wheatley's oeuvre realizes her grand theme in the construction of their intertextual, classical epic.

Wheatley's use of classical materials does not suggest a derivative imitator of British models, but rather identifies an accomplished artist in complete control of her sources. In his history, *American Poetry: The Puritans Through Walt Whitman* (1988), Alan Shucard declares, "There is, in fact, little overt reason to suggest that Phillis Wheatley thought that there was much wrong with the social order" (70). Moreover, he says, "Her work, like most of that of the period, was in couplets, blank verse, and other traditional cadences frequently rife with classical allusions that could do little to support an illusion of originality" (71). We now know that this Early American intellectual was vitally concerned to do what she could to insure that the American quest for freedom included her black brothers and sisters. The products of her pen employed in the service of this objective certainly identify her as a recreative original genius.

I make much of Wheatley's ill use at the hands of latter-day critics and historians because her predicament typifies that of the entire body of marginalized Early American authors, as well as Early American literature and culture as a whole. Indeed, Early American authors before the 1770s generally have been perceived as little concerned "with the social order" or the status quo, and as wholly lacking in originality; they do not qualify to be considered serious artists. Hayden Carruth and George Perkins bluntly state, "One may say two things about colonial poetry in America: all of it copied English models, and almost all of it was bad" (857). As these two do not reproduce any of this completely unoriginal and "bad" poetry they claim to have found, we are left to puzzle over just what may constitute a "bad" form of poetry. Is Early American poetry "bad" because it often is composed in heroic couplets? Phillis Wheatley certainly has been condemned on numerous occasions for this "sin." Or are we dealing here with a dogmatic conviction that any poetry cast in the so-called neoclassical mode must be dismissed out of hand, without a reading? If so, and I strongly suspect this pitiful circumstance does describe the condition here, then where is the logic of such a finally insupportable position?

From the days of Moses Coit Tyler, whose late-nineteenth-century taste for Victorian literature led him to denigrate the entire neoclassical mode, the general trend has been to put down American literature written before 1800 as clearly not like the preferred, later mode. With almost constant repetition of this little-challenged chorus over many years, what once was a general consensus now has become absolute wisdom. Yet the most serious lapse in this accumulated wisdom has been its failure actually to examine the alleged offenders on their own terms.

Philosophic Solitude, by the poet and politician William Livingston, for example, is described by Donald Barlow Stauffer, in his *A Short History of American Poetry* (1974), as "a bland reworking of John Pomfret's widely read 'Choice.'" Upon close scrutiny, however, we find Livingston's long poem to be, in part, a reaction against Pomfret's earlier poem. And the future New Jersey governor's rebellious rejection of Pomfret's preference for monarchy over republicanism is anything but "bland." Without quoting a line, Stauffer concludes of *Philosophic Solitude* that it is "interesting because of the writers he mentions as his choices for his personal library: Milton, Dryden, Pope, and Isaac Watts among the English poets, and Bacon, Boyle, Newton, and Locke among the philosophers" (37). No mention of Vergil, whom Livingston names "prince" of poets, who "shou'd wear the laurel'd crown,/ And other bards pay homage to his throne" (166), the British Milton included. For that matter, we find that Livingston has much more in common with Horace's odes on contentment and country joys, and with the general pastoral mode, than with the British Pomfret.

Obviously, none of these historians of Early American literature has made a serious effort to study the texts whose history they claim to record. Rather, they apparently wish only to perpetuate what we now know to be a fraudulent myth regarding Early American authors: that they were universally derivative and unoriginal; that they imitated British models exclusively; that these models always were superior to the allegedly vapid American imitations; and that Early American authors lacked the recreative energies required to experiment or to rise above the literary conventions of British neoclassicism. *Without doubt, this myth, in one or more ways, accurately characterized some Early American authors—but not all.* This myth of an allegedly universal, derivative literary culture has been largely responsible for the loss of a usable past within the history of Early American letters. Regrettably, few now would question the apparently self-evident veracity of Ruland and Bradbury's proclamation:

> The peaking of American literary power just before the middle of the nineteenth century still seems such a novel and remarkable event that it remains the heartland for *all* discussion of American literature, out of which arises *any* understanding of the originality of American writing, *any* sense of a modern or modernist lineage. (Emphasis mine; 106)

What becomes of the clear, ringing certainty of their proclamation, which excludes any and all possible alternative avenues of approach, following recovery of the Adam and Aeneas dialectic? We discover, for example, that such inarguably great authors as Melville and Hawthorne were not sculpting a wholly new, distinctly American literary idiom out of a vacuum. Rather, each, along with their contemporaries, is keenly and respectfully engaged in responding to an older American literary tradition, one which shaped the United States Constitution and left behind a discernible and dynamic literary legacy.

It may well be that this earlier tradition, beginning with Peter Martyr, does not quite match the energy of Ruland and Bradbury's "peaking of American literary power." However, this suggested contest between the old and the new does not address the salient point to be made here and now: simply put, an earlier period of American literary history witnessed years of a struggle to be free of European literary domination. Contrary to conventional wisdom, those who participated in this struggle for literary independence did not buckle under the pressure, implicit in colonialism, to adopt the literary (and cultural) mode of the oppressors. Rather, these authors, early on, heroically determined to seek their own vehicles of expression. These new paths of expression often were marked by courageous attempts to experiment, to flex and bend the available tools of imaginative literary discourse, in order to create something new—something not British or Continental or even classical, but American.

Before we can set aside the clear, ringing certainty of Ruland and Bradbury's proclamation, we must consider one additional problem it raises. This one is not as troublesome as the denial of an earlier, vigorous American classicism, but it nonetheless serves as a significant premise in the devalorization of Early American literary studies. Implicit within the notion that the authors of the American Renaissance constitute "the heartland for all discussion of American literature" is the perception that all American writing, both before and after, somehow becomes subordinated to this "heartland." While I am content to leave the implications of Ruland's "heartland" notion regarding "a modern or modernist lineage" to specialists in the literature of the late nineteenth and twentieth centuries, I must address the impact this notion has—and for years has had—for Early American literary studies.

If the literature of the American Renaissance is the reference point for all discussion of American literature, then it follows that the literature written by Americans before this energetic moment must be not only subordinate to, but also less than, the literary products of the later era. This thinking leads all too readily to what I think of as the old "X predicts Y" pattern, according to which author "X" and her or his work is only "good" insofar as he or she predicts author "Y" and her or his work. In their discussion of Jonathan Edwards, for example, Ruland and Bradbury appear to "validate" Edwards as a subject in their history insofar as his work serves as an "anticipation of the transcendental Romanticism of the next century" (39).

One of the most renowned literary historians of American poetry also happens to be one of the most prominent progenitors of the "X predicts Y" pattern. Hyatt H. Waggoner, in *American Poets*, his long but selective history, after discussing the poems and poetic career of Edward Taylor for some nine pages, concludes that Taylor should be included as a legitimate member of the American poetry canon (he seems less certain about Anne Bradstreet, who gets less than three pages), only because it is possible, with much effort, to find in his work premonitions of the poetry and poets of the American Renaissance. In Waggoner's own words, "Only when we think of his style in the largest sense—of the purely poetic aspect [whatever *that* is; Waggoner is vague on this point] of his poetry—are we likely to think of him as belonging in the company of the chief American poets." In case we have missed the point, Waggoner elaborates:

> For in his attitude toward language and poetic forms Taylor shows us what will later become recognizable as the peculiarly American attitude, an attitude compounded of perhaps equal parts of Puritan eschatology and Transcendental seeking. Taylor's verbal coinages, archaisms and often personal meanings, his readiness to drop the meter when the thought demands it, his way of twisting, ignoring or distorting any convention that gets in his way—all this and more makes us think of Emerson and later American poets. If his doctrines are Puritan, his attitude toward language and forms of verse might just as well be called Transcendental. (16)

While I am somewhat mystified by the phrase "all this and more," I am left puzzling particularly over the phrase "all this." Can Waggoner seriously be asking his readers to believe that only American authors conjure "verbal coinages," persist in the use of "archaisms," impose upon their texts "personal meanings," alter the regularity of meter as their imaginations demand, or have their way with any convention, no matter how sacrosanct? One has only to stroll casually through Spenser's *Faerie Queen* or Shakespeare's sonnets to witness "all this." The notion that Taylor's "attitude toward language and forms of verse," as described by Waggoner, should be labeled "Transcendental" I find bewildering.

Waggoner nevertheless builds upon this infirm foundation when he repeats his earlier observation, but with an interesting interpolation: "Taylor's anticipations of what was destined to become the main tradition in American poetry—insofar as American poetry is not simply a rather inferior branch of British poetry—are somewhat more apparent in the way he uses language and his attitude toward poetic forms than they are in the substance of his poems" (22–23). After embellishing upon his addition of the remark regarding American poets' dependence upon British models, Waggoner compares Taylor to the English George Herbert and concludes:

> Clearly, Taylor is a lesser poet than either Herbert or Emerson, for entirely different reasons, but comparison of his work with Herbert's tends to lead to the conclusion that Taylor's is hardly worth reading being only a very inferior imitation; while comparison with Emerson makes him seem a sort of poetic pioneer. (24)

Waggoner completes the "X predicts Y" schema by adding, "Comparisons are strategic as well as instructive" (24).

Why must we compare Taylor to either Herbert or Emerson? As supposedly skilled readers of literature, should we not focus our attention first upon Taylor? If we do, we discover that he maintains an acceptance and denial pattern in his poems and sermons, and that he has a fascinating fondness for the classical form of the *meditatio* and for other classical materials, upon which he makes tropes to use like symbols. Perhaps such a reading will help free Taylor's very good poetry from the fetters of not only the detestable "X predicts Y" schema, but also the hegemonic Adamic myth which has prevented us from learning that Edward Taylor, along with other poets treated in this book, is a much more complex, original artist than we have suspected.

Waggoner's British comparison leads directly to consideration of our last literary history, this one a special case. Somewhat disconcerting is the appearance in 1988 of the ninth volume in *The New Pelican Guide to English Literature* series. Boris Ford is general editor of this ninth volume, *American Literature*. Despite centuries of effort to separate English literature from American, Ford writes in his "General Introduction" that *The New Pelican Guide to English Literature* is "not, be it emphasized, a guide to the literature even of England, but to literature in English." Even so, he still calls American literature, as the series's title demands, "a large and important part of English literature" (ix). While I am prompted to quip, "What part of this English literature would Ford dare to identify as unimportant?" I am left to observe the obvious—that Ford relegates American literature to some vague corner under the umbrella term "English literature."

Surely this study has destroyed the myth that Early American literature is derivative of British models; in fact, that body of letters manifests an identifiably American classicism. Our discussion above has just as certainly invalidated the long-practiced "X predicts Y" schema that tries to force us all to consider Early American authors good only if they foreshadow some quality better expressed by an author in the American Renaissance. These results should help present-day Americans understand how Early Americans exerted efforts to secure their literary independence. Rather than causing Americans to feel shame for a so-called derivative and therefore unusable past, destruction of these two fraudulent myths should lead Americans to take pride in their wholly usable Early American past.

Some Consequences of Recovery

In what follows, I am not going to try to answer all questions raised by recovery of the Adam and Aeneas dialectic. Indeed, this paradeictic is so new that I am uncertain what all the questions are or may prove to be, much less how possible answers may evolve. My intention is to suggest, not to foreclose, thought. Perhaps most practical for such an interrogative procedure is the format of a question, followed by a tentative response. Four questions strike me as most urgent. Both the questions and the tentative responses are constructed to encourage lively debate and constructive exchange, and not in any sense to terminate argument. The first query follows upon the heels of taking pride in a wholly usable Early American literary past.

1. *How does recovery of the Adam and Aeneas dialectic re-form our understanding of the American Renaissance and its authors?*

Acknowledging that, for a long period, eighteenth-century America enjoyed a flourishing classicism of its own construction, a period characterized throughout by many concerted efforts to achieve literary independence in anticipation of political independence, reorients the entire era that F. O. Matthiessen has designated the American Renaissance. This reorientation embraces two imperatives: first, that this earlier period be appreciated for itself and on its own terms; and second, that all American authors be reevaluated according to their knowledge of these earlier authors and their praxis of classical discourse. Even though Emerson and Melville (in "Hawthorne and His Mosses"), among other writers, thought it necessary to redeclare literary independence, they themselves were, to a certain extent, victims of the radical shift in discourse, of the post-independence denigration of the writing and discourse of Americans before the 1780s as something not quite yet American. After all, did we not find in chapters 9 and 10 that Hawthorne and Melville display somewhat ambivalent attitudes toward these earlier authors, while at the same time exhibiting a clear reverence for Washington's Adamicized pietas (*pietas instauratio emendata*)? Significantly, both writers appear to be aware of the Adam and the Aeneas dialectic. This reorientation process, brought on by recovery of America's classical origins, urges a general rereading of all authors of this period, and by extension all succeeding American writers, as in varying degrees they address the tenets of the American Aeneas and this discourse's interplay with the American Adam.

The playing out of this reorientation instructs us that the literature of the American Renaissance was not created in a literary vacuum—that is, in an atmosphere of pastlessness. Indeed, reclamation of this usable, classical past validates Matthiessen's term for what many consider to have been the most productive era of American literary history.

Another question, whose response would occupy too much space for investigation here, is simply, "How does recovery of a flourishing classicism upon the American strand reorient our thinking regarding an American Romanticism?"

In any event, if literature is thought to serve as an often reliable touchstone for what develops culturally during the period of its provenance, then transition to a consideration of American culture should follow as a matter of course. The remaining three questions, therefore, take up various facets of the American cultural *selves*.

2. *Is the Adam and Aeneas dialectic multicultural?*

In the construction of this work, I share José David Saldivar's carefully articulated "desire to challenge the narrow Anglocentric concept of 'tradition' and the linear view of history on which it is predicated" (xv). One immediately self-evident result of reclaiming the Adam and Aeneas dialectic is the termination of any possibility of a "linear view of history."

In the beginning of this book, I proposed a metaphor for understanding the dynamic operation of this dialectic: the three-dimensional human DNA molecule. As in human creation itself, wherein two strands of genetic material come together in such a way that an entirely new organism results, so do the two strands of Adam and Aeneas intermingle in tensive interaction to create the American self or selves. The explicit possibility that a self can be always new (or always renewed) is intentional here. This metaphor includes a recognition that these two strands originate from two distinct and identifiable parents. In describing American multicultural society, it is probably best, healthiest, to think of these two strands, Adam and Aeneas, as genetically dissimilar parents of two different races. In consequence, they produce a hybrid progeny. This understanding of the Adam and Aeneas dialectic, in and of itself, explodes the "Anglocentric concept of 'tradition'" and places emphasis upon the multicultural American self or selves.

The Adam and Aeneas dialectic should serve as an enabling dynamic for interpreting America's multicultural society precisely because it excludes no one and includes everyone. All along the way in this work, I have made an effort not merely *not* to ignore multicultural issues, but positively to incorporate them. In consideration of the work by Phillis Wheatley, for example, I have been scrupulous to assess her poetry and prose in terms of her sex and her race—not merely to investigate her superior manipulation of the Adam and Aeneas strands of Americanness. At strategic intervals, I also have emphasized Native American issues. While these obvious multicultural concerns are not accidental, Wheatley has represented my principal career interest to this point. My work on Native American affairs stems from recent probings into my own biological origins among the native peoples of this continent. The point here is that the multicultural concerns evident in this book do not represent responses to trends or fashions; rather, they are motivated by a personal conviction that these concerns are among the most compelling of our era.

The mere presence of multicultural groups brings up the issue of language, an issue that Vergil raises within the *Aeneid*. There, in book XII, Vergil places in the mouth of Juno a request to Jupiter that the Trojans adopt the language already in place—that is, the language of the Latins. Here Vergil is making a clear cultural statement, one designed to support the Roman ideal of cultural cohesiveness, believed to be a consequence of practicing a single, universal language. Explicit in this same passage in the *Aeneid* is Jupiter's requirement that the Roman people arise from a mixing of Trojan and Latin blood. Multicultural concerns, then, are evident in the myth of Aeneas. I submit that, as a result, multicultural concerns always have been present within the secular half of the American self, whether explicit or implicit.

3. How can lifting the siege covering the American Aeneas serve American culture?

In his timely and provocative magnum opus, *Culture and Imperialism*, Edward Said proposes that,

> if you read and interpret modern European and American culture as having had something to do with imperialism, it becomes incumbent upon you also to reinterpret the canon in the light of texts whose place there has been insufficiently linked to, insufficiently weighted toward the expansion of Europe. (60)

Behind this significant interpretation lies the idea that European and American expansion across the globe has been predicated upon the tenets of empire described and taught over the past two thousand years by Vergil's *Aeneid*.[2] I have no quarrel with this premise. Before we can grasp the full impact of Said's probing exhortation and then act upon it, however, we must be convinced that the United States, all along, has been motivated by this turn toward empire. Like Said, I do not find the American people to be so convinced. Said cogently describes this denial:

> "In the United States," according to historian Richard W. Van Alstyne in *The Rising American Empire*, "it is almost heresy to describe the nation as an empire." Yet he shows that the early founders of the Republic, including George Washington, characterized the country as an empire, with a subsequent foreign policy that renounced revolution and promoted imperial growth. He quotes one statesman after another arguing, as Reinhold Niebuhr put it caustically, that the country was "God's American Israel," whose "mission" was to be "trustee under God of the civilization of the world." (295)

What has occurred here has been brought about by an acceptance of what Early Americans viewed as their reading of Vergil's epic when applied to their own predicament and subsequently by a denial, particularly during and after the radical shift, of that classical source, among others. Recovery of America's classical origins, then, should promote the honest reassessment of American motives and aspirations that Said correctly demands. The path toward this reclamation runs through many obstacles, two of which include America's stubborn anti-intellectualism and its tendency to equate its objectives with the Adamic compulsion, in Niebuhr's phrasing, "to be 'trustee under God of the civilization of the world.'"

While we all need to learn tolerance, we also must discourage intolerance. Earlier, in chapters 5 and 7, we spoke of how and when America's faith of rebellion became transformed into a faith in America. This faith in America, brought about by a denigration of classical discourse and a valorizing of Adamic discourse, has been insuring American cultural cohesiveness now for over two hundred years. At the present time, however, this Adamic faith in America frequently serves, as it always has before, as a center for an unreasoning, fanatical motive to action. While such a motive arguably once functioned well to maintain cultural cohesion, it now threatens to widen rifts or divisions within our American cultural selves to the dimensions of an abyss. For example, recent efforts by many well-intentioned intellectuals to celebrate cultural differences increasingly appear to have been sabotaged in the public sector by fanatical groups bent on blowing those points of cultural difference out of all proportion, to the extent that difference, which should be a positive stimulant for growth, is quickly becoming a major rationale for absolute divisiveness.

Both fronts—religious fanaticism and patriotic fanaticism—require a tempering or balancing mechanism. This balancing or tempering can be achieved through lifting the siege that has obscured the Aeneas discourse. Recovery of the classical origins of the American self or selves can assist in creating a better system of checks and balances. In fact, this recovery can become a valuable part of the "theoretical work" which Edward Said insists "must begin to formulate the relationship between empire and culture" (60).

Certainly a system of checks and balances is built into the dialectic of Adam and Aeneas. On the one hand, for example, the classical perspective advances the premise, probably first articulated by the Greek sophist Protagoras, that "man is the measure of all things." On the other hand, Adamic discourse ever subordinates human beings to deity, even when some pompous or misled fanatics—a David Koresh, for example—presume to speak for the deity. The one promotes the notion that human beings can rise to the level of perfection, while the other discourages pride and encourages humility before Awe. Alone, however, either is capable of fostering its own fanaticism. All attempts to achieve perfection are doomed to failure, because human beings finally are only imperfect beings. And all attempts to force human beings into some single, dogmatic conformity inevitably are doomed to the same failure. While it is true that today too many want others to tell them how to believe and act, many others will never capitulate to coercion. The two discourses, then, blend to demand a reexamination of human motives and actions; together they promote self-examination and critical thinking. Together they urge a critical patriotism and a critical religious consciousness. Again, awareness of the Adam and Aeneas dialectic can facilitate constructive human interaction.

What we need now is a patriotism bereft of fanaticism or patriotic fervor. This critical patriotism, one informed regarding the illusions inherent in all ideologies, or what Said calls the narratives of culture and imperialism that are used "to block other narratives from forming and emerging" (xiii), must come about not to destroy the edifice of the faith in America but to repair it, to refurbish it, and to construct an America re-formed according to the present-day imperatives of tolerance and inclusiveness. Said instructs us:

> Loyalty and patriotism should be based on a critical sense of what the facts are, and what, as residents of this shrinking and depleted planet, Americans owe their neighbors and the rest of mankind. Uncritical solidarity with the policy of the moment, especially when it is so unimaginably costly, cannot be allowed to rule. (301)

As it would appear that many of the principal problems Americans create for themselves appear to stem from their propensity to accept cultural forms from other cultures but then to claim these forms as their own property, action cannot move forward in this necessary direction until Americans reclaim their actual identity, centered upon the dialectic of Adam and Aeneas. Edward Said describes quite well the contemporary predicament concerning the naming of an American identity when he remarks, "Before we can agree on what the American identity is made of, we have to concede that as an immigrant settler society superimposed on the ruins of a considerable native presence, American identity is too varied to be a unitary and homogenous thing" (xxv).

Indeed, if the truth be told, no cultural identity is homogeneous; all are heterogeneous hybrids. As Said insists, "Cultural experience or indeed every cultural form is radically, quintessentially hybrid" (58). The notion that there exists, or ever could have existed, some pure American essence arising out of the crucible of an Adamic errand into the wilderness must now, with recovery of Peter Martyr's invention of America in terms of the Aeneas myth, forever be laid to rest.

If all cultures are in fact hybrids, does it follow that the possibility for exceptionalism no longer exists? Even if this cultural principle—that all cultures are hybrids, a premise upon which Said and most other cultural critics today begin their critical investigations—is true, people within the boundaries of a particular nation seem to be compelled to discover to themselves an identity, a means of separating themselves from the rest of the globe, an identity which moves beyond mere political separation. Said exclaims in frustration:

> My impression is that more effort is spent in sustaining the connection, bolstering the idea that to be Syrian, Iraqi, Egyptian, or Saudi is a sufficient end, rather than in thinking critically, even audaciously, about the national program itself. Identity, always identity, over and above knowing about others. (299)

One way to assuage Said's frustration regarding the identity issue may be not to place the question of identity "over and above knowing about others" but simply before any attempt to move beyond national identity. Throughout his work, Said has been scrupulous to place in the foreground his personal identity as an expatriate Palestinian who has become an American citizen. He writes as if from a critical perspective rendered more acute and objective by its locus in the space between two apparently disparate cultural vantage points. In general, Americans are not so sure-footed when trying to explain their identity to others or even to themselves, and this difficulty derives in large part from their denial of one-half of the American self, the classical half. Any people so uncertain of its origins as to have overlooked half of those origins is going to be confused, and frustration will inevitably obfuscate any attempt to move beyond its incomplete identity. Let us first locate our true origins, our true selves; then we can the better muster the stamina and maturity to move toward "knowing about others."

In other words, I think it is human nature to demand a substantial perception of the self; this demand is essentially a healthy one. Only upon this basis can human beings properly or "even audaciously" learn about others. So perhaps a modicum of patience is indicated here. Most would agree that an inaccurate or inadequate perception of self can only lead to uncertainty and excessive suspicion when dealing with others. I say "excessive suspicion" only because I wish to distinguish a cautious, sharply objective regard for others from an incautious, distorted paranoia. Again what is needed is a critical patriotism, one tempered by compassion, when dealing with other nations of our shrinking globe.

If an American identity is to reach its mature potential, it must arise from an informed awareness of the dynamic interplay of two principal, inclusive modes of discourse, the Adamic and the classical. The unique blend of these two modes, highlighted by a Washingtonian pietas, strongly attests something equally unique about the American character. This *something* has become attenuated, not by the many cultural and/or ethnic voices which do deserve to be heard, but by a denial of America's classical multiculturalism. *Once American exceptionalism is redefined as one or more traits within a hybrid identity, then Americans can begin actually to know themselves*. For the most part, this approach is, I think, in accord with Said's recommendations. Such an acknowledgment of self reclaims and/or explains that, from the very beginning, America has "had something to do with imperialism," as Said points out in the quotation at the beginning of this section.

Recovery of our classical origins should, as well, lead to a reinterpretation of the present canon of American literature. This reinterpretation will inevitably bring about a recognition that the American canon, however it may be changed as a result of recovering classical discourse, has always been linked to ancient classical texts, particularly Vergil's *Aeneid*, just as it has always owed an immense debt to the Bible. The implications of this recognition should effect changes in our elementary and secondary school curricula. If the Latin language itself does not begin to play a substantial role in this revision process, certainly classical culture and its history, sociology, and politics must begin to receive serious attention.

Within our public school systems, emphatic attention to classical studies in some form can assist in accomplishing what Said demands: "A new critical consciousness [which] can be achieved only by revised attitudes to education" (330). Such a program should stress how particular classical forms and/or modes of thought influenced certain actions within the development of the American self or selves. Given a program of this sort in the public schools, we will be better able to appreciate, as Said so intelligently urges, "other identities, peoples, cultures," and, in fact, begin "to study how, despite their differences, they always have overlapped one another, through unhierarchical influence, crossing, incorporation, recollection, deliberate forgetfulness, and of course conflict" (330–31).

4. *How does the Adam and Aeneas dialectic interplay with contemporary approaches to American literature and culture?*

Our postmodern age has produced almost universal dissatisfaction with past constructions of American literary and cultural histories. This dissatisfaction is justified, for none of these appears able to stand up to contemporary historiographic and literary scrutiny. As these older representations have been discredited, several attractive and provocative revisionist approaches have been proposed. Sacvan Bercovitch, for example, has asserted that an agreement to engage in *dissensus*, or an agreement to disagree, will lead us out of the mire of uncertainty. Bercovitch's approach, however, is premised largely upon a linear theory of Adamic discourse which this book renders inadequate or obsolete. Other approaches which merit careful scrutiny are those offered by William C. Spengemann in *A New World of Words: Redefining Early American Literature* (1994), Earl E. Fitz in *Rediscovering the New World: Inter-American Literature in a Comparative Context* (1991), and José David Saldivar in *The Dialectics of Our America: Genealogy, Cultural Critique, and Literary History* (1991).

David Saldivar demonstrates that the present Anglocentric conception of American culture is simply too narrow to respond adequately and constructively to the many geographical interconnections and competing political ideologies which obtain in North America, including the Caribbean. What he seeks is a much broader conception of multiculturalism than is possible within the confines of nationalism. The discussion in this book can contribute importantly toward achieving Saldivar's objectives; as we have seen, awareness of the secular, classical origins of the American self or selves inevitably leads to acknowledgment of the multicultural dimensions of American culture. While these never have been far from the surface, they have been obscured through the hegemony of the Adamic myth.

An approach closely related to that of Saldivar is Earl E. Fitz's even more inclusive design, presented in *Rediscovering the New World.* Here Fitz hopes "to feature lesser-known works and works by women" (xii). His primary premise is "that the concept of 'American literature' is not the exclusive province of one nation," but rather "is a concept that would link together all the literatures of the New World" (xiii). Fitz insists that, "inescapably, the colonization of the New World would impose a new identity on everyone involved" (34). We have seen that this certainly was so with the American colonists. As well as treating authors from the areas that became the United States, Fitz gives careful attention to the literatures of French Canada, Spanish America, and Brazil, which he feels "have not yet received the recognition they merit" (234), certainly not as part of an inter-American literature. While he does not ignore connections to Vergil's *Aeneid* in his examination of such New World epics as Alonso de Ercilla y Zúñiga's *The Araucaniad* and Joel Barlow's *The Columbiad,* Fitz does not go far enough in developing the implications of these deep cultural connections (perhaps I should say interconnections). To be sure, Fitz's focus is not cultural but literary. Even so, it seems likely that an awareness of the immense debt America owes to its classical origins would strengthen considerably the argument for an inter-American literature, based upon a common classical heritage. Fitz nonetheless is moved by his reading of New World epics to register this sweeping generalization, which carries many contiguities with *The American Aeneas:*

> It is quite natural that the epic should have been cultivated in the Americas. The entire process of the New World's discovery, conquest, and colonization by the Old World involved a complex struggle of epic proportions. Moreover, writers like Ercilla and [Barlow] had before them wonderful examples of how expressive and adaptive the epic poem could be. These and other New World epicists [although Fitz does not mention them, Cotton Mather, Benjamin Tompson, and Phillis Wheatley qualify for inclusion here] felt the need to enter into the epic tradition but to do so by writing new epics, works that, though deriving from European models, would adapt themselves formally, thematically, and stylistically to both the extraordinary realities and the vast potentialities of the New World experience. These New World epics mark important steps in the ongoing quest for New World identity and expression. (69)

Responding (perhaps inadvertently) to the hegemony of the Adamic myth, Fitz states in his "Afterword," "It is interesting to note, however, that within the Americas it is the United States that has been most laggardly in embracing a significant Inter-American consciousness" (233). Our country's reluctance to free itself from the shackles of an inadequately understood nationalism is hardly surprising.

One important American work which gestures significantly toward both Fitz and Saldivar is the revised edition of *Benet's Reader's Encyclopedia of American Literature*, cited earlier in this chapter. In a new "Preface," the editors explain that, "while emphasizing the literature of the United States, [the *Encyclopedia*] provides extensive coverage of Canada and Latin America" (v). The present volume, too, should be viewed as turning toward this expansive possibility.

One approach which does not so readily gesture toward an inter-American literature and culture is offered by William C. Spengemann in his *A New World of Words*. Lamenting "the invention of Early American literature" by such early nineteenth-century American literary historians as Samuel Knapp and Samuel Kettle, "where none seemed to exist" (2), Spengemann prescribes restoring Early American literature to its English-language roots. I find this project a reasonable one. If pursued properly, it should teach us much about our American linguistic past. What I find objectionable are several of the premises upon which Spengemann plans to construct his project.

Spengemann soundly grounds his plan in the judicious observation that, "cobbled together from historical archives for political purposes, Early American literature has always depended for its identity and value far more upon historical than literary considerations" (4). Certainly the radical shift in discourse, a historical reality of which Spengemann seems unaware, was designed for political reasons; but it was also designed for cultural ones and resulted in the American Way. It is at this point that I think Spengemann's project could be profitably modified, taking the Adam and Aeneas paradeictic into account. For Spengemann insists that:

> by shifting our attention from the imagined nationality of these writings to their indisputable language, we may find ourselves, for the first time, in possession of the ground of historical kinship and continuity that national literary history was designed to provide but that American literary history, sucking its paws for want of an American language, has always had to make do without. (524)

First, recovery of the eighteenth-century poetic genres of the literary independence poem, the subversive pastoral, and the pastoral elegy contradicts the notion of an "imagined nationality" during this period. Most of the authors working within these genres were keenly aware of significant differences between themselves and their British parent nation, differences consciously featured in their texts.

Second, Spengemann's notion of linguistic poverty—seen in the fact that American language was indistinguishable from British English—strikes me as both unsound and finally unnecessary. Regarding this linguistic poverty that he claims characterizes American literary history, Spengemann asserts, "Any concentration by American literary history upon writings in a single tongue automatically robs the subject of that self-evident uniqueness which makes it unnecessary for historians of French and Spanish literature to spend their time, as Americanists must, defining the thing whose development they mean to trace" (30). Peter Martyr wrote his *Decades* in Latin; do we call this writing Roman literature? Do we group Ercilla's *Arancaniad*, the national epic of Chile, with *Don Quixote?* The truth is that much literature has been written in Latin and Spanish, French, German, Italian, Japanese, Chinese, etc., which does not exhibit "the identity, coherence, and historical continuity" that Spengemann maintains characterizes other "national" (30) literatures.

Spengemann's imputation of American linguistic poverty cannot withstand scrutiny. In fact, his argument for American linguistic poverty becomes unnecessary when the Adam and Aeneas paradeictic is allowed to enter the picture. Recovery of America's classical origins helps to explode two premises from which the American linguistic poverty position draws most of its punch. At one point, Spengemann scornfully speaks of an "apparent want of poetic genius" (25), which he claims describes Early American poetry. Surely the identification of nineteen pastoral elegies written by Americans during the eighteenth century will help to dismantle this old saw!

At another point in his essay, Spengemann holds that, "so long as we go on reading texts amid circumstances different from those in which the texts were written, a diachronic link will remain intact, implicit in our ability to read—and in our fate to misread—words set down long ago, in other worlds" (38–39). While I am not at all certain how Spengemann's American linguistic poverty position can help to turn this "diachronic link" into a separate, sufficient historical moment, it seems likely that the archaeology of Early American literature and culture performed in the present volume should promote reclamation of America's early "other worlds."

Another factor which does not recommend Spengemann's focus on English language, even if an American English, is the ever-present possibility that, with increased frequency, American literature may become relegated to an undistinguished corner within some huge schema, as we have observed in *The New Pelican Guide to English Literature*.

Despite all these difficulties, I must applaud Spengemann's determination to make "*Early*" stop "meaning less." As well he strongly urges that the phrase American Literature must come "to describe any selection and arrangement of English words attributable to the writer's efforts to take hold of 'America'" (49). Happily, Spengemann and I share this agenda.

Though fraught with contradictions, the American self or selves, upon reflection, should be rendered less confusing by this recovery of America's classical, secular half. Perhaps the most self-evident consequence of this interrogative procedure has been to demonstrate that the Adam and Aeneas dialectic participates fully in what Cornel West has called "the cultural and political whirlwinds of our present moment." Lifting the siege of America's classical origins will expedite construction of a fully traversable path through these ostensibly chaotic whirlwinds and will lend new dignity to the American self or selves. ▧

Notes

Preface

1. I understand myth to be a distillation of human experience, or *à la* Foucault, a mode of discourse.
2. Some may wish me to engage each of the various Adamic camps—from Bercovitch to Pease, Delbanco to Jay, for example. However, I am not going to do so. First, each submythos partakes of the overarching hegemony of the Adamic mythos; to address each of these submythoi would result in endless repetition. Second, contending with these several submythoi would mire recovery of the American Aeneas in endless argumentation, unnecessarily obscuring the larger key issues. Rather, I suggest that each of these sub-Adamicisms critique the paradeictic of Adam *and* Aeneas. Indeed, I have constructed this book as a deliberate invitation to such engagement.

Introduction

1. Pease apparently understands the term *consensus* as Bercovitch applies it in numerous places in discussing his notion of *dissensus*. Bercovitch, "Problem of Ideology," e.g., describes "consensus history" as that mode of critical thought "through which [Vernon] Parrington defined the main currents of American culture" (633). Bercovitch maintains that succeeding Americanists—including Richard Chase, Leslie Fiedler, Harry Levin, R. W. B. Lewis, F. O. Matthiessen, Henry Nash Smith *(Virgin Land)*, and Robert Spiller—have either concurred with that mode of thought or refined it. This perception of a consensus mode, to which a new generation of Americanists must react, seems to me problematical. Lewis himself says that he welcomes "more stirring implusions," "greater perspectives," and "more penetrating controversies" than those which his *The American Adam* may provoke (*American Adam* 10). In short, I question whether the "consensus" insisted upon by many new Americanists ever really existed.

   Matthiessen's exuberant celebration of the possibilities inherent in his idea of Americanness seems to rule out any "possibility" of consensus. For if

Americanness equals possibilities, how can the idea of Americanness ever arrive at a state in which, at any given moment, all agree on what Americanness is? That Bercovitch and others "agree to disagree" signals, as Pease holds, merely another modality of consensus, a consensus that derives much of its forceful rhetoric from reaction to an alleged "consensus" which, as stated above, probably never existed.

2. See, e.g., Ryder 228ff.
3. The guidelines for this approach may lie in Emerson and in D. H. Lawrence, *Studies in Classic American Literature* (1923). The attributive "Classic" is truly ironic, though Lawrence clearly intends to designate modern "classics." Lewis quotes two passages. One is from Emerson's *Journals:* "Here's for the plain old Adam, the simple genuine self against the whole world." The other is from Lawrence: "That is the true myth of America. She starts old, old, wrinkled and writhing in an old skin. And there is a gradual sloughing off of the old skin, towards a new youth. It is the myth of America" (Lewis vi).
4. The passage is in Silvestris 27. Unlike Silvestris, Landino, in *Quaestiones Camaldulenses* (which also treats only the first six books), presents an exaggerated reading of the *Aeneid* in terms of contemplation—a mode not exactly foreign to the Puritan discipline of piety or praxis of the *meditatio*. As Don Cameron Allen puts it, Aeneas's "character created by Virgil was that of a man who gradually purged himself of many great vices, learned the marvelous ways of virtue, and, in spite of obstacles, reached his *summum bonum*, a feat which no man can achieve without wisdom" (150). Allen provides a thorough discussion of the influence of the commentaries by Silvestris and Landino, among others (135–62). At least by the middle of the seventeenth century, Protestants, in particular, had begun to contest the traditional Catholic holding that Vergil's fourth eclogue amounts to a prediction of the birth of Christ (D. Allen 162n). This Protestant skepticism undoubtedly influenced the second and third generation of Puritan New Englanders.
5. Many consider as standard the first volume of Cremin, *American Education*, a two-volume work tracing the history of American education. In my view, it does not eclipse the more readable Middlekauff, *Ancients and Axioms*. Another still valuable source is Murdock, "Teaching of Latin and Greek." All three provided invaluable background for the above discussion. See esp. Cremin 1: 68–69, 167–95, 206–7, 406–7, 436–37, and 500–509; and Middlekauff 63–65, 75–79, 85–87, 120–23, 134–35, 154–57, 162–69, and 191–95. Two important articles illuminate colonial American and early post–Revolutionary War–era literacy. Monaghan concludes, "From the earliest days of settlement then, and throughout the colonial period, the colonists expected that all children ought to be able to read, no matter how low their station or how poor their circumstances" (30). Nord traces the readership of *New York Magazine; or, Literary Repository* (begun in 1790) to republican artisans or New York tradesmen who sought to continue their Revolutionary War participation in the affairs of state. Nord, however, perpetuates the notion that the classical republican tradition maintained that

all should "sacrifice individual interests to the common good" (43). Consider what Cicero, that lion of republican virtues, says in *De officiis* (a text popular in the grammar schools) about the creation of the state in order to protect the property rights of individual owners (Loeb Classical Library edition of *De officiis* 249 and 255).

6. Foucault, esp. "Preface" and ch. 7.
7. I am aware that this schema resembles the delineation of the epistemes in Foucault: "pre-classical" (Renaissance to mid-seventeenth century), "classical" (to end of the eighteenth century), "modern" (1800–1950), and the "contemporary age" (1950 to the present). Resemblance, however, is as far as it goes. Foucault's epistemes capture neither the subtleties of dynamic movement and interaction which occurred on the American strand, nor the remarkable differences between American and European cultures.

1. Translatio Cultus

1. Concerning the word *hero* and its association with the Bible, Fritz Graf has observed in "Heros," *Dictionary of Deities and Demons in the Bible*, 2d ed., ed. Karel van der Toorn et al. (Grand Rapids, Mich.: Eerdmans, 1999) that, while *hero* does not occur in the Latin Vulgate or in any English translation, "*Heros* [an English transcription of the Greek] occurs only in the toponym 'City of the Heroes,' which is the LXX [Septuagint] rendering for Goshen in Genesis 46:28–29" (412). See Graf 412–15.
2. R. B. Davis, the principal scholar of George Sandys's life and career, finds several verbal parallels to Eden's anthology of New World "histories," including Martyr's *Decades*. See Davis, "America" 297–304, esp. 301–2 and notes. Davis traces Sandys's reference to the fountain of youth to Martyr's "second *Decade*, . . . with Martyr taking Sandys' attitude towards it." Yet I do not find any reference to the fountain of youth or to de León in the second *Decade* of Martyr, though he is mentioned twice in the third *Decade* (Eden 165 and 181). López de Gómara discusses both de León and the fountain of youth as occurring in Martyr's *Decades* (Eden 345–46).
3. R. B. Davis, *George Sandys, Poet-Adventurer*, gives a good overview of Sandys's contribution to the development of the heroic couplet (212–14; see esp. notes on these pages). Perhaps the best assessment of Sandys's contribution to this poetic form is in Piper's substantial *Heroic Couplet*, 69–75 and 222–30.
4. The story of the perception of the imaginative faculty is a fascinating one. Jonathan Edwards, *A Treatise Concerning Religious Affections* (1746), defines this faculty as "that power of the mind, whereby it can have a conception, or idea of things of an external or outward nature (that is, of such sort of things as are the objects of the outward senses), when those things are not present, and be not perceived by the senses" (210–11). I would emphasize the phrase "external or outward nature"; indeed, Edwards's major impetus in writing

Religious Affections was precisely to distinguish those inner affections or emotions, arising from a truly divine source, from the outward or external emotions stirred by the imagination, a wholly false source. The origin of Edwards's concern is the powerfully emotional response of many colonial Americans to the dramatic, evangelical rhetoric of the British minister George Whitefield, often called "the Voice of the Great Awakening." Contrary to what is sometimes thought, Edwards's philosophical temperament made him justifiably suspicious of zealotry. In Edwards's own words, "When persons' affections are founded on imaginations, which is often the case, those affections are merely natural and common, because they are built on a foundation that is not spiritual." These hardly spiritual emotions are "entirely different from gracious affections, which . . . do evermore arise from those operations that are spiritual and divine" (217).

Edwards's final disparagement of imagination comes in his association of this faculty with evil: "The imagination or phantasy seems to be that wherein are formed all those delusions of Satan, which those are carried away with, who are under the influence of false religion, and counterfeit graces and affections" (288). And as if these remarks were not devastating enough, he draws this graphic paradigm of Satan's invasion of the soul: "So that it must be only by the imagination, that Satan has access to the soul, to tempt and delude it, or suggest anything to it" (289).

Edwards's discussion here strikingly parallels several remarks of John Locke in his "[Of Enthusiasm]" essay which he added to the fourth (1696) edition of *An Essay Concerning Human Understanding:* "And what readier way can there be to run ourselves into the most extravagant errors and miscarriages, than thus to set up fancy for our supreme and sole guide" (2: 437). "Light, true light," continues Locke, "in the mind is, or can be, nothing else but the evidence of the truth of any proposition" (2: 437). This line of thought predicts Edwards' "divine and supernatural light." Locke remarks further of light which may be given to falsity by saying, "To talk of any other light in the understanding is to put ourselves in the dark, or in the power of the Prince of Darkness, and, by our own consent, to give ourselves up to delusion to believe a lie. For, if strength of persuasion be the light which must guide us; I ask how shall any one distinguish between the delusions of Satan, and the inspirations of the Holy Ghost?" (2: 438). Edwards and Locke, though certainly not in total agreement here, are hardly in opposition in their thinking.

In *Jonathan Edwards*, Terence Erdt makes a worthy attempt to reconstruct a viable aesthetic from the works of Edwards, surely one of America's greatest original thinkers. Though Erdt avoids citing the passages given above, he adduces much evidence and builds intricate arguments from which he concludes that the imaginative faculty "enables the saint to come as close as is possible, without the intervention of grace, to a glimpse, an *earnest*, of divine beauty." Moving from this premise, Erdt maintains that, "By imagining great natural beauty and the aesthetic feeling it instills, the saint stands in a better position to receive the actual earnest of divine beauty" (56). While this aesthetic promises complete fulfillment for the elect or the saints, it holds none either for the unregenerate or for unbelievers.

This negative attitude is not dead. In a popular journal for ministers, Wierske recently considered seriously whether imagination is friend or enemy of the Protestant Christian faith. He distinguishes fancy from imagination in a way before unknown to me: "Fancy creates a new world for you; imagination gives you new insight into the old world" (23). Subsequently he insists, however, that only that imagination is valid which is "a sanctified imagination" (23, 24, and 25). Even recently, then, Edwards's conservative, guarded posture toward this faculty retains a measure of credibility.

A second recent writer, Perry D. Le Fevre, who has written a book on Edwards, insists that imagination should be used by the believer but that this faculty must be a "loving imagination" originating in sincere supplication to God (12).

5. Bradstreet's singing Mariner could be a reference to Aeneas, considered a "great Master of the seas" (380). Within the context of the Aeneas myth, *must* one read "the white stone" in stanza 33 as a reference to Revelation 2:17? Cannot the white stone be merely a gravestone? If so, this final stanza, devoted to "Time" as "the fatal wrack of mortal things" (381), draws together both the Adamic and the classical modes of discourse; for death, who "draws oblivions curtains over kings" as well as the common man, is the great equalizer of all people.
6. Bornstein, "Captan Perse," discusses and edits this important Early American manuscript poem. Although the quality of Walker's poem does not approach Tompson's more learned performance, it is nonetheless a fascinating work that Bornstein thinks may have been influenced by Tompson's *New Englands Crisis*.

2. Edward Taylor's Classicism

1. In determining this count and others made in this essay, I have not included allusions to Rome or to Romans which, it could be argued, may refer to the biblical Rome or Romans, or to Catholic Rome. Nor do I count such words as *chalybdine* or *smargdine*, because of their probable derivation from medieval alchemy (e.g., the *Tabula Smargdina*, believed to have been written by the Egyptian Hermes Trismegistus or Thoth, god of letters). Taylor well may have construed a neologism in *chalybdine*, which does not appear in the *OED* (although other words related to it, such as *chalybean* [which Milton uses in *Samson Agonistes* l. 133], *chalybeate*, and *chalybite*, do). I have chosen not to include such phrases as *aqua vitae* and *aqua infernales* because they were standard for the day and because they could have come from Taylor's curiosity about alchemy. My purpose is to identify what is distinctly classical and pagan.
2. From "Preface to A *Survey of the Summe of Church-Discipline*," in Perry Miller and Johnson 2: 673. Taylor cites Hooker in both *Treatise* 215–16 and *Christographia* 421. He refers to Calvin many times in each collection of sermons and in the sermons comprising *Upon the Types*.
3. Johnson, *Poetical Works* 201–20, lists the *Epitome* as part of the inventory of Taylor's estate (p. 213, item 106). Quotation, *Epitome* 211.

4. On seventeenth-century offerings at Harvard, see Morison, *Founding* and *Harvard College*. See esp. *Founding* 263–70, for a list of books with which the college library started, including gifts by such noteworthies as John Harvard and Sir Kenelm Digby. For details of the Harvard curriculum, see *Harvard College* 139–284; on history of the college library from 1655 to 1723, see 285–97. Taylor was at Harvard in 1668–71.
5. Sandys, *Ovid's Metamorphosis* 290. I do not mean to suggest that Taylor lacked the creativity to think of the "oares" metaphor on his own; but, if he did read the book, perhaps Sandys's translation (on this same page) of a passage from Seneca's *Hercules Oetaeus* (in which the Daedalus myth is treated) suggested to the poet that Icarus's wings were "oares." Part of Sandys's passage from Seneca reads: "May my small Bark coast by the shore/ Unforct to sea by lofty windes."
6. Taylor may have translated the passage from the *Metamorphoses* as a grammar school exercise. What has been preserved, however, is a later manuscript translation of the *Ars* passage, which Isani describes as a "four-page fragment found lining the homemade binding" of Taylor's *Commonplace Book* (67).
7. Another source for Taylor's adaptation of typology (as applied to nonbiblical, pagan sources) may have been Thomas Godwin's *Romanae Historiae*, a copy of which Taylor owned (Johnson, *Poetical Works* p. 207, item 41). For instance, one of Taylor's early poems, "A Dialogue between the Writer and a Maypole Dresser" (circa 1669), resonates with the enthusiasm of a recent convert. Here the poet describes the Maypole celebration as initiated by "Flora a whorish strumpet in Rome." After becoming wealthy from her profession, Flora "bequeathed to Rome" monies to honor her birthday, "at which the Romans were/ Abashed." So they "called her Goddesse of sweet flowers" and established the Maypole tradition (Taylor, "Earliest Poems" 145). All this recalls Thomas Morton's Maypole at Merrymount. Explicating the many parallels between Roman and English laws and customs, Godwin explains that "the strumpet Flora . . . made the people of Rome heir to those goods which she had gotten by prostituting her body to young Gentlemen, leaving also a certain sum of money to procure a celebration of her birthday: which because of her infamy, the people shaming to do, they feigned her to be a Goddess of flowers" (7). The wording here is similar to that in Taylor's poem. Early in the poem, Taylor sets up a typology between this Roman ritual and the Philistine celebration of the false god Dagon, holding that Dagon and the Maypole "Combine in one God to mock, flout and jeare" ("Earliest Poems," 145). So Taylor already had begun to construct types from the pagan world long before he encountered Samuel Mather's caveat.
8. The *Idylls* of Theocritus, along with much other poetry and some prose, comprised part of Harvard's required Greek curriculum from the college's beginnings. Taylor's Greek grammar by Nicolaus Clenardus was a standard freshman text long before he arrived in New England (Morison, *Harvard College* 1: 194–200).

9. The Apelles Taylor refers to in *Upon the Types* 2.521 and 2.644 is not the Greek painter but the second-century founder of a Gnostic sect, usually referred to as "the heretic."
10. Clement, *Clementis Alexandrini Opera: Graece et Latine*, 210. This folio volume is a bilingual edition, with the Latin and Greek on parallel columns on each page. The year of the volume is close enough to Taylor's own period that he may have consulted one like it. Grabo, *Edward Taylor*, does not identify the source of this anecdote. According to Artz, "Clement's toleration for pagan culture was very great" (70). In book V of his *Miscellanies*, Clement even recommends the Greek virtue of "sophrosyne" ("Nothing in excess"). See Clement, *Writings* 2: 248. Apparently Taylor and this Church Father were kindred spirits.
11. Mingazzini 509 makes no mention of any paintings of Helen by Apelles. Since none of Apelles's paintings survives, we suspect that the attribution to Apelles of a painting of Helen is likely to be spurious.
12. See Elgoods 41–74 and esp. 66, on this Ptolemy's extravagance and his role in preserving priceless manuscripts in the Mouseion.
13. Actually Taylor applies the allusion to a discussion of the authority of the Greek translation in its rendering of a Hebrew word into a Greek word meaning *body*. The text of the sermon is Hebrews 10:5, "A Body hast thou prepared me." As usual, the Westfield minister is employing a conventional type here of Christ's human nature.
14. It should be observed that, even in Taylor's century, the authenticity of the *Letter to Aristeas* was questioned. Taylor owned a copy of Raleigh (see T. H. Johnson, *Poetical Works* p. 204, item 3). In it, Raleigh annotates a reference to the *Aristeas*, observing that "many learned men . . . hold suspition that it is counterfeit" (p. 641, side note "h"). Taylor, however, appears to rely on the testimony of Augustine, whose authority he cites in his sermons more often than that of any other Church Father. In *The City of God* XV.13 and XVIII.42, Augustine defends the manner by which the pseudonymous Aristeas claims the *Septuagint* was made. While Taylor seems to have accepted the *Letter from Aristeas*, since Ptolemy Philadelphus is not considered "biblical" today, I group allusions to him with those to ancient Egypt, exclusive of the Bible.
15. Pliny, in his *Natural History* (XXXVI.13), attributes the construction to a King Petesucus, or Tithoes. George M. Hanfmann identifies the actual historical builder of the Egyptian Labyrinth as Amenemhet III.
16. Morison observes that "the College Library had Demosthenes and Herodotus before 1682" (*Harvard College* 1: 199).
17. I quote from Herodotus, *Famous Hystory* 225. This 1584 edition of the first two books, translated by B. R., was a popular one of the times and may have been seen by Taylor.
18. Raleigh, *History of the World*, speaks of "Lake of Myris," which B. R. spells *Moeris* in his translation of Herodotus; and Raleigh identifies the statues in

the middle of the lake as "Pyramis," which B. R. describes as "Towers called Pyramides" (192). Raleigh speaks of *Psammetichos* (Raleigh spells the name *Psammiticus;* B. R., *Psammitichus*) but does not mention him in connection with the construction of the Labyrinth. Instead he connects its building with Actisanes and with Marus (cf. Diodorus's Marrus). Since Taylor spells the Egyptian ruler's name *Posamnitick,* he obviously has not returned to Raleigh, a book he owned, to check the spelling (1713 *Meditation* 113). This last observation, along with the internal evidence given above, suggests that Raleigh is not his source for references to the pyramids, Lacus Moeris, or Psammetichos, but that Taylor instead drew them from a borrowed copy of Herodotus, perhaps even in B. R.'s translation.

19. It is worth asking whether the poetics Lewalski describes in *Protestant Poetics* originates within a religious tradition, Protestant or Catholic. Since classical sources treating the *meditatio* were so readily available to British and American poets as grammar school texts throughout the seventeenth century, should we not read seventeenth-century religious lyrics, esp. those clearly indebted to the *meditatio,* as poems very likely secular in origin? If we concede the probable secular origins of such meditative poetry, does such redirected reading not then alter our interpretation of what these poems say? Is the poetics which gives shape to these poems so clearly Protestant or Catholic? Would Lewalski so easily have concluded that Edward Taylor's religious commitment so imposes upon his poetic meditations that he "does not actively grapple with his psyche or his art" (391)? Such readings of Taylor, as deriving from a wholly religious context, tend to trivialize Taylor's efforts to create poetry *qua* poetry and inexorably relegate him (and American Puritans in general) to the second or third rank as poets.

20. See C. Plinius Caecilius Secondus, *Panegyricus* (XIII.1); Apuleius, *Florida* (XV); M. Fabius Quintilianus, *Institutio Oratoria* (IV.ii.29 and X.70); and Aulus Gellius, *Noctes Atticae* (XX.V.3). Texts of all these Latin works were printed at least by 1600 and most as early as 1500 (see Bolgar 275–76). For the contention that Gellius and Quintilian formed part of the curriculum in early American grammar schools, see Cremin, 204–5.

21. It can be objected that *only* as a consequence of Loyola's "codification" of the *meditatio* in the 1548 *Exercises* did Renaissance poets take an interest in writing poems exemplifying this praxis. However, the Old English poem *The Seafarer* has been analyzed as a *meditatio* (J. C. Shields, "*Seafarer*" 29–41).

22. Scheick does discuss "Fancie" briefly within the context of the Puritan understanding of the function of the senses and affections. This discussion, however, addresses imagination's functioning according to Edward Reynolds and Jonathan Edwards, not Taylor (Scheick, *Will and Word* 29–33).

23. Bolgar says that Aristotle's *De anima* was translated into Latin as early as 1480 (434). By the late seventeenth century, *De anima* had become a textbook (in Greek) within grammar schools in the American colonies. The unknown author of the immensely popular *Rhetorica ad Herennium* (86–82 B.C.) explicates the ancient *Ars memorativa* as a discipline in which he

locates (discovers a *locus*) the thing (object or idea) to be committed to memory by means of the process of imaging (or associating the memory desired with a placed image). The word *imagines* appears some 36 times within this passage of the *Rhetorica* (205–25). If a poet does not trace images, then surely he does not write poetry, but prose. For a full analysis of the ancient art of memory, see Yates, ch. 1.

24. This tradition of denigrating the faculty of fancy is at least as old as Plato's *Ion*, in which the Greek philosopher cautions against the reliability of poets' "divine madness" (this is essentially why he refuses to admit poets to his ideal *Republic*). During the Renaissance, this tradition was rekindled. Tyndale, *Pentateuch* (1526), translates the Hebrew word *yeçer* (defined in A *Hebrew and English Lexicon* 428 as impulse or tendency toward good or evil in man) as imagination or imaginations (in Gen. 6:5 and 8:21). Part of Gen. 6:5 is rendered, with little change from Tyndale's version, in the Geneva Bible of 1560 (the text of the English and American Puritans until well after 1700) as "all the imaginacions of the thoghts of his [man's] heart were onely evil continually" (Gen. 6:5). A modern English version of the Hebrew *Torah* phrases this same passage as follows: "How every plan devised by his [man's] mind was nothing but evil all the time" (11). Such a Renaissance translation, identifying the imaginative faculty as associated intimately with depravity in man, must have intensified suspicion of this faculty. Indeed, by the early 1600s, William Perkins, one of the great patriarchs of Puritanism, echoes the Genesis passage with this arresting portrait of how this faculty threatens grammar school–age children: parents, masters and tutors "must all joyne hand in betime to stop up or at least to lessen this corrupt fountain" (164–65). Notwithstanding Perkins's superlative use of his own imagination in devising this inversion of the Parnassian spring, Puritan wisdom, at least through Jonathan Edwards, loathed this faculty, which was perceived to be the means by which Satan gained access to the unsanctified soul of mortal man. Taylor's recognition of this faculty as necessary to initiate the meditative process hence contradicts the traditional Puritan position concerning this faculty.

25. For the negative references to imagination, see Taylor, *Christographia*, 341 and 354.

26. Henry Taylor, a descendant of Edward Taylor and, according to Francis Murphy, "an avid historian of his family," claims that the Westfield minister did not wish "his heirs . . . to publish any of his writings" (Henry Taylor to William B. Sprague, quoted by Murphy). When Taylor's humanism is viewed in conjunction with his essentially positive private attitude toward the use of the imagination, this testimony gains credibility. Murphy 393–94 ascertains *only* that Taylor died intestate, but does not *prove* that the poet left no injunction among his heirs not to publish his works still remaining in manuscript. Why would Henry Taylor, only two generations removed from those who knew Edward personally, concoct a tale regarding an injunction not to publish? During Edward Taylor's own lifetime, many of his congregation

would have been shocked not only by the scatological imagery in his poems, but also by his happy use of classicism and his positive use of fancy. These latter two elements form part of the myth of Aeneas, always largely the province of an intellectual elite. As both his use of classicism and his application of the *meditatio* derive from the myth of Aeneas, why would Taylor make himself an object of suspicion by presenting either of these "special domain[s]" to his congregation, steeped almost exclusively in the tenets of the Adamic myth?

3. Cotton Mather's Epic in Prose

1. Three recent works have examined Milton's influence on early America: Stavely, *Puritan Legacies*; Schulman, *Rise of the American Republic*; and K. P. Van Anglen, *New England Milton*. While we would expect to see spirited discussion of Mather in Stavely's work, instead we find him speaking of Mather's *Magnalia* within the context of treating other authors. All three authors refer to Sensabaugh's *Milton in Early America* at least once, and Schulman calls *Milton* "My chief literary inspiration" (ix). Having not found any studies since Sensabaugh's which investigate Milton's influence on Mather, I take Sensabaugh as still authoritative.
2. Quotations from the first two books of *Magnalia* are from Mather, *Cotton Mather: Magnalia Christi Americana*, bks. I and II, ed. Murdock; this first quotation appears on 96. Quotations from the remaining five books are taken from Mather, *Magnalia Christi Americana* (1852, rpt. 1967). The Latin quotations from the *Aeneid* are from Vergil, *Virgil*, trans. Fairclough, Loeb ed. (1935). Leo M. Kaiser has accomplished much toward identifying the sources of Latin passages in *Magnalia* ("Latin Verse" 301–6; and "Six Notes" 297).
3. While most people today probably associate elves with Santa's helpers, those of Mather's time made no such connection. Indeed, the *OED* points out that, before 1800, an elf was distinguished from a fairy "as a more malignant being, an 'imp' [or] 'demon.'" The classic 11th ed. of the *Encyclopaedia Britannica* (1910–11) defines *elf* as "usually of a more or less mischievous and malignant character, causing diseases and evil dreams, stealing children and substituting changelings, and thus somewhat different from the . . . fairy, which usually has less sinister associations" (9: 266). Mather even describes children "stolen" from white settlers by Native Americans.
4. In Milton, *John Milton: Complete*, editor Merritt Y. Hughes traces exactly 37; *Paradise Lost* is pp. 207–469. Milton renders two lines from the *Aeneid* (I, 11 and IV, 554) in his *Paradise Lost* (VI, 788 and IX, 953).
5. Good places to begin a study of the influence of Vergil's *Aeneid* on Milton's composition of *Paradise Lost* are Osgood *passim*, and Hanford and Taaffe 206–7. On classical sources in Milton's entire *oeuvre*, see "Milton and the Dictionaries," in Starnes and Talbert, 226–339; and Harding, *Club of Hercules*.

4. Surge for Cultural Independence

1. This phrase is from Edward Gibbon, *Autobiography*, qtd. in Gay 358.
2. As many earlier and recent scholars of Early America confuse the abuse of classical texts in the hands of would-be eighteenth- and nineteenth-century apologists for the practice of slavery with the actual practice of slavery in the ancient Mediterranean world, I think it necessary to address this issue head-on. In *The Oxford History of the Classical World*, John Boardman et al., eds. (New York: Oxford UP, 1986), for example, Elizabeth Rawson observes that "Marxists, exaggerating the admittedly great importance of slavery in ancient society, have supposed that Roman conquests were fuelled by the need for slaves." Yet, as she continues, "No ancient source hints at this" (425). In the "Introduction" to the just cited volume, Jaspar Griffin states that "Rome was extraordinary among slave owning societies in that slaves were constantly freed in great numbers, and that the moment they were freed they became citizens. More than half of the thousands of epitaphs extant from imperial Rome are of freedmen and freedwomen" (8-9).

   A surprising number of scholars persist in suggesting that slavery in the colonies was motivated in some sense by colonial Americans' effort to emulate imperial Rome. Such a contention distorts the facts of history. Indeed, the high-water mark of the practice of slavery in Rome came in the second and first centuries B.C., *when Rome was still ruled as a republic*. It was during this time that the wealthy Roman patricians enlarged their already sizable estates, or *latifundia*, by introducing slavery on a huge scale to farm their vast lands. Moreover, only during this period did slave revolts occur on a large scale; Spartacus rose in Italy in 73–71 B.C.

   Neither during the Roman republic nor during the era of post-republican Rome did holders of slaves decide, for racist reasons, to target a particular race of people as worthy only for a life of servitude to white masters. David S. Wiesen differentiates the practice of slavery in colonial America from that of antiquity by stating that, in the case of the ancients, "two characteristic elements of modern racism are wanting: scorn for the physical appearance of the outsider and a deep-seated belief in his innate inferiority" (Eadie, *Classical Traditions* 193). In *The Glorious Cause* Middlekauff bolsters the argument that slavery was not peculiar to imperial Rome. Discussing slavery and the Declaration of Independence of 1776, he notes that the members of Congress attempted "to cast the king as the perpetrator of slavery in America as well as the instigator of racial violence." Yet, "as Congress knew," Middlekauff continues, "white Americans—not the king—had instituted slavery and had maintained it" (332). A distinction must be drawn between the actual practice and justification of slavery in America and the abuses Americans were willing to make of the sources, both ancient and modern, that they alleged legitimated this practice. For an excellent overview of the practice of slavery, in both the ancient world and the New World, see "Servitude," *Encyclopaedia Britannica* (1988), 27: 225–38.

3. This quotation and information on East Apthorp are from Sprague, *Annals* 5: 174–80; and Quinlivan (*American Writers Before 1800*, Levernier and Wilmes, eds., I: 57–59).
4. More literary independence poems could have been added to this discussion. However, my intention was not to be comprehensive, but rather to show a pattern of thought, an increasing political alignment of the literary independence poem with the quest for political and socioeconomic independence. Treatment of Nathaniel Evans's fine little poetic declaration of literary independence (see Ruland 10), e.g., would merely expand an already sizable amount of evidence.
5. See Sibley 12–15 and passim.
6. Byles also mentions Belinda in "To Pictorio, on the Sight of His Pictures," a poem from his *Poems on Several Occasions* (1744), in the line "Thy Blush, Belinda, future Hearts shall warm" (91).
7. For a preliminary investigation of Wheatley's African heritage and her debt to that heritage as traceable in her opus, see J. C. Shields, "Phillis Wheatley" in *African American Writers* 473–91, esp. 473–82.
8. On Boston's rejection of Wheatley's 1772 "Proposal" for a volume, see Robinson, *Black New England Letters* 51–52. Nor am I the first to note in print that Wheatley's portrait enacts a sort of rebellion. Baker, e.g., calls Wheatley's portrait "an almost revolutionary" one (6).
9. As this poem is not named in her Boston "Proposal" of 1772, it probably was written after April of that year. If so, it joins a number of other poems (including "Thoughts on the Works of Providence," "On Recollection," hymns to "Morning" and "Evening" "Isaiah LXIII," "To S. M. a Young African Painter," and "On Imagination"), all among her best work. Cumulatively these poems suggest that, in the year preceding publication of *Poems*, Wheatley was at the height of her poetic powers.
10. See Redding 640–42, esp. 641.
11. On a pattern of evolving liberalism regarding Wheatley's early dogmatically Christian views, as expressed in "Atheism" and "An Address to the Deist," see J. C. Shields, "Phillis Wheatley" in *African American Writers* 473–91, esp. 482–83.
12. See my "Phillis Wheatley and Mather Byles: A Study in Literary Relationship," *CLA Journal* 23, no. 4 (June 1980): 377–90.
13. The last two poems—"A Rebus," by another author (perhaps James Bowdoin, who founded Bowdoin College, which later was attended by Hawthorne and Longfellow); and "An Answer to the Rebus"—do not fit the spirit of the volume, appearing to be appended to it for the purpose of extending Wheatley's authenticity. Thus I consider Wheatley's *Poems* to conclude with "A Farewel to America."
14. The translation of the KJV is "how the mighty are fallen," as indicated in the text above, suggesting that Oakes perhaps preferred the KJV to the more

Calvinistic Geneva Bible, where the same line appears as: "how are the mighty overthrowen." If so, Oakes's preference for the KJV, perceived by many as more Anglican, seems unusual for the time. Nevertheless, Oakes incorporates the Geneva passage within his text at least once when he turns the phrase "his great Friends overthrow" (208).

15. These Boston poets could be following Milton's lead in his Latin "Epitaphium Damonis" ("Lament for Damon"), but more likely they emulate Spenser's practice of including an "Argument" for each of his poems in *The Shepeardes Calender: Conteyning Twelve Aeglogues*. Neither Vergil nor Pope (in his pastorals on the seasons) employs the introductory argument.

16. Other representations of the genre of the American pastoral elegy which I have not named in the text include the anonymous "A Pastoral Elegy on the Death of a Young Lady"; Benjamin Church, "XI"; Anonymous ("A first-time author"), "A Pastoral Elegy"; "N. L." and "Hibernicus," "A Pastoral Elegy, on the Death of ADMIRAL WARREN"; "A Youth of His [i.e., the Reverend Joshua Belding of Newington] Parish," "An Elegy on the Death of Mrs. Anne Belding, Late Wife"; Mather Byles, "A Poem On the Death of His Late Majesty King George [I]"; and Stephen Sewall, "V." Recently several more pastoral elegies have come to my attention, bringing to 30 the total number of pastoral elegies I have located composed in America before 1790: "Philantus," "A Pastoral Elegy, on the Death of a Virtuous Young Lady"; and the anonymous "Pastoral Elegy, on a Young Gentleman Lately Deceased," *South Carolina Gazette* 906 (Sept. 23, 1751): 332, e.g., plus others.

17. Paul Alpers is well known and highly respected for his *The Singer of the "Eclogues": A Study of Virgilian Pastoral* before writing *What Is Pastoral?* which has been called "a landmark study" of this genre. In the latter work, Alpers argues that "we will have a far truer idea of pastoral if we take its representative anecdote to be herdsmen and their lives, rather than landscape or idealized nature" (22). By "idealized nature," Alpers has in mind "the Golden Age," which he maintains receives an "extraordinary emphasis . . . in modern accounts of pastoral—far beyond what is justified by ancient or even Renaissance writers" (30; but see discussion on 30–32). Regarding the present study, two points need to be made. We are not investigating works of the Renaissance, but of the 17th and 18th centuries in America. Alpers does not examine pastorals and/or pastoral elegies composed by Early Americans. As I argue in this chapter, in Early American hands, the classical ideal of a golden age meshes neatly with the Judaeo-Christian Edenic paradise; this blending creates an appealing cultural grid against which many, if not most, Early Americans sought to define themselves and their American experience. So, while the value of Alpers's text is unquestionable, I doubt that Alpers, after absorbing the evidence presented in chapter 4, would draw the same conclusions about this evidence that he has presented in *What Is Pastoral?* In fact, in light of this reclamation of America's classicism, Alpers's treatment of such American writers as Sarah Orne Jewett, Robert Frost, and Wallace Stevens may require modification.

5. George Washington and the Vergilian Moment

1. Cotton Mather refers to Machiavelli several times in *Magnalia Christi Americana*. Edward Dacres translated *Il Principe* into English from the Italian as early as 1640 (London).
2. See, e.g., Trumbull, *An Essay on the Uses and Advantages of the Fine Arts* 11–12; and Royall Tyler's comedy *The Contrast, passim*.
3. While some British or American commentary may exist connecting the behavior of Addison's Cato to Vergil's hero Aeneas (who was, of course, first in pietas), such a discovery has eluded me—either in British or American commentary on the play.
4. See Bailyn, *Ideological Origins* 36–37 and 43–44, which discusses the impact of *Cato's Letters*, in conjunction with Addison's *Cato*, in creating "a 'Catonic' image central to the political theory of the time" (44). *Cato's Letters* were written by John Trenchard and Thomas Gordon and published in their *London Journal*. First appearing as a series, they were gathered into four volumes in 1724. In these, the authors launched scathing attacks upon the corruption in British politics surrounding the South Sea Bubble crisis. The name of Rome's hero of republicanism was invoked because of his known stand against the power of the monarch (Caesar) and also because of the impact of Addison's play.
5. On William Parks, see Cook, *Literary Influences* 151–54ff.
6. For a detailed history of performances of *Cato* in Early America, see Litto 435–41.
7. Three of these printing announcements of *Cato* (those of 1750, 1753, and 1780) are taken from bookseller's advertisements (Shipton's *Short Title Catalogue* [of Early American Imprints before 1801] 1: 5). They may never have appeared; but, given Litto's provocative speculation concerning interest in *Cato*, in particular, it is likely that more printings occurred than those advertised or those from which copies survive.
8. On these parallel reactions by Patrick Henry and Nathan Hale to passages in *Cato*, see Litto 444–46 and Furtwangler 43–44. On the likelihood that Hale taught *Cato* just prior to his death, see Seymour 85–87.
9. As well, Syphax's "story" closely parallels Vergil's relation of the tearful farewell that Evander, king of Pallanteum, takes of his son Pallas, whom he entrusts to the care of Aeneas (*Aeneid* VIII, 572–84).
10. On Washington's associations with numerous classical figures other than Cato, see Bryan 145n69 and Wills *passim*.
11. The "newsy" prose piece should interest scholars of the Revolutionary War era, if only because, first, it urges dismissal of Britain's present ministers as a step toward making peace with the American colonies; and, second, it contains this striking assertion: "A French war is not far off, notwithstanding

the peaceful professions from Versailles, but America and England united, might defy all the powers in Europe" (2).

12. The 1786 version of *Cato*, printed at Philadelphia, retains Pope's "Prologue" and Garth's "Epilogue"; nor does this edition print Sewall's "A New Epilogue."
13. John Francis Latimer, editor of the 1976 facsimile edition of *Georgii Washingtonii Vita*, thinks this date for the first edition is spurious, because he was unable to locate any listing of the *Vita* in the Library of Congress or the Union Catalogue for the year 1834. See his discussion of editions in Glass, *Composite Translation* 21–22 and n. 21, pp. 21–22.
14. Rogers gives an excellent survey of American problems with British mistreatment and abuse during the French and Indian War years. Thomas Godfrey, author of the eulogistic pastoral elegy on Gen. James Wolfe discussed in ch. 4, probably had no knowledge of Wolfe's disdain for the colonial militia, revealed in Rogers's quotations from Wolfe's military communiqués of the period. Wolfe had declared, e.g., "The Americans are in general the dirtiest, the most contemptible, cowardly dogs that you can conceive." Rogers offers this final Wolfe observation: "There is no depending upon them in action. They fall down dead in their own dirt and desert by battalions, officers and all" (63). These remarks reflect no notion whatever that Early Americans probably did not find the British struggle for empire precisely in keeping with their own objectives.

6. The American Epic Writ Large

1. Several other verse epics were composed by Americans after the Revolution. For a full listing, see McWilliams 243. On *The Conquest of Canaan*, see Silverman, *A Cultural History* 499–503.
2. In using the term *epyllion* (plural *epyllia*), I am fully aware of the work of Walter Allen Jr. He argues that "there never was such a literary genre as the epyllion, and the name and the genre are errors on the part of comparatively recent classical philology" (515). Even so, the term continues to be used in such authoritative reference works as the *New Princeton Encyclopedia of Poetry and Poetics* (1993 ed.), *The Oxford Classical Dictionary* (1996 ed.), and *A Handbook to Literature* (1996, 7th ed.). In this essay, I use the definition of *epyllion* given in *A Handbook to Literature* (7th ed.): "A NARRATIVE POEM usually presenting an episode from the heroic past and resembling an EPIC but much briefer and more limited" (195). I first described Wheatley's adaptation of the epyllion in J. C. Shields, "Phillis Wheatley's Use of Classicism."
3. This phrase illustrates a henotheistic construct and, as such, suggests Wheatley's recollection of her African religious heritage. It probably represents a syncretized composite of solar worship, primitivism (not unlike the polytheism in the early portions of the Old Testament), and animism or spirit worship (esp. of ancestors). So interpreted, this phrase illustrates her syncretistic tendencies.

4. From early July 1775, Washington had assumed command of the Continental Army at Cambridge, MA. Here he and the army remained, keeping the British troops commanded by Gen. William Howe under siege until mid-April 1776. See Purcell and Burg 52–80. Washington apparently invited Wheatley to visit him at his Cambridge headquarters, and it is believed that she accepted.
5. In the reference to "olive," Wheatley may be alluding to the Olive Branch Petition to King George III, approved by the Continental Congress on July 5, 1775, seeking reconciliation and new grounds for negotiations. On November 9, 1775, less than three weeks after Wheatley had completed "To . . . Washington," Congress received word that George III had rejected the Olive Branch Petition and had "declared the colonies in a state of rebellion" (Purcell and Burg 62; see also 52–53).
6. Wheatley's parents probably practiced some sort of hierophantic solar worship; see J. C. Shields, "Phillis Wheatley" 473–91, esp. 473–74. Since such worship almost invariably is carried out by members of an aristocracy, Wheatley likely recollected an African background in which she herself was a member of the upper class within her particular people.
7. Mason claims that "On Virtue" "is free verse (although she may have intended it for blank verse) ending with a heroic couplet" (19, n. 15). This poem scans regularly as twenty lines of iambic pentameter (two stanzas of ten lines each), followed by a twenty-first line of six feet, an alexandrine. The occasional trochees at the beginning of some lines show that the poet knows how to avoid monotony. The alexandrine is apropos, as it is an extra line in the last of the two stanzas. An amphibrach in line 8 of the second stanza is an acceptable variation. Therefore, this poem is hardly free verse.
8. On the "new world" Wheatley constructs in "On Imagination," see J. C. Shields, "Phillis Wheatley's Subversive Pastoral" 631–47.
9. A recent reading of "On Imagination" robs Wheatley of her agency as regards use of imagination but returns it as regards application of the subordinate fancy. McKay and Scheick fall into difficulty with the statement: "Since Imagination and Fancy are both gendered as female, the phrase 'To tell her glories' presents a pronoun that remains referentially uncertain" (74). As Fancy is not named until the third line *following* this phrase but Imagination has been named in the title, "her" clearly and unambiguously refers to Imagination. Nevertheless, this alleged ambiguity leads McKay and Scheick to uncover other "ambiguities" in this poem, and these cause the authors to conclude: "Imagination represents Anglo-American tradition" (not defined; as Wheatley herself is carving out the African American tradition, I suppose this tradition is that of whites), while Fancy "may serve as a trope for African American experience" (81). Scheick, in his *Authority and Female Authorship*, repeats this interpretation with no additional justification. As if his interpretation is donnée, he simply asserts, "Rather than align herself with Imagination as a means of escape from the world in this poem . . . , the poet identifies with marginalized Fancy" (125).

McKay and Scheick's use of the subjunctive mood in the above phrase, "may serve," proves telling. Frequently recurring phrases such as "may refer to" (74), "may be read," "may be interpreted" (77), and "may be argued" (81) bespeak a weak foundation. At best, such characterizations as "arid neoclassical tradition" (76), "the tawdry ornamentalism of neoclassical tradition" (76), "tyrannical neoclassical culture, the ideals of which suppress human feeling," and "passionless neoclassical verse" (82), announce biased judgment. At worst, they give real offense. What *evidence* do we have that Wheatley disliked American classicism? In fact, she appears to have embraced it with an enthusiasm and an intelligence that enabled her to turn her adopted idiom against itself. Is it not the measure of a gifted poet that she can do just that?

These authors insist that readers accept the incredible: that Wheatley would give up her agency, her power of creativity, or any part of it. Before publication of the 1773 *Poems*, in which "On Imagination" appeared, Wheatley was a slave. Nevertheless, she was permitted by a white society (which viewed Wheatley more as a "side show" freak than as a legitimate artist—a view of which she was painfully aware) to wield a pen with a remarkable degree of flexibility. Why on earth would she present the picture of a divided artistic consciousness, one-half of which she has surrendered to white folks? Does it not make more sense to posit that the power she sees within *her* imagination, *her* recollection, and *her* idea of Providence functions as a direct, conscious manifestation of her own empowerment?

McKay and Scheick are correct, of course, in stating that Wheatley, like W. E. B. Du Bois, displays in her work a "double-consciousness," one which forces her, for her own survival, to see herself "through the eyes of others," while the white world, largely incapable of empathy for her predicament, "looks on in amused contempt and pity." She herself declares, "Some view our sable race with scornful eye" (18). It does not follow, however, that this capable and savvy black woman would ever consider denying the integrity of *her* artistic consciousness. Indeed, her struggle is to maintain it intact and hence to shape a space of her *own* by means of which she can both survive and strike out against those who, in their dispassionate avarice, would and did cause the development of Du Bois's "peculiar sensation."

10. Some precedents existed in America for Wheatley's privileging of the imaginative faculty. Before her, Joseph Seccombe, Samuel Cooper, and William Billings, all Bostonians, had published tracts urging positive regard for the imagination. Joseph Seccombe (1706–1760) was a missionary to Native Americans, poet, and author of several published sermons, who received treatment of his pastoral elegy in chapter 4. Dr. Joseph Sewall, grandson of Samuel Sewall and Phillis Wheatley's spiritual mentor until his death in 1769 (Wheatley composed an elegy on his death), delivered Seccombe's ordination sermon—a fact that ties Seccombe to Wheatley.

    In *Some Occasional Thoughts on the Influence of the Spirit with Seasonable Cautions Against Mistakes and Abuses* (1742), Seccombe quotes from Jonathan Edwards, in order to align himself with those ministers who opposed the "miraculous" and "enthusiastic" conversions of George Whitefield. Wheatley's elegy on Whitefield was her most famous poem published during her lifetime—another reason why she might have been interested in reading Seccombe's sermon. Seccombe does not, however, agree fully with Edwards regarding the imaginative faculty, for Edwards had maintained that this faculty was the root of many specious conversions. Devoting several pages to a consideration of the imagination (and even quoting from Pierre de Charron's treatise, *De la sagesse*), Seccombe concludes, in remarkable disagreement with Edwards, that the imagination is "under the conduct of the Understanding . . . a very useful and powerful Faculty" (7). Unlike Edwards, Seccombe does not require that the imagination, in order to be secured against the invasion of evil, be sanctified by the gift of God's grace; thus we see in Seccombe a move toward the secular in considering this faculty.

Samuel Cooper was the Boston minister who baptized Wheatley on August 18, 1771, and upon whose death she composed her most personal statement of grief, "An Elegy Sacred to the Memory of That Great Divine, The Reverend and Learned Dr. Samuel Cooper" (1784). Cooper is thought to have been the author of the subversive introduction to *Pietas et Gratulatio*, discussed in chapter 4. In addition, Cooper contributed at least two poems to that collection of thirty-one "dedicated" to George III, odes 13 and 28. In "Ode XIII," Cooper has this poignant line: "Imagination! heaven-born maid!" Thus he suggests a parallel between Imagination as goddess and Minerva, or Pallas Athena, virgin goddess of wisdom.

Wheatley's elegy on Cooper was published in early 1784 as the first six pages of an eight-page pamphlet. Its final two pages presented a funeral anthem composed on Cooper's behalf by William Billings, America's first native-born composer, hence establishing a concrete connection between Billings and Wheatley. As Billings had moved within Boston circles for some fifteen years as a composer and director of numerous "singing schools" designed especially for participation by women, we may surmise that this occasion was hardly the first on which Billings and Wheatley met. Billings's first book, *The New-England Psalm-Singer*, published in 1770 by the Boston printers Edes and Gill, includes an anthem entitled simply "Africa," which may have been composed with Wheatley in mind. In the essay "To all Musical Practitioners," comprising part of the prefatory material of *Psalm-Singer*, Billings asserts, regarding the creative process, "Fancy goes first, and strikes out the Work roughly, and Art comes after, and polishes it over" (32). The affinity of thought regarding the imaginative faculty among Wheatley and these three men—Seccombe, Cooper, and Billings—need only be stated to be recognized.

11. Wheatley employs other elements of epic, such as cataloguing (European involvement in the Revolution, 155), further use of the epic simile, use of the chthonic (arguably Wheatley's attempt to relate the obligatory visit to the Underworld for purposes of enlightenment; see elegies in *Collected Works* 84–87), and her frequent depiction of a cosmic setting (see, e.g., "Thoughts

on the Works of Providence" and "On Imagination"). Consideration of these, however, would only have delayed the inevitable conclusion: Wheatley constructs, even if unconsciously, an intertextual epic in her extant works.

7. The Radical Shift in Discourse

1. Perhaps the first American colonist to advance the cause of de-emphasizing Latin studies in favor of promoting English language and grammar studies was Hugh Jones (1671–1760). In his *An Accidence to the English Tongue* (1724), published in England seven years after his immigration to America, Jones advances his theory that the study of Latin in the grammar schools serves no *useful* purpose. Jones's ideas here are certainly in line with those of John Locke in *Some Thoughts Concerning Education*. One of Jones's recent commentators has observed that "there is no evidence that Jones's grammar was ever imported to the colonies or used in colonial classrooms" (see Michael Montgomery 844–46). Nevertheless, Jones traveled frequently to Philadelphia, "where he associated with notables, such as Benjamin Franklin" (845). It is highly probable, therefore, that Jones and Franklin exchanged ideas about their theories of education.
2. For example, Benjamin Rush, a physician and pamphleteer who became one of the best-known educators of the United States before 1800, wrote, in a letter to John Adams on July 21, 1789: "At 22 years of age I read Lowth's *Introduction* to the grammar of our language." Since Rush was born in 1745, the year for his reading of Lowth would have been 1767, some seven years after his receipt of a B.A. degree from the College of New Jersey (now Princeton) and during his two-year stay in Edinburgh while completing his medical studies. Rush 1: 524 and Barnett 3: 1255–58.
3. Lowth's emphasis on the teaching of English grammar *before* the student goes on to Latin reflects the separation of classes in Britain; knowledge of ancient languages was largely the province of the educated, higher class. This tradition of separating the classes by means of education is well articulated in Simpson: "There is a continuing polemical tradition connecting Chaucer's Parson with the author of a study reported in the London *Sunday Times* (December 19, 1982), who argues that teaching Latin to working-class children would be a blow for social and educational equality because class divisions in England are based on two different languages" (14). While it is true that Americans have a very different notion of "equality" than the author of the *Sunday Times* passage, a similar understanding of the function of education existed before and during the Revolutionary era. For that matter, despite the efforts of American cultural levelers, this notion of privileging by virtue of amount of education attained persists in America to the present day—and is a contemporary manifestation of the persistence of the Aeneas myth.
4. The Reinhold essay's lack of familiarity with Early American literature erodes the effectiveness of its argument that "there was no profound influence of

Vergil's poems on American thought and literature" (Reinhold 230). For example, in an effort to show that hostility existed toward the classics, the essay quotes from Francis Hopkinson's letter to Benjamin Franklin, May 24, 1784: "'What would Virgil think could he hear his beautiful poem frittered into its grammatical component parts in one of our schools?'" (Reinhold 223). Further investigation would have turned up another passage from Hopkinson's pen, part of an address given two years later: "What would Horace do if he could be present in a modern school, and hear one of his elegant odes frittered into all the small ware of the syntax? What would he do? He would break the pupils head, and put the tutor to death" (Hopkinson 2: 48). In Hopkinson's mind, then, Horace and Vergil are interchangeable in that his hostility is directed not toward Vergil (or any classical author) but toward a general incompetence among "common School-masters, those Haberdashers of Moods & Tenses, possess'd of the least Feeling or Taste for the Authors they teach" (Hastings 420). Much earlier in Hopkinson's career, just as his scholar-student days ended, at about age 26 (1763), he composed these lines of comic doggerel:

> Thus, learn'd Professors with poetic Bray
> In melting Strains would rigid Rules convey,
> Not half so tuneful Sons of Bitches howl.
> But from such Music, from such heav'nly Squall
> Good Lord deliver *me, him, them, you, us & all.* (Hastings 89)

It is true that Hopkinson came out in favor of trading the pursuit of the "dead languages" in the grammar schools for the more practical subjects of English grammar, arithmetic, geography, etc. Two points need to be made regarding this position, however. First, in the above quotations, Hopkinson was objecting to poor pedagogy and impracticality, not poor or unacceptable culture or authorship. Second, Hopkinson's recommendation that study of classical languages be eliminated from the public grammar schools came in 1786, in the heat of the radical shift, when such a position was becoming popularly held.

5. Warfel records that, in 1786, Noah Webster prepared a new edition of *The New-England Primer*, one which toned down the harsh Puritan catechism, thereby identifying the Puritan forefathers as ideal candidates to assist in the valorization of the myth of Adam.
6. As Rush spent most of his formative years and nearly all of his mature career in Philadelphia, he had ample occasion to carry on intellectual exchange with Anthony Benezet personally. They corresponded until Benezet's death in 1784. Warfel maintains that Webster, early in adulthood, met Benezet during a trip to Philadelphia (214).
7. Warfel 90–92 and illustration on 90 verso.
8. On America's early nationalist period as one in which (contrary to Derrida's position in *Of Grammatology*) "the written is an advance over the spoken," see Simpson, *Politics* 56–57.

9. It never has been my intention even to suggest that the Founding Fathers, in their endeavor to set up a workable, practicable government for the United States, slavishly imitated ancient political theoria. For excellent overviews of how the designers of the Constitution incorporated the thought of classical authors, see first David A. J. Richards and then Carl J. Richard.
10. Craven records that, when the Catholic Charles Carroll, known as the Settler, migrated to the Maryland colony during the Glorious Revolution (1688), he changed his family motto from "Strong in Faith and War" to "Anywhere So Long as There Be Freedom." In so doing, continues Craven, "he revealed his desire to find a place on earth that offered religious toleration" (236). In this example, religious freedom had become the equivalent of freedom in general. This illustration lends credibility to Bender's generalization, that in the minds of many (even among the better educated class), little distinction existed between religious and political freedom. This understanding became established from very early times.
11. This statement is used as a chapter headnote in Graff 209. According to Graff, this quotation derives from Culler's then unpublished essay, "Literary Criticism and the University" (Graff 297).
12. On this problematic issue, see ch. 2, n. 26.
13. Knapp offers a comment on the status of classical studies in America in 1829, asserting that teachers of the time led their "pupils through the paths of miscellaneous and classical literature—and at the present day, even the humblest education partakes of much that is of a classical nature" (4). As Knapp is not more specific, it is unclear whether he means that students read classical authors in translation or that they actually spent hours learning some Latin and less Greek. Had he had in mind a full-scale Latin and Greek program, surely he would have said so. It is true that Latin and Greek (esp. Latin) were not dead, even in the public schools of America, but few (except private schools) retained a classical studies curriculum, and virtually none of the public schools required such studies. In the public sector after the radical shift, when classical studies were retained at all, they were relegated to elective status. Knapp's own classical training becomes evident in his commentary on the many authors he profiles, such as Joseph Green, whom he correctly calls "a wit, a classical scholar, and a poet" (159); Joel Barlow, of whose *Columbiad* he observes that the poet did not keep "constantly within the strict laws of measure, or on the classical top of Pindus" (168); and Francis Hopkinson, of whose satire upon the press Knapp wrote, "Juvenal and Pope could not boast of having produced such an effect with all their fame" (164).
14. Michael Lind, poet of *The Alamo*, kindly urged me to emphasize that the South always has stimulated rearticulation of classicism in American thought. For the suggestion that Emerson, Thoreau, and Whitman should not be ignored in this discussion, I am indebted to Nina Baym.
15. To speak of Whitman as "less formally educated" is not to suggest that he should be considered in any way the intellectual inferior of Emerson or

Thoreau. Rather, Whitman, like Melville, should be considered a self-made intellectual. Kaplan observes that Whitman was "the beneficiary of a thrifty and rational scheme of education devised by an English Quaker, Joseph Lancaster." His tenure in the public school lasted some "five or six years" (Kaplan 67). "At eleven," then, "all the formal schooling he was to have behind him, Walt worked as an office boy for a firm of lawyers, James B. Clarke and his son Edward" (70–71). At age seventeen and continuing intermittently until he was twenty-two, Whitman served as a public schoolmaster, taking his students "through a 'bare and superficial' curriculum of reading, writing, grammar [English], arithmetic and geography" (82). Throughout his long career, Whitman's reading was extensive, esp. in astronomy and world religions. For an overview of how Whitman's intellectual curiosity manifested itself in his reading, see Kaplan 229–31.

16. On the intellectual milieu of alternative mythologies which suffused the period from about 1750 at least until the 1830s, see R. D. Richardson Jr. 3–33. The "Selected Bibliography of Works Pertaining to Myth and Literature in America Between 1760 and 1860" is extremely instructive (R. D. Richardson 267–99). The "two traditions" Richardson describes are the pro-mythological and the anti-mythological.

8. The Persistence of the American Aeneas in Hawthorne

1. R. D. Richardson Jr. offers a learned and provocative study arguing that the major writers of nineteenth-century America—he lists Bronson Alcott, Emerson, Hawthorne, Melville, Theodore Parker, Thoreau, and Whitman—"were equally familiar with the case for myth as a form for imaginative philosophical or religious truth and the case against myth as fraud, illusion and falsehood" (6–7). From these positions for and against myth, Richardson traces two traditions: the pro-mythological and the anti-mythological. While I do not quarrel with Richardson's finding that there were two such traditions, in Europe as well as in America, I think Richardson presses too hard for an anticlassicism, esp. in the work of Hawthorne. In Hawthorne there is a palpable tension between the myths of Aeneas (or classicism) and Adam (or the Judaeo-Christian tradition), with "myth" taken to be, not exactly as Richardson takes it, "as a form for imaginative philosophical or religious truth," but as a distillation of human experience or, a la Foucault, a mode of discourse.

   Significantly, Richardson's discussion of Hawthorne's *A Wonder-Book for Boys and Girls* and *Tanglewood Tales* (168–79 and notes on 256–58) ignores Nina Baym, "Hawthorne's Myths for Children." This cogent, closely argued essay treats first *A Wonder-Book* and then *Tanglewood Tales*, showing that both should be understood "entirely in terms of Hawthorne's perceptions of audience needs and tastes" (35). Thus Baym undermines Richardson's position that both works constitute Hawthorne's attempt to promote his notion of "the Gothic" over that of the classical. According to Baym, "Where Hawthorne faulted the Greek myths in *A Wonder-Book* . . . for their elegant indifference to human life, they are now [in *Tanglewood Tales*] criticized for their lack of restraint, their passionate extremeness. The classic myths are not 'classic' at all—if anything they are overly romantic" (42). In Baym's view, the process Hawthorne adopts in reconstructing the Greek myths is one "of improving a myth by making its most objectionable passages [esp. those which do not reinforce nineteenth-century America's perceptions of moral decorum] the occasion for noble sentiments" (46). Hawthorne's motives for proceeding in this manner Baym attributes to his conscious attempts, *not* to vilify classical thought and culture, but to appeal to a popular reading public, most of it consisting of children. We also should note that Jane F. Dejovine's doctoral dissertation deals with Hawthorne's classicism.

2. Other investigations include Stewart, "Hawthorne and *The Faerie Queene*"; Arner (published seven months after Bush's article, this piece makes no mention of Bush's study); Shroeder; Buford Jones; Schecter; and J. C. Boswell.

Two articles dealing with Hawthorne's serpent metaphor require commentary. Schecter's discussion of Hawthorne's "Bosom Serpent" compares the tale to the recent film *Alien*. Oddly, Schecter makes no reference in either his analysis or his notes (155–56) to Bush's comprehensive study. While his comparison of tale and film is entirely appropriate, Schecter's claim that Hawthorne displays an "uncharacteristic clumsiness" in the composition of "Bosom Serpent" is less tenable. For example, he maintains that "the image of Roderick 'undulat[ing] along the pavement in a curved line' . . . is more suggestive of a rhumba dancer than a man possessed by a 'bosom fiend'" (22). This reading of Hawthorne's description of Elliston suggests that the tale's central character still attempts, at least, to walk erect, yet Hawthorne explicitly states early in the tale that, "instead of walking straight forward with open front, he undulated along the pavement in a curved line," serving "to imitate the motion of a snake" (249–50). Lest there be any doubt, at the tale's end, just after Herkimer, the sculptor, sees "a waving motion through the grass" (as the serpent leaves Elliston's bosom), "Roderick sat up like a man renewed" (263). Obviously this man, so long as he remains possessed by the viper, cannot (or thinks he cannot) walk erect. Such misreading prompts Schecter to conclude of Hawthorne and this tale, "By straining so hard after allegory, Hawthorne drains the central fantasy of its dreamlike (or, more properly, nightmarish) energies and reduces a potent legend to a flat and mechanical sermon" (23). A reader with such an uncharitable attitude toward Hawthorne (one who apparently prefers folklore and legend to conscious artistry) could say the same of most of Hawthorne's fiction.

The only piece of scholarship I have located which asserts that Hawthorne's source for the "Bosom Serpent" lies in classical authors is Boswell's "Bosom Serpents Before Hawthorne: Origin of a Symbol." He names Vergil's book VII of the *Aeneid* and Aesop's *Fables*. Disappointingly, neither attribution is convincing, largely because the discussions are too brief.

Claiming that "extensive investigation of Hawthorne's reading matter leaves little doubt he knew that classical instance in Book Seven of Vergil's *Aeneid* in which a bosom snake figures unforgettably," Boswell then, in a footnote, quotes a listing of several pages from Kesselring's well-known *Hawthorne's Reading* (280). He provides no further information, adducing not a single title from Kesselring's listing and leaving the reader to divine what an "extensive investigation" may consist of. Conducting my own "extensive investigation" into Kesselring's useful listing, I located many titles from classical authors (e.g., Homer's *Epics*, trans. by Alexander Pope, checked out on June 9, 1832; Juvenal's *Satires*, checked out twice, on February 16 and 22, 1831; Persius's *Satires* [which are more homiletic than satirical], checked out on August 25, 1831; Plautus's *Comedies*, May 9, 1829; Pliny's *Histories*, May 21, 1836; Plutarch's *Lives* [Dryden's trans.], August 20, 1838; Tacitus's *Works*, June 2, 1832; and Terence's *Comedies*, October 16, 1827). All these works were in English translations. One searches in vain for a single Vergil listing until this promising entry (no. 147, p. 49): "Dryden, John. *Original Poems and Translations*. London, 1743. 2V," edited by Rev. Thomas Broughton, which Hawthorne took out three times: on January 14 and 24, 1829, and on September 19, 1832. *The National Union Catalog* entry for this collection calls it the first gathering of Dryden's original poems and his translations. As such, one would expect these two volumes to contain Dryden's famous translation of all Vergil's works, including the *Aeneid* (Dryden's translation was considered standard until the *fin de siècle*). Upon inspection, however, such proves not to be the case; this edition contains *some* of Dryden's original pieces and *some* of his translations (parts of Ovid's *Metamorphoses*, parts of Lucretius, parts of others), but not a single translation of anything from Vergil. Broughton himself states on the second and third pages of his "Preface" (these pages are not numbered) that

> There is, indeed, a Collection of *Original Poems and Translations* by Mr. *Dryden*, publish'd for *J. Tonson* in 1701, in a thin *Folio*. But, as it contains not much above half the Pieces, so it does not at all answer the design, of the present Collection; which, with the Author's *Plays*, *Fables*, and *Translations* of *Virgil*, *Juvenal*, and *Persius*, is intended to complete Mr. *Dryden's Works* in *Twelves*.

A check into Hugh Macdonald's *John Dryden* reveals that Broughton is correct in his description of Jacob Tonson's earlier efforts; for, in 1701, Tonson had issued a set of Dryden's *Works* in four folio volumes with the general title *Poems and Translations*. These 1701 volumes included two of plays and operas, a third of some original poems and some translations, and a fourth devoted exclusively to Dryden's translations of Vergil's *Eclogues*, *Georgics*, and the *Aeneid* (Macdonald 149–50).

From my own "extensive investigation of Hawthorne's reading matter," I have ascertained that Hawthorne did *not* see a copy of Dryden's *Aeneid*, at least not one he checked out from the Salem Athenaeum. Of course, he could have borrowed a copy of this popular translation from family and/or friends, or he could have purchased one. It would have been sounder procedure to make a case for Hawthorne's academic classical training, one in which he undoubtedly was expected to memorize lengthy passages from all of Vergil's works (and from other classical authors as well, but esp. from Vergil).

All the above objections recede into the background, however, when one considers Boswell's methodology for asserting Vergil as a source. Assertion consists of quoting a part of the salient passage (not enough for me) and the standard Loeb Library translation, followed only by the comment: "Americanists may well excuse themselves for failing to search for bosom serpent sources in the classics" (281). Boswell makes no attempt to suggest how Hawthorne's source provides hints concerning character motivation or how this source may have worked with others to suggest to Hawthorne a *modus operandi* for his characterization of Elliston.

Boswell's handling of Aesop as a source is even less convincing. He opens this section by asserting that, in Aesop, "we find the progenitor of all bosom snakes" (283). As before, assertion is not followed by proof. Subsequently, Boswell quotes the Latin text of the fable, "A Countryman and a Snake," which he maintains displays "the farmer putting the serpent into his bosom." Without providing a transliteral rendering into English of the Latin passage, Boswell next quotes "John Ogilby's popular verse translation [which is] fanciful in some respects but quite faithful in regard to the bosom" (284). Without burdening the reader with Ogilby's admittedly "fanciful" version, I will give an English rendering of the Latin text Boswell quotes: "Serpens semel iacebat super terram gelatem et multum algebat. Homo quidam hoc videns, pictate motus, accepit serpentem et posuit in sinum suum ad calefaciendum. Serpens calefactus hominem fortiter pungebat" (284; Once a snake lay above the frozen earth and felt particularly cold. A certain man seeing it, moved by pity, took the serpent and put [it] in his bosom [as in a garment or in a place of concealment], to make [it] warm. The snake, having become warm, vigorously bit the man). While it is certainly plausible to maintain that there are some similarities here, as a snake and a human being endure physical intimacy for a brief time, this fable contains no image of an actual physical invasion, as is the case in Vergil. As before, however, Boswell fails to discuss how this fable does or does not constitute an analogy to Hawthorne's tale.

To make his presentation more convincing, Boswell might have pointed out that Aesop's *Fables* contain two additional tales. One is about man and snake living in enmity with one another (perhaps more pertinent to Hawthorne's uses in "Bosom Serpent"). The other is about a raven and a snake; the popular version printed by Samuel Richardson (about 1740) contains his own "Life of Aesop" as a preface. In this version, the tale is followed by this statement of its moral: "Nature has made all the necessaries of life safe and easy to us; but if we will be hankering after things that we neither want nor understand, we must take our fortune, let what will be the event" (109). This last passage, it seems to me, is pregnant with possible applications to Hawthorne's tale. Had Boswell been more thorough, he could have constructed a significant interpretation of this tale.

3. Arlin Turner, *Nathaniel Hawthorne: A Biography*, maintains that in this story Hawthorne declares "the connection of his tale . . . with the allegorical meaning the serpent has had in Western thought from the Book of Genesis onward" (161). Hence Turner places the tale in the larger context of the Western literary imagination from its most ancient times.

4. This is the significant passage from Spenser, in *Edmund Spencer's Poetry*, edited by Hugh Maclean:

   > O hatefull hellish Snake, what furie furst
   > Brought thee from balefull house of Proserpine,
   > Where in her bosome she thee long had nurst,
   > And fostred up with bitter milke of tine [affliction],
   > Fowle Gealosie, that turnest love divine
   > To joylesse dread, and mak'st the loving hart
   > With hatefull thoughts to languish and to pine,
   > And feed it selfe with selfe-consuming smart?
   > Of all the passions in the mind thou vilest art. (327)

   The ties here to Hawthorne's "head of Envy, with her snaky locks" (250) are obvious. At the bottom of the page on which these lines appear (in n. 2), Maclean makes the following parenthetical observation: "probably echoing Virgil's description of the frenzied Alecto, in the *Aeneid*, 7.342–55." If one knows the passage from Vergil, one quickly understands that Spenser intends to draw on the *physical* invasion motif for his own picture of how "Fowle Gealosie" works its evil will on its victims. Thus Spenser could have served Hawthorne as a source of the physical invasion construct. This possibility was overlooked by Bush and others seeking a source of physical, serpentine invasion. Moreover, in volume 3 of *The Works of Edmund Spenser: A Variorum Edition*, editor Padelford records that the first stanza of book III, canto 11, has been associated with Vergil's *Aeneid* VII, 346–51 at least since John Upton's edition of Spenser appeared in 1758. Padelford notes that, in Upton's edition, the eighteenth-century editor remarked in his commentary on this passage: "See how Virgil (*Aeneid* 7.351) has painted the fury Alecto, with her jealous and envious snake, poisoning the Latian [*sic*] Queen, 'viperam inspirans animam'" (288). Earlier than this time, very likely no gloss was necessary.

5. Several critics have remarked upon the similarity between Hawthorne's river crossing and that which occurs in Dante's *La Commedia* (Inferno, canto III). Among these, see Broes 171–84, esp. 174–75; Dennis 250–58 (esp. 253); and Liebman 443–57, esp. 445. In the following text, I too speak of Robin in terms of a conversion of sorts, though not in quite the same terms as Liebman.

6. For a standard interpretation couched in the tenets of the Adamic myth, see Dennis. For a refreshingly different approach to "My Kinsman," see Edwin

H. Miller, "My Kinsman" 145–51. Miller argues that if this tale is read with what he identifies as Hawthorne's "spirit of play," "we may not arrive at intellectual-historical-mythical profundities, which I believe Hawthorne eschews, but we may come closer to the comi-tragic (the elements of the word are deliberately reversed) spirit of his affectionate depiction of a boy-man at the difficult, anxiety-ridden age of eighteen" (146).

7. On "My Kinsman," among others of Hawthorne's tales, see Leverenz, "Historicizing Hell" 101–32. Leverenz insists that, rather than the earlier "evil, malice or the devil's fiery eyes" (*Manhood* 235), *shrewd* now denotes "demonic possession," a definition *not* to be found in my copy of the *OED*. Leverenz also maintains that Hawthorne has constructed "Kinsman" "under the guise of narrating a slightly displaced account of the American Revolution" (109). Hawthorne places the time of action in his story at least forty years *before* the Revolution; why must we claim that Hawthorne *really* meant to write about another time? Why can't his tale be addressing American colonial growing pains as the colonials were evolving toward the maturity of a perspective which, forty years later, demanded that they be free? Moreover, Leverenz draws provocative and judicious connections between Dante's *La Commedia* and "My Kinsman," but he presses so hard for other connections to Dante that he ends by concluding that the tale bears "Dantean contradictions," and these apparently remain unresolved (107–10). Perhaps viewing "My Kinsman" as an inverse response to Vergil's *Aeneid*, esp. to book VI's depiction of Aeneas's trip to the Underworld, would resolve Leverenz's "contradictions."
8. Subsequent discussion of "My Kinsman, Major Molineaux" is based on the idea that, while Aeneas seeks and finds his father Anchises, Robin rejects his kinsman, which constitutes a perversion of the Aeneas myth. I am indebted to my friend and colleague Mary R. Ryder for this insight.

9. The Persistence of the American Aeneas in Melville

1. On Melville's allegedly pro-Christian views in *Billy Budd*, see Matthiessen, Lewis 146–52, and Hillway 138–42. Among these critics, only Matthiessen insists that Melville himself yielded to the tenets of the Gospels (e.g., "And only by profound acceptance of the Gospels was he [Melville] able to make his warmest affirmation of good through a common sailor's act of holy forgiveness," 513). Still, Lewis and Hillway lean heavily toward a Christian interpretation of *Billy Budd*. On Melville's allegedly anti-Christian views in this work (often read within what is taken to be Melville's ironic posture), see James E. Miller 218–28, 241, 248–49, and 251–52; Dillingham, *Melville's Later Novels* 365–99 and 406–7; and esp. Thompson 355–414.
2. Coffler, "Classical Elements" (a dissertation directed by Merton M. Sealts Jr.), concludes of Melville's last novel, "In terms of balance, harmony, and

unity, *Billy Budd, Sailor* is Melville's most purely 'classic' work" (*DAI* [Sept. 1981]: 1148). Classical elements in Melville's works are treated in Coffler, "Form as Resolution" 105–22; Coffler, "Melville's *Billy Budd, Sailor*" 2–3; and Coffler, "*Moby-Dick:* Classicism" 73–84. Another dissertation on Melville's classicism is Small, directed by Nathalia Wright. See abstracts of Small and Coffler, in Hayashi 271 and 422, respectively.

3. Gilman points out that the curriculum at Lansingburgh Academy "included Latin, Greek, and Hebrew," as well as courses in "mathematics, surveying and engineering, natural philosophy, astronomy, intellectual philosophy, logic, rhetoric, and bookkeeping" (103). Such offerings sound like a budding writer's paradise. Coffler reports that Melville *did* study Latin while attending the Albany Classical Academy (2).
4. See Gilman 84–90, 147–48, and 150–51.
5. See Sealts, *Melville's Reading* 51–52 and 51 n. This invaluable source is used most profitably in conjunction with Bercaw, *Melville's Sources* (a revision of Bercaw's dissertation under Harrison Hayford). This work cross-indexes a plethora of possible sources for Melville's poems and prose, along with articles and books in which discussions of Melville's sources have appeared (most reliable through 1980).
6. In a footnote to his identification of the origins of Mardi and Media, Merrell Davis quotes the first two lines (and the first two words of the third) of the "Mardi" entry and the first two lines (and once again the first two words of the third) from the "Media" entry. Then he writes: "No proof exists for Melville's choice of these names, but the combination is striking, even if he changed 'Media' to designate a king rather than a country and applied 'Mardi' to an unknown island archipelago rather than an Asiatic people" (72 n.). Anthon, *Classical,* contains a 17-line entry for "Mardi" and a 106-line entry for "Media." These present ample "proof" of why Melville made Mardi a country and Media a king. The third designation for "Mardi" Anthon gives is "A nation dwelling to the south of Bactriana, and to the north of the chain of Paropamisus. Pliny (VI, 16) says they extended from Caucasus to Bactriana," etc. Here we have Mardi as a nation associated with a chain of islands! Anthon, about halfway through the "Media" entry, identifies (on 808) "the commencement of the Median monarchy B.C. 716," followed by the names of those who comprised that monarchy—hence the suggestion of the name Media as a monarch. Investigators of Melville's work (and that of many other American authors) seem to assume that, since they are not seriously interested in classical sources, Melville himself could not have been. Yet we should all recall that Melville asserted early in his career that he loved minds that dive deep.
7. On the particulars of this and subsequent discussions of astronomical elements, see handbooks on astronomy, such as Tuer 9 and 228, and Satterthwaite 10, 166–69 (article on Sir William Herschel), and 463. Leach is an excellent general reference for astronomical and mythological associations of the names of prominent stars. As for Melville's likely familiarity

with binary stars, Sir William Herschel, *Catalogue of Double Stars* (1781) and *Second Catalogue of Double Stars* (1784), long had been incorporated into the body of knowledge comprising navigational astronomy. Another explanation for Melville's use of *bis* could be much closer to home, at least closer to the American plains of Melville's day. Perhaps *bis* is simply a shortened form for *bison*. If so, Melville imparts to the name of Aeneas's ship a peculiarly American flavor.

8. Throughout this discussion of *Billy Budd*, I assume that Melville performs as his own narrator. In arriving at the conclusion that Melville is telling his story himself, I am responding on three levels. First, Melville's subtitle for the work *(An Inside Narrative)* I take to be, among other possibilities, an indication of the author's intimacy with the text. Second, repeatedly I encounter a first-person narrator who remains ever empathic toward his "fellow" sailors. To take just one instance among many: "The sailor is frankness, the landsman is finesse" (86). Third, I defer to the leading authority on this text, Merton M. Sealts Jr. In "Innocence and Infamy: *Billy Budd, Sailor*," Sealts affirms that "the narrator of *Billy Budd*, it may be observed, sounds very much like the authors of these several earlier headnotes [such as those to "John Marr" and "Tom Deadlight," among others]—which is to say, like Melville himself" (412).

9. Coffler, *Melville's Classical Allusions*, identifies this personification as an implied allusion to Venus (15). Venus long has been associated with the Graces. Anthon's entry on "Gratiae" (i.e., the Graces), identifies these three sisters as "the attendants of Venus," who sometimes were called "the children of Bacchus and Venus" and who presided "over social enjoyment, the banquet . . . and all that tended to inspire gayety [*sic*] and cheerfulness" (562). After Budd has been impressed into service aboard the *Bellipotent*, Melville describes him as having "a sort of genial happy-go-lucky air"; indeed, there was "no merrier man in his mess" (49). This description appears barely a page before Budd's association with "Love and the Graces."

   In *The Faerie Oueene*, Spenser calls the Graces the "Handmaids of Venus" (VI, x, 15). Discussing this work, Starnes and Talbert point out that Servius, Boccaccio, and Natales Comes all draw associations similar to Spenser's; several Renaissance classical dictionaries (e.g., Friar Ambrosius Calepine, *Dictionarium* [1502]; Robert Stephanus, *Thesaurus Linguae Latinae* [1531]; and Charles Stephanus, *Dictionarium historicum ac poeticum* [1553]) also present the intimate association of the Graces to Venus (90). Horace's well-known ode 30 from book I associates the Graces with Venus. In doing so, Melville rests upon long tradition.

10. On this Hercules passage, see Hayford and Sealts' discussion of leaf 38 among Melville's *Billy Budd* manuscript pages (Melville, *Billy Budd* 140–41).

11. On the importance of the sacrificial bull in Old Testament tradition, see the article entitled "Bull" (Buttrick 1: 473–74).

12. See Ferguson 18, 19, and plate 1.

13. See Robertson and Dietriech 589–90.

14. See, e.g., Dillingham, *Melville's Later Novels* 365–99.
15. Dentan states, "The concept of redemption from sin appears nowhere [in the Old Testament] except possibly in Ps. 130:8" (21–22). Rather, in the Old Testament, most of which forms part of the Jewish Holy Scriptures, the idea of redemption usually is not applied to individuals but to delivering entire bodies of the people of Israel from tribulations of various sorts. Dentan points out, however, that, esp. in the case of Job, "God is his personal redeemer *(go el)* and must therefore ultimately vindicate his integrity"—not his sin(s), because Job remains sinless. Dentan also observes that the notion of a personal redeemer appears in Gen. 48:16; II Sam. 4:9; and Ps. 26:11, 49:15, 69:18, and 103:4. But it remains for the New Testament to develop the concept of redemption from one's sins. See, e.g., in Heb. 9:15, where the term "redemption" is applied to forgiveness of sins. Of the New Testament concept of redemption, Dentan concludes, "In its proper Christian theological sense [redemption] always implies deliverance from sin and its effects, rather than merely from death or trouble" (22). On the inadequacy of the Christian myth, see James E. Miller Jr. 251–52.
16. Melville, *Great Short Works* 365. I am certainly not the first to point out Melville's familiarity with *Magnalia*. See Leyda 1:477 and 2:515. For a guide to scholarly discussions of *Magnalia* as a source in *Moby Dick*, "The Lightning-Rod Man," "The Apple-Tree Table," and *The Confidence-Man*, see Bercaw, p. 101, entry 485.
17. See, e.g., Sealts, "Innocence and Infamy," and Dillingham, *Melville's Later Novels*. Dillingham thinks *Vere* connotes *Veritas*, another Latin noun for *truth*, as well as *vir* (369–71).
18. I quote from Goodrich 110 because of the immense popularity of this early American civics text by the creator of the famous Peter Parley textbooks for children. Note that Goodrich authored this text himself, under his own name. While I argue neither that Melville used this book as a text himself (it was written too late) nor that he would have consulted this text as an authority, he could have come across it as a text used by his children.
19. For alternative readings of Melville's handling of the Orpheus myth, see Adler 175–76 and Dillingham, *Melville's Later Novels* 370–71, 376, 377, 379–80, and 387–88.

Conclusion

1. Earlier, Ruland and Bradbury wrote provocatively of Mather's *Magnalia*: "Indeed, it draws not only on the Bible but the Vergilian tale of trials overcome in Rome's founding, the making of the great city" (15). Disappointingly, they carry this observation no further.
2. Quint gives another analysis of the role of empire after the fall of Rome.

Bibliography

Aarsleff, Hans. *The Study of Language in England, 1780–1860*. Minneapolis: University of Minnesota P, 1983.

Abrams, M. H. *The Mirror and the Lamp: Romantic Theory and the Critical Tradition*. New York: Norton, 1958.

Adams, John [1704–1740]. *Poems on Several Occasions*. Boston, 1745.

Adler, Joyce Sparer. *War in Melville's Imagination*. New York: New York UP, 1981.

Ahlstrom, Sydney E. *A Religious History of the American People*. 2 vols. Garden City, NY: Doubleday, 1975.

Akenside, Mark. *The Poetical Works of Mark Akenside*. Ed. Alexander Dyce. London, 1894.

Akers, Charles W. *The Divine Politician: Samuel Cooper and the American Revolution in Boston*. Boston: Northeastern UP, 1982.

Albanese, Catherine L. *Sons of the Fathers: The Civil Religion of the American Revolution*. Philadelphia: Temple UP, 1976.

Aldridge, A. Owen. *Early American Literature: A Comparatist Approach*. Princeton: Princeton UP, 1982.

Allen, Don Cameron. *Mysteriously Meant: The Rediscovery of Pagan Symbolism and Allegorical Interpretation in the Renaissance*. Baltimore: Johns Hopkins UP, 1970.

Allen, Walter, Jr. "The Non-Existent Classical Epyllion." *Studies in Philology* 55 (1958): 515–18.

Allen, William B., ed. *George Washington: A Collection*. Indianapolis: Liberty Classics, 1988.

Alpers, Paul. *The Singer of the "Eclogues": A Study of Virgilian Pastoral*. Berkeley: U of California P, 1979.

———. *What Is Pastoral?* Chicago: U of Chicago P, 1996.

Anderson, Howard, et al., eds. *The Familiar Letter in the Eighteenth Century*. Lawrence: UP of Kansas, 1966.

Anonymous. *Rhetorica ad Herennium*. Trans. Harry Caplan. Cambridge, MA: Harvard UP, 1981.

Anthon, Charles. *A Classical Dictionary*. New York: Harper and Brothers, 1841.

Apthorp, East. *The Felicity of the Times*. Boston, 1763.

———. *Of Sacred Poetry and Music: A Discourse at Christ Church, Cambridge, at the Opening of the Organ*. Boston, 1764.

Aristotle. *The Complete Works of Aristotle: The Revised Oxford Translation*. 2 vols. Ed. Jonathan Barnes. Princeton: Princeton UP, 1984.

———. *De Anima, Books II and III (with Certain Passages from Book I)*. Trans. D. W. Hamlyn. Oxford: Oxford UP, 1968.

Arner, Robert D. "Of Snakes and Those Who Swallow Them: Some Folk Analogues for Hawthorne's 'Egotism; or, The Bosom Serpent.'" *Southern Folklore Quarterly* 35.4 (Dec. 1971): 336–46.

Arnott, D. W. *The Nominal and Verbal Systems of Fula*. Oxford: Oxford UP, 1970.

Artz, Frederich B. *The Mind of the Middle Ages*. 3rd ed. Chicago: U of Chicago P, 1980.

Ash, John. *Grammatical Institutes*. 1785. Delmar, FL: Scholars' Facsimiles and Reprints, 1979.

Atkins, J. W. H. *English Literary Criticism: The Medieval Phase*. London: Cambridge UP, 1943.

Awkward, Michael. *Inspiriting Influences: Tradition, Revision, and Afro-American Women's Novels*. New York: Columbia UP, 1989.

Axtell, James. "The Scholastic Philosophy of the Wilderness." *William and Mary Quarterly* 29.3 (July 1972): 335–66.

Bailyn, Bernard. *The Ideological Origins of the American Revolution*. Cambridge, MA: Harvard UP, 1967.

———, ed. *Pamphlets of the American Revolution, 1750–1776*. Vol. 1. Cambridge, MA: Belknap P of Harvard UP, 1965.

———. *Voyagers to the West: A Passage in the Peopling of America on the Eve of the Revolution*. New York: Vintage Books, 1988.

Baker, Houston A., Jr. *The Journey Back: Issues in Black Literature and Criticism*. Chicago: U of Chicago P, 1980.

Barker, Virgil. *American Painting: History and Interpretation*. New York, NY: Bonanza, 1950.

Barlow, Joel. *Poetry*. Ed. William K. Bottorff and Arthur L. Ford. Gainesville, FL: Scholars' Facsimiles and Reprints, 1970. Vol. 2 of *The Works of Joel Barlow: In Two Volumes*. 1970.

Barnett, Louise K. "Benjamin Rush (1745–1813)." In *American Writers Before 1800: A Biographical and Critical Dictionary*. Ed. James A. Levernier and Douglas R. Wilmes. Vol. 3, 1255–58. Westport, CT: Greenwood, 1983.

Baxter, Richard. *The Saints' Everlasting Rest*. London: 1650.

Baym, Max I. *A History of Literary Aesthetics in America*. New York: Ungar, 1973.

Baym, Nina. "Between Enlightenment and Victorian: Toward a Narrative of American Women Writers Writing History." *Critical Inquiry* 18 (Autumn 1991): 22–41.

———. "Hawthorne's Myths for Children: The Author Versus His Audience." *Studies in Short Fiction* 10.1 (Winter, 1973): 35–46.

———. "Mercy Otis Warren's Gendered Melodrama of Revolution." *South Atlantic Quarterly* 90.3 (Summer, 1991): 531–54.

Bedini, Silvio A., ed. *The Christopher Columbus Encyclopedia*. 2 vols. New York: Simon and Schuster, 1992.

Belknap, Jeremy. "An Eclogue Occasioned by the Death of the Reverend Alexander Cumming." Boston, 1763.

Bender, John, and David E. Wellbery, eds. *The Ends of Rhetoric: History, Theory, Practice*. Stanford, CA: Stanford UP, 1990.

Bender, Thomas. "New York in Theory." *America in Theory*. Ed. Leslie Berlowitz et al. New York: Oxford UP, 1988.

Benezet, Anthony. *The Pennsylvania Spelling-Book; or, Youth's Friendly Instructor and Monitor*. Philadelphia, 1782.

———. *Some Necessary Remarks on the Education of Youth*. Philadelphia, 1778.

Benson, Mary Sumner. *Women in Eighteenth-Century America: A Study of Opinion and Social Usage*. New York: AMS, 1976.

Bercaw, Mary K. *Melville's Sources*. Evanston, IL: Northwestern UP, 1987.

Bercovitch, Sacvan. *The American Jeremiad*. Madison: U of Wisconsin P, 1978.

———, ed. *The American Puritan Imagination: Essays in Revaluation*. Cambridge, Eng.: Cambridge UP, 1974.

———, ed. *The Cambridge History of American Literature*. Vol. 1: *1590–1820*. Cambridge, Eng.: Cambridge UP, 1994.

———. "New England Epic: Cotton Mather's *Magnalia Christi Americana*." *English Literary History* 33.3 (Sept. 1966): 337–50.

———. "The Problem of Ideology in American Literary History." *Critical Inquiry* 12.4 (Summer 1986): 33–44.

———. *The Puritan Origins of the American Self*. New Haven: Yale UP, 1975.

———. "The Puritan Vision of the New World." In *Columbia Literary History of the United States*. Ed. Emory Elliott et al. New York: Columbia UP, 1988. 33–44.

———, ed. *Reconstructing American Literary History*. Cambridge, MA: Harvard UP, 1986.

Bercovitch, Sacvan, and Myra Jehlen, eds. *Ideology and Classic American Literature*. Cambridge, Eng.: Cambridge UP, 1986.

Berlowitz, Leslie, Denis Donoghue, and Louis Menand, eds. *America in Theory*. New York: Oxford UP, 1988.

Berrigen, Joseph R., ed. *Fabulae Aesopicae: Hermolai Barbari et Gregorii Corrarii*. Lawrence, KS: Coronado, 1977.

Beverley, Robert. *The History and Present State of Virginia*. Ed. Louis B. Wright. Chapel Hill: U of North Carolina P, 1947.

Billings, William. *The New England Psalm-Singer (1770)*. Ed. Karl Kroeger. Boston: American Musicological Society and Colonial Society of Massachusetts, 1981. Vol. 1 of *The Complete Works of William Billings*. 1981.

———. *The Singing Master's Assistant (1778); Music in Miniature (1779)*. Ed. Hans Nathan. Boston: American Musicological Society and Colonial Society of Massachusetts, 1977. Vol. 2 of *The Complete Works of William Billings*.

Binger, Carl. *Revolutionary Doctor: Benjamin Rush (1746–1813)*. New York: Norton, 1966.

Blackwell Companion to the Enlightenment. Ed. John W. Yolton. Cambridge, MA: Basil Blackwell, 1991.

Blackwell Encyclopedia of the American Revolution. Ed. Jack P. Greene and J. R. Pole. Cambridge, MA: Basil Blackwell, 1991.

Blake, William. *Complete Poetry and Prose of William Blake*. Ed. David V. Erdman. Berkeley, CA: U California P, 1982.

Blessington, Francis C. "'That Undisturbed Song of Pure Conceit,': Paradise Lost and the Epic-Hymn." In *Renaissance Genres*, ed. Barbara Kiefer Lewalski. Cambridge, MA: Harvard UP, 1986.

Boardman, John, et al., eds. *The Oxford History of the Classical World*. New York: Oxford UP, 1986.

Bolgar, R. R. *The Classical Heritage and Its Beneficiaries*. Cambridge, Eng.: Cambridge UP, 1954.

Bornstein, Diane. "Captan Perse and His Coragios Company: Philip Walker," *Proceedings of the American Antiquarian Society* 83 (1973): 67–102.

Boswell, Jackson Campbell. "Bosom Serpents Before Hawthorne: Origin of a Symbol." *English Language Notes* 12.4 (June 1975): 279–87.

Bowden, Mary Weatherspoon. *Philip Freneau*. Ed. Sylvia E. Bowman. Boston: Twayne, 1976.

Bradford, M. E. *A Worthy Company*. Westchester, IL: Crossway Books, 1982.

Bradford, William. *Of Plymouth Plantation, 1620–1647*. Ed. Samuel Eliot Morison. New York: Knopf, 1952.

Bradstreet, Anne. *The Works of Anne Bradstreet in Prose and Verse*. Ed. John Harvard Ellis. Gloucester, MA, 1867. Rpt. Peter Smith, 1962.

Broes, Arthur T. "Journey into Moral Darkness: 'My Kinsman, Major Molineaux' as Allegory." *Nineteenth-Century Fiction* 19 (Sept. 1964): 171–84.

Breen, T. H. *Puritans and Adventures: Change and Persistence in Early America*. New York: Oxford UP, 1980.

Bridenbaugh, Carl. *Early Americans*. New York: Oxford UP, 1981.

Brookes, George S. *Friend Anthony Benezet*. Philadelphia: U of Pennsylvania P, 1937—to which is appended a collection of Benezet letters.

Bryan, William Alfred. *George Washington in American Literature, 1775–1865*. New York: Columbia UP, 1952.

Bryant, John, ed. *A Companion to Melville Studies*. New York: Greenwood, 1986.

Buell, Lawrence. *New England Literary Culture: From Revolution Through Renaisance*. Cambridge, Eng.: Cambridge UP, 1989.

Burke, Helen M. "The Rhetoric and Politics of Marginality: The Subject of Phillis Wheatley." *Tulsa Studies in Women's Literature* 10.1 (Spring 1991): 31–45.

Burke, Edmund. *The Speeches of Edmund Burke in the House of Commons and Westminster Hall*. 4 vols. Oxford: Oxford UP, 1816.

Burnet, Thomas. *The Sacred Theory of the Earth*. 1691. Carbondale: Southern Illinois UP, 1965.

Bush, Sargent, Jr. "Bosom Serpents Before Hawthorne: The Origins of a Symbol." *American Literature* 43.2 (May 1971): 181–99.

Buttrick, George A., ed. *The Interpreter's Dictionary of the Bible*. Nashville, TN: Abingdon P, 1962.

Byles, Mather. "A Poem On the Death of His Late Majesty King George [I]." Boston: No Printer, 1727.

———. *Poems on Several Occasions*. 1744. Introd. C. Lennart Carlson. New York: Columbia UP, 1940.

———. *Works: Compiled and with an Introduction by Benjamin Franklin V.* Delmar, FL: Scholars' Facsimiles and Reprints, 1978.

Calvin, John. *Epitome* of the *Institutes of the Christian Religion*. London, 1583.

Campbell, Joseph. *Occidental Mythology*. New York: Viking, 1964.

Carr, Patrick. *Crispus Attucks Memorial: A Memorial of Crispus Attucks, Samuel Maverick, James Caldwell, Samuel Gray and Patrick Carr from the City of Boston*. Miami, FL: Mnemosyne, 1969.

Carroll, Frances Laverne, and Mary Meacham. *The Library at Mount Vernon*. Pittsburgh: Beta Phi Mu, 1977.

Carruth, Hayden, and George Perkins. "Poetry: Before 1960." In *Benet's Reader's Encyclopedia of American Literature*. Ed. George Perkins et al. New York: HarperCollins, 1991.

Casey, John. *Pagan Virtue: An Essay in Ethics*. Oxford, Eng.: Clarendon, 1992.

Cheyney, Edward Potts. *European Background of American History, 1300–1600*. New York: Frederick Ungar, 1978.

Church, Benjamin. "XI." In *Pietas et Gratulatio Collegii Cantabrigiensis Apud Novanglos*. Boston: J. Green and J. Russell, 1761. 31–41.

———. "Elegy on the Death of the Reverend Jonathan Mayhew." In "The Devil Undone: The Life of Benjamin Church (1734–1778) to Which Is Added, an Edition of His Complete Poetry" by Jeffrey B. Walker (Diss., 1977), 181–91.

Cicero. *De officiis*. Loeb Classical Library.

Clement. *Clementis Alexandrini Opera: Graece et Latine*. Cologne: Schrey and Meyerum, 1688.

———. *The Writings of Clement of Alexandria*. Trans. William Wilson. London, 1869.

Cochrane, Charles Norris. *Christianity and Classical Culture: A Study of Thought and Action from Augustus to Augustine*. New York: Oxford UP, 1957.

Coffler, Gail H. "Form as Resolution: Classical Elements in Melville's *Battle-Pieces*." In *American Poetry: Between Tradition and Modernism 1865–1914*. Ed. Roland Hagenbuchle. Regensburg, Germany: Pustet, 1984. 105–22.

———. "Melville's *Billy Budd, Sailor*." *Explicator* 40.2 (Winter 1982): 2–3.

———. *Melville's Classical Allusions: A Comprehensive Index and Glossary*. Westport, CT: Greenwood Press, 1985.

———. "*Moby-Dick*: Classicism in Melville's Style." *Essays in Arts and Sciences* 16 (May 1987): 73–84.

Coleridge, Samuel Taylor. *The Collected Works of Samuel Taylor Coleridge: Biographia Literaria; or, Biographical Sketches of My Literary Life and Opinions*. Ed. James Engell and W. Jackson Bate. Princeton: Princeton UP, 1984.

A Collection of Poems by Several Hands. Boston, 1745.

Conte, Gian Biagio. *Latin Literature: A History*. Trans. Joseph B. Solodow. Rev. ed. Baltimore: Johns Hopkins UP, 1994.

Cook, Ebenezer. *The Sotweed Factor*. London, 1708.

Cook, Elizabeth C. *Literary Influences in Colonial Newspapers, 1704–1750*. 2nd ed. Ed. Donald H. Steward. New York: Columbia UP, 1940.

Cowell, Pattie. *Women Poets in Pre-Revolutionary America, 1650–1775: An Anthology*. Troy, NY: Whitston, 1981.

Cradock, Thomas. *The Poetic Writings of Thomas Cradock, 1718–1770*. Ed. David Curtis Skaggs. Newark, NJ: U of Delaware P, 1983.

Craven, Wayne. *Colonial American Portraiture: The Economic, Religious, Social, Cultural, Philosophical, Scientific and Aesthetic Foundations*. Cambridge, Eng.: Cambridge UP, 1986.

Cremin, Lawrence A. *American Education: The Colonial Experience, 1607–1783*. New York: Harper and Row, 1970.

Cressy, David. *Coming Over: Migration and Communication between England and New England in the Seventeenth Century*. Cambridge, Eng.: Cambridge UP, 1987.

Crèvecoeur, J. Hector St. John de. *Letters from an American Farmer and Sketches of Eighteenth-Century America*. Ed. Albert E. Stone. New York, NY: Penguin, 1981.

Crews, Frederick. *The Sins of the Fathers: Hawthorne's Psychological Themes*. Berkeley: U of California P, 1989.

Cunliffe, Marcus. *American Literature to 1900*. New York: Peter Bedrick, 1987.

———. *George Washington: Man and Monument*. Rev. ed. New York: Penguin, 1982.

Daly, Robert. *God's Altar: The World and the Flesh in Puritan Poetry*. Berkeley: U of California P, 1978.

Dathorne, O. R. *The Black Mind: A History of African Literature*. Minneapolis: U of Minnesota P, 1974.

Davidson, Cathy N. *Revolution and the Word: The Rise of the Novel in America*. New York: Oxford UP, 1986.

Davis, Merrell R. *Melville's Mardi: A Chartless Voyage*. 1952. New Haven: Archon, 1967.

Davis, Richard Beale. "America in George Sandys' 'Ovid.'" *William and Mary Quarterly* 4.3 (July 1947): 297–304.

———. *George Sandys, Poet-Adventurer: A Study in Anglo-American Culture in the Seventeenth Century*. London: Bodley Head, 1955.

———. *Intellectual Life in the Colonial South, 1585–1763*. 3 vols. Knoxville: U of Tennessee P, 1978.

———. *Intellectual Life in Jefferson's Virginia, 1790–1830*. Knoxville: U of Tennessee P, 1972.

Davis, Thomas M. *A Reading of Edward Taylor*. Newark, NJ: U of Delaware P, 1992.

Dejovine, Jane F. "Classical Myths and Moral Growth in the Four Major Romances of Nathaniel Hawthorne." Diss., Northern Illinois U, 1977.

Delbanco, Andrew. *The Puritan Ordeal*. Cambridge, MA: Harvard UP, 1989.

Dennis, Carl. "How to Live in Hell: The Bleak Vision of Hawthorne's 'My Kinsman, Major Molineux.'" *University Review* 37.4 (Summer 1971): 250–58.

Dentan, R. C. "Redeem, Redeemer, Redemption." In *The Interpreter's Dictionary of the Bible*. 4 vols. and supplement. Ed. George A. Buttrick. Nashville, TN: Abingdon P, 1962. Vol. 4: 21–22.

Diggins, John Patrick. "Theory and the American Founding." In *America in Theory*. Ed. Lelie Berlowitz et al. New York, NY: Oxford UP, 1988. 3–25.

Dillingham, William B. *An Artist in the Rigging: The Early Work of Herman Melville*. Athens: U of Georgia P, 1972.

———. *Melville's Later Novels*. Athens: U of Georgia P, 1986.

———. *Melville's Short Fiction, 1853–1856*. Athens: U of Georgia P, 1977.

Dryden, John. *The Poems of John Dryden*. Ed. James Kinsley. Vol. 3. Oxford: Oxford UP, 1958.

———. *The Works of John Dryden: Poems: The Works of Virgil in English. 1697*. Vols. 5 and 6. Ed. Alan Roper et al. Berkeley: U of California P, 1987.

Duban, James. *Melville's Major Fiction: Politics, Theology, and Imagination*. DeKalb: Northern Illinois UP, 1983.

Duyckinck, Evert A., and George L. Duyckinck. *Cyclopedia of American Literature Embracing Personal and Critical Notices of Authors, and Selections from Their Writings, from the Earliest Period to the Present Day; with Portraits, Autographs, and Other Illustrations*. Ed. M. Laird Simons. 2 vols. 1855. Philadelphia: Baxter Publishing, 1881.

Dwight, Timothy. *The Conquest of Canaan: A Poem, in Eleven Books*. London: J. Johnson, 1788. Rpt., Westport, CT: Greenwood, 1970.

———. "The Friend, No. IV." *New-Haven Gazette, and the Connecticut Magazine* 9 (June 1789): 564–67.

———. *The Major Poems of Timothy Dwight, 1752–1817: With a Dissertation on the History, Eloquence, and Poetry of the Bible*. Introd. William J. McTaggart and William K. Bottorff. Gainesville, FL: Scholars' Facsimile and Reprints, 1969.

———. *The True Means of Establishing Public Happiness*. New Haven, 1795.

Eadie, John W., ed. *Classical Traditions in Early America*. Ann Arbor: U of Michigan P, 1976.

Eberwein, Jane Donahue. "'In a Book, as in a Glass': Literary Sorcery in Mather's Life of Phips." *Early American Literature* 10.3 (1975-76): 289–300.

Eckstein, Neil T. "Pastoral and the Primitive in Benjamin Tompson's 'Address to Lord Bellamont.'" *Early American Literature Association* 8 (Feb. 1973): 111–16.

Eden, Richard, trans. *The First Three English Books on America*. Ed. Edward Arber. Birmingham, 1885.

Edwards, Jonathan. *A Treatise Concerning the Religious Affections*. 1746. Ed. John E. Smith. New Haven: Yale UP, 1959.

Egan, Jim. *Authorizing Experience: Refigurations of the Body Politic in Seventeenth-Century New England Writing*. 1999. Princeton, NJ: Princeton UP, 1999.

Ehrlich, Heyward. "Evert Augustus Duyckinck." *Dictionary of Literary Biography: American Literary Critics and Scholars, 1850–1880*. Vol. 64. Ed. John W. Rathbun and Monica M. Grecu. Detroit: Bruccoli Clark, 1988.

Eliade, Mircea. *Patterns in Comparative Religion*. Trans. Rosemary Sheed. New York: World, 1958.

Elgoods, P. G. *The Ptolemies of Egypt*. Bristol, Eng., 1938.

Elliott, Emory, et al., eds. *Columbia Literary History of the United States*. New York: Columbia UP, 1988.

———. *Power and the Pulpit in Puritan New England*. Princeton: Princeton UP, 1975.

———. *Revolutionary Writers: Literature and Authority in the New Republic, 1725–1810*. New York: Oxford UP, 1982.

Elson, Ruth Miller. *Guardians of Tradition: American Schoolbooks of the Nineteenth Century*. Lincoln: U of Nebraska P, 1964.

Emerson, Everett, ed. *Major Writers of Early American Literature*. Madison: U of Wisconsin P, 1972.

Emerson, Ralph Waldo. *Essays and Lectures. Nature: Addresses, and Lectures. Essays: First and Second Series. Representative Men. English Traits. The Conduct of Life. Uncollected Prose*. New York: Library of America, 1983.

Engell, James. *The Creative Imagination: Enlightenment to Romanticism*. Cambridge, MA: Harvard UP, 1981.

Encyclopaedia Britannica. 11th ed. 29 Vols. Cambridge: Cambridge UP, 1910–1911.

Encyclopaedia Britannica. 15th ed. 31 Vols. Chicago: Encyclopaedia Britannica Inc., 1988.

Erdt, Terrence. *Jonathan Edwards: Art and the Sense of the Heart*. Amherst, MA: U Massachusetts P, 1980.

Feidelson, Charles, Jr. *Symbolism and American Literature*. Chicago: U of Chicago P, 1953.

Ferguson, George. *Signs and Symbols in Christian Art*. New York: Oxford UP, 1966.

Ferguson, Robert A. "The American Enlightenment, 1750–1820." In *The Cambridge History of American Literature, 1590–1820*. Ed. Sacvan Bercovitch. Cambridge, Eng.: Cambridge UP, 1994. 345–537.

Ferling, John E. *The First of Men: A Life of George Washington*. Knoxville: U of Tennessee P, 1988.

Fiering, Norman. *Moral Philosophy at Seventeenth-Century Harvard: A Discipline in Transition*. Chapel Hill: U of North Carolina P, 1981.

Finkelstein, Dorothee Metlitsky. *Melville's Orienda*. New Haven: Yale UP, 1961.

Finnegan, Ruth. *Oral Literature in Africa*. Oxford: Oxford UP, 1970.

"A first-time author." "A Pastoral Elegy." *New-York Weekly Journal* 264 (Oct. 9, 1738).

Fischer, David Hackett. *Albion's Seed: Four British Folkways in America*. New York: Oxford UP, 1989.

Fitz, Earl E. *Rediscovering the New World: Inter-American Literature in a Comparative Context*. Iowa City: U of Iowa P, 1991.

Flexner, James Thomas. *George Washington: Anguish and Farewell (1793–1799)*. Boston: Little, Brown, 1972.

———. *George Washington in the American Revolution (1775–1783)*. Boston: Little, Brown, 1968.

———. *George Washington: The Forge of Experience (1732–1775)*. Boston: Little, Brown, 1965.

Ford, Boris, ed. *American Literature*. London: Penguin Books, 1991. Vol. 9 of the *New Pelican Guide to English Literature*. 1991.

Foucault, Michel. *The Archaeology of Knowledge and the Discourse on Language (L'ordre du discours)*. Trans. A. M. Sheridan Smith. New York: Pantheon, 1972.

———. *The Order of Things: An Archaeology of the Human Sciences*. Ed. R. D. Laing. New York: Vintage Books, 1973.

Franklin, Benjamin. *The Papers of Benjamin Franklin*. Vol. 3: *January 1, 1745, through June 30, 1750*. Ed. Leonard W. Labaree et al. New Haven: Yale UP, 1961.

———. *The Papers of Benjamin Franklin*. Vol. 4: *July 1, 1750, through June 30, 1753*. Ed. Leonard W. Labaree et al. New Haven: Yale UP, 1961.

Franklin, Benjamin, V. *Mather Byles Works: Compiled with an Introduction by Benjamin Franklin*. New York: Scholar's Facsimiles and Reprints, 1978.

Freneau, Philip. *Poems of Freneau*. Ed. Harry Hayden Clark. New York: Harcourt, Brace, 1929.

———. *The Poems of Philip Freneau: Poet of the American Revolution*. 3 vols. Ed. Fred Lewis Pattee. 1902. New York: Russell and Russell, 1963.

Furtwangler, Albert. "Cato at Valley Forge." *Modern Language Quarterly* 41.1 (Mar. 1980): 38–53.

Garrison, James D. *Pietas from Vergil to Dryden*. University Park: Pennsylvania State UP, 1992.

Gatta, John. *Gracious Laughter: The Meditative Wit of Edward Taylor*. Columbia: U of Missouri P, 1989.

Gay, Peter. *The Enlightenment: An Interpretation: The Rise of Modern Paganism*. New York: Knopf, 1966.

Gellius, Aulus. *Noctes Atticae*. Ed. G. P. Godd. 3 vols. Cambridge, MA: Harvard UP, 1946.

Gelpi, Albert. "American Poetry: The Colonial Period." In *The New Princeton Encyclopedia of Poetry and Poetics*. Ed. Alex Preminger and Terry V. T. Brogan. Princeton, NJ: Princeton UP, 1993.

The Geneva Bible: A Facsimile of the 1560 Edition. Introd. Lloyd E. Berry. Madison: U of Wisconsin P, 1969.

Gilbert, Sandra M. "The American Sexual Politics of Walt Whitman and Emily Dickinson." In *Reconstructing American Literary History*. Ed. Sacvan Bercovitch. Cambridge, MA: Harvard UP, 1986. 123–54.

Gilman, William H. *Melville's Early Life and Redburn*. New York: New York UP, 1951.

Gilmore, Michael T., ed. *Early American Literature: A Collection of Critical Essays*. Englewood Cliffs: Prentice-Hall, 1980.

Glass, Francis. *A Composite Translation of* A Life of George Washington *in Latin Prose*. Ed. John Francis Latimer. Washington, DC: George Washington U, 1976.

———. *A Grammatical and Historical Supplement to* A Life of George Washington *in Latin*. Ed. John Francis Latimer. Washington, DC: George Washington U, 1976.

———. *Georgii Washingtonii Vita: A Life of George Washington in Latin Prose*. Ed. J. N. Reynolds. New York: Harper and Brothers, 1835. Washington, DC: George Washington U, 1976.

———. *Vie de Washington*. Trans. (into the French) A. N. Girault. 4th ed. Philadelphia: Henry Perkins, 1835.

Godfrey, Thomas. "To the Memory of General Wolfe." *Juvenile Poems . . . by . . . Thomas Godfrey*. Philadelphia, PA: Henry Miller, 1765.

Godwin, Thomas. *Romanae Historiae Antholgia Recognita et Aucta: An English Exposition of the Roman Antiquities, Wherein Many Roman and English Offices Are Paralleld, and Diverse Obscure Phrases Explained*. London, 1648.

[Goodrich, Samuel G.] *Fourth Reader, For the Use of Schools*. Louisville, KY: Morton and Griswold, n.d.

Grabo, Norman S. *Edward Taylor*. Ed. Sylvia E. Bowman. New York: Twayne, 1961.

———. "So Who Killed Colonial Literary History?" *William and Mary Quarterly* 45.2 (1988): 342–45.

Graf, Fritz. "Heros." In *Dictionary of Deities and Demons in the Bible*. Ed. Karel van der Toorn et al. 2nd ed. Grand Rapids, MI: William B. Eerdmans, 1999. 412–15.

Graff, Gerald. *Professing Literature: An Institutional History*. Chicago: U of Chicago P, 1987.

Granger, Bruce Ingham. *Benjamin Franklin: An American Man of Letters*. Ithaca: Cornell UP, 1964.

———. *Political Satire in the American Revolution, 1763–1783*. Ithaca, NY: Cornell UP, 1960.

Graves, A. J. *Woman in America: Being an Examination into the Moral and Intellectual Condition of American Female Society*. New York: Harper, 1843.

Green, Joseph. "An Eclogue Sacred to the Memory of . . . Jonathan Mayhew." Boston, MA, 1766.

Greenblatt, Stephen. *New World Encounters*. Berkeley: U of California P, 1993.

Greene, Donald. *The Age of Exuberance: Backgrounds to Eighteenth-Century English Literature*. New York: Random House, 1970.

Greene, Jack P. *The Intellectual Construction of America: Exceptionalism and Identity from 1492 to 1800*. Chapel Hill: U of North Carolina P, 1993.

Greene, Jack P., and J. R. Pole, eds. *The Blackwell Encyclopedia of the American Revolution*. Oxford: Blackwell, 1991.

———, eds. *Colonial British America: Essays in the New History of the Early Modern Era*. Baltimore: Johns Hopkins UP, 1984.

Greene, Lorenzo J. *The Negro in Colonial New England*. New York: Atheneum, 1968.

Grégoire, Henri. *An Enquiry Concerning the Intellectual and Moral Faculties, and Literature of Negroes*. Trans. David Bailie Warden. 1810. Armonk, NY: M. E. Sharpe, 1997.

Griffin, Jaspar. "Introduction" to *The Oxford History of the Classical World*. Ed. John Boardman et al. New York: Oxford UP, 1986. 1–13.

Grimsted, David. "Anglo-American Racism and Phillis Wheatley's 'Sable Veil,' 'Length'ned Chain,' and 'Knitted Heart.'" In *Women in the Age of the American Revolution*. Ed. Ronald Hoffman and Peter J. Albert. Charlottesville: UP of Virginia, 1989. 338–444.

Gummere, Richard M. *The American Colonial Mind and the Classical Tradition: Essays in Comparative Culture*. Cambridge, MA: Harvard UP, 1963.

Gunn, Giles. *The Culture of Criticism and the Criticism of Culture*. New York: Oxford UP, 1987.

Gura, Philip F. "Response." *William and Mary Quarterly* 45.2 (1988): 350–51.

———. "The Study of Colonial American Literature, 1966–1987: A Vade Mecum." *William and Mary Quarterly* 45.2 (1988): 305–42.

———. *The Wisdom of Words: Language, Theology, and Literature in the New England Renaissance*. Middletown, CT: Wesleyan UP, 1985.

Hahn, T. G. "Urian Oakes's *Elegie* on Thomas Shepard and Puritan Poetics." *American Literature* 45.2 (May 1973): 163–81.

Halperin, David M. *Before Pastoral: Theocritus and the Ancient Tradition of Bucolic Poetry*. New Haven: Yale UP, 1983.

Hambrick-Stowe, Charles E. *The Practice of Piety: Puritan Devotional Disciplines in Seventeenth-Century New England*. Chapel Hill: U of North Carolina P, 1982.

Hammond, Jeffrey A. *Edward Taylor: Fifty Years of Scholarship and Criticism*. Columbia, SC: Camden House, 1993.

———. *Sinful Self, Saintly Self: The Puritan Experience of Poetry*. Athens: U of Georgia P, 1993.

Hanfmann, George M. "Labyrinth." In *Oxford Classical Dictionary*, 2nd ed. Oxford: Oxford UP, 1970.

Hanford, James Holly, and James G. Taaffe. *A Milton Handbook*. 5th ed. New York: Meredith, 1970.

Harding, Davis P. *The Club of Hercules: Studies in the Classical Background of* Paradise Lost. Urbana: U of Illinois P, 1962.

Hardison, O. B., Jr., ed. *English Literary Criticism: The Renaissance*. New York: Appleton-Century-Crofts, 1963.

Harrington, James. *The Commonwealth of Oceana*. London, 1656.

Harrison, Thomas Perrin, ed. *The Pastoral Elegy: An Anthology*. 1939. New York: Octagon, 1968.

Hastings, George Everett. *The Life and Works of Francis Hopkinson*. 3rd ed. New York: Russell and Russell, 1968.

Hatch, Nathan O. *The Democratization of American Christianity*. New Haven: Yale UP, 1989.

———. *The Sacred Cause of Liberty: Republican Thought and the Millennium in Revolutionary New England*. New Haven: Yale UP, 1977.

Havens, Raymond Dexter. *The Influence of Milton on English Poetry*. Cambridge, MA: Harvard UP, 1922.

Hawthorne, Nathaniel. *Nathaniel Hawthorne's Tales: Authoritative Texts, Backgrounds, Criticism*. Ed. James McIntosh. New York: Norton, 1987.

———. *Selected Tales and Sketches*. 3rd ed. New York: Holt, Rinehart and Winston, 1970.

Hayashi, Tetsumaro, ed. *Herman Melville: Research Opportunities and Dissertation Abstracts*. Jefferson, NC: McFarland, 1987.

Hayden, Lucy K. "Classical Tidings from the Afric 'Muse': Phillis Wheatley's Use of Greek and Roman Mythology." *College Language Association Journal* 35.4 (June 1992): 432–47.

A *Hebrew and English Lexicon of the Old Testament*. Ed. Francis Brown, S. R. Driver, and C. A. Briggs. Boston: Houghton Mifflin, 1906.

Heimert, Alan. *Religion and the American Mind: From the Great Awakening to the Revolution*. Cambridge, MA: Harvard UP, 1966.

Henson, Robert. "Form and Content of the Puritan Funeral Elegy." *American Literature* 32.1 (Mar. 1960): 11–27.

Herodotus. *The Famous Hystory of Herodotus*. Introd. Leonard Whibley. "Englished by B. R." 1584. Rpt. New York: Peter Smith 1967.

Hillway, Tyrus. *Herman Melville*. 2nd ed. Boston: G. K. Hall, 1979.

Hoffman, Ronald, and Peter J. Albert, eds. *Women in the Age of the American Revolution*. Charlottesville: UP of Virginia, 1989.

Hopkinson, Francis. *Miscellaneous Essays, and Occasional Writings*. Philadelphia, 1792.

Horace. *The Odes and Epodes*. Trans. C. E. Bennet. Cambridge, MA: Harvard UP, 1978.

Hornblower, Simon, and Antony Spawforth, eds. *The Oxford Classical Dictionary*. 3rd ed. New York: Oxford UP, 1996.

Houpt, Charles Theodore. *Mark Akenside: A Biographical and Critical Study*. Diss., U of Pennsylvania, 1944. Folcroft, PA: Folcroft, 1970.

Howard, Leon. "The Influence of Milton on Colonial American Poetry." *Huntington Library Bulletin* 9 (April 1936): 19–36.

Humphreys, David. *The Miscellaneous Works of David Humphreys, 1804: A Facsimile Reproduction*. Introd. William K. Bottorff. Gainesville, FL: Scholars' Facsimiles and Reprints, 1968.

Hutchinson, Thomas. *The History of the Colony and Province of Massachusetts-Bay*. Ed. Lawrence Shaw Mayo. 3 vols. Cambridge, MA: Harvard UP, 1936.

Hyatt, Vera Lawrence, and Rex Nettleford, eds. *Race, Discourse, and the Origin of the Americas: A New World View*. Washington, DC: Smithsonian Institution P, 1995.

Hyneman, Charles S., and Donald S. Lutz. *American Political Writing During the Founding Era: 1760–1805*. 2 vols. Indianapolis: Liberty, 1983.

Imlay, Gilbert. *A Topographical Description of the Western Territory of North America, Containing a Succinct Account of Its Soil, Climate, Natural History, Population, Agriculture, Manners and Customs*. 3rd ed. New York: Reprints of Economic Classics, 1969.

Irving, William Henry. *The Providence of Wit in the English Letter Writers*. Durham, NC: Duke UP, 1955.

Irwin, Terence. *Classical Thought*. New York: Oxford UP, 1989. Vol. 1 of *A History of Western Philosophy*. 1989.

Isani, Mukhtar Ali. "Edward Taylor and Ovid's *Art of Love*: The Text of a Newly Discovered Manuscript." *Early American Literature* 9 (1975): 65–74.

———. "The 'Fragment' as Genre in Early American Literature." *Studies in Short Fiction* 18.1 (Winter 1981): 17–26.

Israel, Calvin, ed. *Discoveries and Considerations: Essays on Early American Literature and Aesthetics. Presented to Harold Jantz*. Albany: State U of New York P, 1976.

Jefferson, Thomas. *The Writings of Thomas Jefferson*. Ed. Andrew A. Lipscomb and A. E. Bergh. 20 vols. Washington, DC: Thomas Jefferson Memorial Association, 1903–4.

Jehlen, Myra, and Michael Warner, eds. *The English Literatures of America, 1500–1800*. New York: Routledge, 1997.

Johnson, Thomas H. *Poetical Works of Edward Taylor*. Princeton: Princeton UP, 1939.

Jones, Buford. "*The Faery Land* of Hawthorne's Romances." *Emerson Society Quarterly* 48 (3rd Qtr., 1967): 113–15.

Jones, Howard Mumford. *O Strange New World: American Culture: The Formative Years*. New York: Viking, 1964.

———. *The Theory of American Literature*. Ithaca, NY: Cornell UP, 1965.

Jones, Hugh. *An Accidence to the English Tongue*. London, 1724.

Jordan, Cynthia S. "'Old Words' in 'New Circumstances': Language and Leadership in Post-Revolutionary America." *American Quarterly* 40 (Dec. 1988): 491–513.

———. *Second Stories: The Politics of Language, Form, and Gender in Early American Fictions*. Chapel Hill: U of North Carolina P, 1989.

Kaiser, Leo M., ed. *Early American Latin Verse, 1625–1825: An Anthology*. Chicago: Bolchazy-Cardiucci, 1984.

———. "On the Latin Verse in Cotton Mather's *Magnalia Christi Americana*." *Early American Literature* 10.3 (1975-76): 301–6.

———. "Six Notes." *Early American Literature* 13.3 (1978-79): 294–98.

Kaplan, Justin. *Walt Whitman: A Life*. New York: Simon and Schuster, 1980.

Keller, Karl. *The Example of Edward Taylor*. Amherst: U of Massachusetts P, 1975.

Kelsall, M. M. "The Meaning of Addison's *Cato*." *Review of English Studies*, new series 17.66 (1966): 149–62.

Kesselring, Marion Louise. "Hawthorne's Reading, 1828–1850." *Bulletin of the New York Public Library* 53 (1949): 55–71. 121–38, 173–94.

———. *Hawthorne's Reading, 1828–1850: A Transcription and Identification of Titles, Recorded in the Charge-Books of the Salem Athenaeum*. New York: New York Public Library, 1949.

Kettell, Samuel, ed. *Specimens of American Poetry*. 3 vols. Boston, 1829.

King, William. *An Historical Account of the Heathen Gods and Heroes*. London, 1710.

Klein, Milton M. *The American Whig: William Livingston of New York*. New York: Garland, 1989.

Knapp, Samuel Lorenzo. *American Cultural History, 1607–1829: A Facsimile Reproduction of Lectures on American Literature (1829)*. 1829. Delmar, FL: Scholars' Facsimiles and Reprints, 1977.

Knight, Denise D. *Cotton Mather's Verse in English*. Newark, NJ: U. of Delaware P, 1989.

Knox, Samuel. *Essay on . . . Liberal Education*. In *Essays on Education in the Early Republic*. Ed. Frederick Rudolph. Cambridge, MA: Harvard UP, 1965. 271–372.

Kupperman, Karen Ordahl. *America in European Consciousness, 1493–1750*. Chapel Hill: U of North Carolina P, 1995.

Lambert, Ellen Zetzel. *Placing Sorrow: A Study of the Pastoral Elegy Convention from Theocritus to Milton*. Chapel Hill: U of North Carolina P, 1976.

Landino, Christoforo. *Quaestiones Camaldulenses*. See Don Cameron Allen. *Mysteriously Meant: The Rediscovery of Pagan Symbolism and Allegorical Interpretation in the Renaissance*. Baltimore: Johns Hopkins UP, 1970. 142–54, *passim*.

Lathrop, Henry Burrowes. *Translations from the Classics into English from Caxton to Chapman, 1477–1620*. Madison: U of Wisconsin Studies in Language and Literature, 1933.

Lawrence, D. H. *Studies in Classic American Literature*. 1923. New York: Viking, 1961.

Leach, Maria, ed. *Funk and Wagnalls Standard Dictionary of Folklore, Mythology and Legend*. New York: Funk and Wagnalls, 1972.

Le Fevre, Perry D. *Chicago Theological Seminary Register*. (1984).

Lemay, J. A. Leo. "Jonson and Milton: Two Influences in Oakes' *Elegie*." *New England Quarterly* 38.1 (Mar. 1965): 90–92.

———. *Men of Letters in Colonial Maryland*. Knoxville: U of Tennessee P, 1972.

Leverenz, David. "Historicizing Hell in Hawthorne's Tales." In *Hawthorne's Major Tales*. Ed. Millicent Bell. New York: Cambridge UP, 1993.

———. *Manhood and the American Renaissance*. Ithaca: Cornell UP, 1989.

Levernier, James A., and Douglas R. Wilmes, eds. *American Writers Before 1800: A Biographical and Critical Dictionary*. 3 Vols. Westport, CT: Greenwood, 1983.

Levin, David. "A Survivor's Tale." *William and Mary Quarterly* 45.2 (1988): 345–48.

Levin, Harry. *The Myth of the Golden Age in the Renaissance*. 1969. New York: Oxford UP, 1972.

Lewalski, Barbara Kiefer. *Protestant Poetics and the Seventeenth-Century Religious Lyric*. Princeton: Princeton UP, 1979.

———, ed. *Renaissance Genres: Essays on Theory, History, and Interpretation*. Cambridge, MA: Harvard UP, 1986.

Lewis, R. W. B. *The American Adam: Innocence, Tragedy and Tradition in the Nineteenth Century*. Chicago: U of Chicago P, 1955.

Leyda, Jay. *The Melville Log: A Documentary Life of Herman Melville, 1819–1891*. 2 Vols. New York: Gordian P, 1969.

Liebman, Sheldon W. "Robin's Conversion: The Design of 'My Kinsman, Major Molineux.'" *Studies in Short Fiction* 8.3 (Summer 1971): 443–57.

Litto, Fredric M. "Addison's *Cato* in the Colonies." *William and Mary Quarterly* 23.3 (July 1966): 431–49.

Livingston, William. *American Poems: Selected and Original*. Ed. Elihu Hubbard Smith. Litchfield, : Collier and Buel, 1793.

Locke, John. *An Essay Concerning Human Understanding*. 4th ed. 2 vols. 1696.

———. *Some Thoughts Concerning Education*. 1693. Menston, Eng.: Scolar P Ltd., 1970.

———. *Two Treatises of Government*. Ed. Peter Laslett. 2nd ed. Cambridge, Eng.: Cambridge UP, 1988.

Lockridge, Kenneth A. *Literacy in Colonial New England: An Enquiry into the Social Context of Literacy in the Early Modern West*. New York: Norton, 1974.

Looby, Christopher. *Voicing America: Language, Literary Form, and the Origins of the United States*. Chicago: U of Chicago P, 1996.

Lowth, Robert. *A Short Introduction to English Grammar*. 1775. Delmar, FL: Scholars' Facsimiles and Reprints, 1979.

Loyola. *Exercitia Spiritualia*. Rome, 1548.

Lucas, Paul. *American Odyssey, 1607–1789*. Englewood Cliffs: Prentice-Hall, 1984.

Macdonald, Hugh. *John Dryden: A Bibliography of Early Editions and of Drydeniana*. London: Oxford UP, 1939,

Marinelli, Peter V. *Pastoral*. Ed. John D. Jump. London: Methuen, 1971.

Martin, Terence. *Nathaniel Hawthorne*. Ed. Lewis Leary. Boston: Twayne, 1983.

Martz, Louis L. *The Poetry of Meditation: A Study in English Religious Literature of the Seventeenth Century*. New Haven: Yale UP, 1954.

Marx, Leo. *The Machine in the Garden: Technology and the Pastoral Ideal in America*. New York: Oxford UP, 1967.

Mason, Julian D., Jr., ed. *The Poems of Phillis Wheatley*. 2nd ed. Chapel Hill: U of North Carolina P, 1989.

Mather, Cotton. *Cotton Mather: Magnalia Christi Americana*. Books I and II. Ed. Kenneth B. Murdock. Cambridge, MA: Harvard UP, 1977.

———. *The Great Works of Christ in America: Magnalia Christi Americana*. Ed. Thomas Robbins. 2 vols. Hartford, CT: Silas Andrus and Son, 1853. Rpt., Banner of Truth Trust, 1979.

Mather, Increase. *The History of King Philip's War, by the Rev. Increase Mather, D.D. Also, A History of the Same War, by the Rev. Cotton Mather, D.D. To Which Are Added an Introduction and Notes by Samuel G. Drake, Late President of the New England Historic-Genealogical Society*. Boston, 1862.

Mather, Samuel. *The Figures or Types of the Old Testament*. 1705. Rpt., New York: Johnson, 1969.

Matthiessen, F. O. *American Renaissance: Art and Expression in the Age of Emerson and Whitman*. New York: Oxford UP, 1941.

May, Henry F. *The Enlightenment in America*. New York: Oxford UP, 1978.

Mayhew, Jonathan. *Discourse Concerning Unlimited Submission*. Boston, MA: D. Fowle and D. Gookin, 1750.

McDonald, Forrest. *E Pluribus Unum: The Formation of the American Republic, 1776–1790*. Indianapolis: Liberty, 1979.

———. *Novus Ordo Seclorum: The Intellectual Origins of the Constitution*. Lawrence: UP of Kansas, 1985.

———. *We the People. The Economic Origins of the Constitution*. New Brunswick, NJ: Transaction, 1992.

McGuffey, William H. *McGuffey's Eclectic Readers: Primer to Sixth*. New York: American Book Company, 1921.

McKay, David P., and Richard Crawford. *William Billings of Boston: Eighteenth-Century Composer*. Princeton: Princeton UP, 1975.

McKay, Michele, and William J. Scheick. "The Other Song in Phillis Wheatley's 'On Imagination.'" *Studies in the Literary Imagination* 27.1 (1994): 71–84.

McMichael, George, gen. ed. *Anthology of American Literature*, 6th ed. 2 vols. Upper Saddle River, NJ: Prentice-Hall, 1997.

McWilliams, John P., Jr. *The American Epic: Transforming a Genre, 1770–1860*. Cambridge, Eng.: Cambridge UP, 1989.

Melville, Herman. *Battle-Pieces and Aspects of the War*. New York: Harper and Brothers, 1866.

———. *Billy Budd, Sailor: An Inside Narrative*. Ed. Harrison Hayford and Merton M. Sealts Jr. Chicago: Phoenix, 1962.

———. *Great Short Works of Herman Melville*. Ed. Warner Berthoff. New York: Harper and Row, 1969.

———. *Mardi and A Voyage Thither*. Ed. Harrison Hayford et al. Evanston, IL: Northwestern UP, 1970.

———. *Moby Dick: An Authoritative Text, Reviews and Letters by Melville, Analogues and Sources, Criticism*. Ed. Harrison Hayford and Hershel Parker. New York: Norton, 1967.

———. *Selected Poems of Herman Melville*. Ed. Henning Cohen. New York: Fordham UP, 1991.

———. *Selected Poems of Herman Melville*. Ed. Robert Penn Warren. New York: Barnes and Noble, 1998.

———. *The Portable Melville*. Ed. Jay Leyda. New York: Viking, 1952.

Meserolc, Harrison T., ed. *American Poetry of the Seventeenth Century*. University Park: Pennsylvania State UP, 1985.

Middlekauff, Robert. *Ancients and Axioms: Secondary Education in Eighteenth-Century New England*. New Haven: Yale UP, 1963.

———. *The Glorious Cause: The American Revolution, 1763–1789*. New York: Oxford UP, 1982.

Middleton, Richard. *Colonial America: A History, 1607–1760*. Oxford: Blackwell, 1992.

Miles, Edwin A. "Classicism in Early American Thought." *Journal of the History of Ideas* 35.2 (April–June 1974): 259–74.

Miller, Edwin H. *Melville*. New York: Venture, 1975.

———. "'My Kinsman, Major Molineux': The Playful Art of Nathaniel Hawthorne." *Emerson Society Quarterly: A Journal of the American Renaissance* 24 (1978): 145–51.

Miller, James E., Jr. *A Reader's Guide to Herman Melville*. New York: Noonday, 1962.

Miller, Perry. *The Life of the Mind in America: From the Revolution to the Civil War*. Books 1–3. New York: Harcourt, Brace and World, 1965.

———. *The New England Mind: From Colony to Province*. Boston: Beacon, 1961.

———. *The New England Mind: The Seventeenth Century*. Boston: Beacon, 1961.

Miller, Perry, and Thomas H. Johnson, eds. *The Puritans: A Sourcebook of Their Writings*. Rev. ed. 2 vols. New York: Harper Torchbooks, 1963.

Milton, John. *Complete Poems and Major Prose*. Ed. Merritt Y. Hughes. New York: Odyssey, 1957.

Mingazzini, Paolino. "Apelles." In *Encyclopedia of World Art*. New York: McGraw Hill, 1959. 509–11.

Monaghan, E. Jennifer. "Literacy Instruction and Gender in Colonial New England." *American Quarterly* 40 (Mar. 1988): 18–41.

Monk, Samuel H. *The Sublime: A Study of Critical Theories in Eighteenth-Century England*. New York: Modern Language Association of America, 1935. Rpt., Ann Arbor: Ann Arbor Paperbacks, 1960.

Montesquieu, Baron de. *The Spirit of the Laws*. Ed. Franz Neumann, Trans. Thomas Nugeat. New York: Macmillan, 1949.

Montgomery, Charles F., and Patricia E. Kane, eds. *American Art, 1750–1800: Towards Independence*. Boston: New York Graphic Society, 1976.

Montgomery, Michael. "Hugh Jones [1671–1760]." In *American Writers Before 1800: A Biographical and Critical Dictionary*. Ed. James A. Levernier and Douglas R. Wilmes. Westport, CT: Greenwood, 1983. Vol. 2: 844–46.

Moore, Maxine. *That Lonely Game: Melville,* Mardi *and the Almanac*. Columbia: U of Missouri P, 1975.

Morgan, Edmund S. *The Birth of the Republic: 1763–89*. 3rd ed. Chicago: U of Chicago P, 1992.

Morison, Samuel Eliot. *Builders of the Bay Colony*. Boston: Northeastern UP, 1981.

———. *The Founding of Harvard College*. Cambridge, MA: Harvard UP, 1963.

———. *Harvard College in the Seventeenth Century*. Part 1. Cambridge, MA: Harvard UP, 1936.

———. *Oxford History of the American People*. New York: Oxford UP, 1965.

Mulford, Carla, ed. *Only for the Eye of a Friend: The Poems of Annis Boudinot Stockton*. Charlottesville: UP of Virginia, 1995.

Murdock, Kenneth Ballard. *Literature and Theology in Colonial New England*. Cambridge, MA: Harvard UP, 1949.

———. "The Teaching of Latin and Greek at the Boston Latin School in 1712." *Publications of the Colonial Society of Massachusetts: Transactions, 1927–1930* 27 (1932): 21–29.

Murphy, Francis. "Edward Taylor's Attitude Toward Publication: A Question Concerning Authority." *American Literature* 34 (1962): 393–94.

Mushabac, Jane. *Melville's Humor: A Critical Study*. Hamden, CT: Archon, 1981.

Myer, Jack, and Michael Simms. *The Longman Dictionary of Poetic Terms*. New York: Longman, 1989.

Myerson, Joel, ed. *Dictionary of Literary Biography*. Vol. 3. Detroit: Bruccoli Clark, 1979.

Newman, John Kevin. *The Classical Epic Tradition*. Madison: U of Wisconsin P, 1986.

"N. L." and "Hibernicus." "A *Pastoral Elegy*, on the *Death* of ADMIRAL WARREN." *New York Gazette* 510 (Nov. 6, 1752).

Nicolson, Marjorie Hope. *Mountain Gloom and Mountain Glory: The Development of the Aesthetics of the Infinite*. New York: Norton, 1963.

Nord, David Paul. "A Republican Literature: A Study of Magazine Reading and Readers in Late-Eighteenth-Century New York." *American Quarterly* 40 (Mar. 1988): 42–64.

Norton, John, II. "A Funeral Elogy Upon . . . Anne Bradstreet." 1672. In *American Poetry of the Seventeenth Century*. Ed. Harrison T. Meserole. University Park: Pennsylvania State UP, 1963.

Nyquist, Mary, and Margaret W. Ferguson, eds. *Re-membering Milton: Essays on the Texts and Traditions*. New York: Methuen, 1987.

Oakes, Urian. "An Elegie Upon . . . Thomas Shepard." 1677. In *American Poetry of the Seventeenth Century*. Ed. Harrison T. Meserole. University Park: Pennsylvania State UP, 1963.

O'Neale, Sondra A. *Jupiter Hammon and the Biblical Beginnings of African-American Literature*. Metuchen, NJ: Scarecrow, 1993.

———. "A Slave's Subtle War: Phillis Wheatley's Use of Biblical Myth and Symbol." *Early American Literature* 21.2 (Fall, 1986): 144–65.

Osgood, Charles Grosvenor. *The Classical Mythology of Milton's English Poems*. 1900. Rpt., New Haven: Yale UP, 1964.

Otten, Robert M. *Joseph Addison*. Ed. Bertram H. Davis. Boston: Twayne, 1982.

Ovid. *Metamorphoses*. Trans. Rolfe Humphries. 2nd ed. Bloomington: Indiana UP, 1955.

———. *Metamorphoses. Books 6–10*. Ed. William S. Anderson. Norman: U of Oklahoma P, 1972.

———. *Ovid's* Metamorphosis*: Englished, Mythologized, and Represented in Figures*. Trans. George Sandys. Ed. Karl K. Hulley and Stanley T. Vandersall. Lincoln: U of Nebraska P, 1970.

Oxford Latin Dictionary. Ed. P. G. W. Glare. Oxford: Oxford UP, 1982.

Parini, Jay, and Brett C. Millier, eds. *The Columbia History of American Poetry*. New York: Columbia UP, 1993.

Parker, Hershel. *Herman Melville: A Biography*. Vol. 1: *1819–1851*. Baltimore: Johns Hopkins UP, 1996.

Parley, Peter [Samuel G. Goodrich]. *Popular Biography*. New York: George A. Leavitt, 1832.

———. *The Young American; or, Book of Government and Law*. New York: W. Robinson, 1842.

"A Pastoral Elegy on the Death of a Young Lady." *American Magazine* [third version with this name], April 1769, pp. 120–22.

"Pastoral Elegy, on a Young Gentleman Lately Deceased." *South Carolina Gazette* 906 (Sept. 23, 1751): 332.

Patrides, C. A., ed. *Milton's Lycidas: The Tradition and the Poem*. Rev. ed. Columbia: U of Missouri P, 1983.

Patterson, Annabel, ed. *Roman Images: Selected Papers from the English Institute, 1982*. New series, no. 8. Baltimore: Johns Hopkins UP, 1984.

Pearce, Roy Harvey, ed. *Colonial American Writing*. 2nd ed. New York: Holt, Rinehart and Winston, 1969.

Pearcy, Lee T. *The Mediated Muse: English Translations of Ovid. 1560–1700*. Hamden, CT: Archon, 1984.

Pease, Donald E. *boundary 2: Special Issue: New Americanists: Revisionist Interventions into the Canon* 17.1 (Spring 1990).

Perkins, William. *A Treatise of Mans Imaginations: Shewing His Naturall Evill Thoughts, His Want of Good Thoughts, The Way to Reforme Them*. Cambridge, Eng.: John Legat, 1607.

"Philantus." "A Pastoral Elegy, on the Death of a Virtuous Young Lady." *New York Weekly Journal* 261 (Sept. 11, 1738).

Pierson, William H., Jr. *American Buildings and Their Architects: The Colonial and Neoclassical Styles*. Vol. 1. New York: Oxford UP, 1970.

Piper, William Bowman. *The Heroic Couplet*. Cleveland, OH: Case Western Reserve UP, 1969.

"A Plain Politician." *Honesty Shewed to be True Policy; or, A General Impost Considered and Defended*. New York, 1786. Pamphlet.

Pocock, J. G. A. *The Machiavellian Moment: Florentine Political Thought and the Atlantic Republican Tradition*. Princeton: Princeton UP, 1975.

Poirier, Richard. *The Renewal of Literature: Emersonian Reflections*. New York: Random House, 1987.

Pomfret, John. "The Choice." 1700. *Eighteenth-Century English Literature*. Ed. Geoffrey Tillotson et al. Chicago: Harcourt, Brace and World, 1969. 790–92.

Pope, Alexander. *Poetry and Prose of Alexander Pope*. Ed. Aubrey Williams. Boston: Houghton Mifflin, 1969.

Porter, Carolyn. "What We Know That We Don't Know: Remapping American Literary Studies." *American Literary History* 6.3 (1994): 467–526.

Potts, Abbie Findlay. *The Elegiac Mode: Poetic Form in Wordsworth and Other Elegists*. Ithaca: Cornell UP, 1967.

Preminger, Alex, and T. V. F. Brogan, eds. *The New Princeton Encyclopedia of Poetry and Poetics*. 3rd ed. Princeton, NJ: Princeton UP, 1993.

Purcell, L. Edward, and David F. Burg, eds. *The World Almanac of the American Revolution*. New York: World Almanac, 1992.

Puttenham, George. *The Arte of English Poesie*. London, 1589.

Quinlivan, Mary E. "East Apthorp (1733–1816)." In *American Writers Before 1800: A Biographical and Critical Dictionary: A–F*. Ed. James A. Levernier and Douglas R. Wilmes. Westport, CT: Greenwood, 1983. Vol. 1: 57–59.

Quint, David. *Epic and Empire: Politics and Generic Form from Virgil to Milton*. Princeton: Princeton UP, 1993.

Quintilianus, M. Fabius. *Institutio Oratoria*. Trans. H. E. Butler. 4 vols. Cambridge, MA: Harvard UP, 1980.

Raleigh, Sir Walter. *The History of the World*. London, 1614.

Randall, Willard Sterne. *George Washington. A Life*. New York: Owl Book, 1997.

Rathbun, John W., and Monica M. Grecu, eds. *Dictionary of Literary Biography*. Vol. 64. Detroit: Bruccoli Clark, 1988.

Redding, J. Saunders. "Wheatley, Phillis." In *Dictionary of American Negro Biography*. Ed. Rayford W. Logan and Michael R. Winston. New York: Norton, 1982.

Regis, Pamela. *Describing Early America: Bartram, Jefferson, Crèvecoeur, and the Rhetoric of Natural History*. DeKalb: Northern Illinois UP, 1992.

Reinhold, Meyer. *Classica Americana: The Greek and Roman Heritage in the United States*. Detroit: Wayne State UP, 1984.

Reising, Russell J. "Trafficking in White: Phillis Wheatley's Semiotics of Racial Representation." *Genre* 22.3 (Fall, 1989): 231–61.

———. *The Unusable Past: Theory and the Study of American Literature*. New York: Methuen, 1986.

Reynolds, Larry J. *European Revolutions and the American Literary Renaissance*. New Haven: Yale UP, 1988.

Rice, Grantland S. *The Transformation of Authorship in America*. Chicago: U of Chicago P, 1997.

Richard, Carl J. *The Founders and the Classics: Greece, Rome, and the American Enlightenment*. Cambridge, MA: Harvard UP, 1994.

Richards, David A. J. "Founders' Intent and Constitutional Interpretation." In *America in Theory*. Ed. Leslie Berlowitz et al. New York: Oxford UP, 1988. 26–52.

Richardson, Robert D., Jr. *Myth and Literature in the American Renaissance*. Bloomington: Indiana UP, 1978.

Richardson, Samuel, ed. *Richardsonana II: Aesop's Fables. 1740*. New York: Garland, 1975.

Richter, David. *The Critical Tradition: Classic Texts and Contemporary Trends*.

Robertson, Noel, and B. C. Dietriech. "Fate." In *The Oxford Classical Dictionary*. Ed. Simon Hornblower and Antony Spawforth. Oxford, Eng.: Oxford UP, 1996. 589–90.

Robertson-Lorant, Laurie. *Melville: A Biography*. New York: Clarkson Potter, 1996.

Robinson, William H. *Black New England Letters*. Boston: Boston Public Library, 1977.

———. *Phillis Wheatley and Her Writings*. New York: Garland, 1984.

Rogers, Alan. *Empire and Liberty: American Resistance to British Authority, 1755–1763*. Berkeley: U of California P, 1974.

Rose, Aquila. *Poems on Several Occasions. To Which Are Prefixed, Some Other Pieces Writ to Him and to His Memory After His Decease. Collected and Published by His Son Joseph Rose of Philadelphia*. Philadelphia, PA: New Printing Office, 1740.

Ross, Alexander. *Mystagogus Poeticus; or, The Muses' Interpreter*. London, 1647.

Rowe, Karen E. *Saint and Singer: Edward Taylor's Typology and the Poetics of Meditation*. Cambridge, Eng.: Cambridge UP, 1986.

Rubin, Deborah. *Ovid's* Metamorphosis *Englished: George Sandys as Translator and Mythographer*. New York: Garland, 1985.

Rudolph, Frederick, ed. *Essays on Education in the Early Republic: Benjamin Rush, Noah Webster, Robert Coram, Simeon Doggett, Samuel Harrison Smith, Amable-Louis-Rose de Lafitte du Corteil, Samuel Knox*. Cambridge, MA: Belknap P of Harvard UP, 1965.

Ruland, Richard, ed. *The Native Muse: Theories of American Literature*. Vol. 1. New York: Dutton, 1976.

Ruland, Richard, and Malcolm Bradbury. *From Puritanism to Postmodernism: A History of American Literature*. New York: Penguin, 1992.

Rush, Benjamin. *The Letters of Benjamin Rush*. 2 vols. Ed. L. H. Butterfield. Princeton: Princeton UP, 1954.

Russell, Gene. *A Concordance to the Poems of Edward Taylor*. Washington, DC: Microcard Editions, 1973.

Ryder, Mary R. *Willa Cather and Classical Myth: The Search for a New Parnassus*. Lewiston, NY: Edwin Mellen Press, 1990.

Said, Edward W. *Culture and Imperialism*. New York: Knopf, 1993.

Saldivar, José David. *The Dialectics of Our America: Genealogy, Cultural Critique, and Literary History*. Durham, NC: Duke UP, 1991.

Sambrook, James. *English Pastoral Poetry*. Ed. Kinley E. Roby. Boston: Twayne, 1983.

Sandys, George. *Ovid's* Metamorphosis *Englished, Mythologized, and Represented in Figures*. Oxford, Eng., 1632.

Sanford, Charles L., ed. *Manifest Destiny and the Imperialism Question*. New York: Wiley, 1974.

Satterthwaite, Gilbert E. *Encyclopedia of Astronomy*. New York: St. Martin's, 1971.

Saunders, Richard H., and Ellen G. Miles. *American Colonial Portraits, 1700–1776*. Washington, DC: Smithsonian Institution P, 1987.

Schechter, Harold. *The Bosom Serpent: Folklore and Popular Art*. Iowa City: U of Iowa P, 1988.

Scheick, William J. *Authority and Female Authorship in Colonial America*. Lexington: UP of Kentucky, 1998.

———. "Standing in the Gap: Urian Oakes' Elegy on Thomas Shepard." *Early American Literature* 9.3 (Winter, 1975): 301–6.

———. *The Will and the Word: The Poetry of Edward Taylor*. Athens: U of Georgia P, 1974.

Schulman, Lydia Dittler. Paradise Lost *and the Rise of the American Republic*. Boston: Northeastern UP, 1992.

Sealts, Merton M., Jr. "Innocence and Infamy: Billy Budd, Sailor." In *A Companion to Melville Studies*. Ed. John Bryant. Westport, CT: Greenwood, 1986. 407–33.

———. *Melville's Reading: A Check-List of Books Owned and Borrowed*. Madison: U of Wisconsin P, 1966.

Seccombe, Joseph. *Business and Diversion . . . in the Fishing Season*. Boston, 1743.

———. "On the Death of the Reverend Benjamin Colman, D.D. An Eclogue." Boston, 1747.

———. *Some Occasional Thoughts on the Influence of the Spirit with Seasonable Cautions Against Mistakes and Abuses*. Boston, 1742.

Seigel, Jerrold E. "*Virtu* in and Since the Renaissance." In *Dictionary of the History of Ideas*. Ed. Philip P. Wiener et al. Vol. 4: 476–86.

Sensabaugh, George F. *Milton in Early America*. Princeton, NJ: Princeton UP, 1964.

Sewall, Stephen. "V." In *Pietas et Gratulatio Collegii Cantabrigiensis Apud Novanglos*. Boston: J. Green and J. Russell, 1761.

Seybolt, Robert F. "Schoolmasters of Colonial Boston." *Publications of the Colonial Society of Massachusetts: Transactions, 1927–1930* 27 (1932): 130–56.

Seymour, George Dudley. *Documentary Life of Nathan Hale*. New Haven: Privately Printed, 1941.

Shields, David S. "Happiness in Society: The Development of an Eighteenth-Century American Poetic Ideal." *American Literature* 55.4 (Dec. 1983): 541–59.

———. "Herbert and Colonial American Poetry: 'Then Shall Religion to America Flee.'" *Like Season'd Timber: New Essays on George Herbert*. Ed. Edmund Miller and Robert DiYanni. New York: Peter Lang, 1987. 281–96.

———. *Oracles of Empire: Poetry, Politics, and Commerce in British America, 1690–1750*. Chicago: U of Chicago P, 1990.

———. "The Wits and Poets of Pennsylvania: New Light on the Rise of Belles Lettres in Provincial Pennsylvania, 1720–1740." *Pennsylvania Magazine of History and Biography* 109.2 (Apr. 1985): 99–143.

Shields, John C., ed. *The Collected Works of Phillis Wheatley*. New York: Oxford UP, 1988.

———. "Jerome in Colonial New England: Edward Taylor's Attitude Toward Classical Paganism." *Studies in Philology* 81.2 (Spring 1984): 161–84.

———. "Phillis Wheatley." In *African American Writers*. Ed. Valerie Smith, Lea Baechler, and A. Walton Litz. New York: Charles Scribner's Sons, 1991. 473–91.

———. "Phillis Wheatley and Mather Byles: A Study in Literary Relationship." *College Language Association Journal* 23.4 (June 1980): 377–90.

———. "Phillis Wheatley and the Sublime." In *Critical Essays on Phillis Wheatley*. Ed. William H. Robinson. Boston: G. K. Hall, 1982. 189–205.

———. "Phillis Wheatley's Struggle for Freedom in Her Poetry and Prose." In *The Collected Works of Phillis Wheatley*. Ed. John C. Shields. New York: Oxford UP, 1988. 229–70; 324–36.

———. "Phillis Wheatley's Subversive Pastoral." *Eighteenth-Century Studies* 27.4 (June 1994): 631–47.

———. "Phillis Wheatley's Use of Classicism." *American Literature* 52.1 (1980): 97–111. Rpt. in *Poetry Criticism: III*. Detroit: Gale Research, 1991. 355–60.

———. "*The Seafarer* as a Meditatio." *Studia Mystica* 3.1 (1980): 29–41.

———, guest ed. Special Issue in *Style: African American Poetics* 27.2 (Summer 1993).

Shipton, Clifford K. *National Index of American Imprints through 1800. The Short-Title Evans*. 2 Vols. Worcester and Boone, MA: American Antiquarian Society and Barre Publishers, 1969.

Shroeder, John W. "Hawthorne's 'Egotism; or, The Bosom Serpent' and Its Sources." *American Literature* 31 (May 1959): 150–62.

Shucard, Alan. *American Poetry: The Puritans Through Walt Whitman*. Boston, MA: G. K. Hall, 1988.

Shuffelton, Frank. "'Philosophic Solitude' and the Pastoral Politics of William Livingston." *Early American Literature* 17.1 (Spring, 1982): 43–53.

Shurtleff, Harold R. *The Log Cabin Myth: A Study of the Early Dwellings of the English Colonists in North America*. Ed. Samuel Eliot Morison. Gloucester, MA: Peter Smith, 1967.

Sibley, Agnes M. *Alexander Pope's Prestige in America, 1725–1835*. New York: Columbia UP, 1949.

Silverman, Kenneth, ed. *Colonial American Poetry*. New York: Hafner Publishing, 1968.

———. *A Cultural History of the American Revolution: Painting, Music, Literature, and the Theatre in the Colonies and the United States, from the Treaty of Paris to the Inauguration of George Washington, 1763–1789*. New York: Crowell, 1976.

———. "From Cotton Mather to Benjamin Franklin." In *Columbia Literary History of the United States*. Ed. Emory Elliott et al. New York: Columbia UP, 1988. 101–12.

———. *The Life and Times of Cotton Mather*. New York: Columbia UP, 1985.

———, comp. *Selected Letters of Cotton Mather*. Baton Rouge: Louisiana State UP, 1971.

Silvestris, Bernardus. *Commentary on the First Six Books of Vergil's Aeneid*. Trans. Earl G. Schreiber and Thomas E. Maresca. Lincoln: U of Nebraska P, 1979.

Simpson, David. "Literary Criticism and the Return to 'History.'" *Critical Inquiry* 14.4 (Summer 1988): 721–47.

———. *The Politics of American English, 1776–1850*. New York: Oxford UP, 1986.

Simpson, Lewis P. *The Dispossessed Garden: Pastoral and History in Southern Literature*. Athens, GA: U of Georgia P, 1975.

Small, Julianne. "Classical Allusions in the Fiction of Herman Melville." Diss., U of Tennessee, Knoxville, 1974.

Smith, Cynthia J. "'To Maecenas': Phillis Wheatley's Invocation of an Idealized Reader." *Black American Literature Forum* 23.3 (Fall, 1989): 579–92.

Smith, Elihu Hubbard, ed. *American Poems*. 1793. Gainesville, FL: Scholars' Facsimiles and Reprints, 1966.

Smith, Henry Nash. *Virgin Land: The American West as Symbol and Myth*. Cambridge, MA: Harvard UP, 1950.

Solberg, Winton U. "Cotton Mather: *The Christian Philosopher* and the Classics." *Proceedings of the American Antiquarian Society* (Annual Meeting Held at Worcester, MA, Oct. 15, 1986) 96, pt. 2 (1987): 323–66.

Sonneck, Oscar G. T. *Francis Hopkinson: The First American Poet-Composer (1737–1791); and James Lyon: Patriot, Preacher, Psalmodist (1735–1794)*. 1905. New York: Da Capo, 1967.

Spenser, Edmund. *Edmund Spencer's Poetry: Authoritative Texts, Criticism*. Ed. Hugh Maclean. New York: Norton, 1968.

———. *The Works of Edmund Spenser: A Variorum Edition*. Ed. Frederick M. Padelford. Baltimore: Johns Hopkins UP, 1934.

Spengemann, William C. *A New World of Words: Redefining Early American Literature*. New Haven: Yale UP, 1994.

Sprague, William B., ed. *Annals of the American Pulpit*. 9 vols. New York: Robert Garter and Brothers, 1857–1869.

Stanford, Donald E. "The Earliest Poems of Edward Taylor." *American Literature* 32 (1960): 141–56.

———. *The Poems of Edward Taylor*. New Haven: Yale UP, 1960.

Stannard, David E. *American Holocaust: The Conquest of the New World*. Manoa, HI: U of Hawaii P, 1976.

Starnes, DeWitt T., and Ernest William Talbert. *Classical Myth and Legend in Renaissance Dictionaries: A Study of Renaissance Dictionaries in Their Relation to the Classical Learning of Contemporary English Writers*. Chapel Hill: U of North Carolina P, 1955.

Stauffer, Donald Barlow. *A Short History of American Poetry*. New York: E. P. Dutton, 1974.

Stavely, Keith W. F. *Puritan Legacies:* Paradise Lost *and the New England Tradition, 1630–1890*. Ithaca: Cornell UP, 1987.

Stedman, Capt. J. G. *Narrative of Five Years' Expedition Against the Revolted Negroes of Surinam in Guiana on the Wild Coast of South America from the Years 1772 to 1777. Elucidating the History of That Country and Describing Its Productions, viz. Quadrupedes, Birds, Reptiles, Trees, Shrubs, Fruits, and Roots; With an Account of the Indians of Guiana and Negroes of Guinea by Captain J. G. Stedman, Illustrated with 80 Elegant Engravings from Drawings Made by the Author*. 1796. Amherst: U of Massachusetts P, 1972.

Stern, Milton R. "Melville, Society and Language." In *A Companion to Melville Studies*. Ed. John Bryant. Westport, CT: Greenwood Press, 1986.

Stewart, Randall. "Hawthorne and *The Faerie Queene*." *Philological Quarterly* 12 (Apr. 1933): 196–206.

———. *Nathaniel Hawthorne. A Biography*. New Haven: Yale UP, 1961.

Stillinger, Jack. ed. *Wordsworth: Selected Poems and Prefaces*. Boston: Houghton Mifflin, 1965.

Tasso, Torquato. *Jerusalem Delivered*. Trans. Ralph Nash. Detroit, MI: Wayne State UP, 1987.

Taylor, Edward. *Diary*. [April 1668–December 1671.] In *Proceedings of the Massachusetts Historical Society* 18 (1880–81): 4–18.

———. *Edward Taylor's Christographia*. Ed. Norman S. Grabo. New Haven: Yale UP, 1962.

———. *Edward Taylor's Minor Poetry*. Ed. Thomas M. Davis and Virginia L. Davis. Boston: Twayne, 1981. Vol. 3 of *The Unpublished Writings of Edward Taylor*. 1981.

———. *Treatise Concerning the Lord's Supper*. Ed. Norman S. Grabo. East Lansing, MI: Michigan State UP, 1966.

———. *Upon the Types of the Old Testament*. Ed. Charles W. Mignon. 2 vols. Lincoln: U of Nebraska P, 1989.

Taylor, Larry E. *Pastoral and Anti-pastoral Patterns in John Updike's Fiction*. Carbondale: Southern Illinois UP, 1971.

Thomas, Isaiah. *The History of Printing in America*. 2nd ed. Ed. Marcus A. McCorison. 2nd ed. 1874. New York: Weathewane Books, 1970.

Thomas, Kyper Peter. *The Significance of Mather Byles in the Literary Tradition of America: A Study of His "Poems on Several Occasions" and His Literary Criticism*. Diss., Auburn U, 1974. Ann Arbor: UMI, 1982.

Thompson, Lawrence. *Melville's Quarrel with God*. Princeton: Princeton UP, 1952.

Thoreau, Henry David. *Walden*. In *Anthology of American Literature*. Ed. George McMichael, et al. 2nd ed. Vol. 1 *Colonial Through Romantic*. New York, NY: Macmillan, 1980.

Toliver, Harold E. *Pastoral Forms and Attitudes*. Berkeley: U California P, 1971.

Tompson, Benjamin. *Benjamin Tompson; Colonial Bard: A Critical Edition*. Ed. Peter White. University Park, PA: Pennsylvania State UP, 1980.

Tooke, John Horne. *The Diversions of Purley*. Vol. 1, 1786. Vol. 2, 1805.

The Torah. Translated according to the Masoretic text. Philadelphia: Jewish Publication Society of America, 1962.

Trenchard, John, and Thomas Gordon. *Cato's Letters: Or, Essays on Liberty, Civil and Religious*. Ed. Ronald Hamowy. 2 vols. Indianapolis: Liberty Fund, 1995.

Trumbull, John. *An Essay on the Uses and Advantages of the Fine Arts*. New Haven: T. & S. Green, 1770.

———. *The Satiric Poems of John Trumbull:* The Progress of Dulness *and* M'Fingal, *with Illustrations from Engravings by E. Tisdale*. Ed. Edwin T. Bowden. Austin: U of Texas P, 1962.

Tuer, David F. *Dictionary of Astronomy, Space, and Atmospheric Phenomena*. New York: Van Nostrand Reinhold, 1979.

Turner, Arlin. *Nathaniel Hawthorne: A Biography*. New York: Oxford UP, 1980.

———. *Nathaniel Hawthorne: An Introduction and Interpretation*. New York: Barnes and Noble, 1961.

Tuttle, Julius Herbert. "The Libraries of the Mathers." *Proceedings of the American Antiquarian Society* (Semi-Annual Meeting Held in Boston, Apr. 20, 1910) 20.2:269–356.

Tyler, Moses Coit. *A History of American Literature, 1607–1765*. 2 vols. 1878. Ithaca: Cornell UP, 1949.

———. *The Literary History of the American Revolution, 1763–1783*. 2 vols. 1897. New York: Burt Franklin, 1970.

Tyndale, William. *Pentateuch*. Cologne, Germany, 1530.

Van Anglen, K. P. *The New England Milton: Literary Reception and Cultural Authority in the Early Republic*. University Park: Pennsylvania State UP, 1993.

Van Cromphout, Gustaaf. "Cotton Mather as Plutarchan Biographer." *American Literature* 46.4 (1975): 465–81.

———. "*Manuductio ad Ministerium:* Cotton Mather as Neoclassicist." *American Literature* 53.3 (Nov. 1981): 361–79.

Vance, William L. *America's Rome*. 2 vols. New Haven: Yale UP, 1989.

Vergil. *Eclogues*. Ed. Robert Coleman. Cambridge, Eng.: Cambridge UP, 1977.

———. *Vergil's Aeneid and Fourth ("Messianic") Eclogue in the Dryden Translation*. Ed. Howard Clark. University Park: Pennsylvania State UP, 1989.

Virgil. *Virgil*. Rev. ed. Trans. H. Rushton Fairclough. Loeb Library edition. 2 Vols. Cambridge, MA: Harvard UP, 1935.

Waggoner, Hyatt H. *American Poets from the Puritans to the Present*. Rev. ed. Baton Rouge: Louisiana State UP, 1984.

Wagner, Henry R. "Peter Martyr and His Works." *Proceedings of the American Antiquarian Society* (Annual Meeting Held in Worcester, MA, Oct. 16, 1946) 56, pt. 2 (1947): 239–88.

Warfel, Harry R. *Noah Webster: Schoolmaster to America*. New York: Macmillan, 1936.

Warren, Austin. *Rage for Order: Essays in Criticism*. Ann Arbor: U of Michigan P, 1948.

Washington, George. *Writings of George Washington, 1745–1799*. Ed. John C. Fitzpatrick. 39 vols. Washington, D.C.: Government Printing Office, 1931–1944.

Wasserman, George R. *John Dryden*. Ed. Sylvia E. Bowman. New York: Twayne, 1964.

Watts, Emily Stipes. *The Poetry of American Women from 1632 to 1945*. Austin: U of Texas P, 1977.

Webb, Stephen Saunders. *1676: The End of American Independence*. New York: Knopf, 1984.

Webster, Noah. *An American Selection of Lessons in Reading and Speaking . . . Being the Third Part of a Grammatical Institute*. Hartford, CT: Hudson and Goodwin, 1789.

———. *A Collection of Essays and Fugitiv Writings*. 1790. Delmar, FL: Scholars' Facsimiles and Reprints, 1977.

———. "On the Education of Youth in America." *American Magazine* [New York] (1787 and 1788).

Weems, Mason Locke. *History of the Life, Death, Virtues, and Exploits of George Washington*. Philadelphia: Mathew Carey, 1800.

Weinbrot, Howard D. *Augustus Caesar in "Augustan" England: The Decline of a Classical Norm*. Princeton: Princeton UP, 1978.

Wharton, Donald P. *Richard Steere, Colonial Merchant Poet*. Pennsylvania University Studies, no. 44. University Park: Pennsylvania State UP, 1979.

White, Peter, ed. *Puritan Poets and Poetics: Seventeenth-Century American Poetry in Theory and Practice*. University Park: Pennsylvania State UP, 1985.

Whitman, Walt. *Leaves of Grass: Authoritative Texts, Prefaces, Whitman on His Art, Criticism*. Ed. Sculley Bradley and Harold W. Blodgett. New York: Norton, 1973.

Wierske, Warren W. "Imagination: The Preacher's Neglected Ally." *Leadership* 4.2 (Spring 1983): 22–27.

Wiesen, David S. "The Contribution of Antiquity to American Racial Thought." In *Classical Traditions in Early America*. Ed. John W. Eadie. Ann Arbor: U of Michigan P, 1976.

Willey, Basil. *The Seventeenth-Century Background: Studies in the Thought of the Age in Relation to Poetry and Religion*. New York: Columbia UP, 1934.

Wills, Garry. *Cincinnatus: George Washington and the Enlightenment*. New York: Doubleday, 1984.

Wilson, Robert. *American Sublime: The Genealogy of a Poetic Genre*. Madison: U of Wisconsin P, 1991.

Wilson, Robert John. *Poetics of the Sublime Poem in America, 1650–1860*. Ann Arbor: UMI, 1982.

Woodberry, George Edward. *America in Literature*. New York: Harper and Brothers, 1903.

———. *Appreciation of Literature, and America in Literature*. 3rd ed. New York: Harcourt, Brace, 1921.

Wordsworth, William. *The Prelude, 1799, 1805, 1850: Authoritative Texts, Context and Reception, Recent Critical Essays*. Ed. Jonathan Wordsworth et al. New York: Norton, 1979.

Yannella, Donald. "Evert Augustus Duyckinck. George L. Duyckinck." In *Dictionary of Literary Biography*. Vol. 3: *Antebellum Writers in New York and the South*. Ed. Joel Myerson. Detroit: Bruccoli Clark, 1979.

Yates, Frances A. *The Art of Memory*. Chicago: U of Chicago P, 1966.

Young, Edward. *The Poetical Works of Edward Young*. Vol. 1. Westport, CT: Greenwood, 1970.

"A Youth of His [i.e., the Reverend Joshua Belding of Newington] Parish." "An Elegy on the Death of Mrs. Anne Belding, Late Wife." Hartford, CT: Eben. Watson, 1774.

Ziff, Larzer. "Text and Context." *William and Mary Quarterly* 45.2 (1988): 348–50.

Zimbardo, Rose, and Benilde Montgomery. *African-American Culture in the Eighteenth Century*. Special issue of *Eighteenth-Century Studies* 27.4 (Summer 1994). Baltimore: Johns Hopkins UP, 1994.

Index

The American Aeneas was designed and typeset on a Macintosh computer system using Quark software. The text and chapter openers are set in Goudy. This book was designed and typeset by Cheryl Carrington and manufactured by Thomson-Shore, Inc. The paper used in this book is designed for an effective life of at least three hundred years.